Current Perspectives on the Anxiety Disorders

Implications for DSM-V and Beyond

Dean McKay, PhD, ABPP, is an associate professor in the Department of Psychology at Fordham University. He currently serves on the editorial boards of *Behaviour Research and Therapy*, the *Journal of Clinical Psychology*, and the *Journal of Anxiety Disorders*, and is Associate Editor of the *Journal of Cognitive Psychotherapy*. He has published over 120 journal articles and book chapters, is the editor or coeditor of 8 published and forthcoming books, and has given over 150 conference presentations. His research has focused primarily on obsessive–compulsive disorder (OCD), body dysmorphic disorder and health anxiety and their link to OCD, and the role of disgust in psychopathology. His research has also focused on mechanisms of information processing bias for anxiety states.

Jonathan S. Abramowitz, PhD, ABPP, is professor and Associate Chair of the Department of Psychology, and Research Professor in the Department of Psychiatry, at the University of North Carolina (UNC) at Chapel Hill. He is also the Founder and Director of the UNC Anxiety and Stress Disorders Clinic. He conducts research on obsessive–compulsive disorder and other anxiety disorders, and has published 10 books and over 100 peer-reviewed research articles and book chapters on these topics. He currently serves as Associate Editor of *Behaviour Research and Therapy* and the *Journal of Cognitive Psychotherapy*, and serves on the editorial boards of several other scientific journals. He regularly presents papers and workshops on anxiety disorders and their treatment at regional, national, and international professional conferences.

Steven Taylor, PhD, ABPP, is a professor and clinical psychologist in the Department of Psychiatry at the University of British Columbia, and is Editor-in-Chief of the *Journal of Cognitive Psychotherapy*. He has published over 220 journal articles and book chapters, and 18 books on anxiety disorders and related topics. His research interests include cognitive-behavioral treatments and mechanisms of anxiety disorders and related conditions, as well as the behavioral genetics of these disorders.

Gordon J. G. Asmundson, PhD, RD Psych, is currently a full-time professor of psychology at the University of Regina, an adjunct professor of psychiatry at the University of Saskatchewan, a Canadian Institutes of Health Research (CIHR)

Investigator, and the leader of a CIHR New Emerging Team focusing on mechanisms and treatment of PTSD. Dr. Asmundson holds several editorial posts, including North American Editor of *Cognitive Behaviour Therapy*, Behavioral Medicine Section Editor for *Cognitive and Behavioral Practice*, PTSD Section Coeditor for *Psychological Injury and Law*, and serves on the editorial board of the *Journal of Anxiety Disorders*. He has published over 210 journal articles and book chapters on anxiety disorders and chronic pain as well as 5 books. He has research and clinical interests in assessment and basic mechanisms of the anxiety disorders, health anxiety (hypochondriasis, disease phobia), acute and chronic pain, and the association of these with disability and behavior change.

Current Perspectives on the Anxiety Disorders

Implications for DSM-V and Beyond

- Dean McKay, PhD, ABPP
- Jonathan S. Abramowitz, PhD, ABPP
- Steven Taylor, PhD, ABPP
- Gordon J. G. Asmundson, PhD, RD Psych

SPRINGER PUBLISHING COMPANY
NEW YORK

Springer Publishing Company, LLC
11 West 42nd Street
New York, NY 10036
www.springerpub.com

Acquisitions Editor: Sheri W. Sussman
Cover design: Mimi Flow
Composition: Six Red Marbles

Ebook ISBN: **978-0-8261-3248-2**

09 10 11 / 5 4 3 2 1

Library of Congress Cataloging-in-Publication Data

Current perspectives on the anxiety disorders : implications for DSM-V and beyond / edited by Dean McKay ... [et al.].
p. ; cm.
Includes bibliographical references and index.
ISBN 978-0-8261-3247-5 (alk. paper)
1. Anxiety disorders—Classification. 2. Diagnostic and statistical manual of mental disorders. I. McKay, Dean, 1966–
[DNLM: 1. Diagnostic and statistical manual of mental disorders. 2. Anxiety Disorders—diagnosis. 3. Anxiety Disorders—classification. WM 172 C9766 2009]
RC531.C875 2009
616.85'22—dc22

2009019937

Printed in the United States of America by Hamilton

DM: For the students, the future of the field

JSA: To Stacy, Emily, and Miriam—with all my love

ST: To Anna, Alex, and Amy, with love

GJGA: To the many dedicated researchers and clinicians, including my friends and coeditors of this volume, who strive to understand and alleviate mental anguish

Contents

Part II: Empirical and Theoretical Perspectives on Diagnosis

Part III: Classification and Specific Anxiety Problems

Contributors

Jonathan S. Abramowitz, PhD, ABPP
Department of Psychology
University of North Carolina
Chapel Hill, NC

Martin M. Antony
Department of Psychology
Ryerson University
Toronto, ON, Canada

Gordon J. G. Asmundson, PhD, RD Psych
Department of Psychology
University of Regina
Regina, Saskatchewan, Canada

Anu Asnanni, PhD
Department of Psychology
Boston University
Boston, MA

Amit Bernstein, PhD
The International Research Collaborative on Anxiety
Department of Psychology
University of Haifa
Haifa, Israel

Timothy A. Brown, PsyD
Center for Anxiety and Related Disorders
Boston University
Boston, MA

Kelsey C. Collimore, PhD
University of Regina
Regina, Saskatchewan, Canada

Jacek Debiec, MD, PhD
Department of Psychiatry
School of Medicine & Center for Neural Science
New York University
New York, NY

Paul M. G. Emmelkamp
Department of Clinical Psychology
University of Amsterdam
Amsterdam, Netherlands

Matthew J. Friedman, MD, PhD
National Center for PTSD
Department of Veterans Affairs
White River Junction, VT

Devon Hinton, PhD
Massachusetts General Hospital
Harvard Medical School
Boston, MA

Stefan Hofmann, PhD
Department of Psychology
Boston University
Boston, MA

Curtis Hsia, PhD
Department of Psychology
Azusa Pacific University
Azusa, CA

Andrew M. Jacobs, PsyD
Anxiety Treatment and Research Centre
St. Joseph's Healthcare & Department of Psychiatry and Behavioral Neurosciences
McMaster University
Hamilton, ON, Canada

Kerry L. Jang, PhD
Department of Psychiatry
University of British Columbia
Vancouver, BC, Canada

Naomi Koerner, PhD
Department of Psychology
Ryerson University
Toronto, ON, Canada

Amy E. Lawrence, PhD
Center for Anxiety and Related Disorders
Boston University
Boston, MA

Joseph E. LeDoux, PhD
Center for Neural Science
New York University
New York, NY

Randi E. McCabe, PhD
Anxiety Treatment and Research Centre
St. Joseph's Healthcare & Department of Psychiatry and Behavioral Neurosciences
McMaster University
Hamilton, ON, Canada

Dean McKay, PhD, ABPP
Department of Psychology
Fordham University
Bronx, NY

Thomas H. Ollendick, PhD
Child Study Center
Department of Psychology
Virginia Polytechnic Institute and State University
Blacksburg, VA

Lawrence Park, PhD
Massachusetts General Hospital
Harvard Medical School
Boston, MA

Wade Pickren, PhD
Department of Psychology
Ryerson University
Toronto, ON, Canada

Brian Pilecki, MA
Department of Psychology
Fordham University
Bronx, NY

Mark Pollack, PhD
Massachusetts General Hospital
Harvard Medical School
Boston, MA

Mark Powers, PhD
Department of Clinical Psychology
University of Amsterdam
Amsterdam, Netherlands

Andrew Rasmussen, PhD
Division of General Internal Medicine
New York University School of Medicine
New York, NY

Christina J. Riccardi, PhD
Department of Psychology
Florida State University
Tallahassee, FL

J. Anthony Richey, PhD
Department of Psychology
Florida State University
Tallahassee, FL
Department of Psychology
Boston University
Boston, MA

Winfried Rief, PhD
Institute of Psychology
University of Marburg
Marburg, Germany

Anthony J. Rosellini, PhD
Center for Anxiety and Related Disorders
Boston University
Boston, MA

Alison Sawyer, PhD
Department of Psychology
Boston University
Boston, MA

Chizuru Shikishima
Keio Advanced Research Centers
Keio University
Tokyo, Japan

Norman B. Schmidt, PhD
Department of Psychology
Florida State University
Tallahassee, FL

Eric A. Storch, PhD
Departments of Pediatrics and Psychiatry
University of South Florida
Tampa, FL

Richard Swinson, MD
Anxiety Treatment and Research Centre
St. Joseph's Healthcare & Department of Psychiatry and Behavioral Neurosciences
McMaster University
Hamilton, ON, Canada

Steven Taylor, PhD, ABPP
Department of Psychiatry
University of British Columbia
Vancouver, BC, Canada

Kiara R. Timpano, PhD
Department of Psychology
Florida State University
Tallahassee, FL

Nathan Thoma, MA
Department of Psychology
Fordham University
Bronx, NY

Warran Tryon, PhD, ABPP
Department of Psychology
Fordham University
Bronx, NY

David Watson
Department of Psychology
University of Iowa
Iowa City, IA

Stephen P. Whiteside, PhD, ABPP
Departments of Psychiatry and Psychology
Mayo Clinic
Rochester, MN

Michael J. Zvolensky, PhD
Department of Psychology
University of Vermont
Burlington, VT

A Look Back at a Quarter Century of the Descriptive Model of Classification

1 Current Perspectives on Anxiety Disorders: Models and Methods in Anticipation of *DSM-V*

Dean McKay
Steven Taylor
Gordon J.G. Asmundson
Jonathan S. Abramowitz

For over a quarter century, classification of mental disorders, including anxiety disorders, has relied on descriptive systems such as the various editions of the *Diagnostic and Statistical Manual of Mental Disorders* (*DSM*; e.g., American Psychiatric Association [APA], 1980). These systems emerged to ensure that patients were reliably diagnosed, which was a major shortcoming of the prior diagnostic systems. Reliance on the descriptive approach of *DSM* resulted in greater reliability in diagnoses when structured interviews are utilized (Segal, Hersen, & Van Hasselt, 1994). This included an increase in the reliability of anxiety disorder diagnoses.

The descriptive approach to diagnosis is consistent with the neo-Kraepelinian technique, which relies on symptoms, signs, clinical course, and family history in determining diagnoses (Kraepelin, 1917).[1] This approach has had much utility over the years, particularly by introducing methodological rigor. In classifying anxiety disorders, it has been particularly useful, setting the occasion for research identifying prevalence of the conditions and specifying distinctions among different behavioral and cognitive manifestations of anxiety conditions. Rich theoretical accounts of different anxiety disorders have emerged that, in turn, have given rise to empirically supported interventions and best practice guidelines. Unprecedented relief from anxiety conditions has been provided to anxiety sufferers as a result, no doubt due in large part to the increased precision accorded clinicians from the improved classification system. At the frontier of this research, specific anxiety problems that were previously underexamined, such as social anxiety disorder and generalized anxiety disorder, now have well-established treatment guidelines.

Recent research, however, has emerged in several anxiety disorders suggesting that the neo-Kraepelinian approach should be augmented with other empirically-driven methods as well as by robust theory-driven approaches to classification. In the case of empirically-driven approaches, considerable research supports an interaction between genetic and environmental factors that contribute to the manifestation of anxiety disorders (Hettema, Neale, & Kendler, 2001). Additionally, the recent widespread use of taxometric methods has taken a purely empirical approach to determining distinct categories of conditions (Waller & Meehl, 1997). The conceptual and methodological developments have lead to a richer base from which to develop a revised classification system for the next edition of the *DSM*.

Multiple Perspectives: Bridging Gaps in Classification Approaches

An assumption underlying the current diagnostic approach (*DSM-IV Text Revision* [*DSM-IV-TR*]; APA, 2000) is that each diagnosis represents a discrete entity. That is, it is assumed that individuals who meet criteria for a specific disorder are categorically different from those without the diagnosis.

Interestingly, the *DSM-IV-TR* (AAPA, 2000) includes a disclaimer that suggests that this long-held assumption may not be true (Widiger & Mullins–Sweatt, 2007). Calls for dimensional approaches to diagnosis have grown in recent years. For example, statistical analyses of the full range of disorders listed in the *DSM* have lead to dimensional schemes. Watson (2005) obtained empirical evidence to distinguish among the following three classes of disorders: bipolar disorders, distress disorders, and fear disorders. Krueger (1999) showed that many of the disorders in the *DSM* may form two broad categories—internalizing and externalizing disorders—with internalizing disorders further classified into anxious–misery and fear conditions.

Dimensional approaches have been widely used in research examining the heritability of different psychiatric problems. Behavioral genetic studies have been conducted to determine the relative contribution of genes versus environment when modeling traits, measured by administering instruments to twins, without necessarily relying on the presence of specific diagnoses (DiLalla, 2004). In addition, many studies have attempted to specify the neural circuitry involved in fear learning. This research has involved brain imaging technology, such as functional magnetic resonance imaging in conjunction with cognitive processing tasks. Research such as this brings together methodology that has been central to biological psychiatry (Malizia & Nutt, 2008) with methods that originated in experimental psychology (Williams, Watts, MacLeod, & Mathews 1997).

Theory and Mechanisms in Diagnosis

Although the descriptive approach has enhanced the science behind classification by improving the reliability of diagnosis, it does not, in itself, provide a link to treatment. The practice guidelines that have developed for a wide range of psychiatric disorders grew from other theoretical traditions built around the existing diagnoses. Recent years have witnessed a growing interest in determining the underlying mechanisms that result in psychiatric conditions. This movement has, in turn, lead to a renewed call for an explicitly theory-based diagnostic system.

An explicitly theory-driven approach to diagnosis in other sciences may function adequately, given the presence of a single or very small set of theories. Psychiatry and psychology, however, are characterized by multiple theories with disparate methodologies. Recently, Kendler (2008) made a compelling case for relying on multiple theories in describing psychiatric disturbance. This would yield a range of possible mechanisms of psychopathology. The examination of any single mechanism may be an effective means of understanding microlevel elements of psychiatric conditions. In their aggregate, the mechanisms may interact in a nonlinear fashion. As a result, Kendler advocated examination of the interactions between psychological and biological mechanisms of psychiatric disturbance.

Overview of This Book

The impetus for this book was the need to examine empirical approaches to conceptualizing and diagnosing anxiety disorders. The past 25 years have witnessed significant growth in how anxiety disorders are understood. These conceptualizations cut across many theoretical perspectives, each with proposed mechanisms of disorder. The goal of the book is to bring together leading authorities from multiple theoretical traditions, and to present updates on the empirical status of the diagnostic system for specific anxiety conditions. The book is organized into three major sections. Part I examines the recent history of the neo-Kraepelinian approach to diagnosis as applied to the *DSM* and International Classification of Diseases systems of diagnosis, and the progress made within specific areas within the anxiety disorders. There have been considerable changes and advances made in the conceptualization of anxiety disorders, and classification in general, since the publication of *DSM-III*. Part II covers the empirical bases of classification within specific theoretical perspectives on the anxiety disorders. Several approaches have become prominent in the anxiety disorders, such as fear circuitry, genetic and behavioral–genetic, neurochemical, and taxometric methods. Part III examines specific topics that relate to anxiety diagnosis. For example, there has recently been considerable discussion in the literature regarding the putative obsessive–compulsive spectrum, and how the candidate disorders for the spectrum may be classified for future revisions of the *DSM*. This section will cover some of the areas that have been the source of controversy in classification and conceptualization.

The past quarter century has been extremely productive in advancing our understanding of anxiety disorders. It is hoped that the perspectives included in the chapters in this volume will help usher in another highly productive quarter century of research on the conceptualization, classification, and treatment of anxious conditions. We anticipate that many of the perspectives contained in this book will be relied on in the planning of the next edition of the *DSM* and will be informative as further refinements are undertaken in the future.

Note

1 Kraepelin is commonly portrayed as someone who was simply interested in descriptive methods of diagnosis. But, in fact, Kraepelin was interested in the possibility of eventually developing an etiology-based classification system.

References

American Psychiatric Association. (1980). *Diagnostic and statistical manual of mental disorders* (3rd ed.). Washington, DC: Author.

American Psychiatric Association. (2000). *Diagnostic and statistical manual of mental disorders* (4th ed., text rev.). Washington, DC: Author.

DiLalla, L. F. (2004). *Behavior genetics principles: Perspectives in development, personality, and psychopathology*. Washington, DC: American Psychological Association.

Hettema, J. M., Neale, M. C., & Kendler, K. S. (2001). A review and meta-analysis of the genetic epidemiology of anxiety disorders. *American Journal of Psychiatry, 158*, 1568–1578.

Kendler, K. S. (2008). Explanatory models of psychiatric disorders. *American Journal of Psychiatry, 165*, 695–702.

Kraepelin, E. (1917). *Lectures on clinical psychiatry* (3rd ed.). New York: William Wood.

Krueger, R. F. (1999). The structure of common mental disorders. *Archives of General Psychiatry, 56*, 921–926.

Malizia, A. L., & Nutt, D. (2008). Principles and findings from human imaging of anxiety disorders. In R. J Blanchard, C. Blanchard, G. Griebel, & D. Nutt (Eds.), *Handbook of anxiety and fear* (pp. 437–454). Amsterdam: Academic Press.

Segal, D. L., Hersen, M., & Van Hasselt, V. B. (1994). Reliability of the structured clinical interview for DSM-III-R: An evaluative review. *Comprehensive Psychiatry, 35,* 316–327.

Waller, N., & Meehl, P. E. (1997). *Multivariate taxometric procedures: Distinguishing types from continua*. Newbury Park, CA: Sage.

Watson, D. (2005). Rethinking the mood and anxiety disorders: A quantitative hierarchical model for DSM-V. *Journal of Abnormal Psychology, 114,* 522–536.

Widiger, T.A., & Mullins-Sweatt, S. (2007). Mental disorders as discrete clinical conditions: Dimensional versus categorical classification. In M. Hersen, S. M. Turner, & D. C. Beidel (Eds.), *Adult psychopathology and diagnosis* (5th ed., pp. 3–33). New York: Wiley.

Williams, J. M. G., Watts, F. N., MacLeod, C., & Mathews, A. (1997). *Cognitive psychology and the emotional disorders* (2nd ed.). Chichester: Wiley.

2

Historical Perspectives on Psychiatric Classification and Anxiety Disorders

Martin M. Antony
Wade Pickren
Naomi Koerner

Introduction

This chapter begins with a review of the history of mental illness classification, providing a broader context in which to understand where our current classification of anxiety disorders originated. This general overview includes a discussion of the roots of psychiatric nomenclature going back to the late 1800s, through the first three editions of the *Diagnostic and Statistical Manual of Mental Disorders* (*DSM*; American Psychiatric Association [APA], 1952, 1968, 1980).

Next, we shift the focus to the classification of anxiety disorders in particular, including a discussion of the ways in which classification of anxiety-based disorders has changed across each edition of the *DSM*, from the first edition of *DSM* (*DSM–I*; APA, 1952) through the most recent text revision of *DSM's* fourth edition (*DSM–IV–TR;* APA, 2000). This discussion is followed by more detailed accounts of the major revisions in diagnostic criteria for each of the anxiety disorders, including the rationale for these revisions. Though we include some discussion of the World Health Organization's *International Classification of Diseases* (*ICD;* World Health Organization [WHO], 1992), the emphasis in this chapter is on the *DSM,* because there is little sound historical scholarship available on the classification of mental disorders in *ICD*.

History of Classification of Mental Illness

In January 1881, the young psychiatrist Emil Kraepelin (1856–1926) wrote to Wilhelm Wundt, founder of modern experimental psychology, "As often before and with your permission I would like to ask for your advice and support and to dedicate myself more and more to psychology, which is really my primary inclination" (Muller, Fletcher, & Steinberg, 2006, p.132). He was asking for support for what we in the 21st century would call a postdoctoral fellowship. Kraepelin had first studied with Wundt in 1877, when he was still a medical student, and sought to return for further studies with Wundt after completing his medical training and briefly serving as an assistant psychiatrist in Wurzburg and Munich. Wundt encouraged his application, and in February 1882, Kraepelin began a nearly 2-year stint in Wundt's laboratory.

Kraepelin took away from his time in Wundt's laboratory a commitment to empirical research and a psychological perspective for understanding a range of human activities, including psychiatric problems, substance abuse, and problems of work life in a rapidly industrializing Germany. Kraepelin is rightly known for his work in developing descriptive psychopathology, especially an innovative system of classification of mental disorders. At the heart of this system was an attempt to understand and classify the disorders in terms of the ways they are experienced psychologically.

In 19th-century psychiatry, diagnostic classification was not considered essential to clinical work. Only a few psychiatrists engaged in research; the great majority were asylum superintendents. In America, they came to call themselves *alienists*, reflecting their belief that their patients had become alienated from their reason. Among those who did conduct research, classification was of minor concern. Nevertheless, some systems did emerge. For example, Richard von Krafft-Ebbing proposed a classification of sexual disorders in his *Psychopathia Sexualis*. Diagnostic categories such as moon madness, circular insanity, masturbatory insanity, and others had been proposed and used during the century (Shorter, 1997). In the 1880s, Carl Wernicke, known for his neurological work on aphasia, proposed a simple classification system using the concept that in all psychiatric disorders there is always one primary feature from which all others arise (Krahl & Schifferdecker, 1998). So, Kraepelin was not the first to develop a nosology for psychiatric disorders. However, he was the pioneer of a classification system that had clinical utility.

Kraepelin developed his nosology over a period of years, based on extensive clinical experience in various psychiatric settings. Kraepelin sought to understand psychiatric disorders through observing their outcome. What, he wondered, does the course of the disorder tell us about its nature? The growth of his understanding can be traced through successive editions of his textbook, *Psychiatrie*. During the course of his work, he described dementia praecox in terms of its outcome and separated it from other disorders. By the 6th edition (1899), Kraepelin had arrived at a comprehensive classification. Mental disorders were now divided into 13 groups, based on their course and outcome.

Kraepelin continued to refine his nosology until his death in 1926. By that time, his classificatory approach was broadly accepted throughout much of Europe. Following Kraepelin, many European psychiatrists pursued a descriptive approach in diagnosing their patients. In North America, Kraepelin's classification system had a favorable reception early in the 20th century, but by the 1920s and 1930s, it was largely out of favor. Instead, the dynamic psychiatry of Adolf Meyer (1866–1950) had become dominant. Meyer was Swiss born and trained at Zurich under the well-known psychiatrist August Forel (Leys, 1991). Meyer moved to the United States in 1892, where he held a series of increasingly salient positions until he finally landed at Johns Hopkins University in 1910, where he remained until he retired in 1941.

Meyer's rise to the leadership of American psychiatry in the pre–World War II era was facilitated by his eclecticism. For better or worse, Meyer drew from often disparate theoretical bases to forge what he called dynamic psychiatry. Early on in America, he was a proponent of Kraepelin's descriptive approach, though he later minimized the importance of descriptive psychiatry. He was also receptive to some of the ideas of Sigmund Freud, especially the role of early life experience and sexuality (Burnham, 1967). But underlying all of Meyer's work was an allegiance to the concept of adaptation, drawn loosely from the work of Charles Darwin (Leys, 1991). Meyer, like such American psychologists as William James, Robert Yerkes, John Dewey, and James Angell, was committed to Darwinian notions of function and purpose in mind and behavior. He used the term *psychobiology* to indicate that human mental functioning, both in health and disorder, was a combination of psychological and biological efforts at adapting to the world (Dewsbury, 1991). Meyer worked closely with psychologists, reflecting a broader trend in the development of American psychiatry to attempt to redefine itself as a medical science through alliances with cognate disciplines based in laboratory approaches (Grob, 1983; Pickren, 2007). Indeed, it was in this move that American psychiatrists renamed themselves *psychiatrists* instead of alienists. Meyer's dynamic psychiatry with its psychobiological focus led to attempts in American psychiatry to understand disordered mental functioning in the full context of each person's life. Meyer proposed that his colleagues draw up a "life chart" for each person they treated. This life chart would then facilitate diagnosis and treatment. Such was Meyer's dominant position within American psychiatry, that the mainstream of the profession spent the prewar years concerned with understanding and treating psychiatric disorders as problems of adaptation and function and paid much less attention to issues of classification of mental disorders than many of their European counterparts.

The other major influence that moved North American psychiatry away from a focus on psychiatric nosology was the work of Sigmund Freud. It has been well documented that Freud's ideas began to circulate in North America in the 1890s; and by the first decade of the 20th century, his work was increasingly known among psychologists, psychiatrists, and neurologists (Burnham, 1967; Shakow & Rapaport, 1964). In this same period, psychiatry was redefining itself as a profession concerned with delivery of services in private office settings (Grob, 1983). By the time of World War II American psychiatry was principally concerned with problems of adjustment, with services conceptualized in an ad hoc mixture of Meyer's dynamic psychiatry and an American adaptation of Freud's psychoanalysis. Increasingly, American psychiatrists worked outside mental hospitals and were less concerned with the treatment of serious mental illness.

The experience of psychiatrists serving in the armed forces during World War II facilitated a greater emphasis on environmental and psychological factors. Many of the young psychiatrists who served in the war became leaders of psychiatry in the two decades after the war. The Menninger brothers, Karl and William, were among this leadership. William Menninger had been chief of military psychiatry during the war. He promoted a psychoanalytic approach to diagnosis and treatment during this time and his influence grew after the war. Because of the influence of the Menningers and the additional influence of many émigré psychoanalysts in American academic departments of psychiatry, the years from 1945 to 1965 were dominated by psychoanalytic theory and praxis (Hale, 1995). This was also the period of the emergence of modern clinical psychology with the growth of clinical training programs based on David Shakow's "Boulder Model," fuelled by generous National Institute of Mental Health (NIMH) funding (Pickren & Schneider, 2005). Popular culture in this period also reflected the influence of psychoanalytic ideas (Hale, 1971). The impact of all these factors was to facilitate the creation of a rich psychologically minded culture that was receptive to psychotherapeutic treatment (Herman, 1995; Pickren, 2005). Practitioners responded to these demands with little emphasis on issues of classification. However, the seeds for change were sown in this period and the document that would reflect that change was published near the beginning of this era.

The first official American classification of mental disorders appeared in 1918 as the *Statistical Manual for the Use of Institutions for the Insane*. It was developed by the American Medico-Psychological Association (immediate precursor to American Psychiatric Association) and the National Committee for Mental Hygiene in response to the needs and demands of the U.S. Census Bureau to enumerate the insane. The first few editions focused almost entirely on the psychoses, but by the tenth edition (1942), various "psychoneuroses," including anxiety states were employed (Grob, 1991b). *DSM* was first published in 1952. It drew upon the earlier manual but its development was guided by the broad, adaptationist perspective of Adolf Meyer's dynamic psychiatry and the more psychoanalytically oriented perspective of psychiatrists who had served in the war, especially William and Karl Menninger (Friedman, 1990). William Menninger had been involved in the development of the U.S. Army manual for diagnosing mental disorders and his influence is seen in the first *DSM*. The manual uses the broad Kraepelinian classification of endogenous mental disorders with the reaction types found in Adolf Meyer's work. Psychoanalytic constructs of neuroses are threaded throughout the manual. For the time period, this made sense, as most practitioners did not place primary emphasis on diagnostic purity.

The second edition or "revision" of the *DSM* (APA, 1968) followed much the same plan. Now, there were more subdivisions of the major disorders; for example, instead of just listing alcoholism *(DSM–I)*, there were now the categories of episodic excessive drinking, habitual excessive drinking, etc. *(DSM–II)*. What was different was the need to integrate the *DSM* with the World Health Organization's *ICD*. The eighth edition of the *ICD* was on the horizon and, by treaty, the United States was obligated to coordinate its system of classifying diseases with that of the World Health Organization.

The coordination with the *ICD* was coincident with other forces that led to the creation of an almost entirely new way of classifying mental disorders in America. Briefly, the increasingly psychological culture of postwar America created a demand for psychological services unprecedented in American life (Cushman, 1995). The NIMH's funding for training of mental health professionals—psychiatrists, clinical psychologists, psychiatric nurses, social workers—greatly increased the numerical and political strength of their respective professions. In the 1960s, the federal government and many large corporations responded to the demands of their employees to provide insurance coverage for mental health outpatient services. By the 1970s, many insurers were beginning to complain that the high cost of ongoing psychological care would bankrupt them. From insurers' perspective, many of the illnesses were vaguely defined with widely varied treatments that seemed to have no specifiable end. The federal government, one of the largest employers paying for such services, soon began to demand an assessment of whether such treatments worked and were worth the cost (Rosner, 2005).

Within psychiatry, the environmentalist and social psychiatry, strongly analytic in tone, that had become dominant after WWII, began to lose its hegemony (Grob, 1991a). By the late 1950s, a small group of psychiatrists had begun to see the need for greatly strengthening the research base of psychiatry. David Hamburg, then at NIMH, left for Stanford University where he revitalized the department of psychiatry, making it one of the most research-oriented programs in North America. A similar movement had begun in the 1950s at Washington University in St. Louis, led by Eli Robbins and Samuel Guze. These psychiatrists helped move the profession toward a focus on research. Because NIMH had always favored the funding of psychiatry over the other mental health disciplines, there were abundant resources to facilitate this reorientation. By the late 1970s, there had been a major shift within psychiatry toward a biological, rather than a psychological or psychosocial, understanding of mental disorders. The development of effective psychotropic medications, beginning in the 1950s, provided an important pressure point on psychiatry and psychology to develop identifiable, measurable, and specific diagnostic classifications of mental disorders that would facilitate clinical trials of pharmacotherapies (Baker & Pickren, 2007). Finally, the pressure to conform to an upcoming revision of the *ICD* provided the proximal impetus to revise the *DSM* again.

All of these factors came together in the 1970s to provide the necessary context for a revision of the *DSM* that would reflect the changed social and policy dynamics of North American psychiatry (Horwitz, 2002; Wilson, 1993). The appointment of Robert Spitzer to chair the American Psychiatric Association Task Force on Nomenclature and Statistics in 1974 provided the critical professional leadership that led to the *DSM–III*. Spitzer had a strong commitment to psychiatry as a research-based profession and had strong ties with the Washington University psychiatry department. He and the Task Force built on the work of Washington University researcher, John Feighner, who had articulated 14 clearly specified criteria for diagnosis of mental disorders (Feighner et al., 1972). Spitzer and the Task Force aimed to redesign the *DSM* in such a way that it could become a manual useful in research as well as diagnosis (Spitzer, 2001). Despite controversy over the elimination (then temporary reinstatement) of such vague terms as neurosis, they were able to win over enough of the American psychiatry establishment to firmly establish their neo-Kraepelin approach to classification.

How does the history of the classification of anxiety disorders fit within this broader history of psychiatric nosologies? Medical writings from the late medieval period until the 19th century made frequent references to what are now termed anxiety disorders, though the specific term is not used. In 1869, American neurologist George Beard first described neurasthenia, or nervous exhaustion, in language that encompassed anxiety as a neurosis. However, it was Sigmund Freud who strongly suggested that anxiety be considered a separate disorder from other neuroses or psychoses (Berrios, 1996). Freud's conceptualization was foundational to the classification system found in the first *DSM*. In the remainder of this chapter, the particular histories of the classification of anxiety disorders are covered.

History of Anxiety Disorders Classification in the *DSM*

Though the term *anxiety disorders* did not appear in the official psychiatric nomenclature until the publication of *DSM–III* (APA, 1980), both *DSM–I* (APA, 1952) and *DSM–II* (APA, 1968) have included categories for anxiety-based problems. *DSM–I* included three conditions that were precursors to anxiety disorders as they are currently classified. The first was called *anxiety reaction*, which referred to a state of anxiety that is "diffuse and not restricted to definite situations or objects" (APA, 1952, p. 32). As is the case with *DSM–I*, overall, the definition was couched in psychoanalytic terms. For example, the definition of anxiety reaction stipulated that it could not be "controlled by any specific psychological defense mechanism as in other psychoneurotic reactions" (APA, 1952, p. 32). The second anxiety-based condition in *DSM–I* was called a *phobic reaction*, in which anxiety "becomes detached from a specific idea, object or situation in the daily life and is displaced to some symbolic idea or situation in the form of a specific neurotic fear... The patient attempts to control his anxiety by avoiding the phobic objects or situation" (APA, 1952, p. 33). The third category of anxiety-based conditions in *DSM–I* was *obsessive–compulsive reaction*, which was the forerunner to what is now known as obsessive–compulsive disorder (OCD), which is discussed later in this chapter. Anxiety reaction, phobic reaction, and obsessive–compulsive reaction were all examples of the broader classification known in *DSM–I* as *psychoneurotic disorders*. *DSM–I* also contained a condition called *gross stress reaction*, which overlapped most closely with what is now referred to as posttraumatic stress disorder (PTSD).

In *DSM–II*, the terminology was revised slightly, though the descriptions continued to be couched in psychoanalytic theory (APA, 1968). The term psychoneurotic disorders was replaced with the term *neuroses*. Anxiety reaction, phobic reaction, and obsessive–compulsive reaction were replaced with the terms *anxiety neurosis, phobic neurosis*, and *obsessive–compulsive neurosis*, respectively. Anxiety neurosis referred to "anxious over-concern extending to panic and frequently associated with somatic symptoms... not restricted to specific situations and objects" (APA, 1968, p. 39). Phobic neurosis was defined as "intense fear of an object or situation which the patient consciously recognizes as no real danger to him" (APA, 1968, p. 40). According to the definition, "phobias are generally attributed to fears displaced to the phobic object or situation from some other object of which the patient is unaware" (APA, 1968, p. 40). Obsessive–compulsive neurosis is described in more detail later in this chapter, in the section on OCD.

In 1970, the psychiatrist Isaac Marks published an influential paper on the classification of phobic disorders (Marks, 1970). In it, he proposed that phobias be classified into two broad categories, *phobias of external stimuli* and *phobias of internal stimuli*. Phobias of external stimuli were further divided into four main groups: (a) agoraphobia, (b) social phobias, (c) animal phobias, and (d) other specific phobias. Phobias of internal stimuli were further classified into (a) illness phobias and (b) obsessive phobias. Marks believed that agoraphobia was the most common phobia type, accounting for 60% of phobic patients at the Maudsley Hospital in London, where he was based. In 1980, *DSM–III* was published, incorporating much of Marks' proposed classification of phobic disorders.

With *DSM–III* (APA, 1980), came the current multiaxial approach to diagnosis. Anxiety disorders were diagnosed on Axis I (of the five axes) and were divided into two broad categories called *phobic disorders* (or phobic neuroses) and *anxiety states* (or anxiety neuroses), which were flowing directly out of the earlier categories in *DSM–I* and *DSM–II*. However, unlike the categories from the earlier editions of *DSM*, these broad categories were subdivided into particular disorders, criteria were much more explicit, and there was an effort to ensure that criteria were not based on any particular theoretical approach. Therefore, all references to psychoanalytic concepts (e.g., defense mechanisms) were avoided. Phobic disorders included (a) agoraphobia with panic attacks, (b) agoraphobia without panic attacks, (c) social phobia, and (5) simple phobia. Anxiety states included (a) panic disorder, (b) generalized anxiety disorder, (c) obsessive–compulsive disorder, and (d) posttraumatic stress disorder. In addition, there was a category called *atypical anxiety disorder,* reserved for anxiety disorders that did not meet criteria for any of the above specified conditions.

In *DSM–III–R* (APA, 1987), anxiety disorders were no longer classified into the broad categories of phobic disorders and anxiety states. In addition, atypical anxiety disorder was renamed *anxiety disorder not otherwise specified*. Otherwise, very little changed in the overall structure of the anxiety disorders section from *DSM–III* to *DSM–III–R*. However, there were important changes to the diagnostic criteria for specific disorders, as reviewed in the remaining sections of this chapter.

In the mid-1990s, the next major revision of the *DSM* was published (*DSM–IV*; APA, 1994). This event coincided with the publication of the *ICD-10* (WHO, 1992), and some efforts were made to minimize inconsistency between these two publications. In addition, more than ever before, there was an attempt to ensure that revisions were grounded in scientific research, rather than simply professional consensus. A series of position papers were published describing empirical advances in anxiety disorders research and advocating for particular changes stemming from these advances (see Widiger et al., 1996). Some of the most important changes included (a) removal of the panic attack definition from the criteria set for panic disorder and listing it separately (recognizing that panic attacks can occur across anxiety disorders and in the absence of an anxiety disorder); (b) removing agoraphobia from the list of codable disorders, and instead recognizing that it is a feature of panic disorder, though it can also occur in the absence of panic; and (c) addition of the new categories of acute stress disorder, anxiety disorder caused by a general medical condition, and substance-induced anxiety disorder. In 2000, the *DSM–IV* text revision was published. Though the diagnostic criteria for all disorders remained unchanged, the background text accompanying the description of each disorder was updated to reflect advances in knowledge.

Panic Disorder and Agoraphobia

DSM–IV–TR defines a *panic attack* as a discrete period of fear or discomfort that reaches a peak within 10 minutes and is accompanied by 4 out of 13 possible symptoms (mostly symptoms of arousal, such as increased heart rate, difficulty breathing, and dizziness). *Panic disorder* is a condition characterized by recurrent panic attacks, at least some of which occur unexpectedly, without any obvious situational trigger. To be diagnosed with panic disorder, an individual must experience a period lasting a month or longer in which he or she is concerned about having additional attacks, is worried about the consequences of the attacks, or changes his or her behavior because of the attacks (for example, beginning to rely on safety behaviors or avoid feared situations). *Agoraphobia* is frequently associated with panic disorder and is defined as fear or avoidance of situations in which escape might be difficult or help unavailable in the event of experiencing an unexpected panic attack or panic-like symptoms. In *DSM–IV–TR*, it is possible to receive a diagnosis of (a) panic disorder without agoraphobia, (b) panic disorder with agoraphobia, or (c) agoraphobia without history of panic disorder.

Although the terms panic attack and panic disorder were not introduced until the publication of *DSM–III*, the term agoraphobia was first used more than a century ago by Carl Friedrich Otto Westphal (1833–1890), a German psychiatrist and neurologist. In his classic account, Westphal (1871) described a series of patients who experienced panic in public squares and empty streets, on bridges, and in crowds. The symptoms were very similar to what people with panic disorder and agoraphobia often report today, including anticipatory anxiety and a fear of sudden incapacitation (Kuch & Swinson, 1992). The term "agoraphobia" was the result of combining the Greek words used to describe the open marketplace (*agora*) and fear (*phobos*).

Although the term agoraphobia has been around for some time, it did not come into frequent use until the past few decades and did not enter the formal psychiatric nomenclature until 1980, with the publication of *DSM–III*. Before the publication of *DSM–III*, an individual who might now receive a diagnosis of panic disorder without agoraphobia would likely have received a diagnosis of anxiety reaction *(DSM–I)* or anxiety neurosis *(DSM–II)*. The terms phobic reaction *(DSM–I)* and phobic neurosis *(DSM–II)* would likely have been used to describe what is now referred to as panic disorder with agoraphobia or agoraphobia without history of panic disorder.

In *DSM–III*, agoraphobia was defined as a fear of being alone or of being in public places from which escape might be difficult or in which help might be unavailable in the case of sudden incapacitation. Fears of experiencing panic attacks or panic-like symptoms were not part of the definition, as they are today. In addition, the relative importance of agoraphobia versus panic attacks in the conceptualization and classification of panic disorder and agoraphobia were exactly the opposite of what they are now. In *DSM–III*, people could receive a diagnosis of agoraphobia with panic attacks, agoraphobia without panic attacks, or panic disorder. For people with both panic attacks and agoraphobia, the agoraphobia was seen as the hallmark symptom, and panic attacks were viewed as a secondary feature. Furthermore, the fact that panic disorder was classified as an anxiety state and both agoraphobia without panic attacks and agoraphobia with panic attacks were classified as phobic states suggests that these conditions were viewed as conceptually unrelated. A diagnosis of panic disorder required at least three panic attacks during a 3-week period, and the definition of a panic attack was similar to what it is today, with some minor differences (e.g., four symptoms required out of a total of 12; no requirement for the attack to peak within 10 minutes).

By the time *DSM–III–R* was being published, studies were emerging to suggest that that panic disorder and agoraphobia were related, and that agoraphobia was probably secondary to a fear of having panic attacks for most individuals (Craske & Barlow, 1988; Turner, Williams, Beidel, & Mezzich, 1986). For example, agoraphobia usually begins after the first panic attack in clinical samples (e.g., Katerndahl & Realini, 1997). The location of the first panic attack (i.e., whether it occurs in a situation typically associated with agoraphobia) is predictive of whether an individual will develop panic disorder alone versus panic disorder with agoraphobia, and the expectation of having a panic attack has been found to predict subsequent avoidance (Craske, Rapee, & Barlow, 1988). With the publication of *DSM–III–R*, agoraphobia was seen as a feature of panic disorder, rather than the other way around. Individuals could receive a diagnosis of panic disorder with agoraphobia, panic disorder without agoraphobia, or agoraphobia without history of panic disorder. Additional changes in *DSM–III–R* included the following:

- A requirement of four panic attacks over 4 weeks or at least 1 attack followed by a month of persistent worry about having another attack (this is the first time that worry about having panic attacks was included in the *DSM* criteria for panic disorder)
- A requirement that 4 out of 13 symptoms be present and that at least some of the panic attacks reach a peak within 10 minutes (to distinguish panic attacks from periods of elevated anxiety that increase in intensity more gradually)
- Changing the definition of agoraphobia to specify that fear and avoidance must be related to anxiety over having a panic attack (panic disorder with agoraphobia) or developing a symptom that could be incapacitating or embarrassing, such as dizziness, depersonalization, etc. (agoraphobia without history of panic disorder)
- A number of exclusions (e.g., not caused by an organic factor) and specifiers (e.g., severity) were added to the criteria.

From *DSM–III–R* to *DSM–IV*, the most important changes in the criteria for panic disorder included the requirement that the individual have recurrent panic attacks (but without specifying a particular number), as well as the explicit requirement that there be a period of at least a month in which the individual is worried about having more attacks or about the consequences of the attacks, or in which the individual changes his or her behavior because of the attacks. The decision to remove any reference to a particular number of required panic attacks was based on findings that many individuals experience panic attacks infrequently, but still experience the other features of panic disorder (Ballenger & Fyer, 1996). Overall, the definition of panic disorder has changed very little from *DSM–III–R* to *DSM–IV*.

In *ICD-10* (WHO, 1992), the organization of panic disorder and agoraphobia is much more similar to the way these conditions are organized in *DSM–III* than more recent versions of *DSM*. Agoraphobia without panic disorder and agoraphobia with panic disorder are listed as examples of *phobic anxiety disorders*. Panic disorder (also called *episodic paroxysmal anxiety*) is listed as an *other anxiety disorder*. The definition of agoraphobia is based on the range of situations avoided (e.g., crowds, public places, etc.), and there is no mention that the avoidance must be caused by a fear of experiencing panic attacks, panic-like symptoms, or incapacitation. The *ICD-10* criteria for these disorders are much less detailed than they are for comparable disorders in recent editions of the *DSM*.

Specific Phobia

In *DSM–IV–TR*, the key feature of a specific phobia is excessive or unrealistic fear and/or avoidance of specific objects or situations, which is severe enough to cause clinically significant distress or functional impairment. Five types of specific phobia are specified in *DSM–IV–TR*: (a) *animal type* (e.g., fear of animals or insects), (b) *natural environment type* (e.g., fear of storms, heights, or water), (c) *blood-injection-injury type* (e.g., fear of seeing blood, receiving injections, undergoing invasive medical procedures), (d) *situational type* (e.g., fear of flying, driving, enclosed places), and (e) *other type* (fears cued by other specific stimuli; e.g., clowns, balloons).

As mentioned earlier, the term *phobia* is derived from the Greek word for fear, *phobos*, which was also the name of the ancient Greek god of terror (the son of mythological deities Ares and Aphrodite). Working with Ares (the god of war), Phobos was believed to strike fear and horror in one's enemies. Although descriptions of morbid fears go back at least to the time of Hippocrates (Marks, 1970), it was not until the 19th century that the term phobia was used in the clinical literature to describe unrealistic fears (e.g., Freud, 1895; Maudsley, 1879; Westphal, 1871).

The first 2 editions of the *DSM* each grouped all phobic disorders together. A specific phobia would have been called a phobic reaction in *DSM–I* and a phobic neurosis in *DSM–II*. With the publication of *DSM–III*, specific phobias were distinguished from other phobic disorders and were referred to as *simple phobias*. Simple phobia was considered a residual category of phobic disorder to be assigned when an individual had a persistent and irrational fear of a specific object or situations and when criteria for agoraphobia and social phobia were not met. To distinguish simple phobias from delusional fears, it was required that the individual recognize that his or her fear is excessive or unreasonable, a criterion that has continued to be included in every edition of *DSM* since *DSM–III*. Although *DSM–III* required that the individual experience distress associated with the phobia, there was no mention of functional impairment until subsequent editions of *DSM*.

DSM–III–R described the criteria for simple phobia in more detail than *DSM–III*, but the definition was otherwise very similar. In *DSM–III–R*, simple phobia was defined as a persistent fear of a circumscribed object or situation that was unrelated to the content of another anxiety disorder (e.g., fear of having panic attacks, fear of social situations, obsessions, trauma, etc.). The anxiety response had to occur immediately upon exposure to the feared object and had to be associated with either functional impairment or distress over having the fear.

In *DSM–IV*, the changes to this diagnosis were relatively minor. First, the category was renamed specific phobia to more accurately describe the focus of the fear. Second, the five specific phobia types were introduced based on research showing that these types vary with respect to age of onset, sex ratio, familial aggregation, physiological response (e.g., panic attacks, fainting), their relationship with agoraphobia, comorbidity, and groupings among phobias in factor analytic studies (Antony & Barlow, 2002; Craske et al., 1996). Finally, the diagnosis was now permitted in the presence of unexpected panic attacks, as long as the attacks were confined to the phobic object or situation. In *ICD-10*, this category is referred to as *specific (isolated) phobia*. The criteria are similar to those in *DSM–IV*, though they are described in less detail.

There has been little discussion in the literature about possible changes to Specific Phobia criteria in *DSM–V*. However, there are reasons to consider a number of changes. For example, there are a significant number of individuals whose symptoms meet all of the diagnostic criteria for specific phobia except for insight into the excessiveness of their fear, and for whom phobic beliefs are not of a delusional intensity (Jones & Menzies, 2000; Menzies & Clarke, 1995; Menzies, Harris, & Jones, 1998). Based on these findings, one might argue that the requirement for recognition that the fear is excessive be removed or replaced with a requirement that the fear not be of a delusional intensity. In addition, we have argued elsewhere (Antony, Brown, & Barlow, 1997) that the specific phobia types be removed from *DSM* because of inconsistencies among the data that are often cited to support these types, practical challenges in assigning phobias to types (e.g., is a fear of the dark a natural environment fear or a situational fear?), and because specifying the specific phobia type (e.g., specific phobia, natural environment type) is less descriptive than simply naming the phobia (e.g., specific phobia of storms). It remains to be seen what changes will happen to the criteria for Specific Phobia in *DSM–V*, if any.

Social Anxiety Disorder

Social anxiety disorder is a condition characterized by a persistent and extreme fear of one or more social or performance situations that cause clinically significant distress or functional impairment. Examples of situations that are often feared by individuals with social anxiety disorder include dating, meeting new people, conversations, being the center of attention, public speaking, and talking to people in authority. In *DSM–IV–TR*, the official name of this disorder is *social phobia*, and the name *social anxiety disorder* appears in parentheses. However, in recent years, the name social anxiety disorder has gained popularity. This change appeared to coincide with the U.S. Food and Drug Administration approving several medications for the treatment of social anxiety disorder and for pharmaceutical companies to use the term social anxiety disorder almost exclusively in their marketing, scientific publications describing clinical trials, and continuing medical education. In addition, a group of prominent social anxiety researchers (including a mix of psychologists and psychiatrists) published a letter in the *Archives of General Psychiatry* calling for social anxiety disorder to be the primary name for this condition, arguing that, compared to the name social phobia, the name social anxiety disorder more strongly conveys a sense of pervasiveness and impairment, and better differentiates the disorder from specific phobia (Liebowitz, Heimberg, Fresco, Travers, & Stein, 2000).

Social anxiety disorder was first introduced (under the name social phobia) in the official psychiatric nomenclature with the publication of *DSM–III*, following Isaac Marks' classic article in which he identified social phobia as a unique phobic disorder (Marks, 1970). Before *DSM–III*, social anxiety disorder would have been called a phobic reaction in *DSM–I* and a phobic neurosis in *DSM–II*. Although it was not included in any formal nomenclature until recently, there were published reports in the clinical literature on individuals with excessive social anxiety for at least a century, including books by French authors Dugas (1898) and Hartenberg (1901). Of these two books, the better known one was *Les Timides et la Timidité* by French psychiatrist Paul Hartenberg (1871–1949). In this book, Hartenberg described a disorder that corresponds very closely to the current *DSM–IV* description of social anxiety disorder (Fairbrother, 2002). For Hartenberg, social phobia was comprised of two basic emotions: fear and shame. This is not unlike the more modern descriptions in *DSM*, which emphasize the roles of fear, humiliation, and embarrassment. Hartenberg also recognized that exposure-based therapy is an effective method effective for overcoming social anxiety.

In *DSM–III*, the definition of social phobia was similar to what it is today. The core feature was a "persistent, irrational fear of, and a compelling desire to avoid, a situation in which the individual is exposed to possible scrutiny by others and fears that he or she may act in a way that will be humiliating or embarrassing" (APA, 1980, p. 228). Criteria also required that individuals be distressed by the disturbance and that they recognize that the fear is excessive or unreasonable. Finally, the fear could not be caused by another mental disorder. Though the disorder was introduced in 1980, it took a number of years before researchers started paying attention to this common condition. As recently as 1985, social phobia was referred to as a "neglected anxiety disorder" and there was very little known about the nature and treatment of social anxiety (Liebowitz, Gorman, Fyer, & Klein, 1985).

The changes to the criteria for social phobia in *DSM–III–R* paralleled those for specific phobia. During some phase of the disturbance, the anxiety response had to occur immediately upon exposure to the feared situations and had to be associated with either functional impairment or distress over having the fear. Additional criteria were included to help distinguish social phobia from other *DSM–III–R* conditions. For example, a diagnosis of social phobia could not be made if the fear was primarily of having a panic attack. In addition, the term *generalized* was now used to describe individuals who experienced anxiety in most social situations. This was added in the context of growing evidence concerning differences between generalized versus nongeneralized forms of the disorder, such as discrete fears of public speaking. For example, individuals with generalized social phobia tend to experience greater levels of functional impairment and have higher levels of anxiety and depression than individuals with discrete social fears (for a review, see Schneier et al., 1996).

In *DSM–IV*, the name social anxiety disorder was added (in parentheses), but the description of the disorder otherwise changed very little. The most important changes focused on further delineating the boundaries between social phobia and other conditions, such as avoidant personality disorder, generalized anxiety disorder, and panic disorder. For example, in *DSM–IV*, a diagnosis of social anxiety disorder is permitted even if the fear was focused on having panic attacks, as long as the panic attacks were confined to social situations. In *ICD-10*, the criteria for social phobia are similar to those in *DSM–IV*, though they are less detailed.

Obsessive–Compulsive Disorder

In *DSM–IV–TR*, OCD is defined by the presence of obsessions or compulsions. Obsessions are recurrent and persistent thoughts, impulses, or images that are experienced as intrusive, inappropriate, and distressing. The individual attempts to ignore or suppress the obsessions or to neutralize them with another thought or action. In addition, the obsession is not simply a worry about real-life problems, and the individual recognizes that the obsession is a product of his or her own mind. Compulsions are repetitive behaviors or mental acts that are performed in response to an obsession or according to rigid rules. Compulsions are meant to reduce distress or to prevent some dreaded event from occurring. The individual recognizes that the obsessions and compulsions are excessive, and these symptoms cause clinically significant distress or impairment. Finally, *DSM–IV–TR* requires that the symptoms of OCD are not better accounted for by another disorder.

As far back as medieval times, terms such as *obsessio, compulsio, impulsio,* and *scrupulus* have been used by the medical community to describe OCD-like phenomena (Berrios, 1989). Throughout the 19th century, several authors published detailed descriptions of individuals suffering from OCD (Berrios). For example, Jean-Etienne Esquirol (1772–1840) described the case of a merchant who feared that she would do wrong to others. Specifically, she feared that she might give too little change to customers and felt compelled to shake her hands vigorously to make sure that nothing stuck to her fingers that did not belong to her (Esquirol, 1838, as cited in Stone, 2002).

In *DSM–I, obsessive–compulsive reaction* was included as one of the psychoneurotic disorders. This condition was described as anxiety that is "associated with the persistence of unwanted ideas and of repetitive impulses to perform acts which may be considered morbid by the patient. The patient himself may regard his ideas and behaviors as unreasonable, but nevertheless is compelled to carry out his rituals" (APA, 1952, p. 33). Examples of symptoms listed in *DSM–I* include touching, counting, ceremonials, hand washing, and thoughts (often accompanied by a compulsion to repeat some action).

In *DSM–II*, the name of the disorder was changed to *obsessive–compulsive neurosis*, and it was included in the broader category of neuroses. The disorder was described as the "persistent intrusion of unwanted thoughts, urges, or actions that the patient is unable to stop. The thoughts may consist of single words or ideas, ruminations, or trains of thought often perceived by the patient as nonsensical" (APA, 1968, p. 40). Hand washing was provided as an example of a repeated action that may occur in people with this disorder. Although the wording was different, the condition described in *DSM–II* was similar to that in *DSM–I*, and the amount of detail in the description was similar (a total of eight lines, to be exact).

In *DSM–III*, obsessions and compulsions were clearly defined for the first time, and the definitions were quite similar to what they are today in *DSM–IV*. In addition, clinically significant distress or impairment was necessary for the diagnosis. The criteria also stipulated that the symptoms could not be caused by another mental disorder. The criteria for OCD changed very little from *DSM–III* to *DSM–III–R*, and again, very little with the publication of *DSM–IV*. The most important changes in *DSM–IV* were the mention of mental/covert compulsions, specification of the boundary between obsessions and worry, and addition of the "with poor insight" specifier to identify individuals who do not recognize their obsessions or compulsions as unreasonable or excessive.

There are several important differences in the definition of OCD in *ICD-10* from the various editions of the *DSM*. First, *ICD* does not list OCD as an anxiety disorder; rather, it is listed as a separate category. Second, the symptoms are required to be present most days for at least 2 weeks, whereas no version of the *DSM* has ever stipulated a required duration of symptoms. In addition, *ICD* specifies that the thought of carrying out the act must not be pleasurable (this criterion is meant to differentiate obsessions from pleasurable fantasies). Finally, the definitions of obsession and compulsion in *ICD-10* are much less detailed than they are in *DSM*.

Generalized Anxiety Disorder

The hallmark feature of *generalized anxiety disorder* (GAD) as defined by *DSM–IV–TR* is worry that is *excessive* and perceived by the individual as *uncontrollable*. Current criteria stipulate that the worry should be about a number of subjects and be present more days than not for a minimum duration of 6 months. In GAD, anxiety and worry are accompanied by the following six symptoms: (a) restlessness or feeling "keyed up" or "on edge," (b) easy fatigability, (c) concentration difficulties, (d) irritability, (e) muscle tension, and (f) sleep disturbance. Of the associated symptoms, at least three are required for the diagnosis, "with at least some" present more days than not. In GAD, the worry and associated symptoms are not restricted to features of another Axis I condition, cause clinically significant distress and functional impairment, and are not caused by the effects of a substance or to a general medical condition.

Although the diagnosis of GAD was not included in the first 2 editions of *DSM*, the categories of anxiety reaction *(DSM–I)* and anxiety neurosis *(DSM–II)* would likely have captured what is now known as GAD. GAD first appeared in the third edition of the *DSM* as a *residual diagnosis* intended for individuals with a presenting complaint of persistent anxiety of a nonspecific (i.e., generalized) nature. Symptoms from three of four of the following categories were required: (a) *motor tension* (e.g., eye twitch, muscle aches), (b) *autonomic hyperactivity* (e.g., sweating, heart pounding), (c) *apprehensive expectation* (worry, anticipation of a negative outcome), and (d) *vigilance and scanning* (e.g., irritability, insomnia). In addition, a minimum duration of 1 month was required for the diagnosis. A GAD diagnosis was assigned when an individual's symptoms were judged not to be consistent with another psychological disorder such as a depressive disorder or schizophrenia. At the time of *DSM–III*, functional impairment was considered "rarely more than mild." Problems associated with GAD that was defined by *DSM–III* were the low specificity of its symptoms and its low diagnostic reliability (Di Nardo, O'Brien, Barlow, Waddell, & Blanchard, 1983). In addition, clinicians found it difficult to distinguish GAD from transient reactions to life stressors (Barlow & Wincze, 1998; Breslau & Davis, 1985; Spitzer & Williams, 1984). It was also hypothesized that the 1-month duration criterion was an explanatory factor in the unusually high lifetime prevalence rate of GAD (Breslau & Davis).

Clinical observations and empirical evidence contributed to several important changes to the GAD criteria in *DSM–III–R*. The cardinal feature of GAD that is defined by *DSM–III–R* became *anxiety and worry* (apprehensive expectation). To better distinguish GAD from other forms of anxiety, the revised criteria stipulated that the anxiety and worry be *unrealistic or excessive* and focus on two or more life circumstances. In addition, the minimum duration was extended from 1 month to 6 months based in part on research by Breslau and Davis (1985) (see Barlow & Wincze, 1998). In their community sample, they found that increasing the duration criterion by 5 months led to a reduction in 6-month and lifetime prevalence estimates to rates that were more comparable to those of other psychological disorders. The independence of GAD from other disorders was reflected in criteria that required that the worry should not pertain to aspects of another disorder (e.g., the anxiety and worry is not about having a panic attack) and that it should not occur exclusively during the course of a mood disorder or a psychotic disorder. Three symptom clusters—motor tension, autonomic hyperactivity, and vigilance and scanning—were retained with the following changes: (a) the symptoms were designated as associated features of GAD, not primary features, as in *DSM–III* and (b) the presence of a minimum of six associated symptoms was required, excluding symptoms that are typically a part of the experience of panic attacks.

The *DSM–III–R* definition raised the status of GAD from residual diagnosis to full-fledged anxiety disorder and gave rise to a marked increase in research on the phenomenology of GAD-type worry. The frequency, temporal characteristics, form, and content of worry were examined extensively (e.g., Borkovec, Shadick, & Hopkins, 1991; Freeston, Dugas, & Ladouceur, 1996; Tallis, Davey, & Capuzzo, 1994). In addition, cognitive–behavioral treatments designed to reduce the frequency and intensity of the condition's main symptom—worry—were developed, which represented a departure from previous treatments that consisted of strategies aimed at reducing tension and anxiety. Nonetheless, problems with the revised definition were noted. Diagnostic agreement was poor to good at best (Di Nardo, Moras, Barlow, Rapee, & Brown, 1993). Furthermore, comorbidity with other forms of anxiety and with mood disorders was exceedingly high (Brown, Di Nardo, Lehman, & Campbell, 2001). Taken collectively, these problems were interpreted as indicators of poor discriminant validity and there was discussion of omitting GAD altogether from subsequent revisions of the *DSM* (Brown et al.).

In an attempt to sharpen the boundaries between GAD and other disorders, the diagnostic criteria were revised for *DSM–IV* (Brown et al., 2001). The surge of research on worry in the 1980s had a significant impact on the revision. Worry was retained as the hallmark feature of GAD. The requirement that the worry must be excessive was also retained but the one stipulating that it should be unrealistic was eliminated. The removal of the "unrealistic" criterion and retention of the "excessive" criterion were based in part on research showing that worry over minor matters distinguishes individuals with GAD from individuals with other anxiety disorders (Craske, Rapee, Jackel, & Barlow, 1989). Based on empirical findings (Abel & Borkovec, 1995; Borkovec, Robinson, Pruzinsky, & DePree, 1983; Craske et al., 1989), the requirement that the worry must be perceived by the individual as uncontrollable was added, as this was shown to be a factor that distinguished clinically significant worry from normative worry. The 6-month duration criterion was retained. The list of associated symptoms was reduced from 18 to 6 based on work by Marten and colleagues (1993), which showed that restlessness or feeling "keyed up or on edge", fatigue, concentration difficulties, irritability, muscle tension, and sleep disturbance were the symptoms that were the most commonly endorsed by individuals with *DSM–III–R* GAD. Symptoms of autonomic hyperarousal were discarded in light of empirical evidence indicating that individuals with GAD endorse these symptoms at a lower rate than symptoms of motor tension and vigilance and scanning (Brown, Marten, & Barlow, 1995). In addition, the autonomic symptoms overlapped considerably with symptoms of panic disorder (Brown et al., 1995). The associated symptom criterion was modified to include a requirement that 3 out of 6 symptoms be present. Brown et al. (1995) expressed concern that the "3 out of 6" criterion was not empirically driven. Research employing the *DSM–IV* criteria substantiated this concern by indicating that the criterion was associated with a low level of specificity, as a very high percentage of individuals with other forms of anxiety endorsed a sufficient number of symptoms to meet the criterion (Brown et al., 1995). Given the problems associated with earlier definitions of GAD, it was particularly important to determine what, if any, impact the modifications had on diagnostic agreement. Brown et al. (2001) reported findings indicating that GAD that was defined by *DSM–IV* was associated with improved reliability; however, their findings also suggested that the overlap with major depressive disorder was still problematic. Although the current *DSM–IV* definition of GAD represents an improvement compared to its predecessors, several features of the diagnosis continue to incite debate, in particular, the 6-month duration criterion (e.g., Kessler et al., 2005) and the "excessive" criterion (Ruscio et al., 2005).

The *ICD-10* definition of GAD is closely aligned with the *DSM–III* definition of the disorder. The critical feature of GAD that is defined by *ICD-10* is *generalized and persistent (i.e., "free-floating") anxiety*. Three symptom clusters are described. The *apprehension* cluster consists of symptoms that correspond with *DSM–III* apprehensive expectation (worry) and vigilance and scanning (difficulty concentrating and feeling "on edge"). The *motor tension* cluster consists of four symptoms: restless fidgeting, tension headaches, trembling, and inability to relax. With the exception of headaches, all of these symptoms also appear in *DSM–III* under the same header. Finally, the *autonomic overactivity* cluster is consistent with *DSM–III* autonomic hyperactivity. The *ICD-10* requires that the anxiety symptoms be present "most days for at least several weeks at a time, and usually for several months" (WHO, 1992, p. 140). There are two noteworthy differences between the *ICD-10* and *DSM–III* criteria. Although the primary criterion of both *ICD-10* and *DSM–III* GAD is generalized and persistent anxiety, worry is also a part of the *ICD-10* definition. In addition, in *ICD-10*, GAD cannot be diagnosed in the presence of a depressive episode, phobic anxiety disorder, panic disorder, or obsessive–compulsive. This requirement is limited to mood disorders and schizophrenia in the *DSM–III*.

Posttraumatic Stress Disorder and Acute Stress Disorder

The diagnosis of PTSD that is defined by *DSM–IV–TR* requires the individual to have been exposed to an extreme stressor in which he or she (a) "experienced, witnessed, or was confronted with an event or events that involved actual or threatened death or serious injury or a threat to the physical integrity of the self or others" and (b) "responded with intense fear, helplessness, or horror" (criterion A).

The symptoms of PTSD are organized into three clusters and the diagnosis requires the presence of symptoms from all three categories. Criterion B stipulates that *at least one* of the following symptoms of persistent reexperiencing must be present: (a) intrusive recollections, (b) nightmares, (c) acting or feeling as if the trauma were recurring, (d) intense psychological distress upon exposure to internal or external cues that represent or are similar to aspects of the trauma, and (e) physiological reactivity upon exposure to external or internal triggers that represent or are similar to aspects of the trauma. Criterion C requires the presence of *at least three* symptoms of persistent avoidance and numbing of responsiveness, not present before the trauma. These include (a) efforts to avoid thoughts, feelings, or discussions of the trauma; (b) efforts to avoid activities, places, or people that trigger memories of the trauma; (c) difficulty recalling aspects of the trauma; (d) an important reduction in interest or participation in activities; (e) feelings of detachment or disengagement from others; (f) restricted emotional range; and (g) a sense of a foreshortened future. Finally, criterion D requires the presence of *at least two* symptoms of hyperarousal, not present before the trauma. These include (a) sleep disturbance, (b) irritability or anger outbursts, (c) concentration difficulties, (e) hypervigilance, and (e) exaggerated startle response.

In order to receive a diagnosis of PTSD, symptoms must be present for more than 1 month and lead to significant distress and functional impairment. Acute PTSD has a duration of less than 3 months and chronic PTSD has a duration of more than 3 months. The current criteria also include a delayed onset specifier for cases in which the onset of PTSD occurs 6 months after exposure to the trauma.

Prior to its entry into the official nomenclature, PTSD was conceptualized as a war-induced syndrome. Charcot (1825–1893) used the terms *névrose traumatique* and *hystérie traumatique* to describe the constellation of symptoms observed in men who had served in the Franco-Prussian War. The term *shell shock* was popularized in the early 1900s and was eventually replaced with *war neurosis* (Jones & Wessely, 2007). Although PTSD first appeared as a formal diagnosis in *DSM–III*, there are precursors to the disorder in the preceding editions (Jones & Wessely). In *DSM–I*, *gross stress reaction* described reactions to extreme stressors and was conceptualized as a *transient situational personality disorder*. In *DSM–II*, the term *transient situational disturbance* was used to describe responses to extreme stressors. Jones and Wessely note that the introduction of PTSD in *DSM–III* was heavily influenced by the sociopolitical climate in the United States as a result of the Vietnam War, making it "one of the few politically-driven psychiatric diagnoses."

Overall, changes to the criteria across editions of the *DSM* have been minimal. The prerequisite for the *DSM–III* diagnosis was exposure to an extreme stressor, defined as an event that would "evoke significant symptoms of distress in almost everyone" (APA, 1980, p. 238). The definition also emphasized that the stressor be an event that is outside the range of stressful experiences that are more commonly encountered, such as chronic illness and marital conflict. Sexual assault, combat, natural disasters, car accidents, and torture were listed as examples of traumatic events. In *DSM–III–R*, this criterion is similar with a more explicit suggestion that the trauma need not have been experienced directly (i.e., witnessing a traumatic event was sufficient). In the text of *DSM–III–R*, subjective responses to trauma (intense fear, terror, and helplessness; APA, 1987, p. 247) are described but are not integrated in the actual diagnostic criteria; whereas in *DSM–IV*, subjective responses are part of criterion A.

Similar to subsequent editions, *DSM–III* required the presence of symptoms from three categories. Criterion B (reexperiencing) is similar to its *DSM–III–R* and *DSM–IV* counterparts. Criterion C referred to symptoms that are consistent with numbing of responsiveness only. Criterion D was more heterogeneous than in subsequent editions and consisted of symptoms of increased arousal, as well as worsening of symptoms upon exposure to trauma cues, avoidance of activities that trigger memories of the trauma, and guilt about surviving the trauma or about behaviors that were engaged in for survival. In the *DSM–III–R*, the list of symptoms increased to 17 (from 12 in the *DSM–III*) and was organized into three clusters. Symptoms of reexperiencing (criterion B) were similar to ones described in *DSM–III* and also included intense psychological distress at exposure to cues resembling the trauma. Criterion C was expanded to encompass symptoms of persistent avoidance in addition to symptoms consistent with numbing of general responsiveness. Persistent avoidance referred not only to avoidance of external reminders of trauma, but also *internal* cues (e.g., thoughts, feelings). Psychogenic amnesia and a sense of a foreshortened future were added to this cluster of symptoms. Criterion D was revised to focus on symptoms of increased arousal. The symptoms are identical to those that appear as part of criterion D in the *DSM–IV* with the exception of physiological reactivity upon exposure to cues of the trauma, which was shifted from criterion D in *DSM–III–R* to criterion B in *DSM–IV*. *DSM–III–R* is similar to *DSM–IV* in that criteria in both editions require the presence of at least one symptom of reexperiencing, three symptoms of avoidance, and two symptoms of arousal.

Interestingly, PTSD that was defined by *DSM–III* had no required minimum duration and the acute specifier applied to cases of PTSD with an onset occurring within 6 months of exposure to the trauma and a duration of less than 6 months.

The delayed specifier applied to cases of PTSD with an onset beyond 6 months after exposure to the trauma and a duration of more than 6 months. The 1-month minimum duration criterion was added in *DSM–III–R* and was retained in *DSM–IV*. In addition, the acute and chronic course specifiers were added to the *DSM–IV* criteria.

A new category, acute stress disorder, was introduced in *DSM–IV*. The diagnosis captures responses to trauma that have a duration between 2 days and 4 weeks, with an onset occurring within 4 weeks of exposure to the event. The main criterion is the same as for PTSD that is defined by *DSM–IV* and the diagnosis requires the presence of symptoms of reexperiencing, persistent avoidance, and hyperarousal. Unlike the PTSD diagnosis, dissociative symptoms such as derealization and depersonalization are emphasized in acute stress disorder.

The main criterion of *ICD-10* PTSD is exposure to (experiencing and/or witnessing) a "stressful event or situation of an exceptionally threatening or catastrophic nature, which is likely to cause pervasive distress in almost anyone" (WHO, 1992, p. 147). The symptoms are not organized into specific clusters as in the *DSM*, but are similar. In addition, the minimum number of symptoms required for the diagnosis is not specified in the *ICD-10*. The *ICD-10* criteria for PTSD differ from the *DSM-IV* criteria in that they apply only to forms of the disorder that have an onset within 6 months from the time of exposure to the trauma. The diagnostic guidelines state that a "probable" diagnosis of delayed PTSD can be assigned only if the individual reports the required symptoms and the symptoms cannot be better accounted for by another disorder (e.g., obsessive–compulsive disorder).

Looking Ahead

Before long, *DSM–IV–TR* and *ICD-10* will be history. *DSM–V* and *ICD-11* are both expected to be published in the year 2011. It is too early to know how the anxiety disorders will change in these new editions. However, there have been some discussions in the literature about possible revisions. For example, there have been suggestions that OCD no longer be grouped with the anxiety disorders, and that instead it be grouped with other conditions often referred to as obsessive–compulsive spectrum disorders (e.g., tic disorders, hypochondriasis, body dysmorphic disorder; Bartz & Hollander, 2006). A recent survey of OCD experts (Mataix-Cols, Pertusa, & Leckman, 2007) found broad support for this proposal, particularly among psychiatrists (as opposed to psychologists and other professional groups). In addition, psychologist David Watson and colleagues (Gamez, Watson, & Doebbeling, 2007; Slade & Watson, 2006) have argued based on factor analytic studies, that GAD and PTSD have more in common with depression than they do with other anxiety disorders, and that perhaps these should be grouped together under the umbrella of "distress disorders," leaving the remaining anxiety disorders to be grouped together as "fear disorders." If *DSM-V* does include three main types of anxiety-based disorders (distress disorders, fear disorders, obsessive–compulsive based disorders), our diagnostic nomenclature will have come full circle with respect to basic structure (recall that *DSM-I* included anxiety reaction, phobic reaction, and obsessive-compulsive reaction). However, this time, the structure would be based on empirical evidence.

References

Abel, J. L., & Borkovec, T. D. (1995). Generalizability of DSM-III-R generalized anxiety disorders to proposed DSM-IV criteria and cross-validation of proposed changes. *Journal of Anxiety Disorders, 9,* 303–315.

American Psychiatric Association. (1952). *Diagnostic and statistical manual of mental disorders.* Washington, DC: Author.

American Psychiatric Association. (1968). *Diagnostic and statistical manual of mental disorders,* (2nd ed.). Washington, DC: Author.

American Psychiatric Association (1980). *Diagnostic and statistical manual of mental disorders,* (3rd ed.). Washington, DC: Author.

American Psychiatric Association (1987). *Diagnostic and statistical manual of mental disorders,* (3rd ed., revised). Washington, DC: Author.

American Psychiatric Association (1994). *Diagnostic and statistical manual of mental disorders,* (4th ed.). Washington, DC: Author.

American Psychiatric Association (2000). *Diagnostic and statistical manual of mental disorders,* (4th ed., text revision). Washington, DC: Author.

Antony, M. M., & Barlow, D. H. (2002). Specific phobia. In D. H. Barlow (Ed.), *Anxiety and its disorders: The nature and treatment of anxiety and panic* (2nd ed., pp. 380–417). New York: Guilford Press.

Antony, M. M., Brown, T. A., & Barlow, D. H. (1997). Heterogeneity among specific phobia types in DSM-IV. *Behaviour Research and Therapy, 35,* 1089–1100.

Baker, R. R., & Pickren, W. E. (2007). *Psychology and the Department of Veterans Affairs: A historical analysis of training, research, practice, and advocacy.* Washington, DC: American Psychological Association.

Ballenger, J.C., & Fyer, A.J. (1996). Panic disorder and agoraphobia. In T.A Widiger, A.J. Frances, H.A. Pincus, R. Ross, M.B. First, & W.W. Davis (Eds.), *DSM-IV sourcebook,* (Vol. 2, pp. 411–471). Washington, DC: American Psychiatric Association.

Barlow, D. H., & Wincze, J. (1998). DSM-IV and beyond: What is generalized anxiety disorder? *Acta Psychiatrica Scandinavica Supplementum, 98,* 23–29.

Bartz, J. A., & Hollander, E. (2006). Is obsessive–compulsive disorder an anxiety disorder? *Progress in Neuropsychopharmacology and Biological Psychiatry, 30,* 338–352.

Berrios, G.E. (1989). Obsessive–compulsive disorder: Its conceptual history in France during the 19th century. *Comprehensive Psychiatry, 30,* 283–295.

Berrios, G. E. (1996). *The history of mental symptoms: Descriptive psychopathology since the nineteenth century.* New York: Cambridge University Press.

Borkovec, T. D., Robinson, E., Pruzinsky, T., & DePree, J. A. (1983). Preliminary exploration of worry: Some characteristics and processes. *Behaviour Research and Therapy, 21,* 9–16.

Borkovec, T. D., Shadick, R., & Hopkins, M. (1991). The nature of normal and pathological worry. In R. M. Rapee & D. H. Barlow (Eds.), *Chronic anxiety: Generalized anxiety disorder and mixed anxiety-depression* (pp. 29–51). New York: Guilford Press.

Breslau, N., & Davis, G. C. (1985). DSM-III generalized anxiety disorder: Investigation of more stringent criteria. *Psychiatry Research, 14,* 231–238.

Brown, T. A., Di Nardo, P. A., Lehman, C. L., & Campbell, L. A. (2001). Reliability of DSM-IV anxiety and mood disorders: Implications for the classification of emotional disorders. *Journal of Abnormal Psychology, 110,* 49–58.

Brown, T. A., Marten, P. A., & Barlow, D. H. (1995). Discriminant validity of the symptoms constituting the DSM-III-R and DSM-IV associated symptom criterion of generalized anxiety disorder. *Journal of Anxiety Disorders, 9,* 317–328.

Burnham, J. C. (1967). *Psychoanalysis and American medicine: 1894–1918.* New York: International Universities.

Craske, M. G., & Barlow, D. H. (1988). A review of the relationship between panic and avoidance. *Clinical Psychology Review, 8,* 667–685.

Craske, M. G., Barlow, D. H., Clark, D. M., Curtis, G. C., Hill, E. M., Himle, J. A., et al. (1996). Specific (simple) phobia. In T. A Widiger, A. J. Frances, H.A. Pincus, R. Ross, M. B. First, & W. W. Davis (Eds.), *DSM-IV sourcebook* (Vol. 2 pp. 473–506). Washington, DC: American Psychiatric Association.

Craske, M. G., Rapee, R. M., & Barlow, D. H. (1988). The significance of panic-expectancy for individual patterns of avoidance. *Behavior Therapy, 19,* 577–592.

Craske, M. G., Rapee, R. M., Jackel, L., & Barlow, D. H. (1989). Qualitative dimensions of worry in DSM-III-R generalized anxiety disorder. *Journal of Anxiety Disorders, 9,* 317–328.

Cushman, P. (1995). *Constructing the self, constructing America: A cultural history of psychotherapy.* New York: Addison-Wesley.

Dewsbury, D.A. (1991). "Psychobiology." *American Psychologist, 46,* 198–205.

Di Nardo, P.A., Moras, K., Barlow, D.H., Rapee, R.M., & Brown, T.A. (1993). Reliability of the DSM-III-R anxiety disorder categories using the Anxiety Disorders Interview Schedule-Revised. *Archives of General Psychiatry, 50,* 251–256.

Di Nardo, P.A., O'Brien, G.T., Barlow, D.H., Waddell, M.T., & Blanchard, E.B. (1983). Reliability of DSM-III anxiety disorder categories using a new structured interview. *Archives of General Psychiatry, 40,* 1070–1074.

Dugas, L. (1898). *Timidité.* Paris: Alcan.

Esquirol, E. (1838). *Des maladies mentales considerées sous les rapports medical, hygienique et medico-legal.* Paris: J.B. Bailliére.

Fairbrother, N. (2002). The treatment of social phobia – 100 years ago. *Behaviour Research and Therapy, 40,* 1291–1304.

Feighner, J. P., Robins, E., Guze, S. B., Woodruff, R. A., Jr., Winokur, G., & Munoz, R. (1972). Diagnostic criteria for use in psychiatric research. *Archives of General Psychiatry, 26,* 57–63.

Freeston, M. H., Dugas, M. J., & Ladouceur, R. (1996). Thoughts, images, worry, and anxiety. *Cognitive Therapy and Research, 20,* 265–273.

Freud, S. (1895). *Review of Neurology 3.* (Translated in *Collected Papers.* Vol. 1, p. 128. London: International Psychoanalytic Press, 1924).

Friedman, L. J. (1990). *Menninger: The family and the clinic.* New York: Alfred Knopf.

Gamez, W., Watson, D., & Doebbeling, B. N. (2007). Abnormal personality and the mood and anxiety disorders: implications for structural models of anxiety and depression. *Journal of Anxiety Disorders, 21,* 526–539.

Grob, G. N. (1983). *Mental illness and American society, 1875–1940.* Princeton, NJ: Princeton University Press.

Grob, G. N. (1991a). *From asylum to community: Mental health policy in modern America.* Princeton, NJ: Princeton University Press.

Grob, G. N. (1991b). Origins of DSM-I: A study in appearance and reality. *American Journal of Psychiatry, 148,* 421–431.

Hale, N.G. Jr. (1971). *Freud and the Americans: The beginnings of psychoanalysis in the United States, 1876–1917.* New York: Oxford University Press.

Hale, N.G. Jr. (1995). *The rise and crisis of psychoanalysis in the United States. Freud and the Americans, 1917–1985.* New York: Oxford University Press.

Hartenberg, P. (1901). *Les timides et la timidité [The socially anxious and social anxiety].* Paris: Félix Alcan.

Herman, E. (1995). *The romance of American psychology: Political culture in the age of experts.* Berkeley, CA: University of California Press.

Horwitz, A. V. (2002). *Creating mental illness.* Chicago: University of Chicago Press.

Jones, E., & Wessely, S. (2007). A paradigm shift in the conceptualization of psychological trauma in the 20th century. *Journal of Anxiety Disorders, 21,* 164–175.

Jones, M. K., & Menzies, R. G. (2000). Danger expectancies, self-efficacy and insight in spider phobia. *Behaviour Research and Therapy, 38,* 585–600.

Katerndahl, D. A., & Realini, J. P. (1997). Quality of life and panic-related work disability in subjects with infrequent panic and panic disorder. *Journal of Clinical Psychiatry, 58,* 153–158.

Kessler, R. C., Brandenburg, N., Lane, M., Roy-Byrne, P., Stang, P. D., Stein, D. J., et al. (2005). Rethinking the duration requirement for generalized anxiety disorder: Evidence from the National Comorbidity Survey Replication. *Psychological Medicine, 35,* 1073–1082.

Krahl, A., Schifferdecker, M., & Beveridge A. (1998). Carl Wernicke and the concept of 'elementary symptom.' *History of Psychiatry, 9,* 503–508.

Kuch, K., & Swinson, R. P. (1992). Agoraphobia: What Westphal really said. *Canadian Journal of Psychiatry, 37,* 133–136.

Leys, R. (1991). Types of one: Adolf Meyer's life chart and the representation of individuality. *Representations, 34,* 1–28.

Liebowitz, M. R., Gorman, J. M., Fyer, A. J., & Klein, D. F. (1985). Social phobia: Review of a neglected anxiety disorder. *Archives of General Psychiatry, 42,* 729–736.

Liebowitz, M. R., Heimberg, R. G., Fresco, D. M., Travers, J., & Stein, M. B. (2000). Social phobia or social anxiety disorder: What's in a name? *Archives of General Psychiatry, 57,* 191–192.

Marks, I. M. (1970). The classification of phobic disorders. *British Journal of Psychiatry, 116,* 377–386.

Marten, P. A., Brown, T. A., Barlow, D. H., Borkovec, T. D., Shear, M. K., & Lydiard, R. B. (1993). Evaluation of the ratings comprising the associated symptom criterion of DSM-III-R generalized anxiety disorder. *Journal of Nervous and Mental Disease, 181,* 676–682.

Mataix-Cols, D., Pertusa, A., & Leckman, J. F. (2007). Issues for DSM-V: How should obsessive-compulsive and related disorders be classified? *American Journal of Psychiatry, 164,* 1313–1314.

Maudsley, H. (1879). *Pathology of mind* (pp. 319, 431). London: Macmillan.

Menzies, R. G., & Clarke, J. C. (1995). Danger expectancies and insight in acrophobia. *Behaviour Research and Therapy, 33,* 215–221.

Menzies, R.G., Harris, L.M., & Jones, M.K. (1998). Evidence from three fearful samples for a poor insight type in specific phobia. *Depression and Anxiety, 8,* 29–32.

Müller, U., Fletcher, P. C., & Steinberg, H. (2006). The origin of pharmacopsychology: Emil Kraepelin's experiments in Leipzig, Dorpat and Heidelberg (1882–1892). *Psychopharmacology, 184,* 131–138.

Pickren, W.E. (2005). Science, practice, and policy: An introduction to the history of psychology and the National Institute of Mental Health. In W. E. Pickren & S. F. Schneider (Eds.), *Psychology and the National Institute of Mental Health: A historical analysis of science, practice, and policy* (pp. 3–15). Washington, DC: American Psychological Association.

Pickren, W. E. (2007). Psychology and medical education: A historical perspective from the United States. *Indian Journal of Psychiatry, 49,* 175–177.

Pickren, W. E., & Schneider, S. F. (2005). *Psychology and the National Institute of Mental Health: A historical analysis of science, practice, and policy.* Washington, DC: American Psychological Association.

Rosner, R. I. (2005). Psychotherapy research and the National Institute of Mental Health, 1948–1980. In W. E. Pickren & S. F. Schneider (Eds.),

Psychology and the National Institute of Mental Health: A historical analysis of science, practice, and policy (pp. 113–150). Washington, DC: American Psychological Association.

Ruscio, A.M., Lane, M., Roy-Byrne, P., Stang, P.E., Stein, D.J., Wittchen, H-U., et al. (2005). Should excessive worry be required for a diagnosis of generalized anxiety disorder? Results from the US National Comorbidity Survey Replication. *Psychological Medicine, 35,* 1761–1772.

Schneier, F.R., Liebowitz, M.R., Beidel, D.C., Fyer, A.J., George, M.S., Heimberg, R.G., et al. (1996). Social phobia. In T.A Widiger, A.J. Frances, H.A. Pincus, R. Ross, M.B. First, & W.W. Davis (Eds.), *DSM-IV sourcebook* (Vol. 2, pp. 507–548). Washington, DC: American Psychiatric Association.

Shakow, D., & Rapaport, D. (1964). *The influence of Freud on American psychology*. New York: International Universities Press.

Shorter, E. (1997). *A history of psychiatry: From the era of the asylum to the age of Prozac.* New York: Wiley.

Slade, T., & Watson, D. (2006). The structure of common DSM-IV and ICD-10 mental disorders in the Australian general population. *Psychological Medicine, 36,* 1593–1600.

Spitzer, R. L. (2001). Values and assumptions in the development of DSM-III and DSM-III-R: An insider's perspective and a belated response to Sadler, Hulgus, and Agich's "On values in recent American psychiatric classification." *Journal of Nervous and Mental Disease, 189,* 351–359.

Spitzer, R. L., & Williams, J. B. W. (1984). Diagnostic issues in the DSM-III classification of the anxiety disorders. In L. Grinspoon (Ed.), *Psychiatry Updates* (Vol. 3, p. 395). Washington, DC: American Psychiatric Press.

Stone, M.H. (2002). History of anxiety disorders. In D.J. Stein & E. Hollander (Eds.), *The American Psychiatric Publishing textbook of anxiety disorders* (pp. 3–11). Washington, DC: American Psychiatric Publishing Inc.

Tallis, F., Davey, G. C. L., & Capuzzo, N. (1994). The phenomenology of non-pathological worry: A preliminary investigation. In G. C. L. Davey & F. Tallis (Eds.), *Worrying: Perspectives on theory, assessment, and treatment* (pp. 61–89). Oxford, UK: Wiley.

Turner, S. M., Williams, S. L., Beidel, D. C., & Mezzich, J. E. (1986). Panic disorder and agoraphobia with panic attacks: Covariation along the dimensions of panic and agoraphobic fear. *Journal of Abnormal Psychology, 95,* 384–388.

Westphal, C. (1871). Die agoraphobie: Eine neuropathische erscheinun [Agoraphobia: A neuropathological symptom]. *Archives für Psychiatrie und Nervenkrankheiten, 3,* 138–161.

Widiger, T. A., Frances, A. J., Pincus, H. A., Ross, R., First, M. B., & Davis, W.W. (Eds.) (1996). *DSM-IV sourcebook* (Vol. 2). Washington, DC: American Psychiatric Association.

Wilson, M. (1993). DSM-III and the transformation of American psychiatry: A history. *American Journal of Psychiatry, 150,* 399–410.

World Health Organization. (1992). *The ICD-10 classification of mental and behavioural disorders: Clinical descriptions and diagnostic guidelines.* Geneva: World Health Organization.

3

Neo-Kraepelinian Diagnosis: Adequacy for Phobias and Panic

Paul M. G. Emmelkamp
Mark B. Powers

The purpose of this chapter is to discuss the current status of research with respect to the clinical features, course, and prognosis of specific phobias, agoraphobia, and panic disorder, and to provide some directions for improvement in the assessment of these disorders.

Specific Phobia

Description of the Disorder

According to almost all epidemiologic community surveys, specific phobias, as defined by *the Diagnostic and Statistical Manual of Mental Disorders, Third Edition, Revised* (*DSM-III-R*) and *DSM-IV* (formerly "simple phobia" in

DSM-III) are, as a group, the most widespread of all anxiety disorders (e.g., Kessler et al., 2005). Specific phobias are intense fears of specific objects or situations, such as animals, heights, storms, darkness, enclosed spaces, or darkness. It is well known that specific phobias can develop in response to almost any type of stimulus (Marks 1987). According to *DSM-IV-TR* (American Psychiatric Association [APA], 2000), specific phobia should be diagnosed in cases of marked and persistent, excessive, or irrational fear that occurs in response to real or anticipated confrontation with a circumscribed object or situation (criterion A) in which all of the following criteria must be met:

- The confrontation almost invariably provokes an immediate anxiety reaction, which might reach the severity threshold of a situationally bound panic attack (criterion B).
- The person recognizes that the anxiety is excessive or unreasonable (criterion C).
- The situations or objects are avoided or endured with intense anxiety (criterion D).
- The fear, associated anticipatory anxiety, or avoidance behavior must interfere significantly with the person's normal life or be associated with clinically significant suffering (criterion E).

To meet diagnostic criteria for specific phobia, the fear, panic, or avoidance should not be better explained by other mental disorders, such obsessive–compulsive disorder, post-traumatic stress disorder, social phobia, or panic disorder (with or without agoraphobia).

In the case of children, the *DSM-IV-TR* criteria for specific phobia are modified in three ways: (a) panic-like features (criterion B) might manifest with different emotional responses, (b) children are not required to consider their fear as irrational or excessive, and (c) the duration in children must be at least 6 months.

The diagnostic criteria of the *International Classification of Diseases and Related Health Problems, 10th edition* (*ICD-10*) are very similar; however, *ICD-10* does not require that the phobia in adults be recognized as unreasonable. *DSM-IV-TR* distinguishes five types of specific phobias, whereas *ICD-10* makes fewer distinctions. The *DSM* subtypes are: animal type (e.g., spiders, dogs, cats, snakes, or birds); natural environment type (e.g., storms, heights, or water); blood–injection–injury type (e.g., dental procedures); a situational type (e.g., tunnels, bridges, elevators, flying, driving, or enclosed places); and a residual category (choking, vomiting, loud sounds, costumed characters). The decision to distinguish different types of phobia arises from research suggesting that each type has sufficiently distinct features; that is, with regard to age of onset, physiological response (e.g., fainting, panic), fear of physiological response, and patterns of comorbidity (Antony, Brown, & Barlow, 1997; Lipsitz, Barlow, Mannuzza, Hofmann, & Fyer, 2002). People with blood–injection–injury phobia exhibit a unique biphasic response pattern of sympathetic activation followed by significant parasympathetic activation. This biphasic process may account for the fact that about three quarters of individuals with blood–injection–injury phobia tend to faint when exposed to phobic stimuli. As we will see later in this chapter, debate continues about the utility and significance of the *DSM* subtyping scheme.

Epidemiology

Despite considerable methodological differences, convergent evidence from many studies around the world suggest a lifetime prevalence of specific phobias in the community of greater than 10%–13% (Emmelkamp & Wittchen, 2008; Kessler et al., 2005) making them the most common of all mental disorders. In the National Epidemiologic Survey on Alcohol and Related Conditions (NESARC) study, however, slightly lower prevalence figures were reported (Stinson et al., 2007). Results of this study indicate that in the United States in 2001–2002, 7.1% of adults met criteria for specific phobia in the prior 12 months, and 9.4% met criteria during their lifetime.

Cultural differences. There are some indications that rates of specific phobia vary by culture. Compared with Caucasians, higher rates have been reported from African Americans and Mexican Americans born in the United States (Brown, Eaton, & Sussman 1990; Karno et al., 1989; Robins & Regier, 1991). Higher rates have also been reported in Brazil compared with the US population (Da Motta et al., 2000). The NESARC epidemiology study reported lower risk among

Asians and Hispanics (Stinson et al., 2007) than among Caucasians. Lower figures were also reported in Japan (Kawakami et al., 2005) compared with western countries. Whether these figures reflect true differences in prevalence of specific phobias across cultures or are the result of methodological confounds is unclear. Potentially important methodological confounds include the following: (a) sample sizes in several surveys were too small to analyze rates among ethnic minorities; (b) different instruments were used across cultures to assess the prevalence of specific phobia; and (c) some instruments may not have been adequately adapted for use in a given culture (e.g., translation problems).

Age and gender differences. Most studies indicate that the prevalence of specific phobias is higher in children, adolescents, and young adults, compared with older adults (Emmelkamp & Wittchen, 2008). Replicating this result, the largest epidemiological study to date on the prevalence of specific phobias (Stinson et al., 2007) found that the prevalence was highest in children, adolescents, and young adults, compared with adults age 65 years and older.

Research has consistently found that particular subtypes of specific phobia (animals, lightning, enclosed spaces, or darkness) are more common in women than men (Fredrickson et al., 1996; Goisman et al., 1998). Smaller gender differences were observed for phobias of heights, flying, injections, and dentistry. Gender differences are less pronounced before the age of 10 (Wittchen, Reed, & Kessler, 1998) and increase with age (Craske, 2003). According to Craske (2003), adolescence is a period in which women develop fears and phobias at a relatively greater rate than men. Several environmental factors in adolescence likely contribute to these sex differences, such as psychosocial stressors and sex-specific socialization. For example, sexual abuse and sexual violence is much more common in females than in males. As to sex-specific socialization, there is ample evidence that girls are less positively reinforced for assertiveness, independence, and activities than are boys. By being encouraged to be more active and independent, boys are likely to build competency and self-efficacy in a wider array of domains than are girls. In addition, repeated exposure to a broad array of activities is likely to facilitate habituation to aversive stimuli (Craske, 2003). Another factor that might mediate gender differences in fears and phobias is disgust sensitivity, to be discussed below.

Specific phobias and subtypes. Few studies have reported data on the prevalence of types of specific phobias. The recent NESARC study is a notable exception. Fears of animals and heights were the most common, with half of all individuals with specific phobia reporting them. About one third of individuals with a specific phobia reported claustrophobia and fear of flying. Fears of blood–injection–injury and fears of storms and water were least frequently reported. Most individuals with specific phobia report multiple fears (Goisman et al., 1998; Lipsitz et al., 2002; Stinton et al., 2007). In the NESARC study, less than one third of individuals with specific phobia reported only a single specific fear. The mean number of fears among respondents with specific phobia was 3.1. About one quarter of respondents with specific phobia reported fear and avoidance of only one object or situation. Having more than one fear, regardless of content, was associated with greater disability and impairment (Stinton et al., 2007). The Stinton et al. (2007) study shows that a substantial number of people with specific phobia have multiple types of phobias.

Impairment

Why do relatively few individuals with specific phobia apply for treatment given the high prevalence of specific phobia in the community and the highly effective psychological treatments that are available (Emmelkamp, 2004)? One reason might be lack of dissemination of information on the availability and effectiveness of treatment (Powers & Emmelkamp, 2008). Another reason might be the low levels of impairment associated with specific phobia. Apart from cases where avoidance might have immediate or severe consequences, such as when a person with blood phobia avoids medical treatment, or a person with claustrophobia refuses to have an MRI scan, avoidance of the phobic object or situation often does not result in clinically significant impairment for most people with specific phobia.

Several studies have specifically addressed the issue of impairment in specific phobias. Zimmerman, Chelminski, and Young (2004) found that adding the criterion of clinically significant impairment substantially reduced the number of specific phobia diagnoses. Studies that directly compared impairment among different anxiety disorders generally found that specific phobia was associated with the least impairment. In a study using the Work and Social Adjustment Scale, for example, specific phobic patients were clearly less impaired than patients with agoraphobia or social phobia, especially in the areas of work and relationships (Mataix–Cols et al., 2005). In a study in Europe, specific phobias were associated with fewer missed work days than panic disorder, agoraphobia, posttraumatic stress disorder, major depressive disorder, and dysthymia (Wittchen & Jacobi, 2005). One study found that the impairment associated with specific phobia was comparable to the impairment associated with other anxiety disorders (Stinton et al., 2007), but less than the impairment associated with mood disorders. In a study of more than 2,000 individuals, Cramer, Torgersen, and Kringlen (2005) found that in contrast to social phobia, panic disorder, and generalized anxiety disorder, specific phobias had only a small effect on quality of life.

One of the major problems with the diagnosis of specific phobia in *DSM-IV-TR* is the lack of a clear definition of clinically significant impairment. In fact, the high prevalence figures of specific phobia in epidemiological studies may be a result of the current definition being overinclusive. Many individuals meeting the *DSM-IV-TR* criteria are not significantly impaired. One of the goals of having a diagnostic system is that having a specific diagnosis has implications for specific treatment. Perhaps the *DSM-IV-TR* is missing the boat with a disorder that is assigned to about 10% of the population with only a small number of these people experiencing so much impairment that they desire treatment. There is a clear need for studies on the relationship between level of impairment of specific phobias and the desire to seek treatment.

Structure of Fear

The high-degree of comorbidity between anxiety and mood disorders has generated research into the common (higher-order) factors involved in these disorders. Many factor-analytic studies of fear and phobia surveys have been conducted, but results are sometimes difficult to interpret because of the non-representative samples used (e.g., students rather than community samples) as well as other methodological problems. More recently, investigators have used the dataset from the National Comorbidity Survey (NCS) to investigate the structure of fears in terms of *DSM* phobias. In a study investigating the structure of the specific phobias listed in *DSM*, some evidence was found in latent class analyses that two types of specific phobias could be distinguished: fear of heights versus blood and animal phobias (Curtis, Magee, Eaton, Wittchen, & Kessler 1998). A more recent study investigated the structure of all phobias in the NCS (Cox, McWilliams, Clara, & Stein,, 2003). Exploratory and confirmatory factor analysis revealed the following structure:

- Agoraphobia: public places, crowds, being away from home, travel by car, train, or bus
- Speaking: public speaking, speaking to a group, talking to others
- Heights or water: flying, heights, crossing a bridge, water
- Being observed: public eating, public toilet use, writing in front of others
- Threat: blood or needles, storms or thunder, snakes or animals, being alone, enclosed spaces

Thus, the original split between two types of specific phobias (fear of heights versus blood and animal phobias, Curtis et al., 1998) was supported in these subsequent analyses. In addition, two types of social fears could be distinguished: speaking and being observed. Higher-order factor analyses revealed two second-order fear factors: social fears and specific fears. At the third-order level, one general fear factor was identified (Cox et al., 2003).

By performing factor analysis of data obtained from 5,491 young adult students from 11 countries, Arrindell et al. (2003) found evidence for separate diagnostic constructs for the blood–injection–injury type, and for the animal type. However, the natural environment type and the situational type represented a single common factor. Similar findings were obtained by Fredrikson et al. (1996). Similarly, in a study of children, Muris, Schmidt, & Merckelbach (1999) showed a single-factor model that pooled the natural environment type and the situational type. Results of these studies suggest that the current distinction of subtypes may need reconsideration.

Another way of determining whether diagnostic categories represent different phenomena is to test if they differ with respect to comorbidity. If different types of specific phobia differ with respect to comorbidity patterns, this could indicate that they have different etiological mechanisms, with different long-term consequences, or that they require subtype-specific treatment. Results of studies assessing comorbidity rates in cases of specific phobia reveal high rates of comorbidity with other anxiety disorders, with mood and somatoform disorders, and to a lesser extent with antisocial and substance use disorders (Emmelkamp & Wittchen, 2008). Some studies investigated comorbidity patterns according to phobia subtype, but this was limited to panic disorder. For example, situational specific phobia was associated with the presence of panic attacks (Lipsitz et al., 2002; Starcevic & Bogojevic, 1997). Both Antony et al. (1997) and Starcevic and Bogojevic (1997) found agoraphobia associated with the natural environment subtype, but not with the other subtypes. Hence, results of studies that tried to delineate subtypes of specific phobia are inconclusive.

Given that various subtypes of specific phobia often co-occur with one another, along with the lack of empirical support for the differentiation among animal type, natural environment type, and situational type, we propose a different "mapping" in future *DSM* editions. Clearly, blood–injury–injection phobia is different from animal and situational phobias, in terms of psychometric findings and psychophysiological reaction patterns. However, there is not enough systematic evidence for justifying a more coherent and clinically useful subtyping.

Genetic Patterns

Family studies have shown moderate degrees of familial aggregation of specific phobias. Positive correlations have been found routinely between the fears of children and their mothers (Emmelkamp & Scholing, 1997). The influence of mothers' and siblings' fears on the fears of children is probably greater for younger than older children. Although these data suggest that social learning factors are important in the development of specific phobias, other factors may also be involved. Like social learning factors (e.g., modeling), the experience of stressful life events (e.g., parental loss or separation, child abuse) may be related to the development of anxiety disorders, but the effects are largely nonspecific across disorders. Genetic factors may also account for the co-occurrence of specific phobias in families.

In a study of over 4,500 twins by Bolton et al. (2006), patterns of genetic and environmental influences on early-onset anxiety disorders were investigated. The heritability estimate for specific phobia was high (60%) for diagnostic status (with associated impairment), with remaining variance attributed to nonshared environment. Although the heritability estimate suggests that the genetic effects on specific phobia are more significant than environmental effects, the investigators did not investigate gene–by-environment interactions, so we cannot draw firm conclusions with respect to the relative contribution of genes versus environment. Research suggests that there is a common genetic factor for anxiety disorders in general, as well as genetic vulnerability that is particular to specific phobia (Kendler, Neale, Kessler, Heath, & Eaves, 1992; Kendler & Prescott, 2006; Skre, Onstad, Torgersen, Lygren, & Kringlen 1993). To illustrate the specific factors, individuals with blood–injury phobia have more relatives with similar problems than other individuals with phobias do (Marks, 1987; Öst, 1992). So it has been suggested that blood–injury phobias stand out as a separate category. However, the Virginia Adult Twin Study of Psychiatric and Substance Use Disorders (VATSPSUD) study (Kendler & Prescott, 2006) found the lowest *specific* heritability for blood–injury phobias.

Hettema, Prescott, Myers, Neale, & Kendler (2005) investigated whether the comorbidity of anxiety disorders in a community sample (twin register) could be explained by underlying genetic and environmental risk factors, using multivariate structural equation modeling. The results of this study suggest that etiologically, the anxiety disorders possess a relatively simple genetic architecture. In the best-fitting model, the genetic influences on anxiety were best explained by two additive genetic factors common across the disorders. The first loaded primarily in generalized anxiety disorder, panic disorder, and agoraphobia, whereas the second loaded strongly in two specific phobias, situational phobia and animal phobia. However, a methodologically more sophisticated analysis of the same data set (Kendler & Prescott, 2006) reveals a slightly different picture. Although they also found evidence for a common genetic factor contributing to all phobias, the contribution was largest for animal (21%) and blood–injury phobia (22%) and weakest for agoraphobia (11%) and social phobia (5%). The disorder-specific genetic factors account for 7% (blood–injury phobia) to 15% (situational phobia) of the variance.

Hettema, Annas, Neale, Kendler, & Fredrikson (2003) investigated the heritability of fear conditioning in same-sex twin pairs. Results reveal that genetic factors play a significant role in the acquisition and extinction of fears. Interestingly, different results were found for evolutionarily relevant stimuli (snakes, spiders) as compared with evolutionary irrelevant stimuli (triangles, circles) thus providing some support for the preparedness theory of phobia acquisition. Implications for the classification of anxiety and mood disorders will be discussed later (Watson, 2005).

Disgust Sensitivity

Disgust sensitivity, defined as the propensity to experience disgust toward a wide range of stimuli, has been described as a genetically based vulnerability factor that may contribute to the development of spider phobia, blood–injury–injection phobia, and obsessive–compulsive disorder (Olatunji & Deacon, 2008). People with spider phobia often report disgust rather than fear reactions to spiders (Davey, 1992). Alternatively, when viewing pictures of spiders, individuals with fear of spiders report experiencing both fear and disgust. The disgust response to picture presentations of spiders has been shown to be independent of fear responses (Olatunji, 2006) and has also been shown on facial electromyographic activity (de Jong, Peters, & Vanderhallen, 2002). The few available studies employing in vivo spider exposure (rather than picture ratings) have confirmed that individuals with spider phobia respond with significantly more fear and disgust than nonphobics (e.g., Olatunji & Deacon, 2008). There is some evidence that disgust is a stronger predictor of avoidance of spiders than anxiety (Olatunji & Deacon, 2008; Woody, McLean, & Klassen, 2005).

Disgust sensitivity is considered as a personality trait that functions to facilitate avoidance of stimuli that may communicate uncleanliness, contamination, and the potential for disease. Not only spiders but also other small animals (e.g., rats, cockroaches, snails) may be avoided because of their perceived disgust, contamination, and disease properties rather than concerns of harm during exposure to the animals (Davey, 1992). Several studies have found support for this disease-avoidance model. When a spider has briefly touched a cookie or a candy bar that is still packaged, substantially more individuals with spider phobia refuse to eat the cookie or candy compared with nonphobic individuals (Olatunji & Deacon, 2008).

Although disgust sensitivity has been described as a genetically based vulnerability factor, evidence for a genetic component to disgust is lacking; correlations for monozygotic and dizygotic twins are very similar to one another ($r = 0.29$ and $r = 0.24$, respectively), which suggests that disgust has a small (if any) genetic component (Rozin, Haidt, & McCauley, 2000). Although the parent–child correlation for disgust or contamination was found to be higher ($r = 0.52$), this can be explained by other than genetic factors such as vicarious and informational transmission pathways. For instance, parents high in disgust sensitivity might be more protective and provide the child with information regarding sources of potential contaminants (e.g., spiders); modeling might play a role as well.

Davey (1994) proposed that the gender differences found in many specific phobias may be a result of gender differences in disgust sensitivity. Earlier studies addressing this issue in blood–injection–injury fears and animal phobias were inconclusive. More recently, Connolly, Olatunji, and Lohr (2008) evaluated the potential role of disgust sensitivity as a mediator of gender differences in blood–injection–injury fears and spider fears while controlling for trait anxiety and negative affect. The results supported the notion that disgust-sensitivity mediates the gender differences in blood–injection–injury fears and spider fears.

What implications would disgust have for *DSM-V*? First, data regarding the role of disgust sensitivity in animal fears are mostly analog in nature. That is, most studies involved volunteers with fears of spiders rather than phobic patients. There is a clear need for replicating these findings with individuals formally diagnosed with spider phobia. Similarly, studies have focused on spider fears only, but disgust sensitivity and associated disease avoidance also have implications for other small animals. Studies are needed to examine the role of disgust in other phobias of small animals. Finally, there is some preliminary evidence that disgust sensitivity is not only restricted to fear of small animals but is also related to blood–injury fears (e.g., Olatunji, Sawchuk, Lohr, & Patten, 2007), contamination fears in obsessive–compulsive disorder (Olatunji, Williams, Lohr & Sawchuk, 2005), health anxiety and hypochondriasis (Davey & Bond, 2006), eating disorders (Troop, Treasure, & Serpell, 2002), and sexual dysfunction (de Jong et al., 2008).

To our knowledge, researchers have yet to directly test the accuracy of the assumption that neurocircuitry of disgust sensitivity is related to neurocircuits in the disorders listed above. There is already some evidence to suggest that the anterior insular cortex and the ventrolateral prefrontal cortex are involved in disgust sensitivity, contamination obsessions, and washing compulsions (Husted, Shapira, & Goodman, 2006; Lawrence et al., 2007). If future studies confirm that disgust sensitivity is related to various psychiatric disorders, this might have implications for future editions of the *DSM*. For example, this may lead not only to a different subtyping of specific phobias, but also to a broadening of the fear circuitry (anxiety) disorders to include health anxiety and some sexual dysfunctions.

Panic Disorder

Description

The major features of panic disorder are recurrent, spontaneous panic attacks, interspersed with anticipatory anxiety of further attacks and, in around 65 % of individuals, agoraphobic avoidance. Panic attacks are discrete periods of intense fear associated with at least four anxiety symptoms, which develop suddenly and peak within 10 minutes. Panic disorder usually arises between late adolescence and the early 30s. In many cases, the first panic attack is triggered by psychosocial stress (e.g., living on one's own), physical illness, childbirth, or medical treatment.

Symptoms of Panic

Before *DSM-III* introduced the category of panic disorder, two syndromes were commonly diagnosed: (a) "hyperventilation" with dyspnea, paraesthesia and fear of dying by choking, and (b) "cardiac neurosis" with symptoms resembling those of angina pectoris such as chest discomfort or pain, palpitations, tachycardia, and fear of dying. Starting with *DSM-III*, both syndromes were classified as panic disorder.

Several studies have tried to investigate how the symptoms currently listed under panic disorder are grouped together using factor analysis or cluster analysis. Bandelow et al. (1996) reported that panic symptoms were composed of two factors: (a) fear of dying, chest pain or discomfort, dyspnea, tingling or numbness, and choking or smothering sensations and (b) fear of losing control or going crazy, flushes or chills, trembling or shaking, nausea or abdominal distress, and palpitations. The symptoms of sweating, dizziness or faintness, and depersonalization or derealization did not load strongly on any of these factors.

In a large sample of patients who had experienced at least one panic attack in their life time ($n = 1{,}213$), the properties of each diagnostic criteria item for panic attack was determined using item-response theory (Ietsugu, Sukigara, & Furukawa, 2007). Results revealed that not all criteria contributed equally to the severity of panic attacks. The best items to predict severity of panic attacks were paresthesia, choking, and fear of dying. Shortness of breath, chest pain, and dizziness were markers of moderate severity. Although palpitations are the most frequently reported panic attack symptom, palpitations only discriminated between cases and noncases at low levels of panic attack severity. Taken together, the Bandelow et al. and Ietssugu et al. findings suggest that several panic symptoms could be omitted to improve diagnostic efficiency.

Peak Anxiety

Another issue that needs some attention is the time it takes for anxiety to reach its peak during a panic attack. The criterion of peak anxiety within 10 minutes as required in the *DSM-IV-TR* may need closer examination. In studies investigating the time to peak (Norton, Zvolensky, Bonn-Miller, Cox, & Norton, 2008; Scupi, Benson, Brown, & Uhde, 1997), more than half of the panickers reported worst-ever attacks reaching peak intensity in longer than 10 minutes; most still classified this longer-onset experience as a panic attack. It should be noted that these studies were retrospective in nature, so it may be that the panickers overestimated the time to peak intensity. However, if this finding is confirmed in prospective studies, it may be that the *DSM-IV-TR* criterion of peak intensity within 10 minutes may not be a valid discriminator between a true panic attack and other anxiety-related experiences. However, given that most panic attacks peak within 20 minutes, some criterion should be retained to distinguish panic attacks from chronic anxiety. The longer the time to peak, the greater the blurring of the distinction between panic attacks and generalized anxiety.

Cognitive Factors in the Phenomenology of Panic

Several authors have emphasized cognitive factors in the phenomenology of panic disorder (Beck, 1988; Beck, Emery, & Greenberg, 1985; Clark, 1986). One such factor is anxiety sensitivity, defined as the fear of benign bodily sensations (heart rate, sweating, etc.) based on beliefs that they may produce harmful consequences (e.g., heart attack, death; Reiss, Peterson, Gursky, & McNally, 1986). Many researchers have suggested that anxiety sensitivity is critical in the development and maintenance of panic disorder (Barlow, 1988; Beck et al., 1985; Bouton, Mineka, & Barlow, 2001; Clark, 1986; Wolpe & Rowan, 1988), and many lines of research support this hypothesis. First, studies show that early learning experiences may influence anxiety sensitivity development (Stewart et al., 2001) that later results in greater emotional responding to panic provocation agents (Brown, Smits, Powers, & Telch, 2003; Eke & McNally, 1996; Holloway & McNally, 1987; McNally & Eke, 1996; Rapee & Medoro, 1994; Telch, Jacquin, Smits, & Powers, 2003). This heightened responding is significantly reduced with repeated exposures to the provocation agent (Schmidt, Trakowski, & Staab, 1997). Second, prospective studies show that people who are high in anxiety sensitivity are at greater risk for naturally occurring panic attacks (Schmidt, Lerew, & Jackson, 1997; Schmidt, Lerew, & Joiner, 1998). Third, patients diagnosed with panic disorder score higher than psychiatric and nonpsychiatric controls on measures of the construct such as the Anxiety Sensitivity Index (Peterson & Heilbronner, 1987; Peterson & Reiss, 1987; Taylor, Koch, & McNally, 1992; Telch et al., 2003). For example, anxiety sensitivity is consistently highest in panic disorder compared to other anxiety disorders (Taylor, Koch, & McNally, 1992; see Figure 1).

3.1

Anxiety sensitivity scores across the anxiety disorders. Data from Taylor et al. (1992). GAD = generalized anxiety disorder; OCD = obsessive–compulsive disorder; PD = panic disorder; PTSD = posttraumatic stress disorder.

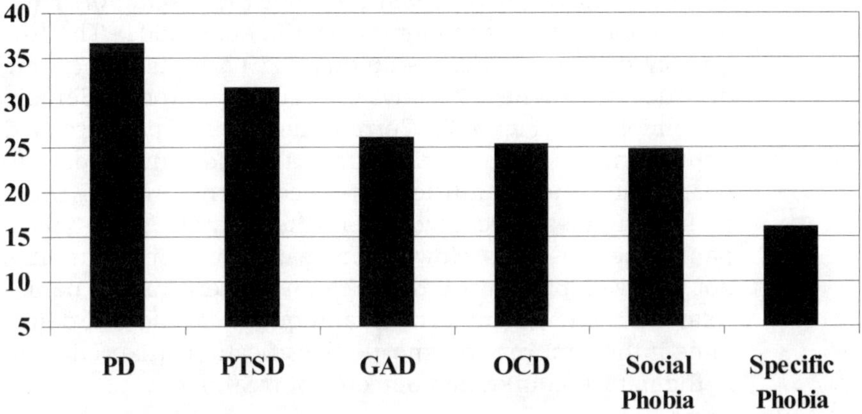

Finally, several studies suggest that anxiety sensitivity mediates improvement in the treatment of panic patients (Cho, Smits, Powers, & Telch, 2007; Hofmann et al., 2007; Smits, Powers, Cho, & Telch, 2004). For example, in a study of cognitive-behavior therapy for panic disorder, anxiety sensitivity fully mediated improvements in disability and partially mediated changes in agoraphobia, anxiety, and panic frequency (Smits, Powers, Cho, & Telch, 2004). Reductions in anxiety sensitivity precede reductions in panic symptoms, thereby showing temporal precedence (Smits et al., in press).

In summary, anxiety sensitivity figures prominently in theories of panic disorder etiology, maintenance, and treatment.

As reflected in the *DSM-IV-TR*, panic-related catastrophic thoughts currently include (a) concern about having future attacks, (b) worry about the implications or consequences of the attacks, or (c) a significant change in behavior because of the attacks. The feared consequences of panic are further divided into (a) fear that something is physically wrong (e.g., having a heart attack), (b) fear of negative social evaluation by others because of the symptoms (e.g., "People may think

I'm weird"), and (c) fear that the symptoms mean they will lose control or go crazy. However, further research identified two additional concerns expressed by patients. First, patients report fear that panic disorder may lead to functional impairment in general or reduced quality of life (Feske & de Beurs, 1997; Raffa, White, & Barlow, 2004; Telch, Brouillard, Telch, Agras, & Taylor, 1989) and that the discomfort from panic attacks will be intolerable (Raffa et al., 2004). The frequency of these concerns among 207 patients with panic disorder was highest for physical and lowest for intolerable discomfort (see Figure 2). Current measures of panic-related apprehension, such as the panic appraisal inventory, do not include these additional two concerns. Adding them to existing measures may help further characterize atypical panic disorder cases. However, research on their addition is not yet available. Future research on concerns about panic-related functional impairment and quality of life will determine if they improve diagnostic classification and prediction of the nature, course, and outcome of treatment.

3.2

Percentage of endorsement of categories of feared consequences of panic attacks. From Raffa et al. (2004).

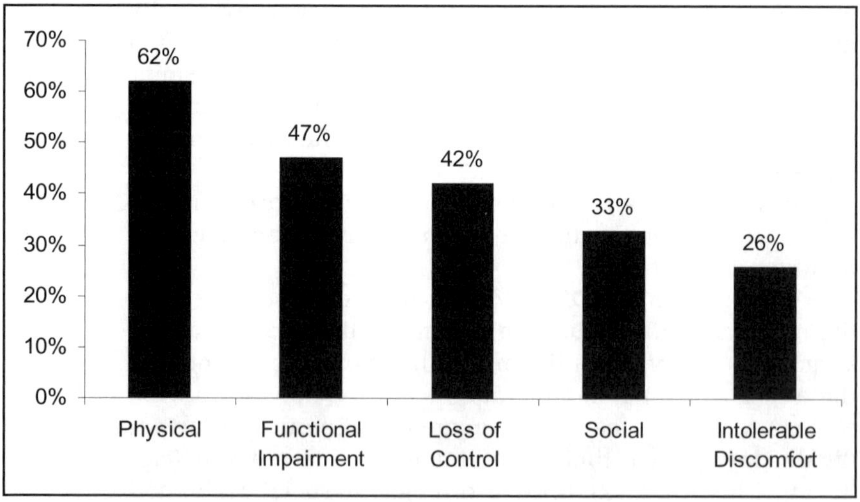

Agoraphobia

Description

The classification of agoraphobia in *DSM* has undergone significant changes over time. Originally in *DSM-III*, agoraphobia was classified as a phobic disorder that could occur with or without panic attacks. Agoraphobia is anxiety about being in situations from which escape might be difficult or in which help may not be available in the event of having a panic attack or panic-like symptoms. This anxiety typically leads to a pervasive avoidance of various situations such as being home alone, being in crowded places, entering shops, and walking and traveling alone. In *DSM-IV-TR*, agoraphobia is defined as:

- Anxiety about being in places or situations from which escape might be difficult (or embarrassing) or help might not be available in the event of having an unexpected or situationally predisposed panic attack or panic-like symptoms. Agoraphobic fears typically involve characteristic clusters of situations that include being outside the home alone, being in a crowd or standing in a line, being on a bridge, and traveling in a bus, train, or automobile.
- The situations are avoided (e.g., travel is restricted) or else are endured with marked distress or with anxiety about having a panic attack or panic-like symptoms, or require the presence of a companion. Phobic avoidance may be motivated by unrealistic fears of the *consequences* of having panic symptoms in particular situations where the person feels trapped or far from help.

There is an important difference with respect to the role played by agoraphobia in *DSM-IV-TR* and *ICD-10*. In the latter, agoraphobia is included among the phobias. Starting with *DSM-III-R*, the *DSM* has reversed the relationship between agoraphobia and panic disorder such that agoraphobia is now considered secondary to panic disorder. Thus, *DSM-IV-TR* emphasizes the priority of the onset of panic disorder toward the onset of agoraphobia, implying that agoraphobia is almost always a consequence of spontaneous panic attacks. Agoraphobia is only coded in the context of either panic disorder or limited-symptom panic attacks.

Epidemiology

If agoraphobia without panic disorder is a rarity, one would expect that it would hardly be observed in the community. In earlier studies using *DSM-III* criteria, the 1-year prevalence of agoraphobia without panic disorder was estimated at 1.7% for men and 3.8% for women, and the lifetime prevalence in both sexes was estimated at between 6% and 10% (Hackman, 2006). Such figures do not support the notion that agoraphobia should be accompanied by a current or past history of panic disorder. However, earlier studies that used the Diagnostic Interview Schedule (DIS) (e.g., Dick, Sowa, Bland, & Newman, 1994; Meyers et al., 1984; Robins et al., 1984) had higher prevalence rates of agoraphobia than later studies. The previous large-scale epidemiologic studies using the DIS may have overestimated the true rates of agoraphobia. For a diagnosis of agoraphobia, the DIS required fear and avoidance of only one situation, although avoidance of a single situation (e.g., public transport) may have represented a specific phobia rather than agoraphobia (Horwath, Lish, Johnson, Hornig, & Weissman, 1993). More recent epidemiological studies have used the Composite International Diagnostic Interview to assess agoraphobia requiring fear of *two or more* specific places or situations, making the diagnosis more likely to be reflective of true agoraphobia. In more recent large epidemiological studies around the world, the lifetime prevalence of agoraphobia (without panic disorder) ranges from 0.9%–1.2% and the 12-month prevalence from 0.3%–0.4% (Kawakamio et al., 2005; The ESEMeD MHEDEA 2000 Investigators, 2004a; Wittchen et al., 2008). However, a recent study in South Africa found a much higher 12-month prevalence of 4.8%, probably because of personal safety issues, given the very high prevalence of violence (Williams et al., 2008). Taking the results of the adult studies together, agoraphobia still does occur without panic disorder, although the prevalence is lower than earlier studies suggested.

Bienvenu et al. (2006) sought to determine how spontaneous panic and agoraphobia relate using a longitudinally assessed general population cohort, with clinical reappraisal at follow-up to assess effects of possible diagnostic misclassification. Results revealed that there were two causal pathways rather than one. Panic predicted later agoraphobia, thus confirming the *DSM* notion, but agoraphobia also appeared to be a risk factor for later panic disorder.

A recent study by Faravelli, Cosci, Rotella, Faravelli, & Catena Dell'Osso (2008) addressed this issue in more detail. Given that the occurrence of agoraphobia without a history of panic disorder could be the result of the assessment methods and the clinical inexperience of the lay interviewers typically used in community studies, Favarelli et al. reevaluated all cases that had been diagnosed with agoraphobia in the community survey of Sesto Fiorentino in Italy. The reassessment was done by psychiatrists with extensive experience in research and treatment of anxiety in community settings. The Structured Clinical Interview for *DSM-IV* and the Composite International Diagnostic Interview were used to make the diagnoses. After the reassessment by an experienced psychiatrist, in 10 out of 12 cases, the criteria for the diagnosis of agoraphobia without panic disorder were confirmed, totaling a lifetime prevalence of 0.4%. Agoraphobia participants with and without panic attacks were compared with regard to sex, age, age of onset, duration of illness, family history for anxiety, or mood disorders. Further, no differences between agoraphobia participants with or without a history of panic attacks were detected with respect to the avoided situations (number and type of situations).

In adolescents in a metropolitan area in the U.S. (Roberts, Ramsay, & Yun Xing, 2007), a substantially higher 1-year prevalence of 4.5% was reported for agoraphobia than in studies among adults, although the prevalence dropped to 1.6% when impairment was taken into account. In this study, agoraphobia was the most prevalent anxiety disorder. Other studies have found a substantial number of adolescents with agoraphobia without a history of panic attacks (Hayward, Killen, & Taylor 2003; Wittchen, Nelson, & Lachner, 1998).

Wittchen et al. (2008) prospectively examined the natural course of panic attacks, panic disorder, and agoraphobia in a large German community sample of adolescents with an age of 14–24 at baseline (n = >3000). Panic attacks or panic disorder had only a moderate increased risk of the development of subsequent agoraphobia. Most importantly, most of the subjects with agoraphobia in this community sample never experienced panic attacks.

Taking the results of these studies together, there is clear empirical support that agoraphobia does exist in cases without a history of panic attacks. Thus, a substantial number of people with severe agoraphobia have never met criteria for panic disorder nor have had any panic-like symptoms. Hackmann (2006) argued that the *DSM-IV-TR* criteria for agoraphobia may have restricted our understanding of the disorder, because they have led some to consider that agoraphobia is a secondary psychological phenomenon and that panic attacks are the principal cause of the disorder. Although *DSM-IV-TR* indeed states that agoraphobia is typically a consequence of panic attacks or panic-like episodes, it should be noted that the latter may include limited symptom panic attacks, paroxysmal episodes of tenesmus (as in irritable bowel syndrome), and other sorts of rapid-onset alarming reactions (e.g., migraines triggered by bright light). Nevertheless, there is now substantial evidence from community studies that agoraphobia exists as a separate category independent from panic attacks or limited panic attacks.

It is notable that agoraphobia is much more common in women than men, whereas panic disorder is more equally distributed between the sexes. A recent meta-analysis (Bekker & van Mens–Verhulst, 2007) provides the following female–male gender ratios: agoraphobia 4:1; panic disorder 2:1. The female–male ratio for patients who suffer from both panic disorder and agoraphobia is 3:1. Findings like this support the notion that panic disorder and agoraphobia are not synonymous but separate disorders.

Finally, another line of research suggests that the diagnosis of agoraphobia has clinical utility. Results of a study by Schmidt and Cromer (2008) indicate that there is a clear incremental validity for the diagnosis of agoraphobia. Analyses revealed that agoraphobia status adds uniquely to the prediction of panic disorder symptoms, impairment, and response to treatment.

There is a clear need for studies addressing why some individuals with panic attacks start avoiding situations while others do not. Some authors have suggested that the addition of agoraphobia represents a more severe form of panic disorder (Noyes, Clancy, Garvey, & Anderson, 1987; Turner,

Williams, Beidel, & Mezzich, 1986). Similarly, it has been proposed that panic disorder with agoraphobia is a two-stage disorder, with stage 1 including panic disorder and stage 2 including the addition of agoraphobia (Garvey & Tuason, 1984; Thyer & Himle 1985). However, there is little evidence for these two hypotheses. For example, data suggest that there is not always a difference in severity between panic disorder alone and panic disorder with agoraphobia (Berle et al., 2008; Craske, Sanderson, & Barlow, 1987; Telch, Brouillard, Telch, Agras, & Taylor1989). Also, not all patients with panic disorder go on to develop agoraphobia, arguing against a two-stage model. Although panic severity does not predict agoraphobic status, other variables are stronger predictors, including exaggerated prediction of panic occurrence likelihood, more catastrophic cognitions about the consequences of panic, and less confidence in personal resources to manage panic (Telch et al., 1989). Of these, patients' exaggerated likelihood estimation of panic occurrence in situations is the best predictor of agoraphobic avoidance, accounting for almost 80% of the variance in avoidance behavior (Rachman, 1994; Telch et al., 1989).

Specific personality traits have also been assumed to predispose individuals to develop agoraphobia. Agoraphobic patients have been described as dependent, shy, anxious, depressive, unassertive, immature, and the like; but there is little empirical evidence that a clear "agoraphobic personality" exists (Chambless, 1982). One of the factors increasing the risk of subsequent agoraphobic avoidance after having a panic attack may be the use of an avoidance-based coping style. There are some studies to suggest that avoidance-based coping strategies are also associated with higher levels of anxious responding and increased distress in response to bodily sensations (Spira, Zvolensky, Eifert, & Feldner, 2004). Indeed, in reviewing the literature, Feldner, Zvolensky, and Leen–Feldner (2004) found that patients with panic disorder utilize more avoidance-based coping strategies when compared with controls.

DSM-V may improve with a de-emphasis of the one-way causal relationship from spontaneous panic to agoraphobia and make agoraphobia itself a stand-alone diagnosis. The position taken by *ICD-10*, which differentiates agoraphobia without history of panic disorder, panic disorder with agoraphobia, and panic disorder without agoraphobia seems to be more empirically valid.

Role of Avoidance

In *DSM-IV-TR*, patients are classified with the diagnosis of agoraphobia when, as a result of panic attacks and/or expectations of having a panic attack, (a) travel is avoided, (b) a companion is needed in to be able to travel, or (c) agoraphobic situations are endured despite intense anxiety (distress). *DSM-IV-TR*'s method of diagnosing agoraphobia may cause potential diagnostic problems, because this criterion is a vague mixture of actual avoidance, anxiety experienced in situations, and use of companions. In contrast to *DSM-III-R*, where situational avoidance was classified across four different levels (none, mild, moderate, severe) in the *DSM-IV-TR*, this is no longer the case.

Schmidt, Salas, Bernert, & Schatschneider (2005) investigated whether clinicians weighted the three criteria for agoraphobia equally (avoidance, use of companions, and endurance of situations with distress). In their study, they used prototypical vignettes of agoraphobic cases with symptom profiles emphasizing each of these three criteria. Results revealed that there was a rather low interrater reliability. In fact, clinicians did no better than chance, in most of the cases, emphasizing only one out of the three criteria. Surprisingly, patients with higher levels of avoidance were less likely to receive an agoraphobia diagnosis. It may be that the current definition of agoraphobia in *DSM-IV-TR* is confusing. One would expect that avoidance of agoraphobic situations would be more central in the definition and classification of agoraphobia. There is a clear need to redefine the role of avoidance in the definition of agoraphobia in future editions of *DSM*.

As suggested by the Schmidt and Cromer (2008) study, it might be wise to revert to a dimensional measure that is specific to situational avoidance (versus distress or use of companions). In their study on patients with panic disorder with or without agoraphobia, the *dimensional* measure of avoidance contributed the most variance beyond that accounted for by severity, frequency, and intensity of panic and *DSM-IV-TR* agoraphobia diagnosis. Taking together the results of several studies, it seems that the diagnostic reliability and clinical utility of agoraphobia may be improved by the use of one specifier only—a dimensional rather than a categorical measure of situational avoidance.

General Medical Conditions

Anxiety disorders appear to be highly prevalent among persons with asthma and may be associated with increased asthma morbidity. Studies in clinical and epidemiological samples have indicated that persons with asthma and other respiratory diseases are more likely to have anxiety disorders than people without respiratory disorders (Weiser, 2007). Taking the results of these studies together, the average prevalence of any anxiety disorder among adults with asthma was 34%, indicating a strong relationship between the two conditions in general. More specifically, the prevalence of panic attacks (25%), panic disorder (12%), and agoraphobia (12%) were considerably higher among adults with asthma than in the general population.

Breathing-related symptoms such as dyspnea or feelings of suffocation are central features of the experience of panic. Presence of asthma may increase the risk of developing panic disorder through various cognitive and behavioral mechanisms, including producing threatening bodily sensations that could trigger panic among susceptible individuals. Thus, panic and associated avoidance behavior may be a conditioned response connected to an earlier aversive or traumatic experience related to asthma; panic attacks may be classically conditioned responses to subtle physiological changes that resemble those occurring with asthma. Such interoceptive conditioning can occur without conscious representation of learning, and it is now generally assumed that implicit emotional memories can activate amygdala-based fear systems without individuals being aware of the reasons (Craske, 2005). This interoceptive conditioning model contrasts with the catastrophic appraisal model, in which misappraisals of bodily sensations (e.g., imminent death, loss of control) are viewed as central and necessary. According to this view, symptoms of asthma tend to be misinterpreted and catastrophized by patients with panic disorder as signs of impending, dire harm. These misinterpretations of bodily sensations lead to a positive feedback loop between anxiety and physical sensations, eventuating in full-blown panic attacks.

Further evidence for a relationship between panic disorder and respiratory diseases is provided by the literature concerned with chronic bronchitis and conditions characterized by irreversible airway obstruction (chronic obstructive pulmonary disease [COPD]). For example, Porzelius, Vest, and Nochomovitz (1991) reported that 37% of a clinical sample with COPD reported having experienced a panic attack. In a large population-based study in Canada in a sample of 36,984 subjects, the prevalence of COPD or lung emphysema and chronic bronchitis were substantially higher among individuals with panic disorder (odds ratio of 2:1 and 3:8, respectively) than in persons without panic disorder (Patten & Williams, 2007). There is a substantial overlap in symptoms between respiratory diseases and panic disorder (e.g., dyspnea, chest tightness), leading to frequent consequent symptom confusion and misattribution. Thus, in individuals with respiratory diseases, there is ample opportunity for interoceptive conditioning, selective attention, and catastrophic interpretation of body sensations.

Although the emphasis here is on respiratory diseases, panic disorder is commonly comorbid with vestibular disorders as well, such as benign paroxysmal positional vertigo (BPPV), acute vestibular neuritis and Menière disease (Heinrichs, Edler, Eskens, Mielczarek, & Moschner, 2007; Mira, 2008). In *DSM–IV-TR*, disturbances of mood and anxiety that are judged to be a result of the direct physiological consequences of a general medical condition are placed in different categories including mood and anxiety disorders because of a general medical condition. However, if respiratory diseases or vestibular disorders play a psychological (rather than a medical) role through a process of interoceptive conditioning in the emergence of panic attacks and avoidance behavior, the question is whether this is justified.

Reliability of Neo-Kraepelinian Diagnosis

Neo-Kraepelinian diagnosis was adopted in an effort to increase the reliability and detection of agreed-upon diagnostic categories by clinicians. If this effort was successful, then multiple clinicians should be able to separately diagnose the same case with the same diagnosis. In practice, this level of agreement is often measured with either a test–retest or interrater reliability approach. The level of agreement is expressed as κ, which can be interpreted as follows: excellent agreement = $\kappa \geq .75$, good agreement = κ between .60 and .74, fair agreement = κ between .40 and .59, and poor agreement = $\kappa < .40$ (Di Nardo, Moras, Barlow, Rapee, & Brown, 1993; Mannuzza et al., 1989). The test–retest reliability for panic disorder and specific phobias are between good and excellent (Williams et al., 1992). Likewise, the interrater reliability is also within the good to excellent range (Brown, Di Nardo, Lehman, & Campbell, 2001). Most encouraging is the increase in reliability from the *DSM-III-R* to the *DSM-IV*. For example, panic disorder diagnostic reliability significantly increased from .43 to .72 (see Table 3.1).

Disagreements in diagnoses can be categorized as threshold (clinicians disagree on the disorder meeting the impairment or distress criteria), differences in patient reports, and interviewer error. In the Brown et al. (2001) study, the most common sources of disagreement for panic disorder and specific phobias were threshold (46% and 46%), differences in patient report (31% and 22%), and interviewer error (23% and 14%). Because the most common reason for disagreement was the threshold criteria, this may be an area for improvement in the *DSM-V*. The current categorical criteria of impairment may well benefit from the addition of a dimensional approach here (Cicchetti, Shoinralter, & Tyrer, 1985). However, one must still keep in mind that reliability in itself may not be the ultimate determinant of the utility of Neo-Kraepelinian diagnosis.

3.1 Interrater Reliability of Panic Disorder and Specific Phobia

	Principal Diagnosis	
	DSM-IV κ	DSM-III-R κ
Panic Disorder	.72	.43
Panic Disorder with Agoraphobia	.77	.72
Specific Phobia	.86	.82

Data from Brown et al., 2001.

Hierarchical Models of Diagnostic Categories

As stated above, reliability in diagnosis may not help estimate the validity of the diagnoses. *DSM-IV-TR* currently groups disorders into categories on the basis of phenomenological features, as illustrated in Figure 3. This classification scheme has met with criticism. For example, it seems inconsistent with the high comorbidity among disorders. Also, each disorder is characterized by significant heterogeneity. This heterogeneity then necessitates the large number of specifiers currently in *DSM-IV*. One proposed solution is to consider a quantitative hierarchical model for the *DSM-V* (Watson, 2005; see Figure 4). This empirically based model incorporates correlational and factor analyses taking into account genotypic and phenotypic results, heterogeneous populations, and cross-cultural replications. Watson (2005) stated that this model relies on actual—not assumed—similarities among different disorders. This model results in a single higher-order factor (emotional disorders) that subsumes both mood and anxiety disorders. Emotional disorders is then further characterized by three subscales including bipolar disorders, distress disorders, and fear disorders. As can be seen in Figure 4, panic disorder and specific phobias fall under the category of fear disorders, which is a subclass

3.3

Schematic structure of current *DSM-IV* anxiety disorders. From Watson (2005). GAD = generalized anxiety disorder; OCD = obsessive–compulsive disorder; PTSD = posttraumatic stress disorder; ASD = acute stress disorder; BII = blood-injection-injury; Natural Environ = natural environment; Avoid/Numb = avoidance/numbing.

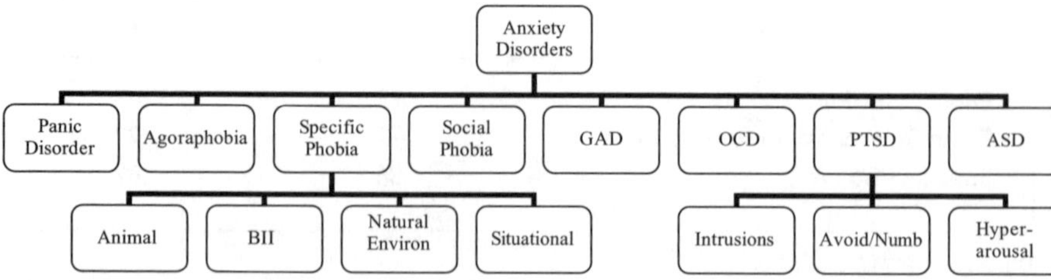

3.4

Revised structure proposed for *DSM-V*. From Watson (2005). BPD I = bipolar I disorder; BPD II = bipolar II disorder; CT = cyclothymia; MDD = major depressive disorder; DD = dysthymic disorder; GAD = generalized anxiety disorder; PTSD = posttraumatic stress disorder.

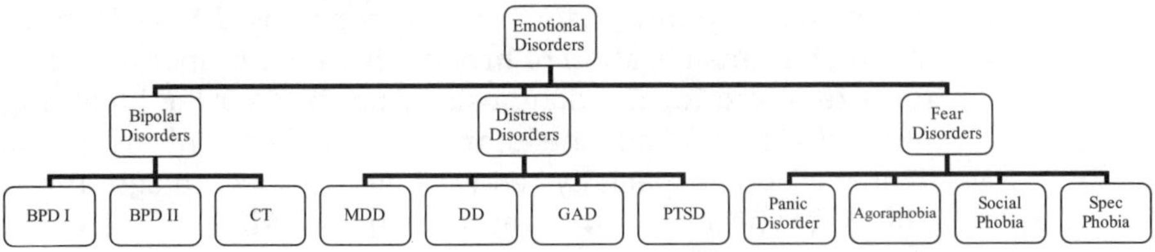

of the overarching class of emotional disorders. One difficulty with this model is the placement of obsessive–compulsive disorder and will be discussed elsewhere in this volume.

Summary

There are several areas identified for improvement in the *DSM-V*. First, the most common reason for diagnostic disagreement for specific phobias and panic disorder is the threshold criteria. The *DSM-IV-TR* currently uses a roughly defined categorical decision that leads to 46% of these disagreements. Diagnostic reliability may improve with a clearer definition of clinically significant impairment.

Second, there is a clear need to redefine the role of avoidance in the definition of agoraphobia in future editions of *DSM*. As suggested by Schmidt and Cromer (2008), it might be wise to revert to a dimensional measure that is specific to situational avoidance (versus distress or use of companions). Therefore, the clinical utility of agoraphobia may be improved by the use of one specifier only: a dimensional rather than a categorical measure of situational avoidance (Cicchetti et al., 1985).

Third, the current distinction among specific phobia subtypes may need reconsideration. Results of studies that tried to delineate subtypes of specific phobia are inconclusive. Given the high overlap between the various subtypes among people with specific phobias, the lack of empirical support for the differentiation between animal type, natural environment type, and situational type, we propose a different "mapping" in future *DSM* editions. Clearly, blood–injury–injection phobia is differentiated from animal and situational phobias, both on psychometric and psychophysiological reaction patterns, but there is not enough systematic evidence for justifying the other subtypes. Therefore, it may be wise to specify only blood–injury–injection phobia and make a further differentiation between (a) simple type, in case of one specific phobia, and (b) generalized type, in case of more than one specific phobia.

Fourth, several adjustments may be indicated for the diagnosis of panic disorder. In preparing *DSM-V*, there should be consideration of broadening the number of symptoms required for the diagnosis of panic disorder, including blurred vision, headache, diarrhea, and frequent urination. This might be especially relevant with respect to agoraphobia. Agoraphobic situations may be avoided by different patients for different reasons, for example, fear of fainting, fear of dying, fear of urinating, or defecating, or fear of panic. Also, *DSM-IV-TR* currently requires symptoms to reach peak intensity within 10 minutes, but given that more than half of the panickers reported worst-ever attacks reaching peak intensity in longer than 10 minutes, it may be that the *DSM-IV-TR* criterion of peak intensity within 10 minutes may not be a valid discriminator between a true panic attack and other anxiety-related experiences. *DSM-IV-TR* also currently describes the feared consequences of panic as including physical, social, or loss of control concerns. However, two additional concerns have been identified. Panic may also lead to functional impairment in general or reduced quality of life or a concern that the discomfort from panic attacks will be intolerable. *DSM-V* may benefit from potential inclusion of these factors. Also, if respiratory diseases or vestibular disorders play a psychological (rather than a medical) role through a process of interoceptive conditioning in the emergence of panic attacks and avoidance behavior, the question is whether classifying them under mood and anxiety disorders because of a general medical condition is justified.

Fifth, *DSM-IV-TR* emphasizes the priority of the onset of panic disorder toward the onset of agoraphobia, implying that agoraphobia is almost always a consequence of spontaneous panic attacks. *DSM-V* may improve with a de-emphasis of the one-way causal relationship from spontaneous panic to agoraphobia and make agoraphobia itself a stand-alone diagnosis, as in *ICD-10*.

Finally, the validity of the current diagnostic categories has been criticized. The current diagnostic scheme results in high comorbidity among disorders, which raises the question of whether the disorders are truly distinct from one another. Also, each disorder is characterized by significant heterogeneity, which necessitates the large number of specifiers currently in *DSM-IV*. One proposed solution is to consider a quantitative hierarchical model for *DSM-V* (Watson, 2005). In this model, panic disorder and specific phobias would fall under the category of fear disorders, which would be a subclass of the overarching class of emotional disorders.

References

American Psychiatric Association (2000). *Diagnostic and statistical manual of mental disorders* (4th ed., text rev.). Washington, DC: Author.

Antony, M. M., Brown, T. A., & Barlow, D. H. (1997). Heterogeneity among specific phobia types in DSM-IV. *Behaviour Research and Therapy, 35,* 1089–1100.

Arrindell, W. A., Eisemann, M., Richter, J., Oei, T. P., Caballo, V. E., van der Ende, J., et al. (2003). Phobic anxiety in 11 nations. Part I: Dimensional constancy of the five-factor model. *Behaviour Research and Therapy, 41,* 461–479.

Bandelow, B., Amering, M., Benkert, O., Marks, I., Nardi, M. E., Osterheider, M., et al. (1996). Cardio-respiratory and other symptom clusters in panic disorder. *Anxiety, 2,* 99–101.

Barlow, D. (1988). *Anxiety and its disorders*. New York: Guilford Press.

Beck, A. T. (1988). Cognitive approaches to panic disorder: Theory and therapy. In S. Rachman & J. Maser (Eds.), *Panic: Psychological perspectives* (pp. 91–109). Hillsdale, NJ: Erlbaum.

Beck, A. T., Emery, G., & Greenberg, R. (1985). *Anxiety disorders and phobias: A cognitive perspective.* New York: Basic Books.

Bekker, M. H. J., & van Mens–Verhulst, J. (2007). Anxiety disorders: Sex differences in prevalence, degree, and background, but gender-neutral treatment. *Journal of Gender Medicine, 4*(Suppl.), S178–S193.

Berle, D., Starcevic, V., Hannan, A., Milicevic, D., Lamplugh, C., & Fenech, P. (2008). Cognitive factors in panic disorder, agoraphobic avoidance, and agoraphobia. *Behaviour Research and Therapy, 46,* 282–291.

Bienvenu, O. J., Onyike, C. U., Stein, M. B., Chen, L. S., Samuels, J., Nestadt, G., et al. (2006). Agoraphobia in adults: Incidence and longitudinal relationship with panic. *British Journal of Psychiatry, 188,* 432–438.

Bolton, D., Eley, T. C., O'Connor, T. G., Perrin, S., Rabe–Hesketh, S., Rijsdijk, et al. (2006). Prevalence and genetic and environmental influences on anxiety disorders in 6-year-old twins. *Psychological Medicine, 36,* 335–344.

Bouton, M. E., Mineka, S., & Barlow, D. H. (2001). A modern learning theory perspective on the etiology of panic disorder. *Psychological Review, 108,* 4–32.

Brown, D. R., Eaton, W. W., & Sussman, L. (1990). Racial differences in prevalence of phobic disorders. *Journal of Nervous and Mental Disease, 178,* 434–441.

Brown, M., Smits, J. A., Powers, M. B., & Telch, M. J. (2003). Differential sensitivity of the three ASI factors in predicting panic disorder patients' subjective and behavioral response to hyperventilation challenge. *Journal of Anxiety Disorders, 17,* 583–591.

Brown, T. A., Di Nardo, P. A., Lehman, C. L., & Campbell, L. A. (2001). Reliability of DSM-IV anxiety and mood disorders: Implications for the classification of emotional disorders. *Journal of Abnormal Psychology, 110,* 49–58.

Chambless, D. L. (1982). Characteristics of agoraphobics. In D. L. Chambless & A. J. Goldstein (Eds.), *Agoraphobia: Multiple perspectives on theory and treatment* (pp. 1–18). New York: Wiley.

Cicchetti, D. V., Shoinralter, D., & Tyrer, P. J. (1985). The effect of number of rating scale categories on levels of interrater reliability: A Monte Carlo investigation. *Applied Psychological Measurement, 9,* 31–36

Cho, Y., Smits, J. A., Powers, M. B., & Telch, M. J. (2007). Do changes in panic appraisal predict improvement in clinical status following cognitive-behavioral treatment of panic disorder? *Cognitive Therapy and Research, 31,* 695–707.

Clark, D. M. (1986). A cognitive approach to panic. *Behaviour Research and Therapy, 24,* 461–470.

Connolly, K. M., Olatunji, B. O., & Lohr, J. M. (2008). Evidence for disgust sensitivity mediating the sex differences found in blood–injection–injury phobia and spider phobia. *Personality and Individual Differences, 44,* 898–908.

Cox, B. J., McWilliams, L. A., Clara, I. P., Stein, M. B. (2003). The structure of feared situations in a nationally representative sample. *Journal of Anxiety Disorders, 17,* 89–101.

Cramer, V., Torgersen, S., & Kringlen, V. (2005) Quality of life and anxiety disorders: A population study. *Journal of Nervous and Mental Disease, 193,* 196–2005.

Craske, M. G., Sanderson, W. C., & Barlow, D. H. (1987). The relationships among panic, fear, and avoidance. *Journal of Anxiety Disorders, 1,* 153–160.

Craske, M.G. (2003). *Origins of phobias and anxiety disorders: Why more women than men?* Oxford, UK: Elsevier.

Craske, M. G., & Waters, A. M. (2005). Panic disorder, phobias, and generalized anxiety disorder. *Annual Review of Clinical Psychology, 1,* 197–225.

Curtis, G. C., Magee, W. J., Eaton, W. W., Wittchen, H. U., & Kessler, R. C. (1998). Specific fears and phobias. Epidemiology and classification. *British Journal of Psychiatry, 173,* 212–217.

Da Motta, W. R., de Lima, M. S., de Oliveira Soares, B. G., Paixao, N. R., & Busnello, E. D. (2000, May). *An epidemic of phobic disorders in Brazil? Results from a population-based cross-sectional survey.* Poster presented at the annual meeting of the American Psychiatric Association, Chicago, IL.

Davey, G. C. L. (1992). Characteristics of individuals with fear of spiders. *Anxiety Research, 4,* 299–314.

Davey, G. C. L. (1994). Self-reported fears to common indigenous animals in an adult UK population: The role of disgust sensitivity. *British Journal of Psychology, 85,* 541–554.

Davey, G. C. L., & Bond, N. (2006). Using controlled comparisons in disgust psychopathology research: The case of disgust, hypochondriasis and health anxiety. *Journal of Behavior Therapy and Experimental Psychiatry, 37,* 4–15.

de Jong, P. J., Peters, M. L., & Vanderhallen, I. (2002). Disgust and disgust sensitivity in spider phobia: Facial EMG in response to spider and oral disgust imagery. *Journal of Anxiety Disorders, 16,* 477–493.

de Jong, P. J., van Overveld, M., Weijmar Schultz, W, Peters, M. L., & Buwalda, F.M. (2008). Disgust and contamination sensitivity in vaginismus and dyspareunia. *Archives of Sexual Behavior, 38,* 255–252.

Dick, C.L., Sowa, B., Bland, R.C., & Newman, S. C. (1994). Phobic disorders. *Acta Psychiatrica Scandinavica, 376,* 36–44.

Di Nardo, P., Moras, K., Barlow, D. H., Rapee, R. M., & Brown, T. A. (1993). Reliability of DSM-III-R anxiety disorder categories: Using the Anxiety Disorders Interview Schedule-Revised (ADIS-R). *Archives of General Psychiatry, 50,* 251–256.

Eke, M., & McNally, R. J. (1996). Anxiety sensitivity, suffocation fear, trait anxiety, and breath holding duration as predictors of response to carbon dioxide challenge. *Behaviour Research and Therapy, 34,* 603–607.

Emmelkamp, P. M. G. (2004). Behavior therapy with adults. In M. Lambert (Ed.), *Bergin and Garfield's handbook of psychotherapy and behavior change* (5th ed., pp. 393–446). New York: Wiley.

Emmelkamp, P. M. G., & Scholing, A. (1997). Anxiety disorders. In C. A. Essau & F. Petermann (Eds.), *Developmental psychopathology* (pp. 219–263). London: Harwood Academic Publishers.

Emmelkamp, P. M. G., & Wittchen, H. U. (in press). Specific phobia. In G. Andrews & D. Charney (Eds.), *Towards DSM-V: Fear circuitry disorders.* American Psychiatric Association.

Faravelli, C., Cosci, F., Rotella, F., Faravelli, L., & Catena Dell'Osso, M. (2008). Agoraphobia between panic and phobias: Clinical epidemiology from the Sesto Fiorentino Study. *Comprehensive Psychiatry 48,* 283–287.

Feldner, M. T., Zvolensky, M. J., & Leen–Feldner, E. W. (2004). A critical review of the empirical literature on coping and panic disorder. *Clinical Psychology Review, 24,* 123–148.

Feske, U., & de Beurs, E. (1997). The Panic Appraisal Inventory: Psychometric properties. *Behaviour Research and Therapy, 35,* 875–882.

Fredrickson, M., Annas, P., Fischer, H., & Wik, G. (1996). Gender and age differences in the prevalence of specific fears and phobias. *Behaviour Research and Therapy, 34,* 33–39.

Garvey, M. J., & Tuason, V. B. (1984). The relationship of panic disorder to agoraphobia. *Comprehensive Psychiatry, 25,* 529–531.

Goisman, R. M., Allworth, B. A., Rogers, M. P., Warshaw, M. G., Goldenberg, I., Vasile, R. G., et al. (1998). Simple phobia as a comorbid anxiety disorder. *Depression and Anxiety, 7,* 105–112.

Hackmann, A. (2006). Agoraphobia: Clinical features and treatment strategies. *Psychiatry, 6,* 254–257.

Hayward, C., Killen, J. D., & Taylor, C. B. (2003). The relationship between agoraphobia symptoms and panic disorder in a non-clinical sample of adolescents. *Psychological Medicine, 33,* 733–738.

Heinrichs, N., Edler, C., Eskens, S., Mielczarek, M. M. & Moschner, C. (2007). Predicting continued dizziness after an acute peripheral vestibular disorder. *Psychosomatic Medicine 69,* 700–707.

Hettema, J. M., Annas, P., Neale, M. C., Kendler, K. S., & Fredrikson, M. (2003). A twin study of the genetics of fear conditioning. *Archives of General Psychiatry, 60,* 702–708.

Hettema, J. M., Prescott, C. A., Myers, J. M., Neale, M. C. & Kendler, K. S. (2005). The structure of genetic and environmental risk factors for anxiety disorders in men and women. *Archives of General Psychiatry, 62,* 182–189.

Hofmann, S. G., Meuret, A. E., Rosenfield, D., Suvak, M. K., Barlow, D. H., Gorman, J. M., et al. (2007). Preliminary evidence for cognitive mediation during cognitive-behavioral therapy of panic disorder. *Journal of Consulting & Clinical Psychology, 75,* 374–379.

Holloway, W., & McNally, R. J. (1987). Effects of anxiety sensitivity on the response to hyperventilation. *Journal of Abnormal Psychology, 96,* 330–334.

Horwath, E., Lish, J. D., Johnson, J., Hornig, C. D., & Weissman, M. M. (1993). Agoraphobia without panic: Clinical reappraisal of an epidemiologic finding. *American Journal of Psychiatry, 150,* 1496–1501.

Husted, D., Shapira, N., & Goodman, W. (2006). The neurocircuitry of obsessive–compulsive disorder and disgust. *Progress in Neuro-Psychopharmacology and Biological Psychiatry, 30,* 389–399.

Ietsugu, T., Sukigara, M., & Furukawa, T. A. (2007). Evaluation of diagnostic criteria for panic attack using item response theory: Findings from the National Comorbidity Survey in USA. *Journal of Affective Disorders, 104,* 197–201.

Karno, M., Golding, J. M., Burnam, M. A., Hough, R. I., Escobar, J. I., Wells, K. M., et al. (1989). Anxiety disorders among Mexican Americans and non-Hispanic Whites in Los Angeles. *Journal of Nervous and Mental Disease, 177,* 202–209.

Kawakami, N., Takeshima, T., Ono, Y., Uda, H., Hata, Y., Nakane, Y., et al. (2005). Twelve-month prevalence, severity, and treatment of common mental disorders in communities in Japan: Preliminary finding from the World Mental Health Japan Survey 2002–2003. *Psychiatry and Clinical Neurosciences, 59,* 441–452.

Kendler, K. S., Neale, M. C., Kessler, R. C., Heath, A. C., & Eaves, L. J. (1992). The genetic epidemiology of phobias in women: The interrelationship of agoraphobia, social phobia, situational phobia, and simple phobia. *Archives of General Psychiatry, 49,* 273–281.

Kendler, K. S., & Prescott, C. A. (2006). *Genes, environment, and psychopathology: Understanding the causes of psychiatric and substance use disorders.* New York: Guilford Press.

Kessler, R. C., Berglund, P., Demler, O., Jin, R., Merikangas, K. R., & Walters, E. E. (2005). Lifetime prevalence and age-of-onset distributions of DSM-IV disorders in the National Comorbidity Survey Replication. *Archives of General Psychiatry, 62,* 593–602.

Lawrence, N. S., Ann, S. K., Mataix-Cols, D., Ruths, F. Speckens, A., & Phillips, M. L. (2007). Neural responses to facial expressions of disgust but not fear are modulated by washing symptoms in OCD. *Biological Psychiatry, 61,* 1072–1080.

Lipsitz, J. D., Barlow, D.H ., Mannuzza, S., Hofmann, S. G., & Fyer, A. J. (2002). Clinical features of four DSM-IV specific phobia subtypes. *Journal of Nervous and Mental Disease, 190,* 471–478.

Mannuzza, S., Fyre, A. J., Martin, L. Y., Gallops, M. S., Endicott, J., Gorman, J., et al. (1989). Reliability of anxiety assessment. I. Diagnostic agreement. *Archives of General Psychiatry, 46,* 1093–1101.

Marks, I. M. (1987). *Fears, phobias and rituals*. New York: Oxford University Press. Mataix-Cols, D., Cowley, A.J., Hankins, M., Schneider, A., Bachofen, M., Kenwright, M., et al. (2005). Reliability and validity of the Work and Social Adjustment Scale in phobic disorders. *Comprehensive Psychiatry, 46,* 223–228.

McNally, R. J., & Eke, M. (1996). Anxiety sensitivity, suffocation fear, and breath-holding duration as predictors of response to carbon dioxide challenge. *Journal of Abnormal Psychology, 105,* 146–149.

Meyers, J. K., Weissman, M. M., Tischler, G. L., Holzer, C. E., Leaf, P. J., Orvaschel, H., et al. (1984). Six-month prevalence of psychiatry disorders in three communities. *Archives of General Psychiatry, 41,* 959–967.

Mira, E. (2008). Improving the quality of life in patients with vestibular disorders: the role of medical treatments and physical rehabilitation. *International Journal of Clinical Practice, 62,* 109–114.

Muris, P., Schmidt, H., & Merckelbach, H. (1999). The structure of specific phobia symptoms among children and adolescents. *Behaviour Research and Therapy, 37,* 863–868.

Norton, P. J., Zvolensky, M. J., Bonn–Miller, M. O., Cox, B. J., & Norton, G. R. (2008). Use of the Panic Attack Questionnaire-IV to assess non-clinical panic attacks and limited symptom panic attacks in student and community samples. *Journal of Anxiety Disorders, 22,* 1159–1171.

Noyes, R., Clancy, J., Garvey, M. J., & Anderson, D. J. (1987). Is agoraphobia a variant of panic disorder or a separate illness? *Journal of Anxiety Disorders, 1,* 3–13.

Olatunji, B. O. (2006). Evaluative learning and emotional responding to fearful and disgusting stimuli in spider phobia. *Journal of Anxiety Disorders, 20,* 858–876.

Olatunji, B.O., & Deacon, B. (2008). Specificity of disgust sensitivity in the prediction of fear and disgust responding to a brief spider exposure. *Journal of Anxiety Disorders, 22,* 328–336.

Olatunji, B. O., Sawchuk, C. N., Lohr, J. M., & Patten, K. (2007). Fear and disgust responding to heterogeneous blood–injection injury stimuli. *Journal of Psychopathology and Behavioral Assessment, 29,* 1–8.

Olatunji, B. O., Williams, N. L., Lohr, J. M., & Sawchuk, C. N. (2005). The structure of disgust: Domain specificity in relation to contamination ideation and excessive washing. *Behaviour Research and Therapy, 43,* 1069–1086.

Öst, L. G. (1992). Blood and injection phobia: Background and cognitive, physiological, and behavioral variables. *Journal of Abnormal Psychology, 101,* 68–74.

Patten, S. B., & Williams, J. V. A. (2007). Chronic obstructive lung diseases and prevalence of mood, anxiety, and substance-use disorders in a large population sample. *Psychosomatics, 48,* 496–501.

Peterson, R. A., & Heilbronner, R. L. (1987). The Anxiety Sensitivity Index: Construct validity and factor analytic structure. *Journal of Anxiety Disorders, 1,* 117–121.

Peterson, R. A., & Reiss, S. (1987). *Anxiety Sensitivity Index manual.* Palos Heights, IL: International Diagnostic Systems.

Porzelius, J., Vest, M., & Nochomovitz, M. (1991). Respiratory function, cognitions, and panic in chronic obstructive pulmonary patients. *Behaviour Research and Therapy, 30,* 75–77.

Powers, M. B. & Emmelkamp, P. (2008). Dissemination of research findings. In D. Richard & S. Huprich (Eds.) *Clinical psychology: Assessment, treatment, and research* (495–525). San Diego, CA: Academic Press.

Rachman, S. (1994). The overprediction of fear: A review. *Behaviour Research and Therapy, 32,* 683–690.

Raffa, S. D., White, K. S., & Barlow, D. H. (2004). Feared consequences of panic attacks in panic disorder: A qualitative and qualitative analysis. *Cognitive Behaviour Therapy, 33,* 199–207.

Rapee, R. M., & Medoro, L. (1994). Fear of physical sensations and trait anxiety as mediators of the response to hyperventilation in non-clinical subjects. *Journal of Abnormal Psychology, 103,* 693–699.

Reiss, S., Peterson, R. A., Gursky, D. M., & McNally, R. J. (1986). Anxiety sensitivity, anxiety frequency, and the prediction of fearfulness. *Behaviour Research and Therapy, 24,* 1–8.

Roberts, R. E., Ramsay, C., & Yun Xing, R. (2007). Rates of DSM-IV psychiatric disorders among adolescents in a large metropolitan area. *Journal of Psychiatric Research, 41,* 959–967.

Robins, L. N., Helzer, J. E., Weissman, M. M., Orvaschel, H., Gruenberg, E., Burke, J. D., et al. (1984). Lifetime prevalence of specific psychiatric disorders in three sites. *Archives of General Psychiatry, 41,* 949–958.

Robins, L. N., & Regier, D. A. (Eds.), (1991). *Psychiatric disorders in America: The Epidemiologic Catchment Area Study.* New York: Free Press.

Rozin, P., Haidt, J., & McCauley, C. R. (2000). Disgust. In M. Lewis & J. M. Haviland (Eds.), *Handbook of emotions* (pp. 637–653). New York: Guilford.

Schmidt, N.B., & Cromer, K. R. (2008). Assessing the clinical utility of agoraphobia in the context of panic disorder. *Depression and Anxiety, 25,* 158–166.

Schmidt, N. B., Lerew, D. R., & Jackson, R. J. (1997). The role of anxiety sensitivity in the pathogenesis of panic: Prospective evaluation of spontaneous panic attacks during acute stress. *Journal of Abnormal Psychology, 106,* 355–364.

Schmidt, N. B., Lerew, D. R., & Joiner, T. E., Jr. (1998). Anxiety sensitivity and the pathogenesis of anxiety and depression: Evidence for symptom specificity. *Behaviour Research and Therapy, 36,* 165–177.

Schmidt, N. B., Salas, D., Bernert, R., & Schatschneider, C. (2005). Diagnosing agoraphobia in the context of panic disorder: Examining the effect of DSM-IV criteria on diagnostic decision-making. *Behaviour Research and Therapy, 43,* 1219–1229.

Schmidt, N. B., Trakowski, J. H., & Staab, J. P. (1997). Extinction of panicogenic effects of a 35% CO_2 challenge in patients with panic disorder. *Journal of Abnormal Psychology, 106,* 630–638.

Scupi, B. S., Benson, B. E., Brown, L. B., &Uhde, T. W. (1997). Rapid onset: A valid panic disorder criterion? *Depression and Anxiety, 5,* 121–126.

Seddon, K., & Nutt, D. (2007). Pharmacological treatment of panic disorder. *Psychiatry, 6,* 198–203.

Skre, L., Onstad, S., Torgersen, J., Lygren, S., & Kringlen, E. (1993). A twin study of DSM-III-R anxiety disorders. *Acta Psychiatrica Scandinavica, 88,* 85–92.

Smits, J. A., Berry, A. C., Rosenfield, D., Powers, M., Behar, E., & Otto, M. W. (2008). Reducing anxiety sensitivity with exercise. *Depression & Anxietym 25,* 689–699.

Smits, J. A., Powers, M. B., Cho, Y., & Telch, M. J. (2004). Mechanism of change in cognitive-behavioral treatment of panic disorder: Evidence for the fear of fear mediational hypothesis. *Journal of Consulting and Clinical Psychology, 72,* 646–652.

Spira, A. P., Zvolensky, M. J., Eifert, G. H., & Feldner, M. T. (2004). Avoidance-oriented coping as a predictor of panic-related distress: A test using biological challenge. *Journal of Anxiety Disorders, 18,* 309–323.

Starcevic, V., & Bogojevic, G. (1997). Comorbidity of panic disorder with agoraphobia and specific phobia: Relationship with the subtypes of specific phobia. *Comprehensive Psychiatry, 38,* 315–320.

Stinson, F. S., Dawson, D. A., Chou, S. P., Smith, S. Goldstein, R. B., Ruan, W. J., et al. (2007). The epidemiology of DSM-IV specific phobia in the USA: Results from the National Epidemiologic Survey on Alcohol and Related Conditions. *Psychological Medicine, 37,* 1047–1059.

Stewart, S. H., Taylor, S., Jang, K. L., Cox, B. J., Watt, M. C., Fedoroff, I. C., et al. (2001). Causal modeling of relations among learning history, anxiety sensitivity, and panic attacks. *Behaviour Research and Therapy, 39,* 443–456.

Taylor, S., Koch, W. J., & McNally, R. J. (1992). How does anxiety sensitivity vary across the anxiety disorders? *Journal of Anxiety Disorders, 6,* 249–259.

Telch, M. J., Brouillard, M., Telch, C. F., Agras, W. S., & Taylor, C. B. (1989). Role of cognitive appraisal in panic-related avoidance. *Behaviour Research and Therapy, 27,* 373–383.

Telch, M. J., Jacquin, K., Smits, J. A., & Powers, M. B. (2003). Emotional responding to hyperventilation as a predictor of agoraphobia status among individuals suffering from panic disorder. *Journal of Behavior Therapy and Experimental Psychiatry, 34,* 161–170.

The ESEMeD MHEDEA 2000 Investigators. (2004a). Prevalence of mental disorders in Europe: Results from the European Study of the Epidemiology of Mental Disorders (ESEMeD) project. *Acta Psychiatrica Scandinavica, 109*(Suppl. 420), 21–27.

Thyer, B. A., & Himle, J. (1985). Temporal relationship between panic attack onset and phobic avoidance in agoraphobia. *Behaviour Research and Therapy, 23,* 607–608.

Troop, N. A., Treasure, J. L., & Serpell, L. (2002). A further exploration of disgust in eating disorders. *European Eating Disorders Review, 10,* 218–226.

Turner, S. M., Williams, S. L., Beidel, D. C., & Mezzich, J. E. (1986). Panic disorder and agoraphobia with panic attacks: Covariation along the dimensions of panic and agoraphobic fear. *Journal of Abnormal Psychology, 95,* 384–388.

Watson, D. (2005). Rethinking the mood and anxiety disorders: A quantitative hierarchical model for DSM-V. *Journal of Abnormal Psychology, 114,* 522–536.

Weiser, E. B. (2007). The prevalence of anxiety disorders among adults with asthma: A meta-analytic review. *Journal of Clinical Psychology in Medical Settings, 14,* 297–307.

Williams, D. R., Herman, A., Stein, D.J., Heeringa, S.G., Jackson, P.B., Moomal, H., et al. (2008).Twelve-month mental disorders in South Africa: Prevalence, service use and demographic correlates in the population-based South African Stress and Health Study. *Psychological Medicine, 38,* 211–220.

Williams, J. B., Gibbon, M., First, M. B., Spitzer, R. L., Davies, M., Borus, J., et al. (1992). The Structured Clinical Interview for DSM-III-R (SCID). II. Multisite test-retest reliability. *Archives of General Psychiatry, 49,* 630–636.

Wittchen, H.U., & Jacobi, F. (2005). Size and burden of mental disorder in Europe: A critical review and appraisal of 27 studies. *European Neuropsychopharmacology, 15,* 357–376.

Wittchen, H. U., Nelson, C. B., & Lachner, G. (1998). Prevalence of mental disorders and psychosocial impairments in adolescents and young adults. *Psychological Medicine, 28,* 109–126.

Wittchen, H. U., Nocon, A., Beesdo, K., Pine, D.S., Hofler, S., Lieb, R., et al. (2008). Agoraphobia and panic: Prospective-longitudinal relations suggest a rethinking of diagnostic concepts. *Psychotherapy & Psychosomatics, 77,* 147–157.

Wittchen, H. U., Reed, V., & Kessler, R. C. (1998). The relationship of agoraphobia and panic disorder in a community sample of adolescents and young adults. *Archives of General Psychiatry, 55,* 1017–1024.

Wolpe, J., & Rowan, V. (1988). Panic disorder: A product of classical conditioning. *Behaviour Research and Therapy, 26,* 441–450.

Woody, S. R., McLean, C., & Klassen, T. (2005). Disgust as a motivator of avoidance of spiders. *Journal of Anxiety Disorders, 19,* 461–475.

Zimmerman, M., Chelminski, I., & Young, D. (2004). On the threshold of disorder: A study of the impact of the DSM-IV clinical significance criterion on diagnosing depressive and anxiety disorders in clinical practice. *Journal of Clinical Psychiatry, 65,* 1400–1405.

4

Neo-Kraepelinian Diagnosis: Adequacy for OCD, GAD, and PTSD

Randi E. McCabe
Richard P. Swinson
Andrew M. Jacobs

In a backlash to the dominance of psychoanalysis in American psychiatry post–World War II, the 1960s and 1970s saw a return to the basic principles of Kraepelin's approach to psychiatry: descriptive classification, observation of the course of mental illness, scientific knowledge through empirical research, and avoidance of etiological speculation (Decker, 2007). The leaders of this approach were termed *neo-Kraepelinians* by Klerman (1978). The neo-Kraepelinian approach was a significant influence on the transformation of the American Psychiatric Association's (APA) *Diagnostic and Statistical Manual* in the *Third Edition* (*DSM-III*), which saw a shift from opinion-based classification heavily influenced by psychoanalytic thought to an atheoretical, data-driven classification based on a medical model of mental illness. For reviews, see Decker, 2007.

The focus of this chapter is on the adequacy of neo-Kraepelinian diagnosis for obsessive–compulsive disorder (OCD), generalized anxiety disorder (GAD), and posttraumatic stress disorder (PTSD). Current diagnostic conceptualizations of these disorders are contained in the *DSM, Fourth Edition, Text Revision* (*DSM-IV-TR*; APA, 2000) and were developed through the *DSM-IV* work groups. Following neo-Kraepelinian principles, the task of the work groups was to develop criteria sets for disorders that were empirically supported. The empirical basis was established through literature reviews, reanalysis of existing data, and field trials to determine the reliability and validity of proposed criteria sets and address questions raised by the literature review (Liebowitz, 1996). Convergence with the *International Classification of Diseases, Tenth revision* (*ICD-10*) by the World Health Organization (WHO, 1992) was also a goal. The present chapter is divided into three sections separated by disorder. Within each section, we described the current diagnostic approach, the empirical basis for the current classification, as well as issues for consideration in *DSM, Fifth Edition* (*DSM-V*).

Obsessive–Compulsive Disorder

Conceptualization of OCD as a disorder characterized by the occurrence of obsessions and/or compulsions has remained remarkably stable across revisions of the *DSM*.

Current Diagnostic Approach

The *DSM-IV-TR* (2000) diagnostic criteria for OCD require the presence of *either* obsessions or compulsions (Criterion A). Obsessions are defined as "recurrent and persistent thoughts, impulses, or images that are experienced, at some time during the disturbance, as intrusive and inappropriate and that cause marked anxiety or distress" (p. 462). The intrusive thoughts, impulses, or images must not be just excessive worries about realistic concerns (to distinguish obsessions from worries seen in GAD). In addition, the individual must engage in efforts to resist (e.g., ignore or suppress) the thoughts, impulses, or images, or attempts to neutralize them with another thought or behavior. Finally, the individual must be aware that the intrusive thoughts, impulses, or images result from his or her own mind. Compulsions are defined as repetitive behaviors or mental acts that an individual "feels driven to perform" in response to an obsession or according to rigid rules.

Criterion B requires that an individual has displayed some insight into the excessive nature of the obsessions or compulsions at some point during the disturbance. However, insight is not required for a diagnosis in children. Criterion C specifies that the obsessions or compulsions cause significant distress or impairment in functioning or are time consuming (greater than 1 hour per day). To distinguish obsessions from preoccupations in the context of other disorders (e.g., illness concerns in hypochondriasis), Criterion D states that the content of the obsessions or compulsions must not be restricted to the content of another Axis I disorder. Finally, Criterion E specifies that the obsessions or compulsions are not accounted for by the effects of a substance or general medical condition. The specifier, "with poor insight" may be used for diagnosis in an individual who does not acknowledge the excessive or unreasonable nature of the obsessions or compulsions for most of the time during the disturbance.

The *ICD-10* definition of obsession includes ideas, images, and impulses that occur in a stereotyped form. The *ICD-10* specifies three categories of OCD differentiated by the dominance of the symptom set based on the rationale of differential treatment response. The three categories include, "predominantly obsessional thoughts or ruminations," "predominantly compulsive acts (obsessional rituals)," and "mixed obsessional thoughts and acts." There are significant differences between the diagnostic criteria for OCD in *DSM-IV* and *ICD-10*. Thus, it is no surprise that diagnostic agreement between the two classification systems is not high. For example, one study found a concordance rate of 64% (Andrews, Slade, & Peters, 1999) and agreement between the two systems was very poor when used in a sample of children and adolescents (Steinberger & Schuch, 2002). The *DSM-IV* criteria have been found to be superior to the *ICD-10* for diagnosing OCD in children and adolescents given the research finding that the diagnostic stability of the *ICD-10* OCD diagnosis was highly dependent on age (Steinberger & Schuch, 2002).

Empirical Basis

Changes to the diagnostic criteria for OCD in *DSM-IV* were based on findings of the literature reviews undertaken by the OCD sub-work group (Foa et al., 1996) and the results of the *DSM-IV* OCD field trial (Foa et al., 1995). The purpose of the field trial was to collect further data regarding three issues: (a) the degree to which individuals with OCD display insight, (b) the presence of mental compulsions and the degree to which they function as a compulsion to neutralize harm or reduce distress, and (c) the validity of the *ICD-10* OCD categories. Findings from the field trial confirmed both clinical observation and previous research. Insight was found to exist on a broad continuum, with 5% of OCD patients lacking insight into the excessive nature of their symptoms. This finding supported the addition of the OCD specifier "with poor insight." The data also supported the notion of mental compulsions, which were found to occur commonly in combination with behavioral compulsions. Mental compulsions served the same function as behavioral compulsions in preventing feared harm or reducing the distress caused by an obsession. Thus, *DSM-IV* included the presence of mental acts in the definition of a compulsion.

Field trial findings on the validity of the three *ICD-10* OCD categories were equivocal. Using data from the Yale-Brown Obsessive–Compulsive Scale (Y-BOCS; Goodman, Price, Rasmussen, Mazure, Delgado et al., 1989; Goodman, Price, Rasmussen, Mazure, Fleischmann et al., 1989) symptom checklist, Foa et al. (1995), found that 96% of patients had both obsessions and compulsions, 2% had predominantly obsessions, and 2% had predominantly compulsions. However, when presented with the three *ICD-10* categories and asked to self-identify, only 49.3% of patients identified predominantly mixed obsessions and compulsions; 29.6% of the patients identified predominantly obsessions; and 21.1% of the patients identified predominantly compulsions.

Reliability for the *DSM-IV* OCD criteria assessed using the Anxiety Disorders Interview Schedule for *DSM-IV*: Lifetime Version (ADIS-IV-L; DiNardo, Brown, & Barlow, 1994) has been found to be excellent for both current (kappa = .75) and lifetime (kappa = .75) disorder with the main source of unreliability because of the disagreement regarding the clinical status of OCD (Brown, DiNardo et al., 2001). Not surprisingly, the addition of the clinical significance criterion in *DSM-IV* has resulted in a significant reduction in OCD prevalence by 65% (Slade & Andrews, 2002).

Issues for *DSM-V*

Several issues arise from the clinical and research literature and should inform future revisions to our conceptualization of OCD for *DSM-V*.

Obsessive–compulsive spectrum disorders (OCSDs). The notion of OCSDs has been proposed based on significant overlap in clinical phenomenology, pathogenesis, and treatment response across a number of disorders, as well as the high frequency of comorbidity among these disorders (Hollander & Evers, 2004). Three basic clusters of OCSDs have been identified: neurological disorders with repetitive behaviors (e.g., Tourette's syndrome), impulse control disorders (e.g., trichotillomania), and body image, body sensation, and body weight concern disorders (e.g., body dysmorphic disorder (BDD) and hypochondriasis) (Hollander, Friedberg, Wasserman, Yeh, & Iyengar, 2005). One proposal for *DSM-V* has been to move OCD out of the anxiety disorders section into a new category along with the OCSDs entitled "Obsessive–Compulsive Behavior Spectrum" (Hollander & Evers, 2004).

For example, the *DSM-IV* OCD sub-work group noted the considerable overlap between OCD and BDD but because of lack of research examining the relation between the two disorders at the time, BDD was not classified as a subgroup of OCD, although the work group recommended that the issue be given reconsideration for *DSM-V* (Foa et al., 1996). In a study comparing the clinical features between BDD and OCD, Phillips and colleagues (2007) found that although there was considerable clinical overlap between the two disorders, differences emerged on variables of insight (BDD was associated with poorer insight), suicidal ideation (BDD was associated with greater lifetime suicidal ideation), and comorbidity (BDD was associated with a higher likelihood of lifetime major depressive disorder and substance use disorder). These differences suggest that BDD may be more appropriately considered within an OCD-spectrum disorders section in *DSM-V* rather than as a subgroup of OCD.

To determine areas of expert consensus and disagreement on the issue of OCD classification, Mataix-Cols, Pertusa, and Leckman (2007) conducted a survey of 303 international OCD experts (individuals identified as corresponding authors on OCD publications between 1996 and 2006) of whom 187 responded. Sixty percent of respondents favored the removal of OCD from the anxiety disorders category based predominantly on obsessions and compulsions rather than anxiety as the central feature of the disorder. Opposition to the removal of OCD from the anxiety disorders category was based primarily on the finding that OCD and other anxiety disorders respond to the same treatments and tend to co-occur. Interestingly, there was a significant difference in the opinions of psychiatrists (75% of whom agreed) compared to other professionals who were comprised primarily of psychologists (40%–45% agreement). If an OCD spectrum disorders category is created, the expert consensus was to favor a narrow category that contains only BDD, trichotillomania, tic disorders, hypochondriasis, and possibly obsessive–compulsive personality disorder (OCPD). In their recommendations, the authors concluded that there was insufficient consensus at this time to recommend the removal of OCD from the category of anxiety disorders.

The expert consensus survey highlights the issue of OCSDs as a contentious one. The opposing view is that the notion of OCSDs is based on a superficial analysis of similarities and OCD should remain within the anxiety disorders category as it shares fundamental features with other anxiety disorders (Abramowitz & Deacon, 2005).

The overlap between OCD and OCPD. Both OCD and OCPD have a number of shared clinical features. Several studies have found OCPD to be more prevalent than other personality disorders in patients with OCD (e.g., Tenney, Schotte, Denys, van Megen, & Westenberg, 2003), suggestive of a unique OCD–OCPD link. However, subsequent research examining the prevalence of OCPD in OCD (23%) and a control anxiety disorder group of individuals with panic disorder (17%) did not find support for a specific OCD–OCPD relation (Albert, Maina, Forner, & Bogetto, 2004). Given the limited research on this issue using *DSM-IV* criteria, further examination is warranted.

Should compulsive hoarding be classified as distinct from OCD? It has been suggested that compulsive hoarding may be more appropriately viewed as a distinct disorder as it is associated with other disorders (e.g., schizophrenia, dementia, autism, mental retardation) and is not specific to OCD (Abramowitz, Wheaton, & Storch, 2008; Saxena, 2007; Stein, Seedat, & Potocnik, 1999). Several other differences between OCD and compulsive hoarding have been documented including the ego-syntonic basis of hoarding, the emergence of hoarding as a separate factor in factor analytic studies using the Y-BOCS symptom checklist, and differential response to treatment (Frost & Tolin, 2008). On the other side of the debate is evidence supporting a link between OCD and hoarding including the high frequency of hoarding in OCD patients (Samuels et al., 2002) and evidence of a genetic linkage to compulsive hoarding behavior in families with OCD (Samuels et al., 2007). Further research is needed before hoarding is reclassified in *DSM-V*.

The search for OCD symptom subtypes and dimensions. In *DSM-IV*, OCD is conceptualized as a unitary disorder. However, clinical practice and research suggest that, in fact, OCD is a heterogeneous disorder with significant variation in symptom profiles across patients. There has been an increasing body of literature examining both dimensional and subtype models of the disorder, with a lack of clear consensus on the best model (Abramowitz, McKay, & Taylor, 2005).

Dimensional models based on factor analyses of various symptom checklists, such as the Y-BOCS generally support four factors (Leckman et al., 1997, Summerfeldt et al., 1999): (a) aggressive, sexual, religious, and somatic obsessions, and checking compulsions, (b) symmetry obsessions and ordering/arranging, counting, and repeating compulsions, (c) contamination obsessions and cleaning compulsions, and (d) hoarding/saving obsessions and hoarding/collecting compulsions.

Various subtype models have been based on the presence or absence of clinical features, such as early age of OCD onset, history of tics, and family history of OCD (Leckman et al., 2000) and OCD-related dysfunctional beliefs (Taylor et al., 2006). Recent evidence supports a combined model with both dimensions and categorical subtypes (Haslam, Williams, Kyrios, McKay, & Taylor, 2005).

The search for OCD subtypes is a complex endeavor that must take into consideration theoretical, conceptual, and practical issues (Radomsky & Taylor, 2005). However, the search may be a fruitful one given the research that specialized cognitive behavioral therapy (CBT) approaches tailored to specific subtypes may augment treatment response (Sookman, Abramowitz, Calamari, Wilhelm, & McKay, 2005).

Differentiation of OCD from other repetitive behavior disorders. It can be challenging for clinicians to differentiate OCD from other repetitive behavior disorders when formulating a diagnosis. Abramowitz and Deacon (2005) identify three limitations of the current *DSM-IV* OCD criteria that contribute to this problem: (a) the wording of the criteria to require *either* obsessions or compulsions neglects the basic phenomenology of OCD and the relation between the two phenomena, thus allowing inclusion of symptoms that are not truly representative of OCD (e.g., compulsive gambling); (b) the lack of reference to the functional relationship between obsessions and compulsions (i.e., that compulsions are performed to reduce distress evoked by obsessions) allows for any disorder characterized by repetitive behaviors (e.g., trichotillomania) to be conceptualized as related to OCD; and (c) the emphasis on the *form* of compulsive behavior as repetitive and stereotyped also neglects the functional properties of the behavior including covert neutralizing strategies that also serve to reduce distress associated with an obsessive thought (e.g., avoidance).

Summary

The neo-Kraepelinian approach to OCD has facilitated the development of our conceptualization of this disorder, the core features of which (i.e., obsessions and compulsions) have remained fairly stable over various revisions of the *DSM*. This approach has ensured that revisions to the criteria set have been based on careful review of the research literature and collection of further data to address identified gaps. Several key issues need to be considered in preparation for *DSM-V*. The issue of where OCD should be classified (anxiety disorder vs OCSD) is a contentious one. Greater focus on the functional basis of OCD symptoms in *DSM-V* would assist in differentiating OCD from other repetitive behavior disorders. Attention should also be directed toward improved differentiation of OCD and OCPD. Research on OCD subtype and dimensional models is newly emerging and no clear model has the support at this time for incorporation into *DSM-V*. However, a recommendation of the expert consensus survey (Mataix–Cols et al., 2007) was to maintain the categorical approach to OCD in *DSM-V*, but to give consideration to the added value of a dimensional approach.

Generalized Anxiety Disorder

GAD was formally recognized as a syndrome in *DSM-III* (APA, 1980) and was originally intended to serve as a "residual" diagnosis for individuals who had chronically elevated anxiety levels, but did not meet full criteria for the acute attacks that were the hallmark of panic disorder (Rickels & Rynn, 2001). To meet criteria for the *DSM-III* diagnosis, the persistent anxiety needed be present for at least 1 month and manifested in three of four symptom categories: motor tension, autonomic hyperactivity, apprehensive expectation, and hypervigilance. Notably, the diagnosis could not be given in the presence of another disorder (APA, 1980). With the development of *DSM-III-R* (APA, 1987), this exclusionary guideline was relaxed to permit comorbid diagnoses if the focus of anxiety was unrelated to the other disorder(s). An exception to this exclusionary criterion was that the symptoms of GAD may not occur exclusively within the context of a major depressive episode—a caveat that remains in the current edition of the *DSM* (APA, 2000). The nature of anxiety was refined to reflect unrealistic and excessive worry about two or more life domains, which would now be accompanied by at least 6 of 18 associated symptoms over a period of at least 6 months.

Current Diagnostic Approach

DSM-IV (APA, 1994) further characterized the excessive worry of GAD as "pervasive" and subjectively uncontrollable. The qualifier of worry being perceived as "unrealistic" was removed to reflect the contemporary understanding that GAD worries tended to focus on real-life concerns (Liebowitz, 1996); however, worries for individuals with GAD are still assessed as being far disproportionate to the actual likelihood or severity of the feared outcome (APA, 2000). The previous exhaustive list of 18 additional symptoms was reduced to 6, 3 of which must be present over a 6-month period: restlessness, being easily fatigued, concentration difficulties, irritability, muscle tension, and disrupted sleep. For children, "overanxious disorder of childhood" diagnosis was subsumed under the heading of GAD, with only 1 of the 6 additional symptoms being required. The *DSM-IV* also modified the degree of distress or impairment required to make a diagnosis; whereas *DSM-III* and *DSM-III-R* noted only the presence of a mild impairment as sufficient to meet diagnostic criteria, *DSM-IV* specifies that the overall experience of worry must lead to marked and severe distress and/or interference with normal functioning (Rickels & Rynn, 2001). These diagnostic modifications have been carried forward in the *DSM-IV-TR* (APA, 2000).

The development of the *DSM-IV* criteria for GAD also aimed to increase compatibility and correspondence with the *ICD-10* (Liebowitz, 1996). Although the two systems do, to a large extent, agree in their description of the disorder, several discrepancies exist. *ICD-10* retains a much broader list of 22 somatic and cognitive symptoms that address domains of autonomic arousal, chest/abdomen symptoms, symptoms involving mental state, general bodily symptoms, symptoms of tension, and other nonspecific symptoms (e.g., hypervigilance, difficulty concentrating, irritability, and sleep difficulties). Unlike the *DSM-IV*, the *ICD-10* diagnosis of GAD does not require that the symptoms cause "clinically significant distress or impairment;" rather, the symptoms need only be "prominent." Perhaps most notably, *ICD-10* does not specify that the worries experienced by an individual with GAD must be excessive or difficult to control. These differences in diagnostic criteria have led to research suggesting that despite the apparent similarities, the *ICD-10* may be diagnosing a less disabling condition than that required to meet the diagnostic criteria in *DSM-IV* (Slade & Andrews, 2001). In one study, the concordance rate between the *DSM-IV* and *ICD-10* systems for GAD diagnosis was 77% (Andrews et al., 1999).

Empirical Basis

In refining the diagnostic criteria for GAD during the development of *DSM-IV*, the problematic reliability in assessing the disorder was targeted as one of the primary areas for research and review (Moras et al., 1996). Several of the criteria were considered to already have adequate interrater reliability, such as the presence of worry and identification of 6 or more associated symptoms (Brown, Barlow, & Liebowitz, 1994). After conducting extensive literature reviews, the work group highlighted the reliability difficulties encountered when assessing the 18-item list of associated symptoms (Moras et al., 1996). In particular, the autonomic hyperactivity cluster of symptoms was identified as being particularly unreliable and infrequently endorsed by individuals with GAD and was therefore suggested for deletion. A smaller set of 7 associated symptoms was found to most reliably identify individuals with GAD (Marten et al., 1993). In light of these findings, the *DSM-IV* reduced the associated list to 6 symptoms, requiring that 3 or more be present for at least 6 months.

The modifications made to GAD diagnostic criteria in *DSM-IV* have led to a significant increase in reliability of diagnosis for the disorder. A large-scale study by Brown, DiNardo, and colleagues (2001) utilizing the ADIS-IV-L found that diagnostic reliability for a principal *DSM-IV* diagnosis of GAD had a kappa value of .67 (good agreement), a marked improvement over the .57 kappa (fair agreement) obtained using the *DSM-III-R*. Similarly pronounced improvements were found when including GAD as a current diagnosis at any clinical level (principal or otherwise), with a kappa value increased to .65 in comparison to the .53 of *DSM-III-R*. Finally, diagnostic reliability for a lifetime diagnosis of GAD was also found to have a kappa value of .65. Most of the interrater disagreement surfaced when differentiating between GAD and another disorder, particularly mood disorders and anxiety disorder not otherwise specified. Also noted as a factor confounding interrater reliability was variation in participants' reporting of their symptoms, which was marginally higher for GAD than for other anxiety disorders (with the exception of posttraumatic stress disorder [PTSD]). Another study by Zanarini et al. (2000), examining the reliability of assessments using the *DSM-IV* version of the Structured Clinical Interview for *DSM* (SCID-IV; First, Spitzer, Gibbon, & Williams, 1996), found the interrater reliability for GAD to be at a kappa level of .63 (on par with that of other anxiety disorders).

Among the more common complaints levied against the validity of *DSM-III-R* GAD was its exceptionally high comorbidity rate and low discriminability from depression and dysthymia. Reviews conducted by the *DSM-IV* anxiety disorders sub-work group noted that insufficient data existed to make clear conclusions regarding the relation of GAD to dysthymia; however, sufficient evidence was found to indicate that certain symptoms of dysthymia (e.g., low mood, suicidality, and feelings of hopelessness) were able to discriminate the condition from GAD. In light of the dearth of evidence suggesting a clear modification that would enhance discriminant validity between GAD and mood disorders, no suggestions were made for criteria revision in this regard (Moras et al., 1996). However, it has been suggested that GAD could also be distinguished by its relative lack of anhedonia and dysphoric symptoms that are assessed in *DSM* criteria for mood disorders (Brown et al., 1994).

As noted above, the decision to omit the autonomic hyperactivity criteria in *DSM-IV* was based on the findings of Marten et al. (1993) that precursors of the current smaller set of associated symptoms were found to be more reliably rated and more frequently endorsed by individuals with GAD. This modification was found to have no adverse impact on discriminative validity (Turvey, Stevens, & Merikangas, 1999). Replication of the findings that motor tension-related associated symptoms were prevalent in GAD led Turvey et al. (1999) to conclude that GAD is a distinct diagnosis on the basis of its element of vigilance and tension, rather than of hyperactive autonomic arousal. As noted by Roemer, Orsillo, and Barlow (2002), this consistent finding may also reflect recent research suggesting that autonomic arousal may actually be *lower* in most people with GAD.

Issues for *DSM-V*

In preparation for *DSM-V* and the potential extension of neo-Kraepelinian classification into the next generation of clinical diagnostics, several areas have been identified as requiring further investigation.

Comorbidity and overlap with depression. As noted above, a key controversy for GAD is the high rate of comorbidity with other anxiety and mood disorders, despite a general research consensus that *DSM-IV* GAD does represent an independent disorder (Roemer et al., 2002). Several recent research findings have suggested that the current criteria for GAD may be too restrictive in permitting the diagnosis. In review of data collected from a large-scale comorbidity study, Kessler et al. (2005) found few differences in impairment, persistence of illness, sociodemographic factors, or comorbidity between individuals who met the 6-month duration criterion of *DSM-IV* and those who experienced clinically significant GAD-like symptoms for episodes lasting from 1 to 5 months. Using the same sample, Ruscio et al. (2005) noted that individuals meeting all but the "excessive worry" criteria experience a clinically significant GAD-like syndrome, albeit in a somewhat milder form. Expanding on these findings, Ruscio et al. (2007) suggest that by broadening diagnostic criteria for GAD (relaxing the 6-month duration, excessive worry, and 3 associated symptoms requirements), validity and clinical utility of the diagnosis may actually be enhanced. Although prevalence rates nearly doubled with the relaxed criteria, rates of comorbid disorders decreased slightly with a more broadly defined GAD. The authors suggest that the use of more relaxed diagnostic criteria may allow for earlier intervention with individuals at greater risk of developing future secondary disorders.

In a similar vein, the retention of the exclusionary criterion from *DSM-III-R* has raised concern that depressed individuals experiencing concurrent GAD symptoms are not being accurately diagnosed in subsuming GAD under the mood diagnosis. A large outpatient study of individuals with major depressive disorder (MDD) found individuals with both *DSM-IV* GAD and a "modified" form of the diagnosis (capturing individuals described in the exclusionary criterion) had increased symptoms across a number of domains compared to individuals who were "purely" depressed. Notably, the *DSM-IV* GAD groups and "modified" GAD groups did not differ from each other on these same domains, suggesting that the exclusionary criterion be considered for deletion in *DSM-V* (Zimmerman & Chelminski, 2003). This argument is bolstered by the results of a prospective study by Moffitt et al. (2007) that found MDD precedes the development of GAD almost as frequently as the reverse suggesting that the current diagnostic hierarchy may be inaccurate in its default primary placement of MDD.

Core features of GAD. The role of pathological worry as a defining feature of GAD has also been brought into question. Rickels and Rynn (2001) cite several studies, which suggest that excessive worry is not necessarily a distinguishing feature of GAD from individuals without the disorder. Additionally, as noted by Purdon and Harrington (2006), worry is a prominent concern in many mental health disorders and may emerge as "uncontrollable," regardless of the diagnosis. Several other constructs may figure more prominently in the phenomenology of GAD than the current focus on excess worry, including intolerance of uncertainty, "worry about worry," emotional avoidance, and deficits in emotional regulation (Mennin, Heimberg, & Turk, 2004).

Summary

GAD has become an increasingly reliable descriptive diagnosis over various revisions in the *DSM*; however, as with any scientific endeavour, several uncertainties remain in the effort to accurately identify GAD as a distinct syndrome. Reliability of the diagnosis has made significant gains; however, validity of the diagnosis itself continues to raise a number of important questions. The ongoing debate regarding high comorbidity rates, potentially restrictive diagnostic criteria, and possible uprooting of "excessive worry" as the core foundation of GAD have led to several exciting developments in our conceptualization of the disorder. The neo-Kraepelinian approach has allowed GAD to be assessed, treated, and researched as a distinct entity; however, many of the questions that have plagued the diagnosis since its conception may ultimately be best answered through a different lens, such as a factor-based, multidimensional approach (e.g., Kubarych, Aggen, Hettema, Kendler, & Neale, 2005).

Posttraumatic Stress Disorder

Clinical syndromes of posttraumatic stress have been documented in the clinical literature since the mid-9th century (Kinzie & Goetz, 1996). Since the entry of PTSD as a formal diagnosis in the category of anxiety disorders in *DSM-III* (1980), PTSD criteria have evolved over subsequent revisions based on clinical experience, empirical research, and efforts to increase specificity with the ultimate goal of acknowledging the psychological impact of trauma and advancing treatment interventions.

Current Diagnostic Approach

The *DSM-IV-TR* (2000) conceptualization of PTSD is based on six criteria, all of which have been the subject of some controversy (e.g., McNally, 2004). Criterion A specifies that an individual must have experienced a traumatic stressor, which is defined as "actual or threatened death or serious injury, or a threat to the physical integrity of self or others" (Criterion A1) to which the individual responds with feelings of intense fear, helplessness, or horror (Criterion A2). Criteria B, C, and D represent the three symptom clusters of PTSD: reexperiencing symptoms (at least 1 of 5 intrusive symptoms required), avoidance and numbing of general responsiveness (at least 3 of 7 symptoms required), and increased arousal (at least 2 of 5 hyperarousal symptoms required). Criterion E specifies that the symptoms must persist for greater than 1 month and Criterion F states that the symptoms must cause clinically significant distress or impairment in functioning. Symptom duration is specified as acute (less than 3 months) or chronic (greater than 3 months). In addition, a delayed onset specifier is used if the symptoms occur more than 6 months following the traumatic stressor.

Acute posttraumatic stress symptoms are diagnosed as acute stress disorder (ASD) in *DSM-IV*. For the diagnosis of ASD, the individual must have experienced a Criterion A traumatic event as defined above. Criterion B requires the presence of at least 3 dissociative symptoms experienced during or after the trauma. Criteria C, D, and E represent the 3 symptom clusters of PTSD above: reexperiencing symptoms (at least 1), avoidance of trauma cues, and symptoms of anxiety or hyperarousal. Similar to PTSD, Criterion F requires clinically significant distress or impairment. Criterion G specifies that the disturbance occurs within 4 weeks of the traumatic event and lasts at least 2 days but not more than 4 weeks.

The focus of this chapter is on PTSD; however, it should be noted that the current conceptualization of ASD has also generated much controversy. ASD may be viewed as an arbitrary dichotomization of PTSD into two different disorders with distinct yet overlapping criteria sets based on symptom duration (less than or greater than 4 weeks) (Marshall, Spitzer, & Liebowitz, 1999). A key criticism of the ASD diagnostic conceptualization is that it does not provide broad-enough coverage for acute posttrauma reactions given the central focus placed on dissociative symptoms (Marshall et al., 1999). This view has also generated much debate (e.g., Marshall, Spitzer, & Liebowitz, 2000).

Comparisons of the conceptualization of PTSD in *DSM-IV* and *ICD-10* reveal many broad commonalities; however, there are also some key differences. *ICD-10* defines PTSD as a delayed and/or prolonged response to a stressful event or situation that is "exceptionally threatening or catastrophic" and would typically cause "pervasive distress in almost anyone." The threshold for diagnosis of PTSD is lower as fewer symptoms must be present and there is no requirement for clinically significant distress and impairment. In *ICD-10*, PTSD is in the category of "reaction to severe stress and adjustment disorders" based on the etiology of the disorder in response to an "exceptionally stressful life event" (p. 145). Although some consideration was given to placing PTSD in a separate category for disorders of extreme stress for *DSM-IV*, the disorder was retained in the anxiety disorders section based on the descriptive rather than etiological approach of *DSM-IV* (Liebowitz, 1996).

Because of the differences between *DSM-IV* and *ICD-10* PTSD conceptualizations, agreement between the two systems is quite poor. One study found a concordance rate for PTSD of 35%, which was among the lowest for all mental disorders (Andrews et al., 1999). In another study comparing *DSM-IV* and *ICD-10* PTSD criteria, Peters, Slade, and Andrews (1999) found that agreement was fair (kappa = .50) and the 12-month prevalence rates of PTSD were higher when *ICD-10* criteria were used (7%) than when *DSM-IV* criteria were used (3%). Discrepancy between the two systems was largely accounted for by the clinically significant distress/impairment criterion (48%) and to a lesser degree by the inclusion of symptoms of general numbing of responsiveness (18%) in *ICD-10*. In contrast to *DSM-IV*, the *ICD-10* diagnostic system has been associated with gender differences in the threshold for diagnosis of PTSD because of the different patterns of symptom endorsement by men and women (Peters, Issakidis,

Slade, & Andrews, 2006). Although both diagnostic systems are designed to facilitate research on PTSD by providing a common language, the differences between the two systems mean that researchers cannot readily compare *DSM-IV* and *ICD-10* PTSD studies as they are not capturing the same clinical phenomenon.

Empirical Basis

Reliability for the *DSM-IV* PTSD criteria assessed using the ADIS-IV-L has been found to be fair (kappa = .59) for current PTSD and good (kappa = .61) for lifetime PTSD, with unreliability arising largely from differences in patient report (Brown, DiNardo et al., 2001). Unreliability may also stem from differences in clinical opinion whether a traumatic event satisfies Criterion A (McNally, 2003). The main issues surrounding the PTSD diagnosis have largely been ones of validity. Does the current criteria set truly capture the core features of PTSD?

Definition of the traumatic event (Criterion A). The stressor criterion has been described as the "gatekeeper to PTSD" (Davidson & Foa, 1991). If an individual has not experienced a stressor as defined by Criterion A, a diagnosis of PTSD is ruled out and a diagnosis of adjustment disorder may be warranted. In *DSM-III-R* (APA, 1987), Criterion A required that the stressor event be "outside the range of usual human experience." No reference was made to an individual's subjective response to the stressor. *DSM-IV* broadened the definition of the trauma to include events that are in the range of all human experience (e.g., hearing about something horrible that has happened to another person). In addition, Criterion A also makes reference to the individual's subjective response to the traumatic event.

In a study examining the impact of the *DSM-IV* two-part stressor criterion, Breslau and Kessler (2001) found that broadening the definition of traumatic event increased the life experiences that were considered traumatic stressors by about 59%, to the point that "almost anyone has experienced a PTSD-level event." The expanded definition resulted in a significant increase in PTSD prevalence, primarily attributed to the inclusion of learning about the sudden unexpected death of a loved one. The broadening of the stressor criterion may have significant consequences. As McNally (2003) points out, capturing very different phenomena within the same diagnostic category may have the negative effect of reducing our ability to understand the true underpinnings of PTSD.

The addition of the subjective response in Criterion A was based on data showing that emotional responses are predictive of PTSD (Brewin, Andrews, & Rose, 2000; Roemer et al., 1998). Breslau and Kessler (2001) found that the events added in *DSM-IV* were just as likely to involve the A2 emotional response but less likely to result in PTSD. Given these findings, it has been proposed that the A2 response may be more appropriate as a separate criterion necessary for the emergence of PTSD rather than a component of the traumatic stressor (Breslau & Kessler, 2001). Other research has found that the early emotions of fear, helplessness, and horror may not be a good predictor of PTSD, and that other emotions, such as shame and anger toward others may also predict later PTSD (Brewin et al., 2000). This has lead to the recommendation that the criteria should be broadened to include other emotions that occur during the trauma or during subsequent cognitive appraisal (Brewin et al., 2000).

PTSD symptom clusters (Criteria B, C, and D). The 3 symptom clusters were initially established using expert consensus. Later empirical research has used exploratory and confirmatory factor analysis of symptoms endorsed on various PTSD symptom rating scales to determine whether these symptom clusters were most representative of the basic underlying features of PTSD (e.g., Taylor, Kuch, Koch, Crockett, & Passey, 1998). These studies found support for alternate models of the PTSD symptom clusters. Asmundson and colleagues (2000) compared models, supported by previous factor-analytic studies, with each other and with models based on the *DSM-IV* using confirmatory factor analysis. Their data supported a four-factor model (re-experiencing, avoidance, numbing, and hyperarousal) subsumed under a higher-order general factor. Collectively, the findings of these studies provide support for the separation of avoidance from numbing in revisions to the PTSD criteria set for *DSM-V*.

Clinically significant distress or impairment (Criterion F). The addition of Criterion F was to ensure that individuals receiving a diagnosis of PTSD were not experiencing normative reactions to psychological stress and that their symptoms were severe enough to warrant a psychiatric diagnosis (Slade & Andrews, 2002). Several studies have been conducted to examine the impact of the addition of the clinical significance criterion to the criteria for PTSD. In a sample of psychiatric outpatients, the inclusion of the clinical significance criterion had little impact, most likely because individuals seeking treatment are motivated to do so because they are experiencing high levels of distress and/or impairment (Zimmerman, Chelminski, & Young, 2004). Research on community samples reveals the criterion to have more of an effect. In a study using data from an Australian epidemiological survey of mental disorders, Slade and Andrews (2002) found that the current prevalence of PTSD was reduced by 24% with the inclusion of the clinical significance criterion.

Breslau and Alvarado (2007) used data from two population samples to evaluate the effect of the clinical significance criterion on the conditional probability of PTSD given trauma exposure and the construct validity of the criterion. They found that the clinical significance criterion reduced the number of PTSD cases by approximately 30%. They also found support for the construct validity of the measurement of the criterion, as individuals who met the criterion exhibited greater disturbance and impaired activity days than did individuals who did not meet the criterion.

Issues for *DSM-V*

In the development of the *DSM-IV* PTSD criteria set, the PTSD sub-work group considered eight issues in their empirical review (Davidson et al., 1996): the definition of the stressor criterion, PTSD symptomatology, where PTSD should be classified (anxiety disorder, dissociative disorder, or stress disorder), biological aspects (e.g., how research developments should influence our understanding of the correct classification of the disorder and the specified criteria), longitudinal course, subtypes and symptom duration (including overlap with adjustment disorder), epidemiology (to provide broader representation of the disorder), and evidence for complex posttraumatic syndrome that results from the effects of prolonged and repeated trauma. More than 10 years later, these same issues should be revisited by the PTSD sub-work group for *DSM-V*.

A significant limitation of the *DSM-IV* is that there is no category to use for complex posttraumatic stress presentations in individuals who have experienced prolonged victimization. Complex PTSD (also referred to as complicated PTSD, disorders of extreme stress, and disorders of extreme stress not otherwise specified) was considered to be a distinct syndrome from PTSD although it warranted further study (Liebowitz, 1996). Despite empirical support for the syndrome in the field trial (Roth, Newman, Pelcovitz, van der Kolk, & Mandel, 1997), the decision was made to make reference to it in the associated features section of *DSM-IV* as a "constellation of symptoms. . .more commonly seen in association with an interpersonal stressor" (p. 465), such as child sexual or physical abuse and domestic abuse. The cluster of symptoms includes impaired affect regulation, self-destructive and impulsive behavior, dissociative symptoms, impaired relationships with others, and change in personality. Serious consideration should be given to providing criteria set for complex PTSD in *DSM-V*, at least within the section on criteria sets for further study. Separate recognition would assist in research efforts to guide treatment.

Modifications to our definition of PTSD in *DSM-V* will also benefit from recent research on the biological mechanisms underlying PTSD. For example, research on the pathophysiology of PTSD and specifically tonic immobility in the acute response to trauma (Marx, Forsyth, Gallup, Fusé, & Lexington, 2008) has led some to suggest that consideration should be given to evolution theory in reconceptualization of PTSD in the *DSM-V* (Bracha & Maser, 2008).

Summary

Neo-Kraepelinian diagnosis has benefited PTSD by providing researchers with a common language to further research aimed at refining our conceptualization of the disorder, identifying the underlying mechanisms, increasing our understanding of risk factors, and developing treatment interventions. The *DSM-IV* PTSD criteria set demonstrates fair to good reliability and benefits mental health professionals in their efforts to identify and treat individuals suffering from this syndrome. Of course, no system is perfect, and the review above reveals that there are many issues that require further study and debate in preparation for future revision of the criteria set in *DSM-V*. Many of these issues relate to the validity of the current criteria set in terms of its ability to truly capture the core features of PTSD. In addition, there are issues related to breadth of coverage ranging from attributing pathological status to events within the realm of normal human experience (i.e., the current definition of traumatic stressor) to the inadequacy of the current system in capturing more complex presentations of posttraumatic stress. Revisions of the criteria set have had direct effects on the prevalence of the disorder and should be undertaken with caution (e.g., Schwarz & Kowalski, 1991).

Conclusion

The strength of the neo-Kraepelinian approach to diagnosis has been the research generated to further our understanding of OCD, GAD, and PTSD. In line with neo-Kraepelinian principles, this research has been used to refine our conceptualization of these disorders with subsequent revisions to the *DSM*. The criteria sets in the most recent iteration of the *DSM* have allowed OCD, GAD, and PTSD researchers to ensure that they are assessing, studying, and treating the same clinical phenomena; however, this approach is not without limitations.

The controversy surrounding the clinical significance criterion in *DSM-IV* underscores a significant limitation of the categorical approach. Spitzer's (1998) view was that mental disorders should be conceptualized in the same way as physical disorders—on a continuum of distress and impairment. Slade and Andrews (2002) echoed this view, noting that milder forms of a disorder may not be associated with significant distress or impairment, and thus our conceptualization of "mental disorder" should be reconsidered in the revision of *DSM-V*. It has been proposed that, similar to *ICD-10*, assessment of impairment or distress should be measured separately in *DSM-V* and should not be a defining feature of the disorder (Spitzer & Wakefield, 1999).

As noted by Brown, Campbell, and colleagues (2001), one of the issues in the reliability of diagnoses based on the *DSM* is not lack of agreement on the defining features of the disorder, but rather the application of categorical cutoffs (presence or absence) to dimensional criteria (i.e., distress and impairment). In addition, the adequacy of the current system for these clinical disorders is limited by the fact that studies to validate the criteria are restricted by the criteria themselves (Brown, 2002). Further, the categorical approach does not truly reflect the dimensional nature of psychopathology, which is cut with arbitrary thresholds (Brown, 2002). Advancement in our understanding of these disorders would benefit from greater empirical examination of shared features (e.g., Slade & Watson, 2006), which may hold greater significance than the unique features of individual disorders (Brown, 2002). The finding that OCD, GAD, and PTSD all have high lifetime comorbidity with other anxiety disorders and with mood disorders (Brown, Campbell et al., 2001) illustrates the point that these disorders have much in common and that their boundaries are not clear cut.

Despite these limitations, the neo-Kraepelinian approach has provided us with a classification system (*DSM-IV*) that demonstrates moderate to good reliability for OCD, GAD, and PTSD. The validity issues reviewed above should direct further modifications to the criteria for *DSM-V*. Any modifications should be undertaken carefully, based on compelling empirical support.

References

Abramowitz, J., & Deacon, B.J. (2005). Obsessive–compulsive disorder: Essential phenomenology and overlap with other anxiety disorders. In J.S. Abramowitz & A.C. Houts (Eds.). *Concepts and controversies in obsessive-compulsive disorder* (pp. 119–135). New York: Springer.

Abramowitz, J., McKay, D., & Taylor, S. (2005). Special series: Subtypes of obsessive–compulsive disorder. *Behavior Therapy, 36,* 367–369.

Abramowitz, J. S., Wheaton, M., G., & Storch, E. A. (2008). The status of hoarding as a symptom of obsessive-compulsive disorder. *Behaviour Research and Therapy, 46,* 1026–1033.

Albert, U., Maina, G., Forner, F., & Bogetto, F. (2004). DSM-IV obsessive–compulsive personality disorder: Prevalence in patients with anxiety disorders and in healthy comparison subjects. *Comprehensive Psychiatry, 45,* 325–332.

American Psychiatric Association. (1980). *Diagnostic and statistical manual of mental disorders* (3rd ed.). Washington, DC: Author.

American Psychiatric Association. (1987). *Diagnostic and statistical manual of mental disorders* (3rd ed., rev.). Washington, DC: Author.

American Psychiatric Association. (1994). *Diagnostic and statistical manual of mental disorders* (4th ed.). Washington, DC: Author.

American Psychiatric Association. (2000). *Diagnostic and statistical manual of mental disorders* (4th ed., text rev.). Washington, DC: Author.

Andrews, G., Slade, T., & Peters, L. (1999). Classification in psychiatry: *ICD-10* versus DSM-IV. *British Journal of Psychiatry, 174,* 3–5.

Asmundson, G.J.G., Frombach, I., McQuaid, J., Pedrelli, P., Lenox, R., & Stein, M.B. (2000). Dimensionality of posttraumatic stress symptoms: A confirmatory factor analysis of DSM-IV symptom clusters and other symptom models. *Behaviour Research and Therapy, 38,* 203–214.

Bracha, H.S., & Maser, J.D. (2008). Anxiety and posttraumatic stress disorder in the context of human brain evolution: A role for theory in DSM-V? *Clinical Psychology: Science and Practice, 15,* 91–97.

Breslau, N., & Alvarado, G. F. (2007). The clinical significance criterion in DSM-IV post-traumatic stress disorder. *Psychological Medicine, 37,* 1437–1444.

Breslau, N., & Kessler, R. C. (2001). The stressor criterion in DSM-IV posttraumatic stress disorder: An empirical investigation. *Biological Psychiatry, 50,* 699–704.

Brewin, C. R., Andrews, B., & Rose, S. (2000). Fear, helplessness, and horror in posttraumatic stress disorder: Investigating DSM-IV criterion A2 in victims of violent crime. *Journal of Traumatic Stress, 13,* 499–509.

Brown, T.A. (2002). Classification of anxiety disorders. In D.J. Stein & E. Hollander (Eds.), *The American Psychiatric Publishing textbook of anxiety disorders.* Washington, DC: American Psychiatric Publishing, Inc.

Brown, T. A., Barlow, D. H., & Liebowitz, M. R. (1994). The empirical basis of generalized anxiety disorder. *American Journal of Psychiatry, 151,* 1272–1280.

Brown, T. A., Campbell, L. A., Lehman, C. L., Grisham, J. R., & Mancill, R. B. (2001). Current and lifetime comorbidity of the DSM-IV anxiety and mood disorders in a large clinical sample. *Journal of Abnormal Psychology, 11,* 585–599.

Brown, T. A., DiNardo, P. A., Lehman, C. L., & Campbell, L. A. (2001). Reliability of DSM-IV anxiety and mood disorders: Implications for the classification of emotional disorders. *Journal of Abnormal Psychology, 110,* 49–58.

Davidson, J. R., & Foa, E. B. (1991). Diagnostic issues in posttraumatic stress disorder: Considerations for the DSM-IV. *Journal of Abnormal Psychology, 100,* 346–355.

Davidson, J., Foa, E.B., Blank, A.S. Brett, E.A., Fairbank, J., Green, B.L. et al. (1996). Posttraumatic stress disorder. In T.A. Widiger, A.J. Francis, H.A. Pincus, R. Ross, M.B. First, & W. W. Davis (Eds.), *DSM-IV sourcebook, Vol. 2* (pp. 577–605). Washington, DC: American Psychiatric Association.

Decker, H.S. (2007). How Kraepelinian was Kraepelin? How Kraepelinian are the neo-Kraepelinians? —from Emil Kraepelin to DSM-III. *History of Psychiatry, 18,* 337–360.

DiNardo, P. A., Brown, T. A., & Barlow, D. H. (1994). *Anxiety Disorders Interview Schedule for DSM-IV: Lifetime version (ADIS-IV-L).* San Antonio, TX: Psychological Corporation.

First, M. B., Spitzer, R. L., Gibbon, M., & Williams, J. B. W. (1996). *Structured Clinical Interview for DSM-IV Axis I Disorders.* New York: Biometric Research Department, New York State Psychiatric Institute.

Foa, E.B., Jenike, M. Kozak, M.J., Joffe, R., Baer, L., Pauls, D. et al. (1996). Obsessive–compulsive disorder. In T.A. Widiger, A.J. Francis, H.A. Pincus, R. Ross, M.B. First, & W. W. Davis (Eds.), *DSM-IV Sourcebook, Vol. 2* (pp. 577–605). Washington, DC: American Psychiatric Association.

Foa, E. B., Kozak, M. J. Goodman, W. K., Hollander, E., Jenike, M.A., & Rasmusussen, S.A. (1995). DSM-IV field trial: Obsessive–compulsive disorder. *American Journal of Psychiatry, 152,* 90–96.

Frost, R.O., & Tolin, D.F. (2008). Compulsive hoarding. In J.S. Abramowitz, D. McKay, D., & S. Taylor (Eds.), *Clinical handbook of obsessive–compulsive disorder and related problems* (pp. 76–94). Baltimore, MD: John Hopkins University Press.

Goodman, W.K., Price, L.H., Rasmussen, S.A., Mazure, C., Delgado, P., Heninger, G.R. et al. (1989). The Yale-Brown Obsessive–Compulsive Scale: II. Validity. *Archives of General Psychiatry, 46,* 1012–1016.

Goodman, W.K., Price, L.H., Rasmussen, S.A., Mazure, C., Fleischmann, R.L., Hill, C.L. et al. (1989). The Yale-Brown Obsessive–Compulsive Scale: I. Development, use, and reliability. *Archives of General Psychiatry, 46,* 1006–1011.

Haslam, N., Williams, B.J., Kyrios, M., McKay, D., & Taylor, S. (2005). Subtyping obsessive-compulsive disorder: A taxometric analysis. *Behavior Therapy, 36,* 381–391.

Hollander, E., & Evers, M. (2004). Review of obsessive-compulsive spectrum disorders: What do we know? Where are we going? *Clinical Neuropsychiatry: Journal of Treatment Evaluation, 1,* 32–51.

Hollander, E., Friedberg, J.P., Wasserman, S., Yeh, C.C., & Iyengar, R. (2005). The case for the OCD spectrum. In J.S. Abramowitz & A.C. Houts (Eds.), *Concepts and controversies in obsessive-compulsive disorder* (pp. 95–118). New York: Springer.

Kessler, R. C., Brandenburg, N., Lane, M., Roy-Byrne, P., Stang, P. D., Stein, D. J. et al. (2005). Rethinking the duration requirement for generalized anxiety disorder: Evidence from the National Comorbidity Survey Replication. *Psychological Medicine, 35,* 1073–1082.

Kinzie, J.D., & Goetz, R.R. (1996). A century of controversy surrounding posttraumatic stress-spectrum syndromes: The impact on DSM-III and DSM-IV. *Journal of Traumatic Stress, 9,* 159–177.

Klerman, G.L. (1978). The evolution of the scientific nosology. In J.D. Shershow (Ed.), *Schizophrenia: Science and practice* (pp. 99–121). Cambridge, MA: Harvard University Press.

Kubarych, T. S., Aggen, S. H., Hettema, J. M., Kendler, K. S., & Neale, M. C. (2005). Endorsement frequencies and factor structure of DSM-III-R and DSM-IV generalized anxiety disorder symptoms in women: Implications for future research, classification, clinical practice, and comorbidity. *International Journal of Methods in Psychiatric Research, 14,* 69–81.

Leckman, J.F., Grice, D.E., Boardman, J., Zhang, H., Vitale, A., Bondi, C. et al. (1997). Symptoms of obsessive-compulsive disorder. *American Journal of Psychiatry, 154,* 911–917.

Leckman, J.F., McDougle, C.J., Pauls, D.L., Peterson, B.S., Grice, D.E., King, R.A. et al. (2000). Tic-related versus non-tic-related obsessive-compulsive disorder. In W.K. Goodman, M.V., Rudorfer, & J.D. Maser (Eds.), *Obsessive-compulsive disorder: Contemporary issues in treatment* (pp. 43–68). Mahwah, NJ: Erlbaum.

Liebowitz, M.R. (1996). Anxiety disorders. In T.A. Widiger, A.J. Francis, H.A. Pincus, R. Ross, M.B. First, & W. W. Davis (Eds.), *DSM-IV sourcebook volume 2* (pp. 397–410). Washington, DC: American Psychiatric Association.

Marshall, R. D., Spitzer, R., & Liebowitz, M. R. (1999). Review and critique of the new DSM-IV diagnosis of acute stress disorder. *American Journal of Psychiatry, 156,* 1677–1685.

Marshall, R. D., Spitzer, R., & Liebowitz, M. (2000). "Review and critique of the new DSM-IV diagnosis of acute stress disorder": Reply. *American Journal of Psychiatry, 157,* 1890–1891.

Marten, P. A., Brown, T. A., Barlow, D. H., Borkovec, T. D., Shear, M. K., & Lydiard, R. B. (1993). Evaluation of the ratings comprising the associated symptom criterion of DSM-III-R generalized anxiety disorder. *Journal of Nervous and Mental Disease, 181,* 676–682.

Marx, B.P., Forsyth, J.P., & Lexington, J. (2008). Tonic immobility as an evolved predator defense: Implications for sexual assault survivors. *Clinical Psychology: Science and Practice, 17,* 74–90.

Mataix-Cols, D., Pertusa, A., & Leckman, J.F. (2007). Issues for DSM-V: How should obsessive–compulsive and related disorders be classified? *American Journal of Psychiatry, 164,* 1313–1314.

McNally, R.J. (2003). Progress and controversy in the study of posttraumatic stress disorder. *Annual Review of Psychology, 54,* 229–252.

McNally, R.J. (2004). Conceptual problems with the DSM-IV criteria for posttraumatic stress disorder. In G.M. Rosen (Ed.), *Posttraumatic stress disorder: Issues and controversies* (pp. 1–14). New York: John Wiley & Sons.

Mennin, D.S., Heimberg, R.G., & Turk, C.L. (2004). Clinical presentation and diagnostic features. In R.G. Heimberg, C.L. Turk, & D.S. Mennin (Eds.), *Generalized anxiety disorder: Advances in research and practice.* New York: Guilford.

Moffitt, T. E., Harrington, H., Caspi, A., Kim-Cohen, J., Goldberg, D., Gregory, A. M. et al. (2007). Depression and generalized anxiety disorder: Cumulative and sequential comorbidity in a birth cohort followed prospectively to age 32 years. *Archives of General Psychiatry, 64,* 651–660.

Moras, K., Borkovec, T. D., DiNardo, P. A., Rapee, R., Riskind, J., & Barlow, D. H. (1996). Generalized anxiety disorder. In T.A. Widiger, A.J. Frances, H.A. Pincus, R. Ross, M.B. First, & W. W. Davis (Eds.), *DSM-IV sourcebook, volume 2.* Washington, DC: American Psychiatric Association.

Peters, L., Issakidis, C., Slade, T., & Andrews, G. (2006). Gender differences in the prevalence of DSM-IV and *ICD-10* PTSD. *Psychological Medicine, 36,* 81–89.

Peters, L., Slade, T., & Andrews, G. (1999). A comparison of ICD10 and DSM-IV criteria for posttraumatic stress disorder. *Journal of Traumatic Stress, 12,* 335–343.

Phillips, K. A., Pinto, A., Menard, W., Eisen, J. L., Mancebo, M., & Rasmussen, S. A. (2007). Obsessive-compulsive disorder versus body dysmorphic disorder: A comparison study of two possibly related disorders. *Depression and Anxiety, 24,* 399–409.

Purdon, C., & Harrington, J. (2006). Worry in psychopathology. In G. C. L. Davey & A. Wells (Eds.), *Worry and its psychological disorders: Theory, assessment, and treatment.* Hoboken, NJ: John Wiley & Sons.

Radomsky, A., & Taylor, S. (2005). Subtyping OCD: Prospects and problems. *Behavior Therapy, 36,* 371–379.

Rickels, K., & Rynn, M. A. (2001). What is generalized anxiety disorder? *Journal of Clinical Psychiatry, 62(Suppl 11),* 4–12.

Roemer, L., Orsillo, S. M., & Barlow, D. H. (2002). Generalized anxiety disorder. In D. H. Barlow (Ed.), *Anxiety and its disorders: The nature and treatment of anxiety and panic* (2nd ed.). New York: Guilford.

Roemer, L., Orsillo, S.M., Borkovec, T.D., & Litz, B.T. (1998). Emotional response at the time of a potentially traumatizing event and PTSD symptomatology: A preliminary retrospective analysis of the DSM-IV criterion A-2. *Journal of Behavior Therapy and Experimental Psychiatry, 29,* 123–130.

Roth, S., Newman, E., Pelcovitz, D., van der Kolk, B., & Mandel, F.S. (1997). Complex PTSD in victims exposed to sexual and physical abuse: Results from the DSM-IV field trial for posttraumatic stress disorder. *Journal of Traumatic Stress, 10,* 539–555.

Ruscio, A. M., Chiu, W. T., Roy-Byrne, P., Stang, P. E., Stein, D. J., Wittchen, H. et al. (2007). Broadening the definition of generalized anxiety disorder: Effects on prevalence and associations with other disorders in the National Comorbidity Study Replication. *Journal of Anxiety Disorders, 21,* 662–676.

Ruscio, A. M., Lane, M., Roy-Byrne, P., Stang, P. E., Stein, D. J., Wittchen, H. et al. (2005). Should excessive worry be required for a diagnosis of generalized anxiety disorder? Results from the US National Comorbidity Survey Replication. *Psychological Medicine, 35,* 1761–1772.

Samuels, J., Bienvenu, O.J., III, Riddle, M.A., Cullen, B.A., Grados, M.A., Liang, K.Y. et al. (2002). Hoarding in obsessive–compulsive disorder: Results from a case-control study. *Behaviour Research and Therapy, 40,* 517–528.

Samuels, J., Wang, Y., Shugart, Y.Y., Pinto, A., Grados, M.A., Fyer, A.J. et al. (2007). Significant linkage to compulsive hoarding on chromosome 14 in families with obsessive-compulsive disorder: Results form the OCD collaborative genetics study. *American Journal of Psychiatry, 164,* 493–499.

Saxena, S. (2007). Is compulsive hoarding a genetically and neurobiologically discrete syndrome? Implications for diagnostic classification. *American Journal of Psychiatry, 164,* 380–384.

Schwarz, E., & Kowalski, J.M. (1991). Posttraumatic stress disorder after a school shooting: Effects of symptom threshold selection and diagnosis by DSM-III, DSM-III-R, or proposed DSM-IV. *American Journal of Psychiatry, 148,* 592–597.

Slade, T., & Andrews, G. (2001). DSM-IV and *ICD-10* generalized anxiety disorder: Discrepant diagnoses and associated disability. *Social Psychiatry and Psychiatric Epidemiology, 36,* 45–51.

Slade, T., & Andrews, G. (2002). Empirical impact of DSM-IV diagnostic criterion for clinical significance. *Journal of Nervous and Mental Disease, 190,* 334–337.

Slade, T., & Watson, D. (2006). The structure of common DSM-IV and *ICD-10* mental disorders in the Australian general population. *Psychological Medicine, 36,* 1593–1600.

Sookman, D., Abramowitz, J.S., Calamari, J.E., Wilhelm, S., & McKay, D. (2005). Subtypes of obsessive–compulsive disorder: Implications for specialized cognitive behavior therapy. *Behavior Therapy, 36,* 393–400.

Spitzer, R.L. (1998). Diagnosis and need for treatment are not the same. *Archives of General Psychiatry, 55,* 120.

Spitzer, R.L., & Wakefield, J.C. (1999). DSM-IV diagnostic criterion for clinical significance: Does it help solve the false positives problem? *American Journal of Psychiatry, 156,* 1856–1864.

Stein, D. J., Seedat, S., & Potocnik, F. (1999). Hoarding: A review. *Israel Journal of Psychiatry and Related Sciences, 36,* 35–46.

Steinberger, K., & Schuch, B. (2002). Classification of obsessive–compulsive disorder in childhood and adolescence. *Acta Psychiatrica Scandinavica, 106,* 97–102.

Summerfeldt, L.J., Richter, M.A., Antony, M.M., & Swinson, R.P. (1999). Symptom structure in obsessive–compulsive disorder: A confirmatory factor-analytic study. *Behaviour Research and Therapy, 37,* 297–311.

Taylor, S., Abramowitz, J.S., McKay, D., Calamari, J.E., Sookman, D., Kyrios, M. et al. (2006). Do dysfunctional beliefs play a role in all types of obsessive–compulsive disorder? *Journal of Anxiety Disorders, 20,* 85–97.

Taylor, S., Kuch, K., Koch, W.J., Crockett, D.J., & Passey, G. (1998). The structure of posttraumatic stress symptoms. *Journal of Abnormal Psychology, 107,* 154–160.

Tenney, N.H., Schotte, C.K.W., Denys, D.A.J.P., van Megen, H.J.G.M., & Westenberg, H.G.M. (2003). Assessment of DSM-IV personality disorders in obsessive-compulsive disorder: Comparison of clinical diagnosis, self-report questionnaire, and semi-structured interview. *Journal of Personality Disorders, 17,* 550–561.

Turvey, C. L., Stevens, D. E., & Merikangas, K. R. (1999). The validity of the associated symptom criteria for DSM-IV generalized anxiety disorder. *International Journal of Methods in Psychiatric Research, 8,* 129–137.

World Health Organization. (1992). *The ICD-10 classification of mental and behavioural disorders.* Geneva: Author.

World Health Organization. (1997). *Composite International Diagnostic Interview (CIDI).* Geneva: Author.

Zanarini, M. C., Skodol, A. E., Bender, D., Dolan, R., Sanislow, C., Schaefer, E. et al. (2000). The collaborative longitudinal personality disorders study: Reliability of Axis I and II diagnoses. *Journal of Personality Disorders, 14,* 291–299.

Zimmerman, M., & Chelminski, I. (2003). Generalized anxiety disorder in patients with major depression: Is DSM-IV's hierarchy correct? *American Journal of Psychiatry, 160,* 504–512.

Zimmerman, M., Chelminski, I., & Young, D. (2004). On the threshold of disorder: A study of the impact of the DSM-IV clinical significance criterion on diagnosing depressive and anxiety disorders in clinical practice. *Journal of Clinical Psychiatry, 65,* 1400–1405.

II

Empirical and Theoretical Perspectives on Diagnosis

The Amygdala Networks of Fear: From Animal Models to Human Psychopathology

Jacek Debiec
Joseph E. LeDoux

Substantial progress has been made in recent decades in characterizing the circuitry and understanding the neural mechanisms underlying fear and anxiety. This has been accomplished in major part through the extensive use of animal models complemented by human pharmacological, imaging, and clinical studies. Animal models have been particularly valuable in providing insights into the microanatomy as well as the cellular and molecular mechanisms of fear and anxiety, which have been so far inaccessible in human research. Animal models also offer suggestions about ways of controlling, especially reducing, fear.

The brain's fear system is an evolutionary-based adaptive system that is activated in response to environmental threats. Its presumed goal is to increase survival in the face of challenges to safety and well-being. This is achieved by the expression of behavioral, autonomic, and endocrine reactions. The behavioral component of fear involves an array of defensive responses, often described as "flight, fight," (Cannon, 1929), or in a more nuanced version, "freeze, flight, fight" (Bracha, Ralston, Matsukawa, Williams, & Bracha, 2004). These behaviors are supported by autonomic and endocrine adjustments that increase blood flow, and hence metabolic energy, to skeletal muscles, especially to muscles in the arms and legs, and to the brain, all at the expense of other organs and tissues, such as the gut and skin that are less involved in the fighting and fleeing (Cannon, 1929).

Fear responses can be categorized as "innate" or "learned." *Innate fear* refers to a preprogrammed reaction to specific environmental factors, such the sight, sound or odor of a predator, species-specific behaviors, facial expressions, or sounds emitted by conspecifics (members of one's own species), painful or other intense stimuli (i.e., loud noise). Information about natural threats appears to have been evolutionary hardwired into animal brains by tuning perceptual processes to relevant informational relationships in the environment (Ohman, 2007).

While innate fears are inherited, learned or acquired fear responses result from a capacity of an organism to learn through experience to recognize cues associated with danger, and especially with innate fear stimuli. One of the most commonly used experimental models of fear learning is fear conditioning, an experimentally controlled learning paradigm wherein a relatively neutral event (a conditioned stimulus, [CS]), such as tone or light is paired with an aversive event (an unconditioned stimulus, [US]), such as electric foot shock (Bouton & Bolles, 1980; Fanselow, 1980; LeDoux, 1996). After pairing with the US, the CS acquires an ability to elicit fear responses (Fig. 5.1). Animal studies using fear conditioning demonstrate the powerful character of fear learning. Very often, a single CS–US pairing is sufficient to establish a memory that may last throughout the lifetime of an animal (Gale et al., 2004).

Animal brains are not only endowed with a set of immediate reactions to threat, but are also capable of initiating and maintaining a state of preparedness for an anticipated danger. Although fear is considered to be a response to an actual threat, anxiety is a state of preparation for a predicted dan-

5.1

In fear conditioning, a neutral stimulus (conditioned stimulus; CS) is paired with an aversive event (unconditioned stimulus; US), often a mild electric shock to the foot pads. As a result, subsequent presentations of the CS trigger fear responses, such as immobility or freezing.

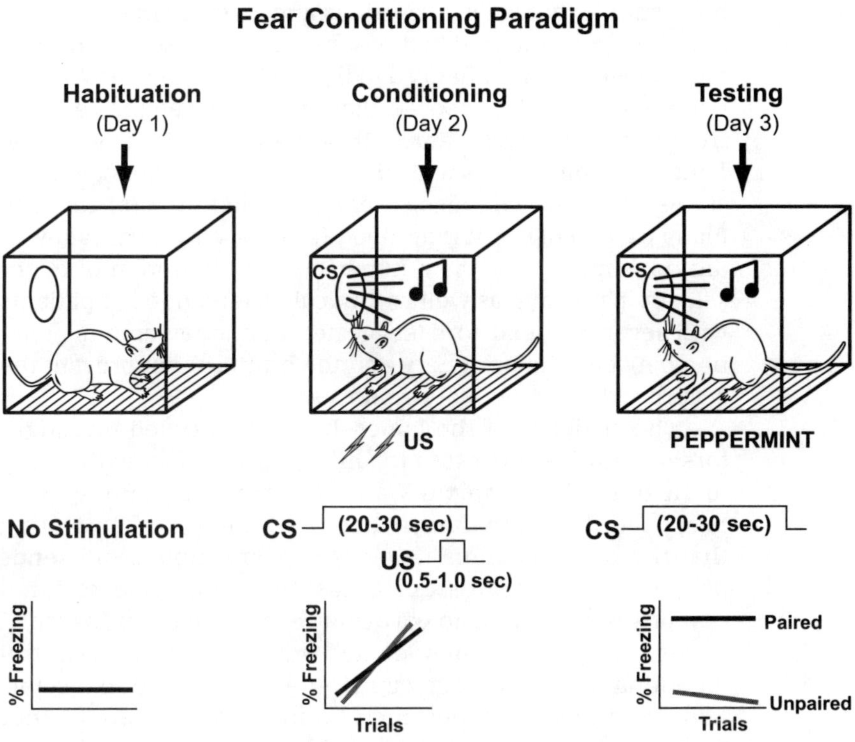

ger, real or imaginary. Thus, fear is typically stimulus-specific, whereas anxiety may be controlled by often undefined possible threats.

Maladaptive fear and anxiety characterize anxiety disorders. Evidence indicates the involvement of fear learning mechanisms in the development of pathological fear and anxiety (LeDoux, 1996; Rosen & Schulkin 1998). Thus, localizing neural circuits, as well as cellular and molecular mechanisms involved in fear learning, is critical for better understanding of pathogenesis, and development of new treatments of anxiety disorders.

Localizing Fear in the Brain: A Historical Perspective

Current developments in the neurobiology of fear and anxiety would not be possible without a prior evolution of concepts and ideas. For centuries, it was commonly accepted that feelings, such as the feeling of fear, trigger emotional responses in the body, such as behavioral reactions and changes in respiration and heart rate, internal bodily sensations, and so on. This traditional view was challenged in the 1890s by the James–Lange hypothesis, which proposed that emotional feelings emerge from bodily changes (James, 1884; Lange, 1885). The James–Lange "peripheral" (as it attributed the initiation of emotional states to bodily changes) theory of emotions appealed to many psychologists at that time. However, empirical evidence did not support this view. Experimental disruption of major sensory pathways, as well as clinical observations of patients with severed spinal cord, suggested that an evident disjunction between the periphery and the brain cannot prevent the occurrence of emotional responses.

The criticism of the James–Lange theory led investigators of emotive processes to shift their focus from the body to the brain. For example, Walter B. Cannon and Philip Bard proposed a hypothalamic theory (Cannon, 1929). Noting that the hypothalamus receives sensory inputs and sends projections to brainstem areas that control emotional responses, as well as to cortical areas involved in "psychic" states, the hypothalamus seemed well-suited to both control emotional responses and contribute to the emotional coloration of subjective experience. Cannon's ideas were further elaborated by James W. Papez (1937), who accepted the role proposed by Cannon for the hypothalamus, but elaborated the circuit of feeling in considerable detail, suggesting that the cingulated cortex was the cortical area involved in the subjective experience of emotional feelings. Although most of the pathways proposed by Papez were later documented, areas like the hippocampus were not found to be significantly involved in emotions.

In 1939, Heinrich Klüver and Paul Bucy published their findings of the impact of the medial temporal lesions on emotions such as fear, in monkeys (Klüuver & Bucy 1939). Almost 2 decades later, in 1956, the critical area located deep inside the medial temporal lobe was identified by Lawrence

Weiskrantz to be the amygdala (Weiskrantz, 1956). Subsequent work provided overwhelming evidence, showing the amygdala as a key player in emotions, especially in fear (Cardinal, Parkinson, Hall, & Everitt, 2002; Davidson, Jackson, & Kalin, 2000; Lang & Davis, 2006; LeDoux 1996; LeDoux 2000; Maren 2001; McGaugh 2004; Paré 2002; Phelps & LeDoux 2005), as well as in the anxiety psychopathologies (Charney, 2004; Etkin & Wager, 2007; Liberzon & Sripada, 2008; Rauch, Shin, & Wright, 2003).

The Amygdala: A Key Interface in Fear Processing

The amygdala was named by the anatomist Karl Burdach for the almond-like (in Greek almond: *amygdale*) shape of one of its subregions (Swanson & Petrovich 1998). It consists of a group of nuclei located bilaterally deep inside the medial temporal lobe (LeDoux, 2007). The role of the amygdala in fear is ubiquitous in vertebrate species (LeDoux, 1996). Although, various criteria have been used to distinguish and categorize areas within the amygdala, the regions of most relevance to fear conditioning are the lateral (LA), basal (B), and central (CE) nuclei of the amygdala, as well as a distinct subgroup of neurons known as *intercalated cells* (ITC) (Fanselow & Poulos, 2005; Lang & Davis, 2006; LeDoux, 2007; Maren, 2005; Paré, Quirk, & LeDoux, 2004) (see Figure 5.2).

The LA is the sensory gateway of the amygdala. It receives inputs from all sensory modalities, including vision, audition, touch and pain, olfaction, and taste (LeDoux, 2000). Although other amygdala nuclei also receive some sensory afferents, the LA is the main sensory input region.

In fear conditioning, the LA is responsible for linking the information about the neutral cue (CS) with that of the noxious stimulus (US). One of the most commonly used variants of fear conditioning is auditory fear conditioning, wherein a CS consists of a single tone. Auditory information is conveyed to the LA through two independent sensory inputs: the "low road" or thalamic pathway provides the amygdala with a rapid but imprecise auditory signal, whereas the "high road" delivers a more complex representation derived from cortical association areas (LeDoux, 1996). The "two roads" model of signal

5.2

Amygdala Inputs, Internal Connections, and Outputs.

The amygdala consists of a group of nuclei. The amygdala nuclei most relevant to fear conditioning are the lateral (LA), basal (B), and central (CE) nuclei of the amygdala, as well as the subgroup of neurons known as intercalated cells (ITC). The LA is the main sensory input area. It receives inputs from the thalamus and the cortex; thus, it is responsible for linking the CS with the US. The B receives projections from the hippocampus, enthorhinal, and polymodal associative cortices, areas that may convey information about the environmental context in which the fearful event is occurring. The C is the common output area controlling expression of behavioral, autonomic, and endocrine fear responses. The LA is connected with the CE in direct and indirect (via the basal nucleus and the intercalated cells) ways. The ITC have the inhibitory control over the CE.

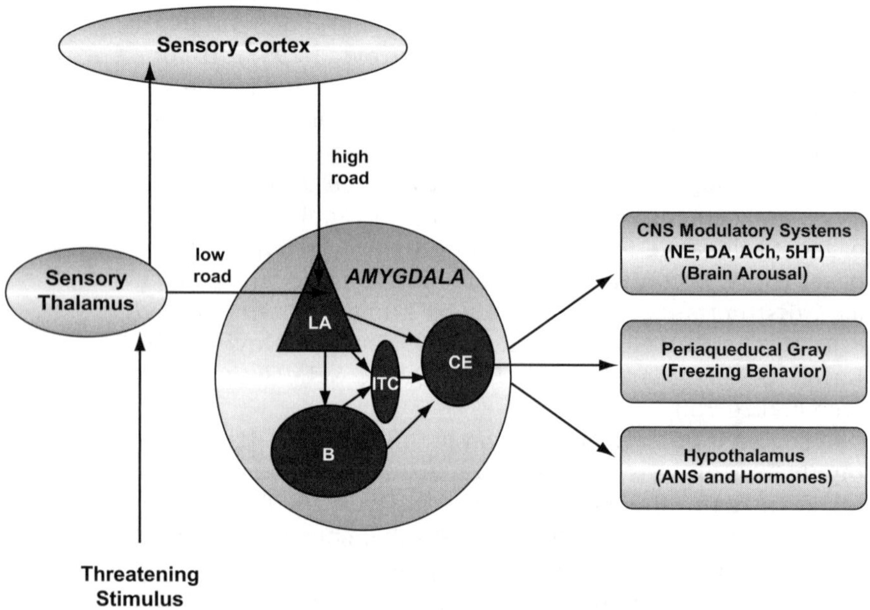

transmission illustrates one way in which fear responses can be initiated (by the direct low road) before we are aware of the eliciting stimulus. Human studies demonstrate that the amygdala may be activated by the stimuli that are not consciously perceived (Ohman 2007; Phelps, 2006; Vuilleumier, Armony, Driver, & Dolan, 2001) (see Figure 5.3).

5.3

Sensory information reaches the LA through two independent sensory inputs: the "low road" or thalamic pathway provides the amygdala with a rapid but imprecise signal, while the "high road" delivers a more complex and detailed representation derived from cortical association areas, responsible in humans for conscious processing. The "two-roads" model of signal transmission illustrates how fear responses can be initiated (by the direct "low road") before we are aware of the eliciting stimulus.

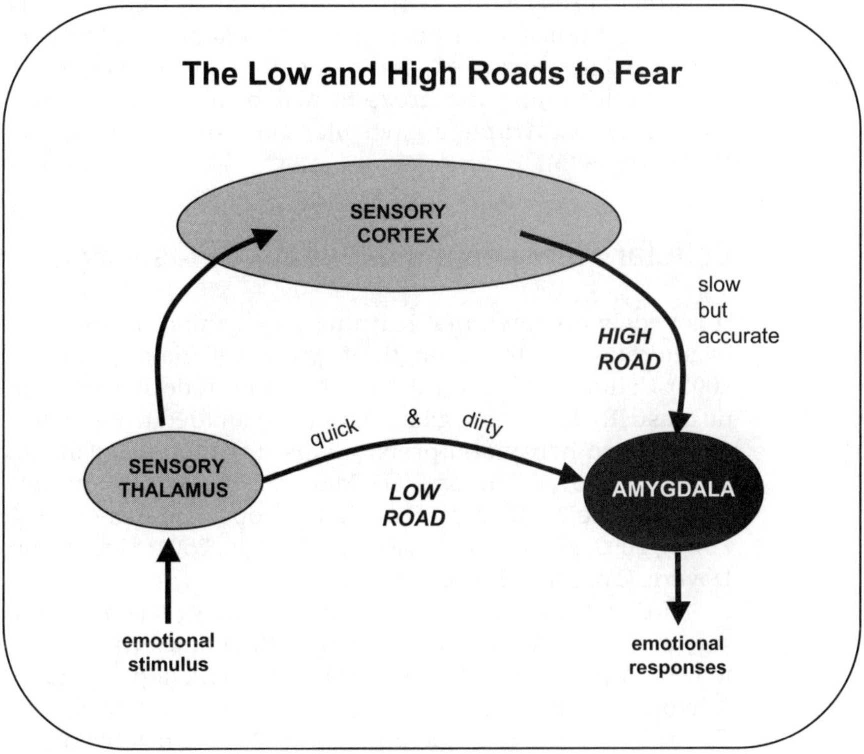

The LA sends direct and indirect (via the basal nucleus and the intercalated cells) projections to the central nucleus. The basal nucleus also receives projections from the hippocampus, enthorhinal, and polymodal associative cortices, areas that may convey information about the environmental context in which threat is occurring (LeDoux, 2007). The intercalated cells consist of clusters of gamma-aminobutyric acid or GABA-ergic neurons, which control the activity of the central nucleus by the mechanism of forward inhibition (Paré, Royer, Smith & Lang, 2003).

The central nucleus is a common output pathway for the expression of fear reactions, including behavioral, autonomic, and endocrine responses, as well as the activation of amine (i.e., adrenergic, serotonergic, dopaminergic, cholinergic) modulatory systems (Lang & Davis, 2006; LeDoux, 2000, 2007). Each class of response is mediated by a distinct output pathway from the central amygdala. Thus, in animal studies it has been shown that damage to the central amygdala impairs expression of all fear responses, while selective lesioning the areas to which the central amygdala projects disrupts a particular class of fear responses (LeDoux, 1996).

Cellular Mechanisms of Synaptic Plasticity

It is widely accepted that learning and memory is mediated by alterations in the strength of synaptic signaling (Kandel, 2001). Cellular and molecular mechanisms underlying synaptic plasticity in the amygdala have been studied using physiological and behavioral preparations (Dityatev & Bolshakov 2005; Fanselow & Poulos, 2005; Maren, 2001, 2005; Rodrigues, Schafe, & LeDoux, 2004; Sah, Faber, Lopez De Armentia, & Power, 2003; Schafe, Nader, Blair, & LeDoux 2001; Sigurdsson, Doyère, Cain, & LeDoux, 2007) (see Figure 5.4).

Most of the fibers projecting onto the amygdala from sensory areas are excitatory and release glutamate, which binds to NMDA (N-methyl D-aspartate) and AMPA (alpha-amino-3-hydroxy-5-methyl-4-isoxazolepropionic acid) receptors. The role of glutamatergic inputs into the LA has been best described. It has been proposed that activation of postsynaptic NMDA receptors in LA neurons, occurring in the context of their depolarization by the projections conveying information about the US, triggers calcium influx (Blair, Schafe, Bauer, Rodrigues, & LeDoux, 2001). This in turn initiates cascades of intracellular processes that involve second messengers and protein kinases, leading to activation of transcription factors, gene expression, new protein synthesis, and synaptic plasticity (Dityatev & Bolshakov 2005; Maren, 2005; Rodrigues et

5.4

Consolidation of fear conditioning is initiated by the activation of receptors at the postsynaptic neuron (1). This, in turn, triggers cascades of intracellular events which regulate the activity of mitogen-activated protein kinase (MAPK)(2). MAPK controls transcription factors, such as CREB (cyclic adenosine monophosphate response element-binding) proteins that regulate transcription of certain genes (3). Gene activation leads to new RNA (ribonucleic acid) and new protein synthesis, and thus structural changes in the postsynaptic neuron (4). Plausible mechanisms of retrograde signaling (5) from the postsynaptic neuron induce changes in the postsynaptic neuron (6).

Signal Transduction Pathways Involved in Fear Conditioning in the Lateral Amygdala

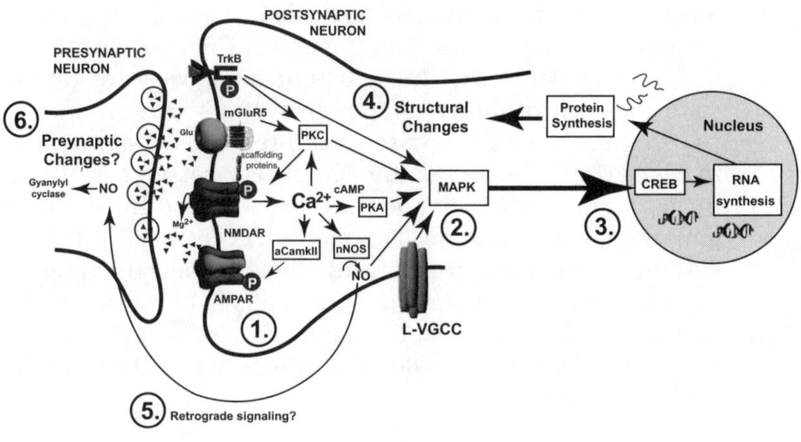

al., 2004; Schafe et al., 2001). Newly synthesized proteins are believed to strengthen synaptic connections in a structural or functional way. For example, recent data demonstrate that fear conditioning stimulates trafficking of AMPA receptors to synapses in LA, which increases the postsynaptic response elicited by presynaptic glutamatergic inputs (Rumpel, LeDoux, Zador, & Malinow, 2005).

Synaptic plasticity and learning in the amygdala is regulated by various neuromodulators, including the catecholamines: noradrenaline (Huang, Wang, & Gean, 1998; Tully, Li, Tsvetkov, & Bolshakov, 2007) and dopamine (Guarraci, Frohardt, Falls, & Kapp, 2000; Kröner, Rosenkranz, Grace, & Barrionuevo, 2005), as well as serotonin (Huang & Kandel, 2007), nitric oxide (Schafe et al., 2005), BDNF (brain-derived neurotrophic factor) (Rattiner, Davis, & Ressler, 2005), endocannabinoids (Azad et al., 2004), and others. These modulators influence either or both principal neurons and inhibitory GABAergic interneurons.

Fear Memory Versus Memory of Fear

The amygdala circuits involved in fear conditioning form implicit memories that are expressed independent of conscious awareness of the stimulus (LeDoux, 1996; Ohman 2007; Phelps, 2006; Vuilleumier et al., 2001). However, during a fearful episode, explicit or conscious memories may be formed in parallel through information storage in the hippocampus and related cortical areas (Phelps, 2006). The former can be thought of as fear memories and the latter as memories of fear. While these memories may be consistent, it is also possible that inconsistent memories are formed such that the stimulus components of a situation that are consciously attended to are attributed causal significance in fear arousal, whereas the actual fear responses elicited through amygdala activation are caused by different components of the situation. The memories formed by the two systems would then be different. This is especially interesting given that amygdala activation leads to hormone release that then strengthens explicit memories formed via the hippocampus (McGaugh, 2000), regardless of whether they are causally accurate.

Active Versus Passive Coping with Fear

A common method for treating fear in humans is exposure (Foa, 2000; Rudd & Joiner, 1998; Shear & Beidel, 1998). This treatment is based on the behavioral process of extinction in which learned fear is reduced, following repeated exposure to the fear-arousing stimulus in a safe or neutral context (Myers & Davis, 2002). Much has been learned about the neural basis of extinction (Barad, 2005; Ji & Maren, 2007; Myers & Davis, 2002; Quirk & Mueller, 2008; Rauch, Shin, & Phelps, 2006; Sotres–Bayon, Bush, & LeDoux, 2004; Sotres–Bayon, Cain, & LeDoux, 2006). In brief, the amygdala, medial prefrontal cortex, and hippocampus are involved. The medial prefrontal cortex and hippocampus are thought to regulate amygdala processing and thereby reduce fear (Corcoran & Quirk, 2007; Ji & Maren, 2007; Milad & Quirk, 2002; Quirk & Beer, 2006; Sotres–Bayon et al., 2004).

Animal studies have shown that the NMDA agonist d-cycloserine facilitates extinction learning via the amygdala (Walker, Ressler, Lu, & Davis, 2002). This prompted human studies, which have shown better outcome when exposure therapy is combined with d-cycloserine (Davis, 2006; Norberg, Krystal, & Tolin, 2008; Ressler et al., 2004).

The subject is passive in extinction and exposure. That is, the stimulus is delivered independent of behavior. It is also possible to create situations in which animals learn to perform active behaviors that reduce fear by eliminating exposure to the fear-arousing stimulus. For example, a rat can learn to press a bar or run to the other side of a chamber or to rear up on its hind legs when a fear stimulus occurs (Cain & LeDoux, 2007). This learning paradigm is referred to as escape from fear (Amorapanth, LeDoux, & Nader, 2000; Cain & LeDoux, 2007). Performance of this response then eliminates the stimulus. The neural basis of this behavior involves a circuit switch in the amygdala that suppresses the central amygdala and its control of fear reactions. Specifically, the LA outputs are directed to the B rather than the CE (Amorapanth et al., 2000). The B then connects with active motor control regions in the striatum and cortex (Cardinal et al., 2002).

One of the problems with exposure and extinction is that the fear often spontaneously recovers. It is particularly interesting that in the active coping task – escape from fear—fear reduction seems less susceptible to recovery (Cain & LeDoux, 2007). Therapies that actively engage the patient may produce more enduring effects (LeDoux & Gorman, 2001).

Reconsolidation and Maintenance of Fear Memories

It was long accepted that memories, once formed and consolidated, persist in an unaltered state (McGaugh, 2000). Memory consolidation, as outlined above, involves activation of receptors at synapses, second messengers, protein kinases, gene expression, and new protein synthesis. New memories are initially labile and susceptible to modifications by interfering with any of these molecular steps of the consolidation processes. The traditional view is that once memory consolidation is completed, synaptic connections become stabilized and memories become immune to alterations.

The traditional view of consolidation was first challenged by studies in the 1960s (Misanin, LeDoux, & Nader, 1968; Schneider & Sherman 1968) followed by other studies, showing that reactivation of a consolidated memory following retrieval renders this memory labile again (Sara, 2000). An interest in postreactivation plasticity, known as *memory reconsolidation* (Alberini, Milekic, & Tronel, 2006; Dudai 2006; Nader, 2003; Sara, 2000), was revived with a demonstration that postreactivation disruption of protein synthesis in the LA permanently impairs auditory fear memory (Nader, Schafe, & LeDoux, 2000). Subsequent studies showed that reconsolidation of auditory fear conditioning in the LA involves NMDA receptor activation (Ben Mamou, Gamache, & Nader, 2006; Lee, Milton, & Everitt, 2006), protein kinases (Doyere, Debiec, Monfils, Schafe, & LeDoux, 2007; Duvarci, Nader, & LeDoux, 2005; Tronson, Wiseman, Olausson, & Taylor, 2006), expression of immediate early gene *Zif268* (Lee, Di Ciano, Thomas, & Everitt, 2005), and new protein synthesis (Debiec, Doyere, Nader, & LeDoux, 2006; Duvarci & Nader, 2004; Nader et al., 2000). These processes may, in turn, be modulated by noradrenergic signaling (Debiec & LeDoux 2004) (see Figure 5.5).

The rediscovery of memory reconsolidation provided new insights into the mechanisms of fear memory storage and offered promises of developing new treatments of fear pathologies. Specifically, it may be possible to reduce the impact of traumatic or otherwise intrusive memories and habits and addictions by blocking reconsolidation after retrieval of a troubling memory or performance of a learned habit (Alberini et al., 2006; Dębiec & Altemus, 2006; Dudai, 2006; Nader, 2003; Sara, 2000; Tronson & Taylor, 2007).

Another implication of reconsolidation research is that as long as the reconsolidation processes are underway, the memory may be altered. In other words, memories recalled during therapy may be modified in an unwanted way after a patient leaves her therapist's office. Furthermore, reconsolidation hypothesis implies that one remembers the last

5.5

Reactivation of the consolidated memory renders it labile and susceptible to interferences. This enables the modification of the existing memory trace by the circumstances accompanying the memory retrieval.

Reconsolidation Processes Enable Modification of the Memory

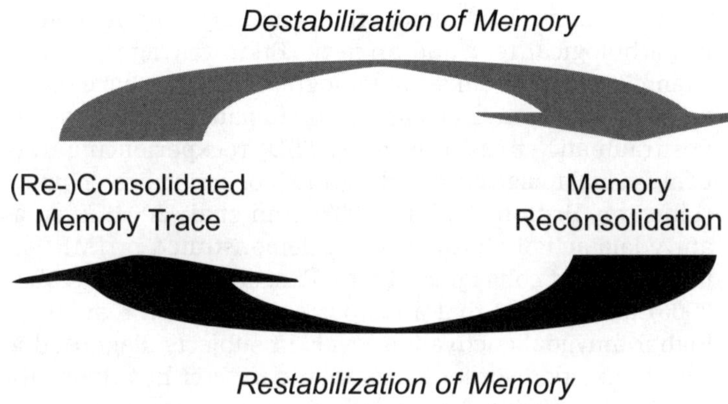

instance of memory more than the original experience. If so, therapists in some instances should attempt to end sessions on a positive note to prevent the storage of the disturbing or dysfunctional memory.

Fear and the Human Amygdala: Evidence from Imaging Studies

Considerable evidence from animal studies has demonstrated the critical role of the amygdala in fear processing. Recent advances in brain imaging techniques have stimulated researchers to explore the involvement of the amygdala in normal fear and anxiety disorders in humans (Charney, 2004; Etkin & Wager, 2007; Liberzon & Sripada, 2008; Phelps & LeDoux, 2005; Pitman, Shin, & Rauch, 2001; Rauch et al., 2003).

Using functional magnetic resonance imaging (fMRI), increased amygdala activity has been observed during fear conditioning in humans (LaBar, Gatenby, Gore, LeDoux, & Phelps, 1998; Morris, Ohman, & Dolan, 1998). Moreover, the degree of this increase was predictive of the intensity of the conditioned fear response (LaBar et al., 1998; Phelps, Delgado, Nearing, & LeDoux, 2004). Parallel to animal studies, human research shows that fear processing in the amygdala is regulated by various neuromodulators, such as norepinephrine (van Stegeren et al., 2005), serotonin (Rhodes et al., 2007), and cannabinoids (Phan et al., 2008).

Clinical studies demonstrate the amygdala involvement in pathological fear and anxiety (Etkin & Wager 2007). For example, positron emission tomography studies have reported an augmented amygdala activation in patients diagnosed with posttraumatic stress disorder (PTSD) reexperiencing trauma using visual images (Shin et al., 1997) or script-driven imagery (Liberzon, Britton, & Phan, 2003; Shin et al., 2004). Increased amygdala activity has also been demonstrated by fMRI studies. Phan and colleagues (Phan, Fitzgerald, Nathan, & Tancer, 2006) have shown that an exposure to social threats triggers higher amygdala activation levels in subjects diagnosed with social anxiety disorder as compared to their healthy controls. Similarly, augmented amygdala responding has been reported in specific phobia (Schienle, Schafer, Walter, Stark, & Vaitl, 2005). Although, at this point, human studies cannot investigate fear processing at the microcircuit and molecular levels they support and extend findings from animal studies.

Conclusions

Research on the amygdala and its involvement in fear and anxiety has advanced considerably in recent decades. Animal models have provided insights into the organization of neural circuits and cellular and molecular mechanisms underlying fear and fear learning. This has formed a solid basis for further studies of fear and anxiety in the human brain. In the years to come, there will undoubtedly be novel, more sophisticated methods that will even further improve understanding of fear and anxiety, and their pathologies, in humans. Animal research has not only revealed basic mechanisms of fear but also provide clues about therapy.

References

Alberini, C. M., Milekic, M. H., & Tronel, S. (2006). Mechanisms of memory stabilization and de-stabilization. *Cellular and Molecular Life Sciences, 63*(9), 999–1008.

Amorapanth, P., LeDoux, J. E., & Nader, K. (2000). Different lateral amygdala outputs mediate reactions and actions elicited by a fear-arousing stimulus. *Nature Neuroscience, 3*(1), 74–79.

Azad, S. C., Monory, K., Marsicano, G., Cravatt, B. F., Lutz, B., Zieglgänsberger, W., et al. (2004). Circuitry for associative plasticity in the amygdala involves endocannabinoid signaling. *The Journal of Neuroscience, 24*(44), 9953–9961.

Barad, M. (2005). Fear extinction in rodents: Basic insight to clinical promise. *Current Opinion in Neurobiology, 15*(6), 710–715.

Ben Mamou, C., Gamache, K., & Nader, K. (2006). NMDA receptors are critical for unleashing consolidated auditory fear memories. *Nature Neuroscience, 9*(10), 1237–1239.

Blair, H. T., Schafe, G. E., Bauer, E. P., Rodrigues, S. M., & LeDoux, J. E. (2001). Synaptic plasticity in the lateral amygdala: A cellular hypothesis of fear conditioning. *Learning and Memory, 8*(5), 229–242.

Bouton, M. E., & Bolles, R. C. (1980). Conditioned fear assessed by freezing and by the suppression of three different baselines. *Animal Learning and Behavior, 8*, 429–434.

Bracha, H. S., Ralston, T. C., Matsukawa, J. M., Williams, A. E., & Bracha, A. S. (2004). Does "fight or flight" need updating? *Psychosomatics, 45*(5), 448–449.

Cain, C. K., & LeDoux, J. E. (2007). Escape from fear: A detailed behavioral analysis of two atypical responses reinforced by CS termination. *Journal of Experimental Psychology Animal Behavior Processes, 33*(4), 451–463.

Cannon, W. B. (1929). *Bodily changes in pain, hunger, fear, and rage* (Vol. 2). New York: Appleton.

Cardinal, R. N., Parkinson, J. A., Hall, J., & Everitt, B. J. (2002). Emotion and motivation: The role of the amygdala, ventral striatum, and prefrontal cortex. *Neuroscience and Biobehavioral Reviews, 26*(3), 321–352.

Charney, D. S. (2004). Psychobiological mechanisms of resilience and vulnerability: Implications for successful adaptation to extreme stress. *American Journal of Psychiatry, 161*(2), 195–216.

Corcoran, K. A., & Quirk, G. J. (2007). Recalling safety: Cooperative functions of the ventromedial prefrontal cortex and the hippocampus in extinction. *CNS Spectrums, 12*(3), 200–206.

Davidson, R. J., Jackson, D. C., & Kalin, N. H. (2000). Emotion, plasticity, context, and regulation: Perspectives from affective neuroscience. *Psychological Bulletin, 126*(6), 890–909.

Davis, M. (2006). Neural systems involved in fear and anxiety measured with fear-potentiated startle. *The American Psychologist 61*(8), 741–756.

Debiec, J., & Altemus, M. (2006). Toward a new treatment for traumatic memories. *Cerebrum*, 2–11.

Debiec, J., Doyere, V., Nader, K., & LeDoux, J. E. (2006). Directly reactivated, but not indirectly reactivated, memories undergo reconsolidation in the amygdala. *Proceedings of the National Academy of Sciences of the United States of America, 103*(9), 3428–3433.

Debiec, J., & Ledoux, J. E. (2004). Disruption of reconsolidation but not consolidation of auditory fear conditioning by noradrenergic blockade in the amygdala. *Neuroscience, 129*(2), 267–272.

Dityatev, A. E., & Bolshakov, V. Y. (2005). Amygdala, long-term potentiation, and fear conditioning. *Neuroscientist, 11*(1), 75–88.

Doyère, V., Debiec, J., Monfils, M. H., Schafe, G. E., & LeDoux, J. E. (2007). Synapse-specific reconsolidation of distinct fear memories in the lateral amygdala. *Nature Neurosci, 10*(4), 414–416.

Dudai, Y. (2006). Reconsolidation: The advantage of being refocused. *Current Opinion in Neurobiology, 16*(2), 174–178.

Duvarci, S., & Nader, K. (2004). Characterization of fear memory reconsolidation. *The Journal of Neuroscience, 24*(42), 9269–9275.

Duvarci, S., Nader, K., & LeDoux, J. E. (2005). Activation of extracellular signal-regulated kinase- mitogen-activated protein kinase cascade in the amygdala is required for memory reconsolidation of auditory fear conditioning. *The European Journal of Neuroscience, 21*(1), 283–289.

Etkin, A., & Wager, T. D. (2007). Functional neuroimaging of anxiety: A meta-analysis of emotional processing in PTSD, social anxiety disorder, and specific phobia. *American Journal of Psychiatry, 164*(10), 1476–1488.

Fanselow, M. S. (1980). Conditional and unconditional components of post-shock freezing. *Pavlovian Journal of Biological Science, 15*, 177–182.

Fanselow, M. S., & Poulos, A. M. (2005). The neuroscience of mammalian associative learning. *Annual Review of Psychology, 56*, 207–234.

Foa, E. B. (2000). Psychosocial treatment of posttraumatic stress disorder. *The Journal of Clinical Psychiatry, 61*(suppl. 5), 43–48; discussion 49–51.

Gale, G. D., Anagnostaras, S. G., Godsil, B. P., Mitchell, S., Nozawa, T., Sage, J. R., et al. (2004). Role of the basolateral amygdala in the storage of fear memories across the adult lifetime of rats. *The Journal of Neuroscience, 24*(15), 3810–3815.

Guarraci, F. A., Frohardt, R. J., Falls, W. A., & Kapp, B. S. (2000). The effects of intra-amygdaloid infusions of a D2 dopamine receptor antagonist on Pavlovian fear conditioning. *Behavioral Neuroscience, 114*(3), 647–651.

Huang, C. C., Wang, S. J., & Gean, P. W. (1998). Selective enhancement of P-type calcium currents by isoproterenol in the rat amygdala. *Journal of Neuroscience, 18*(6), 2276–2282.

Huang, Y. Y., & Kandel, E. R. (2007). 5-hydroxytryptamine induces a protein kinase A/mitogen-activated protein kinase-mediated and macromolecular synthesis-dependent late phase of long-term potentiation in the amygdala. *The Journal of Neuroscience, 27*(12), 3111–3119.

James, W. (1884). What is an emotion? *Mind, 9*, 188–205.

Ji, J., & Maren, S. (2007). Hippocampal involvement in contextual modulation of fear extinction. *Hippocampus, 17*(9), 749–758.

Kandel, E. R. (2001). The molecular biology of memory storage: A dialogue between genes and synapses. *Science, 294*(5544), 1030–1038.

Klüver, H., & Bucy, P. C. (1939). Preliminary analysis of functions of the temporal lobes in monkeys. *Archives of Neurology and Psychiatry, 42*, 979–1000.

Kröner, S., Rosenkranz, J. A., Grace, A. A., & Barrionuevo, G. (2005). Dopamine modulates excitability of basolateral amygdala neurons in vitro. *Journal of Neurophysiology, 93*(3), 1598–1610.

LaBar, K. S., Gatenby, J. C., Gore, J. C., LeDoux, J. E., & Phelps, E. A. (1998). Human amygdala activation during conditioned fear acquisition and extinction: A mixed-trial fMRI study. *Neuron, 20*(5), 937–945.

Lang, P. J., & Davis, M. (2006). Emotion, motivation, and the brain: Reflex foundations in animal and human research. *Progress in Brain Research, 156*, 3–29.

Lange, C. G. (1885). *Om sindsbevaegelser: Et psyko-fysiologisk studie*. Copenhagen: Lunds.

LeDoux, J. (2007). The amygdala. *Current Biology, 17*(20), R868–R874.

LeDoux, J. E. (1996). *The emotional brain*. New York: Simon and Schuster.

LeDoux, J. E. (2000). Emotion circuits in the brain. *Annual Review of Neuroscience, 23*, 155–184.

LeDoux, J. E., & Gorman, J. M. (2001). A call to action: Overcoming anxiety through active coping. *The American Journal of Psychiatry, 158*(12), 1953–1955.

Lee, J. L., Di Ciano, P., Thomas, K. L., & Everitt, B. J. (2005). Disrupting reconsolidation of drug memories reduces cocaine-seeking behavior. *Neuron, 47*(6), 795–801.

Lee, J. L., Milton, A. L., & Everitt, B. J. (2006). Reconsolidation and extinction of conditioned fear: Inhibition and potentiation. *The Journal of Neuroscience, 26*(39), 10051–10056.

Liberzon, I., Britton, J. C., & Phan, K. L. (2003). Neural correlates of traumatic recall in posttraumatic stress disorder. *Stress, 6*(3), 151–156.

Liberzon, I., & Sripada, C. S. (2008). The functional neuroanatomy of PTSD: A critical review. *Progress in Brain Research, 167*, 151–169.

Maren, S. (2001). Neurobiology of Pavlovian fear conditioning. *Annual Review of Neuroscience, 24*, 897–931.

Maren, S. (2005). Synaptic mechanisms of associative memory in the amygdala. *Neuron, 47*(6), 783–786.

McGaugh, J. L. (2000). Memory: a century of consolidation. *Science, 287*(5451), 248–251.

McGaugh, J. L. (2004). The amygdala modulates the consolidation of memories of emotionally arousing experiences. *Annual Review of Neuroscience, 27*, 1–28.

Milad, M. R., & Quirk, G. J. (2002). Neurons in medial prefrontal cortex signal memory for fear extinction. *Nature, 420*(6911), 70–74.

Misanin, J. R., Miller, R. R., & Lewis, D. J. (1968). Retrograde amnesia produced by electroconvulsive shock after reactivation of a consolidated memory trace. *Science, 160*(827), 554–555.

Morris, J. S., Ohman, A., & Dolan, R. J. (1998). Conscious and unconscious emotional learning in the human amygdala. *Nature, 393*(6684), 467–470.

Myers, K. M., & Davis, M. (2002). Behavioral and neural analysis of extinction. *Neuron, 36*(4), 567–584.

Nader, K. (2003). Memory traces unbound. *Trends in Neurosciences, 26*(2), 65–72.

Nader, K., Schafe, G. E., & LeDoux, J. E. (2000). Fear memories require protein synthesis in the amygdala for reconsolidation after retrieval. *Nature, 406*(6797), 722–726.

Norberg, M. M., Krystal, J. H., & Tolin, D. F. (2008). A meta-analysis of D-cycloserine and the facilitation of fear extinction and exposure therapy. *Biological Psychiatry, 63*(12), 1118–1126.

Ohman, A. (2007). Has evolution primed humans to "beware the beast"? *Proceedings of the National Academy of the United States of America, 104*(42), 16396–16397.

Papez, J. W. (1937). A proposed mechanism of emotion. *Archives of Neurology and Psychiatry, 79*, 217–224.

Paré, D. (2002). Mechanisms of Pavlovian fear conditioning: Has the engram been located? *Trends in Neuroscience, 25*(9), 436–437; discussion 437–438.

Paré, D., Quirk, G. J., & LeDoux, J. E. (2004). New vistas on amygdala networks in conditioned fear. *Journal of Neurophysiology, 92*(1), 1–9.

Paré, D., Royer, S., Smith, Y., & Lang, E. J. (2003). Contextual inhibitory gating of impulse traffic in the intra-amygdaloid network. *Annals of the New York Academy of Sciences, 985*, 78–91.

Phan, K. L., Angstadt, M., Golden, J., Onyewuenyi, I., Popovska, A., & de Wit, H. (2008). Cannabinoid modulation of amygdala reactivity to social signals of threat in humans. *The Journal of Neuroscience, 28*(10), 2313–2319.

Phan, K. L., Fitzgerald, D. A., Nathan, P. J., & Tancer, M. E. (2006). Association between amygdala hyperactivity to harsh faces and severity of social anxiety in generalized social phobia. *Biological Psychiatry, 59*(5), 424–429.

Phelps, E. A. (2006). Emotion and cognition: Insights from studies of the human amygdala. *Anuual Review of Psychology, 57*, 27–53.

Phelps, E. A., Delgado, M. R., Nearing, K. I., & LeDoux, J. E. (2004). Extinction learning in humans; role of the amygdala and vmPFC *Neuron, 43*(6), 897–905.

Phelps, E. A., & LeDoux, J. E. (2005). Contributions of the amygdala to emotion processing: From animal models to human behavior. *Neuron, 48*(2), 175–187.

Pitman, R. K., Shin, L. M., & Rauch, S. L. (2001). Investigating the pathogenesis of posttraumatic stress disorder with neuroimaging. *The Journal of Clinical Psychiatry, 62*(suppl. 17), 47–54.

Quirk, G. J., & Beer, J. S. (2006). Prefrontal involvement in the regulation of emotion: Convergence of rat and human studies. *Current Opinion in Neurobiology, 16*(6), 723–727.

Quirk, G. J., & Mueller, D. (2008). Neural mechanisms of extinction learning and retrieval. *Neuropsychopharmacology, 33*(1), 56–72.

Rattiner, L. M., Davis, M., & Ressler, K. J. (2005). Brain-derived neurotrophic factor in amygdala-dependent learning. *Neuroscientist, 11*(4), 323–333.

Rauch, S. L., Shin, L. M., & Phelps, E. A. (2006). Neurocircuitry models of posttraumatic stress disorder and extinction: Human neuroimaging research—past, present, and future. *Biological Psychiatry, 60*(4), 376–382.

Rauch, S. L., Shin, L. M., & Wright, C. I. (2003). Neuroimaging studies of amygdala function in anxiety disorders. *Annals of the New York Academy of Sciences, 985*, 389–410.

Ressler, K. J., Rothbaum, B. O., Tannenbaum, L., Anderson, P., Graap, K., Zimand, E., et al. (2004). Cognitive enhancers as adjuncts to psychotherapy: Use of D-cycloserine in phobic individuals to facilitate extinction of fear. *Archives of General Psychiatry, 61*(11), 1136–1144.

Rhodes, R. A., Murthy, N. V., Dresner, M. A., Selvaraj, S., Stavrakakis, N., Babar, S., et al. (2007). Human 5-HT transporter availability predicts amygdala reactivity in vivo. *The Journal of Neuroscience, 27*(34), 9233–9237.

Rodrigues, S. M., Schafe, G. E., & LeDoux, J. E. (2004). Molecular mechanisms underlying emotional learning and memory in the lateral amygdala. *Neuron, 44*(1), 75–91.

Rosen, J. B., & Schulkin, J. (1998). From normal fear to pathological anxiety. *Psychological Review, 105*(2), 325–350.

Rudd, M. D., & Joiner, T. (1998). The role of symptom induction in the treatment of panic and anxiety. Identifiable domains, conditional properties, and treatment targets. *Behavior Modification, 22*(1), 96–107.

Rumpel, S., LeDoux, J., Zador, A., & Malinow, R. (2005). Postsynaptic receptor trafficking underlying a form of associative learning. *Science, 308*(5718), 83–88.

Sah, P., Faber, E. S., Lopez De Armentia, M., & Power, J. (2003). The amygdaloid complex: Anatomy and physiology. *Physiological Review, 83*(3), 803–834.

Sara, S. J. (2000). Retrieval and reconsolidation: Toward a neurobiology of remembering. *Learning and Memory, 7*(2), 73–84.

Schafe, G. E., Bauer, E. P., Rosis, S., Farb, C. R., Rodrigues, S. M., & LeDoux, J. E. (2005). Memory consolidation of Pavlovian fear conditioning requires nitric oxide signaling in the lateral amygdala. *The European Journal of Neuroscience, 22*(1), 201–211.

Schafe, G. E., Nader, K., Blair, H. T., & LeDoux, J. E. (2001). Memory consolidation of Pavlovian fear conditioning: A cellular and molecular perspective. *Trends in Neurosciences, 24*(9), 540–546.

Schienle, A., Schafer, A., Walter, B., Stark, R., & Vaitl, D. (2005). Brain activation of spider phobics toward disorder-relevant, generally disgust- and fear-inducing pictures. *Neuroscience Letters, 388*(1), 1–6.

Schneider, A. M., & Sherman, W. (1968). Amnesia: A function of the temporal relation of footshock to electroconvulsive shock. *Science, 159*(811), 219–221.

Shear, M. K., & Beidel, D. C. (1998). Psychotherapy in the overall management strategy for social anxiety disorder. *The Journal of Clinical Psychiatry, 59*(suppl. 17), 39–46.

Shin, L. M., Kosslyn, S. M., McNally, R. J., Alpert, N. M., Thompson, W. L., Rauch, S. L., et al. (1997). Visual imagery and perception in posttraumatic stress disorder. A positron emission tomographic investigation. *Archives of General Psychiatry, 54*(3), 233–241.

Shin, L. M., Orr, S. P., Carson, M. A., Rauch, S. L., Macklin, M. L., Lasko, N. B., et al. (2004). Regional cerebral blood flow in the amygdala and medial prefrontal cortex during traumatic imagery in male and female vietnam veterans with PTSD. *Archives of General Psychiatry, 61*(2), 168–176.

Shin, L. M., Wright, C. I., Cannistraro, P. A., Wedig, M. M., McMullin, K., Martis, B., et al. (2005). A functional magnetic resonance imaging study of amygdala and medial prefrontal cortex responses to overtly presented fearful faces in posttraumatic stress disorder. *Archives of General Psychiatry, 62*(3), 273–281.

Sigurdsson, T., Doyère, V., Cain, C. K., & LeDoux, J. E. (2007). Long-term potentiation in the amygdala: A cellular mechanism of fear learning and memory. *Neuropharmacology, 52*(1), 215–227.

Sotres-Bayon, F., Bush, D. E., & LeDoux, J. E. (2004). Emotional perseveration: An update on prefrontal-amygdala interactions in fear extinction. *Learning and Memory, 11*(5), 525–535.

Sotres-Bayon, F., Cain, C. K., & LeDoux, J. E. (2006). Brain mechanisms of fear extinction: Historical perspectives on the contribution of prefrontal cortex. *Biological Psychiatry, 60*(4), 329–336.

Swanson, L. W., & Petrovich, G. D. (1998). What is the amygdala? *Trends in Neuroscience, 21*(8), 323–331.

Tronson, N. C., & Taylor, J. R. (2007). Molecular mechanisms of memory reconsolidation. *Nature Reviews Neuroscience, 8*(4), 262–275.

Tronson, N. C., Wiseman, S. L., Olausson, P., & Taylor, J. R. (2006). Bidirectional behavioral plasticity of memory reconsolidation depends on amygdalar protein kinase A. *Nature Neuroscience, 9*(2), 167–169.

Tully, K., Li, Y., Tsvetkov, E., & Bolshakov, V. Y. (2007). Norepinephrine enables the induction of associative long-term potentiation at thalamo-amygdala synapses. *Proceedings of the National Academy of Sciences of the United States of America, 104*(35), 14146–14150.

van Stegeren, A. H., Goekoop, R., Everaerd, W., Scheltens, P., Barkhof, F., Kuijer, J. P., et al. (2005). Noradrenaline mediates amygdala activation in men and women during encoding of emotional material. *Neuroimage, 24*(3), 898–909.

Vuilleumier, P., Armony, J. L., Driver, J., & Dolan, R. J. (2001). Effects of attention and emotion on face processing in the human brain: An event-related FMRI study. *Neuron, 30*(3), 829–841.

Walker, D. L., Ressler, K. J., Lu, K. T., & Davis, M. (2002). Facilitation of conditioned fear extinction by systemic administration or intra-amygdala infusions of D-cycloserine as assessed with fear-potentiated startle in rats. *The Journal of Neuroscience, 22*(6), 2343–2351.

Weiskrantz, L. (1956). Behavioral changes associated with ablation of the amygdaloid complex in monkeys. *Journal of Comparative Physiological Psychology, 49*, 381–391.

6

Behavioral Genetics: Strategies for Understanding the Anxiety Disorders

Kerry L. Jang
Chizuru Shikishima

An enduring matter of debate and research in the *Diagnostic and Statistical Manual of Mental Disorders* (*DSM*) that cuts across all of the diagnostic categories is the matter of dimensionality—whether or not a disorder is best defined as the extremes of normal behavior or instead best understood as a stand-alone entity with little reference to normal behavioral processes. Inextricably linked to the question of dimensionality is the issue of comorbidity because to investigate one involves examining why two behavioral forms co-occur. For example, one approach to study dimensionality is to establish a relationship, often by correlation coefficient, between normal and abnormal forms of behavior, whereas the same general method is used to estimate the strength of relationship between symptoms such as anxiety and mood to determine if they represent facets of the same or different disorders.

Within the anxiety disorders literature, examples of both kinds of research can be found without difficulty. For example, researchers examining dimensionality have established clear associations between normal fear of negative evaluations and social anxiety disorder, and as much effort has been spent establishing that posttraumatic stress disorder (PTSD) and major depressive disorder are frequently comorbid. The focus has now turned to searching out the bases for these associations, what causes normal behavior to develop into extreme behavior, or why depressive symptoms or feelings of anxiety are found across multiple *DSM* diagnostic categories. Several explanations have been offered to account for these observed relationships, which range from being no more than the consequence of measurement error attributable to criterion overlap to being caused by a shared biology.

It is the latter that is the purview of behavioral genetics, a field devoted to the study of inheritance. Behavioral genetics is best known for conducting twin and adoption studies to estimate *heritability* (the degree to which variation in observed behavior is directly attributable to genetic differences between people—symbolized as h^2) to molecular genetic research that attempts to identify putative genes related to specific disorders. The latter has received the lion's share of attention of late, but given that several genes contribute to the genetic variance of anxiety-related traits or modify the phenotypic expression of pathologic anxiety (Lesch, 2001), any gene or, more specifically, gene variant called a *polymorphism* has, at best, accounted for only a small proportion of the variability in a measure. Adding to the complexity is that the anxiety disorders are multifactorial in that they are caused by multiple genetic and environmental influences and their interactions. These complexities likely account for the limited success researchers have been having in mapping anxiety-related loci in both animals and humans (Gordon & Hen, 2004) from the more than 1.4 million single nucleotide polymorphisms (SNPs) identified in the human genome.

The present state of affairs of genotyping research has had the effect of having researchers returning to classical twin methods because they yield various summary statistics (e.g., h^2) that estimate the total effects of all genes but also different environmental effects and, more recently, their interaction. With this in mind, the purpose of this chapter is to discuss the behavioral genetic research on the causes of comorbidity, but also related questions on the structure and organization of symptoms to more recent questions about the dimensional nature of these disorders, which are of primary concern to the *DSM* system.

The Issue of Comorbidity

Comorbidity is used to describe the co-occurrence of disorders but also broadly used to describe the co-occurrence of symptoms that happen to occur frequently enough that they are grouped together to define a disorder or syndrome. Quantitative genetic theory suggests that the co-occurrence is directly attributable to a common etiological basis, such as a common genetic heritage:

$$r_{x \cdot y} = (h_X \cdot h_Y \cdot r_G) + (e_X \cdot e_Y \cdot r_E) \quad \text{Equation 1}$$

This expression states that the observed or "phenotypic" relationship between two measured variables X and Y, indexed by a correlation coefficient, $r_{x \cdot y}$, is a direct function of the degree to which genetic factors (h_x, h_y) and environmental factors (e_x, e_y) on each measure that is weighted by the degree to which the genetic and environmental influences on X and Y stem from a common source, indexed by the genetic and environmental correlation coefficients r_G and r_E, respectively.

The values of h_x, h_y in Equation 1 is estimated by comparing the similarity (e.g., measured by a correlation coefficient) of identical or monozygotic (MZ) twin pairs to fraternal or dizygotic (DZ) twin pairs. Higher within-pair MZ similarities on each variable and across variables (e.g., $r_{\text{MZ TWIN1} \cdot \text{TWIN2}}$) compared to a within-pair DZ correlation (e.g., $r_{\text{DZ TWIN1} \cdot \text{TWIN2}}$) suggests that genetic influences are implicated because MZ twins share all of their genes whereas DZ twins share half. When, for example, the $r_{\text{MZ TWIN1} \cdot \text{TWIN2}} = r_{\text{DZ TWIN1} \cdot \text{TWIN2}}$, no genetic influences are inferred because despite the twofold greater genetic similarity of MZ twins, their observed similarity is that of DZ twins. Note that h_x, h_y are simply the unstandardized versions of the well-known heritability estimate symbolized as h_X^2 and h_Y^2. The genetic correlation coefficient (r_G) between X and Y is computed much in the same way as h_x and h_y but instead compares MZ to DZ cross-correlations—the correlation between one twin's score on one of the variables and the other twin's score on the other variable.

Two environmental influences are readily estimated from twin data as well. The first is any experience or condition that affects members from the same family in the same way; that is, environmental influences that cause family members to become more similar (c^2) or have the same influence on two variables (r_C). An example of c^2 is socioeconomic status because it is thought to apply to and affect each person within the family equally while differentiating families. The second environmental influence is nonshared family environment (e^2 and r_E). Nonshared environmental influences are defined as any experience, milieu, or circumstance,virtually anything that causes children from the same family to be different from one another, including experiences that systematically differentiate people from one another, such as parental favoritism (Hetherington, Reiss, & Plomin, 1994) and measurement error. Equation 1 thus becomes $r_{x{\cdot}y} = (h_X \cdot h_Y \cdot r_G) + (c_X \cdot c_Y \cdot r_C) + (e_X \cdot e_Y \cdot r_E)$. The actual procedures used to estimate these quantities are explained in detail in many behavioral genetic textbooks (e.g., Jang, 2005; Neale & Cardon, 1992; Plomin, DeFries, McClearn, & McGuffin, 2000) and the details need not be reiterated here.

The computation of the genetic and environmental correlation has been a popular approach applied between various anxiety and other major disorders. One of the most provocative early studies was Eley and Stevenson's (1999) study of 529 twin pairs aged 8–16 years from the Register for Child Twins throughout the British Isles in which the genes underlying symptoms of anxiety measured by the State–Trait Anxiety Inventory for Children and Children's Depression Inventory were virtually identical ($r_G = 1.0$) with genetic correlations of unity between depression and anxiety for younger and older males and female groups. Among adults, a very similar finding was reported by Kendler, Gardner, Gatz, and Pedersen (2007) between a modified version of *DSM-IV* major depression and generalized anxiety disorder (GAD) for men at 0.74 and for women at 1.00, using a sample of 37,296 twins from the population-based Swedish Twin Registry (Gorwood, 2004). A similar finding was found between PTSD and major depression. On a sample of 6744 twins who were veterans from the Vietnam War, Koenen et al. (2008) reported that *DSM-III-R* major depression and PTSD in men substantially shared a common genetic basis $r_G = .77$ (CI: .50–1.00). A broad review of findings such as these is that GAD and major depression are part of the same general disorder, raising the issue of the validity of separate diagnostic categories for each. In contrast, although smoking (nicotine dependence) is frequently observed in individuals with PTSD, Koenen et al. (2005) estimated the genetic correlation at *DSM-III-R* PTSD and nicotine dependence at .45 (CI: .32–.59) in a sample of 6,744 members of the Vietnam Era Twin Registry.

The next two genetic correlational studies are between normal and abnormal forms of behavior and provide support for a dimensional model of the anxiety disorders. Hettema, Prescott, and Kendler (2004) showed that GAD shared all of its genetic etiology with the personality trait neuroticism. The genetic correlations between lifetime GAD assessed through telephone and face-to-face structured psychiatric interviews to *DSM-III-R* and *DSM-IV* criteria was 1.00 (CI: .40–1.00) for men. In contrast, among women, the r_G was estimated at .58 (CI: −1.00–1.00) and was .80 (CI: .52–1.00) in the combined sample. Battaglia, Pesenti–Gritti, Spatola, Ogliari, and Tambs (2008) estimated r_G between self-assessed anxiety post-35% CO_2 to 65% O_2 inhalation and *DSM-IV* lifetime diagnoses panic disorder at .81 (CI: .50–.98) in a sample of 346 young adult twin pairs from the Norwegian Institute of Health Panel.

Structure and Organization of Symptoms and Disorders

An expansion of this approach can be used to test questions of what underlies the organization of anxiety disorder symptoms, as well as test hypotheses about the hierarchical relationship of anxiety disorders with other disorders. For example, is panic disorder a unified entity with its own etiology or is it a special case of some other broader disorder, such as a personality disorder? The two basic forms are illustrated in Figures 6.1 and 6.2. The first is called the independent pathway (IP) model (Figure 6.1). In this model, the observed intercorrelation between symptoms are accounted by the presence of common, and possibly multiple, genetic and experiential factors. Note too that the model makes provision for influences unique to each symptom. In contrast, the model in Figure 6.2 is called the common pathway (CP) model, specifying that the observed relationships between

6.1

Independent pathway model.

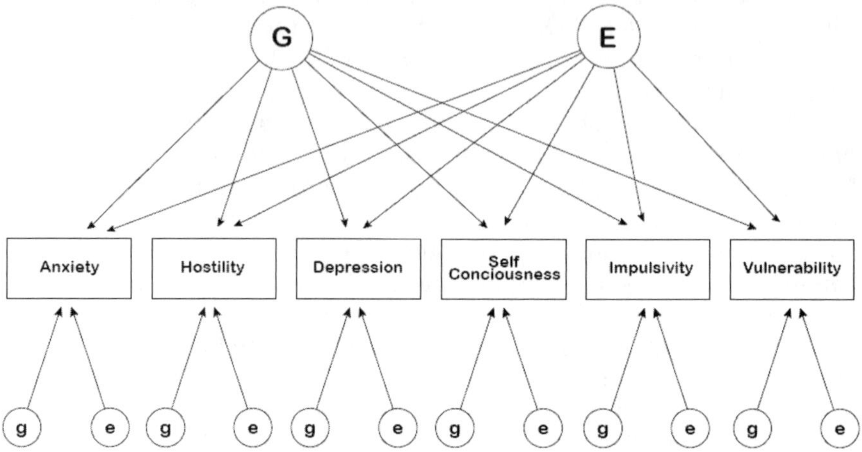

6.2

Common pathway model.

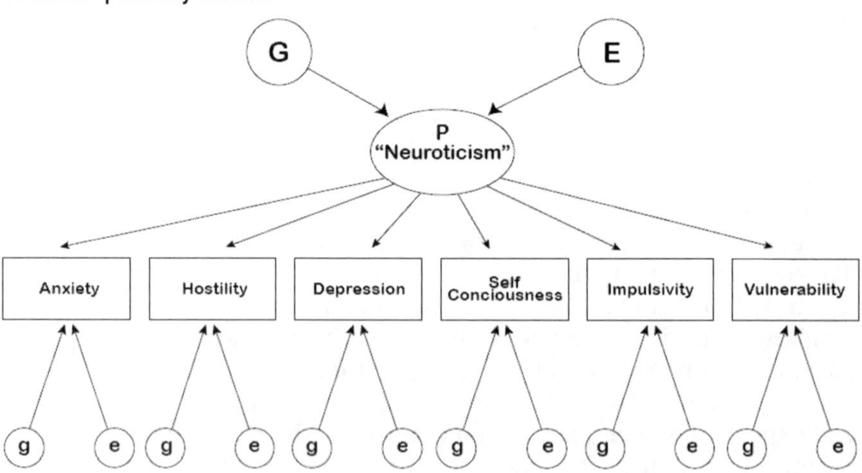

variables are due to the action of a higher-order latent variable (P, which is unmeasured and is inferred by the degree to which the measured variables appear together) in which any and all common genetic and environmental influence is channeled through P. Like the IP model, it makes provision for genetic and environmental influences unique to each symptom. The existence of a genetically and environmentally mediated higher order P trait transforms the latent variable into a veridical entity that has a basis in biology. In practical terms, this means that the higher order construct does represent a specific disease entity and that lower-order symptoms are best understood as exemplars of the higher order construct. Because the IP model does not specify an independently inherited P, diagnostic entities such as "panic disorder" cease to exist as veridical entities and instead are conceptualized as a descriptive term that labels the observed relationship between symptoms.

Knowledge of whether an anxiety disorder diagnosis is structured as defined by an IP or CP model is fundamentally important because each has implications on the search for putative genes. For example, if the CP model is correct, this implies that there are specific genes for the higher order construct. As such, the phenotypic factor score could be computed and used because each facet is an exemplar of the domain that has a common genetic basis with all other aspects of the domain. In contrast, if the IP model is correct, it would mean that either the total summative score across facet traits or phenotypic factor score would not be ideal because it could reflect different, possibly competing etiological influences. Rather, a phenotypic factor score based on only those subsets of facets that share a common genetic basis can be associated with various candidate genes. Both models suggest that it is possible to find a gene for a diagnostic entity (be it real as in the case of the CP model or apparent as in the IP model) as all of the symptoms still share a common etiology to some extent. Rather, the IP model subtly shifts the focus to the treatment and study to individual symptoms.

An excellent example of this approach is Kendler et al.'s (1995) analysis that applied both models to lifetime history of *DSM-III-R* phobia, GAD, panic, bulimia, major depression, and alcoholism. The observed covariance between these diagnoses was best explained by an IP model that specified two additive genetic factors, one shared environmental factor, and one nonshared environmental factor. The two genetic factors appeared to delineate two broad domains of anxiety disorder. The first genetic factor accounted for the largest proportion of heritable influence on phobia (33%), panic disorder (32%), and bulimia (29%) and in total accounted for less than 7% of the variance on the remaining disorders. The second genetic factor was found to influence only GAD and major depression, accounting for 22% and 41% of the variance. This factor only accounted for 12% or less of the variance in the remaining four disorders. Alcoholism was little influenced by either genetic factor. Together, the common factors were found to account for only 7% of the variance on alcoholism, with 45% of the total variance attributable to alcohol-specific genetic factors.

The shared environmental (c^2) factor accounted for 41% of the total variance across all disorders with the exception of bulimia, which accounted for approximately 2%. The single common nonshared environmental factor had the largest influences on GAD and depression, accounting for 38% and 34% of the total variance in each, respectively. Most of the nonshared environmental effects were found to be unique to each disorder, accounting for 29% to 49% of the total variance. These results clearly indicate that what is thought of as a genetically homogenous set of disorders is actually quite an etiologically diverse collection of conditions. The most interesting finding is that GAD has more in common with major depression than any of the other anxiety disorders, suggesting that its classification as an anxiety disorder is incorrect.

In a recent study, van Grootheest, Boomsma, Hettema, and Kendler (in press) fitted IP and CP models to obsessive compulsive (OC) symptoms information collected from a population sample of 1,383 female twins from the Virginia Twin Registry. The symptoms factored into three reliable OC symptom dimensions: rumination, contamination, and checking and covariation was best explained by a CP in which the common factor (which they called obsessive–compulsive behavior) had a heritable component explaining 36% of the variability. Of particular note was their finding that only the contamination dimension was influenced by specific genes and seemed to be a relatively independent dimension. In general, the fit of the CP model suggests that a broad OC behavioral phenotype exists.

Another example of this approach was a recent paper by Taylor, Jang, Stewart, and Stein (in press), in which IP and CP models were fit to measures of physical, cognitive, and social concerns, which are the three primary dimensions of anxiety sensitivity. This paper is particularly interesting because both the IP and CP models provided a satisfactory fit to the covariance between these three dimensions. This is important for two reasons. The first is that it highlights an issue within behavioral genetics that the wise consumer of this research should be aware—how does one choose between equally well-fitting models? The same problem was confronted by Young, Stallings, Corley, Krauter, and Hewitt's (2000) study of behaviors that describe behavioral disinhibition, finding that *either* a one-factor CP model or a one-genetic factor IP provided an equally good explanation of the covariance between these symptoms. In the end, they selected the CP model because "... this is a more parsimonious model than the independent pathway model and shows no significant decrement in fit by χ^2 difference test..." (p. 690–691). This highlights one area of behavioral genetics that probably requires more attention. Specifically, it is necessary to develop criteria to guide selection between equally well-fitting models. Presently, when statistical guidance is lacking, the choice of model becomes (a) arbitrary, (b) based on one's own theoretical preferences, or (c) based on the principle of parsimony, wherein the model with the fewest parameters is the simplest. In short, for the consumer of behavioral genetic research, caveat emptor.

The second reason why the findings of the Taylor et al. (in press) paper is important is it not only highlights the complexity of psychiatric illness such as the anxiety disorders, it also illustrates that although the role of common genetic and environmental factors are significant and frequently large, they rarely approach 1.0; that is, they rarely account for 100% of the total covariation between measures, leaving a significant proportion of the genetic and environmental variability between the measures to etiological factors unique to each. In fact, many of the nonshared environmental correlation coefficients are very small, suggesting that it is the role of environmental experiences, factors, or conditions that determines which set of symptoms that are common features of multiple diagnoses are developed and expressed and, thus, which form of a disease is expressed. How does this happen?

Just what is the role of genetic and environmental effects in differentiating behavior or causing normal anxiety to become extreme enough to be considered an anxiety disorder?

Abnormal From Normal: Dimensional Model of Psychopathology

Clinical research has shown that shyness is predictive of social phobia, and that anxiety sensitivity is predictive of panic attacks (Taylor, 1995). These relationships suggest that the anxiety disorders exist on a continuum of liability and represent an extreme form of normal behavior. Virtually all models of mental illness have assumed a dimensional model of some sort in which abnormal behavior is understood as the extremes of normal range behavior. In a dimensional model, the distribution of scores is bell shaped, and can be split into three (or more) areas that represent what we know about the intensity of a behavior such as self-reported anxiety over its distribution. For example, the range of "normal range" anxiety can be delineated by scores that fall within 1 standard deviation around the mean; the second area representing "subclinical" or "heightened" anxiety might be defined by scores that are greater than 1 standard deviation (perhaps representing what would be observed in people with higher anxiety sensitivity), with scores greater than 1.5 or perhaps 2 standard deviations representing "extreme" anxiety of the kind observed in persons with panic disorder.

One of the challenges of testing dimensional models is that there are few, if any, single measures that assess the full range of behavior across the normal, subclinical, and extreme ranges. Many measures are designed to assess one general area such as the normal range or clinical range behaviors. Research on dimensionality by necessity must employ measures to properly assess the full range of behaviors.[1] This use of multiple measures, each assessing a different level of behavior, allows us to compute and compare h^2, c^2, e^2, and the r_G and r_E between them in a form of test of the dimensional model. For example, a recognized risk factor for panic disorder is anxiety sensitivity. Stein, Jang, and Livesley (1999) estimated at the total score of the Anxiety Sensitivity Index (ASI; Peterson & Reiss, 1992) at 45% in a sample of 179

MZ and 158 DZ general population twin pairs. The next task was to test if the same genetic mechanisms influence normal and extreme range ASI scores. This test required that the heritability of extreme scores (h^2_g) defined by a clinically significant threshold on a quantitative measure to be estimated and compared to the magnitude of genetic influences on the entire range of scores, h^2 (DeFries & Fulker, 1985, 1988; Plomin, Rende, & Rutter, 1991). The clinical threshold for panic disorder on the ASI is a total score of 25. Stein and colleagues estimated h^2_g of the total ASI scores of 25, 27, and 28. Estimates of h^2_g ranged from 45% to 62% that falls within the 95% confidence interval around the 45% h^2 of the total ASI score (lower confidence limit = 33%, upper confidence limit = 59%) estimated from the total sample. The similarity of h^2 and h^2_g estimates suggests that high ASI scores characteristic of panic disorder and those in the subclinical range are influenced by the same genetic factors. In the Taylor et al. (in press) paper mentioned earlier, analyses of anxiety sensitivity by gender were also conducted. This is mentioned here in the context of dimensionality that among women, the heritability significantly increased with anxiety sensitivity scores, indicating that severe forms of anxiety sensitivity, compared to milder forms, are more strongly influenced by genetic factors. These findings provide a clear hint that what causes extreme scores is the activation or influence of specific genetic effects.

Stein, Jang, Taylor, Vernon, and Livesley (2002) used a different approach to testing the dimensionality of PTSD. They reasoned that because traumatic experiences and our responses to them are not limited to war zones, any form of assault, a natural disaster, a car accident, or a negative significant life event can also trigger symptoms of PTSD. A dimensional model would predict that these experiences and our responses to them are equivalent to those experienced by combat veterans. A sample of 406 general population twin pairs was surveyed on lifetime exposure to traumatic events (e.g., car accidents, natural disasters, death of a close family member or friend). Their responses were subjected to factor analysis and two factors were extracted: the first factor described "assaultive events" (robbery, held captive, beat up, sexual assault, other life threat) and the second "nonassaultive events" (sudden family death, motor vehicle accident, fire, and tornado, flood, or earthquake).

Two heritability analyses of assaultive and nonassaultive events factors were conducted. The first estimated the heritable basis of liability of exposure to assaultive trauma using data from all subjects; that is, whether or not they report having experienced any trauma. Additive genetic effects accounted for 20.3%, $c^2 = 21.3\%$ and $e^2 = 58.4\%$. In contrast, a purely environmental model provided the best explanation of liability of exposure to nonassaultive trauma: $c^2 = 38.6\%$ and $e^2 = 61.5\%$. Moreover, the values of r_C and r_E between the types of exposure were estimated at .31 and –.20, suggesting that the environmental influences on assaultive and nonassaultive trauma are largely unrelated. The second analysis estimated the heritable basis of PTSD symptoms conditional upon actual trauma exposure by using data from pairs in which both members of a pair reported experiencing a traumatic event. Those who had reported experience of an event were asked to answer a set of questions in reference to the event that most disturbed them to assess *DSM-IV* PTSD cluster B through D symptoms.

In this subsample of affected twins, additive genetic and nonshared environmental influences best explained the variance in assaultive trauma factor scores and a purely environmental model provided the best explanation for the variance in nonassaultive trauma. Heritability estimates for the symptoms were re-experiencing (36%), avoidance (28%), numbing (36%), hyperarousal (29%), and total symptoms at 38%. Nonshared environmental effects accounted for the remaining variance. Also computed was r_g and r_e between liability to assaultive trauma exposure and PTSD symptoms. The values ranged from .71–.83, suggesting that PTSD symptoms and the experience of trauma are inextricably linked by a common set of genetic factors. It is interesting to note that these estimates for PTSD symptoms and exposure to traumatic events come remarkably close to those derived from an exclusively male sample of combat veterans from the Vietnam Era Twin Registry. This finding is consistent with the hypothesis that the etiological factors underlying PTSD symptoms in the general population are the same as those underlying PTSD in combat veterans.

An extensive literature exists examining what is thought to be the subclinical form of social phobia—the fear of negative evaluation. Of particular interest are the results of the family and community-based research that suggests that social phobia is part of a continuum bounded by mild (i.e., normative) shyness at one end and avoidant personality disorder at the other (Stein & Chavira, 1998; van Velzen, Emmelkamp, & Scholing, 2000; Tillfors, Furmark, Ekselius, & Fredrikson, 2001). Stein, Jang, and Livesley (2002) estimated the genetic correlation between the Fear of Negative Evaluation Scale (FNE: Watson & Friend, 1969) and avoidant personality disorder traits of submissiveness, anxiousness, and social avoidance to range from .78–.80. These results have several implications. First, it suggests that a common set of genes influence vulnerability to these Axis I and Axis II disorders and, if replicated by future studies, would support the growing consensus that social phobia on Axis I and avoidant personality disorder on Axis II are really classifying the same construct. This would provide a good case in point in support of the argument that the division of Axis I and II disorders, although heuristically convenient, is often not empirically supported (e.g., Widiger, 2003).

These research examples show that many different disorders share a common etiological basis but beg the question of what mechanism(s) acts on this basis to create different forms of behavior we observe? Behavioral genetic theory specifies two broad mechanisms. The first is gene–environment interaction where specific environmental factors have been shown to moderate the expression of disease liability genes (Plomin, DeFries & Loehlin, 1977). The second is gene–environment correlations in which genes play a significant role in creating and selecting the environments a person is exposed to.

Going From Normal to Abnormal: Gene–Environment Interaction

As previous research has shown, if the same genes ostensibly influence unique disorders such as GAD and major depression, what causes them to express and manifest as GAD, depression, or both? One explanation is the action of the environment. In many studies, environmental effects are often found to be largely unique to each disorder. For example, Roy, Neale, Pedersen, Mathe, and Kendler (1995) reported that despite finding a common genetic basis to GAD and major depression, major depression appears to be predominantly associated with "loss events" (e.g., death of a relative or loss of a job), whereas GAD was found to be primarily associated with "danger events" such as those "that might elicit future crisis." Behavioral geneticists have long been occupied with identifying specific environmental effects. Turkheimer and Waldron (2000) conducted an extensive meta-analysis of the environmental research on personality and Reiss, Neiderhiser, Hetherington, and Plomin's (2000) book describes one of the most ambitious studies ever conducted to identify environmental effects. Sadly, the main conclusion of these works is that identifying environmental effects as main effects has not been very successful. For example, Turkheimer and Waldron (2000) showed that studies assessing family constellation variables accounted for only 1.1% of the variance on average; differences in maternal and paternal behavior fared slightly better at 2.3% and 1.6%, respectively; differences in sibling interaction accounted for on average 4.1% and differences in peer–teacher interactions a "sizeable" 9.1% on average. They conclude that environmental effects must be cumulative—that it may take many such small effects to accumulate and have a measurable effect on behavior.

In contrast, studies of gene–environment interaction have yielded stunning results. Interaction effects are investigated by stratifying a sample of probands into groups based on levels (usually the presence or absence) of stressor and show that each group is associated with particular polymorphisms implicated in the disorder of interest. Stein, Schork, and Gelernter (2008) used this approach to see if the expression of the serotonin transporter gene (5-HTTLPR) moderated childhood maltreatment to increase susceptibility to anxiety sensitivity in 150 white young adults and in a second ethnically heterogeneous sample ($n = 247$). Linear regression was used to model relationships between 5-HTTLPR, childhood emotional abuse, and anxiety sensitivity. In both samples, they found a statistically significant interaction between levels of childhood emotional (or physical) maltreatment and 5-HTTLPR genotype. Specifically, people who carried two short forms of the serotonin transporter polymorphism (5-HTTLPR) allele and experienced higher levels of maltreatment had significantly higher levels of anxiety sensitivity than subjects in other groups. These results provide evidence of a specific genetic influence on anxiety sensitivity—an intermediate phenotype for anxiety (and depressive) disorders. This effect is modified by severity of childhood maltreatment, and is consistent with the notion that 5-HTTLPR operates broadly to moderate emotional responsibility to stress.

Gunthert et al. (2007) tested whether individuals with at least one copy of the short (S) or long (L) allele of the serotonin transporter polymorphism (5-HTTLPR) exhibit greater reported anxiety, compared with LL individuals under periods of high daily stress. Their sample was 350 college students who recorded their daily stressors and mood for two 30-day periods that were separated by 1 year. The results across both years were remarkably similar—the same patterns were observed for reports of anxious mood as a function of 5-HTTLPR. In particular, individuals with at least one copy of the S or L allele experienced elevated anxiousness on days with more intense stressors compared with those who carried two copies of the long allele. Genotype differences in anxiety were less apparent on low stress days and no consistent allelic association of 5-HTTLPR was found with any other mood states, trait anxiety, or neuroticism.

Using classic twin data, gene–environment interaction was demonstrated by showing that heritability estimates differ across environmental conditions. For example, Silberg, Rutter, Neale, and Eaves (2001) showed that number of life events ("0," "1," or "2 or more") moderates depression and anxiety in adolescent girls. They reported that the heritability of GAD (assessed by the Adolescent Psychiatric Assessment—an investigator-based psychiatric interview providing information for diagnosing the major forms of childhood psychopathology according to *DSM-IV* criteria) becomes larger as a function of number of past-year life events from 19% in the absence of life events, to 34% for one life event, and 44% for two or more life events. Recently, Lau, Gregory, Goldwin, Pine, and Eley (2007) showed that the heritability of separation anxiety symptoms in childhood increases as a function of levels of independent negative life events.

A potential problem with gene–environment interactions to be aware of is that the environmental variable used to stratify the sample could be confounded with several other psychosocial stressors. For example, can estimates of maternal warmth be made independent of maternal care? Thus, any conclusions about the effect of a specific environmental stressor are limited to the extent that other potential moderators have been adequately controlled. Another issue to be aware of is that many stressors (e.g., levels of family conflict) cannot be simply categorized as present or absent. All families experience some level of conflict that varies from low to very high and simple contingency table designs potentially lose important information that can obscure the existence of interaction effects.

Fortunately, recent modifications to the path models (e.g., Dick, Rose, Viken, Kaprio, & Koskenvuo, 2001) used to estimate heritability allows for the analysis of *continuously* measured psychosocial variables (see Figure 6.3). In this model, the psychosocial/environmental experiences reported by each twin are represented by the triangles. The path M_a between A_{TWIN1}, A_{TWIN2} and the psychosocial variable M indexes gene–environment interaction because these influences directly moderate the effect of genetic influences, which is converted to h^2_A. This model is important because now the interplay of environments and experiences are directly estimated using variables that best reflect gradations in environmental effect.

6.3

Moderator model.

G1 and G2 represent genetic influences on Twin 1 (T1) and Twin 2 (T2) measured phenotypes, respectively; C1 and C2 represent common environmental influences on T1 and T2, respectively; and E1, E2 represent nonshared environmental influences on T1 and T2, respectively. M1 and M2 represent the moderator variable for each member of a twin pair.

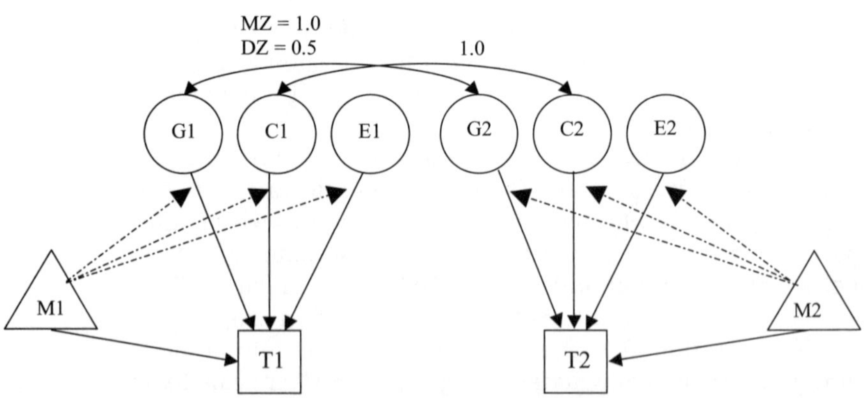

This model is also important because it can estimate experience by environmental interaction (ExE). Just as genetic effects can be influenced by exposure to specific environmental effects, the environment can also be influenced by the occurrence of other nongenetic effects. For example, some people can live in extreme poverty but display no ill effects because the presence of another environmental factor such as an attentive mother that attends to the emotional needs of the child that cancels out the influence of poverty. These kinds of effects are estimated by the path M_c between the triangles and C_{TWIN1}, C_{TWIN2} indexes the degree to which the psychosocial stressors moderate the effect of shared environmental effects (c^2), and the path M_e between the triangles and E_{TWIN1}, E_{TWIN2} indexes the degree to which the psychosocial stressor moderates the effect of nonshared environmental effects (e^2).

Gene by Environment Correlation

The other major form of interplay is what is known as "gene–environment correlation" ($\underline{r}_{ge}$). Theoretically, behavior geneticists discuss three processes: passive, active, and reactive (Plomin et al., 1977). *Passive* genotype–environment correlation occurs because children share heredity and environments with members of their family and can thus passively inherit environments correlated with their genetic propensities. *Reactive* genotype–environment correlation refers to experiences of the child derived from reactions of other people to the child's genetic propensities. *Active* genotype–environment correlation is known as "niche building" or "niche picking" (Plomin, DeFries, & McClearn, 1990, p. 251). This occurs when children actively select or create environments commensurate with their underlying genetic propensities.

The reader should be aware that testing "gene–environment correlation" has taken two forms in the literature. The first way is to correlate a "true" measure of the environment; that is, a scale that assesses a person's perception of external conditions that has no demonstrable heritability, with a measure of psychopathology that is completely heritable. Such an approach could be tested if validated scales with these characteristics existed, but this is typically not the case because as behavior and perceptions of the environment are influenced by both genetic and environmental influences. This limitation has been overcome with the development of methods based on a factor score approach to partition and derive scores that reflect only the genetic portion of a disorder like GAD and only the environmental portion of a measure of a putative event (Sham, et al., 2000; Thomis, et al., 2000 for a description of the computational method). Thus, gene–environment correlation is tested for by regressing the environmentally indexed measure of conditions with the genetically indexed scores on a disorder. Any significant relationship can be interpreted as genetic influences on a disorder, such as GAD creating the necessary environment for its expression. Presently, this approach has not been applied to the anxiety disorders.

However, the next approach has been applied to the anxiety disorders. This approach is somewhat removed from the classical definition outlined above in that it simply accepts a measure of the environment at face value by not requiring the measure to be free of genetic influences as in the previous approach. Instead, it takes advantage of the fact that perceptions of the environment are influenced by genetic influences and measures the strength of this genetic association using r_G with a measure of psychopathology. If r_G is significant, then that is taken as evidence that the environment a person reports as important and behavior are inextricably joined. This approach was used to examine if genetically based personality traits, such as neuroticism, have been implicated in influencing a person's risk for placing oneself in, or creating, potentially hazardous situations that lead to PTSD (e.g., Fauerbach, Lawrence, Schmidt, Munster, & Costa Jr., 2000). Other traits, such as sensation seeking, have been associated with increased risk for being a victim of rape (Kilpatrick, Resnick, Saunders, & Best, 1998). Koenen, et al. (2002) reported that preexisting conduct disorder (which might be considered an early manifestation of antisocial personality traits) was a risk factor for both trauma exposure and subsequent PTSD symptoms using data from male twins who served in the Vietnam War. The same mechanism applies to people in the general population. Jang, Stein, Taylor, Asmundson, and Livesley (2003) examined the relationship between a wide range of normal and abnormal personality traits and exposure to assaultive (e.g., getting beaten up, raped, robbed) and nonassaultive trauma (e.g., car accidents, natural disaster, death of close friend or relative). Multiple regression analysis identified that traits describing antisocial personality characteristics were most predictive of experiencing assaultive trauma and partially accounted for by a modest, but statistically significant, genetic basis (r_G range: .14–.26). In contrast, personality factors were not implicated in exposure to nonassaultative trauma.

Gene–Environment Interaction in the Face of Gene–Environment Correlation

On the face of it, the presence of r_{ge} could pose quite a problem for studies of gene–environment interaction described earlier because differences in environmental conditions may be influenced by genetically based factors. However, it would be wrong to understand gene–environment correlation as mere statistical confound. Recent advances in statistical modeling (e.g., Purcell, 2002) now allow both GxE and r_{ge} to be tested simultaneously. In Figure 6.4 below, the square marked Y represents the intensity of posttraumatic stress symptoms (PTSS) reported by each individual as a result

6.4

Gene–environment interaction in the face of gene–environment correlation.

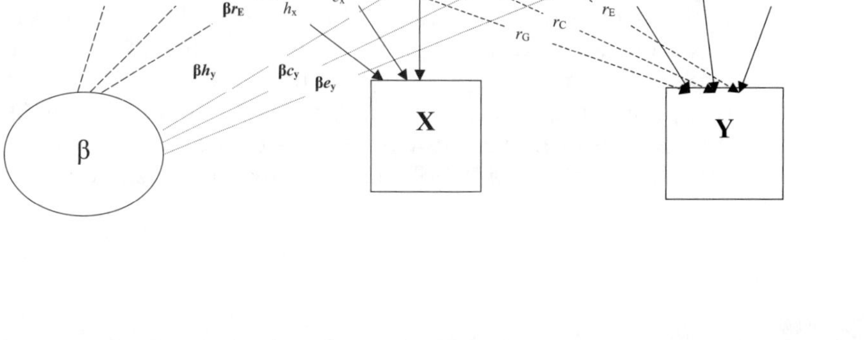

of exposure to either assaultive or nonassaultive trauma (square marked X). The circles labelled G_x and G_y represent genetic influences that are passed directly from parents to offspring along the paths marked h_x and h_y. c_x and c_y represent the general environment of a family that have effects along the path marked c_x and c_y, respectively, of making children within a family more similar (Rowe, 1994). E_x and E_y represent environmental events or conditions that have differential effects transmitted to individual family members along paths e_x and e_y, respectively, in addition to random error variance.

Parameter estimates for h_x, h_y, c_x, c_y, e_x, and e_y are squared and divided by the total variance to compute the familiar standardized proportions of the variance, h^2_x, h^2_y, c^2_x, c^2_y, e^2_x and e^2_y attributable to each source of genetic and environmental influence. The paths labeled r_G, r_C, and r_E index the degree to which PTSS are influenced by the same genetic environmental factors (G_x, C_x, and E_x) that determine frequency of trauma exposure. G_y, C_y, and E_y obviously represent genetic and environmental effects unique to PTSS. To allow testing for the moderation of shared genetic and environmental influences, the number of traumatic exposures, X, is specified in the model for a second time (β). This permits the definition of moderated genetic, shared, and nonshared environmental effects unique to PTSS; βh_y, βc_y, βe_y that index non-shared effects; and βr_G, βr_c, and βr_e that index the moderation of genetic and environmental effects in common to the moderator and PTSS (Purcell, 2002).

This was model applied to data from a sample of 222 MZ and 184 DZ twin pairs who reported on lifetime frequency of assaultive trauma (robbery, held captive, beaten up, and sexual assault) and nonassaultive trauma (sudden family death, motor vehicle, accident fire, and tornado, flood, earthquake) and severity of PTSS (Jang, Taylor, Stein, & Yamagata, 2007). In the case of nonassaultive trauma, variance in PTSS is affected by environmental factors that also influence exposure to nonassaultive traumas indexed by r_E. For example, differences in the total number of motor vehicle accidents experienced by one twin compared to his or her cotwin sibling explains a significant proportion of the reported variability in reexperiencing, avoidance, numbing, and hypervigilance. As the number of nonassaultive traumas experienced increase, the severity of these PTSS increases in a linear fashion.

With assaultive trauma, the results indicated that both genetic and non-shared environmental influences jointly affect PTSS as indexed by r_G and r_E. However, unlike nonassaultive trauma, the number of traumatic events (e.g., sexual abuses, fights) appears to moderate the severity of PTSS. For example, in the cases of reexperiencing, numbing, and hypervigilance, when the number of traumas experienced exceeds 3 or 4 events in total, a significant reduction of genetic covariance is observed. The question that these findings raise is—what is the role of common genetic factors? One interpretation is that they confer some resilience to traumatic events; resilient people are unlikely to report experience of traumatic events because they have suffered less PTSS. However, resilience may not make a difference for those who experienced too many traumatic events.

Just as plausible is that these genetic factors are a liability to PTSS by facilitating the selection of environments (Jang et al., 2003; Stein et al., 2002) that increase risk for experiencing traumatic events; the more one is likely to experience traumatic events, the more one is likely to have PTSS by experiencing the larger number of traumatic events. However, the severity of PTSS becomes unrelated to the number of traumatic events experienced for those who experience too many traumatic events; perhaps what matters for those people is the recency of the traumatic events or other environmental factors, such as social support. The present data are unable to address this question because they are limited to examining aggregate trauma frequency over the lifespan as an index of the trauma dose-response relationship. What is required are specific data on the timing of each trauma and the details of PTSS that followed each traumatic experience.

Dimensionality Revisited

Recent thinking on the model GxE in the face of r_{GE} model described above suggests it can also be used as a means to directly test the assumption of dimensionality underlying related behaviors. Previously, we discussed how r_G computed between measures of normal and extreme scores was used to test this assumption. However, this approach makes a number of assumptions. First, r_G represents an average relationship across the entire range of both scores—and may mask any discontinuity at specific points along the continuum (i.e., genetic effects may be greater or lower for extreme versus less extreme forms). Second, it assumes the transition from normal to abnormal behavior is linear. Third, r_G is not informative on the relative contributions of genetic effects in common to the different behavioral forms and those that are unique as the intensity of behavior in questions moves from normal to extreme levels. For example, just what is the relative role of genetic effects that code for extreme behavior vis-à-vis genetic effects shared between normal and extreme range behavioral forms?

How might such effects be tested? One method would be a variation of the GxE in the face of r_G model illustrated in Figure 6.4 by simply substituting X and Y into the model with measures of behavior thought to be related and occupy different areas under the same curve. For example, X would be a measure of anxiety sensitivity and Y a diagnosis of panic disorder. Another possibility is that X can be a risk factor, such as the personality trait of neuroticism, and Y the diagnosis of PTSD or measure of PTSS. By substituting, for example, trait neuroticism into the square marked X and PTSD in the square marked Y, the paths marked βh_y, βc_y, βe_y will index any moderation of genetic and environmental effects unique to the development of PTSD by preexisting levels of neuroticism. Specifically, these paths represent weights to yield estimates of the heritability of extreme anxiety($h^2{}_y$, $c^2{}_y$, $e^2{}_y$) over systematically increasing levels of neuroticism such that it is possible to determine at what level trait neuroticism has on the development of extreme anxiety, and the mechanism by which it occurs. This is a new use of the model that remains to be examined further.

Conclusions

There is no doubt that recent development in behavioral genetic methodologies makes it possible to examine and test key issues in the development of the *DSM* system. Behavioral genetics has gone beyond simply estimating heritabilities for measured behavior, but the ability to test if the genetic and environmental influences are shared or unique to individual behaviors, traits, or diagnoses permit examination of issues of dimensionality and the structure of mental illness, such as the anxiety disorders. Knowing what causes normal to develop into abnormal behavior and how it is organized are key concepts to any behavioral nosology such as the *DSM*. Classical twin research will continue to play an important role in genotyping research by delineating each behavior's etiologial heritage.

Note

1 A cautionary note for consumers of behavioral genetic research is that it is also important to take into account the sample that was used. This is vital because behavioral genetic research relies on specialized samples of subjects, namely twins, and recruitment of samples with sufficient variability in the behavior of interest may be an issue. At the very least, the twin samples used to study psychopathology need to be a general population sample because with this type of sample, there is sufficient variability in behavior to properly sample the extreme ranges of the behavior of interest. Another issue is gender. Research with twins typically recruits more females, and more MZ twins (Jang, 2005). Given that with some disorders there are marked gender differences in incidence and prevalence, the reader should be aware that some efforts to control for these effects are taken. These measures range from conducting specific analyses that test for gender specific genetic and environmental effects (e.g., sex-limitation analyses), limiting all analyses and subsequent generalizations to samples of one gender or the other, to simply correcting for gender differences in the raw data prior to analyses to examine what could be described as core analyses that are central to both genders.

References

Battaglia, M., Pesenti–Gritti, P., Spatola, C. A., Ogliari, A., & Tambs, K. (2008). A twin study of the common vulnerability between heightened sensitivity to hypercapnia and panic disorder. *American Journal of Medical Genetics. Part B, Neuropsychiatric Genetics, 147B*(5), 586–593.

DeFries, J. C. & Fulker, D. W. (1985). Multiple regression analysis of twin data. *Behavior Genetics, 15*, 467–473.

DeFries, J. C. & Fulker, D. W. (1988). Multiple regression analysis of twin data: Etiology of deviant scores versus individual differences. *Acta Geneticae Medicae et Gemellologiae: Twin Research, 37*, 205–216.

Dick, D. M., Rose, R. J., Viken, R. J., Kaprio, J., & Koskenvuo, M. (2001). Exploring gene-environment interactions: Socioregional moderation of alcohol use. *Journal of Abnormal Psychology, 110*, 625–632.

Eley, T. C. & Stevenson, J. (1999). Exploring the covariation between anxiety and depression symptoms: A genetic analysis of the effects of age and sex. *Journal of Child Psychology and Psychiatry, 40*, 1273–1282.

Fauerbach, J. A., Lawrence, J. W., Schmidt, C. W., Jr., Munster, A. M., & Costa, P. T., Jr. (2000). Personality predictors of injury-related posttraumatic stress disorder. *Journal of Nervous and Mental Disease, 188*, 510–517.

Gordon, J. A. & Hen, R. (2004). Genetic approaches to the study of anxiety. *Annual Review of Neuroscience, 27*, 193–222.

Gorwood, P. (2004). Generalized anxiety disorder and major depressive disorder comorbidity: An example of genetic pleiotropy? *European Psychiatry, 19*, 27–33.

Gunthert, K. C., Conner, T. S., Armeli, S., Tennen, H., Covault, J., & Kranzler, H. R. (2007). Serotonin transporter gene polymorphism (5-HTTLPR) and anxiety reactivity in daily life: A daily process approach to gene-environment interaction. *Psychosomatic Medicine, 69*, 762–768.

Hetherington, E. M., Reiss, D., & Plomin, R. (Eds.). (1994). *Separate social worlds of siblings: Impact of nonshared environment on development*, Hillsdale, NJ: Erlbaum.

Hettema, J. M., Prescott, C. A., & Kendler, K. S. (2004). Genetic and environmental sources of covariation between generalized anxiety disorder and neuroticism. *American Journal of Psychiatry, 161*, 1581–1587.

Jang, K. L. (2005). *The behavioral genetics of psychopathology: A clinical guide*. Mahwah, NJ: Lawrence Erlbaum Associates.

Jang, K. L., Stein, M. B., Taylor, S., Asmundson, G. J., & Livesley, W. J. (2003). Exposure to traumatic events and experience: Aetiological relationships with personality function. *Psychiatry Research, 120*, 61–69.

Jang, K. L., Taylor, S., Stein, M. B., & Yamagata, S. (2007). Trauma exposure and stress response: Exploration of mechanisms of cause and effect. *Twin Research and Human Genetics, 10*, 564–572.

Kendler, K. S., Gardner, C. O., Gatz, M., & Pedersen, N. L. (2007). The sources of co-morbidity between major depression and generalized anxiety disorder in a Swedish national twin sample. *Psychological Medicine, 37*, 453–462.

Kendler, K. S., Walters, E. E., Neale, M. C., Kessler, R. C., Heath, A. C., & Eaves, L. J. (1995). The structure of the genetic and environmental risk factors for six major psychiatric disorders in women: Phobia, generalized anxiety disorder, panic disorder, bulimia, major depression, and alcoholism. *Archives of General Psychiatry, 52*, 374–383.

Kilpatrick, D. G., Resnick, H. S., Saunders, B. E., & Best, C. L. (1998). Rape, other violence against women, and posttraumatic stress disorder. In B. P. Dohrenwend (Ed.), *Adversity, stress, and psychopathology* (pp. 161–176). London: Oxford University Press.

Koenen, K. C., Fu. Q. J., Ertel, K., Lyons, M. J., Eisen, S. A., True, W. R., et al. (2008). Common genetic liability to major depression and posttraumatic stress disorder in men. *Journal of Affective Disorders, 105*, 109–115.

Koenen, K. C., Harley, R., Lyons, M. J., Wolfe, J., Simpson, J. C., Goldberg, J., et al. (2002). A twin registry study of familial and individual risk factors for trauma exposure and posttraumatic stress disorder. *Journal of Nervous and Mental Disease, 190*, 209–218.

Koenen, K. C., Hitsman, B., Lyons, M. J., Niaura, R., McCaffery, J., Goldberg, J., et al. (2005). A twin registry study of the relationship between posttraumatic stress disorder and nicotine dependence in men. *Archives of General Psychiatry, 62*, 1258–1265.

Lau, J. Y. F., Gregory, A. M., Goldwin, M. A., Pine, D. S., & Eley, T. C. (2007). Assessing gene-environment interactions on anxiety symptom subtypes across childhood and adolescence. *Development and Psychopathology, 19*, 1129–1146.

Lesch, K. P. (2001). Molecular foundation of anxiety disorders. *Journal of Neural Transmission, 108*, 717–746.

Neale, M. C. & Cardon, L. R. (Eds.) (1992). *Methodology for genetic studies of twins and families*. Dordrecht, The Netherlands: Kluwer.

Peterson, R. A. & Reiss, S. (1992). *Anxiety Sensitivity Index manual* (2nd ed., rev.). Worthington, OH: International Diagnostic Systems.

Plomin, R., DeFries, J. C., & Loehlin, J. C. (1977). Genotype-environment interaction and correlation in the analysis of human behavior. *Psychological Bulletin, 84*, 309–322.

Plomin, R., DeFries, J. C., & McClearn, G. E. (1990). *Behavioral genetics: A primer* (2nd ed.) New York: Freeman.

Plomin, R., DeFries, J. C., McClearn, G. E., & McGuffin, P. (2000). *Behavioral Genetics* (4th ed.). New York: Worth.

Plomin, R., Rende, R., & Rutter, M. (1991). Quantitative genetics and developmental psychopathology. In D. Cicchetti, & S. L. Toth (Eds.). *Internalizing and externalizing expressions of dysfunction: Rochester Symposium on Developmental Psychopathology* (Vol. 2, pp. 155–202). Hillsdale, NJ: Lawrence Erlbaum Associates.

Purcell, S. (2002). Variance components models for gene-environment interaction in twin analysis. *Twin Research and Human Genetics, 5*, 554–571.

Reiss, D., Neiderhiser, J. M., Hetherington, E. M., & Plomin, R. (2000). *The relationship code: Deciphering genetic and social influences on adolescent development*. Cambirdge, MA: Harvard University Press.

Rowe, D. C. (1994). *The limits of family influence: Genes, experience, and behavior*. New York: Guilford.

Roy, M. A., Neale, M. C., Pedersen, N. L., Mathe, A. A., & Kendler, K. S. (1995). A twin study of generalized anxiety disorder and major depression. *Psychological Medicine, 25*, 1037–1049.

Sham, P. C., Sterne, A., Purcell, S., Cherny, S., Webster, M., Rijsdijk, F., et al. (2000). GENESiS: Creating a composite index of the vulnerability to anxiety and depression in a community-based sample of siblings. *Twin Research and Human Genetics, 3*, 316–322.

Silberg, J., Rutter, M., Neale, M., & Eaves, L. (2001). Genetic moderation of environment risk for depression and anxiety in adolescent girls. *British Journal of Psychiatry, 179*, 116–121.

Stein, M. B. & Chavira, D. A. (1998). Subtypes of social phobia and comorbidity with depression and other anxiety disorders. *Journal of Affective Disorders, 50*(Suppl. 1),S11–S16.

Stein, M. B., Jang, K. L., & Livesley, W. J. (1999). Heritability of anxiety sensitivity: A twin study. *American Journal of Psychiatry, 156*, 246251.

Stein, M. B., Jang, K. L., & Livesley, W. J. (2002). Heritability of social anxiety-related concerns and personality characteristics: A twin study. *Journal of Nervous and Mental Disease, 190*, 219–224.

Stein, M. B., Jang, K. L., Taylor, S., Vernon, P. A., & Livesley, W. J. (2002). Genetic and environmental influences on trauma exposure and posttraumatic stress disorder symptoms: A twin study. *American Journal of Psychiatry, 159*, 1675–1681.

Stein, M. B., Schork, N. J., & Gelernter, J. (2008). Gene-by-environment (serotonin transporter and childhood maltreatment) interaction for anxiety sensitivity, an intermediate phenotype for anxiety disorders. *Neuropsychopharmacology, 33*, 312–319.

Taylor, S. (1995). Anxiety sensitivity: Theoretical perspectives and recent findings. *Behavior Research and Therapy, 33*, 243–258.

Taylor, S., Jang, K. L., Stewart, S. H., & Stein, M. B. (in press). Etiology of the dimensions of anxiety sensitivity: A behavioral–genetic analysis. *Journal of Anxiety Disorders*.

Thomis, M. A., Vlietnick, R. F., Maes, H. H., Blimkie, C. J., van Leemputte, M., Claessens, A. L., et al. (2000). Predictive power of individual genetic and environmental factor scores. *Twin Research and Human Genetics, 3*, 99–108.

Tillfors, M., Furmark, T., Ekselius, L., & Fredrikson, M. (2001). Social phobia and avoidant personality disorder as related to parental history of social anxiety: A general population study. *Behavior Research and Therapy, 39*, 289–298.

Turkheimer, E. & Waldron, M. (2000). Nonshared environment: A theoretical, methodological, and quantitative review. *Psychological Bulletin, 126*, 78–108.

van Grootheest, D. S., Boomsma, D. I., Hettema, J. M., & Kendler, K. S. (in press). Heritability of obsessive-compulsive symptom dimensions. *American Journal of Medical Genetics. Part B, Neuropsychiatric Genetics*.

van Velzen, C. J. M., Emmelkamp, P. M. G., & Scholing, A. (2000). Generalized social phobia versus avoidant personality disorder: Differences in psychopathology, personality traits, and social and occupational functioning. *Journal of Anxiety Disorders, 14*, 395–411.

Watson, D. & Friend, R. (1969). Measurement of social-evaluative anxiety. *Journal Consulting and Clinical Psychology, 33*, 448–457.

Widiger, T. A. (2003). Personality disorder and Axis I psychopathology: The problematic boundary of Axis I and Axis II. *Journal of Personality Disorders, 17*, 90–108.

Young, S. E., Stallings, M. C., Corley, R. P., Krauter, K. S., & Hewitt, J. K. (2000). Genetic and environmental influences on behavioral disinhibition. *American Journal of Medical Genetics, 96*, 684–695.

7

Empirical Approaches to the Study and Classification of Anxiety Psychopathology

Michael J. Zvolensky
Amit Bernstein
Kirsten Johnson

The need to identify and classify anxiety and other forms of psychopathology is a central task for contemporary science and practice. The broad-based goal of the taxonomic study of psychopathology is to validly carve nature at its joints by drawing boundaries between adjacent syndromes, and between these syndromes and normality, where there are genuine discontinuities, either in symptomatology or in etiology (Kendell, 2002, p. 7). Indeed, without accurately delineating specific forms of anxiety disorders or syndromes as well as distinguishing between them and other forms of psychopathology, clinicians are in a critically disadvantaged position in terms of identifying the best way to approach and effectively intervene to meaningfully address the needs of individual clients (Maj, 2005). Likewise, scholars attempting to elucidate underlying etiological, maintenance, or relapse factors require a valid and specific set of anxiety psychopathology phenotypes and related classification system of those syndromes (Maj, 2005). Without such knowledge, the ability to effectively target possible risk and maintenance factors related to a particular disorder or syndrome may be intractable.

Because of the centrality of the study and classification of psychopathology to the ultimate success of science and practice, there has been considerable effort placed into this activity, and perhaps not surprisingly, a long-standing spirited debate as to the best approach(es) for doing so (see e.g., Achenbach, 1995; Joffe, 2004; Lilienfeld, Waldman & Israel, 1994; Meehl, 2001; Rutter, 1994; Widiger & FordBlack, 1994; Zimmerman & Mattia, 1999). This literature overwhelmingly documents the importance of clarifying these nosological (psychiatric classification of psychopathology into taxonic disorders) and taxonomic (science of classification of psychopathology that reflects empirically observed syndromes) issues. Although the scope of the scientific study of classification of psychopathology and anxiety psychopathology may, perhaps at first, seem overwhelming because of the volume and nuance of issues relevant to this domain, several focal questions have guided much of the research and thought on taxonomic research: (a) Is a given form of anxiety psychopathology a categorically distinct, naturally occurring syndrome (taxon), or is that form of anxiety psychopathology more accurately conceptualized as dimensional? (b) Where and how do we identify the boundary(ies) between a disorder and other forms of anxiety disorders or syndromes, normative levels of anxiety, and other forms of psychopathology (e.g., mood disorders)? (c) Is the co-occurrence and multimorbidity between anxiety disorders or syndromes a sign that these nosologically distinct disorders co-occur and may substantively (e.g., causally) relate to one another, or alternatively, an indication that our operational definitions of disorders or syndromes need revision to better account for syndromal phenomenology? (d) Should psychiatric disorders be organized as a function of their descriptive phenomenology or their causes? (e) What approach should be adopted to develop and refine the classification of psychopathology (e.g., a top–down nosological approach or a bottom–up statistical approach)? As we describe in this chapter, some, but not all, of these questions, and others, have begun to be addressed in contemporary anxiety disorder research.

The purpose of this chapter is to provide a synopsis of past and contemporary empirical approaches to the study and classification of anxiety psychopathology. To achieve this aim, the chapter is organized around three sections related to the extant literature. In the first portion of the chapter, we briefly present the historical context for understanding and classifying anxiety psychopathology. In this same section, we present an emerging statistically based hierarchical model of psychopathology (it includes, but is not limited to, anxiety disorders) informed by scholars such as Achenbach, Krueger, Watson, among others. This model is discussed to illustrate an example of innovative empirical work in the area of latent structure and taxonomy. This type of work could be fruitfully incorporated into future taxonomic study of anxiety psychopathology, efforts to empirically guide classification of anxiety psychopathology, as well as to potentially guide broad-based study, assessment, and intervention of anxiety. In the second section, we describe some key statistical methods to answer fundamental taxonomic questions about the latent structure of anxiety and other forms of psychopathology, and that may therefore be important for advances in their classification and study. We conclude with a discussion of the clinical implications of empirical approaches to understanding and classifying anxiety disorders and highlight promising next steps for further scientific pursuit.

Historical Context for the Study and Diagnosis of Anxiety Psychopathology

Anxiety disorders, as well as other types of mental illness, have been the subject of active scientific inquiry over the past few decades (Barlow, 2002). To understand the current status and possible domains for future direction for this area of psychopathology, it is important to clarify the historical basis of approaches employed to study and classify these conditions.

Dominant Model

To date, most anxiety psychopathology research has been driven by conceptual models that posit—even explicitly assume—that discrete mental conditions exist as natural categories (Lilienfeld et al., 1994). This corpus of work has been strongly influenced—sociopolitically and scientifically—by the *Diagnostic and Statistical Manual of Mental Disorders* (*DSM-IV*; American Psychiatric Association [APA], 1994). The basic premise to this type of approach is that in order to meet criteria for a particular disorder, a person must endorse, at a clinically significant level, a specified number of symptoms and related life impairment within a specific period of time, thereby coinciding with preestablished diagnostic criteria. Using this classification approach, there is, by definition, a multitude of permutations of symptoms (or criteria) that could qualify an individual for a specific diagnosis. Thus, two individuals could meet criteria for the same disorder by virtue of endorsing a different constellation of symptoms. This approach is strictly categorical in nature; simply meaning, meeting criteria for a particular disorder is conceptualized on an a priori basis as falling into or out of a category. Because of the various permutations allowed for entry into this (theoretically presumed) category, it is implicitly guided by what has been labeled an underlying *polythetic subtyping* scheme (Clark, Watson, & Reynolds, 1995), a term intended to simply communicate that there are *different ways* to meet criteria for a given disorder.

There can be little doubt that the categorical polythetic approach has been fruitful in many regards (Clark et al., 1995). These successes are particularly evident when one compares the relative inroads made in the study of psychopathology (including anxiety [the focus of the present chapter] and other types of disorders) prior to, and after, the influence of the *DSM* since the 1980s and beyond. For instance, Nathan (1998) observed that the diagnostic labeling of specific conditions derived via the *DSM* system has yielded enhanced communication between clinicians and scholars that would not otherwise be possible. In addition, in the case of anxiety psychopathology, specifically efficacious prevention and treatment, approaches have been developed for a large number of anxiety disorders (e.g., Barlow, Gorman, Shear, & Woods, 2000; Barrett, 1998; Feldner, Zvolensky, & Schmidt, 2004; Hickling & Blanchard, 1997; Wilson, 1996) and key etiological and maintaining factors for particular conditions have been discovered (e.g., Foa & Kozak, 1986). Moreover, integrated theoretical models explicating these conditions have been developed (Barlow, 2002). Thus, at a minimum, the identification and classification of anxiety disorders as discrete entities has served as an organizational framework whereby systematic lines of empirical inquiry can be pursued and critically evaluated. These types of advances, and many others, have surely helped to reduce the public health burden of anxiety and its disorders.

Examples of Gaps in Scientific Knowledge

Despite the noted substantial progress within anxiety disorder research, there are numerous areas where the current scientific knowledge is in need of further development. Indeed, there are tremendous gaps in our existing knowledge of anxiety psychopathology and disorders, and formidable questions remain regarding the best way(s) to conceptualize and study them. For example, extant treatment for anxiety disorders, although often producing meaningful positive behavior change and reduced life impairment, does not necessarily alleviate all instances of human suffering or work for all patients (Barlow, 1996; Eifert, Schulte, Zvolensky, Lejuez, & Lau, 1998; Schulte, 1996; Wilson, 1997). Although this issue may not entirely or solely be driven by problems in classification, numerous scholars have suggested that the complex nature of classification may be playing a key role in hindering success in matching treatments to particular disorders (Eifert et al., 1998; Schulte, 1996). Thus, discrete models of particular anxiety disorders have not uniformly led to advances in clinical care, an issue often lamented by practicing clinicians (Persons, 1991).

As a second example, there are often large amounts of unexplained variance in tests of contemporary models of anxiety psychopathology (Rutter, 1994). Conceivably, we would be better able to account for, and thereby understand, a given form or forms of anxiety psychopathology insofar as our model of its psychopathological architecture best matched its latent structure. Specifically, the more valid the match between our classification of anxiety psychopathology and its putative latent structure, the better the opportunity for models (e.g., etiological models) of such problems (i.e., phenotypes) may be attained. Thus, as an example, enhanced understanding of anxiety phenotypes will permit greater insight into their genotypic origins.

Third, real-world presentations of anxiety symptoms may be clinically and functionally important but may not map isomorphically onto contemporary diagnostic criteria for any one disorder, or be comprehensively accounted for by any single diagnostic category (Eifert, 1992). For example, a person may be experiencing clinically significant impairment across numerous domains of anxiety or disorders, but fail to reach a "diagnostic threshold" for any one of them for various reasons (e.g., exclusion rules used in a diagnosis process; Brown & Barlow, 1992). In other instances, a condition may share features with a range of disorders, and again, not be most accurately accounted for by any one diagnostic category (Hollander & Rosen, 2000). Such inaccuracies may, at a minimum, fuel less than ideal clinical care (e.g., diagnosis and treatment) as a result of the failure in comprehensively capturing the psychopathology of interest (Eifert, 1992).

As a final, and perhaps most notable and well-publicized example, scholars have recognized and actively struggled with the relative degree of overlap between anxiety disorders with one another and other forms of mental illness (Eifert, 1992; Robins, 1994; Spitzer, 1994; Widiger & Ford–Black, 1994).[1] In fact, the empirical literature is replete with findings and discussion of work documenting high rates of co-occurrence and multimorbidity between anxiety and other psychiatric conditions (e.g., Brown, Campbell, Lehman, Grisham, & Mancill, 2001; Mineka, Watson, & Clark, 1998). Although such co-occurrence and multimorbidity is not specific to the anxiety disorders (Giaconia, Reinherz, Paradis, Hauf, & Stashwick, 2001; Kessler et al., 1994; Van Praag, 1996; Widiger & Sankis, 2000), the best way to interpret such co-occurrence(s) and its implications for models of the etiology and maintenance of anxiety psychopathology have yet to be fully delineated (Rutter, 1994; Spitzer, 1994). It is evident from these studies, however, that the study of a particular disorder cannot be completed in isolation from other types of mental illness and is central to debates regarding the classification of anxiety psychopathology.

Together, a key point inferred from the foregoing discussion is that alternative ways to study and classify anxiety psychopatholgy should be explored and systematically evaluated in order to further enhance our understanding of mental illness broadly and anxiety psychopathology specifically. As numerous scholars have argued, competing models of anxiety and other types of psychopathology can be compared to one another, or at a minimum, conducted with more explicit reference to one another (Achenbach, Bernstein, & Dumenci, 2005; Achenbach & Edelbrock, 1984; Jensen, 2003; Klein & Riso, 1993;

Krueger, 1999). In this way, the type of model that can best capture the underlying nature of anxiety psychopathology can be identified and employed in the day-to-day activities of science and practice. This work would, in theory, improve efforts to understand and treat anxiety disorders because of the more accurate elucidation of the latent structure of these conditions. Thus, programmatic study of the taxonomy of anxiety psychopathology promises various theoretical and clinical implications and therefore merits increased scientific attention.

Contemporary Study and Classification of Anxiety Psychopathology: Empirical Advances

In large part, there has been a working assumption that anxiety disorders exist as a discrete class of conditions (APA, 1994), and as a consequence, taxonomically oriented research has predominately aimed to understand their nature and how they relate to other forms of mental illness. Because of this a priori nosological stance, most scientific work has been focused on addressing questions such as: what are the boundary(ies) between anxiety disorders and other forms of anxiety disorders or syndromes and what are the distinctions between clinical and nonclinical presentations of anxiety? The main point here is that the study of anxiety psychopathology and the dominant nosological model has largely assumed that anxiety disorders are a discrete class of presumably related disorders. It also has largely assumed that they are distinct as a class from other forms of psychopathology. Thus, there has been little latent structural work aimed at addressing whether or not anxiety disorders are truly a discrete class of conditions.

Some scholars have astutely observed that the dominant approach currently in place in science and practice has several key limitations (Krueger & Piasecki, 2002). Here, there have been numerous challenges raised, including nosology that is categorically based as opposed to dimensional, not derived from population-based studies that employ representative sampling methods; assigns diagnostic criteria to disorders in a way that may not be ecologically valid; and, draws boundaries in a top–down fashion (Krueger & Piasecki, 2002; Watson, 2005). Perhaps most notably in recent years, dominant models and the approaches used to study them have been challenged because they do not fully account for the full spectrum of phenomenology of co-occurrence, including multimorbidity between anxiety disorders and others forms of psychopathology (i.e., co-occurrence of more than two disorders; Achenbach, 1995; Krueger, 1999; Krueger, McGue, & Iacono, 2001; Krueger & Piasecki, 2002; Watson, 2005). Inspection of this body of work makes clear that the issue of how to best understand the "co-occurrence of disorders" has predominately influenced the type of research questions being addressed—a valid issue at the heart of psychiatric taxonomy. Indeed, prevalence rates of multimorbidity make clear the importance of this issue for critically evaluating the classification of anxiety psychopathology and for understanding co-occurrence. For instance, most individuals with an anxiety disorder meet criteria for more than one additional disorder, a finding apparent in both clinical (Brown et al., 2001) and representative surveys (Kessler et al., 1994). To effectively empirically evaluate and understand such multimorbidity, multivariate models are often powerful tactics.

Historically, there has been far less work using statistical strategies to develop and study a taxonomy of anxiety psychopathology (but see Krueger, 1999; Krueger, Caspi, Moffitt, & Silva, 1998, Middeldorp, Cath, Van Dyck, & Boomsma, 2005; Watson, 2005, for illustrative exceptions). Driven by the groundbreaking work of Achenbach, Krueger, Watson, and others, there is an emerging multivariate perspective of anxiety and other mental disorders (e.g., Achenbach, 1966; Krueger, 1999; Watson, 2005). This approach differs from the dominant top–down nosological system (i.e., *DSM*) in that it attempts to model psychopathology from the bottom-up (Achenbach et al., 2005). Bottom-up is intended to reflect an approach to organize classification and derive a taxonomy of psychopathology based on the empirical co-occurring pattern of disordered behaviors or syndromes as they are observed to occur without any predetermined hypothesis(es) regarding syndrome structure. In contrast to this approach, the current nosological approach is based on classification primarily rooted in expert review of extant literature (APA, 1994).

Although various aspects of a statistically based approach to taxonomy of psychopathology have been evident to varying degrees in the literature for many years (e.g., Achenbach, 1966), these have not always had wide-ranging influence in all domains of anxiety disorder research and practice. In the area of anxiety psychopathology research, *DSM*-based diagnostic categories have largely reflected the dominant unit and operational definitions of study (Barlow, 2002). Indeed, most research in the area of anxiety psychopathology has been focused on the study of nosologically based disorders defined by the *DSM* in contrast to statistically derived internalizing syndromes, or a statistically based taxonomy of anxiety psychopathology (e.g., Achenbach et al., 2005; Krueger, 1999). Yet, this type of multivariate approach to psychopathology, which includes, but is not limited to, anxiety disorders, may arguably represent an intellectually compelling and effective way to understand clinical conditions relative to the traditional, medically based nosological classification system (APA, 1994).

Hierarchical models of psychopathology have been influenced and guided initially by the work of Achenbach and colleagues, and more recently, Watson, Krueger, and their respective colleagues. Although an extensive discussion of this type of modeling of psychopathology is beyond the scope of this chapter (see Achenbach, Dumenci, & Rescorla, 2003; Achenbach & Edelbrock, 1984; Achenbach, Krukowski, Dumenci, & Ivanova, 2005; Krueger, 1999, 2005; Krueger & Piasecki, 2002; Tellegen, Watson, & Clark, 1999; Watson, 2005; Watson & Clark, 1997), we overview one application of this approach to taxonomic study to illustrate the function of such approaches more broadly. It is also important to observe that there are significant distinctions between different empirically derived hierarchical models of psychopathology (Krueger, 2005; Watson, 2005). Our purpose in the present chapter is to portray the commonalities of this type of approach at a broad-based level rather than explicate the distinctions between specific hierarchical models.

Briefly, hierarchical models do not attempt to model psychopathology from a discrete, categorical perspective. Rather, they model psychopathology symptoms along several statistically observed dimensions that relate to specific syndromes—the empirically observed pattern of co-occurrence of symptoms. These syndromes, in turn, are related to a higher-order co-occurring group of syndromes or disorders. That is, syndromes relate to a higher-order factor, and by extension, such hierarchically linked syndromes are related to one another as a function of their common, higher-order dimensional structure (Watson, 2005). A main contribution of this type of approach is that it attempts to model variability in symptom presentation along dimensions. Furthermore, this hierarchical approach does not begin with the assumption that there are necessarily a given number of distinct disorders, be they categorical entities or dimensions, but simply analyzes the actual co-occurring pattern of observable symptoms and identifies these co-occurring dimensions as syndromes. Furthermore, this approach statistically models patterns of comorbidity and multimorbidity observed in nosological study of psychopathology by identifying higher-order factors linking co-occurring but distinct syndromes and includes these higher-order syndromes within the taxonomic system. As a result of this method that is rooted in deriving a taxonomy of psychopathology on the pattern of syndromes as they occur, this approach has the tendency to carve far fewer joints—it is designed to "lump" rather than "split," and thereby, provides an alternative account of co-occurrence and multimorbidity of nosologically based categorical entities. That is, such co-occurrence and multimorbidity of psychopathology is, at least in part, a by-product of invalid distinctions between diagnostic categories (or disorders) that do not validly reflect the latent putatively dimensional structure and relations of psychopathology. Consequently, hierarchical models of classification obviates the "problem" of comorbidity and multimorbidity in the current nosology between anxiety and other disorders that leads to questions about the validity of nosological classification that has, historically, increasingly split rather than lumped (Krueger, 1999, 2005; Krueger & Piasecki, 2002; Tellegen et al., 1999). It is, on the other hand, noteworthy that lumping in favor of splitting too early in the development of a descriptive taxonomic system may result in failure to comprehensively study and clinically measure and treat more narrow syndromes that may be lumped together within this type of broad-based system (Lilienfeld et al., 1994).

Study of psychopathology adopting this statistically based hierarchical model indicates that there are two higher-order factors reflecting internalizing and externalizing symptoms and syndromes (Achenbach, et al., 2003; Achenbach & Edelbrock, 1984; Krueger, 2005; O'Connor, 2002; Watson, 2005). These higher-order factors are indicative of a vulnerability to experience either negative affect (internalizing symptoms) or disinhibition (externalizing symptoms) and consequently elevated levels of one or more syndromes that are lower-order factors. Extant evidence suggests that the internalizing factor corresponds most closely to disorders involving anxiety and depressive features, whereas the externalizing factor reflects substance use disorders and antisocial disorder (Achenbach et al., 2003; O'Connor, 2002; Watson, 2005). In some models, research indicates that the internalizing factor can be further divided into separate lower-order dimensions of distress and fear (Krueger & Markon, 2006). More specific symptom presentations can then be categorized from these distress and fear dimensions (Krueger, 2005). For example, major depression and generalized anxiety disorder (GAD) symptoms tend to fall within the distress category, and panic disorder and specific phobias tend to fall within the fear dimension (Krueger, 2005). On the externalizing side, various conditions involving disinhibition processes such as alcohol and drug use disorders as well as conduct disorder fall within this higher-order dimension (Achenbach & Edelbrock, 1984; Krueger, 2005). It is noteworthy that the cross-national study of psychopathology has indicated a strong degree of consistency in the observed hierarchical model (e.g., Hunt, Issakidis, & Andrews, 2002; Krueger, Chenstova-Dutton, Markon, Goldberg, & Ormel, 2003).

Summary

Overall, a central ongoing and future task for researchers will be to evaluate the fit of empirical observations to a specific model(s) of anxiety and related forms of psychopathology—whether they are categorical or dimensional and hierarchical in nature—when testing the explanatory power of competing theories. To complete such model evaluation work, there is often a need for advanced statistical approaches to answer empirical questions about the latent structure of anxiety psychopathology and its classification. Thus, a practical challenge to moving empirical approaches to the study and classification of anxiety disorders forward in the next decade and beyond will be the implementation of advanced statistical approaches that will be used to evaluate the latent structure of psychopathological conditions from diverse points of view (i.e., comparing different models to one another), as illustrated well by work forwarding a dimensional and hierarchical model of psychopathology. We, therefore, turn to a discussion of some promising technologies that may ultimately offer novel information about anxiety and its disorders.

Statistical Technologies in the Study of the Latent Structure of Anxiety Psychopathology

From an applied perspective, the utility in statistical procedures rests squarely with the type of information they can provide, and by extension, the type of questions they can help answer. Thus, understanding the types of statistical procedures available and the information they can provide is key to forwarding programmatic taxonomic study of anxiety and related psychopathology and, thereby, advancing classification of anxiety disorders. To this end, we now briefly describe some of the major statistical techniques available to answer pressing questions concerning the latent structure of anxiety psychopathology and what information they can provide. This section of the chapter is not intended to represent all possible analytic tools. Rather, it is intended to highlight some key tactics that may be especially relevant to current and future latent structural tests on the anxiety disorders. Please see Table 7.1 for a summary of the data analytic approaches reviewed below.

Factor Analysis

Of the various latent structural statistical tools available, anxiety researchers have largely utilized factor analytic methodology.

7.1 Data Analytic Approach as a Function of Observable Variable and Latent Variable Type

Data Analytic Approach	Observable Variable	Latent Variable
Factor Analysis	Continuous	Continuous
Latent Trait Analysis	Categorical	Continuous
Taxometric (CCK) Analysis	Categorical or Continuous	Categorical
Latent Class Analysis	Categorical	Categorical
Latent Profile Analysis	Continuous	Categorical
Factor Mixture Model Analysis	Categorical or Continuous	Categorical and Continuous

Factor analysis is part of the multiple general linear hypothesis family of procedures (Brown, 2006). In Exploratory Factor Analysis (EFA), the goal is to uncover the underlying structure of a relatively large set of variables (Brown, 2006). In EFA, any indicator may be associated with any factor. EFA is the most common form of factor analysis in anxiety disorder research. There is generally no or limited prior theory guiding this type of work and one uses factor loadings and various factor extraction strategies to intuit the factor structure of the data. In Confirmatory Factor Analysis (CFA), the goal is to determine if the number of factors and the loadings of measured (indicator) variables on them conform to what is expected on the basis of preestablished theory (Brown, 2006). Indicator variables are selected on the basis of a theory and factor analysis is used to see if they load as predicted on the expected number of factors.

There are naturally many ways that factor analysis can be employed to facilitate understanding of latent structure and classification of anxiety psychopathology. In anxiety disorder research and practice, examples of the application of factor analysis have often included tasks such as reducing a large number of variables such as putative symptoms to a smaller number of syndromal factors. Such analysis can thereby be used to empirically define the composition of individual dimensional syndromes, delineate their boundaries with independent and related syndromes, and document the nature of their relations with one another (e.g., hierarchical) and putatively distinct forms of psychopathology (e.g., Watson, 2005). As another example, factor analytic strategies can be used to select a subset of variables, such as diagnostic criteria, from a larger set; to drop proposed diagnostic criteria or putative symptoms that may not discriminate between putatively distinct syndromes; or to validate a syndromal factor by evaluating that its constituent items or putative symptoms load as theoretically or nosologically predicted (e.g., Asmundson, Stapleton, & Taylor, 2004).

Factor analysis, broadly considered, can test questions about the unidimensionality versus multidimensionality of a construct(s) or set of variables or behaviors, and the higher-order structure of a construct or those variables or behaviors. Consequently, factor analytic approaches can help delineate syndromal patterns of symptoms and, thereby, empirically delineate boundaries and relations between dimensional syndromes. Furthermore, factor analytic strategies can help identify the empirical relations, or pattern of co-occurrence, of these syndromes, in relation to one another and in relation to higher-order factors or syndrome spectrum consistent with a hierarchical model of classification. These approaches, however, cannot answer many other fundamental questions relevant to taxonomy. For example, factor analysis cannot test whether a given form of anxiety psychopathology is taxonic or dimensional and, by definition, assumes the latter for all latent variables. Factor analytic strategies also cannot empirically delimit the boundaries between normative levels and syndromal forms of anxiety, but simply reflects dimensions in factor space. As a final example, factor analytic research cannot determine why, theoretically, these specific symptoms and syndromes co-occur. Consequently, theory and other statistical approaches, in addition to factor analytic strategies, are arguably important in a comprehensive programmatic study of anxiety and its classification.

Taxometrics

Taxometrics is a family of statistical procedures that provides a set of tools to investigate the latent class structure of constructs by evaluating whether or not they are taxa, discontinuous dichotomous latent class variables (Haslam, 2007; Meehl, 1973, 1999; Ruscio, Haslam, & Ruscio, 2006; Schmidt, Kotov, & Joiner, 2004). Here, we are highlighting Meehl et al.'s Coherent Cut Kinetic (CCK) taxometric procedures and approach to studying latent structure specifically (Meehl & Golden, 1982; Waller & Meehl, 1998). Meehl's taxometric procedures are designed to test the existence of latent taxonic structure, and indicate nontaxonicity when the latent structure of a construct is either dimensional or composed of more than two discrete classes (e.g., 3 or more classes). In that sense, although potentially less powerful in terms of identifying more complex multiclass models, these CCK taxometric procedures nevertheless provide powerful tests of a specific, taxonic, latent class structure (Waller & Meehl, 1998). Furthermore, the epistemological rigor of taxometrics, involving risky consistency tests of a specific, falsifiable conjecture about the latent taxonic structure of latent variables offered by taxometrics, but not offered by other more inductive, fit-oriented approaches to latent class structure, make taxometrics a uniquely powerful approach (e.g., Meehl, 2004; Schmidt et al., 2004).

In addition to distinguishing between latent anxiety dimensions and taxa and delineating the boundaries between anxiety psychopathology and normative levels and forms of anxiety (e.g., Haslam, 2003; Haslam, 2007; Schmidt et al., 2004 for reviews), taxometric procedures can similarly be utilized to understand comorbidity (Brown, 2001; Meehl, 2001). Taxometrics can similarly be utilized to detect latent comorbidity between two co-occurring taxa such as two categorical anxiety disorders. Specifically, taxometrics can be used to empirically evaluate whether putative taxa (e.g., two anxiety disorders) are indeed distinct taxa that sometimes co-occur, or whether they are not distinct taxa and therefore not, technically speaking in terms of their latent structure, comorbid categorical disorders (cf. dimension(s), single comorbid taxon). Moreover, taxometrics cannot be used to evaluate latent class structures that are more complex than dichotomous taxonic categories. For example, CCK taxometric procedures were not designed to evaluate multiple diagnostic subtypes of a diagnostic category or to detect multiple diagnostic categories from a set of observable indicators (i.e., symptoms) that putatively compose a theoretically related group of discrete disorders (e.g., anxiety disorders). In very recent years, taxometric procedures have been increasingly utilized to evaluate the latent structure of various forms of anxiety psychopathology and nosologically based diagnostic categories (e.g., Broman–Fulks et al., 2006; Kollman, Brown, Liverant, & Hoffman, 2006; Kotov, Schmidt, Lerew, Joiner, Ialongo, 2005; Olatunji, Williams, Haslam, Abramowitz, & Tolin, in press; Schmidt, Kotov, Bernstein, Zvolensky, Joiner, & Lewinsohn, 2007).

Latent Class, Latent Profile, and Latent Trait Analyses

Latent Class Analysis (LCA) shares some conceptual similarity to taxometric procedures in that it is aimed principally at the explication of mutually exclusive underlying classes or groups of cases. LCA is a statistical method for finding subtypes of related cases (latent classes) from multivariate categorical data. Unlike Meehl et al.'s CCK taxometric procedures (Waller & Meehl, 1998), LCA is not constrained to distinguishing between dimensional and taxonic latent structure (dichotomous latent class structure) and instead can be used to detect multiple latent classes (Ruscio et al., 2006). LCA has a similar function to finite mixture estimation, a form of cluster analysis (Day, 1969; Lazarsfeld & Henry, 1968; Titterington, Smith & Makov, 1985; Wolfe, 1970). Latent profile analysis

(LPA) is an extension of LCA, but it is used to model latent class structure using observable *continuous* variables. Latent trait analyses (LTA), in contrast to LCA and LPA, is a form of factor analysis for binary (dichotomous) or ordered-category data that may be used to test latent dimensional structure using observable categorical variables. More recently, there have been advances that build on latent class and common factor analysis, that model categorical *and* continuous latent variable structure concurrently, named factor mixture models (e.g., Lubke & Muthén; 2005). Factor mixture modeling tests the latent categorical structure of a construct(s) and its within-class dimensional structure(s). Thus, unlike traditional LCA and factor analytic approaches, factor mixture modeling evaluates the latent structure of latent variables that are both categorical and continuous and can do so using categorical and continuous observable indicators.

Latent class and latent profile analyses can be used to model the presence, number, and composition of latent classes underlying a set of observable indicators, such as putative diagnostic criteria or symptoms. In comparison, LTA can be used to model the dimensional structure of a latent trait underlying a set of observable indicators, such as putative diagnostic criteria or symptoms. A key distinction between factor analytic strategy compared with taxometric and latent class analytic strategies is that the former is concerned with the structure of variables (i.e., their correlations), whereas the latter is concerned with the structure of cases (i.e., the latent taxonomic structure). Therefore, similar to taxometrics, LCA-related procedures can be used to answer certain taxonomic questions. For example, LCA-related procedures can be used to evaluate the dimensional versus taxonic structure of a putative syndrome. Unlike CCK taxometric procedures, LCA-related procedures can also be used to model putative categorical subtypes of a diagnostic category (e.g., Kessler, Stein, & Berglund, 1998) or multiple diagnostic categories from a set of observable indicators (i.e., symptoms) that putatively compose a theoretically related group of discrete disorders (e.g., anxiety disorders). LCA-related procedures can also be used to identify the boundary(ies) between a taxon or taxa (or latent class(es)) and other forms of anxiety disorders or syndromes, between it and normative levels and forms of anxiety, and between it and other forms of psychopathology (e.g., mood disorders) (e.g., Kessler, Chiu, Demler, & Walters, 2005). Furthermore, LCA-related procedures may similarly be used to evaluate and explicate putative comorbidity and multimorbidity (e.g., Kessler et al., 2005). There are few such studies focused on anxiety psychopathology in the published literature, reflecting an understudied yet promising area for increased research attention. In light of the likelihood that categorical psychopathological constructs also demonstrate substantive within-class dimensionality, factor mixture modeling may be particularly promising in future taxonomic study of anxiety psychopathology.

Contemporary Issues in the Empirical Study and Classification of Anxiety Psychopathology

Although statistical approaches are necessary to address many of the most pressing and clinically important questions about latent structure, the potential of these tools cannot be maximized without attention to extant theoretical and empirical knowledge (Kupfer, First, & Regier, 2002). That is, the relative inroads that can be made in the empirical study and classification of anxiety disorders rest in the larger context of scientific work in this domain. In this final section of the chapter, we explicate some notable issues that future research should address to continue to meaningfully move this body of work forward.

Sequencing Tests of Latent Structure Within a Larger Programmatic Framework for Taxonomic Research

One of the most striking observations of extant latent structural work on the anxiety disorders is that it has proceeded in a manner that does not necessarily consider a macrolevel sequencing of taxonomic questions and tests. Therefore, at a metascientific level, extant work has not been consistently pursued programmatically or systematically across the field. For instance, some research has been conducted with a working premise rooted in an empirically untested assumption that other latent structural questions have been addressed. One broad-based implication of this sort of metascientific problem involves calling for an increasingly unified, comprehensive, and programmatic commitment by researchers to sequentially and systematically evaluate taxonomic questions relevant to the classification of anxiety psychopathology. As an example, it may be helpful to plan research around an organized sequence of taxonomic questions; for example, (a) What symptom-level behaviors co-occur syndromally? (b) Is a putative syndrome dimensional, taxonic, and/or multiclass? (c) What are its boundaries and relations with other syndromes? (d) How do we conceptualize comorbidity and multimorbidity in the context of syndromal structure and relations, and how do we refine classification in light of patterns of co-occurrence?

Connecting Latent Structural Research to Theoretical Models and Other Types of Anxiety Research

At present, evaluation of latent structural research on anxiety and its disorders might lead one to assume that this body of work is being influenced largely by statistical tools more so than theoretical models of anxiety psychopathology. There has been a relative lack of attention paid to linking such latent structural work to more basic areas of science on anxiety and affective states more generally. This relative degree of neglect, although perhaps to be expected at an early developmental stage, is unfortunate. There are large, fast-moving sources of empirical data on the neurobiology and emotional learning directly relevant to understanding anxiety. This problem of the latent structural and taxonomic research alludes to one of the long-standing questions at the heart of taxonomy—whether to develop a descriptive or etiologically based taxonomy of anxiety psychopathology. As noted by scholars in recent conceptual work related to psychiatric taxonomy (Zachar & Kendler, 2007), although a descriptive taxonomy is likely more scientifically feasible and clinically pragmatic, it should nevertheless be directly informed by the broader anxiety research literature. In this regard, the nosological approach used to construct the *DSM* (APA, 1994) that directly incorporates extant literature on psychopathology reviewed by experts, *in combination with* the application of advances in empirically based and statistical strategies used to answer empirical latent structural and taxonomic questions, offer a promising comprehensive metascientific approach to advancing classification.

Over the past decade, for example, basic science has substantially illuminated the physiologic substrates underlying anxiety and other affective states and their disorders

(Davidson, 1998) as well as helped clarify how certain types of learning occur and why (LeDoux, 1996). For instance, differential brain waves have been evident for different mood states, with marked similarities between anxiety and depressive states (e.g., Gotlib, Ranginath, & Rosenfeld, 1998; Heller, Nitschke, Etienne, & Miller, 1997). Such information provides a formative basis by which to develop integrative theoretical models as to why (or why not) a particular anxiety disorder may be similar or different from another. Likewise, different anxiety states have been theorized to serve different functions (e.g., worry as a coping strategy for decreasing anxiety and preparing an individual for the possibility of threat; Craske, 1999; Roemer & Borkovec, 1993). And finally, a plethora of basic learning research suggests that learning-derived plasticity in neural circuitry is central to understanding variation in anxiety vulnerability (Davidson, Jackson, & Kalin, 2000). These and other robust psychophysiological (e.g., autonomic inflexibility) and learning findings provide important clues regarding the nature of anxiety states. Using such information to guide theoretically driven tests of latent structure across and within the anxiety disorders will be a central next step in this line of inquiry. Numerous other examples can similarly be made for understanding how certain types of (presumably adverse) learning influence brain function, psychophysiological responsivity, and cognitive as well as behavioral functioning. The general point here is that this scientific information should inform latent structural research and hypotheses, and latent structural research might also be used to help refine these other areas of study regarding anxiety.

Multimodal Measurement of Multiple Response Systems and Latent Structural Research

Building from the immediately preceding discussion, another key issue of note in the extant latent structural work on anxiety disorders is that it has largely been completed from a unimethod approach. Specifically, self-report or interview-based instruments have been employed to index symptoms. Such study and measurement of anxiety, however, does not comprehensively reflect prevailing theoretical models of the nature of anxiety and fear states in the sense that it fails to include analyses across response (cognitive, physiological, and behavioral) systems (Craske, 1999; Lang, 1994). Thus, there is notable disconnect between theoretical knowledge and empirical support for a multisystemic conceptualization of anxiety and its disorders and how the vast majority of latent structural work in this domain has been developed and evaluated. There are numerous points of substantive concern related to this limitation of extant study including, but not limited to, the possibility that method biases influence observed results; a lack of understanding how one response system relates to another (e.g., self-report anxiety symptoms and psychophysiological responsivity to theoretically relevant stimuli); and the possibility that volitional types of responding may fail to capture and accurately reflect automatic aspects of responding at numerous levels (behavioral, cognitive, and physiological). To the extent multiple response systems are not included in latent structural research (e.g., as observable components of anxiety syndrome phenotypes), it will be difficult to convincingly connect taxonomic work to more basic research on anxiety and fear states.

A Multitaxonomic Approach to Classification of Anxiety Psychopathology

There is also a need to utilize a multitaxonomic approach to classification of anxiety disorders (Achenbach et al., 2005). A multitaxonomic approach to classification operates from the assumption that any single classification system will likely reify *hypotheses* about anxiety and its syndromes or disorders (Achenbach et al., 2005). Consequently, a multitaxonomic approach to the classification of anxiety psychopathology is based on the notion that more than one (competing or complementary) classification system may be used to organize the same set of symptoms. Specifically, the multitaxonomic perspective proposes that we ought to develop, evaluate, and compare various models of latent structure and classification of the same set of symptoms and syndromes (e.g., a nosological system, a statistically based hierarchical system). Doing so will not only protect against taxonomic reification but is theoretically likely to potentiate scientific progress by affording concurrent study of multiple (hypothesized) operational definitions of anxiety psychopathology. As we have noted in this chapter, two or more classification schemes may be more or less likely to lump or split the same set of symptoms and syndromes, conceptualize a syndrome dimensionally or categorically, draw boundaries between syndromes differently, or account for comorbidity and multimorbidity in various ways. Furthermore, from a philosophy of science perspective, multiple scholars have debated the distinctions and merits related to causalism versus descriptivism, essentialism versus nominalism, objectivism versus evaluatism, internalism versus externalism, entities versus agents, categories versus continua, and other philosophical and scientific questions that challenge adherence to a single taxonomic system (Zachar & Kendler, 2007). Consequently, the threat of reification of diagnostic categories or syndromes of anxiety psychopathology is both an important epistemological and scientific point of interest. Thus, multitaxonomic approaches that explicitly relate to diagnostic categories and syndromes as working hypotheses and taxonomy or nosology as a working hypothesized organizational system may merit greater empirical attention and may augment both advances in classification of anxiety psychopathology as well as the study of anxiety and its disorders more broadly.

Summary

The study and classification of anxiety psychopathology is a central task in efforts to explicate the intricate nature of anxiety and its putative syndromes and disorders. There has been substantial progress in the empirical study of anxiety disorders; nevertheless, there is still much work to do. Promising steps forward in latent structural research have been identified including, but not limited to, hierarchical models of psychopathology. Future work in this area needs to continue to apply advanced statistical methods to help facilitate theoretically driven multivariate tests of anxiety disorders and their relation to other conditions. It is likely that such work, as a whole, will be facilitated and better integrated with other domains of work when it takes into consideration a metascientific, programmatic framework for taxonomic research, information from basic areas of science and theory, and explores the potential utility of multitaxonomic approaches.

Note

1 Historically, some scholars refer to the co-occurrence between one or more disorders as "comorbidity," whereas others have argued for the use of terms such as "multimorbidity" or "covariation" or "co-occurrence." From the broadest perspective, all of these terms are intended to reflect the fact that mental disorders are (generally) correlated with one another (see Lilienfeld et al., 1994; Meehl, 2001; Rutter, 1994). In this chapter, we use the term co-occurrence to reflect instances of two clinical conditions and multimorbidity of instances when more than two conditions are present.

References

Achenbach, T. M. (1966). The classification of children's psychiatric symptoms: A factor-analytic study. *Psychological Monographs: General & Applied, 80*, 1–37.

Achenbach, T. M. (1995). Empirically based assessment and taxonomy: Applications to clinical research. *Psychological Assessment, 7*, 261–274.

Achenbach, T. M., & Edelbrock, C. S. (1984). Psychopathology of childhood. *Annual Review of Psychology*, 35, 227–256.

Achenbach, T. M., Bernstein, A., & Dumenci, L. (2005). DSMoriented scales and statistically based syndromes for ages 18 to 59: Linking taxonomic paradigms to facilitate multitaxonomic approaches. *Journal of Personality Assessment, 84*, 49–63.

Achenbach, T. M., Dumenci, L., & Rescorla, L. A. (2003). *DSM*-oriented and empirically based approaches to constructing scales from the same item pools. *Journal of Clinical Child and Adolescent Psychology, 32*, 328–340.

Achenbach, T. A., Krukowski, R. A., Dumenci, L., & Ivanova, M. Y. (2005). Assessment of adult psychopathology: Metaanalyses and implications of cross-informant correlations. *Psychological Bulletin, 131*, 361–382.

American Psychiatric Association. (1994). *Diagnostic and statistical manual of mental disorders* (4th ed.). Washington, DC: Author.

Asmundson, G. J. G., Stapleton, J. A., & Taylor, S. (2004). Are avoidance and numbing distinct PTSD symptom clusters? *Journal of Traumatic Stress, 17*, 467–475.

Barlow, D. H. (1996). Health care policy, psychotherapy research, and the future of psychotherapy. *American Psychologist, 51*, 1050–1058.

Barlow, D. H. (2002). *Anxiety and its disorders: The nature and treatment of anxiety and panic* (2nd ed.). New York: Guilford.

Barlow, D. H., Gorman, J. M., Shear, M. K., & Woods, S. W. (2000). Cognitive–behavioral therapy, imipramine, or their combination for panic disorder: A randomized controlled trial. *Journal of the American Medical Association, 283*, 2529–2536.

Barrett, P. M. (1998). Evaluation of cognitive–behavioral group treatments for childhood anxiety disorders. *Journal of Clinical Child Psychology, 27*, 459–468.

Broman–Fulks, J. J., Ruggiero, K. J., Green, B. A., Kilpatrick, D. G., Danielson, C. K., Resnick, H. S., et al. (2006). Taxometric investigation of PTSD: Data from two nationally representative samples. *Behavior Therapy, 37*, 364–380.

Brown, T. A. (2001). Taxometric methods and the classification and comorbidity of mental disorders: Methodological and conceptual considerations. *Clinical Psychology: Science and Practice, 8*, 534–541.

Brown, T. A. (2006). *Confirmatory factor analysis for applied research*. New York: Guilford.

Brown, T. A., & Barlow, D. H. (1992). Comorbidity among anxiety disorders: Implications for treatment and DSMIV. *Journal of Consulting and Clinical Psychology, 60*, 835–844.

Brown, T. A., Campbell, L. A., Lehman, C. L., Grisham, J. R., & Mancill, R. B. (2001). Current and lifetime comorbidity of the *DSM-IV* anxiety and mood disorders in a large clinical sample. *Journal of Abnormal Psychology, 110*, 585–599.

Clark, L. A., Watson, D., & Reynolds, S. (1995). Diagnosis and classification of psychopathology: Challenges to the current system and future directions. *Annual Review of Psychology, 46*, 121–153.

Craske, M. G. (1999). *Anxiety disorders: Psychological approaches to theory and treatment*. Boulder: Westview Press.

Davidson, R. J. (1998). Affective style and affective disorders: Perspectives from affective neuroscience. *Cognition & Emotion,12*, 307–330.

Davidson, R. J., Jackson, D. C., & Kalin, N. H. (2000). Emotion, plasticity, context, and regulation: Perspectives from affective neuroscience. *Psychological Bulletin, 126*, 890–909.

Day, W. F. (1969). Radical behaviorism in reconciliation with phenomenology. *Journal of the Experimental Analysis of Behavior, 12*, 315–328.

Eifert, G. H. (1992). Cardiophobia: A paradigmatic behavioural model of heart-focused anxiety and nonanginal chest pain. *Behaviour Research and Therapy, 30*, 329–345.

Eifert, G. H., Schulte, D., Zvolensky, M., Lejuez, C. W., & Lau, A. W. (1998). Manualized behavior therapy: Merits and challenges. *Behavior Therapy*, 28, 499–509.

Feldner, M. T., Zvolensky, M. J., & Schmidt, N. B. (2004). Prevention of anxiety psychopathology: A critical review of the empirical literature. *Clinical Psychology: Science and Practice, 11*, 405–424.

Foa, E. B., & Kozak, M. J. (1986). Emotional processing of fear: Exposure to corrective information. *Psychological Bulletin, 99*, 20–35.

Giaconia, R. M., Reinherz, H. Z., Paradis, A. D., Hauf, A. M., C. & Stashwick, C. K. (2001). Major depression and drug disorders in adolescence: General and specific impairments in early adulthood. *Journal of the American Academy of Child & Adolescent Psychiatry, 40*, 1426–1433.

Gotlib, I. A., Ranginath, C., & Rosenfeld, J. P. (1998). Frontal EEG alpha asymmetry, depression, and cognitive functioning. *Cognition & Emotion, 12*, 449–478.

Haslam, N. (2003). Categorical versus dimensional models of mental disorder: The taxometric evidence. *Australian and New Zealand Journal of Psychiatry, 37*, 696–704.

Haslam, N. (2007). The latent structure of mental disorders: A taxometric update on the categorical vs. dimensional debate. *Current Psychiatry Reviews, 3*, 172–177.

Heller, W., Nitschke, J. B., Etienne, M. A., & Miller, G. A. (1997). Patterns of regional brain activity differentiate types of anxiety. *Journal of Abnormal Psychology, 106*, 376–385.

Hickling, E. J., & Blanchard, E. B. (1997). The private practice psychologist and manual-based treatments: Posttraumatic stress disorder secondary to motor vehicle accidents. *Behaviour Research and Therapy, 35*, 191–203.

Hollander, E., & Rosen, J. (2000). *Obsessive–compulsive spectrum disorders: A review*. New York: John Wiley & Sons, Ltd.

Hunt, C., Issakidis, C., & Andrews, G. (2002). *DSM-IV* generalized anxiety disorder in the Australian National Survey of Mental Health and Well-Being. *Psychological Medicine, 32*, 649–659.

Jensen, P. S. (2003). Comorbidity and child psychopathology: Recommendations for the next decade. *Journal of Abnormal Child Psychology, 31*, 293–300.

Joffe, J. M. (2004). Mental disorders: Should our emphasis be on biological or psychosocial factors? An introduction to the special issue. *Journal of Primary Prevention, 24*, 415–418.

Kendell, R. E. (2002). Five criteria for an improved taxonomy of mental disorders. In J. E. Helzer, & J. J. Hudziak, (Eds.). *Defining psychopathology in the 21st century: DSM-V and beyond*. Washington: American Psychiatric Publishing, Inc.

Kessler, R. C., Chiu, W. T., Demler, O., & Walters, E. E. (2005). Prevalence, severity, and comorbidity of 12Month DSMIV disorders in the National Comorbidity Survey replication. *Archives of General Psychiatry, 62*, 617–627.

Kessler, R. C., McGonagle, K. A., Zhao, S., Nelson, C. B., Hughes, M., Eshleman, S., Wittchen, H-U., & Kendler, K. S. (1994). Lifetime and 12-month prevalence of *DSM-III-R* psychiatric disorders in the United States: Results from the National Comorbidity Study. *Archives of General Psychiatry, 51*, 8–19.

Kessler, R. C., Stein, M. B., & Berglund, P. (1998). Social phobia subtypes in the National Comorbidity Survey. *American Journal of Psychiatry, 155*, 613–619.

Klein, D. N., & Riso, L. P. (1993). Psychiatric disorders: Problems of boundaries and comorbidity. In C. G. Costello (Ed.). *Basic issues in psychopathology*. New York: Guilford Press.

Kollman, D. M., Brown, T. A., Liverant, G. I., & Hofmann, S. G. (2006). A taxometric investigation of the latent structure of social anxiety disorder in outpatients with anxiety and mood disorders. *Depression and Anxiety, 23*, 190–199.

Kotov, R., Schmidt, N. B., Lerew, D. R., Joiner, T. E., & Ialongo, N. S. (2005). Latent structure of anxiety: Taxometric exploration. *Psychological Assessment, 7*, 369–374.

Krueger, R. F. (1999). The structure of common mental disorders. *Archives of General Psychiatry, 56*, 921–926.

Krueger, R. F. (2005). Continuity of Axes I and II: Toward a unified model of personality, personality disorders, and clinical disorders. *Journal of Personality Disorders, 19*, 233–261.

Krueger, R. F., Caspi, A., Moffitt, T. E., & Silva, P. A. (1998). The structure and stability of common mental disorders (DSMIIIR): A longitudinal epidemiological study. *Journal of Abnormal Psychology, 107*, 216–227.

Krueger, R. F., Chentsova–Dutton, Y. E., Markon, K. E., Goldberg, D., & Ormel, J. (2003). A cross-cultural study of the structure of comorbidity among common psychopathological syndromes in the general health care setting. *Journal of Abnormal Psychology, 112*, 437–447.

Krueger, R. F., & Markon, K. E. (2006). Reinterpreting comorbidity: A model based approach to understanding and classifying psychopathology. *Annual Review of Clinical Psychology, 2*, 111–133.

Krueger, R. F., McGue, M., & Iacono, W. G. (2001). The higher-order structure of common DSM mental disorders: Internalization, externalization, and their connections to personality. *Personality and Individual Differences, 30*, 1245–1259.

Krueger, R. F., & Piasecki, T. M. (2002). Toward a dimensional and psychometrically informed approach to conceptualizing psychopathology. *Behaviour Research and Therapy, 40*, 485–500.

Kupfer, D. J., First, M. B., & Regier, D. A. (2002). *A research agenda for DSM-V*. Washington, DC: American Psychological Association.

Lang, P. J. (1994). The varieties of emotional experience: A meditation on James–Lange theory. *Psychological Review, 101*, 211–221.

Lazarsfeld, P. F., & Henry, N. W. (1968). *Latent Structure Analysis*. Boston: Houghton Mifflin.

LeDoux, J. E. (1996). *The emotional brain: The mysterious underpinnings of emotional life*. New York: Simon & Schuster.

Lilienfeld, C. O., Waldman, I. D., & Israel, A. C. (1994). A critical examination of the use of the term and concept of comorbidity in psychopathology research. *Clinical Psychology: Science and Practice, 1*, 71–83.

Lubke, G. H., & Muthén, B. O. (2005). Investigating population heterogeneity with factor mixture models. *Psychological Methods, 10*, 21–39.

Maj, M. (2005). Psychiatric research in low- and middle-income countries: The need for concrete action. *Acta Psychiatrica Scandinavica, 111*, 329–330.

Meehl, P. E. (1973). Some methodological reflections on the difficulties of psychoanalytic research. *Psychological Issues, 8*, 104–117.

Meehl, P. E. (1999). Clarifications about taxometric method. *Applied & Preventive Psychology, 8*, 165–174.

Meehl, P. E. (2001). Comorbidity and taxometrics. *Clinical Psychology: Science and Practice, 8*, 507–519.

Meehl, P. E. (2004). What's in a taxon? *Journal of Abnormal Psychology, 113*, 39–43.

Meehl, P. E., & Golden, R. R. (1982). Taxometric methods. In P. C. Kendall, & J. N. Butcher (Eds.). *Handbook of research methods in clinical psychology*. New York: Wiley.

Middeldorp, C. M., Cath, D. C., Van Dyck, R., & Boomsma, D. I. (2005). The comorbidity of anxiety and depression in the perspective of genetic epidemiology: A review of twin and family studies. *Psychological Medicine, 35*, 611–624.

Mineka, S., Watson, D., & Clark, L. A. (1998). Comorbidity of anxiety and unipolar mood disorders. *Annual Review of Psychology, 49*, 377–412.

Nathan, P. E. (1998). Practice guidelines: Not yet ideal. *American Psychologist, 53*, 290–299.

O'Connor, B. P. (2002). The search for dimensional structure differences between normality and abnormality: A statistical review of the published data on personality and psychopathology. *Journal of Personality and Social Psychology, 83*, 962–982.

Olatunji, B., Williams, B., Haslam, N., Abramowitz, J. S., & Tolin, D. F. (in press). The latent structure of obsessive–compulsive symptoms: A taxometric study. *Depression & Anxiety*

Persons, J. B. (1991). Psychotherapy outcome studies do not accurately represent current models of psychotherapy: A proposed remedy. *American Psychologist, 46*, 99–106.

Robins, L. N. (1994). How recognizing "comorbidities" in psychopathology may lead to an improved research nosology. *Clinical Psychology: Science and Practice, 1*, 93–95.

Roemer, L., & Borkovec, T. D. (1993). Worry: Unwanted cognitive activity that controls unwanted somatic experience. In D. M. Wegner, & J. W. Pennebaker (Eds.). *Handbook of mental control.* Englewood Cliffs: Prentice–Hall, Inc.

Ruscio, J., Haslam, N., & Ruscio, A. M. (2006). *Introduction to the taxometric method: A practical guide*. Mahwah: Lawrence Erlbaum Associates Publishers.

Rutter, M. (1994). Comorbidity: Meanings and mechanisms. *Clinical Psychology: Science and Practice, 1*, 100–103.

Schmidt, N. B., Kotov, R., Bernstein, A., Zvolensky, M. J., Joiner, T. E., & Lewinsohn, P. M. (2007). Mixed anxiety depression: Taxometric exploration of the validity of a diagnostic category in youth. *Journal of Affective Disorders, 98*, 83–89.

Schmidt, N. B., Kotov, R., & Joiner, T. E. Jr. (2004). *Taxometrics: Toward a new diagnostic scheme for psychopathology.* Washington, DC: American Psychological Association.

Schulte, D. (1996). Tailor-made and standardized therapy: Complementary tasks in behavior therapy: A contrarian view. *Journal of Behavior Therapy and Experimental Psychiatry, 27*, 119–126.

Spitzer, R. L. (1994). Psychiatric "co-occurrence"? I'll stick with "comorbidity." *Clinical Psychology: Science and Practice, 1*, 88–92.

Tellegen, A., Watson, D., & Clark, L. A. (1999). On the dimensional and hierarchical structure of affect. *Psychological Science, 10*, 297–303.

Titterington, D. M., Smith, A. F. M., & Makov, U. E. (1985). *Statistical analysis of finite mixture distributions*. Chichester: John Wiley & Sons.

Van Praag, H. M. (1996). Serotonin-related, anxiety/aggression-driven, stressor-precipitated depression. A psychobiological hypothesis. *European Psychiatry, 11*, 57–67.

Waller, N. G., & Meehl, P. E. (1998). *Multivariate taxometric procedures: Distinguishing types from continua*. Thousand Oaks: Sage Publications, Inc.

Watson, D. (2005). Rethinking the mood and anxiety disorders: A quantitative hierarchical model for *DSM-V*. *Journal of Abnormal Psychology, 114*, 522–536.

Watson, D., & Clark, L. A. (1997). Measurement and mismeasurement of mood: Recurrent and emergent issues. *Journal of Personality Assessment, 68*, 267–296.

Widiger, T. A., & Ford–Black, M. M. (1994). Diagnoses and disorders. *Clinical Psychology: Science and Practice, 1*, 84–87.

Widiger, T. A., & Sankis, L. M. (2000). Adult psychopathology: Issues and controversies. *Annual Review of Psychology, 51*, 377–404.

Wilson, R. R. (1996). Imaginal desensitization and relaxation training. In C. G. Lindemann (Ed.), *Handbook of the treatment of the anxiety disorders.* Lanham: Jason Aronson.

Wilson, G. T. (1997). Behavior therapy at century close. *Behavior Therapy, 28*, 449–457.

Wolfe, J. H. (1970). Pattern clustering by multivariate mixture analysis. *Multivariate Behavioral Research, 5*, 329–350.

Zachar, P., & Kendler, K. S. (2007). Psychiatric disorders: A conceptual taxonomy. *American Journal of Psychiatry, 164*, 557–565.

Zimmerman, M., & Mattia, J. I. (1999). Psychiatric diagnosis in clinical practice: Is comorbidity being missed? *Comprehensive Psychiatry, 40*, 182–191.

8

The Role of Actigraphy in Diagnosing Anxiety Disorders

Warren W. Tryon

This chapter aims to evaluate the present and possible future role of actigraphy in diagnosing anxiety disorders. Actigraphy refers to the use of computerized accelerometer-based instruments that are attached to a body site, typically the waist or wrist, for extended periods of time while the person behaves in their natural environment. Unlike laboratory measures of activity level that require participants to sit on stabilimeters (cf. Tryon, 1991, pp. 56–58) or behave in special rooms equipped with photoelectric cells or ultrasound devices (Tryon, 1991, pp. 58–60) where generalization from laboratory to the natural environment remains to be demonstrated, actigraphy allows researchers to obtain activity measurements while the person behaves in their natural environment. This makes actigraphy ecologically valid (cf. Barkley, 1991). Although it is possible to have participants wear actigraphs while undergoing psychological testing and/or while behaving in some laboratory setting, the main advantage of actigraphy is to obtain data in natural settings of interest such as home and school or work. The main reason for measuring activity in a standardized setting is that the environment is well defined and the same for everyone. Conversely, the assessment is relatively brief and the ability to generalize to home, school, and/or work is unknown and questionable. Actigraphs have clocks that govern the epoch lengths over which activity measurements are averaged. A 1-minute epoch is quite standard except for sleep research, where the 30-second epoch is frequently chosen. Memory is sufficient to collect data for days, weeks, and even months depending on user selected choices.

The primary advantage of measuring activity in the natural environment is that the data are ecologically valid as they are collected in the situations of interest and can be collected for as long as required to draw firm conclusions about activity in those situations. Conversely, situational variability is confounded with and interacts with person variability. Behavioral diaries can be informative but do not enable one to separate person from situational factors.

Because actigraphs are instruments and because data provided by objective instruments are either not included or are specifically excluded (see below) from diagnostic decisions, this chapter begins by discussing current diagnostic issues before considering the role that instrumented tests might play in clinical assessment and diagnosis. Bias against using instrumented tests for clinical diagnosis and assessment has inhibited empirical research. Interest in alternative objective sleep assessment and evidence that wrist actigraphy is well validated against the gold standard of polysomnography (Tryon, 1996c, 2004) has supported research with anxious adults and children. The second section of this chapter, entitled Actigraphy and Anxiety, reviews the available empirical evidence. The final section of this chapter, entitled Clinical Impressions, contains suggestions for how actigraphy might be used to study anxiety and obsessive–compulsive disorder (OCD).

Diagnosis

Diagnosis is essential to medicine in that treatment is intended to be based on diagnosis. Misdiagnosis can consequently lead to ineffective or inappropriate treatment. Exploring the role of actigraphy in diagnosing anxiety disorders presumes a critical degree of agreement regarding the diagnostic process that does not presently exist. We therefore begin with a consideration of some of the more major current issues regarding diagnosis generally and then focus on the question, "What is the role of instrumented tests in clinical diagnosis and assessment?"

Current Issues

Table 8.1 provides a slightly reordered list of *Diagnostic and Statistical Manual of Mental Disorders, Fourth Edition* (*DSM-IV*) conundrums identified by Frances et al. (1991). The first conundrum identified in Table 8.1 is whether diagnostic categories should be categorical or dimensional. Medical diagnosis has historically been qualitative and categorical. Disease entities have specific characteristics known as symptoms and signs. Teicher (1995), in his seminal article on "new tools for psychiatry", reviewed the classic medical distinction between clinical signs and symptoms. Clinical signs of disease are directly observable and can be measured using instruments. Fever, rash, and irregular pulse are clinical signs. Clinical symptoms are private psychological phenomena. Headache, fatigue, and blurred vision are clinical symptoms. They require patient report and cannot be known by any other means. Activity level is a clinical sign and there are 48 *DSM-IV* (American Psychiatric Association [APA], 1994, 2000) disorders for which activity level is either an inclusion or exclusion criterion (Tryon, 2002, 2006). This chapter will focus on anxiety disorders.

The categorical versus dimensional conundrum identified in Table 8.1 entails the major problem of comorbidity; that is, the high probability that patients presenting with one disorder will also meet diagnostic criteria for one or more other disorders. Patients rarely present with a single disorder. It seems that the diagnostic categories that have been developed to date are fundamentally interrelated and do not represent distinct independent disorders. Patients frequently present with clusters of symptoms that satisfy inclusion criteria for two or

8.1 *DSM-IV* Conundrums Identified by Frances et al. (1991)

Conundrum	Description
Categories vs. Dimensions	The comorbidity problem
Biological and Psychological Test Results	Tests results are currently pertinent only to mental retardation. Instrumented tests play no diagnostic role.
Relation of Axis I to II	No definition of personality disorder distinguishes Axis II conditions from Axis I conditions.
Diagnosis vs. Definition	Should criteria emphasize sensitivity (most characteristic features) or specificity (most discriminating features)?
Education	Emphasizing limitations vs. advantages of the *DSM*
Field Trials	Emphasis on internal vs. external validity
Generalizability	How to include everyone for whom the diagnosis is pertinent while minimizing false positives?
Hierarchies	Should diagnoses be organized hierarchically?
Illness vs. Syndrome	Which mental disorders are diseases and which are not?
Judgment	How rigidly must clinicians adhere to *DSM-IV* criteria when making a diagnosis?
Kultur	Diagnosis must not be culture specific.
Lumping vs. Splitting	Higher level (global) vs. lower level (specific) definitions of disorder
Mental Disorder	The term preserves the unfortunate mind-body distinction.
New Diagnoses	What does it take to get a new disorder into the *DSM*?
Openness	Consensus as scholars vs. advocates of special interests
Prototypes	Are *DSM* disorders prototypes or classical categories?
Quality Control	Consistency concerning implementation of diagnostic criteria
Prevalence and Incidence	Altering diagnostic criteria changes prevalence and incidence rates.
Subthreshold Conditions	Are the current thresholds for each diagnostic disorder optimal?

Conundrum	Description
Theoretical Neutrality	Should diagnostic criteria be theoretically neutral? Should diagnostic criteria extend to relationships?
Users	How to balance the needs of clinicians, researchers, students, administrators, insurance companies, attorneys, etc.?
Validation	How to reconcile conflicting sources of validation (e.g., clinical vs. community (epidemiological) vs. family (genetic) studies)?
When	When is the best time to update a *DSM*?
Xenophilia vs. Xenophobia	*International Classification of Disorders and Related Health Problems (ICD) vs. Diagnostic and Statistical Manual of Mental Disorders*

more disorders. Describing patients along multiple dimensions is one way to solve this problem. Categorizing is replaced by characterizing patients with a score on each of several dimensions. Patients can score low, medium, or high on one or all of these dimensions. There has been much debate over whether mental health diagnosis should move to a dimensional base or retain its categorical approach.

The *Journal of Abnormal Psychology* published two special issues discussing a wide range of diagnostic issues. Barlow (1991) introduced the first special issue of the *Journal of Abnormal Psychology* regarding diagnosis. Millon (1991) discussed general issues of classification with regard to psychopathology. Blashfield and Livesley (1991) explored a psychological testing metaphor. They considered diagnostic criteria as test items, diagnostic categories like scales, and classifications as tests. Maser, Kaelber, and Weise (1991) surveyed 146 mental health professionals, primarily psychiatrists and psychologists, in 42 countries. The results endorsed the multiaxial categorical approach. Widiger, Frances, Pincus, Davis, and First (1991) discussed the need for, and progress toward, placing diagnosis on an empirical basis. Morey (1991) explored viewing psychiatric diagnosis in terms of hypothetical constructs where taxonomic constructs are theoretically grounded. Spitzer (1991) noted that *DSM-IV* (APA, 1994) would be based more on consensus than data. Kendell (1991) observed that the *DSM-IV* is based on a wider range of empirical data than any of the previous editions. Carson (1991) questioned the wisdom of continuing to use a categorical system based on inadequate construct validity and emphasis on clinician acceptance. Nelson–Gray (1991) proposed empirical guidelines from psychometrics to guide *DSM* development. The second special section on diagnosis published by the *Journal of Abnormal Psychology* was introduced by Widiger and Samuel (2005). Brown and Barlow (2005) proposed dimensional severity ratings to existing diagnostic criteria and categories. Krueger, Markdon, Patrick, and Iacono (2005) proposed, and presented supporting data for, an externalizing dimension of psychopathology. Construction of *DSM-V* is well underway. The document entitled "A Research Agenda for *DSM-V*" can be read online at the following URL: http://www.appi.org/book.cfm?id=2292. It remains to be seen how many of the conundrums identified by Frances et al. (1991) will be satisfactorily resolved.

Among the unresolved problems with the dimensional approach are the following: (a) What dimensions should be used? (b) Should these be dimensions of temperament and/or personality such as the Five Factor Model? (c) Should these be dimensions of psychopathology? (d) Should these be dimensions derived from diagnoses given in past using earlier version of the *DSM*? (Kruger, Caspi, Moffitt, & Silva, 1998). (e) How many dimensions should be used? More dimensions will always account for a greater proportion of psychopathologic variation. (f) But, at what point does parsimony dictate that enough dimensions should be used? (g) Should these be orthogonal dimensions? (h) If not, what should the maximum limit be on how correlated these dimensions can be? (i) Are two dimensions that are correlated .7 to .9 really functionally separate?

Practical considerations derive from the dimension versus category debate. The dimensional approach to diagnosis replaces reference to a single category with a profile of scores, one for each dimension of interest. Will this be a list of 5, 10, or 15 numbers? The *DSM* is part statistical manual and enables epidemiologists to compute the incidence (e.g., number of new cases per 100,000 of the population per year) and prevalence (proportion of the population) of specific disorders. How would reporting be done if dimensional profiles replaced diagnostic categories? Investigators currently form work groups around specific disorders like OCD. How would investigators form research groups if vectors of dimensional measurements replaced diagnostic categories? Relatedly, how would one know if two patients were sufficiently similar to be considered to have the same disorder; that is, to be part of the same group? Which dimension scores would have to be similar for two patients to be in the same group? How much could they differ on these dimensions and still be diagnostically equivalent? How would such equivalence be quantified? Would some average discrepancy across all dimensions need to be minimized? These and probably other multidimensional statistical issues will need to be answered before the dimensional approach to diagnosis can become practical.

A hybrid approach might be helpful. Assessment might be based on dimensions but then cutoff scores could be used to categorize persons. This approach would enable dimensional assessment and categorical reporting and thus combine the benefits of both approaches to diagnosis. However, it leaves the problem of what dimensions to assess, how many dimensions there should be, and the permissible degree of correlation among dimensions.

The problems associated with the dimensional versus categorical approach are numerous, complex, and may take many years of research to resolve. As an actigrapher, I favor the dimensional approach because actigraphs measure activity level along an equal interval scale with an absolute zero point; that is, they provide ratio scale measurement. Moreover, the internal clock guarantees that measurements will be taken at equal intervals as required by time series and spectral analyses. The quality of one's basic and applied (clinical) science cannot exceed the quality of the measurement upon which it is based. Actigraphy provides a solid base. More than activity level must be known to properly assess presenting problems and formulate clinical interventions. Hence, actigraph measurements are either indicators of a category or elements of a dimensional description. Actigraphy does not resolve the problems outlined above. I now turn to the role of instruments in diagnostic testing and subsequently consider the role actigraphy currently plays and may play regarding diagnosis.

Evidence-Based Diagnosis

Professional ethics clearly indicate that psychologists must use tests of demonstrated reliability and validity for the designated testing purposes (American Educational Research Association, American Psychological Association, & National Council on Measurement in Education, 1999). Gone are the days that psychologists could use a test of their professional choice based on personal experience and desire. Similar consensus has yet to be reached regarding the ethical practice of psychological intervention. The gap between science and practice is large and little progress has been made to narrow it. Efforts to preserve professional autonomy and choice to practice as they were trained appear to be as or more important than the ethical mandate to provide the most effective treatment available. Legitimate criticisms of existing research including highly select samples that are unrepresentative of clinical populations and complex and lengthy manuals, should set the occasion for conducting better studies rather than dismissing the need for such studies. Commitment to abide by the results of empirical research is in short supply. While some interventions claim effects that go well beyond symptom reduction, ameliorating underlying conflicts should also reduce symptoms given the psychodynamic theory of symptom formation thus rendering the more common outcome measures suitable for evaluating all therapies. The list of empirically supported treatment continues to grow. A current listing can be found at the following APA Division 12 Clinical Psychology Web site: http://www.apa.org/divisions/div12/rev%5Fest/.

What about empirically based diagnosis? Clinical diagnosis consists of relatively easy and difficult parts. The easy part is making a diagnosis given a definitive listing of clinical signs and symptoms. One simply identifies the diagnosis that is most consistent with the evidence. The difficult part is certifying the presence or absence of these clinical signs and symptoms. What is the reliability and validity of various methods for attributing clinical signs and symptoms to people? While the reliability of structured interviews is better than unstructured interviews, empirical studies have shown that reliability coefficients are modest to poor. Shaffer, Fisher, Lucas, Dulcan, and Schwab-Stone (2000) reported *Diagnostic Interview Schedule for Children, Version IV* (*DISC-IV*) test–retest kappa reliability coefficients for 84 parents of a clinical sample of children aged

9–17 years of 0.79 and 0.42 for 82 youth regarding attention deficit hyperactivity disorder (ADHD) for a combined kappa of 0.62. Corresponding *DISC-IV* kappa coefficient data for a community sample of 247 parent–child pairs were .60 for parents, .10 for youth, and .48 for parents and youth. Regarding validity, the authors reported that "to date, there has been no formal validity testing of the NIMH *DISC-IV*" (p. 35). Angold and Costello (2000) did not report reliability data for ADHD. Rather, they reported test–retest kappa coefficients for 77 clinically referred children aged 10–16 years for conduct disorder, a common ADHD comorbid disorder, was 0.55. Ambrosini (2000) reviewed the K-SADS and reported test–retest kappa coefficients ranging from .91 for 26 children to whom the current (vs. past) form of the K-SADS-P IIIR LTR was administered down to .55 for 20 children to whom the K-SADS-P/L LT had been administered.

Reich (2000) presented 1 week test–retest kappa coefficients for 40 children aged 6–12 years. Kappa for children aged 6–12 with ADHD was .32. Kappa for adolescents aged 13–18 with ADHD was .65. Solanto and Alvir (in press) reported kappas for inattentive items that ranged from .38 to .69 for parents and from .31 to .81 for teachers. Kappas for hyperactive–impulsive items ranged from .60 to .76 for parents and from .69 to .81 for teachers. More importantly, they point out that the main question is how consistently children are positively diagnosed on the basis of parent and teacher reports. Their data indicates that "Classification as AD/HD or not AD/HD switched from test to retest in 12% and 10% of all cases, based on ratings by parents and teachers respectively". One indication of the clinical importance of these findings is as follows. The National Institutes of Health (2000) estimates that ADHD effects from 3% to 5% of school-age children. The 2000 census revealed 20,549,505 children aged 5–9 years (http://www.census.gov/population/cen2000/phc-t9/tab01.pdf). The 10% and 12% misclassification rates mean that from 61,648 to 73,978 diagnostic mistakes could have been made assuming that only 3% of school-aged children have ADHD. At 5%, from 102,747 to 123,297 diagnostic mistakes are expected. A 10-year review of ADHD rating scales by Collett, Ohan, and Myers (2003) reported a wide range of reliabilities across rating scales with lower bounds of .08, .12, .13, .18, .30, .35, .40, .47, and .51, all accounting for less than 25% of the variance. Kamphaus and Frick (2005) provide additional information.

Angold and Costello (2000) observed that "The problem with trying to assess the validity of psychiatric interviews is that there is no noninterview test for most psychiatric disorders" (p. 44). This is a very serious limitation. Without validity, reliability is vacuous. Phrenologists reliably measured head size, which is not a valid measure of intelligence and therefore not used as such. Actigraphy provides an objective instrumented methodology for assessing activity level and thus validating teacher and parent reports of hyperactivity at school and home. Progress toward developing empirically based diagnosis will likely entail diagnostic testing.

Doss (2005) advocated incorporating "diagnostic instruments" into clinical practice. She included the *DISC-IV* (Shaffer et al., 2000) and the Schedule for Affective Disorders and Schizophrenia for School-Age Children – Present and Lifetime version (K-SADS-PL) (Kaufman et al., 1997) and the Achenbach System of Empirically Based Assessment (ASEBA) (Achenbach & Rescorla, 2001) (http://www.aseba.org/index.html). The Behavioral Assessment Scale for Children (2nd ed) (BASC) is another empirically based testing system designed to facilitate diagnosis (http://ags.pearsonassessments.com/Group.asp?nGroupInfoID=a30000). The BASC has specific scales for anxiety and hyperactivity. It is beyond the scope of this chapter to review these diagnostic systems in detail. The two main points of interest are (a) that standardized psychological testing has been developed to support clinical diagnosis, and (b) that instrumented tests do not participate in clinical diagnosis.

Diagnostic Testing

The second conundrum regarding diagnoses is that biological and psychological test results currently play no role except for the diagnosis of mental retardation. This is a remarkable departure from the medical model[1] by the APA, a medical organization. Diagnostic testing plays a central role in modern medicine except for psychiatry. The reliance of medicine on diagnostic testing is all too apparent to anyone who has received health care in a hospital setting. For example, a family member of mine with a history of sinusitis who presented to an emergency room with fever had (a) their temperature and (b) blood pressure taken, (c) urine specimen taken, (d) blood drawn and chemistries conducted, and (e) underwent a head X-ray prior to receiving a diagnosis of sinusitis and receiving antibiotics which had worked in the past for prior instances of this disorder. Laboratory testing in this case was relied upon prior to initiating treatment even in the face of a clear cut symptom and therapeutic response history. While it may be argued that all of these tests were not necessary, such experiences verify that medical diagnosis and treatment are highly dependent on diagnostic testing. The title of Davidsohn and Henry's (1974) medical text *Clinical Diagnosis by Laboratory Methods* clearly indicates that diagnosis is to be based on testing by laboratory methods. The preface to their text identifies the following contributions that laboratory methods make to medicine: "(a) diagnosis, (b) confirmation of a clinical impression, (c) screening or detection of disease, (d) prognosis, (e) therapeutic management guideline data" (p. vii). Medical science increasingly uses instruments to record and quantify signs of disease (The Association for the Advancement of Medical Instrumentation; http://www.aami.org/). In this case, diagnostic testing was used to confirm a clinical impression.

The history of scientific medicine is largely a history of instruments and laboratory measurements. More generally, instruments (Tryon, 1996a) and their units of measure (Tryon, 1996b) have driven scientific theory. Likewise, modern medicine understands disease, at least partially, in terms of instrumented measurements. Some disorders are entirely defined in terms of measurements. For example, hypertension and hypotension are completely defined by sphygmomanometer readings. The only way to know if these diseases are present is to measure with a sphygmomanometer. The only way to track the course of this disease is with repeatedly measure with a sphygmomanometer. Likewise, hyperglycemia and hypoglycemia are defined by a laboratory test that determines the number of milligrams of sugar per milliliter of urine. Modern medical practice prefers to measure the patient's temperature with a thermometer. Additional examples could be produced but should not be necessary to illustrate that modern medicine uses laboratory tests and instruments to evaluate and document the patient's clinical condition. Medical diagnoses were derived from clinical configurations of laboratory test results and instrument readings in combination with clinical presentation to inform and guide treatment selection and enable prognostic judgments.

Diagnosis of mental disorder as specified by the APA departs markedly from the medical model in that no laboratory or instrumented tests are used to guide or inform clinical impressions, diagnosis, therapeutic management, and/or outcome assessment. Mainly, the patient is interviewed and, in the case of children, parents and teachers are interviewed, and then a diagnosis is reached. Tests of underlying psychological states are rarely assessed. Objective behavioral samples are rarely taken by trained observers. More to the point of this chapter, instrumented test results are very rarely obtained and as we shall shortly are sometimes prohibited. By way of contrast, cardiologists are interested in their patient's condition as they go about their daily life. They sometimes have patients wear a Holter monitor to record heart function while they behave in their natural environment for several days. Psychiatry and psychology on the other hand do not collect instrumented data from the natural environment despite the availability of actigraphy (Tryon, 1991, Teicher 1995) and its relevance to 48 *DSM-IV* inclusion and/or exclusion criteria (Tryon, 2002) and the availability of other tests such as the continuous performance test (Riccio, Reynolds, & Lowe, 2001).

Psychological Testing

The history of clinical psychology reveals that psychologists began making clinical contributions through diagnostic testing (Tryon, 2007). Psychologists once conducted full test batteries as part of psychodiagnostic and treatment formulation. Unfortunately, psychological testing was never formally linked to diagnostic decisions either in a decisive or advisory way. Undoubtedly, several factors are responsible for this dissociation but almost certainly a primary event was that the APA took charge of the diagnostic nomenclature consistent with their role as medical practitioners, leaving the American Psychological Association and psychologists on the sidelines. Lacking diagnostic tests of their own, psychiatric diagnosis was based, with the exception of mental retardation, solely on interview data. The development of structured interviewing improved the reliability of psychiatric diagnoses but preserved the focus of data collection on self- and other- reports.

People present clinicians with various psychological problems. Diagnosis is intended to facilitate case formulation and treatment selection while diagnostic testing is intended to inform diagnostic decisions. Test selection is clinically driven by the patient's presenting complaint in that physicians order tests depending on the clinical signs and symptoms at hand. People frequently present to mental health professionals with anxiety and depression. Antony, Orsillo, and Roemer (2001) compiled a *Practitioner's Guide to Empirically Based Measures of Anxiety* that reviews more than 200 tests for assessing anxiety disorders that could be administered. They cover self-report and clinician-administered scales for specific anxiety disorders such as panic disorder, specific and social phobias, generalized anxiety disorder (GAD), OCD, and posttraumatic stress disorder (PTSD). They also consider behavioral assessment in the form of behavioral approach tests (Chorpita & Taylor, 2001), psychophysiological tests of heart rate and heart rate variability (Yartz & Hawk Jr., 2001), and biological challenges including CO_2 inhalation (Forsyth & Karekla, 2001). Nezu, Ronan, Meadows, and McClure (2000) have compiled a corresponding list of self- and clinician-administered measures of depression. None of these tests are referred to in *DSM-IV* (APA, 1994) or its text revision (APA, 2000), and none are likely to be included in *DSM-V*. Buros *Mental Measurements Yearbook* and *Tests in Print* (http://www.unl.edu/buros/) reveal an even greater array of psychological tests that have been developed to assess a broad range of psychological traits. Except for intelligence tests, none of these numerous tests is used to guide clinical assessment or inform clinical diagnosis.

Psychologists, like physicians, could prescribe tests as part of working up a clinical case. The practice of selective psychological testing to better characterize and to quantify clinical impressions would enable diagnosis to occur on the basis of clusters or combinations of frequently used tests or categories of tests. For example, a diagnostic category could be assigned for patients who only have elevations on one test scale which given comorbidity would be rare. Separate diagnostic categories could be based for common patterns of high and/or low test scores. Diagnostic nomenclature could be formed to reflect the content of these empirical clusters. One diagnostic number could be assigned to patients with elevated depression scores, a second category for patients who only have elevated anxiety scores, and a third category for patients who have elevated scores on both anxiety and depression tests. Clinical experience would generate patient groups based on test results. This approach to diagnosis is dimensional in that psychological tests provide interval scaling of the psychological construct being measured. This approach answers the question of how many dimensions should be used by identifying the most clinically useful tests; that is, the tests that are given to the majority of patients based on clinical need for the information that the test provides. Perhaps, treatment planning, decisions, and outcome results differ across these three diagnostic categories. The results of treatment studies performed on patients with these test profiles would likely be more acceptable to treating clinicians than treatment studies based on "pure" groups consisting of unusual patients that clinicians rarely if ever see because they would be based on realistic patients. The comorbidity issue would be replaced by test overlap which fortunately does not have the same theoretical implications/problems that comorbidity does because a dimensional rather than categorical approach is taken. Said differently, comorbidity implies two or more separate disorders are present. Test overlap indicates common features. Take medical diagnosis for instance. Infections of various types all raise body temperature. Fever is a sign of various diseases. White blood cell count is also elevated by various infections. Elevations on both measures characterize the clinical presentation and are not an indication that two or more disorders are present but rather reveal the joint effects of infection. This is a test-driven approach to constructing a diagnostic system that is consistent with the use of instrumented tests discussed next. This is a bottom–up clinically driven testing approach to diagnosis that contrasts markedly with the top–down research driven approach where the multidimensional nature of personality must first be solved to determine diagnostic categories. An important difference between these two approaches is that some dimensions that are important to understanding individual differences may be of little clinical interest. For example, the introversion–extraversion personality dimension is a major source of individual difference but does not figure prominently in case formulation and treatment planning. Put generally, answers to basic research questions may not always be relevant to clinical diagnosis and treatment. Clinical consensus regarding which tests should be prescribed for various clinical presentations is a realistic near term goal.

A potential criticism of an instrument driven approach to diagnosis is that the number of test combinations would soon become too numerous to be manageable. However, comorbidity is such that relatively few clusters of tests would more likely result. These empirically based clinically determined clusters would more accurately reflect the types of people being seen by clinicians and therefore would have clinical utility. Successful test construction yields a psychological instrument[2] that is reliable, has internal and temporal stability, is valid (construct and criterion referenced; e.g., concurrent and predictive validity) such that it measures a psychological construct in ways that correlate well with other indicators of the construct in question and contributes to our ability to predict theoretically related events and/or outcomes. Psychometric reliability seems to satisfy the need for consistent diagnostic findings. Psychometric validity seems to address the need for clinically useful correlates. It therefore follows that a psychometrically reliable and valid test of a psychological disorder provides a quantitative assessment of the psychopathological construct of interest. Cut scores to define diagnostic categories could be developed for such tests in the same way as they have been developed for IQ tests. In fact, IQ tests could be taken as the prototype for developing tests of other constructs.

Instrumented tests have no official role in clinical assessment and/or diagnosis. The problem here is more than benign omission. Results from laboratory tests of attention, impulsivity, and activity are not admissible regarding the diagnosis of ADHD on the basis of impaired attention, impulsivity, and hyperactivity. Barkley (1991) explicitly rejected laboratory methods of assessing attention, impulsivity, and activity level when diagnosing ADHD. He based his prohibition on theoretical and empirical grounds. His theoretical argument is based on what he calls ecological validity. Barkley (1991) wrote "The term *ecological validity* (original emphasis) is a rather vague and amorphous concept that most often refers to the degree to which the results of LMs (laboratory measures) represent the actual behaviors of interest as they occur in naturalistic settings. It has been more traditionally referred to as concurrent or predictive validity (Anastasi, 1976)" (p. 150). Predictive validity is part of criterion-referenced validity along with concurrent validity. One or more criteria are used to validate tests. The criterion is contemporary in the case of concurrent validity and can take the form of an independent and previously established test of the same construct. The criterion is future oriented in the case of predictive validity and can take the form of therapeutic outcome or subsequent clinical status. Construct validity is a third validation method where theoretically predicted relationships with other measures of the same (convergent validity) and different (discriminant validity) constructs are provided (Campbell & Fiske, 1959). Barkley (1991) distinguished ecological validity from construct validity as follows: "This is somewhat different than asking whether the LM captures the fundamental behavioral deficit believed to exist in ADHD. That notion requires reference to a theoretical construct of the 'core' deficit(s) which may not always be represented in their purest form in the natural occurrence of ADHD symptoms" (p. 151). Ecological validity can sometimes be the same as construct validity and sometimes not. Therefore, if a laboratory measure were to fully reflect a core deficit then it would sometimes be ecologically valid and other times not depending on whether ADHD was manifested in a pure form or not. No rationale was given to support this conditional perspective nor was any precedent provided for such a position. Are psychological tests ecologically valid? Does the validity of a test of depression or anxiety depend on whether the person being tested manifests depression or anxiety in a pure form or not? It seems that instrumented tests are being treated in an unusual way.

Kamphaus and Frick (1996, p. 354) emphasized Barkley's (1991) reference to "... actual behaviors as they occur in naturalistic settings" as key to understanding ecological validity. An ecologically valid measure reflects the actual way in which the behavior takes place in the classroom. Hence, a laboratory test of attention such as the Continuous Performance Test (CPT) is not ecologically valid because students do not take CPTs as part of their educational experience. By this reasoning, the Wechsler intelligence tests are not ecologically valid measures of intelligence because some of the subscales entail tasks, such as block design, that are not part of everyday classroom experience. Curiously, no concern about the ecological validity of the Wechsler scales has been expressed. By this standard, changing what happens in the classroom can render a previously ecologically valid test invalid.

It remains unclear why the fact that an underlying core deficit that is reflected clinically with some variability makes psychometric construct valid assessments of those core deficits inadmissible regarding clinical diagnosis. Variability of trait expression has not previously been used to render construct valid measures inappropriate for clinical assessment. Such a consideration might well invalidate most, if not all, psychological tests for clinical use. Perhaps, this is why psychological tests are not presently part of the diagnostic process except for intelligence tests, which appear to be open to the same criticism. Actigraphy quantifies acceleration forces at the site of attachment, usually the waist and/or nondominant wrist, and does so as accurately in the classroom as it does in the laboratory. Actigraph data is both highly reliable and valid. No generalization from laboratory to naturalistic setting need be involved. No generalization from assessment task to classroom activity need be involved. To dismiss these data on the basis of "a rather vague and amorphous concept" (Barkley, 1991) such as ecological validity deprives clinicians and investigators of core clinical information.

Barkley's (1991) empirical argument against the ecological validity of laboratory measures is twofold. First, he cited studies that attempted to validate laboratory measures against parent and teacher ratings of ADHD symptoms with the following caveat: "Given so few studies available for comparing LMs with direct observations in natural settings, we are forced to rely primarily on parent and teacher ratings of ADHD symptoms at home or in school as the criteria against which to judge the ecological validity of the LMs reviewed. This is done acknowledging full well that this is not a particularly fair nor scientifically satisfying approach to evaluating ecological validity of the LMs" (p. 154). The author vitiates the empirical evidence presented against LMs by recognizing severe limitations of their data. Barkley did not recognize the possibility that teachers and parents may not accurately rate activity level. Perhaps he assumed that parent and teacher ratings are completely accurate. Or perhaps clinical diagnosis is best accomplished on the basis of perception rather than fact. Perhaps all that matters is if parents and teachers believe that a child is hyperactive. Having been socially categorized in this way may be more important than whether or not the child actually displays motor excess to the degree and in the ways parents and teachers say.

Barkley's second line of evidence is the lack of correlation among laboratory measures of symptoms of ADHD. For example, he cited the lack of a substantial correlation between ankle activity measures and CPT scores. Such an expectation appears to be predicated upon the presumption that diagnostic methods always produce a group of children who are high in both activity level and CPT errors compared to control children who are both low in activity level and CPT errors as this would need to be the case for the required correlation to emerge. This may not be the case for at least two reasons. First, our understanding of ADHD has changed over the last several editions of the *DSM,* which makes children diagnosed with this disorder at one time different from children diagnosed with this disorder at another time. Different clinical definitions can be expected to produce groups with different instrumented test profiles. A second reason why symptoms may not cluster as expected is that teachers and parents may not correctly report behaviors. For example, there is evidence that teachers over report activity level in children (Tryon & Pinto, 1994) and children diagnosed with ADHD (Licht & Tryon, 2007). Hence, the expected covariation in symptoms may not materialize within a diagnostic group. The low correlations among construct valid laboratory measures may reflect the inadequacy of current diagnostic methods.

Even if it were the case that diagnostic methods produced a group of children who are overactive and inattentive, range restriction would attenuate the correlation between activity measurements and CPT scores. Consider basketball players in the National Basketball Association; they are all tall and heavy. They are also all men. Consequently, a correlation of their heights and weights is much smaller than the correlation of all men and/or for all men and women. Only by calculating correlations across ADHD and control children can one obtain an accurate estimate of the real correlation coefficient.

Validation

Inconsistencies between laboratory measures and diagnostic groupings raises a more general issue that also pertains to anxiety disorders and that is the question of how does one validate *DSM* disorders? What methods can one use to show that diagnostic criteria are valid? We say that a test is valid when it measures what it purports to measure. Can this be said of a diagnostic category? Perhaps the validity of a diagnostic category depends upon the validity of the methods used to identify the disorder? If, for example, a reliable and valid method is used to assess anxiety and it is applied to a person suspected of having an anxiety disorder then perhaps one can conclude that the diagnosis of anxiety disorder is reliable and valid. If multiple such methods are administered and they jointly identify an anxiety disorder then perhaps the reliability and validity of that diagnosis is even greater. Given that a diagnosis is a working hypothesis, it follows that the reliability and validity of this conclusion is highly dependent on the methods used to reach it which include the methods used to collect pertinent data and the methods used to combine these data into a decision to support or reject a diagnosis. As mentioned above, with the exception of mental retardation, all *DSM* diagnoses are based on interview data. Angold and Costello (2000) observed that "The problem with trying to assess the validity of psychiatric interviews is that there is no noninterview test for most psychiatric disorders" (p. 44). This is a serious limitation especially since there are no acceptable objective instrumented tests for core deficits and/or symptoms. Diagnosticians rely on parent and teacher reports for practical reasons. Evidence that parents and teachers are valid data sources has yet to be demonstrated. Parents and teachers are not trained observers and do not conduct behavioral assessments that require (a) operational definition of specific target behavior behaviors, (b) training with at least one other rater until high observer reliability has been demonstrated, (c) use of time sampling or other observational technology to sample behavior and an adequate method for recording results, and (d) recalibration of observers as necessary to counteract observer drift as observations extend over time. In short, the veracity of parent and teacher reports remains to be demonstrated.

Absent noninterview data with which to validate structure or open-ended interview data, investigators have mistakenly drawn validity conclusions from reliability studies (Malgady, Rogler, & Tryon, 1992). Showing that two or more diagnosticians can consistently categorize the same patients is evidence of reliability, not validity. The construct they are jointly agreeing on could be seriously flawed. Interviews depend heavily upon patient reports of prior and current symptoms which is highly dependent on memory and motivation for accurate reporting and subject to serious errors

(Rogler, Malgady, & Tryon, 1992). For example, the number of lifetime diagnoses upon retest has been found to be *less than* upon initial testing.

Absent a gold standard or objective instrumented test of the construct at issue, the only remaining way to validate clinical diagnoses is to demonstrate one or more functional relationships between diagnostic grouping and responsiveness to treatment and/or health risk generally. Studies of this sort could not be located. If performed and found positive such research would be clinically useful but would not inform us regarding the underlying mechanism(s) responsible for this disorder. According to http://en.wikipedia.org/wiki/Diagnosis, "In general, *diagnosis* (plural *diagnoses*) has two distinct dictionary definitions. The first definition is "the recognition of a disease or condition by its outward signs and symptoms," while the second definition is "the analysis of the underlying physiological/biochemical cause(s) of a disease or condition." Well-validated instrumented measures of core excesses and/or deficits and/or psychological constructs arguably offer the best chance of making progress in this regard. Medical progress has likely benefited from the use of instrumented measures in the study of disease.

Instrumented Tests

I include laboratory tests as instrumented measures as they typically entail some form of equipment. It is noted again for readers who began with this section that contrary to the medical model, psychiatric diagnosis is, with the exception of intelligence tests, not based on testing of any kind let alone instrumented tests. One possible explanation is that instrumented tests do not assess any clinically relevant psychological constructs and therefore have not been used for diagnostic purposes. The following sections show that instrumented tests of attention, impulsivity, and activity level have been developed and validated.

Attention is a fundamental psychological process and various mental illnesses disrupt it. Perhaps the best known attention disorder is ADHD, the most prevalent child psychiatric disorder affecting 4% to 6% of school-age children between 6 and 12 years old (Brown et al., 2001). An extensive body of evidence has emerged over the past several decades regarding the instrumented measurement of attention and attentional deficits. Riccio, Reynolds, and Lowe (2001) comprehensively reviewed the clinical and research evidence regarding the ability of CPTs to measure attention. Riccio et al. (2001) concluded that: "... a viable use of the CPT is for monitoring outcome of various treatments on aspects of attention and executive control. ... The CPT provides a quick, relatively inexpensive, objective measure of the impact of medications on at least some components of attention as well as processing speed" (p. 312). If CPT tests can inform clinical practice and research regarding treatment outcome, why can't they inform diagnostic formulation?

Teicher, Ito, Glod, and Barber (1996) added infrared motion detection and analysis to a 15-minute CPT known as the McLean – Motion Attention Test™ (M-MAT). Additional details of this test can be found at the following URL: http://www.mclean.harvard.edu/pdf/research/clinicalunit/dbrp/mmat-tech.pdf. It is noteworthy that initial diagnostic norms are available regarding attention and activity level.

Impulsivity is another psychological trait of interest to clinicians diagnosing ADHD. Logan and Cowan (1984) developed a stop-signal method for measuring impulsivity which has subsequently been validated by Logan and Burkell (1986), Schachar and Logan (1990a), and Schachar et al. (1993). Gorlyn et al. (2005) studied impulsivity using a battery of performance tests and concluded that each one taps a different facet of impulsivity which makes each test quite specific in what it measures.

Activity level is perhaps the first personality variable to emerge (Tryon, 2002) in that mothers can reliably and validly detect fetal activity beginning with the 28th week of gestation. Fetal activity appears to increase to a peak at around week 34 and then decrease through week 39 (Eaton & Saudino, 1992). There is near universal agreement that activity level is a fundamental dimension of individual differences among infants (Goldsmith et al., 1987). Other evidence shows that activity level is a prominent trait during middle childhood (Shiner, 1998), and adulthood (Comrey, 1994; Buss & Plomin, 1975, 1984; Buss, 1989). Hence, psychopathology during infancy, middle childhood, or adulthood can be expected to at least temporarily alter personality.

Activity level is a final common pathway for a wide variety of cognitive and affective processes. Most life style decisions influence activity level. For example, to engage in or not engage in specific behaviors like taking a walk, or bowling, shopping for food or clothing, will alter one's activity level for that day. Infections tend to decrease activity level. Basic research on circadian rhythms typically measures either core body temperature or activity level. Actigraphy refers to the use of actigraphs to collect data and enables quantitative studies of circadian rhythm in free living infants, children, and adults. The term *actigraph* properly refers to a device that uses an accelerometer to detect motion. The actigraph is actually measuring its own movement. When firmly attached to the waist, wrist, or ankle actigraphs measure movement of that body site. It is important to keep in mind that actigraph data pertain to a single body site. Multiple actigraphs are required to monitor multiple sites. Acceleration refers to the change in velocity per unit time. Body parts speed up and slow down during movements because they are jointed and therefore move along limited arcs. Accelerometers respond to these velocity changes with voltage changes. An onboard computer chip digitizes the analog voltage signal anywhere from 10 to 32 times a second on a ratio scale with equal measurement intervals and an absolute zero point. These readings are averaged over a user specified epoch that is typically 30 seconds long for sleep studies and 1 minute long otherwise. Epochs as long as 15 minutes have been used in the past when computer memory was bulky and expensive. Modern actigraphs frequently carry a megabyte or more of onboard memory. The computer clock enables actigraphs to be programmed to start at an hour, minute, and second of a specific day of a specified month. This enables delayed start-up to allow a period of habituation where the person gets used to wearing the device. Since the day technically starts at 00 hours, 00 minutes, and 00 seconds—midnight—this is a good time to start data collection. It also enables direct comparison of one record to another as they both start at the same time. Data are transferred from the actigraph to a personal computer for display and analysis.

Infants alternate between periods of rest and/or sleep and waking activity several times during each 24 hour period. They gradually consolidate their sleep into a single period and their waking activity into another single period thus creating a normal circadian rhythm characterized by a measor (average) and acrophase (time of peak activity). A wide variety of personal decisions influence activity level such as choosing to take a walk versus read a book. Psychopathology also alters circadian rhythms. Tryon (2002) documented that activity level is involved in the inclusion and/or exclusion criteria for 48 *DSM-IV* disorders. This includes references to psychomotor retardation, agitation, and sleep disorders. Several sleep variables calculated from wrist actigraphy have been well validated against polysomnography (Tryon, 1996c, 2004). The effects of depression and mania on activity level have been studied more than any other disorder but we shall review research related to anxiety below.

Instrumented tests have certain desirable properties that psychological tests do not have. The first property might be referred to as "*construction validity*" in that devices are engineered to measure one or more quantities and only those quantities. For example, we can be sure that thermometers measure temperature because that it what they were designed to measure. Likewise, we can be sure that accelerometers measure movement because that is what they were engineered to do. Instruments are extremely narrow band devices in that they are constructed to measure a specific physical property. Human observers differ from instruments in that they did not evolve to function as instruments. People possess a variety of psychological properties that compromise their ability to function as instruments.

A second desirable characteristic of instruments not shared with psychological tests is that their reliability and validity can be studied separately from people. Hence, studies can be done that isolate instrument variation from behavioral variation of each person and sampling variability (i.e., who the test people are). This cannot be done with psychological tests. The only way to study the reliability and validity of psychological tests is to give them to people. The literature on validating actigraphs mainly consists of placing them on people who are instructed to perform certain tasks. Measured variability is almost always attributed to actigraph unreliability and by implication lack of validity. Thermistors are used to measure core body temperature but no one uses people to validate whether thermistors reliably and/or validly measure temperature. Why then do investigators question whether accelerometers reliably and validly measure movement? One answer may be that investigators seek clinical repeatability. Tryon (1991, pp. 9–15) distinguished clinical repeatability from instrument reliability. Behavior is inherently variable and disease frequently exacerbates normal variation. Investigators need to measure behavioral variance in order to determine the background measurement variation against which they plan to show systematic change. Longer periods of assessment typically lead to more reproducible average results. Clinical reproducibility studies help investigators select measurement duration. The operational characteristics of instruments are best studied under laboratory conditions. Reliability requires that the same thing be measured repeatedly. Mechanical devices such as pendulums (Tryon, 2005; Tryon & Williams, 1996) and spinners (Tryon & Williams, 1996) can repeat movements far more exactly than humans can. Results to date indicate that reliability and validity coefficients for modern actigraphs equal or exceed approximately .97.

A third desirable characteristic of instruments over psychological tests is their lack of phantom measurement (Tryon & Bernstein, 2002). Phantom measurement occurs to the extent that reliability coefficients exceed validity coefficients. For example, in the case where a reliability coefficient equals .9 and a validity coefficient equals .3 one can say that the device accounts for $.9 \times .9 = .81$ or 81% of measured variation but that only $.3 \times .3 = .09 = 9\%$ of this variation is valid; that is, only 9% measures the construct of interest. Hence, 72% of measured variation pertains to something other than what the test was intended to measure. In this case phantom measurement is nine times greater than valid measurement. Moreover, one rarely knows what factors influence this variation and consequently test score variation. The reliability and validity of actigraphs tested on large pendulums (Tryon & Williams, 1996) and spinners (Tryon & Williams, 1996) are essentially equal and high; they range from .98 to .99. Actigraph data consequently contains little phantom measurement. On the contrary, phantom measurement is common with regard to psychological tests and may also characterize parent and teacher reports.

A fourth desirable characteristic of instruments generally and actigraphs specifically is that they typically provide interval and sometimes ratio scale data. The analog-to-digital conversion chips on board modern actigraphs converts a range of voltage changes emanating from the accelerometer into equal parts thus providing an equal interval scale. Zero volts correspond to no motion and thereby provide an absolute zero point. Time series analyses require that data are collected at equal intervals. On-board clocks aggregate and store measured activity at equal time intervals thus fully satisfying time series data analytic assumptions.

A fifth desirable characteristic of instruments is that their operation characteristics are typically stable over much longer periods of time than are human observer characteristics. Volt meters may need to be recalibrated but trained observers tend to drift much more quickly and require frequent recalibration. The stability of operating characteristics of actigraphs has yet to be empirically established but appear to be stable over weeks and months.

A sixth characteristic of actigraphs is that they can collect data in naturalistic settings; that is, they are ecologically valid. Laboratory instruments that test people under standardized conditions encounter the burden of demonstrating that these laboratory results generalize to real life settings. Actigraphs directly measure behavior in situations of interest (i.e., home, work, and school).

A seventh characteristic of actigraphs is that the behavioral sample can be extended in time as necessary to provide a specified degree of repeatability as measurement repeatability is directly proportional to measurement duration (Epstein, 1979, 1980, 1983, 1986). The *DSM* typically requires that symptoms be present for at least two weeks. Actigraphy can be conducted for 2, 3, 4, or more weeks until the clinician/investigator can be sufficiently certain as to what is happening. For example, concerns that anxiety disrupts sleep can be informed by extended nocturnal wrist actigraphy while the patient sleeps in their own home over as many nights as deemed necessary to reach firm conclusions.

Sleep is typically studied in a laboratory using polysomnography. A typical sleep study entails three nights where data from the first night are usually discarded. Hence, central tendency and variability of sleep laboratory measures are based on two nights of data. How representative can such measures be? Little evidence of generalizability to average levels of sleep in the home, and more importantly, variability in those measures over time at home, is available because suitable home polysomnography is frequently not used. The reactivity of sleeping with many leads attached is another issue with generally unknown effects because electrodes and connecting cables are an integral part of PSG methodology.

Wrist actigraphy provides an alternative method for studying sleep. It provides a completely different perspective on sleep and therefore cannot be expected to exactly duplicate PSG findings. Going to sleep is not a discrete event; we are not awake one instant and asleep the next despite the fact that PSG sleep scoring technology presumes this to be the case. This scoring system has a code for Wake and another for Stage 1 sleep but no codes for the transition between wake and sleep. Tryon (2004) described a sleep-onset spectrum of changes that begin with motor quiescence. People cease moving before they go to sleep. Muscle relaxation occurs next. When PSG was first being validated, the gold standard for defining when sleep first occurred was the dropping of hand-held objects. It was against this behavioral criterion, gold standard, that EEG changes defining Stage 1 sleep were validated. Harui (1999) developed a handheld sleep switch to assess when this occurs. It is a small handheld device. Pressure on a switch keeps it open and allows a watch size clock to run. Muscle relaxation decreases finger pressure to where the clock stops thus recording the time as when first sleep onset occurred. Actigraphy is insensitive to this occurrence. Computer sleep scoring of wrist actigraphy identifies sleep after a prolonged period of inactivity. Persons with insomnia can lie motionless long periods of time. The result is that sleep onset is scored well before concurrent PSG shows that Stage 1 sleep begins. Fortunately, Hauri's (1999) sleep switch provides a good approximation of the onset of Stage 1 sleep.

The sleep onset process continues with additional EEG changes and then the person's auditory threshold increases. This is the point where sleep diaries indicate sleep onset. Subsequent to sleep onset several stages of sleep are defined by EEG changes. Wrist activity cannot discriminate among these EEG defined sleep stages. Actigraphy provides a single channel of data and therefore it cannot be expected to completely duplicate multichannel PSG data. Nevertheless, the validity coefficients against PSG for wrist actigraphy measured Total Sleep Time ranged from .72 to .98, for percent sleep ranged from .82 to .96, for sleep efficiency (time asleep/time in bed) ranged from .56 to .91, and wake after sleep onset ranged from .49 to .87 (Tryon, 1996c). Most of the published literature using actigraphy to assess the effects of anxiety has been via sleep assessment.

Actigraphy and Anxiety

Anxiety tends to disrupt sleep. Wrist actigraphy has been well validated against polysomnography (Tryon, 1996c, 2004). Hence, investigators have studied the sleep of anxious children using wrist actigraphy. Wicklow and Espie (2000) tested the hypothesis that worrisome thoughts can produce insomnia. They obtained voice-activated recordings of spontaneous thoughts and actigraphic data from 21 participants (14 women, 7 men) over 3 consecutive nights. This adult group was on average 36 years of age (range = 16–65) and had sleep problems for an average of 10 years. Content analysis of transcribed audiotapes yielded eight categories of presleep intrusion. The results of their correlation and regression analysis demonstrated that thinking about sleep and anxiety over anticipated consequences of poor sleep significantly predicted sleep latency as measured by actigraphy. Nelson and Harvey (2002) induced stress using image-based and verbal-based methods of stimulating speech related anxiety. The found that the more participants engaged in rehearsing and/or planning and problem solving the longer their actigraphically measured sleep onset latency was.

Kain et al. (2002) reported that children who undergo surgery are thought to develop postoperative sleep problems with some frequency. The purpose of this longitudinal study of 92 children undergoing general anesthesia and outpatient surgery and a community-based sample of 77 children was to empirically test this hypothesis. The children undergoing surgery wore wrist actigraphs to measure their sleep 3 nights before surgery and 5 nights after surgery. The results showed that 43 children who underwent surgery (47%) experienced sleep disturbance versus 13 (14.4%) control children. This difference is statistically significant ($F(1,91) = 4.283$, $p < .047$) thereby supporting the hypothesis that outpatient surgery tends to disrupt children's sleep. While the authors claimed not to understand the clinical significance of their findings it seems reasonable that the trauma associated with the surgery may well have been responsible. Alternatively stated, sleep seems sensitive to anxiety and the distress associated with surgery disrupted sleep enough that actigraphy could detect it. These results appear to validate actigraphy as a clinically relevant sleep measure as much as they validate that outpatient surgery disrupts sleep.

Caldwell–Andrews and Kain (2006) used actigraphy to study postoperative sleep in 52 consecutive children undergoing outpatient surgery. They found sleep problems in 22% of the children. A related study was conducted by Kuo, Chiu, Liao, and Hwang (2006). They used wrist actigraphy to study the extent to which 16 women made anxious by undergoing chemotherapy for Stage I or II breast cancer. Their sleep was assessed on the 8th and 9th days of the third cycle of chemotherapy via wrist actigraphy. Anxiety was assessed with the Hospital Anxiety and Depression Scale. The results were consistent with expectation and demonstrated disrupted sleep.

Children with Asperger's syndrome are known to be more anxious than normal children, resulting in insomnia. Tani et al. (2005) used actigraphs to study 6 nights of sleep for 19 adults with Asperger's syndrome and 10 normal controls. Their self-rated sleep problems were not reflected in the actigraph data. People with insomnia can lie sufficiently still that a wrist actigraph will identify them as asleep. It therefore appears that children with Asperger's sleep normally once asleep. Anxiety at bedtime can produce insomnia.

Kain and Caldwell–Andrews (2003) used actigraphy to evaluate the sleep of 92 adult surgery patients and 35 community controls for 48 hours before and after surgery and found that 23% of the participants getting surgery exhibited significant sleep impairment compared to 2.9% of the controls. This included more night awakenings of more than 5 minutes and less true sleep time. Children undergoing outpatient surgery are understandably anxious.

Kario, Schwartz, Davidson, and Pickering (2001) used actigraphy as a covariate while investigating the relationship between anxiety and depression with blood pressure in a nonpsychiatric sample of 231 working men and women. The simple correlation between depression and the sleep/wake blood pressure ratio in men was $r\ (229) = .24$, $p = .006$. This correlation changed to $r(225) = .25$, $p = .005$ after controlling for age, body mass index, and both waking and sleeping activity. These relations were not found in women.

It is worth noting again that measuring initial sleep onset latency is the sleep index that actigraphy is least accurate in measuring because people suffering from insomnia can and do lay sufficiently still for extended period of time that actigraphs can score them as asleep when by EEG standards they are still awake. Harui's (1999) sleep switch gives initial sleep onset latencies that agree quite well with EEG measures. People who use actigraphs to study activity level are called *actigraphers*. Elsevier has recently launched a new journal entitled *Mental Health and Physical Activity* (http://www.elsevier.com/wps/find/journaldescription.cws_home/714078/description#description) where actigraphers can publish their anxiety-related research.

Clinical Impressions

This section contains my recommendations regarding how actigraphy might be used to further study anxiety and complex disorders such as GAD, OCD, and PTSD. Our first consideration is attachment site. Actigraphs contain accelerometers that generate voltage changes when they are moved. Hence, actigraphs measure their own movement. When firmly strapped to a body site, they measure movement of that body site. The literature cited above regarding sleep measured wrist activity because that is the body site that is most active when people are awake. Prolonged absence of wrist activity commonly occurs during sleep and is the primary basis for how computer algorithms detect nocturnal sleep and daytime napping. Vertical movements at the waist best measure energy expended because the body's center of gravity is just above the waist at the center of the back. Movement at this site is directly proportional to energy expended through activity as the person's body weight is essentially constant over the recording period. What body site is best for measuring anxiety and OCD? Actigraphs can also be attached to ankles. Perhaps ankle measures would best reflect fidgeting in children. Then there is the issue of left or right side. It has become customary to place actigraphs on the nondominant wrist. However, sleep measures taken from the dominant wrist are frequently comparable to measures taken from the nondominant wrist. If performance of an OCD ritual involves one hand more than the other then one would probably want to monitor the more active wrist. With adequate resources, one can simultaneously monitor multiple sites. The data will be time locked because the onboard actigraph clocks will synchronize with the clock in the computer used to initialize them.

Future research should monitor multiple sites in people with varying amounts of anxiety as well as over time in individuals whose anxiety varies substantially. It may be that ideographic methods in conjunction with actigraphy will reveal additional and/or different results than nomothetic methods do.

Investigators must choose between naturalistic and laboratory studies. Actigraphs can be used in both research settings. Naturalistic settings offer the advantage of monitoring behavior in the person's natural environment. If an OCD ritual entails considerable wrist movements then the time that each ritual episode begins and ends can be determined from the actigraph data which is typically stored at one minute intervals from a known start time which typically is 00 hours, 00 minutes, and 00 seconds which corresponds to midnight; the official beginning of each day. For example, persons who repeatedly check the stove or those who retrace their steps out of concern they hit someone while driving may show increased activity level while checking in addition to disrupted sleep. Some actigraphs have enough onboard memory that they can record at 1 minute epochs for at least one month which means that one could determine the frequency, duration, and timing of rituals over as many days as desired. It is prudent to download data every week to guard against accidental loss. Modern memory systems retain data even when battery power is lost. The drawback of naturalistic studies is that the investigator has no control over the person's environment, allowing many variables to vary at will. Diary logs can be used to obtain qualitative data to better interpret the actigraph data but this does not diminish the impact of uncontrolled variables.

It seems reasonable to expect that activity level will increase during acute anxiety and subside as anxiety diminishes. Activity level may also be suppressed as when agoraphobics and panickers attempt to avoid a panic attack by remaining inactive. This combination might give rise to biphasic variations in activity level—heightened when confronted with phobic stimuli, but substantially lowered during avoidance. This pattern may be applicable to disorders characterized by phobia as opposed to chronic anxiety such as OCD/GAD.

Laboratory studies enable investigators to vary the presentation of stimuli that may provoke anxiety and OCD rituals. Actigraphy can still be used to capture these events. In this case the actigraph recording epoch should be set to the shortest possible interval. This can be 1 second down to 1/32 of a second depending upon actigraph model. Most actigraphs are uniaxial and primarily measure movement in one direction. This is fine when vertical movements about the waist are at issue, as they are in counting steps and energy consumption. Other actigraphs are biaxial or triaxial. One triaxial model provides vector summation.

Conclusions

Much of modern medical science rests on instrumentation including measurements made during laboratory assays of specimens and pictures generated by imaging equipment. Psychiatry is the only branch of medicine that does not use instruments for diagnostic purposes with the exception of intelligence tests to diagnose mental retardation. The absence of independent measurement compromises our ability to validate diagnostic entities. Tryon (2002, 2006) has shown that activity level pertains to 48 *DSM-IV* inclusion and exclusion criteria. Actigraphy is an instrumented method for continuously quantifying and integrating waist and/or wrist activity level over user specified epochs, typically 1 min, while the person behaves in their natural environment for as many days, weeks, or months as are required to reach a diagnostic impression and/or evaluate/monitor treatment outcome.

Equipment

Tryon (2008) recently reviewed currently available actigraphs from multiple vendors. This section draws heavily on that article. Vendors are reviewed in alphabetical order. Actigraph LLC (www.theacti-graph.com) sells the GT1M series (http://www.theactigraph.com/productsGT1M.asp) which was developed from the CSA/MTI/Actigraphs. It also has a 30 Hz setting for measuring tremor. Sample data can be seen at http://www.theactigraph.com/actilife.asp.

Ambulatory Monitoring, Inc., (http://www.ambulatory-monitoring.com/) sell a variety of actigraphs including the Basic MotionLogger, the Basic MotionLoggter-L Actigraph which contains a light sensor, the MicroMini-Motionlogger® Actigraph. The Micro-Mini instrument family also includes three other devices: The Micro Light Sensor, the Micro Temperature Sensor, and the Micro Sound Sensor. Their Buzz-Bee Motionlogger is intended to provide an alternative to pharmacological management of hyperactive children.

The accompanying Action 4 software is used to initialize the actigraphs, download, graph, and analyze the data in many different ways.

Cambridge Neurotechnology Limited (http://www.camntech.com/h_ab.html) sells the Actiwatch AW7, the Actiwatch-L that simultaneously monitors light and activity levels, and their Actiwatch Mini. They also sell a Tremorwatch capable of measuring tremors in the 3 Hz to 11 Hz range.

IM Systems, Inc. (http://www.imsystems.net/) sells the Acti-Trac and the Digi-Track (http://www.imsystems.net/digitrac/digitrac.htm), and the Bio-Trainer Pro (http://www.imsystems.net/btpro/btpro.htm).

Mini Mitter (http://www.minimitter.com/) sells three actigraphs. The AW-16 and AW64 are standard actigraphs with event markers. Their Actiwatch-L comes with a light meter.

Pal Technologies Limited (http://www.paltechnologies.com/) makes a leg-worn actigraph (PACTIVPAL™) with software for classifying free-living activity into periods spent sitting, standing, and walking.

Tryon (2008) also reviewed electronic devices that claim to measures calories expended due to activity. They are accelerometer-based devices. Step counters are modern pedometers. They provide an inexpensive means of measuring activity level but require that someone accurately records the time they are put on and taken off so as to be able to compute steps/minute of wearing time. There is no longer any acceptable reason to assess activity level in clinical and/or research settings that does not at least make use of step counters.

Notes

1 Concern that clinical psychology follows the medical model is clearly misplaced regarding diagnosis because, with the exception of intelligence tests relative to the diagnosis of mental retardation, psychological testing is not used to guide or inform diagnoses as codified in the any of the Diagnostic and Statistical Manuals including the current fourth edition (American Psychiatric Association, 1994) and its text revision (American Psychiatric Association, 2000).

2 Psychological tests are frequently called instruments which imply that they are fundamentally the same as old fashioned "brass instruments" and/or modern computerized instruments which is not the case and why separate headings are used in this chapter to discuss important differences.

References

Achenbach, T. M., & Rescorla, L. A. (2001). *Manual for ASEBA School-Age Forms & Profiles.* Burlington: University of Vermont, Research Center for Children, Youth, & Families.

Ambrosini, P. J. (2000). Historical development and present status of the schedule for affective disorders and schizophrenia for school-age-children (K-SADS). *Journal of the American Academy of Child and Adolescent Psychiatry, 39,* 49–58.

American Educational Research Association, American Psychological Association, & National Council on Measurement in Education. (1999). *Standards for educational and psychological testing* (2nd ed.). Washington, DC: American Educational Research Association.

American Psychiatric Association (1994). *Diagnostic and statistical manual of mental disorders* (4th ed.). Washington DC: Author.

American Psychiatric Association. (2000). *Diagnostic and statistical manual of mental disorders* (4th ed., text revision). Washington, DC: Author.

Anastasi, A. (1976). *Psychological testing* (4th ed.). New York: Macmillan.

Angold, A., & Costello, E. J. (2000). The child and adolescent psychiatric assessment (CAPA). *Journal of the American Academy of Child and Adolescent Psychiatry, 39,* 39–48.

Antony, M. M., Orsillo, S. M., & Roemer, L. (Eds.), (2001). *Practitioner's guide to empirically based measures of anxiety.* New York: Kluwer Academic/Plenum Publishers.

Barkley, R. A. (1991). The ecological validity of laboratory and analogue assessment methods of ADHD. *Journal of Abnormal Child Psychology, 19,* 149–178.

Barlow, D. H. (1991). Introduction to the special issue on diagnoses, dimensions, and *DSM-IV*: The science of classification. *Journal of Abnormal Psychology, 100,* 243–244.

Blashfield, R. K., & Livesley, W. J. (1991). Metaphorical analysis of psychiatric classification as a psychological test. *Journal of Abnormal Psychology, 100,* 262–270.

Brown, T. A., & Barlow, D. H. (2005). Dimensional versus categorical classification of mental disorders in the fifth edition of the *Diagnostic and Statistical Manual of Mental Disorders* and beyond: Comment on the special section. *Journal of Abnormal Psychology, 114,* 551–556.

Brown, R. T., Freeman, W. S., Perrin, J. M., Stein, M. T., Amler, R. W., Feldman, H. M., et al. (2001). Prevalence and assessment of attention-deficit/hyperactivity disorder in primary school settings. *Pediatrics, 107*(3), E43.

Buss, A. (1989). Temperaments as personality traits. In G. A. Kohnstamm, J. E. Bates, & M. K. Rothbart (Eds.), *Temperament in childhood* (pp. 49–58). New York: Wiley.

Buss, A. H., & Plomin, R. (1975). *A temperament theory of personality development.* New York: Wiley.

Buss, A., & Plomin, R. (1984). *Temperament: Early developing personality traits.* Hillsdale, NJ: Lawrence Erlbaum.

Caldwell–Andrews, A. A., & Kain, Z. N. (2006). Psychological predictors of postoperative sleep in children undergoing outpatient surgery. *Paediatric Anaesthesia, 16,* 144–151.

Campbell, D. T. & Fiske, D. W. (1959). Convergent and discriminant validity by a multitrait-multimethod matrix. *Psychological Bulletin, 56,* 81–105.

Comrey, A. L. (1994). *Manual and Handbook of Interpretations for the Comrey Personality Scales.* San Diego, CA: EDITs Publishers.

Carson, R. C. (1991). Dilemmas in the pathway of the *DSM-IV*. *Journal of Abnormal Psychology, 100,* 302–307.

Chorpita, B. F., & Taylor, A. A. (2001). Behavioral assessment of anxiety disorders. In M. M., Anthony, S. M. Orsillo, & L. Roemer (Eds.), *Practitioner's guide to empirically based measures of anxiety* (pp. 19–24). New York: Kluwer Academic/Plenum Publishers.

Collett, B. R., Ohan, J. L., & Myers, K. M. (2003). Ten-year review of rating scales: Scales assessing attention-deficit/hyperactivity disorder. *Journal of the American Academy of Child and Adolescent Psychiatry, 42,* 1015–1037.

Clark, L. A. (2005). Temperament as a unifying basis for personality and psychopathology. *Journal of Abnormal Psychology, 114,* 505–521.

Davidsohn, I., & Henry, J. B. (1974). *Todd-Sanford clinical diagnosis by laboratory methods*. Philadelphia: W. B. Saunders Co..

Doss, A. J. (2005). Evidence-based diagnosis: Incorporating diagnostic instruments into clinical practice. *Journal of the American Academy of Child and Adolescent Psychiatry, 44,* 947–952.

Eaton, W. O., & Saudino, K. J. (1992). Prenatal activity level as a temperament dimension? Individual differences and developmental functions in fetal movement. *Infant Behavior and Development, 15,* 57–70.

Epstein, S., (1979). The stability of behavior: I. On predicting most of the people much of the time. *Journal of Personality and Social Psychology, 37,* 1097–1126.

Epstein, S. (1980). The stability of behavior: II. Implications for psychological research. *American Psychologist, 35,* 790–806.

Epstein, S. (1983). Aggregation and beyond: Some basic issues on the prediction of behavior. *Journal of Personality, 51,* 360–392.

Epstein, S. (1986). Does aggregation produce spuriously high estimates of behavior stability? *Journal of Personality and Social Psychology, 50,* 1199–1210.

Forsyth, J. P., & Karekla, M. (2001). Biological challenge in the assessment of anxiety disorders. In M. M., Anthony, S. M. Orsillo, & L. Roemer (Eds.), *Practitioner's guide to empirically based measures of anxiety* (pp. 31–36). New York: Kluwer Academic/Plenum Publishers.

Frances, A. J., First, M. B., Widiger, T. A., Miele, G. M., Tilly, S. M., Davis, W. W., & Pincus, H. A. (1991). An A to Z guide to DSM-IV conundrums. *Journal of Abnormal Psychology, 100,* 407–412.

Goldsmith, H. H., Buss, A. H., Plomin, R., Rothbart, M. K., Thomas, A., Chess, S., et al. (1987). Roundtable: What is temperament? Four approaches. *Child Development, 58,* 505–529.

Gorlyn, M., Keilp, J. G., Tryon, W. W., & Mann, J. J. (2005). Performance test correlates of component factors of impulsivity. *Personality and Individual Differences, 38,* 1549–1559.

Hauri, P. J. (1999). Evaluation of a sleep switch device. *Sleep, 22,* 1110–1117.

Kain, Z. N., Mayes, L. C., Caldwell–Andrews, A. A., Alexander, G. M., Krivutza, D., Teague, B. A., W et al. (2002). Sleeping characteristics of children undergoing outpatient elective surgery. *Anesthesiology 97,* 1093–1101.

Kario, K., Schwartz, J. E., Davidson, K. W., & Pickering, T. G. (2001) Gender differences in associations of diurnal blood pressure variation, awake physical activity, and sleep quality with negative affect: the work site blood pressure study. *Hypertension, 38,* 997–1002.

Kamphaus, R. W., & Frick, P. J. (1996). *Clinical assessment of child and adolescent personality and behavior.* New York: Allyn & Bacon.

Kamphaus, R. W., & Frick, P. J. (2005). *Clinical assessment of child and adolescent personality and behavior* (pp. 255–271, 2nd ed.). New York: Springer.

Kaufman, J., Birmaher, B., Brent, D., Rao, U., Flynn, C., Moreci, P., et al. (1997). Schedule for affective disorders and schizophrenia for school-age children-present and lifetime version (K-SADS-PL): Initial reliability and validity data. *Journal of the American Academy of Child and Adolescent Psychiatry, 36* 980–988.

Kendell, R. E. (1991). Relationship between the *DSM-IV* and the *ICD-10. Journal of Abnormal Psychology, 100,* 297–301.

Kruger, R. F., Caspi, A., Moffitt, T. E., & Silva, P. A. (1998). The structure and stability of common mental disorders (*DSM-III-R*): A longitudinal-Epidemiological study. *Journal of Abnormal Psychology, 107,* 216–227.

Krueger, R. F., Markdon, K. E., Patrick, C. J., & Iacono, W. G. (2005). Externalizing psychopathology in adulthood: A dimensional-spectrum conceptualization and its implications for *DSM-V. Journal of Abnormal Psychology, 114,* 537–550.

Kuo, H. H., Chiu, M. J., Liao, W. C., & Hwang, S. L. (2006). Quality of sleep and related factors during chemotherapy in patients with stage I/II breast cancer. *Journal of Formosan Medical Association, 105,* 64–69.

Logan, G. D. (1994). On the ability to inhibit thought and action. A user's guide to the stop signal paradigm. In D. Dagenbach & T. H. Carr (Eds.), *Inhibitory processes in attention, memory, and language.* San Diego: Academic Press.

Logan, G. D., & Burkell, J. (1986). Dependence and independence in responding to double stimulation: A comparison of stop, change, and dual-task paradigms. *Journal of Experimental Psychology Human Perception and Performance, 12,* 549–563.

Logan, G. D., & Cowan, W. B. (1984). On the ability to inhibit thought and action: A theory of an act of control. *Psychological Review, 91,* 295 327.

Malgady, R., Rogler, L. H., & Tryon, W. W. (1992). Issues of validity in the Diagnostic Interview Schedule. *Journal of Psychiatric Research, 26,* 59–67.

Maser, J. D., Kaelber, C., & Weise, R. E. (1991). International use and attitudes toward *DSM-III* and *DSM-III-R*: Growing consensus in psychiatric classification. *Journal of Abnormal Psychology, 100,* 271–279.

McKay, D., Piacentini, J., Greisberg, S., Graae, F., Jaffer, M., Miller, J., et al. (2003). The Children's Yale-Brown Obsessive-Compulsive Scale: Item structure in an outpatient setting. *Psychological Assessment, 15,* 578–581.

Millon, T. (1991). Classification in psychopathology: Rationale, alternatives, and standards. *Journal of Abnormal Psychology, 100,* 245–261.

Morey, L. C. (1991). Classification of mental disorder as a collection of hypothetical constructs. *Journal of Abnormal Psychology, 100,* 289–293.

Murphy, L. L., Plake, B. S, & Spies, R. A. (Eds). (2006). *Tests in print VII*. Lincoln, NE: Buros Institute of Mental Measurements.

National Institutes of Health (2000). National Institutes of Health consensus development conference statement: Diagnosis and treatment of Attention-Deficit/Hyperactivity Disorder (ADHD). *Journal of the American Academy of Child Adolescent Psychiatry, 39,* 182–193.

Nelson, J., & Harvey, A. G. (2002). The Differential Functions of Imagery and Verbal Thought in Insomnia. *Journal of Abnormal psychology, 111,* 665–669.

Nelson–Gray, R. O. (1991). *DSM-IV*: Empirical guidelines from psychometrics. *Journal of Abnormal Psychology, 100,* 308–315.

Nezu, A. M., Ronan, G. F., Meadows, E. A., & McClure, K. S. (Eds.), (2000). Practitioner's guide to empirically based measures of anxiety. New York: Kluwer Academic/Plenum Publishers.

Plake, B. S., Murphy, L. L., & Spies, R. A. (Eds.) (2005). *The sixteenth mental measurements yearbook*. Lincoln, NE: Buros Institute of Mental Measurements.

Reich, W. (2000). Diagnostic Interview for Children and Adolescents (DICA). *Journal of the American Academy of Child and Adolescent Psychiatry, 39,* 59–66.

Reynolds, C. R., & Kamphaus, R. W. (2006?). *Behavior assessment system for children* (2nd ed.). Bloomington, MN: Pearson Assessments.

Riccio, C. A., Reynolds, C. R., & Lowe, P. A. (2001). *Clinical applications of continuous performance tests: Measuring attention and impulsive responding in children and adults.* New York: Wiley.

Rogler, L. H., Malgady, R. & Tryon, W. W. (1992). Evaluation of mental health issues of memory in the Diagnostic Interview Schedule. *Journal of Nervous and Mental Disease, 180,* 215–222.

Rosvold, H. E., Mirsky, A., Sarason, I., Bransome, E. D. Jr., & Beck, L. H. (1956). A continuous performance test of brain damage. *Journal of Consulting Psychology, 20,* 343–350.

Schachar, R., & Logan, G. D. (1990a). Impulsivity and inhibitory control in normal development and childhood psychopathology. *Developmental Psychology, 26,* 710–720.

Schachar, R., & Logan, G. D. (1990b). Are hyperactive children deficient in attentional capacity? *Journal of Abnormal Child Psychology, 18,* 493–513.

Schachar, R., Tannock, R., & Logan, G. (1993). Inhibitory control, impulsiveness, and attention deficit hyperactivity disorder. *Clinical Psychology Review, 13,* 721–739.

Shaffer, D., Fisher, P., Lucas, C., Dulcan, M., & Schwab–Stone, M. (2000). NIMH Diagnostic Interview Schedule for Children Version IV (NIMH *DISC-IV*): description, differences from previous versions, and reliability of some common diagnoses. *Journal of the American Academy of Child and Adolescent Psychiatry, 39,* 28–38.

Shiner, R. L. (1998). How shall we speak of children's personalities in middle childhood? A preliminary taxonomy. *Psychological Bulletin, 124,* 308–332.

Solanto, M. V., & Alvir, J. M. J. (in press). Reliability of *DSM-IV* Symptom Ratings of AD/HD: Implications for *DSM-V*. *Journal of Attention Disorders.*

Spitzer, R. L. (1991). An outsider-insider's views about revising the *DSMs*. *Journal of Abnormal Psychology, 100*, 294–296.

Tani, P., Lindberg, N., Nieminen–von Wendt, T., von Wendt, L., Alanko, L., Appelberg, B., et al. (2005). Actigraphic assessment of sleep in young adults with Asperger syndrome. *Psychiatry and Clinical Neurosciences, 59(2)*, 206–208.

Teicher, M. H. (1995). Actigraphy and motion analysis: New tools for psychiatry. *Harvard Review of Psychiatry, 3*, 18–35.

Teicher, M. H., Ito, Y., Glod, C. A., & Barber, N. I. (1996). Objective measurement of hyperactivity and attentional problems in ADHD. *Journal of the American Academy of Child & Adolescent Psychiatry, 35*, 334–342.

Tryon, W. W. (1991). *Activity measurement in psychology and medicine*. New York: Plenum.

Tryon, W. W. (1996a). Instrument driven theory. *Journal of Mind and Behavior, 17*, 21–30.

Tryon, W. W. (1996b). Measurement units and theory construction. *Journal of Mind and Behavior, 17*, 213–227.

Tryon, W. W. (1996c). Nocturnal activity and sleep assessment. *Clinical Psychology Review, 16*, 197–213.

Tryon, W. W. (2007) History and theoretical foundations. In M. Hersen & A. M. Gross (Eds.) *Handbook of Clinical Psychology, Volume 1: Adults* (pp. 3-37). New York: John Wiley & Sons.

Tryon, W. W. (2002). Activity level and *DSM-IV*. In S. Turner & M. Hersen (Eds.). *Adult psychopathology and diagnosis* (4th. ed., pp. 547–577). NY: Wiley.

Tryon, W. W. (2004). Issues of validity in actigraphic sleep assessment. *Sleep, 27*, 158–165.

Tryon, W. W. (2005). The reliability and validity of two ambulatory monitoring actigraphs. *Behavior Research Methods Instruments & Computers, 37*, 492–497.

Tryon, W. W. (2006). Activity Measurement. In M. Hersen (Ed.). *Clinician's handbook of adult behavioral assessment* (pp. 85–120). Boston: Elsevier.

Tryon, W. W. (2008) Methods of measuring human activity. *Journal of Behavioral Analysis in Health, Sports, Fitness, and Medicine, 1*, 58–71. http://www.jbahsfm.com/DOCUMENTS/vol1num1/JBAIISFM%20v1n1%20TRYON%2058-71.pdf.

Tryon, W. W., & Bernstein, D. (2002). Understanding measurement. In J. C. Thomas and M. Hersen (Eds.). *Understanding Research in Clinical and Counseling Psychology: A textbook* (pp. 27–68). Mahwah, NJ: Earlbaum.

Tryon, W. W., & Pinto, L. P. (1994). Comparing activity measurements and ratings. *Behavior Modification, 18*, 251–261.

Tryon, W. W., & Williams, R. (1996). Fully proportional actigraphy: A new instrument. *Behavior Research Methods Instruments & Computers, 28*, 392–403.

Widiger, T. A., Frances, A. J., Pincus, H. A., Davis, W. W., & First, M. B. (1991). Toward an empirical classification for the *DSM-IV*. *Journal of Abnormal Psychology, 100*, 280–288.

Yartz, A. R., Hawk, Jr., L. W. (2001). Psychophysiological assessment of anxiety: Tales from the heart. In M. M., Anthony, S. M. Orsillo, & L. Roemer (Eds.), *Practitioner's guide to empirically based measures of anxiety* (pp. 25–30). New York: Kluwer Academic/ Plenum Publishers.

Widiger, T. A., & Samuel, D. B. (2005). Diagnostic categories or dimensions? A question for the *Diagnostic and Statistical Manual of Mental Disorders-Fifth Edition. Journal of Abnormal Psychology, 114,* 494–504.

Wicklow, A., & Espie, C. A. (2000). Intrusive thoughts and their relationship to actigraphic measurement of sleep: toward a cognitive model of insomnia. *Behaviour Research and Therapy, 38,* 679–693.

9

Information Processing and Neuroscience Features of Anxiety: Refining the Bases for Diagnosis

Dean McKay
Nathan Thoma
Brian Pilecki

Across disciplines, research on human emotion has converged on a perspective that views it as an adaptive and protective response which prepares humans for action (Bradley & Lang, 2007; Ekman, 1992; Lang, 1979; Mathews & MacLeod, 1994; Oatley & Johnson-Laird, 1987; Ohman, 1993; Plutchik, 1984; Williams, Watts, MacLeod, & Mathews, 1997). Emotional disorders in this context are seen as adaptive responses which are misplaced, exaggerated, or underdeveloped, with the responses to the environment incorrect in the context of situational constraints. Anxiety disorders in particular are often seen centering on exaggerated fear responses in conjunction with excessively low thresholds for perceiving various types of threat (Barlow, 2002).

Cognitive science approaches to understanding anxiety and anxiety disorders, thus, focus on understanding the cognitive processes, which interact with these emotional responses, ranging from bottom–up perceptual processes to top–down evaluative and attentional control processes. Understanding such inner processes has implications for the etiology, maintenance, and nosology of anxiety disorders. Cognitive science has used a variety of techniques to assess and model the inner workings of the mind with a special focus on the areas of attention, memory, and interpretation. Recent research has extended these basic modeling procedures to include the evaluation of specific brain area activation when engaged in tasks that evaluate cognitive biases. This chapter will examine several methodological approaches to examining different cognitive biases, and consider the degree that these findings support the nosological validity of different diagnoses and the implications of this body of research for diagnosis.

Biases of Attention Processing

The area of attentional bias in emotional disorders has been extensively explored, with numerous experimental studies in the literature focusing on anxiety and anxiety disorders (for a quantitative summary, see Bar-Haim, Pergamin, Bakermans-Kranenberg, & van Ijzendoorn, 2007). The majority of these studies employ four basic paradigms: the emotional Stroop task, the dot-probe task, emotional spatial cueing, and a visual search task. Emotional spatial cueing studies have shown somewhat mixed results (e.g., Broomfield & Turpin, 2005). The Stroop task, and variants of it, has been used extensively, whereas the other differential attention methodologies have been used less frequently.

Emotional Stroop Task and Its Variants

In the emotional Stroop task, a word written in colored ink is shown to a subject for a brief period of time and the subject is asked to name the color of the word as quickly as possible (Stroop, 1935; for a review see C. M. MacLeod, 1991; a detailed description of Stroop task variants is in Williams et al., 1997). Before discussing specific findings related to anxiety conditions, it is worth noting that methodological approaches to designing Stroop tasks can result in significant differences in response latency. For example, a recent meta-analytic review concluded that at longer durations, threat-related words produced a robust response latency with a medium effect ($d = 0.57$, CI = 0.50, 0.64) across persons with various anxiety disorders as well as analogue groups rated high in anxiety (Bar-Haim et al., 2007). In masked presentation, a small effect was detected, but this effect was less robust, with a confidence interval that included zero ($d = 0.23$, CI = –0.10, 0.35). A differential response latency to threat-related words did not occur in normal or low-anxious individuals at either supraliminal or subliminal exposures.

It is interesting to note that even under masked conditions, the content of words disrupts attention when the word types have personal salience. This has been explained by the parallel distributed processing model (Cohen, Dunbar, & McClelland, 1990). Essentially, this model suggests that when confronted with the task of color naming, individuals also automatically read and process the meaning of the word itself, leading to activation of relevant neural connections associated with the specific word type. Among unselected samples, strong cues associated with anxiety lead to attention biases among all participants, whereas more subtle cues lead to delayed color naming only in participants with specific anxious states (Mathews & Mackintosh, 1998). To illustrate, the word 'hepatitis' would lead to biased responses in virtually all respondents. However, the word 'doorknob' would lead to biased responses only in contamination-fearful respondents (owing to the common concern that doorknobs are touched by many individuals and are deemed dirty or contaminated). This suggests that the ability to examine the relevant anxiety construct is determined by the severity of anxious symptoms and specificity of the content of material to be recognized in a Stroop task.

Advances in brain imaging methodology have permitted researchers to examine specific regional activation while engaged in specific attention tasks. Several of these types of investigations have been conducted with anxious participants, as well as those with specific anxiety disorders, using the Stroop task. To illustrate, Engels et al. (2007) found that participants with elevated anxious arousal responded more slowly to threat-related words, and that these responses were associated with activation in the inferior frontal region when evaluated with functional magnetic resonance imaging (fMRI). This region is associated with speech production, which is consistent with the parallel distributed processing model. Additionally, Engels et al. also found activation in the right temporalparietal region, an area previously hypothesized as active in response to immediate threat (i.e., Compton et al., 2003).

While several investigations have examined brain activation in conjunction with emotional Stroop performance for general anxiety, there have also been several studies examining specific anxiety disorder diagnoses and brain area activation while completing an emotional Stroop test. Shin et al. (2001) used fMRI to examine brain area activation during an emotional Stroop among Vietnam combat veterans with posttraumatic stress disorder (PTSD) compared to a group without PTSD. They found reduced activation in the anterior cingulate nucleus among the PTSD participants, which they suggested was supportive of the hypothesis of reduced inhibition of neural systems involved in fear activation via the prefrontal cortex. The hypothesized relation between the anterior cingulate nucleus and reduced inhibition in fear circuitry (see chapter 5 this volume) was examined in individuals with obsessive–compulsive disorder (OCD) by Nakao, et al. (2005). Using a Chinese sample of individuals with OCD, and an emotional Stroop task with Chinese characters, the authors likewise found support for this hypothesis, whereby individuals with OCD had reduced activation in the anterior cingulate nucleus during threat-relevant information. Finally, in a test of the role of the anterior cingulate nucleus, as well as the orbitofrontal and dorsolateral prefrontal cortexes, activation in all areas of interest significantly changed following successful treatment for OCD symptoms using either medication (fluvoxamine) or cognitive–behavior therapy (Nakao et al., 2005). Again, these changes were revealed by subjecting participants to an emotional Stroop task before and after treatment while undergoing fMRI scans.

The utility of investigations examining the conjoint cognitive biases associated with the Stroop task and correlated brain activation is the potential to determine specificity of brain activation associated with particular disorders. This would contribute to a more evolved nosology of anxiety disorders. Such findings are summarized in Table 9.1. As the reviewed studies illustrate, however, some areas of brain

9.1 Emotional Stroop Test and Associated Brain Areas

Authors	Year	N	Female	n	Diagnosis	Imaging	Task	Areas Implicated
Engels et al.	2007	42	57%	11	high PSWQ/ low MASQ	fMRI	emotional Stroop	left inferior frontal gyrus, left inferior temporal gyrus, left inferior parietal lobule
				13	low PSWQ/ high MASQ			right inferior temporal gyrus
				18	control			right cerebellum, left medial frontal gyrus, left superior temporal gyrus,
Nakao et al.	2005	38	63%	24	OCD	fMRI	Stroop (Chinese)	DLPFC, ACC, caudate nucleus, thalamus, parietal cortex, cerebellum
				14	control			(same regions)
Nakao et al.	2004	10	60%	10	OCD (pre vs. post Tx)	fMRI	Sx provocation	less activation in orbitofrontal, DLPFC, & ACC
							Stroop (Chinese)	increased activation in parietal cortex and cerebellum
Shin et al.	2001	16	0%	8	controls	fMRI	emotional Stroop	rostral anterior cingulated
				8	PTSD			no increased activation

Note: PSWQ = Penn State worry questionnaire; MASQ = Mood anxiety symptom questionnaire; fMRI = functional magnetic resonance imaging; OCD = obsessive compulsive disorder; DLPFC = dorsolateral prefrontal cortex; ACC = anterior cingulate cortex; Tx = treatment: either behavioral therapy or pharmacotherapy; Sx = symptom; PTSD = posttraumatic stress disorder.

activation may be more related to specific types of symptoms rather than particular disorders. For example, the anterior cingulate nucleus is implicated in both PTSD and OCD (and possibly other anxiety disorders).

The available literature related to attention bias using the Stroop task, therefore, may not validate the various anxiety disorders. Instead, the findings from this body of research appears to more consistently show that anxious individuals, regardless of diagnosis, show greater response latencies to threatening information, regardless of diagnosis. One plausible potential alternative explanation is that response biases are a function of mood congruence rather than diagnosis. For example, depressed individuals show similar biases when the material presented is related to sad mood or depression themed (i.e., Mitterschiffthaler, et al., 2008). This has also been shown in individuals with elevated worry, whose latencies were observed immediately following a worry-induction interview, but closer to that of nonworriers following a pleasant imagery interview (McKay, 2005, Experiment 2).

Dot-Probe and Other Attention Bias Tasks

The emotional Stroop task has been criticized on the grounds that the results can be considered ambiguous (e.g., Algom, Chajut, & Lev 2004; MacLeod, Mathews, & Tata, 1986; Mathews & MacLeod 2005). The differential latency in response time for threat-related words may not be the result of attentional allotment to threat, but rather the triggering of an emotional response which then disrupts ongoing attentional focus on the task at hand (Mathews & MacLeod, 2005). In the context of brain area activation, this could mask the disorder-specific brain areas by activating more general threat-relevant cortical areas. MacLeod et al. (1986) developed the dot-probe task to further differentiate the processes of threat-related attentional allotment and emotional activation. Similar to the Stroop task, response latencies are the critical variable. In this instance, the participant must examine competing material just prior to indicating the location of a dot, which appears on either the left or right side of the screen after the target material is removed from the screen. Thus, the task is believed to differentiate attentional facilitation from attentional distraction, since response latencies may be faster (i.e., when the dot shows up in place of threatening information) or slower (when the dot replaces other material, and the participant's attention was directed to the other side where threatening information appeared). Bar-Haim et al. (2007) found that clinically anxious and undiagnosed high-anxious subjects showed facilitated attention to threat-related stimuli, using both words and pictures (typically faces). A medium effect size was found in subliminal conditions ($d = 0.65$, CI = 0.42, 0.88), and a small effect in supraliminal conditions ($d = 0.29$, CI = 0.11, 0.47). These findings rule out the hypothesis that the underlying cognitive processes are due solely to disrupted attention, and support the idea that anxiety is related to either exaggerated attention to threat or a lower threshold for threat detection.

Compared to the Stroop task, there have been fewer investigations coupling the dot-probe with brain imaging techniques. However, one investigation showed that rather than a specific dysfunctional brain activation among anxious participants, there was an exaggerated response away from threat among extraverted participants in the right fusiform gyrus, which the authors suggested was a result of increased effort to avoid the negative stimuli and search for neutral or positive stimuli (Amin, Constable, & Canli, 2004).

Despite the small number of imaging studies employing the dot-probe methodology, this approach remains promising for future research due to its value in resolving the ambiguities associated with the more traditional Stroop test, as well as having greater ecological validity. In natural environments, it would be more typical to face a range of stimuli, such as with the dot-probe methodology, rather than only to face threatening stimuli, as with the Stroop. However, at the present time, the findings are again more consistent with a bias toward mood congruent information, rather than disorder specific information. Again, in this case there is some preliminary research supporting this position (McKay, 2005, experiment 3).

Methodological Differences Between Stroop and Dot-Probe Tasks

In the meta-analysis by Bar-Haim et al. (2007) effect sizes for the Stroop and dot probe tasks did not differ significantly between anxiety diagnoses. Attentional bias for normal controls was insignificant, and in general has not been found except in cases where the stimuli are presented in blocked designs and therefore due instead to cumulative effects. Given the similar effect sizes across anxiety disorders and the lack of an effect in normal controls, attentional bias could represent a common cognitive process among those with clinical varieties of anxiety disorders. Specificity of stimuli, geared toward particular disorders in various studies, may play an additional role in producing attentional bias in these different clinical groups. Studies using clinical populations did not differ in effect size from those using high-anxious, but subclinical, subjects for either task. However, clinical populations were typically compared to normals, whereas high-anxious subjects were typically compared to low-anxious subjects. Thus, it is not clear if the tasks are detecting underlying anxiety proneness, or are detecting an effect directly related to anxiety per se.

Stroop and dot-probe studies of attentional bias in anxiety have used a wide variety of subject pools, ranging from normals who self-report high anxiety levels, to various clinical groups; including those with generalized anxiety disorder (GAD), social phobia, specific phobia, panic disorder (PD), OCD, and PTSD. The specificity of the stimuli in relation to the particular concerns of the subjects being studied appears to play an important role in the effect of attentional bias (see Mineka, Rafaeli, & Yovel, 2003; Mathews & MacLeod, 2005). If it can be shown that clinical groups differ from each other in their response to different types of stimuli, this understanding can be of particular interest in building or validating a given nosology of anxiety disorders. However, in most instances a substantial bias for general threat information has also been observed. Therefore, in effect, there is a specificity of bias for disorder specific stimuli, and a general bias for anxiety stimuli. This is not necessarily supportive of specific diagnoses, however. Consider that in studies of attention biases, material related to certain states may also produce strong biases. For example, Jones, Stacy, and Martin (2002) found a strong stroop bias in unselect individuals immediately prior to a dental exam.

Across anxious subjects, stimuli with positive valence do not trigger attention biases as consistently as stimuli with only negative valence. Thus, the general emotionality hypothesis, stating that anxious participants show biases for anxiety-relevant words even if in the positive direction (i.e., relaxed), has not been supported (Mineka et al., 2003). Studies of subjects with GAD, for example, have shown that these participants are responsive to a wide variety of negative stimuli, ranging from angry faces to threat-related words such as "emergency," "hostile," and "attack," as well as depression-related words such as "sadness," "dejected," and "worthless" (see Mogg & Bradley, 2005). There is also evidence that there is a greater effect within GAD groups for words that address their particular concerns, such as words related to social threat for those with social anxiety or words related to physical illness for those with health worries (e.g., Mathews & MacLeod, 1985; Mogg, Mathews, & Eysenck, 1992). So, while there is a general bias toward negative valence words, there is also evidence of disorder specific biases in some cases. This illustrates a problem in the literature on attention biases for threatening information: that in many instances there is limited specificity of effect. As illustrated here, this could be taken as support for the uniqueness of GAD, or alternatively it could be supportive of GAD forming part of an anxious-misery class of disorders, placing it in a class with depression as much as with other anxiety disorders (i.e., Mennin et al., 2008).

The evidence is somewhat mixed for the specificity of attentional bias toward socially threatening words for social phobics (see Bogels & Mansell, 2004). Some studies do show that individuals with social anxiety disorder (SAD) demonstrate greater response latency in the emotional Stroop task for social threatening words than physically threatening words (e.g., Becker, Rinck, Margraf, & Roth, 2001; Lundh & Ost, 1996). One study even showed specificity of socially threatening cues for subtypes of SAD within an SAD sample (McNeil et al., 1995). Additionally, evidence has been found for greater attention to socially threatening stimuli for social phobics vs attention to physically threatening words for subjects with PD (Hope, Rapee, Heimberg, Dombeck, 1990). However, other studies have failed to find evidence for greater attention to socially threatening words among socially anxious individuals (e.g., Amir, Elias, Klumpp, & Przeworski, 2003; Horenstein & Segui, 1997). Subjects with specific phobias have shown attentional bias toward stimuli related to their specific phobic objects, including spiders (Watts, McKenna, Sharrock, & Trezise, 1986) and snakes (Mathews & Sebastian, 1993). Subjects with PD have shown greater attention to threatening bodily sensation words (e.g., Lang & Sarmiento, 2004). However PD subjects, as well as subjects with hypochondriasis, have also shown attentional bias toward panic-related and OCD-related words, while OCD subjects did not show any attentional bias (van den Heuvel et al., 2005). There is some support, however, for specificity in attentional bias in OCD, though there are also studies which have failed to replicate results in which OCD subjects respond differentially to OCD-related stimuli (see Muller & Roberts, 2005). Studies of subjects with PTSD have shown evidence for specificity of attentional bias to trauma-related words, although some contradictory studies failed to find any specificity (see Constans, 2005).

Taken together, these studies of different clinical populations only partially support the specificity hypothesis. The difficulties inherent in obtaining "pure" diagnoses are likely to be one of the confounds underlying the inconsistent results, as comorbidities are common among the anxiety disorders, and it is even unclear if the wide range of disorders in the *Diagnostic And Statistical Manual Of Mental Disorders* (*DSM*) are really unique, taxometrically valid entities (i.e., Krueger, 1999). Whether pure diagnoses confound the findings or not, there is a fundamental difficulty in that the most consistent finding involving attention bias is toward general threat information. There is the additional problem that most studies of clinical subjects attempting to test the specificity of attentional biases do not test clinical groups against each other directly, but rather, use normal controls for comparisons. Because each study tends to vary the experimental parameters to lesser and greater degrees, comparisons between clinical groups from different studies are not necessarily valid. Further research is needed to clarify this picture.

It is likely that both a general attentional bias across the anxiety disorders, as well as specific attentional biases relevant to particular groups' concerns, play roles in generating the emotional Stroop and dot-probe effects. It is also likely that the more idiographic the stimuli, the more consistent and specific the results will be. Indeed, even nonclinical control participants have shown the attentional bias effect when words that are personally relevant to their concerns have been elicited (Riemann & McNally, 1995). To use attentional bias studies, to fully inform the formation of a nosology of emotional disorders, it may be necessary to conduct a large-scale study of persons with a wide variety of emotional disorders incorporating the elicitation of idiographic stimuli from each subject. Subjects showing attentional bias could be included in a cluster analysis to derive groupings according to commonalities in the stimuli they find threatening. It is likely that this would validate other factor-analytic approaches to nosology formation (i.e., Krueger, 1999; Watson, 2005). The main conclusion that can currently be drawn from studies in attentional bias that may relate to nosology is that persons with anxiety disorders share a heightened attention to perceived threat, which can be considered an exaggerated response that functions adaptively in normals.

Distinct and Overlapping Aspects of Anxiety and Depression

Although threat-related attentional bias has been found across the anxiety disorders, very few studies have found attentional biases in depressed subjects (see Mineka et al., 2003; Mogg & Bradley, 2005). Studies have failed to find attentional biases in depressed subjects even when compared directly to subjects with GAD in whom the bias is reliably detected (e.g., Mogg, Bradley, Williams, & Mathews, 1993). This finding holds even when the depressed group also has comorbid GAD (Bradley, Mogg, Millar, & White, 1995). In the few studies in which an attentional bias for mood-congruent material has been found in depressed subjects, the exposure times have generally been long (e.g., 2000 milliseconds), which may allow for elaborative processing to take place (e.g., Gotlib & Cane, 1987; Segal, Truchon, Gemar, Guirguis, & Horowitz, 1995). The distinct findings for anxiety disorders versus depression indicate that despite the common comorbidity of anxiety and depression, they can be considered separable phenomena, with distinct cognitive signatures. This is an important finding in light of the difficulty in distinguishing these disorders through self-report measures, and may help to inform recent writing suggesting that GAD and major depressive disorders (MDD) share common features (e.g., Krueger & Markon, 2006; Mennin et al., 2008; Watson, 2005). This may be so for other anxiety disorders and MDD, but the data has not adequately borne this out. The larger category of negative affect can be seen as containing both anxiety and depression. Exaggerated attention to threat may go along with such tendencies for negative affect, and depression can then be seen as an additive process which overlays and suppresses the active attentional vigilance.

Some have suggested that the distinction between depression and anxiety can be understood as being underpinned by a cognitive focus on the past in depression, through rumination and/or elaboration of cognitive stimuli, versus a focus on the future with anxiety, through worry and/or attention toward potential threat stimuli (e.g., Mineka et al., 2003). This may be true for the types of attentional processes assessed by such paradigms as the Stroop and the dot-probe. However, ongoing cognitive processes such as rumination and worry would appear to lump anxiety and depression together, rather than further split them apart. Just as comorbidity is common between depression and anxiety, rumination and worry each appear to be equally associated with depression and anxiety (Fresco, Frankel, Mennin, Turk, & Heimberg, 2002). A larger factor of repetitive negative ideation has been identified as a common cognitive process subsuming both rumination and worry (Segerstrom, Tsao, Alden, & Craske, 2000; Segerstrom, Stanton, Alden, & Shortridge, 2003). Thus, some cognitive aspects of depression and anxiety do overlap, again pointing to the utility of a superordinate category of distress (cf. Watson, 2005).

Memory and Information Processing in Anxiety

Cognitive science investigations into the area of memory tend to show distinctions between anxiety and depression. Investigations into biased memory in the emotional disorders have included the study of autobiographical memory, explicit memory, and implicit memory. Depressed persons have been found to have mood-congruent biases in all three areas. When asked to freely recall a personal memory in response to a word or phrase, depressed persons respond with overgeneralized memories rather than specific episodes of their lives (see Healy & Williams, 1999). Depression is also associated with better recall for negative material than neutral or positive stimuli that are learned in experimental settings, with or without mood induction (see Matt, Vazquez, & Campbell, 1992). Studies have shown that depression is associated with implicit memory biases as well [see Table 9.2] (see Ruiz–Caballero & Gonzalez, 1994). Studies of memory bias in anxiety, whether general or disorder specific, have been less consistent. For example, investigations of autobiographical memory in anxious subjects have been mixed (cf. Burke & Mathews, 1992; Levy & Mineka, 1998). Studies of explicit memory tasks involving recall and recognition across the anxiety disorders have also received mixed support, with the exception of PD (see C. MacLeod, 1999; Mathews & MacLeod, 2005). Subjects with PD have been shown to consistently recall a greater amount of panic-related as well as general threat-related material. Such a distinction suggests unique cognitive processes in PD, possibly validating PD as a diagnostic category. The nature of the cognitive processes which elicit memory effects in PD, but not in other anxiety disorders, is not known. Studies of implicit memory across the anxiety disorders have been inconsistent, with some reviewers concluding a lack of support (e.g., Mineka et al., 2003) and other reviewers concluding that there is modest support for such a bias (e.g., Coles & Heimberg, 2002). Mathews & MacLeod (2005) have made a compelling case that the few memory biases that have been found in the anxiety disorders are due to biased encoding rather than biased retrieval. This again emphasizes the importance of attention toward threat in the anxiety disorders.

Research examining the neural substrates associated with memory biases in anxiety disorders has primarily concentrated on PTSD. Consistent with the research on attention, the anterior cingulate nucleus appears involved in memory functioning and content biases in PTSD (i.e., Geuze et al., 2007; Hou et al., 2007; Lanius et al., 2003, 2004). Aside from the focus on memory in PTSD, there has been little research into brain localization for emotionally related memory formation. However, one study was conducted that involved auditory presentation of threatening words and recall while undergoing fMRI (Maddock and Buonocore, 1997). It was found that the left posterior cingulate nucleus was more activated for threat related words among participants who scored in the significant range for trait anxiety.

Does memory bias research hold promise for determining specific brain mechanisms involved in different anxiety disorders? While a large body of research has examined information processing biases among different anxiety disorders, the inclusion of brain imaging methodology in research on memory bias has been limited. Whereas the aforementioned research on brain area involvement in PTSD, where several different brain areas have been implicated in individual studies, the only one that has

9.2 Memory Bias and Associated Brain Areas

Authors	Year	N	Female	n	Diagnosis	Imaging	Task	Areas Implicated
Geuze et al.	2008	24	0%	12	PTSD	fMRI	neutral word-pairs, encoding	decreased activity in frontal cortex, increased activity in temporal cortex
				12	controls		neutral word-pairs, retrieval	decreased activity in right frontal cortex, bilateral middle temporal gyri, left posterior hippocampus
				12	controls			no increased activation
Hou et al.	2007	28	0%	10	PTSD	fMRI	trauma-related STM recall	inferior frontal gyrus, middle frontal gyrus, right parahippocampal gyrus
				7	controls			
Lanius et al.	2003	20	N/A	10	trauma w/ PTSD	fMRI	Sx provocation	decreased activation in thalamus, anterior cingulate gyrus
				10	trauma w/o PTSD			increased activation in thalamus, anterior cingulate gyrus
Lanius et al.	2004	24	N/A	11	trauma w/ PTSD	fMRI	Sx provocation	right posterior cingulate gyrus, right caudate, right parietal lobe, right occipital lobe

				13	trauma w/o PTSD			left superior frontal gyrus, left anterior cingulate gyrus, left striatum, left parietal lobe, left insula
Maddock & Buonocore	1997	10	50%	10	normals	fMRI	auditory presentation, threat-related words	left posterior cingulate gyrus
Maddock et al.	2003	14	64%	6	panic disorder	fMRI	threat-related words	left posterior cingulate, left middle frontal cortices, greater right>left asymmetry in mid-parahippocampal region
				8	normals			(same regions, less activation)
van den Heuvel et al.	2005	44	59%	22	OCD	fMRI	modified ToL	decreased activity in dorsolateral prefrontal cortex and caudate nucleus; increased activity in anterior cingulate, ventrolateral prefrontal, and para-hippocampal cortices
				22	normals			
van der Wee, Nic J.A. et al.	2006	14	50%	14	OCD	fMRI	working memory task	medial frontal lobe, anterior cingulate, dorsa-lateral prefrontal, parietal cortex

Note: STM = short-term memory; Sx = symptom; OCD = obsessive–compulsive disorder; ToL = Tower of London task been consistently observed across studies is the cingulated nucleus. This is noteworthy as the cingulate nucleus is associated with anxiety activation generally. Finally, it appears that memory bias in anxiety is a highly specific component of information processing. In a summary of the memory bias research, Mitte (2008) found that there were no differences for implicit and recognition memory. Instead, the most consistent finding has centered on a bias toward threatening information, regardless of anxiety disorder under study. However, individuals with anxiety showed situation specific threat-related memory biases. That is, the specific experiences of individuals with anxiety disorders are more likely to be recalled as threatening, akin to biases in biographical memory observed in depression.

Judgment and Reasoning in Anxiety

Cognitive science investigations into the area of interpretation and judgment have shown that both anxious and depressed subjects show a bias toward negative interpretation relative to normal controls. Studies of the judgment of the probability of future events show that anxiety and depression are both associated with the belief in increased likelihood of negative events (MacLeod, 1999).This adds convergent validity to findings indicating that anxiety and depression are both associated with negative affect. Studies of the interpretation of ambiguous words, sentences, and narratives have shown that anxious and depressed subjects tend to interpret ambiguity negatively when assessed "off-line" (i.e., while not currently anxious), through verbal, self-report methods (e.g., Butler & Mathews, 1983; Eysenck, Mogg, May, Richards, & Mathews, 1991). This is particularly true for anxious subjects if the stimuli match their concerns, such as descriptions of bodily sensations for subjects with PD, or descriptions of social situations for subjects with social phobia (e.g., Richards, Austin, & Alvarenga, 2001; Stopa & Clark, 2000). Few online assessments, which tap the interpretation process as it is occurring, have been made of depressed individuals. Subjects with anxiety disorders have shown a negative bias in such studies (e.g., MacLeod & Cohen, 1993), supporting the idea that bias occurs during initial interpretation rather than afterward in elaboration or retrieval.

Models of Information Processing Bias

Taken together, cognitive science investigations have found robust evidence for an attentional bias across the anxiety disorders, but not in depression or in comorbid anxiety and depression. Evidence supports the specificity of this attentional bias toward the particular concerns of individuals with various anxiety disorders, as well as a more general attentional bias toward threat across the anxiety disorders. Biased memory effects are consistently found in depressed persons, but not in anxious persons, except in the case of PD. Depression and anxiety are both associated with bias toward negative interpretations, particularly if ambiguous stimuli are either mood-congruent or are related to specific anxieties. Depression and anxiety are both associated with ongoing negative ideation, including worry about the future and rumination about recent events.

Various cognitive models have been proposed over the years to account for these findings. Schema theories (e.g., Beck, 1967, 1976; Beck & Clark, 1997; Bower, 1981, 1987) predict that characteristic cognitive biases should be present at every stage of processing in each of the emotional disorders, including attention, interpretation, and memory. These theories are not well-supported, due to the lack of attentional bias in depression and the general lack of disorder-specific memory bias in the anxiety disorders. More recent models attempt to take into account different kinds of processing at different stages (e.g., Bar-Haim et al., 2007; Eysenck, 1992; Fox, Russo, & Dutton, 2002; Mansell, 2000; Mogg & Bradley, 1998, 2005; Williams, Watts, MacLeod, & Mathews 1997; Yiend & Mathews, 2001). Each of these models differs from the others, sometimes in starkly contradictory ways. The basic structure that they all share is the division of cognitive processes into two basic types: fast, automatic orienting responses and slower, more strategic processes of elaboration and resource allocation. This parallels the common distinction in cognitive psychology of bottom–up processing versus top–down processing. The proponents of the various models disagree primarily as to the precise definition of each of these two processes, as well as to the relative emphasis of causal role in the etiology and maintenance of the disorders. It is likely that there are complex reciprocal relationships involved, as a good deal of brain functioning occurs in parallel, and "higher" strategic cognitive processes are increasingly seen as having interactive, reciprocal relationships with "lower" automatic, emotional processing (e.g., Forgas, 2008). The exact nature of these reciprocal relationships has yet to be disentangled. Indeed, it has been suggested that a part of the difficulty lies in conceptual grounding of the definitions of the various identified conditions (Glas, 2004). Whereas imaging methodologies have been promising for showing a small set of neural pathways for anxiety generally, overlooked has been the role of environmental factors in shaping these same neural systems.

Implications for *DSM-V* and for Brain Mechanisms of Anxiety Disorders

Cognitive science, and the recent incorporation of brain imaging methods, has held the promise of uncovering mechanisms of the anxiety disorders. Whereas this has been the great hope of brain imaging methodology, the research has not yet matched the expectations. Aside from connecting established cognitive processing methodologies, some research has accrued to show links between anxiety disorders and the amygdala, insula, and the ventromedial prefrontal cortex (as summarized in an fMRI meta-analysis by Etkin & Wager, 2007). This line of work illustrates the anatomical structures affected by classical conditioning, but does not show differential activation based on environmental exposure.

In many ways, we are at the point of re-evaluating what should be included in a good model of any particular disorder. Whereas the anxiety disorders are unified by elevated anxiety as a central and common feature, the unique features of each diagnosis have not yet been adequately or reliably described via information processing methods when conducted with brain scanning methods. However, the research incorporating brain imaging procedures with well-established information processing approaches is still in its infancy, and the findings in support of disorder-specific biases have been few. Instead, it has been more consistently found that anxiety in general leads to biased processing toward threat information.

Surprisingly, consistencies have been observed for certain complex anxiety states. In the case of OCD, a complex and highly heterogeneous condition, fMRI research has consistently implicated the orbital gyrus and caudate nucleus (Whiteside, Port, & Abramowitz, 2004). As more research accumulates, it is likely that some conditions will be subsumed under other more robust categories within which some functional brain mechanisms may be so similar as to make them indistinguishable.

Recently, some have challenged the notion that findings from neuroscience can inform diagnostic classification (e.g., Hyman, 2007). Part of the argument against relying on the current state of research on anxiety disorders from neuroscience may be derived from the assumed validity of the existing diagnostic categories. As we have detailed in this chapter, much of the existing research on attention, memory and other cognitive biases support a general tendency toward threatening information, with no corresponding specificity that would lend strong support toward the diagnostic validity of any single disorder. Instead, the findings show greater support for dimensional views that would support the presence of anxiety in conditions named anxiety disorders. The addition brain imaging techniques, while promising for the potential of mapping out neural connections associated with reactions to environmental stimuli, have not yet bore fruit. The brain areas associated with different disorders have been highly varied. Whiteside, Port, and Abramowitz (2004) found that, for OCD, there has been only a few consistently identified brain areas associated with the condition. As we have shown here, the brain imaging research on other anxiety disorders suggests a small set of consistently identified areas that are more suggesting of the involvement for anxiety generally, not necessarily for any specific condition.

The full impact of neuroscience research in diagnosis may lie in mechanisms associated with treatment instead of categorizing disorders themselves. For example, neuroscience research has shown that there is greater neuroplasticity than previously suspected, and that changes in neural systems frequently occur following successful treatment (Fuchs, 2004). At the present time, it appears that neuroscience may contribute to diagnosis by sharing an empirical position with other theoretical approaches. This would be consistent with the position advocated by Kendler (2008), whereby he indicates that the processes underlying psychiatric conditions are inherently multiply determined and require multiple theoretical perspectives.

References

Algom, D., Chajut, E., & Lev, S. (2004). A rational look at the emotional Stroop phenomenon: A generic slowdown, not a Stroop effect. *Journal of Experimental Psychology: General, 133*, 323–338.

Amin, Z., Constable, R. T., & Canli, T. (2004). Attentional bias for valenced stimuli as a function of personality in the dot-probe task. *Journal of Research in Personality, 38*, 15–23.

Amir, N., Elias, J., Klumpp, H., & Przeworski, A. (2003). Attentional bias to threat in social phobia: Facilitated processing of threat or difficulty disengaging attention from threat? *Behaviour Research and Therapy, 41*, 1325–1335.

Bar–Haim, Y., Lamy, D., Pergamin, L., Bakermans-Kranenburg, M. J., & van Ijzendoorn, M. H. (2007). Threat-related attentional bias in anxious and nonanxious individuals: A meta-analytic study. *Psychological Bulletin, 133*, 1–24.

Barlow, D. H. (2002). *Anxiety and its disorders: The nature and treatment of anxiety and panic (2nd ed.)*. New York, US: Guilford Press.

Beck, A. T. (1967). *Depression*. Harper and Row: New York.

Beck, A. T. (1976). *Cognitive therapy and the emotional disorders*. Cognitive therapy and the emotional disorders. Oxford, England: International Universities Press

Beck, A. T., & Clark, D. A. (1997). An information processing model of anxiety: Automatic and strategic processes. *Behaviour Research and Therapy, 35*, 49–58.

Becker, E. S., Rinck, M., Margraf, J., & Roth, W. T. (2001). The emotional Stroop effect in anxiety disorders: General emotionality or disorder specificity? *Journal of Anxiety Disorders, 15*, 147–159.

Bogels, S. M., & Mansell, W. (2004). Attention processes in the maintenance and treatment of social phobia: Hypervigilance, avoidance and self-focused attention. *Clinical Psychology Review, 24*, 827–856.

Bower, G. H. (1981). Mood and memory. *American Psychologist, 36*, 129–148.

Bower, G. H. (1987). Commentary on mood and memory. *Behaviour Research and Therapy, 25*, 443–455.

Bradley, M. M., & Lang, P. J. (2007). Emotion and motivation. In J. T. Cacioppo, L. G. Tassinary & G. G. Berntson (Eds.), *Handbook of psychophysiology (3rd ed.)* (pp. 581–607). London: Cambridge University Press.

Bradley, B. P., Mogg, K., Millar, N., & White, J. (1995). Selective processing of negative information: Effects of clinical anxiety, concurrent depression, and awareness. *Journal of Abnormal Psychology, 104*, 532–536.

Broomfield, N. M., & Turpin, G. (2005). Covert and overt attention in trait anxiety: A cognitive psychophysiological analysis. *Biological Psychology, 68*, 179–200.

Burke, M., & Mathews, A. (1992). Autobiographical memory and clinical anxiety. *Cognition & Emotion, 6*, 23–35.

Butler, G., & Mathews, A. (1983). Cognitive processes in anxiety. *Advances in Behaviour Research & Therapy, 5*, 51–62.

Cohen, J. D., Dunbar, K., & McClelland, J. L. (1990). On the control of automatic processes: A parallel distributed processing account of the Stroop effect. *Psychological Review, 97*, 332-361.

Coles, M. E., & Heimberg, R. G. (2002). Memory biases in the anxiety disorders: Current status. *Clinical Psychology Review, 22*, 587–627.

Compton, R. J., Banich, M.T., Mohanty, A., Milham, M.P., Miller, G.A., Scalf, P.E., et al. (2003). Paying attention to emotion: An fMRI investigation of cognitive and emotional Stroop tasks. *Cognitive, Affective, and Behavioral Neuroscience, 3,* 81–96.

Constans, J. I. (2005). Information-Processing Biases in PTSD. In J. J. Vasterling & C. R. Brewin (Eds.), *Neuropsychology of PTSD: Biological, cognitive, and clinical perspectives* (pp. 105–130). New York, Guilford Press.

Ekman, P. (1992). An argument for basic emotions. *Cognition & Emotion, 6,* 169–200.

Engels, A. S., Heller, W., Mohanty, A., Herrington, J.D., Banich, M.T., & Webb, A. G., & Miller, G.A. (2007). Specificity of regional brain activity in anxiety types during emotional processing. *Psychophysiology, 44,* 352–363.

Etkin, A., & Wager, T. D. (2007). Functional neuroimaging of anxiety: A meta-analysis of emotional processing in PTSD, social anxiety disorder, and specific phobia. *American Journal of Psychiatry, 164,* 1476–1488.

Eysenck, M. W. (1992). *Anxiety: The cognitive perspective. Essays in cognitive psychology series.* Anxiety: The cognitive perspective Hillsdale, NJ: Lawrence Erlbaum Associates, Inc.

Eysenck, M. W., Mogg, K., May, J., Richards, A., & Mathews, A. (1991). Bias in interpretation of ambiguous sentences related to threat in anxiety. *Journal of Abnormal Psychology, 100,* 144–150.

Forgas, J. P. (2008). Affect and cognition. *Perspectives on Psychological Science, 3,* 94–101.

Fox, E., Russo, R., & Dutton, K. (2002). Attentional bias for threat: Evidence for delayed disengagement from emotional faces. *Cognition & Emotion, 16,* 355–379.

Fresco, D. M., Frankel, A. N., Mennin, D. S., Turk, C. L., & Heimberg, R. G. (2002). Distinct and overlapping features of rumination and worry: The relationship of cognitive production to negative affective states. *Cognitive Therapy and Research, 26,* 179–188.

Fuchs, T. (2004). Neurobiology and psychotherapy: An emerging dialogue. *Current Opinion in Psychiatry, 17,* 479–485.

Geuze, E., Vermetten, E., Ruf, M., de Kloet, C.S., & Westenberg, H. G. M. (2007). Neural correlates of associative learning and memory in veterans with posttraumatic stress disorder. *Journal of Psychiatric Research, 42,* 659–669.

Glas, G. (2004). Philosophical aspects of neurobiological research on anxiety and anxiety disorders. *Current Opinion in Psychiatry, 17,* 457–464.

Gotlib, I. H., & Cane, D. B. (1987). Construct accessibility and clinical depression: A longitudinal investigation. *Journal of Abnormal Psychology, 96,* 199–204.

Hadwin, J. A., Donnelly, N., French, C. C., Richards, A., Watts, A., & Daley, D. (2003). The influence of children's self-report trait anxiety and depression on visual search for emotional faces. *Journal of Child Psychology and Psychiatry, 44,* 432–444.

Healy, H., & Williams, M. G. (1999). Autobiographical memory. In T. Dalgleish & M. J. Power (Eds.), *Handbook of cognition and emotion* (pp. 229–242). New York, John Wiley & Sons Ltd.

Hope, D. A., Rapee, R. M., Heimberg, R. G., & Dombeck, M. J. (1990). Representations of the self in social phobia: Vulnerability to social threat. *Cognitive Therapy and Research, 14,* 177–189.

Horenstein, M., & Segui, J. (1997). Chronometrics of attentional processes in anxiety disorders. *Psychopathology, 30*, 25–35.

Hou, C., Liu, J., Wang, K., Li, L., Liang, M., He, Z., Liu, Y., Zhang, Y., Li, W., & Jiang, T. (2007). Brain responses to symptom provocation and trauma-related short-term memory recall in coal mining accident survivors with acute severe PTSD. *Brain Research, 1144*, 165–174.

Hyman, S. E. (2007). Can neuroscience be integrated into the *DSM-V*? *Nature Reviews: Neuroscience, 8*, 725–732.

Jones, G.V., Stacy, H., & Martin, M. (2002). Exploring the intensity paradox in emotional stroop interference. *Cognitive Therapy and Research, 26*, 831–839.

Kendler, K. S. (2008). Explanatory models for psychiatric illness. *American Journal of Psychiatry, 165*, 695–702.

Kendler, K. S., Neale, M. C., Kessler, R., Heath, A. C., & et al. (1993). A twin study of recent life events and difficulties. *Archives of General Psychiatry, 50*, 789–796.

Krueger, R. F. (1999). The structure of common mental disorders. *Archives of General Psychiatry, 56*, 921–926.

Krueger, R. F., & Markon, K. E. (2006). Reinterpreting comorbidity: A model-based Approach to Understanding and Classifying Psychopathology. *Annual Review of Clinical Psychology, 2, 111–133.*

Lang, A. J., & Sarmiento, J. (2004). Relationship of Attentional Bias to Anxiety Sensitivity and Panic. *Depression and Anxiety, 20*, 190–194.

Lang, P. J. (1979). A bio-informational theory of emotional imagery. *Psychophysiology, 16*, 495–512.

Lanius, R. A., Williamson, P. C., Densmore, M., Boksman, K., Neufeld, R.W., Gati, J.S., et al. (2004). The nature of traumatic memories: A 4-T fMRI Functional connectivity analysis. *American Journal of Psychiatry, 161*, 36–44.

Lanius R.A., Williamson, P.C., Hopper, J., Densmore, M., Boksman, K., Gupta, M.A., et al. (2003). Recall of emotional states in posttraumatic stress disorder: An fMRI investigation. *Biological Psychiatry, 53*, 204–210.

Levy, E. A., & Mineka, S. (1998). Anxiety and mood-congruent autobiographical memory: A conceptual failure to replicate. *Cognition & Emotion, 12*, 625–634.

Lundh, L.-G., & Ost, L.-G. (1996). Stroop interference, self-focus and perfectionism in social phobics. *Personality and Individual Differences, 20*, 725–731.

MacLeod, C. (1999). Anxiety and anxiety disorders. In T. Dalgleish & M. J. Power (Eds.), *Handbook of cognition and emotion* (pp. 447–477). New York: John Wiley & Sons.

MacLeod, C. M. (1991). Half a century of research on the Stroop effect: An integrative review. *Psychological Bulletin, 109*, 163–203.

MacLeod, C., & Cohen, I. L. (1993). Anxiety and the interpretation of ambiguity: A text comprehension study. *Journal of Abnormal Psychology, 102*, 238–247.

MacLeod, C., & Mathews, A. (2004). Selective Memory Effects in Anxiety Disorders: An Overview of Research Findings and Their Implications. In D. Reisberg & P. Hertel (Eds.), *Memory and emotion* (pp. 155–185). New York: Oxford University Press.

MacLeod, C., Mathews, A., & Tata, P. (1986). Attentional bias in emotional disorders. *Journal of Abnormal Psychology, 95*, 15–20.

Maddock, R. J. Buonocore, M.H. (1997). Activation of left posterior cingulated gyrus by the auditory presentation of threat words: An fMRI study. *Psychiatry Research: Neuroimaging, 75*, 1–14.

Mansell, W. (2000). Conscious appraisal and the modification of automatic processes in anxiety. *Behavioural and Cognitive Psychotherapy, 28*, 99–120.

Mathews, A., & Mackintosh, B. (1998). A cognitive model of selective processing in anxiety. *Cognitive Therapy and Research, 22*, 539–560.

Mathews, A., & MacLeod, C. (1985). Selective processing of threat cues in anxiety states. *Behaviour Research and Therapy, 23*, 563–569.

Mathews, A., & MacLeod, C. (1994). Cognitive approaches to emotion and emotional disorders. *Annual Review of Psychology. 45, 25–50.*

Mathews, A., & MacLeod, C. (2005). Cognitive vulnerability to emotional disorders. *Annual Review of Clinical Psychology, 1*, 167–195.

Mathews, A. M., & Sebastian, S. (1993). Suppression of emotional Stroop effects by fear-arousal. *Cognition & Emotion, 7*, 517–530.

Matt, G. E., Vazquez, C., & Campbell, W. K. (1992). Mood-congruent recall of affectively toned stimuli: A meta-analytic review. *Clinical Psychology Review, 12*, 227–255.

McKay, D. (2005). Studies in cognitive processing during worry. *Cognitive Therapy and Research, 29*, 359–376.

McNeil, D. W., Ries, B. J., Taylor, L. J., Boone, M. L., & et al. (1995). Comparison of social phobia subtypes using Stroop tests. *Journal of Anxiety Disorders, 9*, 47–57.

Mennin, D. S., Heimberg, R.G., Fresco, D.M., & Ritter, M. R. (2008). Is generalized anxiety disorder an anxiety or mood disorder? Considering multiple factors as we ponder the fate of GAD. *Depression and Anxiety, 25*, 289–299.

Mineka, S., Rafaeli, E., & Yovel, I. (2003). Cognitive biases in emotional disorders: Information processing and social-cognitive perspectives. In R. J. Davidson, K. R. Scherer, & H. H. Goldsmith (Eds.) *Handbook of affective sciences*. Oxford; New York: Oxford University Press.

Mitte, K. (2008). Memory bias for threatening information in anxiety and anxiety disorders: A meta-analytic review. *Psychological Bulletin, 134*, 886–911.

Mitterschiffthaler, M. T., Williams, S. C. R., Walsh, N.D., Cleare, A.J., Donaldson, C., Scott, J., et al. (2008). Neural basis of the emotional Stroop interference effect in major depression. *Psychological Medicine, 38*, 247–256.

Mogg, K., & Bradley, B. P. (1998). A cognitive-motivational analysis of anxiety. *Behaviour Research and Therapy, 36*, 809–848.

Mogg, K., & Bradley, B. P. (2005). Attentional bias in generalized anxiety disorder versus depressive disorder. *Cognitive Therapy and Research, 29*, 29–45.

Mogg, K., Bradley, B. P., Williams, R., & Mathews, A. (1993). Subliminal processing of emotional information in anxiety and depression. *Journal of Abnormal Psychology, 102*, 304–311.

Mogg, K., Mathews, A., & Eysenck, M. (1992). Attentional bias to threat in clinical anxiety states. *Cognition & Emotion, 6*, 149–159.

Muller, J., & Roberts, J. E. (2005). Memory and attention in Obsessive-Compulsive Disorder: A review. *Journal of Anxiety Disorders, 19*, 1–28.

Nakao, T., Nakagawa, A., Yoshiura., T., Nakatani, E., Nabeyama, M., Yoshizato, C., et al. (2005). A functional MRI comparison of patients with obsessive-compulsive disorder and normal controls during a Chinese character Stroop task. *Psychiatry Research: Neuroimaging, 139*, 101–114.

Oatley, K., & Johnson-Laird, P. N. (1987). Towards a cognitive theory of emotions. *Cognition & Emotion, 1*, 29–50.

Ohman, A. (1993). Fear and anxiety as emotional phenomena: Clinical phenomenology, evolutionary perspectives, and information-processing mechanisms. In M. Lewis & J. M. Haviland (Eds.), *Handbook of emotions* (pp. 511–536). New York, Guilford Press.

Plutchik, R. (1984). Emotions: a general psychoevolutionary theory. In K. Scherer & P. Ekman (Eds.), *Approaches to emotion* (pp. 197–219). Hilsdale, NJ: Erlbaum.

Richards, J. C., Austin, D. W., & Alvarenga, M. E. (2001). Interpretation of ambiguous interoceptive stimuli in panic disorder and nonclinical panic. *Cognitive Therapy and Research, 25*, 235–246.

Riemann, B. C., & McNally, R. J. (1995). Cognitive processing of personally relevant information. *Cognition & Emotion, 9*, 325–340.

Rinck, M., Becker, E. S., Kellermann, J., & Roth, W. T. (2003). Selective attention in anxiety: Distraction and enhancement in visual search. *Depression and Anxiety, 18*, 18–28.

Ruiz–Caballero, J. A., & Gonzalez, P. (1994). Implicit and explicit memory bias in depressed and nondepressed subjects. Year of Publication 1994. *Cognition & Emotion, 8*, 555–569.

Segal, Z. V., Gemar, M., Truchon, C., Guirguis, M., & Horowitz, L. M. (1995). A priming methodology for studying self-representation in major depressive disorder. *Journal of Abnormal Psychology, 104*, 205–213.

Segerstrom, S. C., Stanton, A. L., Alden, L. E., & Shortridge, B. E. (2003). A Multidimensional Structure for Repetitive Thought: What's on Your Mind, and How, and How Much? *Journal of Personality and Social Psychology, 85*, 909–921.

Segerstrom, S. C., Tsao, J. C. I., Alden, L. E., & Craske, M. G. (2000). Worry and rumination: Repetitive thought as a concomitant and predictor of negative mood. *Cognitive Therapy and Research, 24*, 671–688.

Shin, L. M., Whalen, P. J., Pitman, R. K., Bush, G., Macklin, M. L., Lasko, N. B., et al. (2001). An fMRI study of anterior cingulated function in posttraumatic stress disorder. *Biological Psychiatry, 50*, 932–942.

Stopa, L., & Clark, D. M. (2000). Social phobia and interpretation of social events. *Behaviour Research and Therapy, 38*, 273–283.

Stroop, J. R. (1935). Studies of interference in serial verbal reactions. *Journal of Experimental Psychology, 18*, 643–662.

van den Heuvel, O. A., Veltman, D. J., Groenewegen, H. J., Witter, M. P., Merkelbach, J., Cath, D. C., et al. (2005). Disorder-specific neuroanatomical correlates of attentional bias in obsessive-compulsive disorder, panic disorder, and hypochondriasis. *Archives of General Psychiatry, 62*, 922–933.

van der Wee, N. J. A., Ramsey, N. F., van Megen, H. J. G. M., Denys, D., Westenberg, H. G. M., & Kahn, R. S. (2006). Spatial working memory in obsessive-compulsive disorder improves with clinical response: A functional MRI study. *European Neuropsychopharmacology*, 17, 12–23.

Watts, F. N., McKenna, F. P., Sharrock, R., & Trezise, L. (1986). Colour naming of phobia-related words. *British Journal of Psychology, 77,* 97–108.

Watson, D. (2005). Rethinking the Mood and Anxiety Disorders: A Quantitative Hierarchical Model for DSM-V. *Journal of Abnormal Psychology, 114,* 522–536.

Whiteside, S. P., Port, J. D., & Abramowitz, J. S. (2004). A meta-analysis of functional neuroimaging in obsessive-compulsive disorder. *Psychiatry Research: Neuroimaging, 132,* 69–79.

Williams, J. M. G., Mathews, A., & MacLeod, C. (1996). The emotional Stroop task and psychopathology. *Psychological Bulletin, 120,* 3–24.

Williams, J. M. G., Watts, F. N., MacLeod, C., & Mathews, A. (1997). *Cognitive psychology and emotional disorders* (2nd Ed.). Chichester, England: Wiley.

Yiend, J., & Mathews, A. (2001). Anxiety and attention to threatening pictures. *The Quarterly Journal of Experimental Psychology A: Human Experimental Psychology, 54A,* 665–681.

10

Cultural Anthropology and Anxiety Diagnoses

Devon E. Hinton
Curtis Hsia
Lawrence Park
Andrew Rasmussen
Mark H. Pollack

The current chapter examines the *Diagnostic and Statistical Manual of Mental Disorders* (*DSM*)-defined anxiety disorders from an anthropological perspective, and tries to determine their applicability to other cultural groups and how findings in other cultural groups might be used to better understand how anxiety disorders are produced and classified. In this review, we will focus on three anxiety disorders: panic disorder (PD), generalized anxiety disorder (GAD), and posttraumatic stress disorder (PTSD). In our analysis, we will examine current psychological models of how those disorders are generated in order to explore possible cross-cultural variation, using primarily Cambodian examples.

Panic Disorder in Cross-Cultural Perspective

According to many psychological theories of PD, catastrophic cognitions about somatic sensations play a key role in the generation of the disorder. In the 1980s, cognitive theorists increasingly argued that the *DSM*'s "out of the blue" criterion that true panic attacks are unprovoked should be eliminated (for reviews, see Beck, 1988; Craske, 1991; McNally, 1994; Rapee et al., 1995; Street et al., 1989). Instead, they argued that catastrophic cognitions about bodily sensations constitute a core process in provoking panic attacks, and that the feared bodily sensations that provoke panic may be induced by a wide range of triggers.

Clark (1986) summarized the *catastrophic cognitions theory of panic* as follows:

> *The trigger for an attack often seems to be the perception of a bodily sensation which itself is caused by a different emotional state (excitement, anger) or by some quite innocuous event such as suddenly getting up from the sitting position (dizziness), exercise (breathlessness, palpitations), or drinking coffee (palpitations). Once perceived, the body sensation is interpreted in a catastrophic fashion, and then a panic attack results. (p. 462)*

Other common ways in which sensations might be induced and then trigger panic attacks were also identified: hyperventilation that produces a host of bodily sensations, including blurry vision and hand numbness (Beck, 1988), and temperature and humidity changes—for example, those resulting from entering a sauna or moving from a warm to a cold space—that cause somatic symptoms such as sweating or cold extremities (Rapee et al., 1995).

If the catastrophic cognitions theory of panic is valid, it has important implications concerning the nature of PD and its cross-cultural variability. Below we describe some hypotheses that emerge from the *catastrophic cognitions theory of the generation of PD* about the cross-cultural variation of PD, and we examine the cross-cultural literature to see if such variation has indeed been noted (on these issues, see too, Hinton & Good, in press).

Hypothesis #1: The rate and severity of panic disorder will vary across cultural groups depending on the extent of catastrophic cognitions about anxiety-related sensations.

According to the catastrophic cognitions theory of panic, the more severe a person's catastrophic cognitions about sensations, particularly anxiety-related sensations (e.g., dizziness, palpitations, chest tightness), the greater will be the frequency and severity of panic attacks. In support of this hypothesis, multiple studies demonstrate that the severity of catastrophic cognitions about panic sensations is strongly related to the severity and frequency of PD panic attacks (for a review, see Hinton et al., 2006a). This would suggest a close relationship between cultural interpretations of the danger of particular sensations and rates of PD associated with those sensations. It appears that certain cultural groups having extensive catastrophic cognitions about anxiety symptoms, such as Cambodian refugees, have very high rates of PD-type panic attacks, and that culturally specific catastrophic cognitions about somatic sensations generate panic (Hinton et al., 2006a; Hinton, Ba, Peou, & Um, 2000; Hinton, Chhean, Fama, Pollack, & McNally, 2007a; Hinton, Um, & Ba, 2001a, 2001b, 2001c).

Hypothesis #2: PD catastrophic cognitions will vary across cultural groups.

According to the catastrophic cognitions theory of panic, the catastrophic cognitions associated with panic attacks (about the somatic and psychological symptoms in those panic attacks) would be expected to vary depending on local ideas about the meaning and physiological significance of symptoms (Hinton, Chong, Pollack, Barlow, & McNally, in press). Because of cultural variations in syndromes and ethnophysiology, catastrophic cognitions will vary significantly across culture, cultural subgroup, and even time period (see Fig.10.1).

Two important conclusions in catastrophic cognitions follow from cultural variation : (a) PD patients from two different cultures may have a different degree of fear about each of the anxiety-related somatic symptoms, and (b) even if PD patients from two cultures have the same degree of fear about a certain somatic symptom, for example, dizziness, the reason for fearing that symptom may greatly vary depending on a culture's conceptualization of how that

10.1

The role of cultural syndromes and ethnophysiology in generating catastrophic cognitions and starting a vicious cycle of worsening.

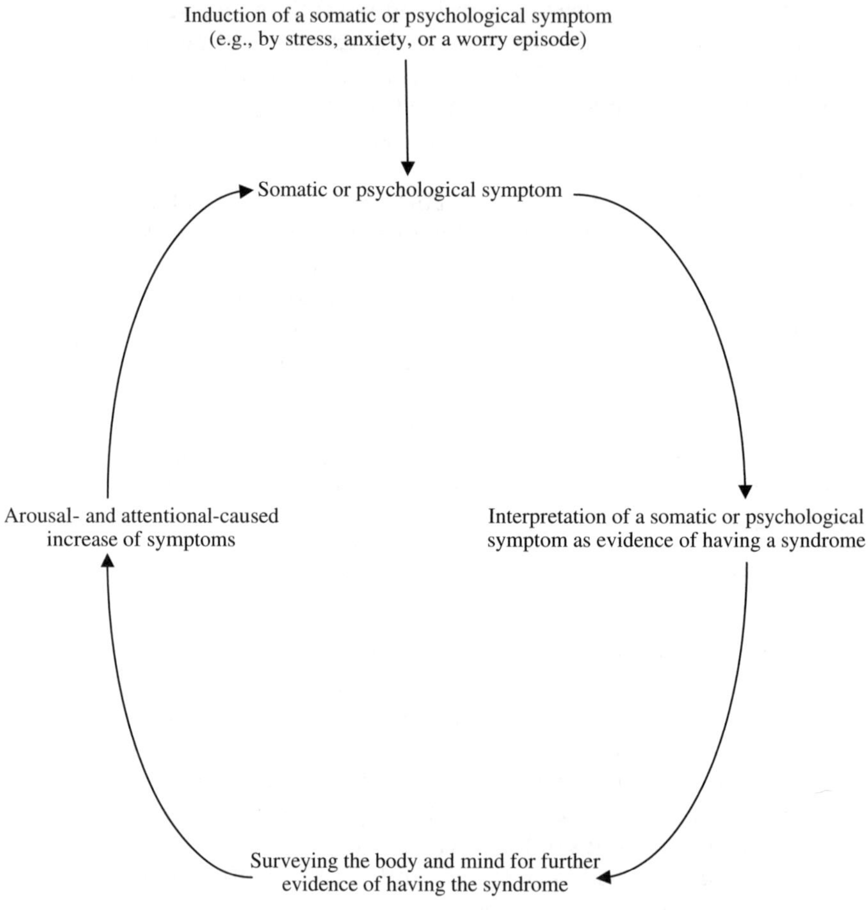

symptom is generated, its associated physiology, and cultural syndromes that it indicates (on cultural syndromes, see Guarnaccia & Rogler, 1999; Hsia & Barlow, 2001; Kirmayer & Sartorius, 2007).

In the United States, fear of heart attack is a frequent catastrophic cognition during panic (Katon, 1984, 1989). In this case, we would refer to current layperson understanding of the heart and heart attacks, and the symptoms of and risk factors for heart attack in a particular social and cultural group in the United States, as a cultural syndrome, or a layperson-type cultural syndrome. This may simply be the knowledge that fatty foods and cigarettes predispose to heart attack, the idea that chest tightness means a heart attack, and the concern that stress may predispose to the disorder. Cambodians have multiple anxiety-related syndromes that are based on fears of disturbed "wind" and blood flow, and we use several of these to illustrate how somatic and psychological symptoms have culturally specific meanings that differ from those in Western medicine. These syndromes give rise to extensive catastrophic cognitions about anxiety-generated somatic sensations.

One of these is the "limb blockage" syndrome (*slap day slap ceung*). Cambodians consider that tightness and soreness in the legs, especially at the knees and elbows, result from blockage of "tubes" (*sâsai*) that carry blood and wind (an air-like substance called *khyâl*) along the limbs, and that coldness in the feet and hands indicates poor blood perfusion (Hinton et al., 2001a, 2001b, 2001c). Blockage of the flow of wind and blood may result in (a) the "death" of the limb because of lack of blood flow (what a Westerner would call a stroke) and (b) the ascent of wind and blood—first, into the trunk of the body, possibly causing asphyxia and cardiac arrest; second, into the neck, possibly causing rupture of the vessels; and third, into the cranium, possibly causing multiple adverse events such syncope, blindness, or death. For these reasons, Cambodian patients greatly fear cold extremities.

Cambodians have a "sore neck" syndrome. Catastrophic cognitions about neck sensations often lead to panic attacks, that is, to neck-focused panic attacks. In a neck-focused panic attack (Hinton et al., 2001c, 2006a; Hinton, Pich, Chhean, Safren, & Pollack, 2007b), a Cambodian fears death from rupture of neck vessels, with prominent symptoms including a sore neck (*rooy kâ*), head symptoms (e.g., headache, tinnitus, blurry vision, and dizziness), and general symptoms of autonomic arousal (e.g., cold extremities, palpitations, and shortness of breath). Cambodians attribute neck soreness to excessive wind and blood pressure at the neck that may rupture vessels at that location, and attribute other symptoms present in a sore neck episode, such as tinnitus and blurry vision, to an upward rising of wind and blood. For these reasons, Cambodian patients greatly fear neck soreness.

Cambodians also have an "abdominal wind" syndrome (Hinton et al., 2005a, 2007a). This syndrome gives rise to catastrophic cognitions about gastrointestinal sensations that often leads to a GI-focused panic attack. In a GI-focused panic attack, Cambodians worry that wind will move upward into the body and cause various bodily disasters. Whereas North Americans often complain of "butterflies in the stomach" or a "sinking sensation" in the stomach when anxious (Chambless et al., 1984; Noyes & Hoehn-Saric, 1998), Cambodians worry that abdominal sensations indicate the occurrence of an upward hitting wind (*khyâl theau laeung leu*). As noted above, the rising wind is believed to potentially cause catastrophic consequences (e.g., syncope, cardiac arrest, or bursting of the neck vessels), with these wind-ascent fears being heightened if symptoms indicative of increased wind pressure also occur (e.g., tinnitus, dizziness, or a sore neck). So, like cold extremities and neck soreness, Cambodian patients also fear stomach distention and sensations.

Cambodians also have great fears of "wind overload" (*khyâl ko*). This is a syndrome that produces catastrophic cognitions about any sensations (e.g., dizziness, palpitations, cold extremities) felt upon standing, and results in orthostatic panic, that is, panic upon rising from lying or sitting to standing (Hinton et al., 2001a, 2001b, 2005a; Hinton, Hofmann, Pitman, Pollack, & Barlow, in press; Hinton, et al., 2004). It is thought that a surge of "wind" and blood upward in the body toward the head may occur upon standing, a condition called wind overload. For this reason, upon standing, Cambodians anxiously assess the bodily state for symptoms that would indicate a pressurized rise of wind and blood toward and into the head: a sore neck (from wind and blood distending the neck vessels), dizziness (from excessive wind and blood entering the head), blurry vision (from wind exiting the eyes), or tinnitus (from wind escaping from the auditory canals, analogous to the sound made by steam exiting the spout of a tea kettle).

Hypothesis #3: The events or actions that trigger the sensations causing PD-related panic attacks will vary across cultural groups.

According to the catastrophic cognitions theory of panic, what induces the feared sensations and triggers PD-type panic attacks may vary in different individuals and cultural groups. Given local illness concepts and syndromes, specific bodily sensations will be viewed with more fear in certain situations. For example, because of syndrome-generated catastrophic cognitions, dizziness upon standing causes much greater fear for a Cambodian (e.g., "Wind will exit my ears and I will die") than for an American (e.g., "I'm very dizzy, and if I do not sit down I will fall."). The frequency with which certain sensation-inducers bring about panic varies by culture: common triggers of panic among Cambodian refugees include standing and feeling dizzy, seeing a spinning object, smelling car-exhaust fumes, or getting neck tightness (Hinton, Chea, Ba, & Pollack, 2004; Hinton, Pich, Chhean, Pollack, & Barlow, 2004); or among Vietnamese refugees, common panic triggers include standing and feeling dizzy, a cold wind hitting the body, or urination (Hinton, Chau, et al., 2001; Hinton & Hinton, et al., 2003).

Hypothesis #4: The emphasized symptoms of PD-related panic attacks will vary across cultural groups.

According to the catastrophic cognitions theory of panic, the sensations most prominent in PD panic attacks will vary, depending on which sensations are viewed as potentially catastrophic by members of a society or social group. Given local illness concepts and syndromes, certain bodily sensations will be viewed with more fear, and those symptoms will form the critical symptoms associated with panic in those contexts. The main symptoms focused on by persons suffering PD panic attacks vary by cultural group; the catastrophic cognitions about a somatic symptom will often be generated by a cultural syndrome specific to that group. Catastrophic cognitions will be produced by a group's understanding of the physiology of anxiety symptoms—its ethnophysiology. The hypothesis that the catastrophic cognitions in a particular group will lead to certain symptoms being emphasized in panic attacks is clearly supported by the fact that certain somatic symptoms not of concern to Westerners give rise to catastrophic cognitions among Cambodian refugees, and that those somatic symptoms are prominent in the panic attacks of Cambodian refugees. Examples of this include neck complaints (see above for a description of neck-related catastrophic cognitions) and tinnitus, which is referred to as "wind shooting from the ears," and is greatly feared as an indicator of wind and blood surging into the head (Hinton et al., 2006b).

Hypothesis #5: The crescendo period of a particular PD panic-attack episode may be relatively prolonged.

According to the catastrophic cognitions theory of panic, episodes of PD-related panic attacks are not seizure-like events. They may crescendo rapidly (in less than 10 minutes, as specified in the *DSM–IV* criteria) or they may crescendo more slowly, even over several hours, worsening as the patient's catastrophic cognitions worsen. Results from at least one study raise the issue of whether the 10-minute diagnostic criterion should be applied to English-speaking North Americans (see Scupi et al., 1997). As we will discuss below, PD-related panic attacks among non-Western populations often develop over more than 10 minutes and start as worry episodes.

Hypothesis #6: Hybrid panic attacks combining PD and PTSD characteristics should occur.

According to the catastrophic cognitions theory of panic, PD-related panic attacks should frequently co-occur with trauma-related panic. Thinking about a trauma or encountering a trauma-evocative stimulus (the location of the event) may trigger various sensations. Those sensations may, in turn, be interpreted as potentially catastrophic: palpitations may recall a trauma event in which the person had experienced strong palpitations, and palpitations may concurrently evoke catastrophic cognitions (e.g., of a heart attack). Or a somatic symptom that is experienced for some reason other than trauma recall, for example, chest tightness owing to hyperventilation, may trigger both catastrophic cognitions and trauma associations.

Such hybrid panic attacks are common among Cambodian populations (see, e.g., Hinton, Hofmann, et al., in press), and within the various panic subtypes (e.g., neck-focused panic, GI-focused panic, orthostatic-triggered panic), the severity of panic is predicted by both catastrophic cognitions and trauma associations that occur during the panic episodes (Hinton et al., 2006a, 2007a; Hinton, Hofmann, et al., in press). Among Cambodian refugees, neck sensations often give rise to catastrophic cognitions, for example, of the bursting of a neck vessel and trigger flashbacks: of slave labor experience during the Pol Pot regime, during which Cambodians were forced to carry dirt-filled buckets suspended at either end of a pole balanced across a shoulder, resulting in extreme neck and shoulder discomfort (Hinton et al., 2001c; Hinton et al., 2006a). Among Cambodian refugees, stomach sensations give rise both to catastrophic cognitions (e.g., of rising wind) and trauma associations: of starvation-related experiences during the Pol Pot regime—hunger-induced peristalsis that caused severe abdominal pain. Orthostasis-induced dizziness, among Cambodian refugees, may trigger both catastrophic cognitions (e.g., of wind overload) and flashbacks of syncopal and near-syncopal episodes during the Pol Pot regime resulting from overwork and starvation.

Generalized Anxiety Disorder in Cross-Cultural Perspective

In our work we have found a modified version of Wells's model (see Fig.10.2) useful to explain the workings of generalized anxiety disorder (GAD) in cross-cultural context, particularly why GAD rates are very high among Southeast Asian refugees and why their GAD-type worry episodes often escalate to panic. Key aspects of Wells's (2000, 2005) model include the following: (a) that catastrophic cognitions about the negative consequences of worry will worsen GAD (i.e., the application of *Clark's fear of fear model* to GAD); (b) that somatic and psychological symptoms form a key aspect of worry episodes; (c) that attempts at self-treatment infl0uence worry perpetuation; and (d) that worry episodes may escalate to panic. Let us now use Wells's model to explore how GAD may vary cross-culturally, using Cambodian examples.

Worry Domains: Cross-Cultural Differences

Individuals from a particular cultural group or subgroup may have a great many reasons to worry, which might be expected

10.2

A model of worry-episode generation and worry-induced panic.

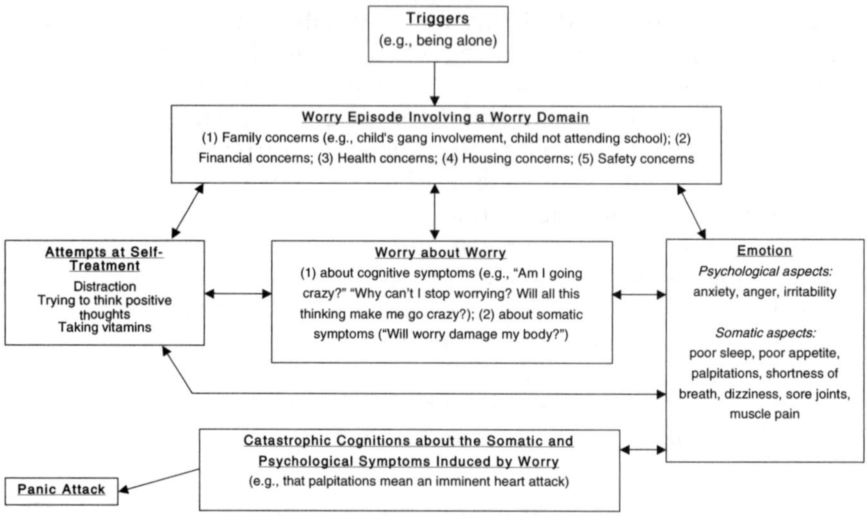

to increase GAD rates, and the type of worry may vary across cultural groups. Cambodian refugees have multiple worry domains. They worry about the following areas:

- *Financial, health, and safety status of family members*: Relatives in Cambodia who have great financial need and receive poor medical care
- *Spiritual status of deceased relatives*: Concerns about the spiritual status of relatives who died during the Cambodian genocide, for example, to assure a good rebirth for the deceased, expensive death rituals may need to be performed, ideally in Cambodia (Hinton & Otto, 2006)
- *Acting-out behaviors of children*: Living in impoverished urban environments, the children of Cambodian patients commonly skip school, fail to complete schoolwork, and become gang involved
- *Personal safety*: Living in poor urban areas, Cambodians are often exposed to violence, including personal assaults, fights, and gunfire in the streets

- *Health*: Because of (a) elevated rates of diabetes and high blood pressure; (b) multiple somatic symptoms generated by high rates of anxiety disorders, including PD and PTSD; (c) a catastrophic-cognitions-producing ethnophysiology (e.g., the wind ethnophysiology) that creates fear of anxiety-related somatic symptoms; and (d) multiple catastrophic-cognitions-producing cultural syndromes (e.g., the so-called weak heart, wind attacks, and hot inside) that also create fear of anxiety-related somatic symptoms

Catastrophic Cognitions About the Somatic and Psychological Consequences of Worry: Cross-Cultural Differences

Cultural groups may vary in respect to the type and total severity of catastrophic cognitions about the psychological and somatic consequences of worry. Let us examine some Cambodian examples.

Cambodian refugees have prominent concerns *about the negative psychological consequences of worry*: Being Buddhists, (a) they place great value on a centered and tranquil state of mind, as exemplified by meditation, and consider the agitated cognitions of a worry episode to be the antithesis of that cultural ideal, and (b) they fear excessive worry to be a dangerous mental agitation that may lead to insanity.

Cambodians have prominent catastrophic cognitions *about the negative somatic consequences of worry*:

- That worry will cause damage to the brain by overheating it—analogous to an overworked machine, and so result in (a) poor memory, (b) insanity, and (c) a predisposition to worry itself, creating a vicious cycle of worsening
- That worry will weaken the mind, which will predispose to worry, again creating a vicious cycle of worsening
- That worry will weaken the body that may possibly result in (a) poor sleep, leading to depletion; (b) poor appetite, leading to depletion; (c) death from depletion; (d) dizziness, especially on standing; (e) a predisposition to wind and fever attacks; (f) poor circulation that may cause stroke; (g) cardiac arrest owing to heart

weakness; and (h) stroke that is thought to be caused by poor perfusion of the limbs, resulting from a weakened heart

Cambodians consider engaging in worry to be both a cause of weakness (a weakness causative) and an indicator of being weak (a weakness indicator). This is true of other worry symptoms such as poor sleep and appetite. In this way, vicious cycles of worsening occur: the patient thinking that worry is causing poor sleep, and that poor sleep will weaken the body and cause more worry.

Symptoms Induced by the Worry Episode: Cross-Cultural Differences

The symptoms induced by a worry episode would be expected to vary across cultures for several reasons. Below we explore the processes that may result in such cross-cultural differences, and how each of those processes may explain the frequency and prominence of dizziness during the worry-episodes of Cambodian refugees.

1. *Inherited biology*. Asian individuals appear to be more predisposed to experience motion sickness than Europeans and Americans as demonstrated by rigorous experimental paradigms (using rotating drums; for a review, see Hinton & Hinton, 2002). Studies indicate that motion sickness is associated with a more general conditionality to dizziness. These same neurobiological structures may contribute to dizziness being induced during anxiety states among Asian populations (for a review and alternative cultural explanation of the motion sickness sensitivity of Asian populations, see Hinton & Hinton, 2002).
2. *Brain-based arousal mechanisms*. In states of arousal, related to trauma and current stresses, worry may induce more symptoms, including dizziness (Bouton, Mineka, & Barlow, 2001). Cambodians often have great arousal due to high rates of anxiety disorders and exposure to stressors including poverty and living in dangerous urban environments; a worry episode may then increase arousal to the point that dizziness and others symptoms are induced. (It is unknown whether brain-based arousal

mechanisms lead to more or different kinds of symptoms [e.g., more dizziness] in different cultures.)

3. *Easily triggered sensation memories*. If a person had past trauma or traumas during which a certain somatic symptom was strongly experienced, that symptom may subsequently be more easily induced during states of distress and anxiety, such as those produced by worry episodes. This symptom inducibility resulting from a previous experiencing of the symptoms (what used to be called "kindling") is probably best explained by the notion of an easily activated cortical-based memory of the symptom (for a review, see Hinton, Howes, & Kirmayer, in press). Cambodians experienced severe dizziness in the Pol Pot period as a result of starvation, malarial episodes, and other traumas (for a review, see Hinton, Howes, & Kirmayer, in press) that may explain in part the salience of dizziness during worry episodes.
4. *Metaphor-guided somatization*. The somatic symptoms may vary as a result of the process of metaphor-induced somatization, that is, the words and phrases used to describe worry and distress may emphasize certain somatic-symptom-related metaphors, leading to the experiencing of that sensation during emotional states (for a review, see Hinton, Howes, & Kirmayer, in press). Multiple Cambodian metaphors configure distress and worry in dizziness-type imagery that is expected to result in worry and distress being somaticized as dizziness. In the Cambodian language, if someone causes you to worry, for instance, a child who skips school, one may well say that the child "shakes me like a pill that is shaken in a bottle" (*greulok ok lok khnyom*). In Cambodian, worry is configured as a turning of the head ("Think here, think there"; *kut pii nih pii nuh*) or mental agitation ("Think a lot"; *kut caraeun*). In addition, if one is exasperated by many problems, one may say that "My brain is spinning." (*wul khue*), which is sometimes meant in a literal sense.
5. *Anxiety-caused attentional amplification*. High arousal (from past trauma, anxiety disorders, and current stresses) may lead to a hypervigilant state. This hypervigilance will be not only for external threats but also interior ones, and thus leads to an examination of the body for an evidence of dangerous symptoms—e.g., dizziness (Barlow, 2002; Craske, 2003; Gorman, 2004). We described above why Cambodians have elevated arousal.

6. *Cultural-syndrome-caused attentional amplification*. If members of a cultural group believe that a certain somatic symptom, such as dizziness, may be induced by worry, and that the symptom indicates a dangerous disorder of physiology, the person will be hypervigilant to that symptom upon engaging in worry. And if even slight dizziness is noted, it will cause fear, and that fear will result in autonomic arousal and increased attentional scrutiny of that symptom, creating a vicious cycle of worsening. As described above, Cambodians consider dizziness to be commonly induced by worry, and that it is a symptom indicating a dangerous dysregulation of physiology.
7. *Anxiety-caused catastrophizing*. High arousal (from past trauma, anxiety disorders, and current stresses) may cause catastrophic-cognitions-type schemas about somatic symptoms (e.g., dizziness) to be more prominent. This is because high arousal causes negative interpretive bias that is an increased salience of threat schemas (Barlow, 2002; Craske, 2003; Gorman, 2004). Cambodian refugees have elevated arousal as described above.

Self-Treatment of Worry Episodes: Cross-Cultural Differences

How others in the family view the worry episode, and how affected individuals treat the worry episode, will have important effects on the course of GAD. Cambodians may use Buddhist practices such as meditation to reduce worry. They may also use various tonics to directly increase bodily energy or medicines to increase energy-restorative processes such as sleep and appetite. If the worry episode causes any anxiety-type symptoms (e.g., dizziness, palpitations, cold extremities, muscle soreness), which is usually the case, they will consider the worry episode to indicate a dysregulation of wind (*khyâl*) and blood flow (a dysregulation that Cambodians often refer to as a wind attack, their term for the sudden onset of anxiety-type somatic symptoms) and will implement culturally indicated treatments. To restore wind and blood flow, many methods may be used, most commonly "coining," a practice which is common to several East and Southeast Asian medical traditions. To coin, (after first dipping a coin in wind oil, a substance thought to promote the release of wind from the skin pores and to provide heat that dissolves blockages), one presses down the edge of a coin on the skin and drags it along a limb, chest or back, resulting in linear marks. Frequently family members will perform the coining. Various tonics may be used to directly strengthen the body, or various medications will be taken to promote sleep and appetite, which will in turn increase energy levels in the body. In some cases, the patient may consider the cause to be bad luck, a condition thought to result in multiple problems and an inability to resolve them, and the patient may consult with priests and other ritual experts who may recommend Buddhists ceremonies to remove bad luck (*krueh*).

Worry Episodes Escalating to Panic: Cross-Cultural Differences

As described above, Cambodian refugees have many catastrophic cognitions about somatic symptoms. These cognitions may cause a worry episode to escalate to panic. For example, if a Cambodian refugee worries about a problem (such as a child skipping school), that anxiety may cause muscular tension that produces neck sensations. These neck sensations will be amplified by the mechanisms outlined above: attentional amplification—because the patient expects to have neck tension upon worrying. The patient will then worry that the neck sensations indicate that wind and blood are rising upward in the body, and that this upward surge may cause the neck vessels to burst and produce dizziness, tinnitus, and syncope. In addition, the patient will scan the body for other symptoms considered to produce or indicate a surge of wind and blood. One example is cold hands, believed to indicate that wind and blood are not moving along the limbs that may cause death of arms and legs and an upsurge in wind and blood.

Trauma-Related Disorder and PTSD in Cross-Cultural Perspective

Our model of trauma-related disorder among different cultural groups is based on current cognitive-behavioral theories of the generation of PTSD. Our model is based on current theories about the structure of PTSD and its comorbidity with other disorders (Watson, 2005), and it emphasizes two aspects of current theories of PTSD production and perpetuation: the key role of the catastrophic interpretation of trauma symptoms (another iteration of the fear of fear model, but here fear of trauma-related symptoms) and of dysfunctional *self* and *world schemas*,to which we add *spiritual schema* (e.g., see Bryant & Guthrie, 2005; Clark & Ehlers, 2004; Dunmore, Clark, & Ehlers, 2001; Foa & Rothbaum, 1998; Halligan, Michael, Clark, & Ehlers, 2003; Michael, Ehlers, Halligan, & Clark, 2005; Southerland & Bryant, 2005). In our model (see Fig.10.3), several psychopathological processes form feedback loops that produce distress and maintain PTSD.

Below we outline those psychopathological processes and illustrate their cultural variability by using Cambodian examples.

1. *Unwanted recall of trauma events and the cultural interpretation of that recall.* For example, believing flashbacks indicate imminent insanity (Halligan et al., 2003; Michael et al., 2005). Cambodian refugees often have trauma recall in nightmares, and upon awakening from nightmares, trauma recall is triggered by encountering exteroceptive cues, such as seeing someone resembling a perpetrator, interoceptive cues, such as dizziness evocative of the trauma, and anger-associated arousal. Trauma recall is often catastrophically interpreted as indicating insanity, physical and mental weakness (e.g., to the point of having the cultural syndrome weak heart), low spiritual strength, or being assaulted by a dead spirit (such as by that of the person who died in the original trauma event) who forces you to relive the event.
2. *Startle and hypervigilance and their cultural interpretation.* Cambodian patients worry that startle indicates a weakened heart that may cause cardiac arrest, and that startle may dislodge the soul and so cause death or insanity (Hinton, Hinton, Um, Chea, & Sak, 2002). They often attribute hypervigilance to weakness or to certain kinds of spiritual attack. These attacks may be made by an enemy using spells to send various objects, such as hair or leather, into the body to produce symptoms like hypervigilance and fear that may cause grave bodily dysfunction.
3. *Poor sleep and its cultural interpretation* (Germain et al., 2004; Zayfert & DeViva, 2004). Cambodian patients

10.3

Psychopathological mechanisms generating trauma-related disorder and PTSD.

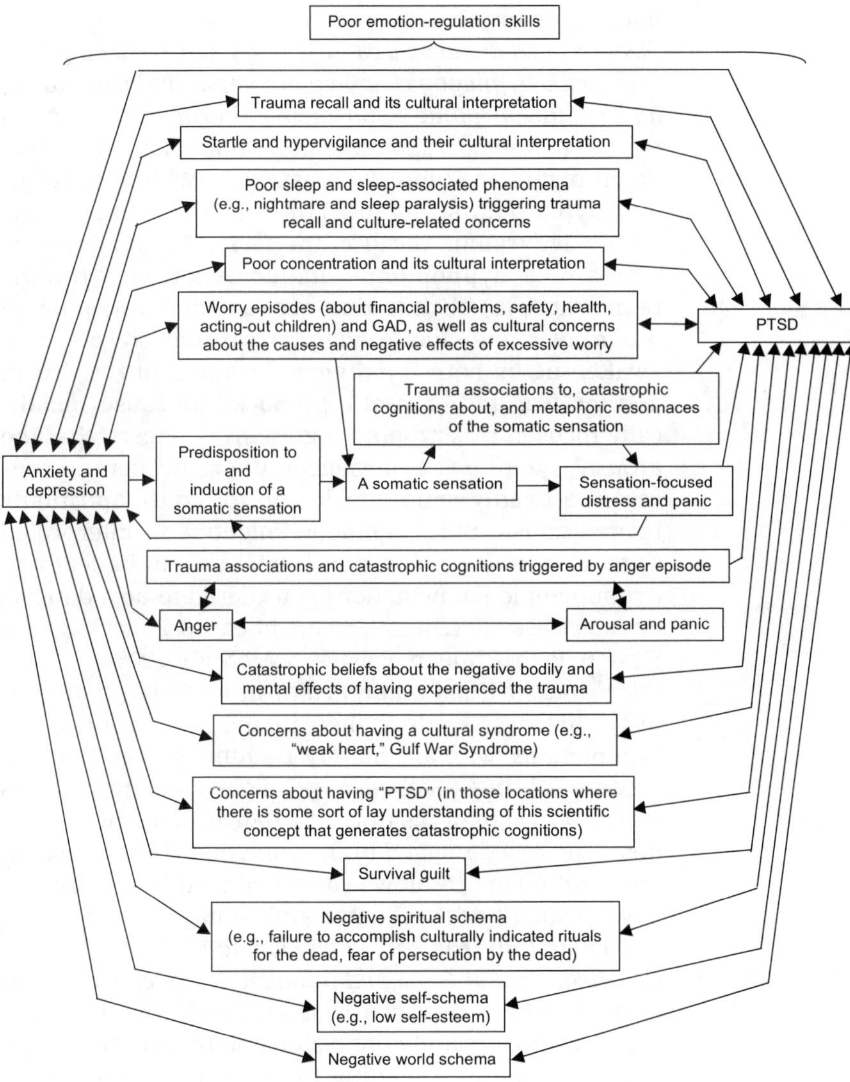

commonly present for treatment with the complaint of sleeping only a few hours each night. They often attribute poor sleep to weakness, and further consider that poor sleep will increase weakness. Sleep is usually disturbed by sleep-associated disorders such as nightmares (see number 4).

4. *Sleep-related disturbances—e.g., nightmares, sleep paralysis (with hypnagogic or hypnopompic hallucinations), and nocturnal panic—and their cultural interpretation and elicitation of trauma events.* Cambodians have frequent nightmares and sleep paralysis (with hypnagogic and hypnopompic hallucinations), and these events (a) involve trauma recall in the form of reliving nightmares or a hypnopompic hallucination of a trauma perpetrator, (b) elicit trauma recall upon awakening—a dream of being chased triggering trauma recall upon awakening by both the thematic content of the dream and the fear and arousal it produces, (c) cause somatically focused catastrophic cognitions—concern that the arousal symptoms experienced upon awakening represent a deadly wind attack, and (d) cause spiritually related catastrophic cognitions—nightmares interpreted as the soul being stolen, which might result in death, or hypnopompic hallucinations considered to be a dangerous spirit assault (Hinton, Pich, Chhean, & Pollack, 2005b; Hinton, Pich, Chhean, Pollack, & McNally, 2005c).
5. *Poor concentration and its cultural interpretation* produce distress. As described in the section on GAD, Cambodians, who are mainly Buddhists, greatly value a centered and focused mind. Poor concentration is feared as a sign of insanity, of a dangerous inner weakness, and of a damaged brain—one that is too "loose" in the skull owing to blows sustained in the past (*rolung khue khabaal*) or overheated and damaged from excessive cogitation (*roulieuk khue khabaal*).
6. *Elevated rates of GAD and frequent worry episodes,* for example, about financial problems and poverty, which increase anxiety and depression and frequently trigger somatic symptoms leading to panic. (See above for a description using Cambodian examples of the cultural variation in worry and GAD.)
7. *Panic attacks that combine PD (viz., catastrophic cognitions) and PTSD (viz., flashback) characteristics,* with

those panic attacks often being triggered by somatic sensations that are induced by multiple processes such as exertion, orthostasis, and trauma recall (Barlow, 2002; Falsetti & Resnick, 2000; Jones & Barlow, 1990; for a review, see Brewin & Holmes, 2003). The commonality of these panic attacks among Cambodian refugees was described above.

8. *Anger, including trauma recall triggered by anger and catastrophic cognitions about anger-induced arousal* (Cloitre, Koenen, Cohen, & Han, 2002; Koenen, Stellman, Stellman, & Sommer, 2003). Cambodians have culturally specific interpretation and treatment of anger episodes, with the anger episode triggering both catastrophic cognitions, for example, that anger-associated heat in the body means a dangerous inner boiling, and trauma recall, for example, when a child's talking disrespectfully evokes memories of abuse in the Pol Pot period (Hinton, Hsia, Um, & Otto, 2003).
9. *The attribution of trauma-related symptoms to a cultural syndrome* such as Gulf War Syndrome, leading to catastrophic cognitions about somatic and psychological symptoms and increased anxiety and distress. Cambodians attribute trauma symptoms to multiple syndromes, including weak heart, upward hitting wind, and wind attacks, and anxious Cambodians often have motion-type sickness when traveling or when in complex sensory environments such as a large shopping mall, labeling these conditions as the so-called car sickness (*pul laan*) and people sickness (*pul menuh*), respectively. These syndromes are thought to result from weakness. (Often, the trauma symptoms may be ascribed to a disorder that may more parsimoniously be described as a disturbed ethnophysiology, as in nerves, *nervios*, or wind.) Also, as described below, trauma symptoms are often attributed to spiritual causes, such as low spiritual energy or the failure to perform burial rites. (These might be called spiritual syndromes.)
10. *Concerns about having PTSD in those locations where the lay understanding of the disorder generates catastrophic cognitions*. If the cultural group has some understanding of the category of PTSD, their understanding of PTSD and its scientific syndrome will have important implications for PTSD severity if members of that group attribute

symptoms to that cultural syndrome. One needs to distinguish PTSD as a scientific syndrome (as understood by a psychologist) from PTSD as a popular syndrome (as understood by a layperson), what might be called a *scientific-syndrome PTSD* versus *popular-syndrome PTSD* (as elaborated in self-help books, commercials, the media, and conversation). If a cultural group has considerable catastrophic cognitions about PTSD, or if a group tends to self-diagnose this disorder with even minimal PTSD-type symptoms, this will increase disability. (The lay understanding of PTSD is another cultural syndrome, but here we give it its own category.)

11. *Survival guilt,* for example, from having witnessed others dying from starvation, being tortured, or being killed (Henning & Frueh, 1997; Lee, Scragg, & Turner, 2001; Resick & Schnicke, 1992). Among Cambodian refugees, who often watched relatives die from starvation and other preventable causes, survival guilt is heightened by cultural ideas about the effects of neglecting death rites and fears about the ability of the deceased to afflict the living (Hinton & Otto, 2006). That is, survival guilt often involves spiritual schemas (see below).
12. *Catastrophic beliefs about the bodily and mental effects of trauma,* for example, that one's body or mind has been permanently damaged (Clark & Ehlers, 2004; Dunmore et al., 2001; Halligan et al., 2003). Often Cambodian refugees worry that trauma has caused irreparable harming of the vascular vessels of the body, predisposing to stroke and other disorders, and that it has caused a permanent weakening of the body, so that like a depleted battery, it can never be fully recharged again (Hinton & Hinton, 2002); or as described above, poor concentration may be ascribed to having received a blow to the head in the past that has caused the brain to become too loose in the skull, with some patients claiming to hear it move upon turning the head. As these examples suggest, catastrophic cognitions about the long term effects of trauma will involve cultural syndromes and ideas about ethnophysiology, and will relate to the local ethnopsychology.
13. *Negative spiritual schemas* about the meaning of the trauma and its related symptoms, which produce distress. Cambodian patients worry about being assaulted by demons and the spirits of the deceased, especially

if they consider themselves to be in a weakened spiritual or physical state: for instance, if someone died during the Pol Pot period without proper burial rites being performed, the deceased may attack the living in nightmares or at other times; if the improperly buried person is a relative, his or her aggrieved spirit may decrease the patient's spiritual strength and so allow attack by various hostile forces.

14. *Negative self-schemas* that result in low self-esteem and other effects (Beck, 1996; Benight & Bandura, 2004; DuBois, Lopez, & Parra, 2004; Foa, Ehlers, Clark, Tolin, & Orsillo, 1999; Foa et al., 2004; Kangas, Henry, & Bryant, 2005; Southerland & Bryant, 2005). For many individuals, living through the Pol Pot period created a sense of helplessness and low self-efficacy as a result of being treated as slaves for many years by the Khmer Rouge. Other processes like survival guilt and inability to work will also create negative self-schemas.
15. *Negative world-schemas* that create a feeling of hopelessness, a lack of meaning, and a sense of deep injustice (Beck, 1996; Benight & Bandura, 2004; DuBois, Lopez, & Parra, 2004; Foa, Ehlers, Clark, Tolin, & Orsillo,1999; Foa et al., 2004; Kangas, Henry, & Bryant, 2005). For many individuals, living through the Pol Pot period created a deep sense of the world being an unjust place. For these individuals, the Cambodian genocide calls into question the very nature of Cambodian culture and Buddhism itself.
16. *Anxiety and depression,* which will induce somatic symptoms and increase arousal, hypervigilance, negative interpretive bias, and amygdala reactivity (Barlow, 2002), with these anxiety-and-depression-caused processes worsening all the psychopathological processes outlined above.
17. *Poor emotional regulation,* reflected in a decreased ability to distance and distract from affects as well as change effects (Cloitre et al., 2002; Wolfsdorf & Zlotnick, 2001); poor emotional regulation leads to all the emotion-related processes outlined above. Cambodians have impaired emotion regulation (e.g., of anger), with many patients utilizing emotion-regulation techniques taught in the context of Buddhism. An important area of research concerns whether local healing traditions can improve the ability to emotionally regulate.

Concluding Remarks

In this chapter we have explored the applicability to other cultural groups of certain anxiety disorders (PAD, GAD, and PTSD), as defined in the *DSM*, by using a certain analytic approach. The current chapter suggests that to examine an anxiety disorder in cross-cultural perspective, one should evaluate not only if it can be diagnosed, but also if its features are found in other cultural contexts, and additionally how that particular type of disorder is generated in other cultural contexts. This might be called the *cross-cultural study of psychopathological mechanisms*, as compared to the *cross-cultural study of diagnostic entities*. Clearly, these two fields are closely linked, but to avoid cultural bias, both approaches should be simultaneously utilized. We consider below the implications of the current chapter in respect to possible changes in the diagnostic criteria of the anxiety disorders in the *DSM*, and also suggest future research directions.

Psychological theorists have put forth theories of how anxiety disorders are generated, and those theories can be tested by examining cross-cultural data. Using such an approach, that is, examining psychopathological mechanisms in cross-cultural perspective, we have provided further evidence of the role of catastrophic cognitions in the anxiety disorders. Building on this finding, and in light of the cross-cultural evidence, we argue that it is important to investigate a group's ethnophysiology and cultural syndromes, its ethnophysiology-caused and cultural-syndrome-caused catastrophic cognitions. For instance, if a patient has a certain symptom in a panic attack, one must determine whether the patient attributes the symptom to a disorder of physiology or to a cultural syndrome; that is, examine the symptom-related cultural syndromes and ethnophysiology. Expanding the notion of catastrophic cognitions to include an examination of ethnophysiology and cultural syndromes allows a more culturally sensitive understanding of the anxiety disorders.

At present, the *DSM–IV* criteria for a panic attack include three catastrophic cognitions, considered at a very abstract level, namely, numbers 9 through 11, which are fear of losing control or going crazy, fear of dying, and derealization and depersonalization. We would suggest that these diagnostic criteria be clearly labeled as catastrophic cognitions in the *DSM*, and that the other symptoms listed in the panic attack criteria, which are sensations, be specifically labeled as such. Additionally, in respect to catastrophic cognitions, we would suggest that the criteria state the following: that the clinician should ask why "insanity" is feared, the nature of the feared mental derangement, and why "death is feared," and in both cases, that the clinician should determine the associated catastrophic cognitions, including feared cultural syndromes and dysregulations of ethnophysiology. (In respect to the third catastrophic cognition, it is not clear that *derealization* and *depersonalization* are identifiable in other cultural groups, though often a similar phenomenon is described as "soul loss" in many cultures; (see Hinton & Good, in press.)

Based on the findings of the current chapter, we would suggest the need for a more elaborated version of the *Glossary of Culture-Bound Syndromes and Idioms of Distress than in the DSM–IV*, the need for one that lists cultural syndromes, cultural-specific ethnophysiologies, and related catastrophic cognitions. Ideally, this would be a supplementary volume, not just a glossary. As outlined in this chapter, syndromes and ethnophysiologies are not just idioms of distress—they give rise to catastrophic cognitions that play a key role in anxiety disorder, including panic disorder (PD), generalized anxiety disorder (GAD), and posttraumatic stress disorder (PTSD). Such a supplement might be labeled *A List of Ethnophysiologies, Cultural Syndromes, and Related Catastrophic Cognitions*, and the clinician could use it to indicate the ethnophysiology or cultural syndrome, as well as catastrophic cognitions, that seem to play a role in the generation of the anxiety disorder in question for a particular patient; or at the very least, the relevant ethnophysiology and/or cultural syndrome could be indicated using a diagnostic code, and the catastrophic cognitions would be clear from the specified ethnophysiology and/or cultural syndrome, and would be discussed in the section in the supplement that describes the ethnophysiology and/or cultural syndrome.

We have also noted that there may be great cultural variability in the anxiety disorders owing to the specific nature of past traumas. Those trauma histories may result in reactivity and sensitivity to certain sensations owing to kindling and trauma recall, may result in a sensitivity to certain sensations; consequently, the occurrence of those anxiety sensations may trigger a rapid escalation of anxiety. Clearly trauma associations will play a key role in the generation and escalation of various anxiety disorders, not just PTSD. In support of such a view, as we have shown in this chapter, hybrid panic attacks that combine PTSD and PD characteristics would seem to be common in many cultural contexts.

More generally, the current review suggests that it is arbitrary to consider PD and PTSD to be totally separate entities. When the putative psychological mechanisms generating these disorders are carefully examined in cross-cultural context, hybrid entities are often seen to occur. It might be more useful to have diagnostic category for panic attacks, with an optional qualification as to whether the attacks feature catastrophic cognitions (CC-type panic attacks), trauma associations (TA-type panic attacks), or both (CC-TA-type panic attacks). This is a phenomenological description that gives importance to cognitions and may help guide therapeutic approaches.

In addition, it might be useful to have a diagnostic category for *worry episodes*, and that the category allow one to indicate the worry-episode-induced symptoms (e.g., dizziness, muscle tension, cold extremities) and whether the episode sometimes escalates to panic—and a way to classify the panic in respect to the three types mentioned above (i.e., a CC-, TA-, or CC-TA-panic attack). As indicated for Cambodian refugees, GAD-type worry episodes often trigger PD-type catastrophic cognitions and PTSD-type trauma associations, which in turn increase anxiety, depression, and health concerns, so producing a vicious cycle of worsening. This model of anxiety psychopathology gives clues as to how comorbidity commonly occurs between GAD and other disorders, such as PD and PTSD, a comorbidity that is commonly observed in other cultural contexts, and this model gives clues as to how such comorbidity is perpetuated. This model of worry-related psychopathology can be investigated by examining its validity in other cultural contexts.

The current review also has important implications for *anxiety sensitivity*, a construct that predicts the predisposition to and severity of anxiety disorders such as PD and PTSD. We would also argue that trauma associations and catastrophic cognitions are a major source of anxiety sensitivity, that is, reactivity to anxiety-related somatic and psychological symptoms (Hinton, Chong, et al., in press; Hinton & Otto, 2006; Hinton, Pich, Safren, Pollack, & McNally, 2006d). Consequently, anxiety sensitivity would be expected to vary greatly across cultures, depending on the trauma associations to and catastrophic cognitions about anxiety-related somatic symptoms and psychological symptoms. There is evidence that is the case (Hinton et al., 2005a, 2006d; Hinton, Chong, et al., in press), which has important implications in respect to the cross-cultural predisposition to anxiety disorders.

The construct of anxiety sensitivity would lead one to expect great comorbidity among the *DSM* anxiety disorders, another reason to encourage a comorbid diagnostic approach, such as allowing the diagnosis of panic attacks in the context of many disorders (e.g., PD, GAD, PTSD, social phobia, phobias more generally). And in cultures or groups with high levels of anxiety sensitivity, high rates of anxiety disorders, and high rates of comorbidity, would be expected.

As suggested in the current review, an adequate examination of the presentation of anxiety disorders in other cultures requires multiple analytic approaches:

- Conducting surveys using an extensive list of symptoms related to the anxiety category in order to minimize excluding symptoms important in that context (e.g., because of being part of local syndromes)
- Determining that group's understanding of the disorder and dimensions of that disorder (e.g., a group may attribute uncontrollable worry to spirit possession, high levels of bad luck, or a weak heart)
- Determining that group's ethnophysiological understanding of how anxiety symptoms are produced (including ethnophysiology-generated catastrophic cognitions)
- Determining the cultural syndromes to which anxiety symptoms are attributed (including cultural-syndrome-generated catastrophic cognitions)
- Determining the trauma events recalled by somatic symptoms
- Determining the metaphors associated with anxiety-related somatic symptoms (e.g., metaphors involving dizziness), because those metaphors may result in worry episodes inducing certain symptoms, may contribute to the affective valences of symptoms, and may impact on *symptom sensitivity*, that is, reactivity to symptoms (Hinton & Otto, 2006; Hinton et al., 2007a)

- Investigating the applicability of current psychological models of how specific anxiety disorders are produced

Such research has implications beyond diagnostic considerations. Only through such investigation can adequate treatments of anxiety disorders in other cultural contexts be developed (Hinton et al., 2004, 2005d; Hinton & Otto, 2006). It is critical to determine the local psychological mechanisms that produce the disorder in question in order to address those processes in treatment. In addition, such research will provide insights into the validity of the *DSM* as applied to other cultures, will give insights into how the *DSM* might be revised to reflect true, basic psychopathological processes, valid for all cultures, rather than being a somewhat arbitrary set of categories, and will give insights into the exact workings of psychopathological processes in other cultural contexts.

References

Bagilishya, D. (2000). Mourning and recovery from trauma in Rwanda, tears flow within. *Transcultural Psychiatry, 37*, 337–353.

Barlow, D. H. (2002). *Anxiety and its disorders: The nature and treatment of anxiety and panic*, (2nd ed.). New York: Guilford Press.

Beck, A. T. (1988). Cognitive approaches to panic disorder: Theory and therapy. In S. Rachman, & J. Maser (Eds.), *Panic, psychological perspectives*. (pp. 33–54). Hillsdale: Lawrence Erlbaum.

Beck, A. T. (1996). Beyond belief: A theory of modes, personality, and psychopathology. In P. M. Salkovskis (Ed.), *Frontiers of cognitive therapy* (pp. 1–25). New York: The Guilford Press.

Benight, C. C., & Bandura, A. (2004). Social cognitive theory of posttraumatic recovery: The role of perceived self-efficacy. *Behaviour Research and Therapy, 42*, 1129–1148.

Bouton, M., Mineka, S., & Barlow, D. H. (2001). A modern learning theory perspective on the etiology of panic disorder. *Psychological Review, 108*, 4–32.

Brewin. C. R., & Holmes, E. A. (2003). Psychological theories of posttraumatic stress disorder. *Clinical Psychological Review, 23*, 339–376.

Bryant, R. A., & Guthrie, R. M. (2005). Maladaptive appraisals as a risk factor for posttraumatic stress: A study of trainee firefighters. *Psychological Science, 16*, 749–752.

Chambless, D. L., Caputo, G. C., Bright, P., & Gallagher, R. (1984). Assessment of fear of fear in agoraphobics: The body sensations questionnaire and the agoraphobic cognitions questionnaire. *Journal of Counseling and Clinical Psychology, 6*, 1090–1097.

Clark, D. (1986). A cognitive approach to panic. *Behaviour Research and Therapy,24*, 461–470.

Clark, D. M., & Ehlers, A. (2004). Posttraumatic stress disorder: From cognitive theory to therapy. In R. L. Leahy (Ed.), *Contemporary cognitive therapy* (pp. 141–160). New York: Guilford.

Cloitre, M., Koenen, K. C., Cohen, L. R., & Han, H. (2002). Skills training in affective and interpersonal regulation followed by exposure: A phase-based treatment for PTSD related to childhood abuse. *Journal of Consulting and Clinical Psychology, 70*, 1067–1074.

Craske, M. G. (1991). Phobic fear and panic attacks: The same emotional states triggered by different cues? *Clinical Psychology Review, 11*, 599–620.

Craske, M. G. (2003). *Origins of phobias and anxiety disorders: Why more women than men?* Amsterdam:Elsevier.

DuBois, D. L., Lopez, C., & Parra, G. R. (2004). Cognitive therapy and the self. In M.A. Reinecke, & D. A. Clark (Eds.), *Cognitive therapy across the lifespan.* (pp. 202–230). Cambridge, England: Cambridge University Press.

Dunmore, E., Clark, D. M., & Ehlers, A. (2001). A prospective investigation of the role of cognitive factors in persistent posttraumatic stress disorder (PTSD) after physical and sexual assault. *Behaviour Research and Therapy, 39*, 1063–1084.

Falsetti, S. A., & Resnick, H. S. (2000). Cognitive–behavioral treatment for PTSD with comorbid panic attacks. *Journal of Contemporary Psychotherapy, 30*, 163–179.

Foa, E. B., Ehlers, A., Clark, D. M., Tolin, D. F., & Orsillo, S. M. (1999). The posttraumatic cognitions inventory (PTCI): Development and validation. *Psychological Assessment, 11*, 303–314.

Foa, E. B., & Rauch, S. A. (2004). Cognitive changes during prolonged exposure versus prolonged exposure plus cognitive restructuring in female assault survivors with posttraumatic stress disorder. *Journal of Consulting and Clinical Psychology, 72*, 879–884.

Foa, E. B., & Rothbaum, B. O. (1998). *Treating the trauma of rape: Cognitive–behavioral therapy for PTSD.* New York: Guilford.

Germain, A., Buysse, D. J., Shear, M. K., Fayyad, R., & Austin, C. (2004). Clinical correlates of poor sleep quality in posttraumatic stress disorder. *Journal of Traumatic Stress, 17*, 477–484.

Gorman, J. M. (Ed.). (2004). *Fear & anxiety: The benefits of translational research.* Washington, DC: American Psychiatric Publishing.

Guarnaccia, P. J., & Rogler, L. H. (1999). Research on cultural-bound syndromes. *American Journal of Psychiatry, 156*, 1322–1327.

Halligan, S. L., Michael, T., Clark, D. M., & Ehlers, A. (2003). Posttraumatic stress disorder following assault: The role of cognitive processing, trauma memory, and appraisals. *Journal of Consulting and Clinical Psychology, 71*, 410–431.

Henning, K. R., & Frueh, B. C. (1997). Combat guilt and its relationship to PTSD symptoms. *Journal of Clinical Psychology, 53*, 801–808.

Henry, D. (2006). Violence and the body: Somatic expressions of trauma and vulnerability during war. *Medical Anthropology Quarterly, 20*, 379–415.

Hinton, D. E., Ba, P., Peou, S., & Um, K. (2000). Panic disorder among Cambodian refugees attending a psychiatric clinic: Prevalence and subtypes. *General Hospital Psychiatry, 22*, 437–444.

Hinton, D. E., Chau, H., Nguyen, L., Nguyen, M., Pham, T., Quinn, S., & Tran, M. (2001). Panic disorder among Vietnamese refugees attending a psychiatric clinic: Prevalence and subtypes. *General Hospital Psychiatry, 23*, 337–344.

Hinton, D. E., Chea, A., Ba, P., & Pollack, M. H. (2004). Olfactory panic among Cambodian refugees: A contextual approach. *Transcultural Psychiatry, 41*,155199.

Hinton, D. E., Chhean, D., Fama, J. M., Pollack, M. H., & McNally, R. J. (2007a). Gastrointestinal-focused panic attacks among Cambodian refugees: Associated psychopathology, flashbacks, and catastrophic cognitions. *Journal of Anxiety Disorders, 21*, 42–58.

Hinton, D. E., Chhean, D., Pich, V., Hofmann, S. G., & Barlow, D. H. (2006b). Tinnitus among Cambodian refugees: Relationship to PTSD severity. *Journal of Traumatic Stress. 19*, 541–546

Hinton, D. E., Chhean, D., Pich, V., Safren, S. A., Hofmann, S. G., & Pollack, M. H. (2005d). A randomized controlled trial of CBT for Cambodian refugees with treatment-resistant PTSD and panic attacks: A cross-over design. *Journal of Traumatic Stress, 18*, 617–629.

Hinton, D. E., Chhean, D., Pich, V., Um, K., Fama, J. M., & Pollack, M. H. (2006a). Neck-focused panic attacks among Cambodian refugees: A logistic and linear regression analysis. *Journal of Anxiety Disorders, 20*, 119–138.

Hinton, D. E., Chong, R., Pollack, M. H., Barlow D. H., & McNally, R. J. (in press). *Ataque de nervios*: Relationship to anxiety sensitivity and dissociation predisposition. *Depression and Anxiety*.

Hinton, D. E., & Good, B. G. (in press). *Culture and panic disorder*. Stanford: Stanford University Press.

Hinton, D. E., & Hinton, S. D. (2002). Panic disorder, somatization, and the new cross-cultural psychiatry: The seven bodies of a medical anthropology of panic. *Culture, Medicine, and Psychiatry, 26*, 155–178.

Hinton, D. E., Hinton, S. D., Pham, T., Chau, H., & Tran, M. (2003). "Hit by the wind and temperature-shift panic among Vietnamese refugees. *Transcultural Psychiatry, 40*, 342–376.

Hinton, D. E., Hinton, S. D., Um, K., Chea, A., & Sak, S. (2002). The Khmer "weak heart" syndrome: Fear of death from palpitations. *Transcultural Psychiatry, 39*, 323–344.

Hinton, D. E., Hofmann, S. G., Pitman, R. K., Pollack, M. H., & Barlow. D. H. (in press). The panic attack–PTSD model: Applicability to orthostatic panic among Cambodian refugees. *Cognitive Behaviour Therapy*.

Hinton, D. E., Howes, D., Kirmayer, L. J. (in press). Towards a medical anthropology of sensation: Definitions and research agendas. *Transcultural Psychiatry*.

Hinton, D. E., Hsia, C., Um, K., & Otto, M. W. (2003). Anger-associated panic attacks in Cambodian refugees with PTSD: A multiple baseline examination of clinical data. *Behaviour Research and Therapy, 41*, 647–654.

Hinton, D. E., & Otto, M. W. (2006). Symptom presentation and symptom meaning among traumatized Cambodian refugees: Relevance to a somatically focused cognitive-behavior therapy. *Cognitive and Behavioral Practice, 13*, 249–260.

Hinton, D. E., Pham, T., Tran, M., Safren, S. A., Otto, M. W., & Pollack, M. H. (2004). CBT for Vietnamese with treatment-resistant PTSD and panic attacks. *Journal of Traumatic Stress, 17*, 429–433.

Hinton, D. E., Pich, V., Chhean, D., & Pollack, M. H. (2005b). "The ghost pushes you down": Sleep paralysis-type panic attacks in a Khmer refugee population. *Transcultural Psychiatry, 42,* 46–78.

Hinton, D. E., Pich, V., Chhean, D., Pollack, M. H., & Barlow, D. H. (2004). Olfactory-triggered panic attacks among Cambodian refugees attending a psychiatric clinic. *General Hospital Psychiatry, 26,* 390–397.

Hinton, D. E., Pich, V, Chhean D, Safren S. A., Pollack, M. H. (2007b) Cognitive-behavior therapy for Cambodian refugees with PTSD and neck-focused panic attacks. *Psychotherapy: Theory, Research, Practice, Training, 43,* 491–505.

Hinton, D., Pich, V., Chhean, D., Pollack, M. H., & McNally, R. J. (2005c). Sleep paralysis among Cambodian refugees: Association with PTSD diagnosis and severity. *Depression and Anxiety, 22,* 47–51.

Hinton, D. E., Pich, V., Safren, S. A., Pollack, M. H., & McNally, R. J. (2005a). Anxiety sensitivity among Cambodian refugees with panic disorder: A discriminant function and factor analytic investigation. *Behaviour Research and Therapy, 43,* 1631–1643.

Hinton, D. E., Pich, V., Safren, S. A., Pollack, M. H., & McNally, R. J. (2006d). Anxiety sensitivity among Cambodian refugees with panic disorder: A factor analytic investigation. *Journal of Anxiety Disorders, 20,* 119–138.

Hinton, D. E., So, V., Pollack, M. H., Pitman, R. K., & Orr, S. P. (2004). The psychophysiology of orthostatic panic in Cambodian refugees attending a psychiatric clinic. *Journal of Psychopathology and Behavioral Assessment, 26,* 1–13.

Hinton, D. E., Um, K., & Ba, P. (2001a). *Kyol goeu* (wind overload) part I: A cultural syndrome of orthostatic panic among Khmer refugees. *Transcultural Psychiatry, 38,* 403–432.

Hinton, D. E., Um, K., & Ba, P. (2001b). *Kyol goeu* (wind overload) part II: Prevalence, characteristics and mechanisms of *kyol goeu* and near-*kyol goeu* episodes of Khmer patients attending a psychiatric clinic. *Transcultural Psychiatry, 38,* 433–460.

Hinton, D. E., Um, K., & Ba, P. (2001c). A unique panic disorder presentation among Khmer refugees: The sore neck syndrome. *Culture, Medicine, and Psychiatry, 25,* 297–316.

Hsia, C. & Barlow, D. H. (2001). On the natural culturally bounded syndromes in the nosology of mental disorders. *Transcultural Psychiatry, 38,* 81–82.

Jones, J. C., & Barlow, D. H. (1990). The etiology of posttraumatic stress disorder. *Clinical Psychology Review, 10,* 299–328.

Kangas, M., Henry, J. L., & Bryant, R. A. (2005). A prospective study of autobiographical memory and posttraumatic stress disorder following cancer. *Journal of Consulting and Clinical Psychology, 73,* 293–299.

Katon, W. (1984). Panic disorder and somatization: Review of 55 cases. *American Journal of Medicine, 77,* 101–106.

Katon, W. (1989). *Panic disorder in the medical setting.* Washington, D. C.: U.S. Department of Health and Human Services.

Kirmayer, L. J., & Sartorius, N. (2007). Cultural models and somatic syndromes. *Psychosomatic Medicine, 69,* 832–840.

Koenen, K. C., Stellman, J. M., Stellman S. D., & Sommer, J. F. (2003). Risk factors for course of posttraumatic stress disorder among Vietnam veterans: A 14-year follow-up of American Legionnaires. *Journal of Consulting and Clinical Psychology, 71,* 980–986.

Lee, D. A., Scragg, P., & Turner, S. (2001). The role of shame and guilt in traumatic events: A clinical model of shame-based and guilt-based PTSD. *British Journal of Medical Psychology, 74*, 451–466.

McNally, R. J. (1994). *Panic disorder: A critical analysis*. New York: The Guilford Press.

Michael, T., Ehlers, A., Halligan, S. L., & Clark, D. M. (2005). Unwanted memories of assault: What intrusion characteristics are associated with PTSD. *Behaviour Research and Therapy, 43*, 613–628.

Noyes, R., & Hoehn-Saric, R. (1998). *The anxiety disorders*. Cambridge, England: Cambridge University Press.

Rapee, R., Craske, M. G., & Barlow, D. H. (1995). Assessment instrument for panic disorder that include fear of sensation-producing activities: The Albany panic and phobia questionnaire. *Anxiety, 1*, 114–144.

Resick, P. A., & Schnicke, M. K. (1992). Cognitive processing therapy for sexual assault victims. *Journal of Consulting and Clinical Psychology, 60*, 748–756.

Scupi, B., Benson, B., Brown, L. & Uhde, T. (1997). Rapid onset: A valid panic disorder criterion? *Depression and Anxiety, 5*, 121–126.

Southerland, K., & Bryant, R. A. (2005). Self-defining memories in post-traumatic stress disorder. *British Journal of Clinical Psychology, 44*, 591–598.

Street, L., Craske, M. G., & Barlow, D. H. (1989). Sensations, cognitions, and the perception of cues associated with expected and unexpected attacks. *Behaviour Research and Therapy, 27*, 189–198.

Watson, D. (2005). Rethinking the mood and anxiety disorders: A quantitative hierarchical model for DSM–IV. *Journal of Abnormal Psychology, 4*, 522–536.

Wells, A. (2000). *Emotional disorder and metacognitions: Innovative cognitive therapy*. West Sussex, England: Wiley.

Wells, A., & Papageorgiou, C. (2004). Metacognitive therapy for depressive rumination. In C. Papageorgiou, & A. Wells (Eds.), *Depressive rumination, Nature, theory, and treatment* (pp. 259–273). West Sussex, England: Wiley.

Wolfsdorf, B. A., & Zlotnick, C. (2001). Affect management in group therapy for women with posttraumatic stress disorder and histories of childhood sexual abuse. *Journal of Clinical Psychology, 57*, 169–181.

Zayfert, C., & DeViva, J. C. (2004). Residual insomnia following cognitive behavioral therapy for PTSD. *Journal of Traumatic Stress, 17*, 69–73.

11

Rethinking the Anxiety Disorders in *DSM-V* and Beyond: Quantitative Dimensional Models of Anxiety and Related Psychopathology

David Watson

A large and rapidly growing body of research has sought to explicate the underlying dimensional structure of the anxiety disorders and closely related types of psychopathology (especially major depression and other mood disorders). This research has been stimulated by two key taxonomic problems—comorbidity and heterogeneity—that have plagued successive editions of the *Diagnostic and Statistical Manual of Mental Disorders* (*DSM*; American Psychiatric Association, 1980, 1987, 1994), including the current *DSM-IV*. The goal of this chapter is to review this structural evidence and to examine its broader implications for the classification of the anxiety and mood disorders in the forthcoming *DSM-V*.

My central argument is that a revised taxonomy that incorporates this quantitative structural evidence can help to address the problems of comorbidity and heterogeneity, and produce a system that better suits the needs of clinical research and treatment.

The Current *DSM-IV* Taxonomy

The Current Diagnostic Classes

DSM-III (American Psychiatric Association, 1980) represented a radical change in the classification of mental disorders. One of its major innovations was the creation of a series of diagnostic classes. These diagnostic classes are rationally based. That is, "the organizing principle . . . is to group disorders based on their shared phenomenological features in order to facilitate differential diagnosis." (*DSM-IV*, p. 10). In other words, disorders are grouped together if they "seem to belong together" because they share phenotypically similar symptoms.

What are these "shared phenomenological features"? The core features of the anxiety disorders "are symptoms of anxiety and avoidance behavior" (*DSM-III-R*, p. 235). In contrast, major depression and other mood disorders "have a disturbance of mood as the predominant feature" (*DSM-IV*, p. 317). Thus, the current separation among the two diagnostic classes essentially rests on the distinction between sad/depressed mood (the organizing principle underlying the mood disorders) and anxious mood/avoidance behavior (the core symptoms of the anxiety disorders) (see Watson, 2005).

A Quantitative Alternative

Extensive evidence indicates that (a) anxious mood is strongly correlated with sad, depressed mood across both normal range and clinical samples, such that (b) the current diagnostic classes do not provide an optimal arrangement of these disorders (see Watson, 2005; Watson, O'Hara, & Stuart, 2008). More fundamentally, we now have sufficient data to eliminate this rational phenomenological system and replace it with an empirically based quantitative structure that reflects the actual—rather than the perceived—similarities among different types of psychopathology. Put differently, we can construct a more valid taxonomy by grouping together disorders that are strongly comorbid and that present significant diagnostic problems.

A quantitatively based taxonomy offers two fundamental advantages over the current rational scheme. First, unlike the current diagnostic classes, it models comorbidity data directly. In a quantitative structure, strongly correlated syndromes are located together within the same basic group, whereas more weakly related disorders are placed in different classes. Accordingly, a quantitatively based taxonomy directly communicates observable patterns of diagnostic co-occurrence in an easily understandable form. Thus, it actually serves the stated goal of facilitating differential diagnosis better than the existing diagnostic classes. Second, genotypic (e.g., twin studies) and phenotypic analyses generally parallel one another and typically lead to similar structural conclusions (Mineka, Watson, & Clark, 1998; Watson, 2005). Consequently, a quantitatively oriented structure would facilitate the ultimate development of a taxonomy based on core underlying etiological features, such as common genetic diatheses.

The Problem of Comorbidity

Comorbidity—that is, the co-occurrence beyond chance of different disorders within the same individual (Lilienfeld, Waldman, & Israel, 1994)—now is widely recognized to be a pervasive problem throughout the *DSM* (Clark, Watson, & Reynolds, 1995; Mineka et al., 1998; Widiger & Clark, 2000). We can view this evidence at three different levels. First, individual anxiety disorders are strongly comorbid with one another (Brown & Barlow, 1992; Brown, Campbell, Lehman, Grisham, & Mancil, 2001). For instance, using lifetime diagnoses in the National Comorbidity Survey (NCS) data, Magee, Eaton, Wittchen, McGonagle, and Kessler (1996) reported that 74.1% of those with agoraphobia, 68.7% of those with simple phobia, and 56.9% of those with social phobia also met criteria for another anxiety disorder. Similarly, in analyses of hierarchy-free 12-month diagnoses in the NCS Replication (NCS-R) data, Kessler, Chu, Demler, and Walters (2005) reported that agoraphobia had tetrachoric correlations of .68 with social phobia, .64 with panic disorder, and .57 with specific phobia.

Second, the anxiety disorders are strongly comorbid with the mood disorders, and vice versa (Clark & Watson, 1991,

2006; Mineka et al., 1998). For example, in analyses of lifetime diagnoses in the NCS data, Kessler et al. (1996) reported that 58% of individuals with major depression also met criteria for a comorbid anxiety disorder; the comorbidity rate was only slightly reduced to 51.2% when 12-month diagnoses were used. Conversely, most individuals with diagnosed anxiety disorders also meet criteria for depression, although comorbidity rates vary widely across disorders (Mineka et al., 1998). For instance, in the NCS data, major depression had very different comorbidity rates with various anxiety disorders, ranging from an odds ratio of 6 with generalized anxiety disorder (GAD) to 4 with panic disorder and 3 for simple and social phobia (Kessler et al., 1996). These differential comorbidity patterns are both highly systematic and quite robust across multiple studies (Kessler et al., 2005; Krueger & Markon, 2006; Slade & Watson, 2006; Vollebergh et al., 2001), and provide the basis for a revised, quantitatively based taxonomy.

Third, the anxiety and mood disorders both show extensive comorbidity with other types of psychopathology, including the substance use disorders, eating disorders, somatoform disorders, and personality disorders (Clark et al., 1995; Mineka et al., 1998; Widiger & Clark, 2000). These data demonstrate that a comprehensive structural scheme need not be restricted to the anxiety and mood disorders but also can subsume syndromes that are currently placed in other diagnostic classes. However, the articulation of a comprehensive structural scheme is beyond the scope of this chapter.

Earlier Structural Models

The Two-Factor Affective Model

How can we explain the extensive comorbidity between the anxiety and mood disorders? My colleagues and I originally developed a model that drew on key findings from the basic mood literature. Extensive data establish the existence of two dominant dimensions of emotional experience: negative affect (or negative activation; NA) and positive affect (or positive activation; PA) (Watson, 2000; Watson & Tellegen, 1985; Watson, Wiese, Vaidya, & Tellegen, 1999). NA is a general dimension of subjective distress and dissatisfaction that subsumes a broad range of mood states—including fear, anger, sadness, guilt, and disgust. Its emergence in structural analyses indicates that these various negative emotions co-occur both within and across individuals (e.g., an individual who reports feeling sad is likely to report substantial levels of anger, fear, guilt, etc.). In parallel fashion, the PA dimension reflects significant co-occurrences among various positive mood states (e.g., someone who reports feeling happy tends to feel interested, excited, confident, and alert).

Extrapolating from these data, we argued that this general NA dimension was largely responsible for the substantial comorbidity between depression and anxiety (Watson, Clark, & Carey, 1988). Put differently, this higher order NA factor produces strong correlations among different types of negative emotion, including sad/depressed affect and fearful/anxious affect (see also Watson, 2000; Watson et al., 2008).

How, then, can anxiety and depression be distinguished? Other findings established that the higher order PA factor has stronger and more consistent (negative) associations with depression than with anxiety (see Watson, 2000; Watson et al., 1988, 1999). We therefore proposed that low levels of PA (i.e., anhedonia) are a specific feature of depression that distinguishes it from the anxiety disorders. Thus, in this two-factor model, NA represents a nonspecific factor common to depression and anxiety, whereas PA is a specific factor that is related primarily to depression. This model has received support in a number of studies (e.g., Mineka et al., 1998; Watson et al., 1988; Watson, 2000, 2005).

The Tripartite Model

Clark and Watson (1991) extended this two-factor model by proposing a second specific factor—physiological hyperarousal—that is relatively unique to anxiety. They therefore argued that a tripartite model more accurately captures this domain. This model classifies symptoms of anxiety and depression into three basic groups. First, many symptoms are strong indicators of the general NA dimension; this nonspecific group includes both anxious and depressed mood, as well as other symptoms that are prevalent in both mood and anxiety disorders (e.g., insomnia, concentration, and memory problems). In addition, each syndrome has its own specific symptom cluster: Somatic tension and hyperarousal (e.g., dizziness, shortness of breath) are specific to anxiety, whereas anhedonia/low PA (e.g., loss of interest; feeling that nothing is enjoyable) is unique to depression. This model also has received support in a number of studies (e.g., Brown, Chorpita, & Barlow, 1998; see Mineka et al., 1998, for a review).

The Integrative Hierarchical Model

Although aspects of the tripartite model worked quite well, the accumulating evidence exposed two significant problems. First, the model fails to account for the substantial heterogeneity within the anxiety disorders. Most notably, Brown et al. (1998) found that the anxious arousal component of the tripartite model was not broadly characteristic of the anxiety disorders but instead represented the specific component of panic disorder; subsequent data also linked anxious arousal to posttraumatic stress disorder (PTSD; Brown, Campbell et al., 2001). Second, several studies have established that the PA dimension is not only unique to depression but also shows consistent negative associations with social phobia (Brown et al., 1998; Watson et al., 1988; Watson, Gamez, & Simms, 2005).

To address these problems, Mineka et al. (1998) proposed an integrative hierarchical model that incorporated elements from both the tripartite model and Barlow's (1991; Zinbarg & Barlow, 1996) hierarchical structure of the anxiety disorders. In this expanded scheme, each individual syndrome is hypothesized to contain a both common and unique component. Consistent with the earlier models, the shared component represents broad individual differences in NA; it is a pervasive higher order factor that is common to both anxiety and mood disorders, and primarily is responsible for the pervasive comorbidity problem. In addition, each disorder also includes unique features that differentiate it from all of the others. Thus, anxious arousal is no longer viewed as broadly characteristic of the anxiety disorders, but instead assumes a more limited role as a specific element in syndromes such as panic disorder.

Furthermore, Mineka et al. (1998) reviewed evidence indicating that the size of these general and specific components differs markedly across disorders. Specifically, both major depression and GAD are distress-laden disorders that clearly contain an enormous amount of this general factor variance; in contrast, most of the other anxiety disorders (such as social phobia and specific phobia) contain a more modest component of nonspecific negative affectivity (see Gamez, Watson, & Doebbeling, 2007; Watson et al., 2005).

Unfortunately, although the integrative hierarchical model represents an improvement over its predecessors, it also has crucial limitations of its own. The key problem is that the model posits a single general factor—that is, general distress or NA—that is responsible for observed patterns of comorbidity. Specifically, it predicts (a) a high level of comorbidity between two disorders that have strong components of negative affectivity, but (b) a weaker level of comorbidity among syndromes containing less of this general factor variance. The former proposition has received substantial support in the literature. Most notably, consistent with this scheme, major depression and GAD—two disorders that are strongly saturated with general factor variance—are highly comorbid with one another (e.g., Krueger, 1999; Mineka et al., 1998; Vollebergh et al., 2001; Watson et al., 2008). The latter prediction has proven to be much more problematic, however. For instance, specific phobia and social phobia—disorders containing a lesser amount of nonspecific variance—also are strongly comorbid (e.g., Krueger, 1999; Krueger & Markon, 2006). These data establish that more than one nonspecific factor is ultimately needed to model comorbidity adequately.

The model's ability to capture observed comorbidities could be improved by taking into account the influence of the PA and anxious arousal dimensions. For instance, the shared component of low PA likely contributes to the comorbidity between major depression and social phobia, whereas a common element of anxious arousal may be partly responsible for the observed co-occurrence between panic disorder and PTSD (Brown, Campbell et al., 2001; Brown et al., 1998). However, the model still fails to account fully for the overlap among lower distress disorders such as specific phobia and social phobia. Of course, we could further enhance the model by positing additional dimensions that will help to account for the comorbidity data more adequately. It is more parsimonious, however, to analyze the comorbidity data directly and then create a structural model that captures these covariations as accurately as possible. This is the strategy I consider next.

A Quantitative Hierarchical Model of the Anxiety and Mood Disorders

The Necessity of a New "Superclass"

As I have discussed, extensive comorbidity data demonstrate that the anxiety disorders are substantially related to the mood disorders—or at least, the unipolar syndromes of major depression and dysthymic disorder (Mineka et al., 1998; Watson, 2005). Moreover, evidence from the basic affect literature establishes that this problem cannot be eliminated through some careful tweaking of the diagnostic criteria; rather, it is inherent in the defining characteristics of these diagnostic classes.

It is time to end the artificial separation between the mood and anxiety disorders, and to formally recognize the strong links between them. The easiest way to accomplish this in *DSM-V* and *ICD-11* would be to create an overarching "superclass" that subsumes most of the current mood and anxiety disorders (Clark & Watson, 2006; Krueger & Markon, 2006; Watson, 2005). This superclass should be given a nonspecific label, such as "emotional disorders". This nonspecific name would formally recognize the fact that this superclass subsumes different types of negative affect, including both depression and anxiety. This superclass easily could be expanded to include other types of negative affect, such as anger-based disorders (e.g., Feindler, 2006; Kassinove, 1995; Watson et al., 2008).

The Necessity of Reorganization

How should individual disorders be arranged within this new superclass? The most conservative approach would be to keep the current organization largely intact and to reconceptualize the mood and anxiety disorders as separate subclasses within the emotional disorders. However, it is now clear that the current diagnostic classes do not provide an optimal arrangement of the disorders; that is, they do not accurately reflect the actual empirical similarities among these disorders, based on comorbidity evidence and other data. The most obvious problem involves the current placement of GAD within the anxiety disorders. GAD is very strongly linked to the unipolar mood disorders, both phenotypically and genotypically (Kendler, Prescott, Meyers, & Neale, 2003; Mineka et al., 1998; Watson, 2005). For instance, analyses of twin data consistently have found that major depression and GAD are genetically indistinguishable, indicating that they reflect a single, common genetic diathesis (Kendler, 1996; Roy, Neale, Pedersen, Mathé, & Kendler, 1995).

Moreover, extensive structural data establish that GAD actually is more strongly related to the unipolar mood disorders than to other anxiety disorders (Watson, 2005). Krueger (1999) conducted extensive structural analyses of *DSM-III-R* diagnoses in the NCS data. He found evidence of a broad internalizing factor that could be decomposed into two subfactors: anxious–misery (defined by major depression, dysthymia, and GAD) and fear (marked by panic disorder, agoraphobia, social phobia, and simple phobia). Moreover, this model fit the data significantly better than a structure based on the traditional *DSM* classification, in which the anxiety disorders marked one factor, and depression and dysthymia defined the other. Thus, the structural evidence clearly demonstrated that GAD was more closely related to the unipolar mood disorders than to other anxiety disorders. Cox, Clara, and Enns (2002) subsequently extended this model by showing that PTSD also loaded on the anxious–misery factor in the NCS data.

Vollebergh et al. (2001) obtained very similar results in confirmatory factor analyses of the two waves of the Netherlands Mental Health Survey and Incidence Study (NEMESIS). Once again, the model fits were better when GAD was grouped with depression and dysthymia than with the other anxiety disorders.

In their analyses of the Australian National Survey of Mental Health and Well-Being, Slade and Watson (2006) extended this evidence in two ways. First, they demonstrated that the same basic structure also characterized *DSM-IV* and *ICD-10* diagnoses. Second, they modeled an expanded set of disorders. Specifically, they demonstrated that major depression, dysthymic disorder, GAD, and PTSD all defined the anxious–misery factor (neurasthenia also loaded on this factor in the *ICD-10* analyses), whereas panic disorder, agoraphobia, social phobia, and obsessive–compulsive disorder (OCD) were markers of Fear.

Finally, Kendler et al. (2003) examined major sources of genetic risk that give rise to common psychiatric disorders. They concluded that "the structure of these genetic risk factors bears a conspicuous resemblance to the phenotypic structure of adult psychiatric disorders proposed by Krueger et al. and Vollebergh et al." (p. 935). Most notably, their proposed structural model of these genetic risk factors again emphasized the basic distinction between anxious–misery (defined here by major depression and GAD, with a lesser link to panic disorder) and fear (defined by situational phobia, animal phobia, and panic disorder).

An Alternative Arrangement of the Disorders

Watson (2005; see also Clark & Watson, 2006) used this structural evidence as the basis for a proposed reorganization of the current mood and anxiety disorders (see also Krueger and Markon, 2006). In its basic form, this new structural scheme consists of an emotional disorders superclass with three subsumed subclasses. The first subclass consists of disorders that have been found to define the anxious–misery factor in the structural analyses; it would include major depression, dysthymic disorder, GAD (as well as overanxious disorder of childhood; see Clark & Watson, 2006), and PTSD. Watson (2005) labeled these syndromes the "distress disorders" to emphasize that they all involve the experience of pervasive subjective distress and they all contain a large component of nonspecific NA (Mineka et al., 1998; Watson et al., 2005).

The second subclass consists of disorders that have been found to define the Fear factor in structural analyses. This would include panic disorder, agoraphobia, social phobia, and specific phobia. Watson (2005) labeled this group the "fear disorders".

Finally, Watson (2005) tentatively suggested that the bipolar disorders—bipolar I, bipolar II, and cyclothymia—would constitute the third subclass. However, structural investigations of the bipolar disorders have been hampered by (a) their very low base rates in the general population and (b) the frequent application of hierarchical exclusion rules (i.e., the occurrence of mania or hypomania precludes the diagnosis of major depression; see *DSM-IV*, pp. 342–343). Consequently, this aspect of the structure needs to be explicated in future research.

The Problem of Obsessive–Compulsive Disorder (OCD)

OCD shows a relatively low base rate in the general population and therefore, often has been excluded from structural analyses. Moreover, the limited data that are available have been somewhat inconsistent (see Watson, 2005, for a discussion).

OCD shares important features with a range of related syndromes that fall outside of the current mood and anxiety disorders. These overlapping features include similar symptoms, common etiological factors, and responsiveness to the same types of pharmacologic treatments. Collectively, this family of related syndromes has been labeled the "obsessive–compulsive spectrum disorders" (e.g., Hollander & Benzaquen, 1997). In a recent survey of 187 OCD experts from around the world (Mataix–Cols, Pertusa, & Leckman, 2007), the majority felt that OCD should be removed from the anxiety disorders and placed in a new class of OCD spectrum disorders. Most OCD experts supported the inclusion of body dysmorphic disorder (72% agreed), trichotillomania (70% agreed), tic disorders (61% agreed), and hypochondriasis (57% agreed) within this new diagnostic class (Mataix-Cols et al., 2007). Consequently, OCD might be removed from the "emotional disorders" in *DSM-V* and form a core component of a new diagnostic class.

Limitations of Diagnosis-Based Analyses

Although this quantitative hierarchical model has many attractive features, it is limited by the fact that it is based on dichotomous indicators (i.e., the presence versus absence of diagnoses). One faces several problems when conducting analyses based on formal diagnoses (see also Brown, Campbell et al., 2001; Watson, 2005). First, many disorders are relatively rare and show very low base rates in community samples, thereby rendering statistical analyses problematic or impossible. For instance, as noted earlier, although OCD symptomatology is quite common in the general population (see Watson, Wu, & Cutshall, 2004), the full syndrome shows a low prevalence rate and often is excluded from structural analyses. Similarly, bipolar disorder has been excluded from structural analyses of both the NCS (Krueger, 1999) and the NEMESIS (Vollebergh et al., 2001) data because of its very low base rate in the general population.

Second, analyses of diagnoses are complicated by hierarchical exclusion rules; these are criteria stipulating that certain disorders should not be diagnosed if they are judged to occur only during the course of a coexisting disorder (one that occupies a higher, more privileged place in the hierarchy; see Brown & Barlow, 1992; Clark et al., 1995). This has proven to be a particular problem in the anxiety disorders. *DSM-III* (APA, 1980) included an extensive set of exclusionary criteria that had the general effect of making it difficult to diagnose anxiety disorders in the presence of significant depression (Mineka et al., 1998). Many of these exclusion rules subsequently were dropped in *DSM-III-R* and *DSM-IV*, but some remain in modified form, and they have been applied inconsistently across different studies. Brown, Campbell et al. (2001), for example, discuss the problem that a *DSM-IV* diagnosis of GAD should not be assigned if its features occur exclusively within the course of a mood disorder. Because GAD is highly comorbid with the mood disorders (e.g., Brown, Campbell et al., 2001; Brown et al., 1998; Mineka et al., 1998), the strict application of this exclusion rule would drastically lower the base rate of GAD in a sample and necessarily would attenuate its associations with syndromes such as major depression.

Third, diagnostic criteria change significantly with each succeeding edition of the *DSM*; some of these changes may affect the strength of their associations with other syndromes. For instance, to improve differential diagnosis vis-à-vis panic disorder, symptoms of autonomic arousal (e.g., accelerated heart rate, shortness of breath) were eliminated from the *DSM-IV* criteria for GAD (see Brown, DiNardo, Lehman, & Campbell, 2001). The net effect of these changes was to enhance the general distress component in GAD, which in turn has led to greater comorbidity with major depression (Brown, DiNardo, et al., 2001; Mineka et al., 1998). Thus, diagnosis-based structural analyses can be substantially influenced by relatively minor and specific changes in the diagnostic criteria.

Fourth, diagnosis-based structural analyses fail to address the second general problem in the existing taxonomy, namely, *heterogeneity* (Watson, 2003, 2005). Many of the current anxiety and mood disorders can be decomposed into distinct symptom groups. For example, structural analyses consistently have repeatedly identified multiple symptom dimensions within OCD (e.g., Mataix–Cols, Rosario–Campos, Leckman, 2005; Watson & Wu, 2005), PTSD (e.g., McWilliams, Cox, & Asmundson, 2005; Palmieri, Weathers, Difede, & King, 2007; Simms, Watson, & Doebbeling, 2002), and specific phobia (e.g., Arrindell, Pickersgill, Merckelbach, Ardon, & Cornet, 1991; Cutshall & Watson, 2004). These symptom dimensions may correlate quite differently with other syndromes, thereby complicating structural analyses and hampering the creation of an adequate taxonomy.

The Next Step: A Symptom-Based Hierarchical Model

Basic Considerations

A quantitative, disorder-based hierarchical model easily could be implemented in *DSM-V*, as it essentially would involve (a) rethinking and replacing the existing diagnostic classes and then (b) reorganizing the current diagnoses without fundamentally changing them. Put differently, it would fundamentally transform the diagnostic classes but would leave the diagnoses themselves intact. In light of the advantages I discussed earlier, it merits serious consideration as an organizing basis for *DSM-V*.

As noted, however, this type of model is limited in a number of ways and it fails to account for the substantial heterogeneity of many current disorders. Consequently, I believe we ultimately need to construct a fully quantitative hierarchical model that decomposes psychopathology into homogeneous symptom clusters. A hierarchical symptom-based scheme requires two basic steps. First, we need to identify all the important, distinguishable symptom dimensions within the current mood and anxiety disorders (as discussed previously, this scheme easily could be expanded to subsume symptoms currently placed in other diagnostic classes). Second, we need to establish replicable patterns of covariation among these symptom clusters in order to organize them hierarchically.

Similar to a disorder-based hierarchical model, this symptom-based structure would address the problem of comorbidity by modeling it directly. In addition, it would neatly solve the problem of heterogeneity by identifying the basic homogeneous building blocks—that is, the distinguishable symptom elements—of psychopathology and then organizing them into a coherent multilevel structure.

Another key advantage of this type of model is that it nicely balances the competing interests of parsimony (which would argue for small number of broad constructs) and descriptive accuracy (which favors more complex schemes incorporating a large number of narrower constructs). Both are captured in a fully articulated hierarchical structure. Thus, depending on the requirements of the situation, researchers and clinicians would have the option of focusing on (a) a few broad higher order factors, (b) several specific lower order dimensions, or (c) some combination of the two.

Given the limited state of our current knowledge, it is not possible to implement a more radically different symptom-based taxonomy in *DSM-V*. Nevertheless, it represents a worthwhile goal for *DSM-VI* and beyond. In order to facilitate this process, I will review the available structural evidence establishing the existence of distinct symptom dimensions within major depression and several current anxiety disorders.

Because there is no clear structural evidence suggesting important, replicable symptom heterogeneity within GAD, panic, and agoraphobia, I will not discuss these areas here.

Obsessive–Compulsive Disorder (OCD)

It now is clearly recognized that OCD is heterogeneous and can be decomposed into several distinguishable symptom clusters. Mataix-Cols et al. (2005) reviewed 12 major factor analytic studies (involving more than 2,000 patients) and established the existence of four highly replicable symptom dimensions: (a) symmetry and ordering, (b) cleaning and contamination, (c) obsessions and checking, and (d) hoarding. These same four symptom factors also have emerged consistently in item-level analyses of the Obsessive–Compulsive Inventory (OCI; Foa, Kozak, Salkovskis, Coles, & Amir, 1998), the OCI Revised (OCI-R; Foa et al., 2002), and the Schedule of Compulsions, Obsessions, and Pathological Impulses (SCOPI; Watson & Wu, 2005) (see Foa et al., 2002; Watson & Wu, 2005; Wu & Watson, 2003). In an international survey of OCD experts (Mataix-Cols et al., 2007), the large majority (89%) agreed with the statement that OCD is heterogeneous and consists of distinct symptom dimensions. Moreover, the experts explicitly acknowledged the existence of these same four symptom dimensions (cleaning 92%; symmetry/order 87%; hoarding 87%; obsessions and checking 85%). Many experts (69%) also supported the existence of a fifth dimension related to sexual and religious obsessions, but this factor has not consistently emerged in structural analyses.

Thus, we can posit at least four differentiable symptom dimensions within OCD. Furthermore, these symptom dimensions are associated with distinct patterns of comorbidity, as well as differential treatment response, and different neural substrates, and genetic diatheses (Mataix-Cols et al., 2005). For instance, ordering/symmetry symptoms show a particularly strong association with Tourette's syndrome (Baer, 1994; Eapen, Robertson, Alsobrook, & Pauls, 1997). In a related vein, Watson et al. (2004) found that dissociation measures correlated much more strongly with obsessions and checking than with cleaning, ordering, and hoarding. More generally, checking symptoms appear to be somewhat more nonspecific and show greater overlap with general distress/NA (Watson et al., 2005) and other types of psychopathology (including depression) than the other dimensions (Watson et al., 2004; Wu & Watson, 2003). These distinctive patterns demonstrate the importance of assessing and modeling these symptom dimensions separately.

Posttraumatic Stress Disorder (PTSD)

The *DSM-IV* criteria for PTSD include three distinct clusters of symptoms: criterion B (intrusions and persistent reexperiencing of the trauma), criterion C (numbing and avoidance of stimuli associated with the trauma), and criterion D (symptoms of increased arousal). This tripartite organization has generated an extensive factor analytic literature on the structure of PTSD symptoms (e.g., King, Leskin, King, & Weathers, 1998; McWilliams et al., 2005; Palmieri et al., 2007; Simms et al., 2002; Taylor, Kuch, Koch, Crockett & Passey, 1998). Although the results have varied across studies, most analyses have failed to support the three-factor structure articulated in *DSM-IV*. Instead, the data have provided the strongest support for two similar four-factor structures. The first model, which initially was identified by King et al. (1998), follows the tripartite *DSM-IV* organization, except that the criterion C symptoms are split into separate avoidance and numbing factors. The second model, which initially was proposed by Simms et al. (2002), also includes intrusions, avoidance, and hyperarousal factors, although this last dimension is defined by a much smaller set of symptoms (only two, as opposed to five in the King et al. model). The fourth factor in the Simms et al. structure—dysphoria—consists of the five criterion C numbing symptoms and three of the criterion D hyperarousal symptoms.

Thus, three symptom factors—intrusions, avoidance, and hyperarousal—are highly replicable and common to both models. The intrusions and avoidance factors both appear to be specific to PTSD and should be included in any comprehensive structural analysis. In contrast, the content of the hyperarousal factor suggests that it basically taps anxious arousal (in the Simms et al. structure, it is defined by the symptoms "feeling jumpy or easily startled" and "being 'superalert' or watchful and on guard"), which has been identified as the core, distinctive symptom feature of panic disorder (Brown et al., 1998; Mineka et al., 1998). Consequently, it seems likely that the variance associated with this factor already is modeled within panic, so that it would be unnecessary to include it separately within PTSD.

The status of the fourth factor is less clear. The numbing factor of the King et al. (1998) model has not been extensively investigated, but it certainly is possible that it represents a distinguishable dimension that merits inclusion in a comprehensive hierarchical scheme. In contrast, the dysphoria factor in the Simms et al. (2002) structure is a nonspecific measure of general NA. Simms et al. reported that their dysphoria scale correlated .80 and .63 with scales assessing depression and generalized anxiety, respectively; moreover, it actually correlated much more strongly with depression than with scales assessing the other three PTSD symptom factors (*r*s ranged from .51 to .61). On the basis of these data, it seems reasonable to conclude that the content of this dysphoria dimension already is well-captured (e.g., by major depression and GAD) by other elements in the hierarchy, so that it need not be added as a separate dimension within PTSD.

In conclusion, the extensive structural literature on PTSD symptoms reveals the existence of at least two distinctive dimensions—intrusions and avoidance—that would need to be included in any comprehensive structural analysis. There is more limited support for an additional Numbing dimension, but this issue needs to be clarified in future research.

Social Phobia

The structural data in this area are more limited than for OCD or PTSD. Nevertheless, there is replicated evidence for two distinguishable types of social anxiety: (a) a social interaction factor centered around fears related to directly interacting with others (e.g., initiating a conversation, making eye contact) and (b) a performance/scrutiny factor that focuses on fears of being watched by others, as well as engaging in activities (such as public speaking, writing, and eating) that would not be stressful if performed in private (Habke, Hewitt, Norton, & Asmundson, 1997; Hughes et al., 2006; Safren, Turk, & Heimberg, 1998; Safren et al., 1999). Moreover, the available data demonstrate that these subfactors show distinctive correlates. For example, Habke et al. (1997) found that the performance/scrutiny factor was more strongly related to other types of psychopathology than the social interaction factor. Furthermore, Hughes et al. (2006) examined these factors in relation to the three basic symptom groups of the tripartite model. They found that performance/scrutiny anxiety was more strongly related to anxious arousal, whereas social interaction fears were more strongly linked to anhedonia/low PA. On the basis of these data, it seems reasonable to propose that social interaction fears and performance/scrutiny anxiety should be included as separate dimensions in future structural analyses.

Specific Phobia

Previous structural evidence. *DSM-IV* formally recognizes four subtypes of specific phobia: animal, natural environment (e.g., storms, heights, water), blood-injection–injury, and situational (e.g., tunnels, bridges, elevators, enclosed spaces). It must be emphasized, however, that this quadripartite scheme was not specifically derived from—nor was it supported by—any explicit structural evidence. Indeed, the *DSM* Specific Phobia Work Group actually recommended a simpler tripartite structure in which animal and natural environment fears were collapsed into a single subtype (Craske et al., 1994).

What do these structural data show? Investigators have conducted dozens of factor analyses of multi-item phobia measures such as the Fear Survey Schedule-III (FSS-III; Wolpe & Lang, 1974). Although the results have been somewhat inconsistent, the data broadly converge on a four-factor solution (Arrindell et al., 1991; J. Beck, Carmin, & Henninger, 1998; Muris, Schmidt, & Merckelbach, 1999). Three of these dimensions represent potential subtypes of specific phobia (the fourth factor typically assesses social anxiety/social phobia): (a) animal fears, (b) blood-injection fears, and (c) some combination of situational and/or agoraphobic fears. Thus, the evidence broadly supports the existence of three of the *DSM-IV* subtypes; the one obvious discrepancy is the failure to identify a distinct dimension corresponding to the natural environment subtype.

Our structural data. These studies are limited, however, in that older instruments such as the FSS-III do not assess the full range of phobias, and may not include enough potential markers to define a distinct natural environment factor. To address this limitation, Cynthia Cutshall and I created a new instrument, the phobic stimuli response scales (PSRS; Cutshall & Watson, 2004). The PSRS item pool contains a range of content relevant to all four *DSM-IV* specific phobia subtypes, and so provides the first direct test of the current quadripartite classification scheme. Cutshall and Watson factor analyzed the PSRS items in two large student samples, obtaining four distinct specific phobia dimensions in each case (as well as a fifth factor related to social phobia). Two of these factors clearly represent the animal and blood-injection–injury subtypes of *DSM-IV*, which further supports their validity. The third factor (bodily harm) was defined by items reflecting environmental fears (e.g., "I get nervous during thunderstorms," "I would never swim in deep water"), as well as an array of health-related concerns (e.g., "I fear that I will suffer an early death"). This factor subsumes the current natural environment subtype, but ultimately reflects a broader construct. Finally, although the fourth factor differed somewhat across the two samples, it tapped an array of situational/agoraphobic concerns in both solutions. It was labeled "physical confinement" in Sample 2, and was marked by such items as "I dislike crowded places" and "I would be terrified if locked in a small, dark room."

These initial data were based on student responses, but we recently have replicated this PSRS factor structure in a sample of 623 outpatients (for recruitment details, see Watson et al., 2007, 2008). Responses to the 46 PSRS items were subjected to a principal factor analysis with squared multiple correlations in the diagonal. Consistent with our earlier results, five large and clear factors emerged that jointly accounted for 91.3% of the common variance; these factors were rotated to oblique simple structure using promax. Table 11.1 presents these rotated loadings. Replicating our previous findings, these five factors clearly can be identified as social phobia, blood–injection phobia, physical confinement fears, animal phobia, and bodily harm fears, respectively.

Summary. Thus, two *DSM-IV* subtypes—animal phobia and blood-injection phobia—have received extensive structural support in the literature. Accordingly, these symptom dimensions need to be included in any comprehensive hierarchical scheme. However, the data are inconclusive. Today, little support has been found for a natural environment factor, although we consistently have obtained evidence of a broader dimension related to bodily harm and health-related concerns.

11.1 Promax–Rotated Factor Loadings of the PSRS Items in an Outpatient Sample

Paraphrased Item	I	II	III	IV	V
get nervous knowing others are watching me	.82	–.03	.06	.05	.00
can't perform if others are watching me	.75	.02	–.01	.04	.08
dislike being watched by others	.70	.02	.08	.04	.00
afraid of looking foolish	.63	–.07	–.05	.05	.10
feel that everyone is watching me	.62	–.04	.12	–.02	.09
public speaking makes me nervous	.60	.06	.01	.06	.02
hate places in which I don't know anyone	.54	.06	.23	.02	.00
uncomfortable around those I find attractive	.48	.11	–.01	–.05	–.02
don't like others watch me eat	.37	.06	.18	.01	.02
dislike strange, unfamiliar places	.35	.07	.29	–.04	.11
not shy around people I've just met	–.48	.04	.05	.09	.12
feel faint at the sight of blood	–.03	.77	–.03	–.09	.06
don't like to look at hypodermic needles	.07	.70	.03	–.02	–.09
turn away from the sight of blood	–.03	.68	–.05	.12	–.04
hate getting shots	.02	.64	.02	.03	–.03
hard for me to prick my own finger	.07	.59	–.07	.02	–.04
would hate to have an IV in my arm	.02	.58	.08	.00	–.01
sight of blood upset me as a child	–.02	.56	.00	–.02	.10
would feel faint witnessing childbirth	.01	.49	.00	–.11	.10
would feel woozy watching a dissection	.01	.42	–.04	.24	.05
gory movies make me queasy	–.04	.29	–.02	.18	.10
dislike crowded places	.16	–.01	.75	–.08	–.13
hate being trapped in a crowd	.15	–.01	.74	–.08	–.05
do not like riding in crowded buses	.10	–.01	.72	–.07	–.03
dislike being in crowded airplanes	.08	.03	.68	–.01	.01
uncomfortable in tight, enclosed spaces	–.04	.05	.68	.01	.09

(continued)

11.1 Promax–Rotated Factor Loadings of the PSRS Items in an Outpatient Sample (continued)

Paraphrased Item	I	II	III	IV	V
hate sitting in a long row of people	.17	–.10	.60	.10	–.06
very afraid of suffocating	–.09	–.08	.46	.03	.38
terrified to be in a small dark room	–.04	.01	.45	.26	.13
would not like to hold a snail	–.03	.00	–.03	.78	–.08
dislike handling slimy things	.09	–.01	–.02	.75	.01
would not like to hold a lizard	–.03	.00	–.02	.72	.04
do not like worms	–.01	.06	–.03	.63	–.07
would never hold a spider	.01	.02	.05	.60	.00
rats and mice bother me	–.01	–.04	.02	.56	.09
would hate to touch a cockroach	.02	.02	.04	.54	.04
it would not bother me to hold a snake	–.03	.03	.05	–.37	.09
afraid I will get cancer	.04	.01	–.11	.02	.72
worry about natural disasters	–.07	.05	.10	–.09	.68
fear an early death	.11	–.03	–.14	.01	.67
worry about a terminal illness	.15	–.04	–.10	–.04	.62
concerned about contracting HIV	.09	.04	.00	–.14	.48
lightning terrifies me	–.15	.11	.13	.17	.46
get nervous during thunderstorms	–.09	.10	.14	.04	.43
terrified at being buried alive	–.02	–.01	.23	.09	.37
would never swim in deep water	–.03	.06	.10	.15	.16

Note. $N = 623$. Loadings of $|.30|$ and greater are underscored. PSRS = Phobic Stimuli Response Scales.

Finally, although many analyses have extracted a dimension that is broadly relevant to the current situational subtype, the content of this factor has varied substantially across studies. Moreover, this dimension typically contains items reflecting classic agoraphobic situations (e.g., crowds, bridges, automobiles), which raises the further issue of whether it can be distinguished from agoraphobia (see Craske et al., 1994). Further research is needed to resolve these issues and to establish the existence of any additional symptom dimensions within specific phobia.

Depression

Previous structural evidence. The situation here closely parallels the one described earlier for specific phobia. Many researchers have argued that meaningful symptom dimensions can be identified within depression, and that it would be clinically advantageous to assess them separately. This has stimulated a large—and rapidly growing—literature on the underlying structure of depressive symptoms. The bulk of this evidence comes from factor analyses of items contained in already developed instruments, such as the original Beck Depression Inventory (BDI; A. Beck, Ward, Mendelson, Mock, & Erbaugh, 1961), the Beck Depression Inventory-II (BDI-II; A. Beck, Steer, & Brown, 1996), and the Center for Epidemiological Studies Depression Scale (CES-D; Radloff, 1977). Two broad conclusions can be drawn from this extensive literature (for a more detailed review, see Watson et al., 2007). First, most investigators have found evidence of additional content dimensions beyond a general depression factor. Second, analyses of the most frequently examined instruments have failed to identify consistent, replicable factor structures.

These results hardly are surprising. Instruments such as the BDI, BDI-II and CES-D originally were created to be general measures of depression and were not explicitly constructed to yield meaningful content factors or subscales. Thus, they lack the range and sampling of item content necessary to produce replicable symptom dimensions.

Our structural data. To address this problem, my colleagues and I created a greatly expanded item pool to provide more definitive analyses of the underlying structure of depressive symptoms. Our basic strategy in creating this pool was to include multiple markers (a minimum of eight) to define all of the symptom dimensions that potentially could emerge in a structural analysis. To ensure that sufficient markers were included for each potential dimension, we rationally organized the candidate items into 12 homogeneous item composites, or HICs. Nine of these HICs corresponded to the basic symptom criteria for major depression in *DSM-IV* (e.g., depressed mood, diminished interest or pleasure, significant weight loss or weight gain, insomnia). The three remaining HICs tapped hopelessness/pessimism, symptom features of melancholic depression, and markers of high energy and positive mood.

We initially administered this item pool to three large samples: college students, psychiatric patients, and community-dwelling adults. We subsequently have replicated our structural findings in several additional samples, including high school students, young adults, postpartum women, and older adults (see Watson et al., 2007, 2008). Our analyses consistently have identified five distinctive symptom factors within depression: insomnia (e.g., difficulties falling asleep and staying asleep), lassitude (i.e., lethargy, anergia, and hypersomnia), suicidality (i.e., thoughts of death and self-harm), appetite loss (i.e., decreased appetite and weight loss), and appetite gain (i.e., increased appetite and weight gain). We also have identified a separate well-being factor (i.e., feelings of energy and high positive affect) that essentially represents the PA dimension of the two-factor, tripartite, and integrative hierarchical models; consistent with these models, this dimension shows stronger correlations with depression than with anxiety.

In addition to these specific content dimensions, our analyses consistently have revealed a large, nonspecific dysphoria factor. This factor subsumes a broad range of content, including depressed mood, loss of interest, worthlessness and guilt, hopelessness, cognitive problems (e.g., poor concentration), psychomotor disturbance, anxious mood, and worry (see Watson et al., 2007; Table 1). This dimension essentially represents the general distress/NA factor of the two-factor, tripartite and integrative hierarchical models. Indeed, the dysphoria scale that was derived from this nonspecific factor correlated .88 with the *General Distress: Depressed Symptoms* scale of the Mood and Anxiety Symptom Questionnaire (MASQ; Watson & Clark, 1991) in a sample of 382 community adults. So this dimension lies at the very heart of distress disorders such as major depression and GAD, and clearly needs to be modeled in any comprehensive symptom structure.

Summary. Thus, our structural analyses have established the existence of seven differentiable symptom dimensions that fall broadly within depression. Five of these dimensions—insomnia, lassitude, suicidality, appetite loss, and appetite gain—represent specific symptoms of depression. The sixth factor (well-being) reflects the PA dimension that—consistent with the two-factor, tripartite, and integrative hierarchical models—is relatively specific to depression. Finally, the broad dysphoria factor captures the general distress/NA dimension of these models.

Conclusion

The central argument in this chapter is that a taxonomy based on quantitative structural evidence can help to address the problems of comorbidity and heterogeneity and produce a system that better suits the needs of clinical research and treatment. A good starting point would be to replace the current rationally derived diagnostic classes with empirically based clusters that reflect the actual—rather than the perceived—similarities among different disorders. I have proposed a revised taxonomy that consists of an emotional disorders superclass with three subsumed subclasses: distress disorders, fear disorders, and bipolar disorders (see Clark & Watson, 2006; Watson, 2005). A structure along these lines could easily be implemented in *DSM-V*. It would help to resolve the problem of comorbidity (by modeling it directly) and would facilitate the ultimate development of a taxonomy based on core underlying etiological features.

However, a diagnosis-based model fails to resolve the problem of heterogeneity. Consequently, I believe we ultimately need to construct a fully quantitative hierarchical model that decomposes psychopathology into homogeneous symptom clusters. A hierarchical symptom-based scheme requires two basic steps. First, we need to identify all the important and distinguishable symptom dimensions that comprise the current *DSM* mood and anxiety disorders. Second, we need to establish replicable patterns of associations among these symptom clusters in order to organize them hierarchically.

We already have replicable evidence of specific symptom dimensions within OCD (obsessions and checking; contamination and cleaning; symmetry and ordering; hoarding), PTSD (intrusions and avoidance), social phobia (social interaction anxiety and performance/scrutiny fears), specific phobia (animal phobia and blood-injection phobia), and depression (insomnia, lassitude, suicidality, appetite loss and gain, well-being), plus a broad, nonspecific dysphoria factor. Further research is needed to explicate the symptom structures in these domains, as well as other areas within the anxiety and mood disorders. Once sufficient structural evidence has accrued to resolve these remaining issues, we will be in a position to implement a more radical symptom-based taxonomy. This important goal should motivate future structural work in this area as we move toward *DSM-VI* and beyond.

References

American Psychiatric Association. (1980). *Diagnostic and statistical manual of mental disorders* (3rd ed.) Washington, DC: Author.

American Psychiatric Association. (1987). *Diagnostic and statistical manual of mental disorders* (3rd ed., rev.) Washington, DC: Author.

American Psychiatric Association. (1994). *Diagnostic and statistical manual of mental disorders* (4th ed.) Washington, DC: Author.

Arrindell, W. A., Pickersgill, M. J., Merckelbach, H., Ardon, M. A., & Cornet, F. C. (1991). Phobic dimensions: III. Factor analytic approaches to the study of common phobic fears; an updated review of findings obtained with adult subjects. *Advances in Behaviour Research and Therapy, 13,* 73–130.

Baer, L. (1994). Factor analysis of symptom subtypes of obsessive–compulsive disorder and their relation to personality and tic disorders. *Journal of Clinical Psychiatry, 55* (Suppl. 3), 18–23.

Barlow, D. H. (1991). The nature of anxiety: Anxiety, depression, and emotional disorders. In R. M. Rapee & D. H. Barlow (Eds.), *Chronic anxiety: Generalized anxiety disorder and mixed anxiety-depression* (pp. 1–28). New York: Guilford.

Beck, A. T., Steer, R. A., & Brown, G. K. (1996). *Beck Depression Inventory manual* (2nd ed.). San Antonio, TX: Psychological Corporation.

Beck, A. T., Ward, C. H., Mendelson, M., Mock, J., & Erbaugh, J. (1961). An inventory for measuring depression. *Archives of General Psychiatry, 4,* 561–569.

Beck, J. G., Carmin, C. N., & Henninger, N. J. (1998). The utility of the Fear Survey Schedule-III: An extended replication. *Journal of Anxiety Disorders, 12,* 177–182.

Brown, T. A., & Barlow, D. H. (1992). Comorbidity among anxiety disorders: Implications for treatment and *DSM-IV*. *Journal of Consulting and Clinical Psychology, 60,* 835–844.

Brown, T. A., Campbell, L. A., Lehman, C. L., Grisham, G. R., & Mancill, R. B. (2001). Current and lifetime comorbidity of the *DSM-IV* anxiety and mood disorders in a large clinical sample. *Journal of Abnormal Psychology, 110,* 585–599.

Brown, T. A., Chorpita, B. F., & Barlow, D. H. (1998). Structured relationships among dimensions of the *DSM-IV* anxiety and mood disorders and dimensions of negative affect, positive affect, and autonomic arousal. *Journal of Abnormal Psychology, 107,* 179–192.

Brown, T. A., DiNardo, P. A., Lehman, C. L., & Campbell, L. A. (2001). Reliability of *DSM-IV* anxiety and mood disorders: Implications for the classification of emotional disorders. *Journal of Abnormal Psychology, 110,* 49–58.

Clark, L. A., & Watson, D. (1991). Tripartite model of anxiety and depression: Psychometric evidence and taxonomic implications. *Journal of Abnormal Psychology, 100,* 316–336.

Clark, L. A., & Watson, D. (2006). Distress and fear disorders: An alternative empirically based taxonomy of the "mood" and "anxiety" disorders. *British Journal of Psychiatry, 189,* 481–483.

Clark, L. A., Watson, D., & Reynolds, S. (1995). Diagnosis and classification of psychopathology: Challenges to the current system and future directions. *Annual Review of Psychology, 46,* 121–153.

Cox, B. J., Clara, I. P., & Enns, M. W. (2002). Posttraumatic stress disorder and the structure of common mental disorders. *Depression and Anxiety, 15,* 168–171.

Craske, M. G., Barlow, D. H., Clark, D. M., Curtis, G. C., Hill, E. M., Himle, J. A., et al. Specific (simple) phobia. (1994) In T. A. Widiger, A. J. Frances, H. A. Pincus, R. Ross, M. B. First, & W. W. Davis (Eds.), *DSM-IV Sourcebook* (Vol 2, pp. 473–506). Washington DC: American Psychiatric Press.

Cutshall, C., & Watson, D. (2004). The Phobic Stimuli Response Scales: A new self-report measure of fear. *Behaviour Research and Therapy, 42,* 1193–1201.

Eapen, V., Robertson, M. M., Alsobrook, J. P., & Pauls, D. L. (1997). Obsessive–compulsive symptoms in Gilles de le Tourette syndrome and obsessive–compulsive disorder: Differences by diagnosis and family history. *American Journal of Medical Genetics, 74,* 432–438.

Feindler, E. L. (Ed.) (2006). *Anger related disorders: A practitioner's guide to comparative treatments.* New York: Springer.

Foa, E. B., Kozak, M. J., Salkovskis, P. M., Coles, M. E., & Amir, N. (1998). The validation of a new obsessive–compulsive disorder scale: The Obsessive–Compulsive Inventory. *Psychological Assessment, 10,* 206–214.

Foa, E. B., Huppert, J. D., Leiberg, S., Langner, R., Kichic, R., Hajcak, G., & Salkovskis, P. M. . (2002). The Obsessive–Compulsive Inventory: Development and validation of a short version. *Psychological Assessment,* 14, 485–496.

Gamez, W., Watson, D., & Doebbeling, B. N. (2007). Abnormal personality and the mood and anxiety disorders: Implications for structural models of anxiety and depression. *Journal of Anxiety Disorders, 21,* 526–539.

Habke, A. M., Hewitt, P. L., Norton, G. R., & Asmundson, G. (1997). The Social Phobia and Social Interaction Anxiety Scales: An exploration of the dimensions of social anxiety and sex differences in structure and relations with pathology. *Journal of Psychopathology and Behavioral Assessment, 19,* 21–39.

Hollander, E., & Benzaquen, S. (1997). The obsessive–compulsive spectrum disorders. *International Review of Psychiatry, 9,* 99–110.

Hughes, A. A., Heimberg, R. G., Coles, M. E., Gibb, B. E., Liebowitz, M. R., & Schneier, F. R. (2006). Relations of the factors of the tripartite model of anxiety and depression to types of social anxiety. *Behaviour Research and Therapy, 44,* 1629–1641.

Kassinove, H. (Ed). (1995). *Anger disorders: Definition, diagnosis, and treatment.* Philadelphia, PA: Taylor & Francis.

Kendler, K. S. (1996). Major depression and generalised anxiety disorder: Same genes, (partly) different environments—revisited. *British Journal of Psychiatry, 168 (Suppl. 30),* 68–75.

Kendler, K. S., Prescott, C. A., Myers, J., & Neale, M. C. (2003). The structure of genetic and environmental risk factors for common psychiatric and substance use disorders in men and women. *Archives of General Psychiatry, 60,* 929–937.

Kessler, R. C., Chiu, W. T., Demler, O., & Walters, E. E. (2005). Prevalence, severity, and comorbidity of 12-month *DSM-IV* disorders in the National Comorbidity Survey Replication. *Archives of General Psychiatry, 62,* 617–627.

Kessler, R. C., Nelson, C. B., McGonagle, K. A., Liu, J., Swartz, M., & Blazer, D. G. (1996). Comorbidity of *DSM-III-R* major depressive disorder in the general population: Results from the US National Comorbidity Survey. *British Journal of Psychiatry, 168 (Suppl. 30),* 17–30.

King, D. W., Leskin, G. A., King, L. A., & Weathers, F. W. (1998). Confirmatory factor analysis of the Clinician-Administered PTSD Scale: Evidence for the dimensionality of posttraumatic stress disorder. *Psychological Assessment, 10,* 90–96.

Krueger, R. F. (1999). The structure of common mental disorders. *Archives of General Psychiatry, 56,* 921–926.

Krueger, R.F., & Markon, K.E. (2006). Reinterpreting comorbidity: A model based approach to understanding and classifying psychopathology. *Annual Review of Clinical Psychology, 2,* 111–133.

Lilienfeld, S. O., Waldman, I. D., & Israel, A. C. (1994). Critical examination of the use of the term and concept of comorbidity in psychopathology research. *Clinical Psychology: Science and Practice, 1,* 71–83.

Magee, W. J., Eaton, W. W., Wittchen, H. U., McGonagle, K. A., & Kessler, R. C. (1996). Agoraphobia, simple phobia, and social phobia in the National Comorbidity Survey. *Archives of General Psychiatry, 53,* 159–168.

Mataix-Cols, D., Pertusa, A., & Leckman, J. F. (2007). Issues for *DSM-V*: How should obsessive–compulsive and related disorders be classified? *American Journal of Psychiatry, 164,* 1313–1314.

Mataix-Cols, D., Rosario–Campos, M. C., & Leckman, J. F. (2005). A multidimensional model of obsessive–compulsive disorder. *American Journal of Psychiatry, 162,* 228–238.

McWilliams, L. A., Box, B. J., & Asmundson, G. J. G. (2005). Symptom structure of posttraumatic stress disorder in a nationally representative sample. *Journal of Anxiety Disorders, 19,* 626–641.

Muris, P., Schmidt, H., & Merckelbach, H. (1999). The structure of specific phobic symptoms among children and adolescents. *Behaviour Research and Therapy, 37,* 863–868.

Mineka, S., Watson, D., & Clark, L. A. (1998). Comorbidity of anxiety and unipolar mood disorders. *Annual Review of Psychology, 49,* 377–412.

Palmieri, P., Weathers, F. W., Difede, J., & King, D. W. (2007). Confirmatory factor analysis of the PTSD Checklist and the Clinician-Administered PTSD Scale in disaster workers exposed to the World Trade Center Ground Zero. *Journal of Abnormal Psychology, 116,* 329–341.

Radloff, L. S. (1977). The CES-D: A self-report depression scale for research in the general population. *Applied Psychological Measurement, 1,* 385–401.

Roy, M.-A., Neale, M. C., Pedersen, N. L., Mathé, A. A., & Kendler, K. S. (1995). A twin study of generalized anxiety disorder and major depression. *Psychological Medicine, 25,* 1037–1049.

Safren, S. A., Heimberg, R. G., Horner, K. J., Juster, H. R., Schneier, F. R., & Liebowitz, M. R. (1999). Factor structure of social fears: The Liebowitz Social Anxiety Scale. *Journal of Anxiety Disorders, 13,* 253–270.

Safren, S. A., Turk, C. L., & Heimberg, R. G. (1998). Factor structure of the Social Interaction Anxiety Scale and the Social Phobia Scale. *Behaviour Research and Therapy, 36,* 443–453.

Simms, L. J., Watson, D., & Doebbeling, B. N. (2002). Confirmatory factor analyses of posttraumatic stress symptoms in deployed and non-deployed veterans of the Gulf War. *Journal of Abnormal Psychology, 111,* 637–647.

Slade, T., & Watson, D. (2006). The structure of common *DSM-IV* and *ICD-10* mental disorders in the Australian general population. *Psychological Medicine, 36,* 1593–1600.

Taylor, S., Kuch, K., Koch, W. J., Crockett, D. J., & Passey, G. (1998). The structure of posttraumatic stress symptoms. *Journal of Abnormal Psychology, 107,* 154–160.

Vollebergh, W. A. M., Iedema, J., Bijl, R. V., de Graaf, R., Smit, F., & Ormel, J. (2001). The structure and stability of common mental disorders: The NEMESIS Study. *Archives of General Psychiatry, 58,* 597–603.

Watson, D. (2000). *Mood and temperament.* New York: Guilford Press.

Watson, D. (2003). Subtypes, specifiers, epicycles, and eccentrics: Toward a more parsimonious taxonomy of psychopathology. *Clinical Psychology: Science and Practice, 10,* 233–238.

Watson, D. (2005). Rethinking the mood and anxiety disorders: A quantitative hierarchical model for *DSM-V. Journal of Abnormal Psychology, 114,* 522–536.

Watson, D., & Clark, L. A. (1991). *The Mood and Anxiety Symptom Questionnaire.* Unpublished manuscript, University of Iowa, Iowa City, IA.

Watson, D., Clark, L. A., & Carey, G. (1988). Positive and negative affectivity and their relation to anxiety and depressive disorders. *Journal of Abnormal Psychology, 97,* 346–353.

Watson, D., Gamez, W., & Simms, L. J. (2005). Basic dimensions of temperament and their relation to anxiety and depression: A symptom-based perspective. *Journal of Research in Personality, 39,* 46–66.

Watson, D., O'Hara, M. W., Simms, L. J., Kotov, R., Chmielewski, M., McDade-Montez, E., Gamez, W., & Stuart, S. (2007). Development and validation of the Inventory of Depression and Anxiety Symptoms (IDAS). *Psychological Assessment, 19,* 253–268.

Watson, D., O'Hara, M. W., & Stuart, S. (2008). *Hierarchical structures of affect and psychopathology and their implications for the classification of emotional disorders.* Manuscript submitted for publication.

Watson, D., & Tellegen, A. (1985). Toward a consensual structure of mood. *Psychological Bulletin, 98,* 219–235.

Watson, D., Wiese, D., Vaidya, J., & Tellegen, A. (1999). The two general activation systems of affect: Structural findings, evolutionary considerations, and psychobiological evidence. *Journal of Personality and Social Psychology, 76,* 820–838.

Watson, D., & Wu, K. D. (2005). Development and Validation of the Schedule of Compulsions, Obsessions, and Pathological Impulses (SCOPI). *Assessment, 12,* 50–65.

Watson, D., Wu, K. D., & Cutshall, C. (2004). Symptom subtypes of obsessive–compulsive disorder and their relation to dissociation. *Journal of Anxiety Disorders, 18,* 435–458.

Widiger, T. A., & Clark, L. A. (2000). Toward *DSM-V* and the classification of psychopathology. *Psychological Bulletin, 126,* 946–963.
Wolpe, J. & Lang, P.J. (1974). A fear survey for use in behavior therapy. In T.J. Edwin (Ed.), *Behavior Modification Procedures: A sourcebook (pp. 228–232)*. New Brunswick, NJ: Aldine Transaction.
Wu, K. D., & Watson, D. (2003). Further investigation of the Obsessive–Compulsive Inventory: Psychometric analysis in two nonclinical samples. *Journal of Anxiety Disorders, 17,* 305–319 .
Zinbarg, R., E., & Barlow, D. H. (1996). Structure of anxiety and the anxiety disorders: A hierarchical model. *Journal of Abnormal Psychology, 105,* 181–193.

12

Developmental Perspectives on Anxiety Classification

Stephen P. Whiteside
Thomas H. Ollendick

Deciding what constitutes "anxiety" and what anxiety problems are intense or frequent enough to require treatment relies on a developmental perspective. Some anxiety is normal and coincides with typical developmental processes associated with growth. In fact, for the most part, anxiety is highly adaptive and possesses clear evolutionary value. Determining when anxiety is maladaptive requires an understanding of what behaviors and emotions are in the normal range, an answer that changes over the lifespan from infancy to older adulthood (Achenbach, 1999). In this chapter we examine the implications that a developmental perspective on psychopathology has for the study and classification of the anxiety disorders.

Defining a Developmental Perspective

Before analyzing the anxiety diagnoses in childhood, it is necessary to provide a developmental psychopathology context for this discussion. Within this broad field, theorists have long debated which developmental model best addresses the many changes that occur in individuals throughout their development and across their lifespan. Early debates centered on issues of autonomy and organization and were tied to two major Western worldviews encapsulated in "mechanistic" and "organismic" models. According to the mechanistic view (Bijou, 1976; Morris et al., 1982; Skinner, 1938), organisms were passive recipients of information. Furthermore, it was believed that changes in behavior over time reflected gradual modifications in antecedent and consequent stimuli with explanations for development deriving largely from principles of learning theory. As a result, development and developmental processes were viewed by many behaviorally oriented clinicians and researchers as possessing relatively little clinical significance (see Gelfand & Peterson, 1985; Holmbeck & Kendall, 1991; Ollendick & Cerny, 1981) for extended discussions of this point.

In contrast to passive qualities of the organism inherent in the mechanistic view, proponents of the organismic model of development (Erikson, 1968; Freud, 1949; Piaget, 1950) suggested that organisms were active agents involved in the construction of their environment. Furthermore, organismic theorists often described development through stages (e.g., Piaget's stages of cognitive development, Freud's psychosexual stages, and Erickson's stages of identity development). These various theories maintained that basic structures and functions changed across age and that they reflected emerging, qualitatively different ways of interacting with the environment. In its purest form, this model asserted that change resulted largely from maturational processes that were determined by intrinsic organismic factors rather than by environmental forces.

Decades of debate among proponents of these two models, as well as recognition of their limitations, led to the advent of a third model of development; namely, the "transactional" model. Also known as "developmental contextualism," the transactional model represented an integration of the two previously described models (Lerner, Hess, & Nitz, 1990, 1991; Sameroff, 1975, 1995) and was highly consistent with the tenets of social learning/social cognitive theory (Bandura, 1977, 1989; Ollendick & Cerny, 1981). According to this model, developmental changes were proposed to occur as a result of continuous reciprocal interactions (i.e., reciprocal determinism, transactions) between an active organism and its active environmental context. Organisms were said to affect their own development by being both producers and products of their environments (Lerner et al.; Ollendick & Cerny).

Although some differences in theory and philosophy remain to this day, most developmental psychologists agree that development involves systematic, successive, and adaptive changes within and across life periods in the structure, function, and content of the individual's mental, behavioral, social, and interpersonal characteristics (Lease & Ollendick, 1993b; Ollendick, Lease, & Cooper, 1993; Ollendick & Vasey, 1999; Sameroff, 1975, 1995). Because developmental changes, for the most part, occur in an orderly fashion (i.e., they are systematic and successive), it is inferred that changes observed at one point in time will influence subsequent events (although not necessarily in a linear fashion). In this sense, development is not viewed as random or capricious or, for that matter, disconnected. Changes that occur at one point in time have an impact on subsequent development. Thus, the diversity or variety of changes possible at a later point in time is constrained by those that occur at an earlier point in time.

Developmental psychopathology is concerned with development and developmental deviations or distortions (i.e., clinical perturbations) that occur throughout and across the lifespan and the processes associated with those maladaptations (Rutter & Garmezy, 1983). The study of psychopathology, from this perspective, is organized around milestones, transitions, and sequences in physical, cognitive, and social–emotional development. Thus, development is viewed as a series of qualitative reorganizations determined by factors at various levels of analysis (e.g., genetic, constitutional, physiological, behavioral, psychological, environmental, and sociological) that are in dynamic transaction with one another (Cicchetti, 1989a, 1989b; Lewis, 1990a, 1990b). Pathological development is understood then as a lack of integration among these systems that contributes synergistically to adaptation at particular developmental levels.

Although development at one level is assumed to affect later functioning, isomorphic continuity of behavior is not necessarily implied. Rather, multiple pathways through which developmental outcomes may occur are suggested based on the notion that both healthy and pathological development result from individually distinct and unique transactions between a changing organism and its ever-changing environmental context (i.e., the principle of equifinality). It is therefore important to identify and understand intra- and extra-individual characteristics that promote or inhibit early deviations or maintain or disrupt early adaptation and development. Toward this end, the field of developmental psychopathology is primarily concerned with the origins and course of a given disorder, its precursors and sequelae, its variations in manifestation with development, and, more broadly, its relations to nondisordered behavior patterns (Lease & Ollendick, 1993a; Rutter, 1985; Toth & Cicchetti, 1999).

As can be seen from this brief review, any taxonomy of anxiety disorders must incorporate the manner in which psychopathology changes over time and how the individual impacts, and is impacted by, the environment. In the current chapter, we will use the transactional model of developmental psychopathology to (a) evaluate the current system for classifying anxiety disorders, (b) review research that has been undertaken with children since the most recent revision to the diagnostic system, and (c) explore future directions for the pending revision of the classification of childhood anxiety disorders.

Development and Classification of Anxiety Disorders

The Diagnostic and Statistical Manual of Mental Disorders

Although early nosological approaches to psychopathology were relatively successful in capturing the diverse ailments of adulthood, there was little attention paid to the developmental aspects of these disorders and how they were manifested in childhood. The *Diagnostic and Statistical Manual of Mental Disorders (DSM)*, the most widely used diagnostic classification system in the world, possesses both strengths and weaknesses (Jensen & Hoagwood, 1997; Jensen, Knapp, & Mrazek, 2004). As a largely descriptive categorical system that provides a list of symptoms specific to a variety of disorders, it has undergone several revisions in recent years with increasing attention to developmental issues. However, although the number of childhood disorders has increased significantly from two in the initial version, the description and utility of these "new" disorders lag behind those for adults. For example, although the *DSM–III* (APA, 1980) introduced diagnostic criteria specific to several adult diagnoses, these criteria were not modified for the childhood disorders, which, perhaps not surprisingly, contributed to their low reliability (Achenbach, 1999).

Although the most recent version of the *DSM* (*DSM–IV–TR*; APA, 1994) includes developmental considerations, the criteria continue to be predominately based on conceptualizations embedded in adult psychopathology. However, and importantly, developmental considerations are addressed in three aspects of the diagnostic system. To begin with, there is a section devoted solely to disorders usually first diagnosed in infancy, childhood, or adolescence. The existence of this section is clear acknowledgment of psychiatric problems that are evident in early childhood. However, and somewhat telling, the inclusion of this separate section for childhood diagnoses does not really address the "developmental" aspects of these disorders; rather, it simply asserts that these disorders are most likely to have their origins in childhood and to manifest themselves early in development.

In addition to a childhood section, development is addressed in two other areas throughout the *DSM* compendium: the text descriptions and the diagnostic criteria. The text descriptions for each diagnosis include brief sections on the age features and on the illness course of the disorder. These sections include, to varying degrees, information about age of onset and the manner in which the disorder is manifested at different ages. For example, the text on social phobia (SoP) includes the developmentally relevant information that the onset of symptoms is typically in midadolescence and that children often do not have the option of avoiding the many social and interpersonal situations that occasion such anxiety. Finally, to aid in diagnoses, some disorders include age qualifiers within the criteria. These statements indicate how a particular criterion may be applied differently to children compared to adults. For example, the requirement that the individual must recognize that fear is excessive is waived for SoP in children. Similar modifications are made for several other disorders.

Although these features of *DSM–IV* represent meaningful steps toward addressing the developmental aspects of psychopathology, there are limitations to the current structure. To begin with, although having a section devoted to disorders of childhood increases the focus on these conditions, it creates an artificial dichotomy between child and adult disorders rather than addressing how these disorders might change and manifest themselves with development. Furthermore, a separate section does not address the characteristics of "adult disorders," such as panic disorder (PD), that can and do occur in children, nor does it describe "child disorders," such as separation anxiety disorder (SAD), in adults (Cyranowski et al., 2002; Ollendick et al., 1993).

At a minimum, a developmentally informed approach would encompass how psychiatric disorders present themselves at different ages. Although some of this information is presented in the text portion of each disorder, it is unclear how much of an impact this information has on the field. The most influential aspects of the *DSM* are the diagnostic criteria, as seen by their inclusion sans text in the Quick Reference Guide to the Diagnostic Criteria for *DSM–IV–TR* (APA, 2000), a common clinical tool. For developmental information to truly have an impact on the categorization of the various anxiety disorders, it seems to us that it needs to be included prominently in the diagnostic criteria. Unfortunately, in the present version, there are relatively few criteria that differ for children. In addition, developmentally specific information sufficient to differentiate normal from clinically significant rates of behavior is not provided for symptoms of childhood disorders in *DSM–IV* (Eyberg, Schuhmann, & Rey, 1998).

The above critique of developmental sensitivity in the *DSM* aptly applies to the anxiety disorders more broadly. With the introduction of the third edition of the *DSM*, three anxiety disorders specific to childhood were recognized: SAD, overanxious disorder (OAD), and avoidant disorder (AD). However, with the publication of *DSM–IV*, some have argued that the *DSM* anxiety disorders have become more a developmental (Daleiden, Vasey, & Brown, 1999). In this version, two of the three anxiety disorders that were introduced to capture symptoms evident in childhood—OAD and AD—were subsumed into the adult categories of generalized anxiety disorder (GAD) and SoP respectively. Instead of separate and more developmentally sensitive diagnoses, *DSM–IV* generally addresses development in the anxiety disorders through qualifiers for children, such as requiring less somatic symptoms in GAD or waiving the insight criteria for SoP.

Although the criteria for both GAD and SoP have some accommodations for children, the wisdom of replacing OAD and AD has been debated. For instance, it remains unclear whether the AD is best conceptualized as a developmentally earlier form of SoP or as a distinct disorder characterized by meaningfully different phobic objects (i.e., unfamiliar people vs. negative social evaluation; Francis, Last, & Strauss, 1992). Although these disorders are similar on global characteristics of sex, race, and comorbid diagnoses, they differ on age of onset (Cantwell & Baker, 1987; Francis et al., 1992; Giaconia et al., 1994). In the absence of longitudinal data potentially linking AD and SoP, the decision to subsume the former into the latter may have been premature. In terms of GAD, qualifiers of the criteria for children significantly lower the threshold for diagnosis in children compared to adults. However, this decision has lead to overlap in symptom presentation with major depressive disorder (MDD) and attention deficit hyperactivity disorder (ADHD; Seligman & Ollendick, 1998). Overall, despite the occasional pockets of developmental considerations, the *DSM* anxiety disorders continue to be based primarily on adult models of anxiety without sufficient research indicating that the models are appropriate for children.

Continuity from Childhood to Adulthood

In applying an adult model of psychopathology to children, the *DSM–IV* tacitly accepted the assumption that these disorders have the same underlying structure at different levels of development. Part of this assumption resides in the notion that the clustering of symptoms in adults reflects a similar clustering in children, leading to the presence of parallel diagnostic categories. In fact, this assumption has been supported in recent studies with young children. For instance, Sterba and colleagues (2007) found that internalizing symptoms in preschoolers could be categorized into three primary areas similar to those found in adults (SoP, separation anxiety, and generalized anxiety/major depression). Overall, this categorization is generally consistent with the structure of *DSM–IV*, with the exception of the combination of GAD and depression. The association between GAD and depression may be a function of the limited symptom criteria for GAD and its similarity to MDD. Such a finding is also consistent with such linkages in adulthood (e.g., Moffitt et al., 2007).

Other patterns of comorbidity are also similar within child and adult populations. For instance, the high rates of cormorbidity among the anxiety disorders in adults (47% to 87%, depending on the primary anxiety diagnoses, Gregory et al., 2007) are also found in children (Jensen & Hoagwood, 1997; Nottelmann & Jensen, 1995). Moreover, the connections among anxiety disorders are also similar between children and adults. Within child samples, the phobias (specific, social, and agora) tend to cluster together, with SoP being related to OAD (Costello, Egger, & Angold, 2005). Studies of adults have found similarly high levels of comorbidity between the phobias and between SoP and GAD (Magee, Eaton, Wittchen, McGonagle, & Kessler, 1996). However, although GAD has been found to be related to specific phobia in adults (Magee et al., 1996), this connection has not been found in children (Costello et al., 2005), further suggesting that OAD and GAD may not be the same disorders.

However, even if the structure of anxiety disorders is similar in children and adults, it does not necessarily follow that anxiety disorders are consistent over time and demonstrate continuity from childhood to adulthood. To date, longitudinal research has tended to support the continuity of the broad class of anxiety disorders, but not of the individual diagnoses. At the macro level, general measures of behavioral inhibition or anxious/withdrawn symptoms in young children have been found to relate to anxiety disorders in later childhood, adolescence, and early adulthood (Costello, Mustillo, Erkanli, Keeler, & Angold, 2003; Goodwin, Fergusson, & Horwood, 2004; Hirshfeld et al., 1992). In addition, adults with anxiety diagnoses typically report experiencing anxiety disorders in adolescence (Gregory et al., 2007).

However, whereas most adulthood disorders were preceded by childhood and adolescent disorders, most childhood disorders do not persist into young adulthood (Pine, Cohen, Gurley, Brook, & Ma, 1998).

The support for the specificity of individual diagnoses within the overall class of the anxiety disorders is mixed. Currently, there is emerging support for homotypic continuity (the same diagnosis at different assessments) for the *DSM–IV* anxiety diagnoses from childhood to adolescence (Costello et al., 2003). However, there is less support for continuity into adulthood, where all forms of adult anxiety appear to be similarly associated with childhood OAD, SAD, and SoPs (Gregory et al., 2007). In addition, there is variation among the anxiety disorders with some diagnoses (PD and posttraumatic stress disorder [PTSD]) appearing to have higher homotypic continuity than others (specific phobia and generalized anxiety disorder). Moreover, patterns of continuity within diagnoses appear to differ depending on the age range studied. For example, although specific phobia appears to have little continuity from childhood to adolescence (Costello et al., 2003), it has strong continuity from adolescence to adulthood (Gregory et al., 2007). Unfortunately, the cobbling of data from separate studies with methodological differences precludes any firm conclusions.

In sum, several developmental issues present themselves in the diagnosis and classification of psychiatric disorders that are not fully addressed by *DSM*. Although existing data suggest that the *DSM–IV* diagnostic categories fit anxiety within childhood to a similar degree as adulthood, high comorbidity remains a problem and the connection between GAD and depression needs to be addressed. In addition, limited support for homotypic continuity, as well as many childhood disorders not progressing into adulthood, raises the probability that the anxiety disorders have complex developmental trajectories, consistent with a developmental psychopathology perspective. Although *DSM–IV* provides some developmental categories and qualifiers, the decision to combine child and adult diagnoses is questionable, and the diagnostic guidelines are insufficient to fully inform the practicing clinician. The following sections examine how developmental issues raise questions that need to be addressed in the revision of *DSM–IV* in the three primary areas of anxiety symptoms: somatic, cognitive, and behavioral.

Anxiety Symptoms and Development

Development and Somatic Symptoms of Anxiety

The importance of somatic symptoms, such as restlessness, stomachaches, palpitations, difficulties breathing, and dizziness can be seen in their inclusion in some of the *DSM–IV* anxiety diagnoses and in etiologic theories of anxiety and its disorder. These symptoms are required for a diagnosis of GAD, PTSD, and PD. In addition, physiological hyperarousal is considered causal in many models of anxiety disorders (Barlow, 1988). An emphasis on somatic symptoms in both adults and children can be seen in the assessment instruments used with these populations, including the Beck Anxiety Inventory (Beck & Steer, 1990) and the Multidimensional Anxiety Scale for Children (MASC; March, 1997).

As noted, somatic symptoms play a central role in the diagnoses of GAD and PD. Although the criteria for these disorders have their origins in adult psychopathology, there is one concession to the possibility that these disorders may present differently in children; in GAD, children only have to experience one, rather than three, of the core physical symptoms (restlessness, easily fatigued, difficulty concentrating, irritability, muscle tension, and sleep disturbance). Panic disorder, on the other hand, has no alterations for children. Although physical symptoms are required of children for these diagnoses, a recent study in children with SoP, SAD, and GAD suggests that the list of physiological symptoms may not apply as readily to children as to adults (Ginsburg, Riddle, & Davies, 2006). In this study restlessness, stomachaches, blushing, palpitations, muscles tension, sweating, and trembling/shaking were found to be the most common somatic symptoms reported by children with these anxiety disorders. Of this list, three are included in PD and only two correspond to the list of six symptoms in GAD. Moreover, of the three somatic symptoms that differentiated children with GAD from those without (restlessness, stomachaches, and chills or hot flashes), only one is included in the criteria for GAD. It is interesting to note that all three of these symptoms are included in the criteria for GAD in the latest version of the *International Classification of the Disorders* (*ICD-10*; WHO, 1992).

In addition to reconsidering the type and number of somatic symptoms for GAD, Ginsburg and colleagues (2006) recommend that *DSM–V* include somatic symptoms, such as "feels sick to stomach," to the criteria for other anxiety disorders. For instance, Ginsburg and colleagues found that separation anxiety disorder was associated with higher rates of restlessness, stomachaches, and palpitations, whereas SoP was associated with more frequent sweating. Currently, *DSM* does not specify any somatic symptoms for either diagnosis in children and only one of the symptoms associated with SAD is listed as an example for criterion eight that refers to physical complaints. Overall, it appears that the somatic symptoms experienced by children with anxiety disorders do not correspond fully to the symptoms included in the current version of the *DSM*. Headaches, a common symptom reported by children, are not addressed at all.

Although direct measures of physiological symptoms are used in research centers, the identification of somatic symptoms is based solely on verbal report in most clinical settings. This raises particular concerns when working with children due to the sometimes questionable reliability of their report and the presence of multiple, and often conflicting, sources of information (Grills & Ollendick, 2003). Rarely do children come into treatment of their own accord. Rather, children are typically brought in by their parents, who believe their child has a "problem." As such, much of the information used to make a diagnosis is based on parent report. Unfortunately, informant agreement (child, mother, father) has been found to be no better than chance and even extremely poor for some anxiety disorders (i.e., separation anxiety disorder and overanxious disorder; Foley et al., 2004; Foley et al., 2005; Grills & Ollendick, 2003). When looking at somatic symptoms in particular, parent and child reports differ significantly (Kendall & Pimentel, 2003).

With disagreements being commonplace, it is difficult to determine which source of information should be considered primary when making a diagnosis. Supporting the utility of child report is the fact that parent report is typically more accurate for externalizing behaviors than for internalizing symptoms (Achenbach, 1999). In addition, children have been found to be able to provide reliable information about internalizing symptoms as early as first grade (Ialongo, Edelsohn, Werthamer-Larsson, Crockett, & Kellam, 1993). However, the fact that older children have been found to report more symptoms than younger children, whereas parent report is consistent across development (Ginsburg et al., 2006; Kendall & Pimentel, 2003), suggests that as children age, their self-reports become more consistent with reports of parents, and presumably more reliable. Parent report is also favored by findings that parent–child agreement increases with age and that parent report tends to agree more with clinician impressions (Edelbrock, Costello, Dulcan, Conover, & Kala, 1986; Grills & Ollendick, 2003). Unfortunately, there are also some data to suggest that diagnoses of internalizing disorders are more reliable in younger children than older children and that child reports may be more reliable than parent reports (Daleiden et al., 1999). Given these conflicting findings, until further research can illuminate the relative value of child and parent report of somatic symptoms, what seems most clear is that report of somatic symptoms will likely differ depending on age and that some acknowledgment of these issues should be included in the criteria for somatic symptoms.

Development and Cognitive Symptoms of Anxiety

Cognitions play a prominent role and are a mainstay for three of the anxiety disorders GAD, OCD, and SoP. These symptoms take the form of apprehensive expectations, recurrent thoughts, and fears of acting in a way that will be humiliating, in these disorders, respectively. The utility of cognitive criteria for the childhood anxiety disorders is unclear, but it is likely affected by developmental maturity (Daleiden et al., 1999). For instance, a certain level of cognitive ability has been theorized to be necessary for developing generalized worry or catastrophic panic interpretations (Barlow & Nelles, 1988; Ollendick & King, 1994).

Some developmental considerations regarding cognition are currently incorporated into the *DSM–IV*. For instance, the criteria for SoP, OCD, and specific phobia include a caveat stating that children do not need to recognize that their fears are excessive or unrealistic. In other disorders, such as SAD, the breadth of the symptom criteria allows for coverage of multiple developmental levels. Even if young children are unable to express their anxiety in terms of specific threats to their parents or to themselves, they can meet the criteria through the presence of nighttime fears of the dark or fears of spending the night at a friend's house. Older children and adolescents, on the other hand, may deny fears of separation and show their fears through avoidance of independent activities and various somatic complaints. In fact, the most common symptoms in 5- to 8-year-old children with SAD are nightmares, in contrast to somatic complaints in 9- to 12-year-olds, and school refusal and wariness of independent activities in adolescents (Francis, Last, & Strauss, 1987).

Unfortunately, in other areas of the *DSM* the cognitive requirements have increased without consideration of developmental factors. Two of the three disorders that require cognitive criteria, GAD and SoP, subsumed childhood disorders and increased the emphasis on thoughts compared to the disorders they replaced (OAD and AD). Under *DSM–III–R*, AD did not include any items related to cognitions, and it was possible for children to receive a diagnosis of OAD without endorsing any of the three criteria that referenced worry. In addition to departing from the previous version, *DSM–IV's* reliance on cognitions in GAD and SoP differs from the criteria in the *ICD-10*. *ICD-10* addresses developmental concerns by providing separate criteria for SoP and GAD in childhood. Under the *ICD-10* criteria, it is possible to receive a diagnosis of GAD without endorsing any cognitive symptoms and a diagnosis of SoP without fear of negative evaluation, an essential feature of SoP in *DSM* which is likely to be absent or at least not as evident in children. Thus, although *DSM–IV* has increased its emphasis on thoughts in childhood anxiety disorders, there appear to be viable alternatives, such as the *ICD-10*, that place less of a focus on these symptoms.

The increased emphasis on cognition resulting from the decision to subsume OAD into GAD has been questioned (Daleiden et al., 1999) and is worth further exploration. To begin with, it is not clear that children who would have received a diagnosis of OAD are being captured by GAD as intended. Studies examining OAD and GAD in children have found that the two disorders correlate only modestly and that within children who had either GAD or OAD, and not depression; only 16% meet the criteria for both disorders (Costello et al., 2005; Pine et al., 1998). These results indicate that the specific symptoms in these disorders identify relatively unique groups of children. Moreover, the developmental continuity of GAD has also been questioned. In a longitudinal study, a general measure of anxiety symptoms in childhood was found to be related to all forms of anxiety disorders, *except* GAD, in adolescence and early adulthood (Goodwin et al., 2004). Finally, in the most direct test of the relation between OAD and GAD, childhood OAD was found to have continuity and was associated with adolescent OAD, but childhood GAD was only related to later conduct disorder (Bittner et al, 2007). The authors concluded that GAD was missing an important subset of anxious children and recommended reconsidering OAD in any revision to the system. In summary, evidence is accumulating which fails to support the decision to subsume OAD into GAD. Whether or not these difficulties reflect a developmentally inappropriate focus on cognition remains to be seen.

Despite the efforts to address developmental variables in disorders such as SoP, GAD, and SAD, some disorders continue to have no such accommodations. For example, no alterations to the criteria for PD have been included in *DSM–IV* despite considerable evidence that PD exists in childhood and that it is necessary to take important developmental features into consideration when determining its presence and expression (Mattis & Ollendick, 1997a, 1997b; Ollendick, 1998; Ollendick, Mattis, & King, 1994). All in all, considerable research continues to need to be done regarding the applicability of cognitive symptoms in the diagnoses of anxiety disorders in children and adolescents.

Development and Behavioral Symptoms of Anxiety

Some of the obstacles to measuring cognitive and somatic symptoms can be circumvented with behavioral symptoms because they can be observed by another individual, such as a parent or a teacher. Thus, it is possible to measure these symptoms at a very young age. For instance, behavioral inhibition (avoidance, fear of unfamiliar situations, crying, and distressful vocalizations) has at least a limited relation to later anxiety disorders and can be measured by behavioral and parent report measures before 2 years of age (Turner, Beidel, & Wolff, 1996). Behavioral inhibition varies over development with infants displaying high motor activity and irritability that give way to withdrawn, passive, avoidant behavior as the infant matures, and finally fearful avoidance of unfamiliar people in childhood (Ollendick & Hirshfeld-Becker, 2002; Pine, 2007).

The current version of *DSM–IV* acknowledges that some behavioral manifestations of anxiety differ depending on developmental level. For example, in the case of specific and social phobias, *DSM–IV* specifies that anxiety may be expressed by crying, tantrums, freezing, or clinging/shrinking from social situations. In addition, the text provides additional description of potential behaviors of young children with SoP including that they "may appear excessively timid in unfamiliar settings, shrink from contact with others, refuse to participate in group play, typically stay on the periphery of social activities, and attempt to remain close to familiar adults" (p. 413). The criteria for PTSD also include a developmentally sensitive approach to describing the expression of anxiety. To begin with, children's response to the trauma can reflect disorganization or agitation rather than intense fear. Moreover, two of the three special notes for reexperiencing symptoms allow for differences in behavioral expression. Specifically, "recurrent and intrusive thoughts" may be exhibited through repetitive play and "acting or feeling as if the event were recurring" may be expressed though trauma-specific reenactment. No further alterations in the behavioral expression of anxiety symptoms in other disorders are included in the current *DSM*.

In addition to the expression of anxiety, the *DSM* provides additional behaviorally related considerations, particularly for SoP. These developmental accommodations include that children must show capacity for normal social relationships with familiar people and that they must be anxious around unfamiliar *peers* as well as adults. In addition, the text regarding SoP includes additional information about the context in which behaviors should be evaluated. For instance, interference in children tends to take the form of failure to show expected gains rather than a decline in functioning. In addition, the *DSM* also acknowledges that children have much less control over their lives than adults, thus children are often not able to avoid the feared situations completely.

Unfortunately, much of this information is contained in the text for SoP, rather than within the diagnostic criteria, likely reducing its impact and use by clinicians.

Developmental Recommendations for Future Categorization of Anxiety Disorders

As we have noted above, the *DSM–IV* has made important strides in incorporating developmental theory and developmental psychopathology into its categorization of the anxiety disorders in childhood. However, its reach has been incomplete and much remains to be done. On a broad level, the *DSM* has failed to incorporate a transactional approach especially in its consideration of the causes and expression of the disorders. For the most part, the anxiety disorders are multiply determined, if not overdetermined (Ollendick & March, 2004). That is, the disorders result from various factors only some of which are internal to the child. Considerable evidence suggests that bioecological and ecobehavioral influences are evident (Bronfenbrenner, 1977) and that these additional factors have important implications for the "location" of the anxiety "disorder." Children are highly dependent on their families, schools, and communities and, not infrequently, these contextual influences occasion and maintain anxiety in them. Thus, one of the first recommendations for *DSM–V* is that a more ecological approach that is sensitive to both development and relationships-in-context be pursued (Jensen et al., 2004; Ollendick & March, 2004; Pine et al., 2002). It is recommended that these factors be considered in Axis IV of the Multiaxial System (Psychosocial and Environmental Problems). Such problems are presently considered in *DSM–IV* but rarely are they enlisted to qualify the diagnosis. In some instances at least, the diagnosis will reside in the environment, not in the child.

A second major recommendation evolves out of the observation that the *DSM* does not take into consideration developmental variations of presenting problems. In this regard *DSM–V* might borrow from a different diagnostic system—the Diagnostic and Statistical Manual for Primary Care–Child and Adolescent Version (*DSM–PC*; Wolraich, Felice, & Drotar, 1997). This system not only includes diagnostic categories from *DSM–IV* that are applicable to children but also a wide range of psychosocial problems that do not meet criteria for a specific disorder but still necessitate treatment. Its major section is organized into behavioral manifestations or clusters, such as "negative/antisocial behaviors," that are described in three categories reflecting the spectrum from normal *developmental variation* (e.g., engaging in brief arguments) through *problem* (e.g., frequently grabbing toys, shouting, punching siblings), to *disorder* (e.g., meets criteria for ODD). The spectrum categories also provide developmental guidelines for determining the significance of specific behaviors for that category within four identified age periods: infancy (birth to age 2), early childhood (3–5 years), middle childhood (6–12 years), and adolescence (13 years and older). As can be seen, this system appears to be a truly developmental one—that is, it is organized around important developmental periods and transitions and provides clear developmental guidelines for the appropriateness of the designated cluster of behaviors. Ollendick and Vasey (1999) as well as Masten and Braswell (1991) and Garber (1984) have recommended use of a similar developmentally based system for the diagnosis of other childhood psychopathologies.

A third recommendation is that *DSM–V* incorporate recent findings related to the somatic, cognitive, and behavioral expressions of anxiety in children. Clearly, somatic symptoms need to be considered for *all* of the anxiety disorders not just GAD and PD. Moreover, the somatic symptoms that are included need to be based on the available research regarding the physical expression of anxiety by children at different ages. Similarly, the role of cognitive factors needs to be carefully reconsidered, especially for younger children. Children are not miniature adults and they express their worries differently and oftentimes in behaviors, not thoughts. This notion is amply demonstrated in the area of panic where children frequently report noncatastrophic and external thoughts associated with their distress and do not generate internal and catastrophic thoughts (Mattis & Ollendick, 1997a, 1997b). Potential models for addressing cognitive variables are provided by the *ICD-10* and the criteria for SAD within the *DSM*. So, too, *DSM–V* should continue its inclusions of behaviors such as clinging and crying to describe the various responses to anxiety situations. We should not expect the symptoms of anxiety for children to be the same as they are with adults.

A fourth recommendation is that *DSM–V* reinstitute OAD and AD in its nomenclature for the anxiety disorders. Accumulating evidence suggests that these are not isomorphic disorders with GAD and SoP, and they may be developmental precursors to GAD and SoP, respectively. In doing so, it will be important to include more somatic symptoms in these disorders, including the commonly occurring childhood symptoms of headaches and stomachaches.

Finally, it is recommended that *DSM–V* take a lifespan approach and recognize that anxiety disorders "usually first diagnosed in infancy, childhood, or adolescence" can and do occur in adulthood. Separation anxiety, for example, can develop in adulthood (Cyranowski et al., 2002; Ollendick et al., 1993) although *DSM–IV* indicates that the "onset is before age 18." However, there does not appear to be any empirical support for this decision as many adults experience separation anxiety *for the first time* as they transition from adolescence into adulthood and from early adulthood into later stages in life. As noted, the categorization of this disorder and others (e.g., ADHD, learning disorders) into their separate category suggests that they are inherently different and somehow less applicable to adults. The *DSM* should incorporate existing research regarding the progression of anxiety disorders over time, as well as encourage further research into the temporal relations between anxiety symptoms in childhood and adulthood. Identification of signs and symptoms in childhood that are predictive of continued psychopathology and adult disorders will be a major achievement for the field of developmental psychopathology.

In sum, the task ahead for *DSM–V* is a formidable one; yet, it must respond to the challenges that await it and take a fresh, developmentally sensitive and contextually rich approach to advance to the next level of excellence. Surely the children and the families we serve deserve such advances.

References

Achenbach, T. M. (1999). Developmental taxonomy. In W. K. Silverman & T. Ollendick (Eds.), *Developmental issues in the clinical treatment of children* (pp. 31–43). Needham Heights, MA: Allyn & Bacon.

American Psychiatric Association (1980). *Diagnostic and statistical manual of mental disorders* (3rd ed.). Washington, DC: Author.

American Psychiatric Association (1994). *Diagnostic and statistical manual of mental disorders* (4th ed.). Washington, DC: Author.

American Psychiatric Association (2000). *Quick reference to the diagnostic criteria from DSM–IV–TR*. Washington, DC: Author.

Bandura, A. J. (1977). *Social learning theory*. Englewood Cliffs, NJ: Prentice Hall.

Bandura, A. (1989). Social cognitive theory. In R. Vasta (Ed.), *Annals of child development* (Vol. 6). Greenwich, CT: JAI Press.

Barlow, D. H. (1988). *Anxiety and its disorders*. New York: Guilford Press.

Barlow, D. H., & Nelles, W. B. (1988). Do children panic? *Clinical Psychology Review, 8*, 359–372.

Beck, A. T., & Steer, R. A. (1990). *Beck Anxiety Inventory: Manual*. San Antonio: The Psychological Corporation.

Bijou, S. (1976). *Child development: The basic stage of early childhood*. Englewood Cliffs, NJ: Prentice Hall.

Bittner, A., Egger, H. L., Erkanli, A. Costello, E. J., Foley D. L., & Angold, A. (2007). What do childhood anxiety disorders predict? *Journal of Child Psychology and Psychiatry, 48*, 1174–1183.

Bronfenbrenner, U. (1977). Toward an experimental ecology of human development. *American Psychologist, 32*, 513–531.

Cantwell, D. P., & Baker, L. (1987). Prevalence of anxiety in children with communication disorders. *Journal of Anxiety Disorders, 1*, 239–248.

Cicchetti, D. (1989a). Developmental psychopathology: Past, present, and future. In D. Cicchetti (Ed.), *The emergence of a discipline: The Rochester symposium on developmental psychopathology* (Vol. 1, pp. 1–12). Hillsdale, NJ: Erlbaum.

Cicchetti, D. (1989b). Developmental psychopathology: Some thoughts on its evolution. *Development and Psychopathology, 1*, 1–4.

Costello, E. J., Egger, H. L., & Angold, A. (2005). The developmental epidemiology of anxiety disorders: phenomenology, prevalence, and comorbidity. *Child and Adolescent Psychiatric Clinics of North America, 14*, 631–648.

Costello, E. J., Mustillo, S., Erkanli, A., Keeler, G., & Angold, A. (2003). Prevalence and development of psychiatric disorders in childhood and adolescence [see comment]. *Archives of General Psychiatry, 60*, 837–844.

Cyranowski, J. M., Shear, M. K., Rucci, P., Fagiolini, A., Frank, E., Grochocinski, V. J., et al. (2002). Adult separation anxiety: psychometric properties of a new structured clinical interview. *Journal of Psychiatric Research, 36*, 77–86.

Daleiden, E. L., Vasey, M. W., & Brown, L. M. (1999). Internalizing disorders. In W. K. Silverman & T. H. Ollendick (Eds.), *Developmental issues in the clinical treatment of children* (pp. 261–278). Needham Heights, MA: Allyn & Bacon.

Edelbrock, C., Costello, A. J., Dulcan, M. K., Conover, N. C., & Kala, R. (1986). Parent–child agreement on child psychiatric symptoms assessed via structured interview. *Journal of Child Psychology and Psychiatry and Allied Disciplines, 27*, 181–190.

Erikson, E. H. (1968). *Identity: Youth and crisis*. New York: Norton.

Eyberg, S. M., Schuhmann, E. M., & Rey, J. (1998). Child and adolescent psychotherapy research: developmental issues. *Journal of Abnormal Child Psychology, 26*, 71–82.

Foley, D., Rutter, M., Pickles, A., Angold, A., Maes, H., Silberg, J., et al. (2004). Informant disagreement for separation anxiety disorder. *Journal of the American Academy of Child and Adolescent Psychiatry, 43*, 452–460.

Foley, D. L., Rutter, M., Angold, A., Pickles, A., Maes, H. M., Silberg, J. L., et al. (2005). Making sense of informant disagreement for overanxious disorder. *Journal of Anxiety Disorders, 19*, 193–210.

Francis, G., Last, C. G., & Strauss, C. C. (1987). Expression of separation anxiety disorder: the roles of age and gender. *Child Psychiatry and Human Development, 18*, 82–89.

Francis, G., Last, C. G., & Strauss, C. C. (1992). Avoidant disorder and social phobia in children and adolescents. *Journal of the American Academy of Child and Adolescent Psychiatry, 31*, 1086–1089.

Freud, S. (1949). *An outline of psycho-analysis*. New York: Norton.

Garber, J. (1984). Classification of childhood psychopathology: a developmental perspective. *Child Development, 55*, 30–48.

Gelfand, D. M., & Peterson, L. (1985). *Child development and psychopathology*. Beverly Hills, CA: Sage.

Giaconia, R. M., Reinherz, H. Z., Silverman, A. B., Pakiz, B., Frost, A. K., & Cohen, E. (1994). Ages of onset of psychiatric disorders in a community population of older adolescents. *Journal of the American Academy of Child and Adolescent Psychiatry, 33*, 706–717.

Ginsburg, G. S., Riddle, M. A., & Davies, M. (2006). Somatic symptoms in children and adolescents with anxiety disorders. *Journal of the American Academy of Child and Adolescent Psychiatry, 45*, 1179–1187.

Goodwin, R. D., Fergusson, D. M., & Horwood, L. J. (2004). Early anxious/withdrawn behaviours predict later internalising disorders. *Journal of Child Psychology and Psychiatry and Allied Disciplines, 45*, 874–883.

Gregory, A. M., Caspi, A., Moffitt, T. E., Koenen, K., Eley, T. C., & Poulton, R. (2007). Juvenile mental health histories of adults with anxiety disorders. *American Journal of Psychiatry, 164*, 301–308.

Grills, A. E., & Ollendick, T. H. (2003). Multiple informant agreement and the anxiety disorders interview schedule for parents and children. *Journal of the American Academy of Child and Adolescent Psychiatry, 42*, 30–40.

Hirshfeld, D. R., Rosenbaum, J. F., Biederman, J., Bolduc, E. A., Faraone, S. V., Snidman, N., et al. (1992). Stable behavioral inhibition and its association with anxiety disorder. *Journal of the American Academy of Child and Adolescent Psychiatry, 31*, 103–111.

Holmbeck, G. N., & Kendall, P. C. (1991). Clinical-childhood-developmental interface: Implications for treatment. In P. R. Martin (Ed.), *Handbook of behavior therapy and psychological science: An integrative approach* (pp. 73–99). New York: Pergamon Press.

Ialongo, N., Edelsohn, G., Werthamer-Larsson, L., Crockett, L., & Kellam, S. (1993). Are self-reported depressive symptoms in first-grade children developmentally transient phenomena? A further look. *Development and Psychopathology, 5*, 433–457.

Jensen, P. S., & Hoagwood, K. (1997). The book of names: *DSM–IV* in context. *Development and Psychopathology, 9*, 231–249.

Jensen, P. S., Knapp, P., & Mrazek, D. (Eds.). (2004). *Beyond DSM–IV: Evolutionary and developmental approaches to clinical diagnosis*. New York: Guilford Press. Kendall, P. C., & Pimentel, S. S. (2003). On the physiological symptom constellation in youth with Generalized Anxiety Disorder (GAD). *Journal of Anxiety Disorders, 17*, 211–221.

Lease, C. A., & Ollendick, T. (Eds.). (1993a). *Developmental and psychopathology*. New York: Pergamon Press.

Lease, C. A., & Ollendick, T., H. (1993b). Development and psychopathology. In A. S. Bellack & M. Hersen (Eds.), *Psychopathology in adulthood: An advanced text* (pp. 89–103). New York: Pergamon Press.

Lerner, R. M., Hess, L. E., & Nitz, K. (1990). Toward the integration of human developmental and therapeutic change. In P. M. Martin (Ed.), *Handbook of behavior therapy and psychological science: An integrative approach* (pp. 13–34). New York: Pergamon Press.

Lerner, R. M., Hess, L. E., & Nitz, K. (1991). A developmental perspective on psychopathology. In M. Hersen & C. G. Last (Eds.), *Handbook of child and adult psychopathology: A longitudinal perspective* (pp. 9–32). Elmsford, NY: Pergamon Press.

Lewis, M. (1990a). Challenges to the study of developmental psychopathology. In M. Lewis & S. M. Miller (Eds.), *Handbook of developmental psychopathology* (pp. 29–40). New York: Plenum Press.

Lewis, M. (1990b). Models of developmental psychopathology. In M. Lewis & S. M. Miller (Eds.), *Handbook of developmental psychopathology* (pp. 15–27). New York: Plenum Press.

Magee, W. J., Eaton, W. W., Wittchen, H. U., McGonagle, K. A., & Kessler, R. C. (1996). Agoraphobia, simple phobia, and social phobia in the National Comorbidity Survey. *Archives of General Psychiatry, 53*, 159–168.

March, J. S. (1997). *Multidimensional anxiety scale for children: Technical manual*. Toronto: Multi-Health Systems Inc.

Masten, A. S., & Braswell, L. (1991). Developmental psychopathology: An integrative framework. In P. R. Martin (Ed.), *Handbook of behavior therapy and psychological science: An integrative approach* (pp. 35–56). New York: Pergamon Press.

Mattis, S. G., & Ollendick, T. H. (1997a). Children's cognitive responses to the somatic symptoms of panic. *Journal of Abnormal Child Psychology, 25*, 47–57.

Mattis, S. G., & Ollendick, T. H. (1997b). Panic in children and adolescents: A developmental analysis. In T. H. Ollendick & R. J. Prinz (Eds.), *Advances in clinical child psychology* (Vol. 19, pp. 27–74). New York: Plenum.

Moffitt, T. E., Harrington, H., Caspi, A., Kim-Cohen, J., Goldberg, D., Gregory, A. M., et al. (2007). Depression and generalized anxiety disorder: cumulative and sequential comorbidity in a birth cohort followed prospectively to age 32 years. *Archives of General Psychiatry, 64*, 651–660.

Morris, E. K., Hursh, D. E., Winston, A. S., Gelfand, D. M., Hartmann, D. P., Reese, H. W., et al. (1982). Behavior analysis and developmental psychology. *Human Development, 25*, 340–364.

Nottelmann, E. D., & Jensen, P. S. (1995). Comorbidity of disorders in children and adolescents: Developmental perspective. In T. H. Ollendick & R. J. Prinz (Eds.), *Advances in clinical child psychology* (Vol. 17, pp. 109–155). New York: Plenum Press.

Ollendick, T., & Cerny, J. A. (1981). *Clinical behavior therapy with children*. New York: Plenum.

Ollendick, T., H., & March, J. S. (Eds.). (2004). *Phobic and anxiety disorders: A clinician's guide to effective psychosocial and pharmacological interventions*. New York: Oxford University Press.

Ollendick, T. H. (1998). Panic disorder in children and adolescents: new developments, new directions. *Journal of Clinical Child Psychology, 27*, 234–245.

Ollendick, T. H., & Hirshfeld-Becker, D. R. (2002). The developmental psychopathology of social anxiety disorder. *Biological Psychiatry, 51*, 44–58.

Ollendick, T. H., & King, N. J. (1994). Diagnosis, assessment, and treatment of internalizing problems in children: the role of longitudinal data. *Journal of Consulting and Clinical Psychology, 62*, 918–927.

Ollendick, T. H., Lease, C. A., & Cooper, C. (1993). Separation anxiety in young adults: A preliminary examination. *Journal of Anxiety Disorders, 7*, 293–305.

Ollendick, T. H., Mattis, S. G., & King, N. J. (1994). Panic in children and adolescents: a review. *Journal of Child Psychology and Psychiatry and Allied Disciplines, 35*, 113–134.

Ollendick, T. H., & Vasey, M. W. (1999). Developmental theory and the practice of clinical child psychology. *Journal of Clinical Child Psychology, 28*, 457–466.

World Health Organization (1992). *International Classification of Diseases, 10th Rev*. Geneva: Author.

Piaget, J. (1950). *The psychology of intelligence*. New York: Harcourt Brace.

Pine, D. S. (2007). Research review: a neuroscience framework for pediatric anxiety disorders. *Journal of Child Psychology and Psychiatry and Allied Disciplines, 48*, 631–648.

Pine, D. S., Alegría, M., Cook, E. H., Costello, E. J., Dahl, R. E., Koretz, D., et al. (2002). Advances in developmental science and *DSM–V*. In D. J. Kupfer, M. B. First & D. A. Regier (Eds.), *A research agenda for DSM–V* (Vol. 1, pp. 332): American Psychiatric Publishing, Inc.

Pine, D. S., Cohen, P., Gurley, D., Brook, J., & Ma, Y. (1998). The risk for early-adulthood anxiety and depressive disorders in adolescents with anxiety and depressive disorders. *Archives of General Psychiatry, 55*, 56–64.

Rutter, M. (1985). Resilience in the face of adversity. Protective factors and resistance to psychiatric disorder. *British Journal of Psychiatry, 147*, 598–611.

Rutter, M., & Garmezy, N. (1983). Developmental psychopathology. In E. M. Hetherington (Ed.), *Socialization, personality, and social development* (Vol. 4). New York: Wiley & Sons.

Sameroff, A. (1975). Transactional models in early social relations. *Human Development, 18*, 65–79.

Sameroff, A. (1995). General systems theories and developmental psychopathology. *Developmental Psychopathology, 1*, 659–695.

Seligman, L. D., & Ollendick, T. H. (1998). Comorbidity of anxiety and depression in children and adolescents: an integrative review. *Clinical Child and Family Psychology Review, 1*, 125–144.

Skinner, B., F. (1938). *The behavior of organisms*. New York: Plenum.

Sterba, S., Egger, H. L., & Angold, A. (2007). Diagnostic specificity and nonspecificity in the dimensions of preschool psychopathology. *Journal of Child Psychology and Psychiatry, 48*, 1005–1013.

Toth, S. L., & Cicchetti, D. (1999). Developmental psychopathology and child psychotherapy. In S. W. Russ & T. H. Ollendick (Eds.), *Handbook of psychotherapies with children and families* (pp. 15–43). New York: Kluwer Academic/Plenum Publishers.

Turner, S. M., Beidel, D. C., & Wolff, P. L. (1996). Is behavioral inhibition related to the anxiety disorders? *Clinical Psychology Review, 16*, 157–172.

Wolraich, M. L., Felice, M. E., & Drotar, D. (1997). *The classification of child and adolescent mental diagnoses in primary care*. Elk Grove Village, IL: American Academy of Pediatrics.

III

Classification and Specific Anxiety Problems

13

The Obsessive–Compulsive Spectrum: A Critical Review

Jonathan S. Abramowitz
Eric A. Storch
Dean McKay
Steven Taylor
Gordon J. G. Asmundson

A reclassification of obsessive–compulsive disorder (OCD) into a group of "obsessive–compulsive spectrum disorders" (OCSDs) has been proposed with considerable debate (e.g., Mataix–Cols, Pertusa, & Leckman, 2007) for the forthcoming *Diagnostic and Statistical Manual, Fifth Edition* (*DSM-V*) (Hollander & Evers, 2004). According to the OCSD model, the putative spectrum disorders occur on a compulsivity–impulsivity dimension with the compulsive anchor characterized by behaviors aimed at harm avoidance and anxiety reduction, and the impulsive anchor characterized by pleasure-seeking and gratification behaviors (Hollander & Zohar, 2004). Specifically, the following disorders have been proposed as OCSDs: OCD, body dysmorphic disorder (BDD), hypochondriasis, chronic tic disorders (e.g., Tourette's syndrome), numerous impulse control disorders (*ICDs*; e.g., trichotillomania, pathological gambling, compulsive shopping, pyromania), eating disorders, addictions, and autism (Hollander & Zohar, 2004). In light of the extensive range of potential disorders falling in this class, it has been proposed that the OCSDs form their own category separate from anxiety disorders (Hollander, Braun, & Simeon, 2008).

When the OCSD model was first proposed (Hollander, 1993), it was argued that these disorders were related to OCD on the basis of phenotypic similarities (i.e., *repetitive* thinking and behavior). However, the basis for the OCSD model has been updated. The primary arguments for considering shifting OCD from the anxiety disorders into a new OCSD classification are as follows (Bartz & Hollander, 2006; Hollander et al., 2008; Hollander & Zohar, 2004; Stein & Lochner, 2006):

(a) The symptoms of OCD and OCSDs share a core feature, namely repetitive thoughts and behaviors.
(b) There are similarities in associated features (e.g., comorbidity, familial loading) between OCD and OCSDs.
(c) OCD and the proposed OCSDs share common genetic factors, brain circuitry, and neurotransmitter abnormalities.
(d) OCD and the proposed OCSDs share similar treatment response profiles.

In this chapter, we will critically examine the arguments listed above using the available empirical research.

The Appeal to Repetitive Thoughts and Behaviors

Proponents of the OCSD approach assert that OCD and the proposed spectrum disorders are linked on a "core repetitive behavior domain" characterized by the inability to delay or inhibit repetitive behaviors. This assertion is modeled on the assumption that uncontrolled behaviors fall along a continuum from risk aversion (compulsions) to risk-taking (impulsivity). Thus, at one end of the continuum are "compulsive disorders" such as OCD, hypochondriasis, BDD, and anorexia nervosa, which are characterized by repetitive behaviors aimed to reduce or avoid anxiety, risk, and harm. Impulse control disorders (e.g., sexual compulsions, addictions) in contrast, represent the other anchor, as these conditions are characterized by pleasure-seeking (and sometimes risky) behaviors. To this end, the unifying factor among the proposed OCSDs is the presence of *repetition*. Yet, the proposal that repetitive behaviors link disorders along a spectrum encounters many important problems.

Behavioral Ecology of OCD and the OCSDs

By emphasizing the presence of repetitive behaviors as a fundamental criterion for inclusion in the OCD spectrum, the OCSD approach overlooks other essential (and arguably more fundamental) features of OCD phenomenology. Perhaps some "blame" for focusing on repetitive behaviors in the OCSD approach can be attributed to the *DSM*'s approach to taxonomy, wherein disorders are defined merely by lists of signs and symptoms rather than by etiological factors derived from models that incorporate empirically validated constructs (e.g., motivation and cognition). This is especially the case in OCD where, due to its emphasis on symptom form as opposed to symptom function, the *DSM-IV/DSM-IV-TR* (American Psychiatric Association [APA], 1994, 2000) definition and diagnostic criteria overlook important empirically established aspects of the nature of obsessions and compulsions. Most critical to the current discussion is that, according to the *DSM*, either obsessions *or* compulsions are necessary and sufficient for a diagnosis of OCD. The difficulty here is that this leaves the impression that obsessions and compulsions are independent from each other. Whereas this conceptualization of OCD is unsupported by the literature (as we discuss below), it could lead to drawing parallels between OCD symptoms and other disorders that involve repetitious behavior. Examples include "compulsive" gambling, "compulsive" stealing, "compulsive" use of pornography, "obsessive" jealousy, and even excessive nail biting, which clinicians frequently subsume under the OCD umbrella.

This superficial conceptual approach is at odds with research findings on the phenomenology of OCD. For example, Foa et al. (1995) found that 96% of 411 OCD patients reported both obsessions *and* compulsions on the Yale–Brown Obsessive Compulsive symptom checklist, whereas only 2.1% reported predominantly obsessions and only 1.7% reported predominantly compulsions. Moreover, a growing literature has identified dimensions and "subtypes" of OCD in which obsessions and compulsions load together on the same symptom-based factors and clusters (e.g., Leckman et al., 1997) as well as on measures of symptom severity (Amir, 1997; Deacon & Abramowitz, 2005). Thus, as much as the distinction between obsessions and compulsions is intuitively appealing and endorsed by the *DSM*, research suggests that OCD phenomenology does not necessarily distill neatly into these two categories.

OCD rather is characterized by an internally consistent link between obsessions and compulsions. Initially, individuals experience involuntary thoughts and doubts (obsessions) that they find unacceptable and anxiety evoking. Often but not always, the obsessions are triggered by environmental stimuli. To alleviate obsessional distress, patients resort to deliberate and purposeful behaviors (including sometimes, mental activity) aimed at reducing distress and bringing about a sense of safety. Therefore, one can conceptualize OCD as a problem in which an individual is fearful of certain situations and stimuli which are the focus of the obsessions. Compulsive behavior is performed with the purpose of alleviating obsessional and emotional distress, a phenomenon that unifies OCD with other anxiety disorders (as we discuss further below).

A series of elegant, yet simple laboratory studies have closely examined the relationship between obsessions and compulsions in OCD. The research paradigm included exposing patients to stimuli that provoked urges to engage in compulsive behavior and recording subjective levels of anxiety and urges to "ritualize" before and after exposure, and after performing the compulsive "ritual." The findings of these studies can be summarized as follows: For patients with washing rituals evoked by fears of germs, exposure to contaminants led to an increase in subjective anxiety and urges to ritualize, whereas completion of a washing ritual rapidly reduced the distress and urges. A more gradual spontaneous reduction in both anxiety and compulsive urges was observed when the performance of rituals was delayed for 30 minutes (Hodgson & Rachman, 1972). Similar results were obtained in two studies of patients with checking rituals evoked by exposure to potentially harmful stimuli such as knives (Roper & Rachman, 1976; Roper, Rachman, & Hodgson, 1973), and in a study of patients with mental compulsions evoked by intrusive unacceptable thoughts (de Silva, Menzies, & Shafran, 2003).

The above findings show that in OCD, compulsive behavior is performed in response to specific cues, such as particular personally relevant situations or thoughts that evoke anxiety concerning feared outcomes. Moreover, anxiety and compulsive urges typically (although not always) subside after completion of the ritual. The evocation of compulsive urges by obsessional fear, the immediate reduction in anxiety following compulsive behavior, and the eventual reduction of anxiety and compulsive urges (even if the ritual is not performed) are the hallmarks of OCD, but not the other OCSDs (e.g., compulsive gambling, paraphilias).

In contrast, impulsive behavior such as that which characterizes *ICD* is pleasure-seeking. The person feels an intrinsically reinforcing rush of excitement when the behavior is performed (Grant & Potenza, 2004). There are no data to suggest that the anxiety-reducing compulsive behavior observed in OCD and the positively reinforced impulsive behavior observed in *ICD*s exist on a spectrum. In fact, it is unclear exactly what kind of data would demonstrate whether such a spectrum is present or not, and it may be that impulsivity and compulsivity are best viewed as dimensions that can co-occur in any given person regardless of their diagnosis of OCD. In support of this, the extant evidence suggests the lack of any specific relationship between impulsivity and compulsivity for a number of reasons. First, *ICD*s occur at low rates among patients with OCD (Bienvenu et al., 2000). Second, people with OCD do not necessarily evidence greater levels of impulsivity than individuals with other sorts of psychiatric disorders do (Summerfeldt et al., 2004). Third, the effective behavioral treatment approaches for OCD and the *ICD*s are very different (e.g., Abramowitz & Houts, 2002). Finally, in its current form, OCD itself is a highly heterogeneous disorder that lacks a single compelling model to account for the diversity (i.e., Taylor, McKay, & Abramowitz, 2005). Without a single framework to describe OCD per se, it is unlikely that a compulsive–impulsive continuum of disorders could be organized around any one central variable, let alone the ambitious list of explanatory variables advanced by proponents of the spectrum (McKay, Abramowitz, & Taylor, 2008).

The Appeal to Associated Features

Comorbidity

Proponents of the OCSD approach propose that high comorbidity between OCD and the OCSDs supports a new category of OCSDs in *DSM-V*. Results of large-scale comorbidity studies, however, do not support this proposition. For example, in the Johns Hopkins OCD family study, Bienvenu et al. (2000) reported generally low rates of OCSDs among 80 individuals with OCD: hypochondriasis = 16%, BDD = 15%, anorexia nervosa = 9%, bulimia = 4%, trichotillomania = 4%, kleptomania = 3%, pathologic gambling = 0%, and pyromania = 0%. In a study of 98 adults with OCD, Richter et al. (2003) found comorbidity rates of 13% for a tic disorder, 9% for trichotillomania, 5% for an eating disorder, and 15% for clinical skin picking. Similar results have been found by others (Barsky, Wyshak, & Klerman, 1992; Savron et al., 1996).

The findings presented above indicate that OCSDs are rather *uncommon* among patients with OCD. The exceptions are BDD and hypochondriasis, which are considered by many researchers to be anxiety-motivated disorders (Abramowitz, 2005; Abramowitz & Braddock, 2006; Noyes, 1999; Phillips, Kim, & Hudson, 1995). The generally low comorbidity of OCD and OCSDs is most dramatically illustrated by noting that among OCD patients in the Bienvenu et al. (2000) study, 96% *did not* have trichotillomania, whereas in the Richter et al. (2003) study, 87% *did not* have a tic disorder. Even if it is granted that OCSD comorbidity rates are higher than chance in OCD, and even if comorbidity is a useful basis for lumping disorders in *DSM-V* (an issue we consider further below), the bigger problem for this argument is that comorbidity rates between OCD and other anxiety and mood disorders are considerably higher than the rates for putative OCSDs. For example, data from the John Hopkins Study indicate that 13% of OCD patients also met criteria for generalized anxiety disorder, 21% met criteria for panic disorder, 17% for agoraphobia, 36% for social phobia, 31% for specific phobias, and 54% for recurrent major depression (Nestadt et al., 2001). So, the comorbidity argument that OCSD proponents (e.g., Hollander, Friedberg, & Wasserman, 2005) use to support their contention that OCSDs are related to OCD is actually more in line with the view that OCD is more closely related to other anxiety disorders (on the order of 2- to 3-fold closer).

Family History

Similar arguments apply to OCSD proponents' assertion that OCD has a familial or genetic association with OCSDs, which suggests that a spectrum exists. Not only are there no data on this issue for most of the proposed OCSDs, but the available data show that rates of other anxiety disorders among first degree relatives of people with OCD are far higher than the rates of OCSDs among relatives of people with OCD (e.g., Bienvenu et al., 2000; Nestadt et al., 2001). For example, Nestadt et al. reported the following rates of anxiety disorders in first-degree relatives of adults with OCD: 16% OCD, 16% generalized anxiety disorder, 9% panic disorder, 23% social phobia, 25% specific phobia, and 13% separation anxiety disorder (Nestadt et al.). In the same dataset, however, lifetime prevalence rates of *ICDs* in first-degree relatives of adults with OCD were: 1% trichotillomania, 0% kleptomania, 9% pathological gambling, 0% pyromania, 4% "any" eating disorder, 17% any "grooming" disorder (Bienvenu et al.). So the assertion that familial pattern is good evidence for a relationship between OCD and other disorders again ends up supporting the view that OCD is more strongly related to other anxiety disorders than to the proposed OCSDs. These data are also more consistent with the notion of shared genetic vulnerability among OCD and the other anxiety disorders, as opposed to a genetic link between OCD and the putative OCSDs.

The Appeal to Brain Circuitry and Neurotransmitter Abnormalities

Brain Circuitry

While most proponents of the OCSD model concede that existing data on the brain circuitry of OCD and OCSDs remain equivocal, commonalities in brain circuitry are hypothesized to exist between OCD and many of the OCSDs on the basis of the available data (Bartz & Hollander, 2006). Most of the research on brain circuitry in OCD has used neuroimaging techniques to examine functional aspects of various brain regions thought to be involved in obsessions and compulsions. An important limitation of this research is that results across studies have not been consistent. In a meta-analysis of neuroimaging studies, for example, Whiteside, Port, and Abramowitz (2004) found that differences between OCD patients and controls were not replicated across studies for the orbitofrontal cortex, caudate nucleus, frontal cortex, parietal, left temporal, right temporal, anterior cingulate, or thalamus. This review included only 13 methodologically rigorous studies, indicating the preliminary nature of this literature. Other authors have also suggested it is too early to base diagnostic reclassifications on neurobiology findings (e.g., Hyman, 2007; Mataix-Cols et al., 2007). However, it is reasonable to use these data to develop well controlled studies that can more conclusively answer the question of commonalities and differences among disorders. In the absence of such studies, it is premature to bring neurobiology into the formal classification of mental disorders that will form the core of the *DSM-V* (Hyman, pp. 731).

Another limitation is that the *specificity* of brain structures and functions to OCD has not been studied. That is, there are few (if any) controlled studies in which people with OCD and those with other anxiety disorders have been directly compared on neurocircuitry variables. This problem of lack of evidence for specificity is perhaps the most limiting factor in our ability to infer that OCD is characterized by differences in neurocircuitry from other anxiety disorders. Similarly, very little data exist comparing patients with OCD relative to those with proposed OCSDs. In the absence of such data, it is premature to make a decision to restructure the *DSM-V* based on biological variables.

Neurotransmitter Abnormalities

Perhaps the most consistent finding in the biological literature on OCD is that obsessive–compulsive symptoms respond specifically to pharmacotherapy by selective serotonin reuptake inhibitors (SSRIs; e.g., fluoxetine, sertraline), as opposed to antidepressants with other mechanisms of action (e.g., desipramine, imipramine). On the basis of these findings, the "serotonin hypothesis" has been proposed. This hypothesis states that OCD is caused by abnormalities in the serotonergic system (Barr et al., 1992). A logical problem with this hypothesis is that specific models of etiology cannot be derived solely from knowledge of successful treatment response. This is a logical error known as *ex juvantibus* reasoning or "reasoning backward from what helps," a variation of the fallacy known as *post hoc ergo propter hoc* or "after this therefore because of this." The logical fallacy is clear if you consider the following example: "When I take aspirin, my headache goes away. Thus, the reason I get headaches is because my aspirin level is too low."

Just as there may be many possible mechanisms by which aspirin makes headaches go away, there may be many possible mechanisms by which SSRIs decrease OCD symptoms. For example, because neurotransmitter systems do not work in isolation, serotonergic neurons in one area of the brain may have synaptic relationships with, say, dopaminergic neurons elsewhere in the brain. Therefore, increasing serotonin levels in one region (e.g., by administration of SSRIs) may effectively increase or decrease (depending on the relationship) dopamine levels elsewhere. From an epistemological standpoint, successful response to a treatment derived from a particular conceptual framework may in some instances provide clues to etiology; however, definitive conclusions regarding causes of disorders are generally not warranted on the basis of treatment response alone. As we describe further below, this is a particular problem with treatment by SSRIs.

One of the great scientific, as opposed to practical, problems with the SSRI drugs is that they seem to work for a wide variety of disorders. Thus, there is not much chance of meaningful pharmacological dissection of disorders with the SSRIs—they seem to improve so many conditions that they are unlikely to lead to any useful information about mechanisms that characterize or distinguish OCD from other disorders. The fact that OCD responds to SSRI, but not to other types of antidepressant medicine, is not convincing evidence that serotonin is the culprit in OCD.

Over the last few decades considerable energy has been devoted to studies of biological markers (e.g., Zohar et al., 1987) and pharmacological challenge paradigms (e.g., Goodman et al., 1995) to test such hypotheses. Collectively, the findings from these investigations have been remarkably inconsistent (for a review, see Barr et al., 1992). Some have interpreted the highly discrepant results from this body of literature to support the serotonin hypothesis. However, researchers have not identified specific underlying abnormalities in serotonergic functioning that, if present at all, generate OCD symptoms. It may be that for OCD, serotonin is dysregulated in different ways in different brain areas although this remains to be demonstrated. Similarly, there is a rare research on the question of whether serotonin is dysregulated in the various OCSDs.

Even if OCD is associated with serotonin dysregulation, this does not mean that OCD is *caused* by an abnormally functioning serotonin system. A problem with lumping together a group of disorders (such as those in the proposed OCSD model) on the basis of their relationship with serotonin, is that serotonin is involved with many aspects of human behavior such as emotion, temperature regulation, memory, motor activity, pain, sleep, digestion, and hunger. Thus, the argument that OCSDs are all related to serotonin dysfunction does not reveal anything specific about these conditions.

The Appeal to Treatment Response

Proponents of the concept of OCSDs claim that these disorders respond to the same treatments that have been shown to be effective with OCD (Hollander et al., 2008). This line of reasoning however has been primarily focused on pharmacological interventions, unfortunately minimizing the role of effective psychological treatments (see Abramowitz, Whiteside, & Deacon, 2005, and Storch & Merlo, 2006, for reviews). Nonetheless, a number of rigorous and randomized controlled studies have demonstrated the effectiveness of serotonin reuptake inhibitors (SRIs), which include clomipramine and SSRIs, in adults and children with OCD (e.g., DeVeaugh-Geiss, et al., 1992; Foa et al., 2005; Geller et al., 2003; Goodman et al., 1989; Greist et al., 1995; Tollefson et al., 1994). These studies show that about 50%–60% of patients undergo a positive outcome with these agents.

In contrast to data in OCD patients, SRI response in OCSDs is more modest and varied in terms of efficacy and the amount of available data. For example, several studies have shown no beneficial effect of SSRIs in adults with trichotillomania relative to placebo (Christenson, Mackenzie, Mitchell, & Callies, 1991; Ninan, Rothbaum, Marsteller, Knight, & Eccard, 2000; Streichenwein & Thronby, 1995; van Minnen et al., 2003), whereas others have found efficacy (Dougherty, 2006). In a methodologically rigorous trial of trichotillomania, van Minnen et al. (2003) found that both behavioral psychotherapy and a waitlist control were superior to fluoxetine. Data are seriously limited regarding other disorders that would be included in the proposed OCSD (e.g., paraphilias, sexual addictions). A small number of uncontrolled trials have shown a moderate response to SRI therapy in patients with non-paraphilic sexual addictions (Kafka, 1994; Stein et al., 1992); but, as noted by Mataix–Cols et al. (2007), there are insufficient data at present to support any linkage among putative OCSDs as a function of treatment response.

Treatment response ought to be the litmus test for any OCSD proposals as it is an ultimately successful treatment that is sought by dealing with matters of phenomenology and etiology. Tests of the underlying mechanisms proposed for the OCSD would support similar treatment outcome across disorders. That is, therapies that target the underlying compulsive-impulsive continuum would have beneficial effect and imply a common etiological basis. However, as argued above, there is little to suggest a common etiological mechanism. Proponents of the spectrum conceptualization therefore may even lead people with OCD *away from* the best treatment for their condition. OCSD proponents (e.g., Hollander et al., 2005; Lochner & Stein, 2006) strongly tout evidence for a preferential response to medication in OCD and the OCSDs as supporting the spectrum conceptualization. However, the appeal to this preferential response is only clinically useful in delineating an OCD spectrum if three conditions are met: (a) preferential response to SRIs is observed uniformly in OCD and the OCSDs, (b) the preferential response to SRIs is not observed in other disorders that are not characterized as OCSDs, and (c) SRIs are the best treatment available for OCD and OCSDs. Unfortunately, none of these propositions have empirical support.

First, whereas OCD responds preferentially to SRIs, the claim of a similar preferential response across the OCSDs is not supported by the data. Very few controlled double-blind studies in which an SRI and non-SRI are directly compared have been reported for the various proposed OCSDs. This means that the assertion of preferential treatment response in most OCSDs is based on open-trial study results that are inadequate for answering the question of relative efficacy of medication. We find it troubling that such broad speculations about treatment response are made given the lack of convincing data and implications for clinical management. Evidence even suggests that non-SRIs are helpful for many of the proposed OCSDs, such as kleptomania (McElroy, Keck, Pope, & Hudson, 1989), compulsive shopping (McElroy et al., 1991), and pathological gambling (Moskowitz, 1980), to name a few. Also, antipsychotic medications (e.g., haloperidol) that are ineffective as monotherapies for OCD are often used in the treatment of Tourette's syndrome (Leckman et al., 1991).

Second, in addition to OCD, the SRIs are efficacious in the treatment of mood disorders (e.g., Nemeroff & Shatzberg, 1998) and various anxiety disorders, including those that are not part of the putative OCD spectrum (e.g., panic disorder; Boyer, 1995). Again, the spectrum argument runs into the lack of specificity problem: Because SRIs help so many disorders, the observation that a group of problems respond preferentially to these drugs does not tell us anything special about these disorders. Just because *preliminary* data support their use in OCSDs does not mean this is evidence of a common linkage. If that were true, a vast number of psychiatric disorders (e.g., major depression, bipolar disorder, some personality disorders, non-OCD anxiety disorders) not considered within the OCSD model would be implicated for their linkage. Furthermore, many patients with *ICD*s who benefit from SSRIs have comorbid anxiety or depressive disorders, which may explain treatment associated benefits (Grossman et al., 1999).

Third, ignored within the OCSD conceptualization is the highly effective psychological treatment for OCD, namely cognitive-behavior therapy (CBT). It is now well acknowledged that CBT, involving the procedures of exposure and response prevention (ERP), is the most effective treatment for OCD (Abramowitz et al., 2005; Foa et al., 2005; Jenike, 2004). Not only is ERP more effective than SRIs (average symptom reduction rates for ERP are 60%–70% versus only 20%–40% with SRIs; Jenike, 2004), but ERP was developed from a specific and empirically demonstrated conceptualization of OCD as an anxiety disorder in which compulsive rituals are performed to reduce inappropriate fear of obsessional stimuli.

When one considers the outcome of exposure-based CBT, a pattern emerges that links OCD with the other anxiety disorders. Outcome for this form of treatment in varied anxiety disorders across the age range are quite consistent. For example, between 54%–84% of adults with social phobia are considered responders to CBT (Clark et al., 2003, 2006; Taylor, 1996), a figure comparable to OCD outcome data (e.g., Abramowitz et al., 2005; Foa et al., 2005; Storch et al., 2007). This is in stark contrast to the outcomes of CBT protocols for *ICD*s. Currently, very few randomized trials have been conducted that examine CBT for OCSDs. Whereas some positive results have been found (e.g., Mitchell, Burgard, Faber, Crosby, & de Zwaan, 2006; Burgard, Faber, Crosby, & de Zwaan, 2006), many studies report on small samples and are vulnerable to the bias that positive results are more likely to be published than negative results. Further, many of these trials involve treatment protocols that differ significantly from those adopted for OCD. For example, whereas effective treatment for trichotillomania has been developed, these trials do not typically involve exposure-based procedures, but instead center on impulse control (Woods, Wetterneck, & Flessner, 2005). This is true of other *ICD* treatment (i.e., Grant & Odlaug, in press). This again points to differing mechanisms underlying compulsive and anxious conditions compared to impulsive conditions. Other studies are limited to subjects who comply with treatment, which is a significant factor when considering the pleasure-seeking nature of *ICD*s (e.g., only very motivated individuals seek treatment). Given the large dropout rates of many treatments, this practice exerts a sampling bias in favor of positive results.

Because CBT is based on the specific relationship between obsessional fear and compulsive behavior, this treatment is irrelevant for most of the putative OCSDs. For example, because trichotillomania involves neither obsessional fears nor urges to perform compulsive rituals designed to escape or neutralize anxiety, there would be no logic in using exposure or response prevention in the treatment of this disorder. Hair pulling in trichotillomania is not evoked by obsessional anxiety but rather by general tension, fatigue, or boredom. Hair pulling in trichotillomania is also not performed to reduce the probability of danger, as is observed with compulsions in OCD.

As can be seen, trichotillomania involves considerably different behavioral mechanisms than does OCD. Thus, the therapeutic procedures used in reducing this behavior are necessarily different. Functional analysis logically leads to the use of treatment procedures that hinder attempts to pull (stimulus control), such as wearing mittens, covering hair, or remaining around other people (Himle, Woods, Piacentini, & Walkup, 2006). Procedures that compete with pulling, such as handling a rubber ball, are also implemented along with repeated practice in "high-risk" situations. Finally, procedures that help patients avoid strong urges to pull (e.g., avoidance of cues, relaxation training) are employed. Similar procedures that aim to complicate the performance of specific undesirable behaviors are used to reduce other disorders of impulse control such as binge eating, pathological gambling, pathological sexual behavior, and substance abuse disorders.

Where Does OCD Belong in *DSM-V*?

One aim of diagnostic classification is to organize clinical problems into groups sharing common characteristics, including treatment response. Recent data (Mataix–Cols et al., 2007) illustrates that experts remain mixed in opinion as to whether OCD should remain classified as an anxiety disorder; specifically, 60% of a sample of primarily psychiatrists and psychologists who were listed as corresponding authors on OCD papers published between 1996 and 2006 endorsed *removal* of OCD from the anxiety disorders. Psychiatrists were more likely (75%) than psychologists and other professionals (40%–45%) to endorse removal. Some authors have raised this issue as a matter of debate by asserting that OCD is *more* closely linked to OCSDs due to the presence of repetitive behavior as the primary symptom, as well as similarities in clinical presentation, neurobiology, and treatment response. Authors who envision OCD as distinct from other anxiety disorders also point to the presence of strange, intrusive, and repetitious obsessions and compulsions which, while present in OCD, are not apparent in other anxiety disorders. Furthermore, the *DSM-IV/DSM-IV-TR* includes a specifier for "poor insight" in OCD, but not for the other anxiety conditions. Below, we assert that OCD *is* an anxiety disorder on the basis of shared fundamental phenomenology and similar responses to specific treatments for anxiety and fear.

OCD as an Anxiety Disorder

Although an examination of the current *DSM* criteria might lead one to see topographical differences between OCD and other anxiety disorders, the *DSM* criteria are merely meant to be descriptive; it is an atheoretical document (APA, 2000). In contrast, empirical research on the psychological experiences of those with OCD indicates clearly that there are strong similarities with other anxiety states. An in-depth review of this research is beyond the scope of this chapter (indeed, entire books have been written on the subject; e.g., Barlow, 2002); yet, the main conclusions of this work are summarized in Table 13.1. The table shows that OCD, specific phobia, social phobia, panic, and posttraumatic stress disorder (PTSD) all involve fear that occurs in the context of more or less disorder-specific situations or stimuli. Research also demonstrates that across disorders, this fear is maintained by distorted perceptions regarding the dangerousness of such situations, sensations, or mental events (also shown in Table 13.1).

There is also phenomenological similarity in how patients with different anxiety disorders respond when confronted with feared stimuli or with the prospect of exposure to feared situations. In a broad sense, when danger is perceived, taking action to avoid or escape from the potential threat is normal and adaptive (i.e., the "fight or flight" response). Indeed, this kind of avoidance and "safety-seeking" behavior is observed across the anxiety disorders (e.g., Clark, 1999). Examples include resting to prevent heart attacks during panic episodes, the agoraphobic's use of a "safety person" to avoid losing control, over-rehearsal of a speech by someone with social anxiety who fears that any mistake would result in public humiliation, and (of course) phobic avoidance of disorder-specific feared stimuli. Likewise, in OCD the same type of phobic avoidance of situations that trigger obsessional fear is apparent (e.g., public bathrooms, knives, "unlucky" numbers, cemeteries). Yet, because many obsessional fears are ubiquitous or unavoidable (e.g., using the bathroom, intrusive violent thoughts), the patient resorts to compulsive rituals to escape from anxiety—washing behavior because of feared contact with "urine germs," repeated checking motivated by thoughts of having "hit a pedestrian with one's car." These rituals are essentially the same as the behavior of a person with social phobia who finds him or herself in a social situation and consumes alcohol to reduce distress, or a person with panic who goes to the emergency room because he or she feels a panic attack beginning.

Although the excessive avoidance and escape behaviors in OCD and in the other anxiety disorders might appear topographically diverse, each is phenomenologically linked to a feared stimulus and a belief (i.e., overestimation of threat)

13.1 Empirically Established Features of OCD and other Anxiety Disorders

Disorder	Characteristic fear evoking stimuli	Prototypic beliefs	Typical safety signals and safety behaviors
OCD	Intrusive thoughts and related triggers	Thoughts are equivalent to actions, inflated responsibility for preventing harm (e.g., Obsessive–Compulsive Cognitions Working Group, 1997)	Avoidance, checking, hoarding, washing, ordering/arranging, covert neutralizing
Specific phobia	Snakes, heights, injections, storms, etc.	Overestimation of the likelihood or severity of danger from the feared stimulus (Beck & Emery, 1985)	Avoidance, drinking alcohol before flying, distraction during storms
Social phobia	Social situations, embarrassment, etc.	Other people are highly judgmental, negative evaluation is intolerable (Clark & Wells, 1995)	Avoidance of social situations, speaking softly, using alcohol
Panic disorder and agoraphobia	Arousal-related body sensations	Heart palpitations lead to heart attacks, dizziness leads to fainting (Clark, 1986)	Agoraphobic avoidance, sitting down, going to an emergency room, drinking water, calling a safe person, carrying the therapist's business card in purse or wallet
PTSD	Memories and reminders of traumatic events	Nowhere is safe, people can't be trusted, I am vulnerable (Taylor, 2006)	Avoidance of triggers, distraction, relying on others for safety, carrying some form of protection (e.g., pepper spray)

that are characteristic of each disorder. To the patient, the safety response functions to reduce the perceived probability of feared consequences. Put another way, there is an internal logic to the types of compulsive rituals performed by people with OCD; and this is the same "logic" that is observed across the anxiety disorders (but not in many of the putative OCSD conditions such as *ICD*s or Tourette's disorder). The far right column in Table 13.1 displays examples of so-called safety behaviors observed in the various anxiety disorders. Although it may be tempting to view compulsive rituals as unique from the safety behaviors in other anxiety disorders, any differences in repetitiveness, strangeness, or degree of functional impairment they engender are merely topographical differences that are less important than the fundamental psychological purpose of these behaviors, which are the same. All of this is to point out that the fundamental phenomenology of OCD is threat detection-based, and the same as that in the other anxiety disorders.

OCD as a Heterogeneous Condition

Although the above conceptualization applies to the majority of patients with OCD, it is noteworthy that recent research has shown that symptoms of OCD may be motivated by factors other than fear. Several examples are relevant and these may represent distinct disorder subtypes. First, some people exhibit contamination symptoms that are primarily driven by disgust rather than feared outcomes (McKay & Moretz, 2009; Stein, Liu, Shapira, & Goodman, 2001). Second, some patients with OCD experience feelings of incompleteness or "just right" feelings rather than a specific fear (e.g., Leckman et al., 1995). Finally, a considerable literature has debated the inclusion of hoarding as an OCD subtype (e.g., Abramowitz, Wheaton, & Storch, 2008; Grisham, Brown, Liverant, & Campbell–Sills, 2005), given the often ego-syntonic nature of hoarding symptoms among other characteristics that distinguish it from more "classic" OCD symptoms (Lochner et al., 2005), and emerging evidence suggesting that most cases of compulsive hoarding comprise a syndrome that is distinct from OCD (Pertusa et al., 2008).

Perhaps the perception that OCD on the whole does not fit well with either the anxiety disorders or OCSDs is a result of the considerable heterogeneity of OCD as it is currently conceptualized. Some OCD symptoms (e.g., contamination fears, fears of unwanted impulses) share many features with other anxiety disorders. On the other hand, OCD symptoms involving symmetry, ordering, and hoarding can sometimes share features with other sorts of disorders proposed as OCSDs (e.g., *ICD*s). Perhaps a resolution to the present debate over where OCD belongs in future editions of the *DSM* would be to parse OCD into more homogeneous categories, some of which overlap with other anxiety disorders, and some of which are more similar to *ICD*s, tic disorders, and neurological conditions with repetitive behaviors. We hope researchers will take up this issue of trying to better "carve OCD at its joints" rather than continuing to study and treat the disorders as if it were a homogeneous entity.

Conclusion

In this chapter we provide a critical review of the research related to proposals that OCD be removed from the anxiety disorders and into a new OCSD category in the *DSM-V*. As noted, there is inadequate empirical support for such a marked conceptual and nosological shift. Furthermore, incorrect conclusions have been drawn from existing data and cited to support the OCSD shift. Pragmatically, the OCSD model has limited heuristic and practical value when compared to a phenotypic or functional model of diagnostic classification. For example, diagnosing an OCSD on the basis of common etiological factors is problematic given that there is no reliable and valid laboratory test for OCD (or, for that matter, any other psychological disorder; Hyman, 2007). We suggest that it is premature to make the proposed OCSD shift given the absence of supporting empirical data, a lack of consensus among experts in the field, and further conceptual issues that must be better understood and integrated.

References

Abramowitz, J. S. (2005). Hypochondriasis: Conceptualization, treatment, and relationship to obsessive–compulsive disorder. *Annals of Clinical Psychiatry, 17,* 211–217.

Abramowitz, J. S., & Braddock, A. E. (2006). Hypochondriasis: Conceptualization, treatment, and relationship to obsessive–compulsive disorder. *Psychiatric Clinics of North America, 29,* 503–519.

Abramowitz, J.S., & Houts, A.C. (2002). What is OCD and what is not? Problems with the OCD spectrum concept. *The Scientific Review of Mental Health, 1,* 139–156.

Abramowitz, J. S., & Houts A. C. (2005). *Concepts and controversies in obsessive–compulsive disorder.* New York: Springer Science.

Abramowitz, J. S., Wheaton, M., & Storch, E. A. (2008). The status of hoarding as a symptom of obsessive–compulsive disorder. *Behaviour Research and Therapy, 46,* 1026–1033.

Abramowitz, J., Whiteside, S. P., & Deacon, B. J. (2005). The effectiveness of treatment for pediatric obsessive–compulsive disorder: A meta-analysis. *Behavior Therapy, 36,* 55–63.

American Psychiatric Association. (1994). *Diagnostic and statistical manual of mental disorders* (4th ed.). Washington, DC: Author.

American Psychiatric Association. (2000). *Diagnostic and statistical manual of mental disorders* (4th ed., text rev.). Washington, DC: Author.

Amir, N., Foa, E., & Coles, M. (1997). Factor structure of the Yale–Brown Obsessive Compulsive Scale. *Psychological Assessment, 9,* 312–316.

Barlow, D. H. (2002). *Anxiety and its disorders: The nature and treatment of anxiety and panic (2nd ed.).* New York: Guilford Press.

Barr, L. C., Goodman, W. K., Price, L. H., & McDougle, C. J. (1992). The serotonin hypothesis of obsessive-compulsive disorder: Implications of pharmacologic studies. *Journal of Clinical Psychiatry, 53S,* 17–28.

Barsky, A. J., Wyshak, G., & Klerman, G. L. (1992). Psychiatric comorbidity in DSM-III-R hypochondriasis. *Archives of General Psychiatry, 49,* 101–108.

Bartz, J. A., & Hollander, E. (2006). Is obsessive-compulsive disorder an anxiety disorder? *Progress in Neuro-Psychopharmacology and Biological Psychiatry, 30,* 338–352.

Beck, A. T., & Emery, G. (1985). *Anxiety disorders and phobias: A cognitive perspective.* New York: Basic Books.

Bienvenu, O. J., Samuels, J. F., Riddle, M. A., Hoehn–Saric, R., Liang, K. Y., Cullen, B. A., et al. (2000). The relationship of obsessive-compulsive disorder to possible spectrum disorders: results from a family study. *Biological Psychiatry, 48,* 287–293.

Christenson, G. A., Mackenzie, T. B., Mitchell, J. E., & Callies, A. L. (1991). A placebo controlled, double-blind crossover study of fluoxetine in trichotillomania. *American Journal of Psychiatry, 148,* 1566–1571.

Clark, D. M. (1986). A cognitive approach to panic. *Behaviour Research and Therapy, 24,* 461–470.

Clark, D. M. (1999). Anxiety disorders: Why they persist and how to treat them. *Behaviour Research and Therapy, 37,* S5–S27.

Clark, D. M., Ehlers, A., Hackmann, A., McManus, F., Fennell, M., Grey, N., et al. (2006). Cognitive therapy versus exposure and applied relaxation in social phobia: A randomized controlled trial. *Journal of Consulting and Clinical Psychology, 74,* 568–578.

Clark, D. M., Ehlers, A., McManus, F., Hackmann, A., Fennell, M., Campbell, H., Flower, T., et al. (2003). Cognitive therapy versus fluoxetine in generalized social phobia: A randomized placebo-controlled trial. *Journal of Consulting and Clinical Psychology, 71,* 1058–1067.

Clark, D. M., & Wells, A. (1995). A cognitive model of social phobia. In R. G. Heimberg, M. R. Liebowitz, D. A. Hope, & F. R. Schneier (Eds.), *Social phobia: Diagnosis, assessment, and treatment* (pp. 69–93). New York: Guilford.

de Silva, P., Menzies, R. G., & Shafran, R. (2003). Spontaneous decay of compulsive urges: The case of covert compulsions. *Behaviour Research and Therapy, 41*, 129–137.

Deacon, B. & Abramowitz, J. (2005). The Yale-Brown Obsessive-Compulsive Scale: Factor analysis, construct validity, and suggestions for refinement. *Journal of Anxiety Disorders, 19*, 575–583.

Deacon, B., & Abramowitz, J. (2006). Anxiety sensitivity and its dimensions across the anxiety disorders. *Journal of Anxiety Disorders, 20*, 837–857.

DeVeaugh–Geiss, J., Moroz, G., Biederman, J. B., Cantwell, D., Fontaine, R., Greist, J. H., et al. (1992). Clomipramine hydrochloride in childhood and adolescent obsessive-compulsive disorder: A multicenter trial. *Journal of the American Academy of Child and Adolescent Psychiatry, 31*, 45–49.

Dougherty, D. D., Loh, R., Jenike, M. A., & Keuthen, N. J. (2006). Single modality versus dual modality treatment for trichotillomania: Sertraline, behavioral therapy, or both? *Journal of Clinical Psychiatry, 67*, 1086–1092.

Foa, E. B., Kozak, M. J., Goodman, W. K., Hollander, E., Jenike, M. A., & Rasmussen, S. A. (1995). DSM-IV field trial: Obsessive-compulsive disorder. *American Journal of Psychiatry, 152*, 90–96.

Foa, E. B., Liebowitz, M. R., Kozak, M. J., Davies, S., Campeas, R., Franklin, M. E., et al. (2005). Randomized, placebo-controlled trial of exposure and ritual prevention, clomipramine, and their combination in the treatment of obsessive compulsive disorder. *American Journal Psychiatry, 162*, 151–161.

Geller, D. A., Biederman, J., Stewart, S. E., Mullin, B., Martin, A., Spencer, T., et al. (2003). Which SSRI? A meta-analysis of pharmacotherapy trials in pediatric obsessive-compulsive disorder. *American Journal of Psychiatry, 160*, 1919–1928.

Goodman, W. K., McDougle, C., Price, L., Barr, L., Hills, O., Caplik, J., et al. (1995). M-Chlorophenylpiperazine in patients with obsessive-compulsive disorder: Absence of symptom exacerbation. *Biological Psychiatry, 38*, 138–149.

Goodman, W. K., Price, L. H., Rasmussen, S. A., Delgado, P. L., Heninger, G. R., & Charney, D. S. (1989). Efficacy of fluvoxamine in obsessive-compulsive disorder: A double-blind comparison with placebo. *Archives of General Psychiatry, 46*, 36–44.

Grant, J. E., & Odlaug, B. L. (in press). Cognitive behavior therapy for impulse control disorders. In D. McKay, J.S. Abramowitz, & S. Taylor (Eds.), *The expanded scope of cognitive-behavior therapy: Lessons learned from refractory cases*. Washington, DC: American Psychological Association.

Grant, J. E., & Potenza, M. N. (2004). Impulse control disorders: Clinical characteristics and pharmacological management. *Annals of Clinical Psychiatry, 16*, 27–34.

Greist, J., Chouinard, G., DuBoff, E., Halaris, A., Kim, S. W., Koran, L., et al. (1995). Double-blind parallel comparison of three dosages of sertraline and placebo in outpatients with obsessive-compulsive disorder. *Archives of General Psychiatry, 52*, 289–295.

Grisham, J. R., Brown, T. A., Liverant, G. I., & Campbell-Sills, L. (2005). The distinctiveness of compulsive hoarding from obsessive–compulsive disorder. *Journal of Anxiety Disorders, 19*, 767–779.

Himle, M. B., Woods, D. W., Piacentini, J. C., & Walkup, J. T. (2006). Brief review of habit reversal training for Tourette syndrome. *Journal of Child Neurology, 21*, 719–725.

Hodgson, R., & Rachman, S. (1972). The effects of contamination and washing in obsessional patients. *Behaviour Research and Therapy, 10*, 111–117.

Hollander, E. (1993). Obsessive–compulsive spectrum disorders: An overview. *Psychiatric Annals, 23*, 355–358.

Hollander, E., Braun, A., & Simeon, D. (2008). Should OCD leave the anxiety disorders in the DSM-V? The case for obsessive–compulsive related disorders. *Depression and Anxiety, 25*, 317–329.

Hollander, E., & Evers, M. (2004). Review of obsessive–compulsive spectrum disorders: What do we know? Where are we going? *Clinical Neuropsychiatry, 1*, 32–51.

Hollander, E., Friedberg, J. P., & Wasserman, S. (2005). The Case for the OCD Spectrum. In J. S. Abramowitz & A. C. Houts (Eds.), *Concepts and controversies in obsessive–compulsive disorder* (pp. 95–118). New York: Springer Science.

Hollander, E., Kim, S., Khanna, S., & Pallanti, S. (2007). Obsessive–compulsive disorder and obsessive–compulsive spectrum disorders: Diagnostic and dimensional issues. *CNS Spectrums, 12*, 5–13.

Hollander, E., & Zohar, J. (2004). Beyond refractory obsessions and anxiety states: Toward remission. *Journal of Clinical Psychiatry, 14*, 3–5.

Hyman, S. E. (2007). Can neuroscience be integrated into the DSM-V? *Nature Reviews: Neuroscience, 8*, 725–732.

Kafka, M. P. (1994). Sertraline pharmacotherapy for paraphilias and paraphilia-related disorders: An open trial. *Annuals of Clinical Psychiatry, 6*, 189–195.

Ladouceur, R., Freeston, M. H., Rheaume, J., Dugas, M. J., Gagnon, F., Thibodeau, N., et al. (2000). Strategies used with intrusive thoughts: A comparison of OCD patients with anxious and community controls. *Journal of Abnormal Psychology, 109*, 179–187.

Leckman, J. F., Grice, D. E., Barr, L. C., de Vries, A. L. C., Martin, C., Cohen, D. J., et al. (1995). Tic-related vs. non-tic-related obsessive–compulsive disorder, *Anxiety, 1*, 208–215.

Leckman, J. F., Hardin, M. T., Riddle, M. A., Stevenson, J., Ort, S. I., & Cohen, D. J. (1991). Clonidine treatment of Gilles de la Tourette's syndrome. *Archives of General Psychiatry, 48*, 324–328.

Lochner, C., Kinnear, C. J., Hemmings, S. M., Seller, C., Niehaus, D. J., Knowles, J. A., et al. (2005). Hoarding in obsessive–compulsive disorder: Clinical and genetic correlates. *Journal of Clinical Psychiatry, 66*, 1155–1160.

Lochner, C., & Stein, D. J. (2006). Does work on obsessive–compulsive spectrum disorders contribute to understanding the heterogeneity of obsessive–compulsive disorder? *Progress in Neuro-psychopharmacology and Biological Psychiatry, 30,* 353–361.

Mataix–Cols, D., Cullen, S., Lange, K., Zelaya, F., Andrew, C., Amaro, E., et al. (2003). Neural correlates of anxiety associated with obsessive–compulsive symptom dimensions in normal volunteers. *Biological Psychiatry, 53,* 482–493.

Mataix–Cols, D., Pertusa, A., & Leckman, J. F. (2007). Issues for DSM-V: How should obsessive-compulsive and related disorders be classified? *American Journal of Psychiatry, 164,* 1313–1314.

McElroy, S. L., Hudson, J. I., Pope, H. G. Jr., & Keck, P. E. (1991). Kleptomania: Clinical characteristics and associated psychopathology. *Psychological Medicine, 21,* 93–108.

McElroy, S. L., Keck, P. E. Jr., Pope, H. G. Jr., & Hudson, J. I. (1989). Pharmacological treatment of kleptomania and bulimia nervosa. *Journal of Clinical Psychopharmacology, 9,* 358–360.

McKay, D., Abramowitz, J.S., & Taylor, S. (2008). Discussion: The obsessive-compulsive spectrum. In J.S. Abramowitz, D. McKay, & S. Taylor (Eds.), *Obsessive–compulsive disorder: Subtypes and spectrum conditions (pp. 287–300)*. Amsterdam: Elsevier.

McKay, D., & Moretz, M.W. (2009). The intersection of disgust and contamination fear. In B.O. Olatunji & D. McKay (Eds.), *Disgust and its disorders: Theory, assessment, and treatment implications (pp. 211–227)*. Washington, DC: American Psychological Association.

Mitchell, J. E., Burgard, M., Faber, R., Crosby, R. D., & de Zwaan, M. (2006). Cognitive behavioral therapy for compulsive buying disorder. *Behaviour Research Therapy, 44,* 859–1865.

Nakatani, E., Nakagawa, A., Nakao, T., Yoshizato, C., Nabeyama, M., Kudo, A., et al. (2005). A randomized controlled trial of Japanese patients with obsessive-compulsive disorder: Effectiveness of behavior therapy and fluvoxamine. *Psychotherapy and Psychosomatics, 74,* 269–276.

Nestadt, G., Samuels, J., Riddle, M. A., Liang, K. Y., Bienvenu, O. J., Hoehn-Saric, R., et al. (2001). The relationship between obsessive–compulsive disorder and anxiety and affective disorders: Results from the Johns Hopkins OCD Family Study. *Psychological Medicine, 31,* 481–487.

Ninan, P. T., Rothbaum, B. O., Marsteller, F. A., Knight, B. T., & Eccard, M. B. (2000). A placebo-controlled trial of cognitive-behavioral therapy and clomipramine in trichotillomania. *Journal of Clinical Psychiatry, 61,* 47–50.

Noyes, R. Jr. (1999). The relationship of hypochondriasis to anxiety disorders. *General Hospital Psychiatry, 21,* 8–17.

Obsessive–Compulsive Cognitions Working Group. (2003). Psychometric validation of the Obsessive Beliefs Questionnaire and the Interpretation of Intrusions Inventory: Part I. *Behaviour Research and Therapy, 41,* 863–878.

Pertusa, A., Fullana, M. A., Singh, S., Alonso, P., Menchon, J. M., & Mataix–Cols, D. (2008). Compulsive hoarding: OCD symptom, distinct clinical syndrome, or both? *American Journal of Psychiatry, 165,* 1289–1298.

Phillips, K. A., Kim, J. M., & Hudson, J. I. (1995). Body image disturbance in body dysmorphic disorder and eating disorders. *Psychiatric Clinics of North America, 18,* 317–334.

Roper, G., & Rachman, S. (1976). Obsessional-compulsive checking: Experimental replication and development. *Behaviour Research and Therapy, 14,* 25–32.

Roper, G., Rachman, S., & Hodgson, R. (1973). An experiment on obsessional checking. *Behaviour Research and Therapy, 11,* 271–277.

Savron, G., Fava, G. A., Grandi, S., Rafanelli, C., Raffi A. R., & Belluardo, P. (1996). Hypochondriacal fears and beliefs in obsessive-compulsive disorder. *Acta Psychiatrica Scandinavica, 93,* 345–348.

Stein, D. J., Hollander, E., Anthony, D. T., Schneier, F. R., Fallon, B. A., Liebowitz, M. R., et al. (1992). Serotonergic medications for sexual obsessions, sexual addictions, and paraphilias. *Journal of Clinical Psychiatry, 53,* 267–271.

Stein, D. J., Liu, Y., Shapira, N. A., & Goodman, W. K. (2001). The psychobiology of obsessive-compulsive disorder: How important is the role of disgust? *Current Psychiatry Reports, 3,* 281–287.

Stein, D. J., & Lochner, C. (2006). Obsessive–compulsive spectrum disorders: A multidimensional approach. *Psychiatric Clinics of North American, 29,* 343–351.

Storch, E. A., Geffken, G.R., Merlo, L. J., Mann, G., Duke, D., Munson, M., et al. (2007). Family-based cognitive-behavioral therapy for pediatric obsessive–compulsive disorder: comparison of intensive and weekly approaches. *Journal of the American Academy of Child and Adolescent Psychiatry,* 46, 469–478.

Storch, E. A., & Merlo, L. (2006). Obsessive-compulsive disorder: strategies for using CBT and pharmacotherapy. *The Journal of family practice,* 55, 329–333.

Streichenwein, S. M., & Thornby, J. I. (1995). A long-term, double-blind, placebo-controlled crossover trial of the efficacy of fluoxetine for trichotillomania. *American Journal of Psychiatry, 152,* 1192–1196.

Summerfeldt, L., Hood, K., Antony, M., Richter, M., & Swinson, R. (2004). Impulsivity in obsessive-compulsive disorder: Comparisons with other anxiety disorders and within tic-related subgroups. *Personality and Individual Differences, 36,* 539–553.

Taylor, S. (1996). Meta-analysis of cognitive-behavioral treatments for social phobia. *Journal of Behavior Therapy and Experimental Psychiatry, 27,* 1–9.

Taylor, S. (2006). *Clinician's guide to PTSD.* New York: Guilford.

Taylor, S., McKay, D., & Abramowitz, J. S. (2005). Is obsessive–compulsive disorder a disturbance of security motivation? Comment on Szechtman & Woody (2004). *Psychological Review, 112,* 650–656.

Tollefson, G. D., Rampey, A. H. Jr., Potvin, J. H., Jenike, M. A., Rush, A. J., Kominguez, R. A., et al. (1994). A multicenter investigation of fixed-dose fluoxetine in the treatment of obsessive compulsive disorder. *Archives of General Psychiatry, 51,* 559–567.

van Minnen, A., Hoogduin, K. A., Keijsers, G. P., Hellenbrand, I., & Hendriks, G. J. (2003). Treatment of trichotillomania with behavioral therapy or fluoxetine: A randomized, waiting-list controlled study. *Archives of General Psychiatry, 60,* 517–522.

Whiteside, S. P., Port, J. D., & Abramowitz, J. S. (2004). A meta-analysis of functional neuroimaging in obsessive–compulsive disorder. *Psychiatry Research, 32*, 69–79.

Woods, D. W., Wetterneck, C. T., & Flessner, C. A. (2005). A controlled evaluation of acceptance and commitment therapy plus habit reversal for trichotillomania. *Behaviour Research and Therapy, 44*, 639–656.

Zohar, J., Mueller, E., Insel, T., Zohar-Kadouch, R., & Murphy, D. (1987). Serotonergic responsivity in obsessive-compulsive disorder: Comparison of patients to healthy controls. *Archives of General Psychiatry, 44*, 946–951.

14

Classification of Worry and Associated Psychopathology

Norman B. Schmidt
Christina J. Riccardi
J. Anthony Richey
Kiara R. Timpano

The past several decades have seen a number of changes in the conceptualization and classification of generalized anxiety disorder (GAD). Despite considerable advances in the understanding of GAD, the development of a reliable diagnostic system remains somewhat elusive. The purpose of this chapter is two fold. First, we will provide a review of the empirical advances in the understanding of GAD. This review includes current classification systems and alternative conceptualizations of the disorder. Second, we will discuss taxometrics as a method of addressing some of the questions and criticisms about the current diagnostic systems of GAD. The implications of these analyses for the *Diagnostic and Statistical Manual of Mental Disorders* (*DSM-V*) are discussed.

Nosologic Evolution of GAD

Humans have always experienced anxiety, but it was not until the 1950s that official efforts were made to classify anxiety disorders, and many revisions to the nosology have occurred since then. What we now consider GAD was initially captured by the construct of *neurosis*. In the *DSM-III* (American Psychiatric Association [APA], 1980), neurotic disorders were redefined and a distinct anxiety disorders classification was created. The disorders where anxiety was experienced as the primary symptom, including GAD, were grouped together. This change marked the first step toward our current conceptualizations of anxiety disorders.

Although we have made significant strides in developing a valid and reliable nosology of anxiety psychopathology, the classification of GAD has been more complex, with significant questions and problems remaining. When GAD first appeared in the *DSM-III* (APA, 1980), the diagnosis required at least 1 month of generalized, persistent anxiety marked by symptoms from at least 3 of 4 clusters: motor tension (muscle aches, shakiness, inability to relax, jumpiness), autonomic hyperactivity (sweating, racing heart, dizziness, nausea), apprehensive expectation (worry, fear, anxiety, rumination), and vigilance and scanning (difficulty concentrating, insomnia, feeling on edge, irritability). In the *DSM-III*, GAD was considered a "residual category" and could only be diagnosed if the patient did not meet criteria for another mental disorder and was generally only used when no other diagnosis could be made. Thus, GAD was initially assigned to cases presenting a significant anxiety that was not clearly defined within other anxiety disorder categories, reminiscent of our current anxiety not otherwise specified (NOS) diagnosis.

Due to the residual, "catch-all" nature of this conceptualization of GAD, it is not surprising that concerns were raised about the *DSM-III* criteria for its diagnosis. Critics questioned, for example, whether the duration criterion (i.e., one month) and necessity of relatively few symptoms could differentiate between relatively brief stress reactions and excessive worry over various domain characteristics of GAD (Spitzer & Williams, 1984). These concerns were echoed by DiNardo et al. (1983) who reported low interrater reliability among GAD diagnoses and identified a number of possibilities for this discrepancy. In particular, many individuals endorsed symptoms of GAD lasting one month or more (per the *DSM-III* criteria), but clinicians tended to disagree about the level at which the impairment and severity of symptoms was sufficiently distressing to warrant a diagnosis. The ambiguities and difficulties relating to the symptom impairment threshold significantly contributed to early GAD diagnostic problems (DiNardo, O'Brien, Barlow, Waddell, & Blanchard, 1983). Additional concerns were raised about the residual category label of GAD and critics suggested GAD would better be classified as a unique disorder. Support for a distinct, nonresidual GAD diagnosis initially came from clinical trials where some individuals successfully treated for other anxiety disorders continued to experience generalized anxiety; this suggested that GAD might constitute a separate disorder (Barlow & DiNardo, 1991).

Revisions to GAD in the *DSM-III-R* (APA, 1987) sought to address many of these concerns. The residual category label was removed and the key feature of GAD is now defined as an excessive and/or unrealistic worry in two or more areas unrelated to another Axis I disorder. Moreover, the duration criterion was substantially increased to a minimum of six months. The symptom criteria were redefined and required 6 or more of 18 somatic symptoms to diagnose GAD. Finally, there were changes to the symptom domains or clusters. Specifically, the anxious apprehension cluster was removed and the 18 symptoms (e.g., trembling or feeling shaky, restlessness, shortness of breath, sweating, dry mouth, feeling on edge, trouble sleeping and irritability) were divided into three remaining clusters (i.e., motor tension, autonomic hyperactivity, and vigilance and scanning).

Despite these revisions, research focused on the reliability of the *DSM-III-R* criteria continued to show low diagnostic agreement for GAD (e.g., DiNardo, Moras, Barlow, Rapee, & Brown, 1993; Mannuzza et al., 1989). Mannuzza et al. (1989), for example, reported poor reliability for current GAD diagnosis ($\kappa = .27$) compared with other anxiety disorders such as panic disorder ($\kappa = .79$), Social Phobia ($\kappa = .68$), and Obsessive–Compulsive Disorder ($\kappa = .91$). One possible reason for the low diagnostic reliability of GAD is the ubiquity of its core characteristic-excessive/unrealistic worry. In fact, all *DSM-III-R* anxiety disorders are characterized by the presence of worry or anxious apprehension. As a result, this key diagnostic criterion for GAD may be less unique than those of other anxiety disorders. Examination of the content of worry suggests GAD can be differentiated from other anxiety disorders by the types of things people worry about. Worry in anticipation of specific objects or situations (e.g., worry about the next encounter with a snake or about the next panic attack) is common among anxiety disorders. Worry across various life situations (e.g., apprehensive expectation) is unique to GAD (Barlow et al., 1986); however, patients may have difficulty specifying the nature of their anxious apprehension, and clinicians may have difficulty identifying this as well. These factors appear to contribute to lower diagnostic reliability in this diagnosis (Brown & Barlow, 1992).

The associated symptom criteria of GAD were another possible source of diagnostic disagreement. An initial research on the 18 symptoms outlined in the *DSM-III-R* suggested that individual symptom ratings were unreliable (Barlow & DiNardo, 1991). Marten and colleagues (1993) also investigated the individual symptoms and generated a list of "satisfactory" symptoms based on reliability and endorsement criteria (interrater agreement of at least 70% and have endorsement of 50% or more in at least 3 of 4 sites). All symptoms in the Vigilance and Scanning cluster and majority of those in the Tension cluster were found to be satisfactory. However, no symptom in the autonomic hyperactivity cluster met the reliability and endorsement criteria. Largely because of these results, the GAD criteria were reconsidered and revised once again in the *DSM-IV* (APA, 1994).

High rates of comorbidity also raised concerns about the *DSM-III-R* GAD diagnostic criteria. Comorbidity was rarely considered in previous versions of the *DSM* because of hierarchical exclusionary rules. Prior to the *DSM-III-R*, diagnoses were excluded if symptoms were present during the course of another disorder. For example, mood disorders such as depression ranked above anxiety disorders in the hierarchy, so an anxiety disorder would generally not be diagnosed if the patient also experienced depression. The exclusionary rules affected GAD diagnosis more than other anxiety disorders because of the residual nature of this category (Brown & Barlow, 1992); that is, a GAD diagnosis could not be made in the presence of another Axis I disorder (e.g., depression or another anxiety disorder).

After the hierarchical decision rules were lifted in the *DSM-III-R*, GAD was the most commonly given additional diagnosis among patients with primary anxiety or mood disorders (Sanderson, Beck & Beck, 1990; Brown & Barlow, 1992). Similarly, when GAD was the primary diagnosis, it was associated with high rates of comorbidity (Massion, Warshaw, & Keller, 1993; Brawman–Mintzer et al., 1993). Sanderson, DiNardo, Rapee, and Barlow (1990) reported that 91% of GAD patients received at least one additional Axis I diagnosis. The most common comorbid disorders were social phobia, panic disorder, dysthymia, and simple phobia. These unusually high rates of comorbidity were considered evidence for poor discriminant validity of the GAD diagnostic criteria that continued to feed earlier concerns whether GAD represented a unique diagnostic category. Further refinement of the diagnostic criteria was needed to sharpen the definition of GAD to features distinct from other anxiety disorders.

The Current Classification Systems

DSM-IV Model of GAD

The *DSM-IV* brought additional revision of the associated symptom criteria of GAD. This criterion was dramatically reduced from 18 to 6 symptoms, but now required endorsement of half of the symptoms rather than the one third (6 of 18 symptoms) required by the *DSM-III-R*. Reduction in the number of symptoms, while requiring the presence of a larger percentage of possible symptoms, suggests researchers were honing in on the key features of GAD.

Unfortunately, empirical support for changing the symptom criteria in the *DSM-IV* was limited and relied heavily on a single study—the six symptoms selected for inclusion in the *DSM-IV* were those identified by Marten et al. (1993) as the most commonly endorsed by patients with *DSM-III-R* GAD diagnoses. The modest literature supporting these changes fueled concern about the validity of the symptoms and questions about the effects of removing the autonomic hyperactivity symptoms. In a study relevant to these concerns, Brown, Marten, and Barlow (1995) found out that more than 98% of patients diagnosed with GAD met the *DSM-IV* criteria of 3 of 6 symptoms; however, a large percentage of individuals with other diagnoses also met these criteria (as high as 92.9% in major depression). When the threshold was raised to 4 of 6 symptoms, specificity was increased from .31 to .48 with minimal change in sensitivity.

Requiring 5 of 6 symptoms further increased specificity (.69) but negatively affected sensitivity (Brown et al., 1995). These results suggested that greater diagnostic specificity would be achieved by raising the threshold from 3 to 4 key symptoms.

The *DSM-IV* revised criteria also required that worry was excessive and difficult to control. Support for these changes came from studies such as that conducted by Abel and Borkovec (1995) indicating that 95% of individuals with GAD reported excessive worry and 82.5% reported difficulty controlling worry (Abel & Borkovec, 1995). Of note, none of the control participants endorsed either symptom, suggesting that these characteristics of worry could reliably differentiate between those with and without GAD. This study also supported the removal of the unrealistic description of worry in the *DSM-IV*. Individuals with GAD were more likely to describe their worry as excessive and uncontrollable rather than unrealistic, whereas control subjects were more likely to describe worry as unrealistic rather than uncontrollable or excessive.

Despite the extensive revisions to our conceptualization of GAD, the debate about the correct nosology for this disorder continues to the present day. While some suggest that more rigorous diagnostic criteria are needed, others believe the current criteria may be too strict and missing a large number of people suffering from GAD who are marked by more transient, somatic symptoms (Rickles & Rynn, 2001). For example, a high number of individuals with subclinical GAD symptoms present for treatment at primary care settings (Olfson et al., 1996). Compared with those meeting full *DSM-IV* criteria for GAD, these subclinical patients are twice as numerous and demonstrate marked social impairment (Marcus, Olfson, Pincus, Shear, & Zarin, 1997). These findings suggest that subthreshold GAD symptoms may create significant distress and impairment, and should potentially be accounted for in the *DSM*.

ICD-10 Model of GAD

The *International Classification of Disease, tenth revision* (*ICD-10*; World Health Organization 1993) represents the other predominant psychiatric nosology. The *ICD-10* lists the key feature of GAD as a generalized and persistent anxiety that is not restricted to particular or environmental circumstances.

The key, free-floating symptoms are described as highly variable and include apprehension, difficulty concentrating, motor tension, and autonomic overactivity.

The *ICD-10* classification system is very similar to the *DSM-IV*. Many, including the American Psychiatric Association, consider the models equivalent. The international version of the *DSM* (APA, 1995) lists *ICD-10* diagnostic codes and the *DSM-IV* diagnostic criteria without consideration of the differences between the models. The key feature of GAD, the presence of worry about various everyday events for more days than not over a period of at least 6 months, is present in both classification systems. Both models include a list of core symptoms associated with GAD, though the content and severity of the symptoms vary somewhat.

Though the models are generally similar, the specific diagnostic criteria differ to some degree. The *DSM-IV* criteria require that worry be excessive in nature and difficult to control, characteristics not found in the *ICD-10*. In addition to differences in the quality o f worry, the associated symptoms of GAD also differ between the two models. The *ICD-10* identifies more symptoms and emphasizes an Autonomic Arousal cluster (e.g., heart palpitations) much like the *DSM-III-R*. This is a potential weakness of the *ICD-10* model because autonomic arousal symptoms are endorsed less frequently (43%–53%) than other symptoms (Slade & Andrews, 2001), and when they do occur, the symptoms are usually mild and contribute minimally in symptom expression (Starcevic, Fallon, & Uhlenhuth, 1994). In contrast, the *DSM-IV* criteria consist of fewer symptoms, the most important of which are those related to Vigilance and Scanning (e.g., feeling keyed up). These are endorsed most frequently among individuals with GAD (88%; Slade & Andrews, 2001), consistent with the research of Marten and colleagues (1993). Research on the discriminant validity of GAD has demonstrated that symptoms in the Vigilance and Scanning cluster are strongly correlated with measures of GAD, and those of the Autonomic Arousal cluster are not (Brown et al., 1995). This suggests that the autonomic arousal symptoms of the *ICD-10* should be less important in diagnosing GAD. The *ICD-10* diagnostic criteria are less well delineated relative to the *DSM* in that a necessary number of symptoms are not specified and the duration criterion is somewhat vague (e.g., several months).

Slade and Andrews (2001) compared GAD diagnostic criteria and found similar 12-month prevalence rates between the *DSM-IV* (2.6 %) and the *ICD-10* (3.0%). However, more than half of those diagnosed with one system were not diagnosed using the other, indicating a considerable discrepancy between the two divergent approaches. Diagnostic inconsistencies between positive *DSM-IV* and negative *ICD-10* diagnoses were attributed primarily to comorbid disorders and a failure to endorse autonomic arousal symptoms.

The *DSM-IV* requires that GAD symptoms cause clinically significant impairment or distress. This criterion is absent in the *ICD-10* and accounts for a significant amount of diagnostic discrepancy between the models (Slade & Andrews, 2001). As a result, the less rigid definition of GAD found in the *ICD-10* appears to yield diagnoses that include a milder, less impairing form of the disorder (Wittchen, Zhao, Kessler, & Eaton, 1994). *ICD-10* diagnosis would also include individuals who suffer from generalized anxiety that is more transient and somatic in its focus and who would be missed using the *DSM-IV* criteria. These individuals appear to be more likely to be present in a primary care setting (Rickles & Rynn, 2001) where the prevalence of GAD is twice than found in the community (Schweizer & Rickles, 1997). This pattern of findings suggests that the *ICD-10* may be sensitive to capturing a broader population of worriers relative to the *DSM-IV* (Rickels & Rynn, 2001).

Both models acknowledge high rates of comorbidity among patients with GAD and require that symptoms occur independent of other disorders. The *DSM-IV* specifies that symptoms of GAD must not occur solely during a mood disorder, but it does not place any limitations on comorbidity. In contrast, according to *ICD-10* criteria, GAD cannot be diagnosed if diagnostic criteria are met for panic disorder, phobic anxiety disorder, or obsessive–compulsive disorder. This specification is particularly important in the *ICD-10* because the symptom profiles are very similar between GAD and panic disorder. Disallowing the diagnosis of GAD in the presence of panic disorder is also likely to contribute to discrepancy in diagnosis between the two models.

Slade and Andrews (2001) compared the GAD diagnostic criteria and found similar 12-month prevalence rates between the *DSM-IV* (2.6%) and the *ICD-10* (3.0%). However, more than half of those diagnosed with one system were not diagnosed using the other, indicating a considerable discrepancy between the two divergent approaches. Diagnostic inconsistencies between positive *DSM-IV* and negative *ICD-10* diagnoses were attributed primarily to comorbid disorders and a failure to endorse autonomic arousal symptoms.

Despite similarities between the *DSM* and *ICD* systems, the consequential differences in the nature of GAD that is diagnosed by these systems point to ongoing issues with the classification of this condition. We see from the development of GAD in these nosologies that clarity regarding the narrowness or breadth of criteria continues to be controversial. In the *DSM*, we have created a system that is progressively narrower. This has increased reliability, but there is a significant question regarding subclinical individuals who often present for treatment and appear to exhibit clinically significant distress. Indeed, the *ICD-10* appears to capture individuals suffering from this mild form of GAD. A related issue is the best approach to dealing with comorbidity. Once again, the diagnostic systems have taken somewhat different approaches in opposite directions. The *DSM-IV* is more liberal in this regard as it allows for comorbidity, whereas the *ICD-10* has specific exclusionary diagnoses. Evaluation of the development of these two diagnostic systems shows an interesting evolution involving adjustments to the system to capture more or fewer patients within this diagnostic category. This struggle is highly relevant to our understanding of the underlying nature of GAD, which we will discuss below in the section on taxometrics.

Alternative Conceptualizations

The *DSM-IV* and the *ICD-10* are the two dominant systems for identification and diagnosis of mental illness, including GAD. In addition to these models, we think it is relevant to include some discussion of alternative conceptualizations that are meant to compliment these systems. In the sections that immediately follow, we highlight several alternative models that provide additional insights into the way GAD symptoms develop and are maintained and have implications for the way we categorize and treat GAD.

Metacognitive Model of GAD

Metacognition is defined by Adrian Wells and Christine Purdon (1999) as "the aspect of the information processing system that monitors, interprets, evaluates and regulates the contents and processes of its own organization" (p. 71). The metacognitive model of GAD is focused on the idea that negative metacognitive beliefs contribute to the development and maintenance of GAD (Wells, 1994). Two distinct types of worry are unidentified in this model, including Type I and Type II. Type I worry refers to worry about external events and noncognitive internal events (i.e., physical symptoms). Concerns about physical health, finances, and specific physical symptoms such as racing heart or dizziness would be classified as Type I worry. Worry about cognitive events or processes is considered Type II. Type II worry is also called worry-about-worry or metaworry. Negative metacognitive beliefs about the nature and consequences of Type I worry lead to the development of Type II worry (Wells, 1994).

Individuals diagnosed with GAD according to the *DSM* classification system have positive beliefs about worry and use worry as a coping strategy for chains of catastrophizing "what-if" questions. The act of worrying allows these individuals to arrive at the feeling that all bases are covered. Worry may, therefore, relieve anxiety (reinforcing positive beliefs). But, it can also perpetuate anxiety as an individual begins to catastrophize (creating negative beliefs). Type II worry occurs when individuals begin to worry about the effects of worrying. A shift toward negative assessment may develop from negative emotions or difficulty controlling emotions caused by worry. Once the belief that worry is uncontrollable or dangerous has been established, it contributes to increased anxiety (more Type II worry) and maintenance of worry behavior.

The metacognitive model also suggests that GAD is maintained by behavioral strategies and thought control. Behaviors such as avoidance, reassurance seeking, and distraction preserve worry by eliminating opportunities for beliefs to be dispelled. Another method of managing worry is thought control. Trying to control thoughts and avoid worrying is very difficult. When an individual with GAD is unsuccessful in attempts to control worry, it is taken as evidence of the uncontrollable nature of worry, reinforcing and perpetuating GAD symptoms.

Identification of different types of worry could have positive implications for GAD diagnosis. The nature of worry reliably differentiates between individuals with GAD and subclinical populations (Barlow, Blanchard, Vermilyea, & DiNardo, 1986). Further classification of the types of worry (Type I versus Type II) predicts the clinical nature or impairment of worry symptoms. Type II worry predicts the development of pathological worry above and beyond that of Type I (Wells & Carter, 1999). Furthermore, increased metaworry differentiates individuals with GAD from those suffering from other anxiety disorders (including panic disorder and social phobia) and nonclinical controls (Wells & Carter, 2001). Negative and positive beliefs about worry are associated with a vulnerability to clinically significant worry symptoms associated with GAD (Cartwright–Hatton & Wells, 1997). This is compelling evidence for considering the incorporation of Type II worry in the GAD diagnostic criteria. Further investigation of the nature of worry symptoms could aid in creating a clearer picture of GAD symptomatology and a more accurate diagnosis within the *DSM-IV* framework.

Cognitive Behavioral Model of GAD

Dugas, Gagnon, Ladouceur, and Freeston (1998) proposed a conceptual model of GAD centered on intolerance of uncertainty. Intolerance of uncertainty is defined as the way a person interprets information in ambiguous situations (Ladouceur, Talbot, & Dugas, 1997). Intolerance of uncertainty is a strong predictor of trait worry (Dugas, Freeston, & Ladouceur, 1997) and distinguishes individuals with GAD from nonclinical worriers (Freeston, Rheaume, Letarte, Dugas, & Ladouceur, 1994; Ladouceur, Blais, Freeston, & Dugas, 1998). Uncertainty intolerance likely intensifies what-if questions and leads to pathological worry. According to this model, individuals with GAD differ from controls and moderate worriers in their belief that worry can help uncover solutions and prevent negative consequences (Ladouceur et al., 1998). Those with stronger beliefs about worry (both positive and negative) are also more likely to worry (Davey, Tallis & Capuzzo, 1996). Individuals with GAD report that worry functions as a distraction from more emotional topics (Borkovec & Roemer, 1995) and helps prepare for negative outcomes (Brown, Moras, Simbarg & Barlow, 1993). Worry is negatively reinforced for patients with GAD when the feared event does not occur.

Similar to the metacognitive model, this model includes a feature of metacognitive processes concerning awareness and appraisal of problems and personal problem-solving ability. These processes are referred to as problem orientation. Worry is associated with indicators of poor problem orientation, including low problem-solving confidence and low perceived control over problem solving (Davey, 1994). Despite low confidence and poor problem orientation, those with GAD have similar knowledge of problem solving skills (Dugas, Letarte, Rheaume, Freeston, & Ladouceur, 1995).

The final key feature of this model is cognitive avoidance. Worry is primarily composed of thoughts rather than images (Borkovec & Inz, 1990; Freeston, Dugas, & Ladouceur, 1996), and the avoidance of mental images is believed to lead to a decrease in the emotional processing about threatening subjects (Borkovec & Lyonfields, 1993).

Unreliable discrimination among the anxious apprehension symptoms present in all anxiety disorders and worries specific to GAD has been an important criticism of the GAD diagnosis. Though further research is needed, incorporating worry related to intolerance of uncertainty into the diagnostic criteria of GAD may aid in distinguishing GAD from other anxiety disorders and lead to lower comorbidity rates among anxiety disorders. This model also has promising clinical implications. Treatment focused on the increasing tolerance of uncertainty and examination and remediation of beliefs is a promising approach to the treatment of GAD (Dugas, Freeston, & Ladouceur, 1997; Dugas et al., 1998).

Summary

The diagnostic definition of GAD has been debated since it first appeared in the *DSM-III*. This is unsurprising given the difficulty in reliably differentiating between GAD and other anxiety and mood disorders. The diagnostic criteria have changed significantly with each new edition of the *DSM* as researchers and clinicians continue to refine the classification of the disorder.

Changes in the *DSM-IV* criteria have contributed to increased diagnostic reliability (Brown, DiNardo, Lehman, & Campbell, 2001), but concerns continue to be raised about the validity of the current GAD characterization. There is continued debate about how broad or narrow the GAD diagnostic criteria should be. Those with GAD symptoms lasting 1 month versus 6 months appear to be comparable on sociodemographic, clinical characteristics (Kessler et al.,

2005), and heritability rates (Kendler, Neale, Kessler, Heath, & Eaves, 1992). Furthermore, individuals who do not describe their worry as excessive, but meet all other *DSM-IV* diagnostic criteria, report rates of treatment presentation, functional impairment, and anxiety comparable to that of excessive worriers (Ruscio et al., 2005). These data support a more relaxed definition of GAD that would include populations currently considered subclinical. In contrast, there is evidence for a narrowed conceptualization of GAD. Increasing the associated symptoms threshold from 3 to 4 symptoms increases the reliability with which individuals suffering from stable and impairing GAD symptoms are identified (Brown et al., 1995). The excessive and uncontrollable feature of worry has also reliably differentiated between clinical and subclinical GAD populations (Abel & Borkovec, 1995).

It appears that one of the key questions for future conceptualization of GAD concerns whether or not subclinical cases should be included in the diagnosis. Broadening the definition of GAD would more than double the prevalence rate (Ruscio et al., 2007) and, because subclinical worry is present among many other disorders (Maser, 1998), it is likely that it would also significantly increase comorbidity and diminish diagnostic reliability. Further research is needed to establish the optimal cut point for a GAD diagnosis. We believe that this key issue can be meaningfully addressed through the use of taxometrics, a set of statistical procedures designed to ascertain whether psychopathological constructs are best represented as categorical or dimensional phenomena.

The Application of Taxometric Methods to GAD and Worry

Worry is the central feature of GAD. Many believe that worry, like most other psychopathological phenomena, resides along a continuum that is adaptive at some level but maladaptive at the other extreme. For example, worry can be an adaptive strategy for coping with stressful life events by facilitating active problem-solving strategies (Davey, 1994). On the other hand, patients with GAD who worry excessively do not show evidence of productive or enhanced problem solving. This raises an interesting question regarding whether worry is simply an individual difference variable that differs by degree across individuals, or whether worry in an extreme form is better thought of as a different kind or type than that evidenced by most individuals. This is exactly the type of question that taxometric procedures are designed to answer.

A taxonomy is often considered to be a specific form of classification in that it is concerned with arranging entities into *natural categories* on the basis of similar features. This distinction pertains to a fundamental issue that is necessary to consider in relation to psychiatric classification. The issue is essentially whether we believe that psychiatric classification is arbitrary or reflective of underlying naturally occurring entities. The term *taxon* is typically used to refer to these natural, nonarbitrary categories. Taxons are described by sets of objects like biological species or organic diseases. Dogs, cats, and mice could be considered taxons. Taxons represent meaningful elements in nature that can be discriminated. In reference to Plato, if we could somehow successfully "carve nature at its joints," what we would be left with is a series of taxons. So a taxon is something that naturally exists whether or not we are currently capable of accurately identifying it. Something is not a taxon when it is arbitrary or dimensional.

The *DSM* is a taxonomy that is implicitly interested in reflecting the taxons that represent mental illnesses. An important question that arises is whether or to what degree the taxonicity of mental illnesses has been tested. Despite the central nature of taxons to the *DSM*, the taxonicity of diagnostic entities has not been adequately assessed in most cases. So, we are not currently in a position to know the degree to which the *DSM* accurately represents natural categories.

To date, we are not aware of a taxometric study focused on GAD. We are aware of only one study that has assessed whether normal and pathological worries are qualitatively distinct. In a study of college students, Ruscio, Borkovec, and Ruscio (2001) found preliminary evidence supporting a dimensional structure of worry. Thus, the underlying structure of worry has received very little attention. Investigation of the taxonicity of worry and/or GAD could be extremely helpful in ascertaining the best cut point for diagnosis, which we have indicated is a central controversy in the literature. Moreover, taxometric analyses have the capacity to identify and refine individual diagnostic criteria through a process of bootstrapping (for more details, see Schmidt et al., 2007). In the final sections of this chapter, we apply taxometric procedures to several large data sets with the intent of identifying whether worry is best conceptualized as dimensional or categorical.

Taxometric Findings for Worry

Two independent samples were used. Sample 1 participants included a total of 780 (57.4% female) undergraduate students who received research credit for participation. Ages ranged from 17–29 ($M = 19.18$, $SD = 2.4$). The racial/ethnic composition of the sample was as follows: African American (6.7%), Asian American (4.1%), Caucasian (74.9%), Hispanic/Latino (9.1%), and other (5.2%). Sample 2 ($n = 397$) consisted of individuals from the Columbus, Ohio Metropolitan Area school system ($n = 46$), the Ohio State University ($n = 263$), and the Columbus, Ohio community ($n = 96$). The demographic make-up of the sample at entry was, by design, relatively young (age $M = 19.3$, $SD = 3.9$) with the majority being female (61%). The sample was also primarily White (74%) with 10% African American, 9% Asian American, 2% Hispanic, and 3% Other.

All participants completed the Penn State Worry Questionnaire (PSWQ), a 16-item self-report measure indexing the general tendency to worry (Myer, Miller, Metzger, & Borkovec, 1990). The PSWQ utilizes a five-point Likert-type scale that reflects the extent to which the individual believes each item is true, and has generally favorable psychometric properties (Brown, Antony, & Barlow, 1992).

After reverse scoring the appropriate items (1, 3, 8, 10, and 11), the first taxometric analysis focused on sample 1 and employed a Short Scale Maximum Covariance (SSMAXCOV) approach (Gangestad & Snyder, 1985). This procedure is computationally similar to the traditional Maximum Covariance (MAXCOV) analyses, with one important exception. Whereas MAXCOV requires three continuous or semicontinuous indicators, SSMAXCOV can operate when these requirements are not met. For instance, in the current dataset, because the factor structure of the PSWQ does not generally support the presence of at least three factors, we were forced to use items as indicators, which is well suited to the SSMAXCOV approach. Specifically, this procedure utilizes two randomly selected indicators (in this case, items) and assigns them the role of "input." The remaining indicators (i-2) are labeled "output" indicators.

The SSMAXCOV algorithm then scans for conditional covariance at each slice in the range of summed scores for input, as a function of the sum of *all-remaining* indicators. SSMAXCOV then repeats this process with another randomly drawn pair of indicators and calculates conditional covariance in a similar fashion, repeating this process until all possible combination of indicators has been exhausted. A composite plot of all results is generally inspected at the end of this process, with interpretation rules identical to the traditional MAXCOV.

Within sample 1 ($N = 780$) a total of 16 indicators (corresponding to individual items) were used, resulting in a total output of 120 curves. An average (composite) plot was produced for the research data, simulated taxonic data, and simulated dimensional data. Ten samples of each type of simulated data were created, and averaged plots for simulated data were produced and compared with the research data. Note that simulated data was matched to the research data in terms of skew, nuisance correlation, and indicator validity. All composite plots were submitted to three raters blinded to the type of data (research, simulated taxonic, simulated dimensional), who were then instructed to rate each plot as taxonic, dimensional, or ambiguous. Simulated data types were correctly identified by all raters ($\kappa = 1.0$), thereby satisfying suitability requirements of SSMAXCOV (Ruscio & Ruscio, 2004). The research data was identified as taxonic by all three raters. Figure 14.1

14.1

Composite SSMAXCOV results, sample 1.

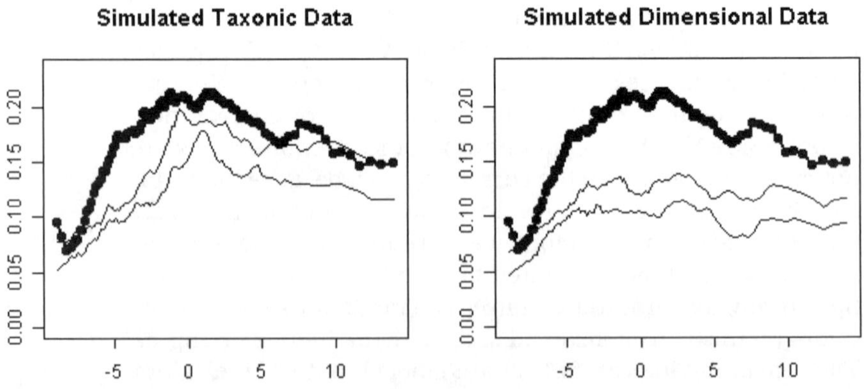

displays superimposed averaged curves for research data versus simulated taxonic and dimensional data.

Interestingly, the base rate for the putative taxon was fairly high with a suggestion that 42% of individuals may fall into this group. However, the standard deviation of this estimate was also high and above normally accepted tolerance limits for these procedures. This may have been due to marginal validity of input indicators. In other words, taxon indicators did not appear to be particularly strong at discriminating between taxon members and nonmembers.

Because some variability was observed in initial analyses for sample 1, we attempted to replicate the results reported above in a separate, independent sample. An identical analytic approach was used wherein the SSMAXCOV algorithm was applied to all 16 individual items for use as input and output indicators. Results across 120 curves produced by SSMAXCOV were averaged into a composite plot and later evaluated against simulated taxonic and simulated dimensional data (see Fig.14.2). Again, all simulated data were parameter matched to ensure that results were not attributable to imperfections in the research data. Composite plots for each were submitted to blinded raters who again rated each plot as taxonic, dimensional, or ambiguous. Interrater agreement was perfect ($\kappa = 1.0$) for all three plots, indicating not only suitability of SSMAXCOV within sample 2, but also taxonicity in the research data (i.e.,

14.2

Composite SSMAXCOV results, sample 2.

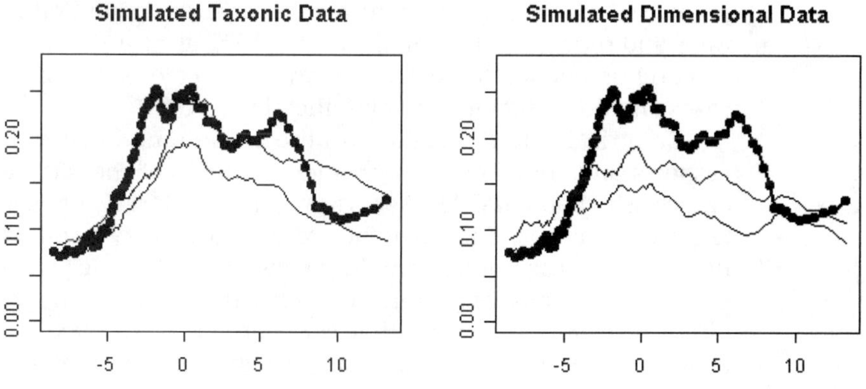

research data was rated as taxonic by blinded raters). Mean base rate (.39) was similar to sample 1 (.41), although the standard deviation in sample 2 (.15) was also higher than is typically desirable, suggesting some variability in the base rate estimates of the putative taxon. Mean indicator validity for the research data was low (1.1, SD = 0.9).

Overall, preliminary results were indicative, but not conclusively in favor of taxonicity, that is, there is some suggestion that worry may be best represented as a discrete category. Base rate estimates (although variable within samples) were consistent across independent samples, as was the overall taxonic shape. Additional research is necessary to replicate our findings; however, we also recommend that future studies extend this approach into the realm of construct validation to ascertain the general nature of the putative taxon reflected in the PSWQ. Although it seems reasonable at this point to assume that a latent class of worriers may be subsumed in overall scores, the current study is methodologically limited in the extent to which these cases can be shown to differ from nonworriers on other relevant measures.

General Discussion

Each revision of the *DSM* has brought changes to the definition of GAD. The diagnostic reliability of the diagnosis has improved, but there continues to be a debate over the validity of the GAD diagnosis. There is evidence for both more stringent and relaxed diagnostic criteria, but it is unclear which classification of the disorder will best represent clinically significant populations. Individuals suffering from subclinical presentations of GAD present for treatment at comparable rates and report similar impairment as clinical cases. Further research is needed to determine whether or not subclinical cases should be included in classification of GAD.

Empirical findings reported here are unique in several respects and contribute to our understanding of the nature and classification of GAD. Across two separate large samples, taxometric analyses indicated the presence of a worry taxon. At first glance, these findings would suggest that a discrete group of individuals possess a form of worry that is qualitatively different from most worry that is experienced. The taxonic conjecture passed several consistency tests, with the analyses converging on a taxon base rate of approximately 40%. Base rate consistency across the data sets was high and adds to our confidence in the taxonic conceptualization, though this high base rate is certainly discrepant with base rate estimates of GAD. These data are suggestive of a categorical variant of pathological worry that encompasses a much broader spectrum of worry than what we typically consider for a GAD diagnosis but which may be more in line with data suggesting a broader inclusion of individuals (i.e., subclinical cases). On the other hand, both studies relied on the same measure for deriving indicators of GAD (i.e., PSWQ). This is an obvious limitation that needs to be addressed in future work through inclusion of other measures of worry. It is also worth noting that the identification of a taxon tells us very little about its nature. In other words, this investigation has identified something that could represent a discreet syndrome, but it did not assess severity/impairment required for a *DSM* diagnosis. Additional work is required to address construct validity of this taxon and whether it is likely to represent a diagnostic group.

Despite the current findings being suggestive of taxonicity, they run counter to the only other published report on the categorical nature of GAD utilizing these techniques. Ruscio et al. (2001) found evidence for a dimensional structure of worry. Both the Ruscio sample and our sample comprised primarily college students. Also, both samples used self-report measures and utilized the PSWQ to construct indicators; however, Ruscio et al., used dichotomous indicators, potentially compromising the analyses by producing range restrictions.

When a taxon is identified, bootstrapping procedures can be employed to evaluate and refine the criteria used to identify the construct or, in this case, diagnosis (Schmidt et al., 2007). The identification of better indicators is extremely helpful in providing empirical guidance regarding the best symptoms to utilize to identify those with this diagnosis. A detailed discussion of this process is beyond the scope of this chapter, but it may be useful to outline the steps. Bootstrapping can be accomplished through construction of a scale (e.g., GAD-T) that can be used to identify GAD taxon members. The GAD-T items can be derived from any instrument or set of instruments that is available to the investigator. Next, items from the scales are selected based on their association with taxon membership. In this selection process, it is desirable to maximize the correlation of the scale with taxon membership while maintaining the internal consistency of the scale. In the case of GAD, each individual symptom (i.e., *DSM* criteria) can be evaluated in relation to taxon membership. At this point, better and poorer indicators of the taxon are derived that can be scrutinized in additional studies, thereby further refining our knowledge.

The diagnosis of GAD continues to evolve. This diagnosis is perhaps the least understood of all of the anxiety disorders, and we certainly have considerable work to do in order to clarify our understanding of its nature and treatment. Because many key issues surrounding GAD focus on correctly capturing people who might have this diagnosis, we have recommended that one approach is the use of taxometric procedures. Taxometrics cannot answer all of these questions and, if a latent discontinuity is ultimately not identified, then these procedures are even more limited in terms of what they can provide us, beyond indicating that this phenomenon is likely to be continuous and inadequately represented in a nosology utilizing categories; yet, the preliminary results reported herein provided convincing and converging evidence of GAD taxonicity. The knowledge gained about the latent structure of GAD will have a number of important theoretical, empirical, and practical implications including its future operationalization in the *DSM*.

References

Abel, J. L., & Borkovec, T. D. (1995). Generalizability of DSM-III-R generalized anxiety disorders to proposed DSM-IV criteria and cross validation of proposed changes. *Journal of Anxiety Disorders, 9*, 303–315.

American Psychiatric Association (1980). *Diagnostic and statistical manual of mental disorders* (3rd ed.). Washington, DC: Author.

American Psychiatric Association (1987). *Diagnostic and statistical manual of mental disorders* (3rd ed., rev.). Washington, DC: Author.

American Psychiatric Association (1994). *Diagnostic and statistical manual of mental disorders* (4th ed. International Version with ICD-10 Codes). Washington, DC: Author.

American Psychiatric Association (1995). *Diagnostic and statistical manual of mental disorders* (4th ed.). Washington, DC: Author.

Andrews, G., Slade, T., & Peters, L. (1999). Classification in psychiatry: ICD-10 versus *DSM-IV*. *British Journal of Psychiatry, 174*, 3–5.

Barlow, D. H., Blanchard, E. B., Vermilyea, J. A., & DiNardo, P. A. (1986). Generalized anxiety and generalized anxiety disorder: description and reconceptualization. *American Journal of Psychiatry, 143*, 40–44.

Barlow, D. H., & DiNardo, P. A. (1991). The diagnosis of generalized anxiety disorder: Development, current status, and future directions. In R.M. Rapee & D.H. Barlow (Eds.), *Chronic Anxiety: Generalized anxiety disorder and mixed anxiety depression*. New York: Guilford Press.

Borkovec, T. D., & Inz, J. (1990). The nature of worry in generalized anxiety disorder: A predominance of thought activity. *Behavior Research and Therapy, 28,* 53–158.

Borkovec, T. D., & Lyonfields, J. D. (1993). Worry: Thought suppression of emotional processing. In H.W. Krohne (Ed.), *Attention and avoidance.* Seattle: Hogrefe & Huber Publishers.

Borkovec, T. D., & Roemer, L. (1995). Perceived functions of worry among generalized anxiety subjects: Distraction from more emotionally distressing topics? *Behavior Therapy and Experimental Psychiatry, 26,* 25–30.

Brawman-Mintzer, O., Lydiard, R. B., Emmanuel, N., Payeur, R., Johnson, M., Roberts, J. et al. (1993). Psychiatric comorbidity in patients with generalized anxiety disorder. *American Journal of Psychiatry, 150,* 1216–1218.

Brown, T. A., Antony, M. M., & Barlow, D. H (1992). Psychometric properties of the Penn tate worry questionnaire in a clinical anxiety disorders sample. *Behavior Research and Therapy, 30,* 33–37.

Brown, T. A., & Barlow, D. H. (1992). Comorbidity among anxiety disorders: Implications for treatment and *DSM-IV. Journal of Consulting and Clinical Psychology, 60,* 835–844.

Brown, T. A., DiNardo, P. A., Lehman, C. L., & Campbell, L. A. (2001). Reliability of *DSM-IV* anxiety and mood disorders: implications for the classification of emotional disorders. *Journal of Abnormal Psychology, 100,* 49–58.

Brown, T. A., Marten, P. A., & Barlow, D. H. (1995). Discriminant validity of the symptoms constituting the *DSM-III-R* and *DSM-IV* associated symptom criterion of generalized anxiety disorder. *Journal of Anxiety Disorders,* 9, 317–328.

Brown, T. A., Moras, K., Simbarg, R. E., & Barlow, D. H. (1993). Diagnostic and symptom distinguishability of generalized anxiety and obsessive-compulsive disorder. *Behavior Therapy, 24,* 227–240.

Cartwright-Hatton, S., & Wells, A. (1997). Beliefs about worry and intrusions: The metacognitions questionnaire. *Journal of Anxiety Disorders, 11,* 279–276.

Davey, G. C. L. (1994). Worrying, social problem solving abilities, and problem solving confidence. *Behaviour research and Therapy, 32,* 327–330.

Davey, G. C. L., Tallis, F., & Capuzzo, N. (1996) Beliefs about the consequences of worrying. *Cognitive Therapy and Research, 5,* 499–520.

DiNardo, P. A., Moras, K., Barlow, D.H., Rapee, R. M., & Brown, T. A. (1993). Reliability of the *DSM-III_R* anxiety disorder categories using the Anxiety Disorders Interview Schedule-Revised. *Archives of General Psychiatry, 50,* 251–256.

DiNardo, P. A., O'Brien, G. T., Barlow, D. H., Waddell, M. T., & Blanchard, E. B. (1983). Reliability of *DSM-III* anxiety disorder categories using a new structured interview. *Archives of General Psychiatry, 40,* 1070–1074.

Dugas, M. J., Freeston, M. H., & Ladouceur, R. (1997). Intolerance of uncertainty and problem orientation in worry. *Cognitive Therapy and Research, 21,* 593–606.

Dugas, M. J., Gagnon, F., Ladouceur, R., & Freeston, M. H. (1998). Generalized anxiety disorder: A preliminary test of a conceptual model. *Behaviour Research and Therapy, 36,* 215–226.

Dugas, M. J., Letarte, H., Rheaume, J., Freeston, M. H., & Ladouceur, R. (1995). Worry and problem solving: Evidence of a specific relationship. *Cognitive Therapy and Research, 19,* 109–120.

Freeston, M. H., Dugas, M. J., & Ladouceur, R. (1996). Thoughts, images, worry and anxiety. *Cognitive Therapy and Research, 20*, 265–273.

Freeston, M. H., Rheaume, J., Letarte, H., Dugas, M. J., & Ladouceur, R. (1994). Why do people worry? *Personality and Individual Differences, 17*, 791–802.

Gangestad, S., & Snyder M. (1985). To carve nature at its joints: On the existence of discrete classes in personality. *Psychological Review, 92*, 317–349.

Kendler, K. S., Neale, M. C., Kessler, R. C., Heath, A. C., & Eaves, L. J. (1992). Generalized anxiety disorder in women. *Archives of General Psychiatry, 49*, 267–271.

Kessler, R. C., Brandenburg, N., Lane, M., Roy–Byrne, P., Stang, P. D., Stein, D. J., et al. (2005). Rethinking the duration requirement for generalized anxiety disorder: evidence form the national comorbidity survey replication. *Psychological Medicine, 35*, 1073–1082.

Ladouceur, R., Blais, F., Freeston, M. H., & Dugas, M. J. (1998). Problem solving and problem orientation in generalized anxiety disorder. *Journal of Anxiety Disorders, 12*, 139–152.

Ladouceur, R., Freeston, M. H., Dugas, M. J., Rheaume, J., Gagnon, F., Thibodeal, N. et al. (1995). *Specific association between generalized anxiety disorder and intolerance of uncertainty among anxiety disorder patients*. Poster presented at the Annual Convention of the Association for Advancement of Behavior Therapy, Washington, DC.

Ladouceur, R., Talbot, F., & Dugas, M. J. (1997). Behavioral expressions of intolerance of uncertainty in worry: Experimental findings. *Behavior Modification, 21*, 355–371.

Maier, W., Gansike, M., Freyberger, H. J., Linz, M., Heun, R., & Lecrubier, Y. (2000). Generalized anxiety disorder (ICD-10) in primary care from a cross-cultural perspective: A valid diagnostic entity? *Acta Psychiatrica Scandinavica*, 101, 29–36

Mannuzza, S., Fryer, A. J., Martin, M. S. Gallops, M. S., Endicott, J., Gorman, J. M., et al. (1989) Reliability of anxiety assessment I: Diagnostic agreement. *Archives of General Psychiatry, 46*, 1093–1101.

Marcus, S. C., Olfson, M., Pincus, H. A., Shear, M. K., & Zarin, D. A. (1997). Self-reported anxiety, general medical conditions, and disability bed days. *American Journal of Psychiatry, 154*, 1766–1768.

Marten, P. A., Brown, T. A., Barlow, D. H., Borkoveck, T. D., Shear, M. K., & Lydiard, R. B. (1993). Evaluation of the ratings comprising the associated symptom criterion of *DSM-III-R* generalized anxiety disorder. *Journal of Nervous and Mental Disease, 181*, 676–682.

Maser, J. D. (1998). Generalized anxiety disorder and its comorbidities: Disputes at the boundaries. *Acta Psychiatrica Scandinavica, Supplementum, 393*, 12–22.

Massion, A. O., Warshaw, M. G., & Keller, M. B. (1993). Quality of life and psychiatric morbidity in panic disorder and generalized anxiety disorder. *American Journal of Psychiatry, 150*, 600–607.

Myer, T. J., Miller, M. L., Metzger, R. L., & Borkovec, T. D. (1990). Development and validation of the Penn State worry questionnaire. *Behavior Research and Therapy, 28*, 487–495.

Newman, S., & Bland, R. (2006). A population-based family study of *DSM-III* generalized anxiety disorder. *Psychological Medicine, 36*, 1275–1281.

Olfson, M., Broadhead, W. E., Weissman, M. M., Leon, A. C., Farber, L., Hoven, C., et al., (1996). Subthreshold psychiatric symptoms in a primary care group practice. *Archives of General Psychology, 53*, 880–886.

Rickles, K., & Rynn, M. (2001). What is generalized anxiety disorder? *Journal of Clinical Psychiatry, 62*, 4–12.

Ruscio, A. M., Borkovec, T. D., & Ruscio, J. (2001). A taxometric investigation of the latent structure of worry. *Journal of Abnormal Psychology, 110*, 413–422.

Ruscio, A. M., Chiu, W. T., Roy–Byrne, P., Stang, P. E., Stein, D. J., Wittchen, H. U., et al. (2007). Broadening the definition of generalized anxiety disorder: Effects on prevalence and association with other disorders in the National Comorbidity Survey Replication. *Journal of Anxiety Disorders, 21*, 662–676.

Ruscio, A. M., Lane, M., Roy–Byrne, Stang, P. E., Stein, D. J., Witchen, H. U., et al. (2005). Should excessive worry be required for diagnosis of generalized anxiety disorder? Results from the US National Comorbidity Survey Replication. *Psychological Medicine, 35*, 1761–1772.

Ruscio, J., & Ruscio, A. M. (2004). A conceptual and methodological checklist for conducting a taxometric investigation. *Behavior Therapy*, 35, 403–447.

Sanderson, W. C., & Barlow, D. H. (1990). A description of patients diagnosed with *DSM-III-R* generalized anxiety disorder. *Journal of Nervous and Mental Disease, 178*, 588–591.

Sanderson, W. C., Beck, A. T., & Beck, J. (1990). Syndrome comorbidity in patients with major depression or dysthymia: Prevalence and temporal relationships. *American Journal of Psychiatry, 147*, 1025–1028.

Sanderson, W. C. DiNardo, P. A., Rapee, R. M., & Barlow, D. H. (1990). Syndrome comorbidity in patients diagnosed with a *DSM-III-R* anxiety disorder. *Journal of Abnormal Psychology, 99*, 308–312.

Schmidt, N. B., Kotov, R., Bernstein, A., Zvolensky, M. J., Joiner, T. E., & Lewinsohn, P.M. (2007). Mixed anxiety depression: Taxometric exploration of the validity of a diagnostic category in youth. *Journal of Affective Disorders, 98*, 83–89.

Schweizer, E., & Rickels K. (1997). Strategies for treatment of generalized anxiety in the primary care setting. *Journal of Clinical Psychiatry, 58*(suppl 3), 27–33.

Slade, T., & Andrews, G. (2001). DSM-IV and ICD-10 generalized anxiety disorder: discrepant diagnosis and associated disability. *Social Psychiatry and Psychiatric Epidemiology*, 36, 45–51.

Spitzer, R. L., & Williams, J. B. W. (1984). Diagnostic issues in the DSM-III classification of the anxiety disorders. In L. Grinspoon (Ed.), *Psychiatry update*, vol. III. (pp. 392–402). Washington, DC: American Psychiatric Press.

Starcevic, V., Fallon, S., & Uhlenhuth, E. H. (1994). The frequency and severity of generalized anxiety disorder symptoms: Toward a less cumbersome conceptualization. *Journal of Nervous and Mental Disease, 182*, 80–84.

Wells, A. (1994). Attention and the control of worry. In G.C.L. Daveys & F. Tallis (Eds.), *Worrying perspectives on theory, assessment, and treatment*. Chichester, UK: Wiley.

Wells, A. (1999). A metacognitive model and therapy of generalized anxiety disorder. *Clinical Psychology and Psychotherapy*, 6, 86–95.

Wells, A., & Carter, K. (1999). Preliminary tests of a cognitive model of generalized anxiety disorder. *Behaviour Research and Therapy, 37*, 585–594.

Wells, A., & Carter, K. (2001). Further tests of a cognitive model of generalized anxiety disorder: Metacognitions and worry in GAD, panic disorder, social phobia, depression, and nonpatients. *Behavior Therapy, 32*, 85–102.

Wells, A., & Purdon, C. (1999). Metacognition and cognitive-behaviour therapy: A special issue. *Clinical Psychology and Psychotherapy, 6*, 71–72.

Wittchen, H-U., Zhao, S., Kessler, R. C., & Eaton, W. W. (1994). DSM-III-R generalized anxiety disorder in the national comorbidity survey. *Archives of General Psychiatry, 51*, 355–364

World Health Organization (1980). International Classification of Impairments, Disabilities, and Handicaps. World Health Organization, Geneva.

World Health Organization (1993). The ICD-10 Classification of Mental and behavioral Disorders – Diagnostic Criteria for Research. World Health Organization, Geneva.

15

PTSD and Other Posttraumatic Syndromes

Matthew J. Friedman

As we move forward with the development of The American Psychiatric Association's (APA's) fifth *Diagnostic and Statistical Manual of Mental Disorders* (*DSM–V*), posttraumatic stress disorder (PTSD) is being reconsidered from at least three different perspectives: (a) where does it fit in the overall classification scheme, (b) should its current diagnostic criteria be retained, and (c) how does it compare with other proposed posttraumatic syndromes? As we consider these questions, it will be useful to discuss dimensional versus categorical issues, cross-cultural influences, and developmental factors.

Where Does PTSD Fit?

Background

Before the mid-19th century, what we now call posttraumatic stress disorder (PTSD) was described in literature by Homer, Shakespeare, Dickens, and others. For example, Shay (1994, 2002) has suggested that Homer was probably a veteran whose Trojan War heroes, Achilles and Odysseus, exhibited symptoms and behaviors consistent with modern PTSD diagnostic criteria. Starting in the 19th century, psychiatrists on both sides of the Atlantic described syndromes among combat veterans (e.g., soldier's heart, Da Costa's syndrome, traumatic neurosis, shell shock, combat fatigue, neurocirculatory asthenia) and civilians (e.g., railway spine) that embody many, if not all, current PTSD symptoms (see review by van der Kolk, 2007). Explanatory models explicating the trajectory from catastrophic exposure to altered cognitions, feelings, and behaviors have been provided by psychoanalytic theory, Pavlovian fear conditioning models, Mowrer's two-factor theory, Selye's theories of stress and adaptation, and neurobiology (see Charney, 2004; Monson, Friedman, & La Bash, 2007; van der Kolk).

In *DSM–I* (APA, 1952), "gross stress reaction" was an ill-defined diagnosis for classifying individuals who had been psychologically altered by exposure to military or civilian experiences. It was a useful diagnosis for classifying military veterans, ex-prisoners of war, rape victims, and Nazi Holocaust survivors. From a PTSD perspective, however, the major problem was that gross stress reaction was considered a "temporary diagnosis," which would be changed to a "neurotic reaction" if the condition persisted.

Paradoxically, during the height of the Vietnam War, *DSM–II* (APA, 1968) eliminated this diagnosis, leaving practitioners with no diagnostic option by which to classify clinically significant reactions to catastrophic experiences. "Situational reaction" was the only diagnostic alternative. It was an ambiguous category that included the full spectrum of adverse events, from traumatic events to unpleasant experiences. Besides trivializing the impact of traumatic exposure, situational reaction was also considered a temporary and reversible clinical condition. By the mid-1970s to late 1970s, many mental health clinicians recognized the need for a new diagnostic category that characterized the severe, chronic, and sometimes irreversible psychological impact of catastrophic events. Several syndromes had appeared in the professional literature by that time, all named after the traumatic event itself—rape trauma syndrome, post-Vietnam syndrome, prisoner-of-war syndrome, concentration camp syndrome, war sailor syndrome, child abuse syndrome, battered women's syndrome, and so forth. During the *DSM–III* (APA, 1980) process, it became apparent that there was so much overlap between these various syndromes that they could all be adequately characterized by the constellation of symptoms proposed in the PTSD diagnostic criteria.

There have been some alterations of the original *DSM–III* PTSD criteria. The number of possible symptoms has increased from 12 to 17. The original three-symptom clusters (e.g., reexperiencing, numbering, miscellaneous) have been shuffled slightly to the present triad (e.g., reexperiencing, avoidant/numbering, hyperarousal—see Table 15.1). But the fundamental etiological construct, built into the diagnostic criteria, that overwhelming stress can produce clinically significant and persistent alterations in cognitions, feelings, and behavior has endured.

We will consider the specific diagnostic criteria subsequently. Before plunging into such details, it is useful to step back and acknowledge the wealth of conceptual, scientific, and clinical advances since 1980 that would not have been possible without inclusion of PTSD in the *DSM–III*. First, with adoption of PTSD, we have accepted the proposition that environmental events can produce enduring and clinically significant alterations of psychological processes, brain function, and behavior. This has not only influenced clinical practice but opened up new approaches to prevention at both the individual and collective level. The PTSD construct has spawned important advances in epidemiology, risk factor research, psychological theory and practice, biological theory and practice, and the overlapping fields of resilience, prevention, and public health. It is important to acknowledge, at the same time, that PTSD is no stranger to controversy. Among major controversies that remain pertinent are assertions that PTSD is not a legitimate diagnosis, PTSD needlessly pathologizes normal reactions to abusive violence, PTSD is a European American culture bound syndrome,

15.1 *DSM–IV–TR* Diagnostic Criteria for PTSD

A1. Exposure to catastrophic stressor
A2. Intense emotional reaction to stressor
B. Reexperiencing Symptoms
(Requires one or more of)
- B1. Intrusive recollections
- B2. Distressing nightmares
- B3. Acting/feeling as though event were recurring (flashbacks)
- B4. Psychological distress when exposed to traumatic reminders
- B5. Physiological reactivity when exposed to traumatic reminders

C. Avoidant/Numbing Symptoms:
(Requires three or more of)
- C1. Avoidance of thoughts, feelings, or conversations associated with the stressor
- C2. Avoidance of activities, places, or people associated with the stressor
- C3. Inability to recall important aspects of traumatic event
- C4. Diminished interest in significant activities
- C5. Detachment from others
- C6. Restricted range of affect
- C7. Sense of foreshortened future

D. Hyperarousal Symptoms
(Requires two or more of)
- D1. Sleep problems
- D2. Irritability
- D3. Concentration problems
- D4. Hypervigilance
- D5. Exaggerated startle response

E. Duration of the disturbance is at least 1 month
F. Requires significant distress or functional impairment

Note. From *Diagnostic and Statistical Manual of Mental Disorders, Text Revision*, by American Psychiatric Association (APA), 2000, Washington, DC: Author. Copyright 2000 by the APA. Adapted with permission.

PTSD primarily serves a litigious rather than clinical purpose, traumatic memories are not valid, and verbal memories are unreliable. (A fuller discussion of PTSD-related progress and challenges can be found in Friedman, Resick, & Keane, 2007a). With this as context, we now begin our discussion of the PTSD diagnosis, itself.

PTSD as an Anxiety Disorder

PTSD was labeled an anxiety disorder in *DSM–III* and has remained thus classified, ever since. Phenomenologically, it certainly shares several symptoms (especially from its hyperarousal/D criterion cluster) with other anxiety disorders, such as insomnia, irritability, poor concentration, and startle. It is primarily a disorder of reactivity along with simple and social phobia, rather than a syndrome with a consistent alteration of the tonic/basal state, such as depression. PTSD avoidant behavior has some similarity to phobic and anxious avoidance. Physiological arousal and dissociation also occur in panic disorder. Persistent reexperiencing symptoms, especially intrusive recollections, bear a superficial resemblance to the obsessional thoughts seen in obsessive–compulsive disorder (OCD). And hypervigilance is superficially similar to the persistent apprehension seen in general anxiety disorder (GAD), although in PTSD, it has a clear focus whereas in GAD, it is usually unrealistic worry that generalizes to most situations. Finally, Jones and Barlow (1990) have argued that PTSD is most closely linked to other anxiety disorders because of "the presence of alarms and the general process of anxious apprehension" (p. 323).

On the other hand, the numbing, alienation, and detachment seen in PTSD appear to have more in common with depression than with other anxiety disorders. Extreme hypervigilance may sometimes be indistinguishable from ideas of reference or a paranoid delusion. In addition, PTSD flashbacks have variously been categorized as either dissociative or brief psychotic episodes. For all these reasons, questions have been raised about the appropriateness of classifying PTSD as an anxiety disorder. Perhaps most important, what distinguishes PTSD from most other psychiatric disorders is the presumed causal relationship between exposure to overwhelming environmental events and the development of the clinical profile explicated in *DSM–III/DSM–IV* and shown in Table 15.1. This unique characteristic has prompted the suggestion that a new category (or subcategory) of stress-induced psychiatric syndromes be created in *DSM–V*. Within such a framework, PTSD would be one of several psychiatric syndromes (including adjustment and, possibly, dissociative disorders) presumed to have developed because of inability to cope successfully with some adverse environmental experience.

Is PTSD a Stress-Related Fear Circuitry Disorder?

In preparing for the *DSM–V* process, APA created several novel initiatives to consider new ways to understand and classify *DSM–IV* disorders. One such initiative was to examine the evidence favoring a diagnostic cluster characterized by abnormalities in the neurocircuitry that mediates the processing of threatening or fearful stimuli. There is a long tradition of psychological theory and research supporting the centrality of Pavlovian fear conditioning as an appropriate model for PTSD (Foa & Kozak, 1986; Keane, Zimering, & Caddell, 1985; Kolb, Ciccone, Bustein, & Greenstein, 1989; Lang, 1977; Monson et al., 2007). Other disorders considered for this diagnostic group (or subgroup) are panic disorder, simple phobia, and social phobia.

The neurocircuitry argument for this proposal is set forth in a recent book (Andrews, Charney, Sirovatca, & Regier, 2009). In brief, the rationale is based on the key role played by the amygdala in processing threatening, fearful, or intense emotional stimuli. Amygdala activation precipitates outputs to the hippocampus, medial prefrontal cortex (mPFC), locus coeruleus, thalamus, insula, hypothalamus, and striatum. The neurocircuitry coordinates the brain's reaction to such stimuli and (with respect to PTSD) mediates and moderates the afferent processing, appraisal, encoding, and retrieval of trauma-related information (see Davis & Whalen, 2001; Neumeister, Henry, & Krystal, 2007). The pathophysiological problem in PTSD is currently understood as disinhibition of the amygdala from normal mPFC restraint. Indeed, evidence that shows disrupted anterior cingulate and orbitofrontal function is completely consistent with this model (Charney, 2004; Vermetten & Bremner, 2002; Woodward et al., 2006). Thus, unrestrained amygdala activity is understood to increase the likelihood of recurrent fear conditioning, threat appraisals, and maladaptive protective behaviors (Charney; Neumeister et al.).

A problem with the stress-related fear circuitry formulation is that by focusing entirely on fear, it neglects other emotions associated with PTSD, such as sadness, grief, anger, guilt, shame, and disgust. Furthermore, a fear-conditioning model may not readily apply to people who were never in any direct danger themselves, but who are overwhelmed by horror or feelings of helplessness during and after a traumatic event. This would not only apply to people who safely witnessed or were confronted by a traumatic event but also by medical personnel, first responders, families, bystanders, or graves registration personnel. Finally, the fact that PTSD is most frequently comorbid with depression, might suggest a different classification scheme in which PTSD is understood as an internalizing disorder (also see Friedman, Resick, & Keane, 2007b).

Is PTSD an Internalizing Disorder, an Externalizing Disorder, or Both?

Watson (2005) has argued that there is a lack of coherence in the current affective and anxiety disorders, which is one reason why there is so much comorbidity within and between these two diagnostic categories. He has proposed collapsing mood and anxiety disorders into an overarching class of "internalizing" disorders that contains three subclasses: the bipolar disorders (bipolar I, bipolar II, cyclothymia), the distress or "anxious–misery" disorders (major depression, dysthymia, GAD, PTSD), and the fear disorders (panic, agoraphobia, social phobia, and specific phobia). A fourth cluster—"externalizing" disorders (Krueger & Markon, 2006)—consists of alcohol dependence, drug dependence, adult antisocial personality disorder, and childhood conduct disorder.

PTSD was omitted from the original analyses that contributed to the development of this scheme. However, based on a reanalysis of *DSM–III–R* data from the National Comorbidity Study (Cox, Clara, & Enns, 2002), as well as analysis of *DSM–IV* data from the Australian National Survey of Mental Health and Well-Being (Slade & Watson, 2006), it has been suggested that PTSD should be grouped with the distress/anxious–misery disorders rather than the fear disorders (Watson). In both the American and Australian data, however, PTSD loaded less strongly on the distress/anxious–misery dimension than depression, dysthymia, or GAD. On the other hand, and contrary to what might be expected from the fear-circuitry argument outlined previously, it did not load significantly on the fear dimension. Clearly more research is needed.

Considering PTSD as an internalizing disorder within the distress/anxious–misery domain has the heuristic advantage of providing a rationale for the high comorbidity between PTSD and depression. Furthermore, when we consider data from confirmatory factor analysis (see below), this formulation is consonant with the finding, in some studies, of a dysphoria factor within the latent structure of PTSD.

It is noteworthy that depending on the choice of model, one comes to very different conclusions with regard to PTSD's proper place within the anxiety or anxiety/affective disorders. A stress-related fear circuitry model places PTSD alongside panic disorder, simple phobia, and social phobia, whereas an internalizing model places PTSD within the distress/anxious–misery cluster alongside depression, dysthymia, and GAD. There is also evidence to suggest that PTSD may be expressed either as an internalizing or as an externalizing disorder. Miller and colleagues (Miller, Grief, & Smith, 2003; Miller, Kaloupek, Dillon, & Keane, 2004; Miller & Resick, 2007), drawing on results from three-cluster analytic studies of personality inventories completed by people with PTSD, have found evidence for both internalizing and externalizing PTSD subtypes among both men and women. As might be expected, internalizers exhibited high rates of comorbid depression and panic disorder, schizoid and avoidant personality characteristics, and personality profiles defined by high negative emotionality combined with low positive emotionality. Externalizers, on the other hand, tended to be impulsive, emotionally labile, easily upset, aggressive, and feeling chronically betrayed and mistreated by others. To summarize, it is by no means obvious where PTSD fits best within the current and proposed classification schemes.

The A (Stressor) Criterion

A distinctive feature of the diagnostic criteria for PTSD is the presumptive etiological role of traumatic exposure as stipulated in the A (stressor) criterion. An excellent comprehensive review of this hotly debated matter can be found elsewhere (Weathers & Keane, 2007). Indeed, in *DSM–III*, criterion A was defined as "a recognizable stressor that would evoke significant symptoms of distress in almost anyone." Drawing on general beliefs in the 1970s, it was thought that such experiences (e.g., rape, war, the Nazi Holocaust) were generally outside the range of usual human experiences.

The *DSM–III–R* (APA, 1987) revision of *DSM–III* retained this language but stated in the clarifying text that traumatic exposure "is usually experienced with intense fear, terror, and helplessness." *DSM–III–R* also widened traumatic exposure to include learning about serious threat or harm to a friend or relative.

By the time *DSM–IV* (APA, 1994) was published, there was sufficient epidemiological research indicating that traumatic exposure was, unfortunately, not unusual but a relatively common occurrence among men, women, and children. The *DSM–IV* A criterion was divided into objective (A_1) and subjective (A_2) components. The A_1 criterion resembled the *DSM–III–R* A criterion, except that a greater number of events were approved as stressor events. These included being diagnosed with a life-threatening illness, child sexual abuse (without threatened or actual violence), learning about the sudden unexpected death of a family member or close friend, and learning that one's child has a life-threatening illness. In addition to exposure to an A_1 event, it was necessary in *DSM–IV* that exposed individuals experience an intense emotional reaction (criterion A_2) characterized as "fear, helplessness, or horror." Although this had been foreshadowed in the *DSM–III–R* text description, the subjective response was now made an explicit (A_2) criterion.

There were also distinctions between PTSD and adjustment disorder that are worth noting. First, it was stated in *DSM–III* that adjustment disorder results from a less severe (nontraumatic) stressor and does not include the PTSD reexperiencing (B), avoidant/numbing (C), and hyperarousal (D) symptoms. In contrast, *DSM–IV* states that individuals who develop B, C, and D symptoms following a low-magnitude (non-A_1) stressor should be diagnosed as having an adjustment disorder. An important difference, however, is that adjustment disorder is considered a time-limited event that will resolve when the environmental precipitant has disappeared, whereas PTSD may persist for decades or a lifetime.

The A_1 Criterion

As noted by Kilpatrick et al. (1998) when summarizing findings from the *DSM–IV* field trials, the argument over how to operationalize criterion A boiled down to a debate over how broad versus how narrow it should be. Proponents of the broad definition argued that criterion A should include any event that can produce PTSD symptoms. Advocates for a more restrictive definition feared that it would trivialize the PTSD diagnosis and defeat the purpose of the original *DSM–III* PTSD construct by permitting people exposed to less stressful events to meet the A criterion. The *DSM–IV* field trials appeared to allay this concern because few people (12%) developed PTSD unless they experienced extremely stressful life events. On the other hand, Breslau and Kessler (2001) tested the implications of the broad *DSM–IV* A_1 criterion that stipulated events not included in *DSM–III*. A nationally representative sample of 2,181 individuals was interviewed about lifetime history of traumatic events and PTSD diagnosis. Lifetime exposure to traumatic events was 68.1% when estimated by a narrow set of qualifying A_1 events that included seven events of "assaultive violence" (e.g., combat, rape, assault) and seven "other injury events" (e.g., serious accident, natural disaster, witnessing death/serious injury). When the A_1 criterion was expanded to include five events from the expanded *DSM–IV* A_1 definition, such as "learning about" traumatic events to close relatives (e.g., rape, assault, accident), lifetime prevalence of exposure to traumatic events increased to 89.6%. These investigators conclude that there was a 59.2% increase in lifetime exposure to a traumatic event because of the expanded A_1 criterion. A problem with these results is that these lifetime exposure estimates are considerably higher than estimates from other studies (Kessler, Sonnega, Bromet, Hughes, & Nelson, 1995).

Weathers and Keane (2007) have suggested that the wide discrepancy between Kilpatrick et al. (1998) and Breslau and Kessler (2001) regarding lifetime exposure to traumatic events (e.g., 50.7% versus 68.1%, respectively) may have more to do with methodology than with the A_1 criterion itself. Because the two studies used different methodological approaches, they cannot be directly compared. Kilpatrick et al. (1998) required that all symptoms be endorsed in two separate interviews whereas Breslau and Kessler required that symptoms be linked to a specific event. Furthermore, Weathers and Keane point out that the five expanded A_1 ("learning about") events analyzed separately by Breslau and Kessler were not new additions in *DSM–IV* but clearly included within the *DSM–III–R* clarifying text.

Thus, the question is how to preserve the original intent of *DSM–III*. It appears that much of the presumed expansion of A_1 in *DSM–IV* was actually a carry over from *DSM–III–R*, although perhaps much more explicitly than before. On the other hand, as noted by Weathers and Keane (2007), the *DSM–IV* language is ambiguous in places and some A_1 events do appear to excessively broaden the stressor criterion (e.g., "confronted with," "threat to physical integrity," "inappropriate sexual experiences"). Hopefully, *DSM-V* will reduce such ambiguity about what events should or should not be considered A_1 events.

Others have argued that it does not matter whether a broad or a narrow definition is set for A_1. They suggest that what really matters is whether people meet criteria B, C, D, E, and F for PTSD and that it would make no difference if the A_1 criterion were completely eliminated. For example, a recent unpublished study of 1,543 adults exposed to one of four Florida hurricanes found a PTSD prevalence of 11.6% (179 out of 1,543) with no A_1 (or A_2) requirement and 11.2% (173 out of 1,543) with requirement for A_1 (but not A_2) (D. G. Kilpatrick, personal communication, February 6, 2008).

The *DSM–IV* PTSD Task Force also considered complete elimination of criterion A. Although it acknowledged the possibility that someone might meet B, C, and D criteria without meeting the A criterion, this option was rejected for fear "that the loosening of criterion A may lead to widespread and frivolous use of the concept" (Davidson & Foa, 1993, p. 347). Several articles suggest that the full PTSD syndrome may be expressed following nontraumatic events. These include Dutch adults exposed to adverse life events (Mol et al., 2005), American college undergraduates (Gold, Marx, Soler-Baillo, & Sloan, 2005), individuals with social anxiety disorder (Erwin, Heimberg, Marx, & Franklin, 2006), and spouses dealing with their partners' infidelity (Dattilio, 2004). Despite the fact that B, C, and D symptom severity among some of these cohorts exceeded that of cohorts with bona fide PTSD, the proper diagnosis for all is adjustment reaction. The A_1 criterion is a sine qua non.

The A_2 Criterion

As noted above, the *DSM–IV* Task Force stipulated that exposure to an A_1 event per se, was not a sufficient condition for meeting the stressor criterion. Instead, individuals exposed must also experience an intense subjective reaction characterized as "fear, helplessness, or horror." It was expected that imposition of the A_2 criterion would ensure that people would not be eligible for the PTSD diagnosis unless they had reacted strongly to a threatening event. It was also expected that imposition of the A_2 criterion would minimize any "frivolous" PTSD diagnoses because of broadening the A_1 criterion. Finally, based on data from the *DSM–IV* field trials (Kilpatrick et al., 1998), it was expected that few people exposed to low-magnitude (nontraumatic) events would meet the A_2 criterion and, therefore, would not be eligible for the PTSD diagnosis.

The utility of the A_2 criterion has been questioned. Brewin and associates (Brewin, Andrews, & Rose, 2000) found that intense levels of immediate postexposure fear, helplessness, and horror were weakly predictive of PTSD 6 months later. They also found evidence that other posttraumatic emotional reactions (e.g., anger, shame) also predicted PTSD. There were, however, a small number of people who denied postexposure A_2 emotions who also met PTSD criteria at 6 months. Creamer, McFarlane, and Burgess (2005) examined a community sample of 6,104 adults with a history of trauma exposure and found that most (76% males and 81% females) met criterion A_2. Roemer, Orsillo, Borkovec, and Litz (1998) reported that only helplessness, but not fear or horror, correlated with posttraumatic symptomatology. They also reported that peritraumatic emotional numbing predicted subsequent PTSD.

Two negative studies found no effect of A_2 on PTSD prevalence (Kilpatrick et al., 1998; Schnurr, et al., 2000). Although the presence of A_2 did not predict PTSD diagnosis, those people who reported an A_2 reaction exhibited the greatest PTSD severity. On the other hand, a consistent finding from three studies (Brewin et al., 2000; Kilpatrick et al., 1998; Schnurr, Spiro, Vielhauer, Findler, & Hamblen, 2002) concerns the negative predictive value of A_2. In other words, people who do not exhibit an intense posttraumatic emotional reaction are unlikely to develop PTSD. Schnurr et al. (2002) suggest that A_2 may be most useful to screen out individuals unlikely to develop PTSD. Although this may be useful in postdisaster screening, it does not appear to have a major bearing on improving diagnostic accuracy.

In the *DSM–IV* field trials, Kilpatrick et al. (1998) reported that, rather than A_2 symptoms, most of the variance of posttraumatic distress was accounted for by a panic reaction consisting of two components: "panic-physiological arousal" and "other panic symptoms" (e.g., trembling, shaking, tachycardia, fear of dying). Fikretoglu et al. (2007) have suggested that the physical and cognitive symptoms of panic mediate both fear, helplessness, and horror as well as dissociation. Other investigators have emphasized the positive predictive value of a fright reaction (Tarquinio & Constanti, 2003; Vaiva et al., 2003) or peritraumatic autonomic activation (Bracha et al., 2004). Finally, Friedman et al. (2007b) have argued that other strong peritraumatic emotions are also associated with PTSD, such as sadness, grief, anger, guilt, shame, and disgust. Taken together, these findings suggest that more research is needed to (a) determine the positive predictive value of a peritraumatic emotional/physiological response for the later development of PTSD, and (b) determine whether the nature of such a response conforms to current A_2 fear, helplessness, and horror.

Summarizing A_1 and A_2 Criteria

It is clear that *DSM–V* will have to address some of the current concerns regarding the A criterion. For A_1, it will have to reduce the ambiguity about what is and what is not a traumatic event. For A_2, it will have to consider the utility of this criterion in making the PTSD diagnosis and whether "fear, helplessness, or horror" should be expanded to include peritraumatic dissociation, panic, and other intense peritraumatic emotions. It has also been suggested (Weathers & Keane, 2007) that instead of including A_2 as part of the stressor criterion, it might be more useful as a separate criterion that encompasses the intense peritraumatic response that precipitates PTSD.

I agree with Weathers and Keane (2007) that the stressor criterion serves as an important "gatekeeper" to PTSD because it rules out people who may exhibit B, C, and D symptoms without ever having been exposed to a traumatic event. The spirit of the A criterion is that a qualifying event must be one that entails "personal involvement with, if not direct exposure to catastrophic life events" (Weathers & Keane, 2007, p. 115). Finally, given the above discussion about the A criterion, we must reconsider the distinction between PTSD and adjustment reactions.

The B, C, and D Criteria: Factor Structure of PTSD and Occurrence of Syptoms

Factor Structure of PTSD

The *DSM–IV* PTSD construct consists of three-symptom clusters: B, reexperiencing; C, avoidant/numbing; and D, hyperarousal (see Table 15.1). Questions have been raised about how well this construct has held together in practice. In other words, what is the latent structure of PTSD? Are there three distinct symptom clusters? And are these three clusters subsumed by an overarching construct, the PTSD diagnosis?

Many studies have utilized confirmatory factor analysis to test whether the three *DSM–IV* symptom clusters or other models provide a better fit to the data. With this method, it has been possible to test several different models. Different investigators have found two-, three-, or four-factor models as the best fit for the data. As we review these findings, it is important to note that different PTSD assessment instruments were used by different investigators and that these instruments were administered to individuals whose PTSD developed from different types of traumatic experiences.

Very few studies have supported the *DSM–IV* three-factor model. Foy, Wood, King, King, and Resnick (1997), utilizing the Los Angeles Symptom Checklist with various adult trauma populations, identified three highly correlated factors representing the *DSM–IV* symptom categories of reexperiencing, avoidance/numbing, and arousal. A second study with 5,664 child and adolescent survivors of hurricane Hugo assessed with the PTSD Reaction Index suggested a different three-factor model—reexperiencing/active avoidance, numbing/passive avoidance, and arousal (Anthony, Lonigan, & Hecht, 1999). Elhai, Gray, Docherty, Kashdan, and Kose (2007), utilizing the PTSD Checklist with 510 college students, found similar results. Finally, Griesel, Wessa, and Herta (2006), utilizing a German version of the Posttraumatic Diagnostic Scale with 143 trauma survivors, identified a three-factor solution that differed from *DSM–IV*. Their data loaded on three factors, including reexperiencing/avoidance, emotional numbing/hyperarousal, and hypervigilance/exaggerated startle. As we shall see subsequently, the first two factors obtained by Giesel et al. are consistent with most two-factor solutions.

Most studies have supported a four-factor model. Reexperiencing, avoidance, and arousal have emerged as distinct clusters in all of these studies. There has been some disagreement, however, about the fourth factor. In many studies, "numbing" has been identified as the fourth factor, whereas a "dysphoria" factor has emerged elsewhere. From a *DSM–IV* perspective, what is most notable is that none of these studies support a single avoidance/numbing cluster.

To briefly summarize the four-factor models in which "numbing" emerged as a distinct cluster, they have been conducted on various populations, including primary care patients, male military veterans, adult survivors of community violence, National Comorbidity Study participants, Cambodian refugees, elderly hurricane survivors, cancer survivors, and sexually harassed women (Asmundson et al., 2000; Duhamel et al., 2004; King, Leskin, King, & Weathers, 1998; McWilliams, Cox, & Asmundson, 2005; Marshall, 2004; Palmieri & Fitzgerald, 2005; Palmieri, Marshall, & Schell, 2007; Schinka, Brown, Borenstein, & Mortimer, 2007). In addition, Andrews, Joseph, Shevlin, and Troop (2006) reported that the model of best fit among a cohort of emergency personal was a four-factor solution alongside a general PTSD factor.

There are also a few studies in which "dysphoria" rather than "numbing" emerged as the fourth factor following analysis of data on Gulf War veterans (Simms, Watson, & Doebbling, 2002) and on disaster workers exposed to the World Trade Center destruction after the 9/11 attacks (Palmieri, Weathers, Difiede, & King, 2007). Furthermore, McWilliams et al. (2005) reported that, although their initial four-factor solution included a "numbing" factor, there was better goodness of fit with a four-factor model consisting of dysphoria, cued reexperiencing/avoidance, uncued reexperiencing/hyperarousal, and trauma-related rumination. In view of our previous discussion about PTSD as an internalizing disorder, this general dysphoria factor may be related to the distress/anxious–misery component of disorders frequently comorbid with PTSD.

An interesting study with African refugees reported a very different four-factor model with distinct numbing and avoidance factors alongside reexperiencing/arousal and hypervigilance. According to these authors, traditional

Mandinka nosology also has four factors for nonpsychotic posttraumatic reactions—extreme fear, heart shakes (somatization), thinking sickness (reexperiencing symptoms), and brain out of place (dissociation) (Rasmussen, Smith, & Keller, 2007).

Finally, five studies support a two-factor solution, although the specific factors have differed between studies. In four studies, the factors were characterized as reexperiencing/avoidance and hyperarousal/numbing. These results were obtained with motor vehicle accident survivors, United Nations peacekeepers, Bosnian refugees, and HIV/AIDS patients (Buckley, Blanchard, & Hickling, 1998; Charney & Keane, 2007; Cuevas et al., 2006; Taylor, Kuch, Koch, Crockett, & Passey, 1998). The fifth study, with United Nations peacekeepers, found that a two-factor model in which reexperiencing/avoidance and numbing/hyperarousal factors offered the best solution (Asmundson, Wright, McCreary, & Pedlar, 2003). It was noted in two of these studies that four-factor models also fit the data quite well and, perhaps, provided richer detail about symptoms (Asmundson et al.; Cuevas et al.).

To summarize, the confirmatory factor analytic literature does not support the three-factor *DSM–IV* model. Avoidance and numbing are consistently distinct from one another in both the four- and two-factor solutions, suggesting that serious consideration should be given to including a fourth "numbing" symptom cluster in *DSM–V*. In light of considering PTSD as an internalizing disorder, the emergence of "dysphoria" as a distinct factor in some studies is of interest. Finally, the two-factor solutions support the assertion of Foa, Zinbarg, and Rothbaum (1992) that numbing occurs in response to hyperarousal whereas avoidance occurs in response to reexperiencing symptoms. As noted by Cuevas et al. (2006), such distinct linkages between symptoms clusters may have clinical implications.

The E (Duration) Criterion

In *DSM–IV*, PTSD may be diagnosed at any time after a traumatic event, except during the first month. The *DSM–IV* rationale is that a one-month window must be allowed before diagnosing PTSD in order to permit normal recovery to occur and to avoid pathologizing normal acute posttraumatic distress. Furthermore, *DSM–IV* recognizes delayed-onset PTSD. Sometimes the interval between trauma and positive diagnosis may be of many years duration. This aspect of *DSM–IV* has had a significant impact on compensation claims where the claimant may not have exhibited PTSD symptoms for many years. Delayed onset may represent unrecognized PTSD, subsyndromal PTSD that later escalates to the full syndrome, or a true delay of syndrome onset. Whatever the trajectory, it is clear that delayed-onset PTSD does occur (Bryant & Harvey, 2002; Solomon & Mikulincer, 2006; Wolfe, Erickson, Sharkansky, King, & King, 1999). It is unclear whether it is more likely to occur following military, civilian accident, or natural disaster trauma (where it appears to be very uncommon; Norris, Murphy, Baker, & Perilla, 2003).

The F (Functional Impairment) Criterion

DSM–IV added a functional impairment criterion for PTSD. This means that a person who meets the requisite A–E criteria would not receive a PTSD diagnosis unless he or she also exhibited clinically significant distress or functional impairment. Functional status also appears to have predictive value, because evidence from the disaster field suggests that acute posttraumatic functional impairment is a better prognostic indicator of subsequent PTSD than acute symptom severity (Norris, Friedman, & Watson, 2002a; Norris, Friedman, & Watson, 2002b). Norris et al. (2003) have also shown that functional impairment was the best single predictor of duration of PTSD symptoms. If functional status is to receive appropriate emphasis in *DSM–V*, it will be necessary to revise the current assessment approach, which relies entirely on the 0–100 Global Assessment of Function (GAF) scale. One possibility would be to assess functional capacity across many pertinent domains that are clinically significant, including marriage, family, interpersonal/social, vocational/scholastic, self-care, dangerousness to self or others, disability status, activities of daily living, quality of life, and so forth. Thorp and Stein (2005) have recently written an excellent guide to the published literature on PTSD and functioning.

Should *DSM–IV* Include Other Posttraumatic Syndromes?

Partial/Subsyndromal PTSD

Although approximately 60 publications have reported on the prevalence and morbidity of "partial" (or "subsyndromal") PTSD among a wide assortment of traumatized individuals, no such diagnosis was operationalized in either *DSM–III* or *DSM–IV*. Because of this lack of standardization, partial PTSD has been defined differently by different investigators. For example, partial PTSD has variously been determined by an adjudication procedure (Weiss et al., 1992) or by hard and fast criteria that have differed from one investigator to the next (Breslau, Lucia, & Davis, 2004; Favaro, Tenconi, Columbo, & Santonastaso, 2006; Schnurr et al., 2000) to name only a few.

In order to be considered a candidate diagnosis for *DSM–V*, partial PTSD should be a clinically significant disorder that is distinguishable both from full PTSD on the one hand and no PTSD on the other. It should have a similar relationship to full PTSD that dysthymia has to major depressive disorder or cyclothymia has to bipolar disorder. Several reports indicate that people with partial PTSD exhibit significantly less symptom severity and functional impairment than those with the full syndrome but exhibit significantly more than those with no PTSD cohorts (Breslau et al., 2004; Carlier & Gersons, 1995; Lipschitz, Rasmusson, Anyan, Gueorguieva, Billingslea et al., 2000; Schnurr et al., 2000; Stein, Walker, Hazen, & Forde, 1997; Taylor & Koch, 1995; Weiss et al., 1992; Zlotnick et al., 2004). There have also been negative findings in which few differences were detected between partial and no PTSD cohorts, whereas both differed significantly from full PTSD (Favaro et al., 2006; Maia et al., 2007).

Given the differences in diagnostic criteria for partial PTSD in these studies, it is hard to know what to make of these findings. On the other hand, despite such variations, the weight of evidence suggests that partial PTSD is both clinically significant and generally distinct from both full and no PTSD. It is arguable whether the evidence at this time is strong enough to warrant inclusion of partial PTSD as a distinct diagnosis in *DSM–V*. In my opinion, a standard set of diagnostic criteria must be developed so that research on this question can proceed and be analyzed properly.

I agree with Mylle and Maes (2004) that if partial PTSD becomes a *DSM–V* diagnosis, it should meet the F criterion and should cause significant distress or functional impairment. As mentioned above, I also believe that there must be hard and fast criteria for partial PTSD. I personally favor the criteria developed by Schnurr, Friedman, and Rosenberg (1993) in which an individual must meet the A (exposure), B (reexperiencing), E (duration), and F (impairment–distress) criteria as well as either (a) the D (hyperarousal), or (b) at least one C (avoidant/numbing) and one D (hyperarousal) symptom; but, this is a matter for the *DSM–V* work group to decide. Because there is only one posttraumatic diagnosis in *DSM–IV*, in contrast to the nine affective spectrum disorders, and given the apparent clinical relevance of partial PTSD, this matter merits serious attention from APA's *DSM–V* work group.

Disorders of Extreme Stress Not Otherwise Specified (DESNOS)/Complex PTSD

Dissatisfaction with the PTSD construct has been expressed by many investigators and clinicians. The major complaint is that the PTSD symptom clusters fail to characterize clinically significant problems often exhibited by individuals exposed to severe and protracted traumatic exposure (most notably childhood sexual abuse and torture within the context of political incarceration). They argue that the most significant clinical sequelae are not delineated by the PTSD construct. Although acknowledging that such individuals often do meet *DSM–IV* PTSD criteria, their most debilitating symptoms often include behavioral difficulties (e.g., impulsivity, aggression, sexual acting out, alcohol/drug misuse, self-destructive actions), emotional difficulties (e.g., affective lability, rage, depression, panic), cognitive difficulties (e.g., dissociation, amnesia, pathological changes in personal identity—dissociative identity disorder), interpersonal difficulties, and somatization (Herman, 1992; Linehan, Tutek, Heard, & Armstrong, 1994, van der Kolk, Roth, Pelcovitz, Sunday, & Spinazzola, 2005).

During the *DSM–IV* process, a field trial was designed to determine whether there was empirical support for including DESNOS as a unique diagnosis. Because only 8% of individuals with DESNOS did not also meet PTSD diagnostic criteria, it was considered too rare an occurrence to be classified as a separate diagnostic entity. During recent years, there has been some research designed to clarify the prevalence and construct validity of DESNOS. Almost all of this work has focused on Western adults (mostly female Caucasians who had been sexually traumatized as children). This research draws on the important conceptual work of Judith Herman (1992). Based on her work with women who had been exposed to prolonged childhood sexual abuse, she coined the term "complex PTSD" as a clinical disorder that encompassed three non-PTSD posttraumatic disorders—dissociative identity disorder, borderline personality disorder, and somatization disorder. It should be noted that there is also enthusiasm for the DESNOS construct among mental health professionals who have worked with non-Western patients exposed to forced migration or torture (de Jong, Komproe, Spinazzola, van der Kolk, & van Ommeren, 2005; Sochting, Carrado, Cohen, Ley, & Brasfield, 2007), although there has been little research in this area.

One problem may be that most researches on DESNOS have utilized the Structured Interview for DESNOS (SIDES; Pelcovitz et al., 1997) which gives equal weight to all seven DESNOS symptom clusters. Ford, Stockton, Kaltman, and Green (2006) have concluded that although the SIDES has shown evidence of reliability, there are serious questions about which symptoms to include as well as the construct validity of its subscales. These investigators found that the DESNOS symptoms that are most likely to occur among individuals with DESNOS without PTSD are dissociation, altered relationships, and disrupted systems of meaning, whereas individuals with DESNOS and PTSD were most likely to exhibit affect dysregulation, loss of impulse control, dissociative, somatization, and severe character pathology. Another study by this group of investigators (Zucker, Blaustein, & van der Kolk, 2006) reported significant elevations in dissociation among PTSD and DESNOS participants in contrast to PTSD alone participants.

The DESNOS issue raises important questions about posttraumatic syndromes. Are there different posttraumatic trajectories based on age and/or nature of traumatic exposure? Is the DESNOS model useful in a cross-cultural context because it emphasizes both dissociation and somatization, two symptoms not included in the *DSM–IV* PTSD diagnostic criteria that are frequently observed in traumatized non-Western cohorts (Kirmayer, 1996)? Is it useful in clarifying the relationship between traumatic exposure and borderline personality disorder (Classen, Pain, Field, & Woods, 2006; Herman, 1992; Sansone, Songer, & Miller, 2005) or alexithymia (McLean, Toner, Jackson, Desrocher, & Stuckless, 2006)?

Finally, Cantor and Price (2007), extrapolating from evolutionary theory and cross-species comparisons, suggest that there might be a different psychobiological model for DESNOS than for PTSD. In contrast to PTSD fear-conditioning models, they propose that DESNOS results when escape is impossible and under conditions of "traumatic entrapment," or "appeasement" (which they report is a time-honored mammalian defense that has been observed in many species). According to these authors, examples of traumatic entrapment or appeasement have been observed among former hostages (e.g., the Stockholm syndrome), following protracted child sexual abuse, or during ongoing domestic violence. Such conditions, they argue, might promote many characteristic DESNOS symptoms, such as affect dysregulation alterations in consciousness, alterations in self-perception (e.g., ineffectiveness, permanent damage, guilt, responsibility), and especially alterations in perception of the preceptor. The possibility that there might be a different psychobiological endophenotype for DESNOS than for PTSD is an intriguing question with a direct bearing on whether DESNOS might be a specific dimension of PTSD or a unique entity unto itself.

Other Post-(Traumatic/Nontraumatic) Stress Syndromes

Shifting from a psychiatric to a medical focus, it is noteworthy that in medicine, the major emphasis is on "stress" per se, rather than "traumatic stress." Dating back to the seminal work of Selye (1946), there is rich literature showing how chronic stress is associated with medical illness (Chrousos & Gold, 1992; McEwen, 1998). McEwen and Steller (1993) proposed the concept of "allostatic load" as an explanatory model for how the biological alterations associated with chronic stress (especially the downstream consequences of heightened hypothalamic–pituitary–adrenal [HPA] axis function) might increase the risk for medical illness. Friedman and McEwen (2004) later showed the applicability of the allostatic load model to PTSD because there is considerable, but not complete, overlap between biological alterations observed in chronic stress syndromes and those detected in PTSD. Schnurr and Green (2004) have presented the wealth of scientific evidence showing that prevalence of medical illness is greater among people with PTSD than among those without the disorder.

This raises two diagnostic questions: (a) should there be a category of posttraumatic medical disorders, and (b) should there be a psychiatric chronic stress disorder in which "chronic stress" is not restricted to "traumatic stress" as defined by the A criterion?

As for posttraumatic medical disorders, there is emerging data showing higher prevalence of cardiovascular, gastrointestinal, endocrinological, musculoskeletal, and immunological disorders associated with PTSD (see Schnurr and Green, 2004). Importantly, it is not trauma exposure per se but trauma exposure followed by the development of PTSD that accounts for such medical abnormalities. Furthermore, there are recognized diseases, such as chronic fatigue syndrome and fibromyalgia, which defy traditional mind–body distinctions between medical and psychiatric diagnoses where exposure to stress is clearly a precipitating factor and where the syndrome exhibits a combination of traditional medical and traditional psychiatric symptoms. One difference between adverse medical outcomes associated with PTSD and those associated with chronic stress might have to do with the duration of exposure. Although a chronic stress syndrome results from protracted exposure, PTSD-related medical disorders might only require a brief period of traumatization that is sufficient to precipitate a full-fledged PTSD syndrome. Indeed, further explication of this issue should distinguish between brief and prolonged traumatic stressors to determine whether there is a difference in the pattern of posttraumatic medical problems.

The second question concerns the legitimacy of nontraumatic stress as a precipitant for a psychiatric syndrome that might be called "post–severe stress syndrome." It would be distinguished from time-limited adjustment disorders by its ongoing chronicity. There is evidence to support such a proposal. First, as discussed previously, two recent studies have reported high PTSD symptom severity among individuals with nontraumatic life events (e.g., chronic illness, death of a loved one, marital discord, unemployment) (Mol et al., 2005; Gold et al., 2005). Second, the full PTSD syndrome has been observed in medical patients in whom the stressful event was a nontraumatic illness such as AIDS (Martinez, Israeliski, Walker, Koopman, 2002), breast cancer (Amir & Ramati, 2002), cancer (Redd et al., 2001), and lymphoma (Geffen, Blaustein, Amir, & Cohen, 2003). Finally, many clinicians who have treated patients with PTSD will attest that some identify divorce, academic failure, business setbacks, and the like as much more distressing and life changing than the traumatic event which precipitated their PTSD.

Cross-Cultural Factors

The PTSD diagnosis has been criticized from a cross-cultural perspective as a European American construct that has little relevance to posttraumatic syndromes encountered in traditional societies (Summerfield, 2004). Kirmayer (1996) has argued that somatization and dissociation, two cardinal symptoms of posttraumatic reactions in traditional societies, are missing from *DSM–IV* diagnostic criteria for PTSD (although they are present in DESNOS). Acknowledging that there may be culture-specific idioms of distress that provide a better characterization of posttraumatic distress syndromes found in one ethnocultural context or another, PTSD has been documented throughout the world (Green et al., 2003; Marsella, Friedman, Gerrity, & Scurfield, 1996). High prevalence rates have been reported in non-Western nations subjected to war or internal conflict, such as Algeria, Cambodia, Lebanon, Palestine, Nepal, and the former Yugoslavia (de Jong, et al., 2001; Hinton, et al., 2006; Thapa & Hauff, 2005). Furthermore, comparable PTSD prevalence has been found among Russian and American adolescents (Ruchkin, et al., 2005). One problem with this issue is that it has been difficult to find similar traumatic events affecting people from widely different cultures. North and coworkers (North, et al., 2005) compared psychiatric morbidity among Kenyan survivors of the bombing of the American embassy in Nairobi with American survivors of the bombing of the Federal Building in Oklahoma City. Both events were remarkably similar with respect to death, injury, destruction, and other consequences.

Similar too was PTSD prevalence among Africans and Americans exposed to each traumatic event, respectively.

Culture is a major filter through which people appraise, cope with, and make meaning out of catastrophic events. Most of the current instruments used to assess posttraumatic sequelae in non-Western, traditional cultures were initially developed in a Euro-American context. Such instruments must be carefully evaluated and revised to establish cultural equivalence and cultural sensitivity. Methodological approaches such as back translation, committee consensus, and decentering are needed if we are to make progress in this important area. Otherwise, we risk underdiagnosis, overdiagnosis, or misdiagnosis (Osterman & de Jong, 2007; Joyce & Berger, 2006; Smit, van den Berg, Bakker, Deedat, & Stein, 2006). For example, a study of DESNOS among individuals from Algeria, Ethiopia, and Gaza found that the primary assessment instrument, the SIDES, did not appear to be valid in these cross-cultural settings (de Jong et al., 2005).

I agree with Osterman and de Jong (2007) that we need a "culturally competent model of traumatic stress" that addresses how culture may differentially influence explanatory models, how it is implicated in the appraisal of risk/protective factors, and how such understanding might contribute to diagnosis and treatment.

Developmental Issues

A thorough discussion of PTSD at either end of the life span is beyond the scope of the present chapter. Consideration of this topic must address how maturational, biological, and psychological changes affect the appraisal of and reaction to traumatic events as well as to differences in expression of posttraumatic distress. For understanding the problems of children who have experienced traumatic events, the developmental context must incorporate the dynamic and evolving relationship between experience, neurological processing, brain development, and self-regulation (Saxe, MacDonald, & Ellis, 2007). Furthermore, Scheeringa and associates (Scheeringa, Zeanah, Drell, & Larrieu, 1995) reported on the inadequacy of *DSM–IV* PTSD criteria to adequately characterize posttraumatic symptoms in infants and children younger than 4 years old. They suggest that criteria anchored in observable behaviors should replace reports of subjective experiences or behaviors. For elderly individuals, a developmental approach must address age-specific psychosocial, behavioral, and neurobiological factors that mediate and moderate trauma-related symptom expression and clinical course (Cook & Niederehe, 2007). An important question with regard to PTSD among the elderly is how it is associated with negative health perceptions, primary care utilization, and suicidal ideation (Rauch, Morales, Zubritsky, Knott, & Oslin, 2006). A comprehensive, longitudinal developmental approach is also needed to explicate how memories for traumatic events are differentially encoded, stored, and retrieved by the immature and developing brain, on the one hand, and by the aging brain, on the other.

Summary

The following points summarize the information provided above. These are issues that, in my opinion, warrant careful consideration as we move toward the *DSM–V* and in future research endeavors.

1. There are arguments for and against classifying PTSD as an anxiety disorder, a stress-related fear-circuitry, or an internalizing disorder. The latter possibility might provide a useful heuristic with which to understand high prevalence of comorbidity between PTSD and other internalizing disorders, although it neglects evidence suggesting that there is an externalizing subtype of PTSD.
2. Any revisions in PTSD diagnostic criteria need to reconsider what to include in the A criterion, apparent failure of the A_2 criterion to improve diagnostic precision, the lack of evidence for a coherent avoidant/numbing cluster, and how best to operationalize the F criterion.
3. There is sufficient evidence to merit consideration of a unique category of posttraumatic and post–nontraumatic stress syndromes. It might be called something like "event-related psychiatric disorders" and would span the spectrum from PTSD to adjustment disorders.
4. Although there are culture-specific posttraumatic idioms of distress, PTSD appears to characterize a universal human response to trauma that may be influenced by cultural factors.

5. Our understanding of PTSD is based mostly on evidence obtained with young and middle-aged adults. There are developmental issues at either end of the life span that should inform diagnostic assessment.

References

American Psychiatric Association. (1952). *Diagnostic and statistical manual of mental disorders.* Washington, DC: Author.

American Psychiatric Association. (1968). *Diagnostic and statistical manual of mental disorders* (2nd ed.). Washington, DC: Author.

American Psychiatric Association. (1980). *Diagnostic and statistical manual of mental disorders* (3rd ed.). Washington, DC: Author.

American Psychiatric Association. (1987). *Diagnostic and statistical manual of mental disorders* (3rd ed., rev.). Washington, DC: Author.

American Psychiatric Association. (1994). *Diagnostic and statistical manual of mental disorders* (4th ed.). Washington, DC: Author.

American Psychiatric Association. (2000). *Diagnostic and statistical manual of mental disorders* (4th ed., text revision). Washington, DC: Author.

Amir, M., & Ramati, A. (2002). Post-traumatic symptoms emotional distress and quality of life in long-term survivors of breast cancer: A preliminary research. *Journal of Anxiety Disorder, 16,* 191–206.

Andrews, G., Charney, D., Sirovatka, P., & Regier, D. (Eds.). (2009). *Stress-induced fear circuitry disorders: Refining the research agenda for DSM–V.* Arlington, VA: American Psychiatric Publishing, Inc.

Andrews, L., Joseph, S., Shevlin, M., & Troop, N. (2006). Confirmatory factor analysis of posttraumatic stress symptoms in emergency personnel: An examination of seven alternative models. *Personality and Individual Differences, 41,* 213–224.

Anthony, J. L., Lonigan, C. J., & Hecht, S. A. (1999). Dimensionality of posttraumatic stress disorder symptoms in children exposed to disaster: Results from confirmatory factory analysis. *Journal of Abnormal Psychology, 108,* 326–336.

Asmundson, G. J. G., Frombach, I., McQuaid, J. R., Pedrilli, P., Lenox, R. J., & Stein, M.B. (2000). Dimensionality of posttraumatic stress symptoms: A confirmatory factor analysis of DSM-IV symptom clusters and other symptom models. *Behaviour Research and Therapy, 38,* 203–214.

Asmundson, G. J. G., Wright, K. D., McCreary, D. R., & Pedlar, D. (2003). Post-traumatic stress disorder symptoms in United Nations peacekeepers: An examination of factor structure in peacekeepers with and without chronic pain. *Cognitive Behaviour Therapy, 32,* 26–37.

Bracha, H. S., Williams, A. E, Haynes, S. N., Kubany, E. S., Ralston, T. C., & Yamashita, J. M. (2004). The STRS (shortness of breath, tremulousness, racing heart, and sweating): A brief checklist for acute distress, with panic-like sympathetic indicators; development and factor structure. *Annals of General Hospital Psychiatry, 3,* 1–8.

Breslau, N., & Kessler, R. C. (2001). The stressor criterion in DSM-IV posttraumatic stress disorder: An empirical investigation. *Biological Psychiatry, 50,* 699–704.

Breslau, N., Lucia, V. C., & Davis, G. C. (2004). Partial PTSD versus full PTSD: An empirical examination of associated impairment. *Psychological Medicine, 34,* 1205–1214.

Brewin, C. R., Andrews, B., & Rose, S. (2000). Fear, helplessness, and horror in posttraumatic stress disorder: Investigating DSM-IV criterion A2 in victims of violent crime. *Journal of Traumatic Stress, 13*, 499–509.

Bryant, R. A., & Harvey, A. G. (2002). Delayed-onset posttraumatic stress disorder: A prospective evaluation. *Australian and New Zealand Journal of Psychiatry 36*, 205–209.

Buckley, T. C., Blanchard, E. B., & Hickling, E. J. (1998) A confirmatory factor analysis of posttraumatic stress symptoms. *Behaviour Research and Therapy, 36*, 1091–1099.

Cantor, C., & Price, J. (2007). Traumatic entrapment, appeasement and complex post-traumatic stress disorder: Evolutionary perspectives of hostage reactions, domestic abuse and the Stockholm syndrome. *Australian and New Zealand Journal of Psychiatry, 41*, 377–384.

Carlier, I. V. E., & Gersons, B. P. R. (1995) . Partial posttraumatic stress disorder (PTSD): The issue of psychological scars and the occurrence of PTSD symptoms. *Journal of Nervous and Mental Disease, 183*, 107–109.

Charney, D. S. (2004). Psychobiological mechanisms of resilience and vulnerability: Implications for successful adaptation to extreme stress. *American Journal of Psychiatry, 161*, 195–216.

Charney, M. E., & Keane, T. M. (2007). Psychometric analyses of the Clinician-Administered PTSD Scale (CAPS) – Bosnian translation. *Cultural Diversity and Ethnic Minority Psychology, 13*, 161–168.

Chrousos, G. P., & Gold, P. W. (1992). The concepts of stress and stress system disorders: Overview of physical and behavioral homeostasis. *Journal of the American Medical Association, 267*, 1244–1252.

Classen, C. C., Pain, C., Field, N. P., & Woods, P. (2006). Posttraumatic personality disorder: A reformulation of complex posttraumatic stress disorder and borderline personality disorder. *Psychiatric Clinics of North America, 29*, 87–112.

Cook, J.M. & Niederehe, G. (2007). Trauma in older adults. In M.J. Friedman, T.M. Keane, & P.A. Resick (Eds.), *Handbook of PTSD: Science and practice (pp. 252-276)*. New York: Guilford.

Cox, B. J., Clara, I. P., & Enns, M. W. (2002). Posttraumatic stress disorder and the structure of common mental disorders. *Depression and Anxiety, 15*,168–171.

Creamer, M., McFarlane, A. C., & Burgess, P. (2005). Psychopathology following trauma: The role of subjective experience. *Journal of Affective Disorders, 86*, 175–182.

Cuevas, C. A., Bollinger, A. R., Vielhauer, M. J., Morgan, E. E., Sohler, N. L., Brief, D. J., et al. (2006). HIV/AIDS Cost Study: Construct validity and factor structure of the PTSD Checklist in dually diagnosed HIV-seropositive adults. *Journal of Trauma Practice, 5*, 29–51.

Dattilio, F. M. (2004). Extramarital affairs: The much-overlooked PTSD. *Behavior Therapist, 27*, 76–78.

Davidson, J. R. T., & Foa, E. B. (Eds). (1993). *Posttraumatic stress disorder: DSM–IV and beyond* (1st ed.). Washington, DC: American Psychiatric Press.

Davis, M., & Whalen, P. J. (2001). The amygdala: Vigilance and emotion. *Molecular Psychiatry, 6*, 13–34.

de Jong, J. T. V. M., Komproe, I. H., Spinazzola, J., van der Kolk, B. A., & Van Ommeren, M. H. (2005). DESNOS in three postconflict settings: Assessing cross-cultural construct equivalence. *Journal of Traumatic Stress, 18*, 13–21.

de Jong, J. T. V. M., Komproe, I. H., Van Ommeren, M., El Masri, M., Araya, M., Khaled, N., et al. (2001). Lifetime events and posttraumatic stress disorder in 4 postconflict settings. *Journal of the American Medical Association, 286,* 555–562.

Duhamel, K. N., Ostroff, J. S., Ashman, T., Winkel, G., Mundy, E. A., Keane, T. M., et al. (2004). Construct validity of the Posttraumatic Stress Disorder Checklist in cancer survivors: Analyses based on two samples. *Psychological Assessment, 16,* 255–266.

Elhai, J. D., Gray, M. J., Docherty, A. R., Kashdan, T. B., & Kose, S. (2007). Structural validity of the Posttraumatic Stress Disorder Checklist among college students with a trauma history. *Journal of Interpersonal Violence, 22,* 1471–1478.

Erwin, B. A., Heimberg, R. G., Marx, B. P., & Franklin, M. E. (2006). Traumatic and socially stressful life events among persons with social anxiety disorder. *Journal of Anxiety Disorders, 20,* 896–914.

Foa, E. B., & Kozak, M. J. (1986). Emotional processing of fear: Exposure to corrective information. *Psychological Bulletin, 99,* 20–35.

Foa, E. B, Zinbarg, R., & Rothbaum, B. O. (1992). Uncontrollability and unpredictability in post-traumatic stress disorder: An animal model. *Psychological Bulletin, 112,* 218–238.

Favaro, A., Tenconi, E., Colombo, G., & Santonastaso, P. (2006). Full and partial post-traumatic stress disorder among World War II prisoners of war. *Psychopathology, 39,* 187–191.

Fikretoglu, D., Brunet, A., Best, S. R., Metzler, T. J., Delucchi, K., Weiss, D. S., et al. (2007). Peritraumatic fear, helplessness and horror and peritraumatic dissociation: Do physical and cognitive symptoms of panic mediate the relationship between the two? *Behaviour Research and Therapy, 45,* 39–47.

Ford, J. D., Stockton, P., Kaltman, S., & Green B. L. (2006). Disorders of extreme stress (DESNOS) symptoms are associated with type and severity of interpersonal trauma exposure in a sample of healthy young women. *Journal of Interpersonal Violence, 21,* 1399–1416.

Foy, D. W., Wood, J. L., King, D. W., King, L. A., & Resnick, H. S. (1997). Los Angeles Symptom Checklist: Psychometric evidence with an adolescent sample. *Assessment, 4,* 377–384.

Friedman, M. J., & McEwen, B. S. (2004). PTSD, allostatic load, and medical illness. In P.P. Schnurr & B.L. Green (Eds.). *Trauma and health: Physical health consequences of exposure to extreme stress* (pp. 157–188) Washington, DC: American Psychological Association.

Friedman, M. J. Resick, P. A., & Keane, T. M. (2007a). Key questions and an agenda for future research. In M.J. Friedman, P.A. Resick, & T.M. Keane (Eds.). *Handbook of PTSD: Science and practice* (pp. 540–561). New York: Guilford Press.

Friedman, M. J., Resick, P. A., & Keane, T. M. (2007b). PTSD: Twenty-five years of progress and challenges. In M.J. Friedman, P.A. Resick, & T.M. Keane (Eds.). *Handbook of PTSD: Science and practice* (pp. 3–18) New York: Guilford Press.

Geffen, D. B., Blaustein, A., Amir, M., & Cohen, Y. (2003). Post-traumatic stress disorder and quality of life in long-term survivors of Hodgkin's disease and non-Hodgkin's lymphoma in Israel. *Leukemia and Lymphoma, 44,* 1925–1929.

Gold, S. D., Marx, B. P., Soler-Baillo, J. M., & Sloan, D. M. (2005). Is life stress more traumatic than traumatic stress? *Journal of Anxiety Disorders, 19*, 687–698.

Green, B. L., Friedman, M. J., de Jong, J. T. V. M., Solomon, S. D., Keane, T. M., Fairbank, J. A., et al. (2003). *Trauma interventions in war and peace: Prevention, practice, and policy.* New York: Kluwer Academic/Plenum Publishers.

Griesel, D., Wessa, M., & Herta, F. (2006) . Psychometric qualities of the German version of the Posttraumatic Diagnostic Scale (PTDS). *Psychological Assessment, 18*, 262–268.

Herman, J. L. (1992). Complex PTSD: A syndrome in survivors of prolonged and repeated trauma. *Journal of Traumatic Stress, 5*, 377–391.

Hinton, D. E., Chhean, D., Pich, V., Pollack, M. H., Orr, S. P., & Pitman, R. K. (2006). Assessment of posttraumatic stress disorder in Cambodian refugees using the Clinician-Administered PTSD Scale: Psychometric properties and symptom severity. *Journal of Traumatic Stress, 19*, 405–409.

Jones, J. C., & Barlow, D. H. (1990). The etiology of posttraumatic stress disorder. *Clinical Psychology Review, 10*, 299–328.

Joyce, P. A., & Berger, R. (2006). Which language does PTSD speak? The "Westernization" of Mr. Sanchez. *Journal of Trauma Practice, 5*, 53–67.

Keane, T. M., Zimering, R. T., & Caddell, J. M. (1985). A behavioral formulation of posttraumatic stress disorder in Vietnam veterans. *Behavior Therapist, 8*, 9–12.

Kessler, R. C., Sonnega, A., Bromet, E., Hughes, M., & Nelson, C. B. (1995). Posttraumatic stress disorder in the National Comorbidity Survey. *Archives of General Psychiatry, 52*, 1048–1060.

Kilpatrick, D. G., Resnick, H. S., Freedy, J. R., Pelcovitz, D., Resick, P. A., Roth, S., et al. (1998). Posttraumatic stress disorder field trial: Evaluation of the PTSD construct—criteria A through E. In T.A. Widiger, A.J. Frances, H.A. Pincus, R. Ross, M.B. First, W.W. Davis, et al. (Eds.). *DSM-IV Sourcebook* (pp. 803–838). Washington, DC: American Psychiatric Association.

King, D. W., Leskin, G. A., King, L. A., & Weathers, F. W. (1998) Confirmatory factor analysis of the Clinician-Administered PTSD Scale: Evidence for the dimensionality of posttraumatic stress disorder. *Psychological Assessment,* 10, 90–96.

Kirmayer, L. J. (1996). Confusion of the senses: Implications of ethnocultural variations in somatoform and dissociative disorders for PTSD. In A.J. Marsella, M.J. Friedman, E.T. Gerrity, & R.M. Scurfield (Eds.), *Ethnocultural aspects of posttraumatic stress disorder: Issues, research, and clinical applications* (pp. 131–163). Washington, DC: American Psychological Association.

Kolb, L. C., Ciccone, P. E., Burstein, A., & Greenstein, R. A. (1989). Heterogeneity of PTSD. Letter to the editor. *American Journal of Psychiatry, 146*, 811–812.

Krueger, R. F., & Markon, K. E. (2006). Reinterpreting comorbidity: A model-based approach to understanding and classifying psychopathology. *Annual Review of Clinical Psychology, 2*, 111–133.

Lang, P. J. (1977). Imagery in therapy: An information processing analysis of fear. *Behavior Therapy, 8*, 862–886.

Linehan, M. M., Tutek, D. A., Heard, H. L., Armstrong, H. E. (1994). Interpersonal outcome of cognitive behavioral treatment for chronically suicidal borderline patients. *American Journal of Psychiatry, 151*, 1771–1776.

Lipschitz, D. S., Rasmusson, A. M., Anyan, W., Cromwell, P. F., & Southwick, S. M. (2000) Clinical and functional correlates of posttraumatic stress disorder in urban adolescent girls at a primary care clinic. *Journal of the American Academy of Child & Adolescent Psychiatry, 39,* 1104–1111.

Maia, D. B., Marmar, C. R., Metzler, T. Nobrega, A., Berger, W., Mendlowicz, M. V., et al. (2007). Post-traumatic stress symptoms in an elite unit of Brazilian police officers: Prevalence and impact on psychosocial functioning and on physical and mental health. *Journal of Affective Disorders, 97*, 241–245.

Marsella, A. J., Friedman, M. J., Gerrity, E. T., & Scurfield, R. M., (Eds). (1996). *Ethnocultural aspects of post-traumatic stress disorder: Issues, research and clinical applications*. Washington, DC: American Psychological Association.

Marshall, G. N. (2004). Posttraumatic stress disorder symptom checklist: Factor structure and English-Spanish measurement invariance. *Journal of Traumatic Stress, 17*, 223–230.

Martinez, A., Israeliski, D., Walker, C., Koopman, C. (2002). Posttraumatic stress disorder in women attending human immunodeficiency virus outpatient clinics. *AIDS Patient Care and STDs, 16*, 283–291.

McEwen, B. S. (1998). Protective and damaging effects of stress mediators. *New England Journal of Medicine, 338*, 171–179.

McEwen, B. S., & Stellar, E. (1993). Stress and the individual: Mechanisms leading to disease. *Archives of Internal Medicine, 153*, 2093–2101.

McLean, L. M., Toner, B., Jackson, J., Desrocher, M., & Stuckless, N. (2006). The relationship between childhood sexual abuse, complex posttraumatic stress disorder and alexithymia in two outpatient samples: Examination of women treated in community and institutional clinics. *Journal of Child Sexual Abuse, 15*, 1–17.

McWilliams, L. A., Cox, B. J., & Asmundson, G. J. G. (2005). Symptom structure of posttraumatic stress disorder in a nationally representative sample. *Journal of Anxiety Disorders, 19*, 626–641.

Miller, M. W., Greif, J. L., & Smith, A. A. (2003). Multidimensional personality Questionnaire profiles of veterans with traumatic combat exposure: Internalizing and externalizing subtypes. *Psychological Assessment, 15*, 205–215.

Miller, M. W., Kaloupek, D. G., Dillon, A. L., & Keane, T. M. (2004). Externalizing and internalizing subtypes of combat-related PTSD: A replication and extension using the PSY-5 scales. *Journal of Abnormal Psychology, 112*, 636–645.

Miller, M. W., & Resick, P. A. (2007). Internalizing and externalizing subtypes in female sexual assault survivors: Implications for the understanding of complex PTSD. *Behavior Therapy, 38*, 58–71.

Mol, S. S. L., Arntz, A., Metsemakers, J. F. M., Dinant, G.-J., Vilters-Van Montfort, P. A., & Knottnerus, J.A. (2005). Symptoms of post-traumatic stress disorder after non-traumatic events: Evidence from an open population study. *British Journal of Psychiatry, 186*, 494–499.

Monson, C. M., Friedman, M. J., & La Bash, H. (2007). A psychological history of posttraumatic stress disorder. In M.J. Friedman, T.M. Keane, & P.A. Resick (Eds.), *PTSD, science & practice: A comprehensive handbook* (pp. 37–52). New York: Guilford Press.

Neumeister, A., Henry, S., & Krystal, J. H. (2007). Neurocircuitry and neuroplasticity in PTSD. In M.J. Friedman, T.M. Keane, & P.A. Resick. (Eds.), *Handbook of PTSD* (pp. 151–165). New York: Guilford Press.

Norris, F. H., Friedman, M. J., & Watson, P. J. (2002a). 60,000 disaster victims speak, part I: An empirical review of the empirical literature, 1981–2001. *Psychiatry, 65,* 207–239.

Norris, F. H., Friedman, M. J., & Watson, P. J. (2002b). 60,000 disaster victims speak, part II: Summary and implications of the disaster mental health research. *Psychiatry, 65*, 240–260.

Norris, F. H., Murphy, A. D., Baker, C. K., & Perilla, J. L. (2003). Severity, timing, and duration of reactions to trauma in the population: An example from Mexico. *Biological Psychiatry, 53*, 769–778.

North, C. S., Pfefferbaum, B., Narayanan, P., Thielman, S. B., McCoy, G., Dumont, C. E. et al. (2005). Comparison of post-disaster psychiatric disorders after terrorist bombings in Nairobi and Oklahoma City. *British Journal of Psychiatry, 186*, 487–493.

Palmieri, P. A., & Fitzgerald, L. F. (2005). Confirmatory factor snalysis of posttraumatic stress symptoms in sexually harassed women. *Journal of Traumatic Stress. 18*, 657–666.

Palmieri, P. A., Marshall, G. N., & Schell, T. L. (2007). Confirmatory factor analysis of posttraumatic stress symptoms in Cambodian refugees. *Journal of Traumatic Stress, 20*, 207–216.

Palmieri, P. A., Weathers, F. W., Difede, J., & King, D. W. (2007). Confirmatory factor analysis of the PTSD Checklist and the Clinician-Administered PTSD Scale in disaster workers exposed to the World Trade Center Ground Zero. *Journal of Abnormal Psychology, 116*, 329–341.

Pelcovitz, D., van der Kolk, B. A., Roth, S., Mandel, F., Kaplan, S., & Resick, P. (1997). Development of a criteria set and a structured interview for disorders of extreme stress (SIDES). *Journal of Traumatic Stress, 10,* 3–16.

Rasmussen, A., Smith, H., & Keller, A. S. (2007). Factor structure of PTSD symptoms among West and Central African Refugees. *Journal of Traumatic Stress, 20*, 271–280.

Rauch, S. A., Morales, K. H., Zubritsky, C., Knott, K., & Oslin, D. (2006). Posttraumatic stress, depression, and health among adults in primary care. *American Journal of Geriatric Psychiatry, 14(4),* 316–324.

Redd, W. H., DuHamel, K. N., Vickberg, S. M. J., Johnson, S. M., Ostroff, J. S., Smith, M. Y., et al. (2001). Long-term adjustment in cancer survivors: Integration of classical-conditioning and cognitive-processing models. In A. S. Baum & B. L. Andersen (Eds.). *Psychosocial interventions for cancer* (pp. 77–97). Washington, DC: American Psychological Association.

Roemer, L., Orsillo, S. M., Borkovec, T. D., & Litz, B. T. (1998). Emotional response at the time of a potentially traumatizing event and PTSD symptomatology: A preliminary retrospective analysis of the DSM-IV criterion A-2. *Journal of Behavior Therapy and Experimental Psychiatry, 29*, 123–130.

Ruchkin, V., Schwab-Stone, M., Jones, S., Cichetti, D. V., Kiposov, R., & Vermeiren, R. (2005). Is posttraumatic stress in youth a culture-bound phenomenon? A comparison of symptom trends in selected U.S. and Russian communities. *American Journal of Psychiatry, 162*(3), 538–544.

Sansone, R. A., Songer, D. A., & Miller, K. A. (2005). Childhood abuse, mental healthcare utilization, self-harm behavior, and multiple psychiatric diagnoses among inpatients with and without a borderline diagnosis. *Comprehensive Psychiatry, 26*, 117–120.

Saxe, G. N., MacDonald, H. Z., & Ellis, H. (2007). Psychosocial approaches for children with posttraumatic stress disorder. In M.J. Friedman, T.M. Keane, & P.A. Resick (Eds.). *PTSD, science & practice: A comprehensive handbook* (pp. 359–375). New York: Guilford Publications.

Scheeringa, M. S., Zeanah, C. H., Drell, M. J., & Larrieu, J. A. (1995). Two approaches to the diagnosis of posttraumatic stress disorder in infancy and early childhood. *Journal of the American Academy of Child & Adolescent Psychiatry, 34*, 191–200.

Schinka, J. A., Brown, L. M., Borenstein, A. R., Mortimer, J. A. (2007). Confirmatory factor analysis of the PTSD Checklist in the Elderly (2007). *Journal of Traumatic Stress, 20*, 281–289.

Schnurr, P. P., Ford, J. D., Friedman, M. J. Green B. L., Dain, B. J., & Sengupta, A. (2000). Predictors and outcomes of posttraumatic stress disorder in World War II veterans exposed to mustard gas. *Journal of Consulting and Clinical Psychology, 68*, 258–268.

Schnurr, P. P., Friedman, M. J., & Rosenberg, S. D. (1993). Premilitary MMPI scores as predictors of combat-related PTSD symptoms. *American Journal of Psychiatry, 150*, 479–483.

Schnurr, P. P., & Green, B. L. (Eds). (2004). *Trauma and health: Physical health consequences of exposure to extreme stress*. Washington, DC: American Psychological Association.

Schnurr, P. P., Spiro, A., Vielhauer, M. J., Findler, M. N., & Hamblen, J. L. (2002). Trauma in the lives of older men: findings from the Normative Aging Study. *Journal of Clinical Geropsychology, 8*, 175–187.

Selye, H. (1946). The general adaptation syndrome and the diseases of adaptation. *Journal of Clinical Endocrinology & Metabolism, 6*, 117–230.

Shay, J. (1994). *Achilles in Vietnam: Combat trauma and the undoing of character*. New York: Atheneum.

Shay, J. (2002). *Odysseus in America: Combat trauma and the trials of homecoming*. New York: Scribner.

Simms, L. J., Watson, D., & Doebbeling, B. N. (2002). Confirmatory factor analyses of posttraumatic stress symptoms in deployed and non-deployed veterans of the Gulf war. *Journal of Abnormal Psychology, 111*, 637–647.

Slade, T., & Watson, D. (2006). The structure of common DSM–IV and ICD-10 mental disorders in the Australian general population. *Psychological Medicine, 36*, 1593–1600.

Smit, J., van den Berg, C. E., Bekker, L.G., Seedat, S., & Stein, D. J. (2006). Translation and cross-cultural adaptation of a mental health battery in an African setting. *African Health Sciences, 6*, 215–222.

Sochting, I., Corrado, R., Cohen, I. M., Ley, R. G., & Brasfield, C. (2007). Traumatic pasts in Canadian Aboriginal people: Further support for a complex trauma conceptualization? *BC Medical Journal, 49*, 320–326.

Solomon, Z., & Mikulincer, M. (2006). Trajectories of PTSD: A 20-year longitudinal study. *American Journal of Psychiatry, 163*, 659–666.

Stein, M. B., Walker, J. R., Hazen, A. L., Forde, D. R. (1997). Full and partial posttraumatic stress disorder: Findings from a community survey. *American Journal of Psychiatry, 154*, 1114–1119.

Summerfield, D.A. (2004). Cross-cultural perspectives on the medicalization of human suffering. In G. M. Rosen (Ed.) *Posttraumatic stress disorder: Issues and controversies* (pp. 233–245). West Sussex, England: Wiley.

Tarquinio, C., Tarquinio, P., & Costantini, M. L. (2003). Sentiment d'effroi, ESPT et alteration du Soi chez des victimes de hold-up. [Fright reaction, PTSD and self concept among employees victims of a hold-up.]. *Revue Francophone due Stress et du Trauma, 3,* 99–109.

Taylor, S., & Koch, W. J. (1995). Anxiety disorders due to motor vehicle accidents: Nature and treatment. *Clinical Psychology Review, 15,* 721–738.

Taylor, S., Kuch, K., Koch, W. J., Crockett, D. J., & Passey, G. (1998). The structure of posttraumatic stress symptoms. *Journal of Abnormal Psychology, 107,* 154–160.

Thapa, S. B., & Hauff, E. (2005). Psychological distress among displaced persons during an armed conflict in Nepal. *Social Psychiatry and Psychiatric Epidemiology, 40,* 672–679.

Thorp, S. R., & Stein, M. B. (2005). Posttraumatic stress disorder and functioning. *PTSD Research Quarterly, 16,* 1–7.

Vaiva, G., Brunet, A., Lebigot, F. Boss, V., Ducrocq, F., Devos, P. et al. (2003). Fright (Effroi) and other peritraumatic responses after a serious motor vehicle accident: prospective influence on acute PTSD development. *Canadian Journal of Psychiatry, 48,* 395–401.

van der Kolk, B. A. (2007). The history of trauma in psychiatry. In M.J. Friedman, T.M. Keane, & T.A. Resick (Eds.). *Handbook of PTSD: Science and practice* (pp. 19–35). New York: Guilford Press.

van der Kolk, B. A., Roth, S., Pelcovitz, D., Sunday, S., & Spinazzola, J. (2005). Disorders of Extreme Stress: The empirical foundation of a complex adaptation to trauma. *Journal of Traumatic Stress, 18,* 389–399.

Vermetten, E., & Bremner, J. D. (2002). Circuits and systems in stress. II. Applications to neurobiology and treatment in posttraumatic stress disorder. *Depression & Anxiety, 16,* 14–38.

Watson, D. (2005). Rethinking the mood and anxiety disorders: A quantitative hierarchical model for DSM-V. *Journal of Abnormal Psychology, 114,* 522–536.

Weathers, F. W., & Keane, T. M. (2007). The Criterion A problem revisited: Controversies and challenges in defining and measuring psychological trauma. *Journal of Traumatic Stress, 20(2),* 107–121.

Weiss, D. S., Marmar, C. R., Schlenger, W. E., Fairbank, J. A., Jordan, K. B., Hough, R. L., et al. (1992). The prevalence of lifetime and partial post-traumatic stress disorder in Vietnam theater veterans. *Journal of Traumatic Stress, 5,* 365–376.

Woodward, S. H., Kaloupek, D. G., Streeter, C. C., Martinez, C., Schaer, M., & Eliez, S. (2006). Decreased anterior cingulate volume in combat-related PTSD. *Biological Psychiatry, 59,* 582–587.

Wolfe, J., Erickson, D. J., Sharkansky, E. J., King, D. W., & King, L. A. (1999). Course and predictors of posttraumatic stress disorder among Gulf War veterans: A prospective analysis. *Journal of Consulting and Clinical Psychology, 67,* 520–528.

Zlotnick, C., Rodriguez, B. F., Weisberg, R. B., Bruc, S. E., Spencer, M. A., Culpepper, L., et al. (2004). Chronicity in posttraumatic stress disorder and predictors of the course of posttraumatic stress disorder among primary care patients. *Journal of Nervous and Mental Disease, 192,* 153–159.

Zucker, M., Spinazzola, J., Blaustein, M., & van der Kolk, B. A. (2006). Dissociative symptomatology in posttraumatic stress disorder and disorders of extreme stress. *Journal of Trauma & Dissociation, 7,* 19–31.

16

Social Anxiety Disorder and the *DSM-V*

Stefan G. Hofmann
J. Anthony Richey
Alison Sawyer
Anu Asnaani
Winfried Rief

Social anxiety disorder (social phobia) dates back only to 1966 when Marks and Gelder (1966) described an emotional state of anxiety when subjected to scrutiny by others while performing a specific task. Today, social anxiety disorder (SAD) is a recognized and frequently diagnosed psychiatric condition. The diagnosis can be assigned at any age, but is most often first given in the midteens, with the core feature being the fear of negative evaluations by others. Situations that can cue social anxiety include performing, speaking, eating, or writing in public, initiating or maintaining conversations, going to parties, dating, meeting strangers, or interacting with authority figures. Public speaking is the most commonly feared social situation (e.g., Pollard & Henderson, 1988). During childhood, SAD is frequently associated with shyness, behavioral inhibition, overanxious disorder, mutism, school refusal, and separation anxiety. The problem is chronic and persistent, and it leads to substantial impairments in social and vocational functioning.

The objective of this chapter is to critically examine the current *Diagnostic and Statistical Manual of Mental Disorders, Fourth Edition* (*DSM-IV*) criteria for SAD, examine the nature and expression of individuals assigned a diagnosis of SAD, and to discuss a possible classification system that may serve as an organizational framework for the various facets and complexities of this disorder for the *DSM-V*. During the first part of this review, we will discuss the diagnostic subtypes of SAD and explore the differences between them. In the second part, we will examine the heterogeneity of SAD with regard to empirically and theoretically derived dimensions. These dimensions include fearfulness, anxiousness, shyness, self-perception, submissiveness, and anger. We will explore how these dimensions may function as a framework for classifying SAD in a way that captures the heterogeneous nature of the disorder more adequately than the current *DSM-IV* subtyping system (see Hofmann, Heimrichs, & Moscovitch, 2004, for a more detailed discussion).

History of *DSM*–SAD Diagnosis

SAD was first officially recognized with the publication of the *DSM-III* (American Psychiatric Association [APA], 1980). The essential feature of SAD was then defined as a persistent, irrational fear of, and compelling desire to avoid, situations in which the individual may be exposed to scrutiny by others. There is also fear that the individual may behave in a manner that will be humiliating or embarrassing (p. 227). The disorder was conceptualized as a form of specific phobia. The *DSM-III* stated that both social and simple phobias generally involve a circumscribed stimulus. When more than one type is present, multiple diagnoses should be made. (p. 225). The *DSM-III* did not acknowledge the fact that most individuals with SAD fear multiple social situations, and stated that generally, an individual has only one social phobia (p. 227). Moreover, the diagnosis of SAD was ruled out if the individual met diagnostic criteria for avoidant personality disorder

(APD). The essential feature of this Axis II disorder was defined as a hypersensitivity to potential rejection, humiliation, or shame; an unwillingness to enter into relationships unless given unusually strong guarantees of uncritical acceptance; social withdrawal in spite of desire for affection and acceptance; and low self-esteem (p. 323).

These diagnostic criteria underwent substantial changes in the *DSM-III-R* (APA, 1987). The disorder was then defined as a persistent fear of one or more situations (the social phobic situations) in which the person is exposed to possible scrutiny by others and fears that he or she may do something or act in a way that will be humiliating or embarrassing (p. 241). This new edition introduced the *generalized subtype* specifier if the person feared "most or all" social situations (p. 417). Furthermore, SAD was no longer ruled out if the criteria for APD were met.

Finally, the *DSM-IV* (APA, 1994) defined SAD as a marked and persistent fear of social or performance situation in which embarrassment may occur (p. 411). The *DSM-IV* noted that the anxiety response may take the form of a situationally bound or situationally predisposed panic attack. The diagnostic criteria for APD were further changed. Six of the seven diagnostic criteria for APD now refer to social interactional situations, and one of the nonsocial-specific criteria for APD was removed in the transition from *DSM-III-R* to *DSM-IV* (APA, 1994). Because of the high overlap between the two diagnoses, many researchers have questioned the utility of maintaining two diagnostic categories on two separate *DSM-IV* Axes (e.g., Reich, 2001; Schneier, Spitzer, Gibbon, Fyer, & Liebowitz, 1991; Tilfors, Furmark, Ekselius, & Fredrikson, 2001).

Definitions of *DSM-IV* Subtypes

The *DSM-IV* instructs clinicians to assign a generalized subtype of SAD when the (individual's) fears are related to most social situations (APA, 1994, p. 451). However, the *DSM* does not specify the number and type of social situations that comprise the generalized subtype. As a result, different research groups have developed slightly different operational definitions for the generalized subtype and the residual subgroup (see Hofmann et al., 2004, for a review).

The *DSM* subtypes are defined based on the number of feared social situations. Therefore, it is important to explore the nature of the feared social situations in more detail and to examine whether the diagnostic subtypes correspond to empirical groups that are formed based on the nature or number of feared social situation.

When working with SAD patients, it soon becomes apparent that there is a considerable degree of variance among individuals in the number and type of feared social situations, as well as in a number of other features, which will be discussed in more details below. As mentioned earlier, the most commonly feared social situation is public speaking. Other feared performance situations include eating, writing, or urinating in public, while commonly feared social situations include initiating or maintaining conversations, going to parties, dating, and meeting strangers. These situations can be reliably measured with the 24-item Liebowitz Social Anxiety Scale (LSAS; Liebowitz, 1987). Some investigators have attempted to quantify the number and type of feared social situations on the basis of items of the LSAS. For example, Holt, Heimberg, Hope, and Liebowitz (1992) proposed four different situational domains based on their inspection of the LSAS: (a) formal speaking or interaction, (b) informal speaking or interaction, (c) assertive interaction, and (d) observation by others. Factor analytic techniques, however, provided mixed support for this classification (Baker, Heinrichs, Kim, & Hofmann, 2002; Safren et al., 1999). Other investigators have employed latent class analysis (Kessler, Stein, & Berglund, 1998) and cluster analysis (Eng, Heimberg, Coles, Schneier, & Liebowitz, 2000) to examine the situational subtypes of SAD. The results of the latent class analysis showed that one-third of the individuals with SAD reported speaking fears only, while the other two-thirds had speaking fears with at least one other social fear.

Although these statistical procedures are useful for identifying groups of participants who have similar fears in common (as in the case of cluster analysis), or for identifying underlying dimensions of feared social situations (as in the case of latent class analysis), there are also some limitations. As pointed out by Meehl (1992), these techniques cannot be used to identify qualitative subgroups of individuals. Therefore, they are ill-suited to study the taxonic structure of SAD. More specifically, several assumptions must be made for these analyses to yield goodness-of-fit statistics (e.g., the same latent distributions within classes and independence between indicators within classes). Because these assumptions constitute auxiliary hypotheses in the test of a taxonic conjecture, rejection of a particular taxonic conjecture may, therefore, be the result of deviations from these assumptions rather than from the hypothesized taxonic structure per se. Moreover, goodness-of-fit tests in latent class analysis are designed to be sensitive to assumption departures, rather than robust. Therefore, most cluster algorithms always uncover clusters, even if the latent structure is dimensional (e.g., Meehl & Yonce, 1996).

To our knowledge, only one study has examined the latent structure of SAD (Kollman, Brown, Liverant, & Hofmann, 2006). This study performed three taxometric procedures as described by Meehl (1992) based on a large sample of patients (N = 2,035) with anxiety and mood disorder. To adequately represent the range of situations that are typically associated with SAD, indicators were constructed from dimensional clinical interview ratings of fear of social situations and questionnaire measures of social anxiety symptoms. These indicators represented the experience of social anxiety in situations that involve assertiveness, authority interaction, dating, public speaking, and social interaction. The results supported the notion that the latent structure of SAD is dimensional, as defined by the chosen indicators. However, the results of these analyses depend on the indicator set that is selected for the analyses. Other indicators may very well suggest a taxonic structure. Some of these possible, theoretically derived indicators will be discussed further below.

Differences Between Diagnostic Subtypes

Studies have found that the generalized subtype of SAD and APD are both associated with high levels of social anxiety, poor overall psychosocial functioning, greater overall psychopathology, high trait anxiety, and depression (e.g., Boone et al., 1999; Brown, Heimberg, & Juster, 1995; Herbert, Hope, & Bellack, 1992; Hofmann et al., 2004; Holt, et al., 1992; Tran & Chambless, 1995; Turner, Beidel, & Townsley, 1992). Therefore, it has been suggested that these diagnoses may simply represent increasingly more severe manifestations of social anxiety, which range on a continuum from specific (non-generalized) subtype of SAD, to generalized SAD without APD, to generalized SAD with APD (McNeil, 2001). In contrast, other studies suggest that not all differences in these diagnostic groupings can be easily explained by differences in social anxiety severity (see Hofmann et al., 2004, for a review). Empirical studies on the difference between diagnostic subtypes in several important variables, including prevalence, demographics, clinical severity, developmental characteristics, psychophysiological response during exposure, and treatment response report mixed findings (Alden & Capreol, 1993; Brown et al., 1995; Dreessen & Arntz, 1998; Feske, Perry, Chambless, Renneberg, & Goldstein, 1996; Heimberg, Hope, Dodge, & Becker, 1990; Herbert et al., 1992; Hofmann & Bitran, 2007; Hofmann, Newman, Becker, Taylor, & Roth, 1995; Hofmann & Roth, 1996; Holt et al., 1992; Hope, Herbert, & White, 1995; Mersch, Jansen, & Arntz, 1995; Van Velzen, Emmelkamp, & Scholing, 1997; Levin et al., 1993; Mannuzza et al., 1995; McNeil et al., 1995; Stein & Chavira, 1998; Stemberger, Turner, Beidel, & Calhoun, 1995; Turner et al., 1992). In sum, the findings suggest that non-generalized SAD, generalized SAD, and APD are different on a dimensional, rather than categorical level (Hofmann et al., 2004; Hook & Valentiner, 2002). The following section of this review will discuss a dimensional classification system of SAD.

Dimensions of SAD

Theoretical Foundation

We will review next the clinical, developmental, personality, and social literature on social anxiety in an attempt to account for the heterogeneity among individuals diagnosed with SAD. Emotion theorists distinguish between *fear* and *anxiety*. Fear is a primitive alarm response to present danger that is characterized by strong arousal and action tendencies, whereas anxiety is an anticipatory emotional response that is characterized by perceptions of unpredictability and uncontrollability over potentially aversive events. We believe that the fear–anxiety distinction is a useful dimension for individuals with SAD. Other SAD dimensions include *shyness, self-perception, submissiveness,* and *anger*. Below we present preliminary evidence for fearfulness, anxiousness, shyness, self-consciousness, submissiveness, and anger as dimensions of SAD.

Fearfulness

In the context of Barlow's (2002) anxiety model, *fearful* individuals with SAD are likely to develop SAD via "true" or "false" alarms (i.e., uncued or situationally bound panic attacks) in social situations, depending on the contribution of specific types of biological risk factors. This manifestation of SAD is associated with high anxiety sensitivity (which refers to the tendency to respond fearfully to symptoms of anxiety) and heightened reactivity to social stress (e.g., Hofmann & Barlow, 2002; McNeil, Vrana, Melamed, Cuthbert, & Lang, 1993). The prediction of Barlow's model is consistent with the observation that a significant number of individuals with SAD attribute their fear of public speaking to "panic attacks" (Hofmann et al., 1995). Although concern about having panic attacks was very common, only few patients met the diagnostic criteria for panic disorder. Consistent with this notion is the idea of a *physiological subtype* of SAD (Öst, Jerremalm, & Johannson, 1980). Individuals with this subtype showed stronger physiological than cognitive or behavioral reactions to a challenging social task than others.

Anxiousness

In contrast to fear, anxiety is a multidimensional, anticipatory, and cognitively mediated response that does not follow the general pattern of a basic emotional reaction (e.g., Barlow, 2002). Because of its anticipatory nature, anxiety is often seen as closely related with worrying. Worrying involves primarily verbal thought processes that are characterized by negative valence and reduced concreteness (Borkovec & Inz, 1990). It has been suggested that some individuals with anxiety disorders use this strategy for abstraction and disengagement to decrease sympathetic arousal in response to aversive material (e.g., Borkovec & Roemer, 1995). Research suggests that the verbal system is less closely connected to the affective, physiological, and behavioral systems than images are, and might, therefore, be a poor vehicle for processing emotional information (Borkovec, Ray, & Stöber, 1998) and solving problems (Davey, Jubb, & Cameron, 1996; Stöber, 1998). Thus, some theorists assume that worrying functions as a cognitive avoidance strategy that leads to the suppression, or inhibition, of psychophysiological response (Borkovec et al., 1998).

Evidence for this inhibitory effect of worrying on cardiovascular activity comes from a study by Borkovec and Hu (1990). In this study, a group of undergraduate speech anxious students, while being measured for changes in heart rate response from baseline, were instructed to engage in relaxed, neutral, or worrisome thinking just prior to visualizing a public speaking situation. Participants in the worry group displayed less heart rate response than those in the neutral condition, who showed less response than those who engaged in relaxation prior to the phobic imagery. Moreover, the groups differed in their self-reported anxiety ratings during the phobic imagery. Participants who engaged in worrying reported greater anxiety than those in the neutral condition, whereas the relaxed group's anxiety was near the level of the worry group and not significantly different from either of the other two groups. More recent studies using clinical samples further suggest that worry induction may reduce vasovagal tone in patients with generalized anxiety disorder (Thayer, Friedman, & Borkovec, 1996).

Similar findings have also been reported in subgroups of SAD individuals who were exposed to a public speaking situation (Hofmann et al., 1995). In this study, individuals with SAD and APD (who are assumed to show more of an anxiety than a fear response; Hofmann & Barlow, 2002) reported greater distress and worrisome cognitions, but lower cardiac response, than SAD individuals without APD during a public speaking challenge test. These findings seem to suggest that some individuals with SAD (those with a generalized subtype) are more likely to exhibit an anxiety response to social threat, whereas others are more likely to respond with fear and panic. This hypothesis was tested more directly in a study conducted by McNeil et al. (1993). This study suggested that only the *fearful* group showed a significant covariation among physiological responses, imagery vividness, and severity of phobic disorders. Fearful participants showed increased autonomic arousal to phobic imagery as imagery vividness increased.

Shyness

Shyness is one of the most heritable temperament characteristics and is closely associated with social anxiety and SAD. Childhood shyness has been extensively studied as behavioral inhibition by Kagan and his colleagues (e.g., Kagan, 2001). Behavioral inhibition refers to the child's fearfulness, timidity, and weariness when encountering novel people, objects, or events. Kagan (1994) posits that the activation threshold of these brain structures, and specifically the amygdala, to unfamiliarity or challenge is tonically lower in inhibited than in uninhibited children. In support of this hypothesis, Schwartz, Snidman and Kagan (1999) followed children through their first 13 years and found that 61% of children who were inhibited during infancy developed symptoms of social anxiety compared with only 21% of children who were uninhibited infants. Behaviorally inhibited and uninhibited individuals appear to form two qualitatively different subgroups (Woodward, Lenzenweger, Kagan, Snidman, & Arcus, 2000).

In contrast to childhood shyness, shyness in adulthood is less well researched. With the exception of some more recent studies (Chavira, Stein, & Malcarne, 2002; Heiser, Turner & Beidel, 2003; Hofmann & Bitran, 2007), the relationship between SAD, shyness, and related constructs has been largely unexplored. Chavira et al. (2002) showed that 49% of individuals in the highly shy group met diagnostic criteria for SAD, compared with only 18% of individuals in the normative shy group. The highly shy group was also more likely to meet criteria for generalized SAD (36% vs. 4%) and APD (14% vs. 4%). Heiser et al. (2003) conducted a similar study using a much smaller sample and reported similar results. These findings suggest that behavioral inhibition and childhood shyness are related to social anxiety disorder in adulthood. It is further possible that sensory processing sensitivity is the underling risk factors for behavioral inhibition, shyness, and SAD. This temperamental construct is conceptualized as a unidimensional personality trait that manifests itself in the form of avoidance of overstimulation (Aron & Aron, 1997). It is assumed that sensory processing sensitivity is a heritable vulnerability factor to develop shyness under certain environmental conditions. Partially consistent with this notion are recent results suggesting that this trait is uniquely associated with the generalized subtype of SAD (Hofmann & Bitran, 2007). This study further showed that sensory processing sensitivity is separate from social anxiety, but it is highly correlated with harm avoidance and agoraphobic avoidance.

Self-perception

Self-perception is an important maintaining factor of SAD (e.g., Clark, 2001; Hofmann, 2007; Leary, 2001; Rapee & Heimberg, 1997; Mansell & Clark, 1999). The cognitive model assumes that, when confronted with social threat, socially anxious individuals shift their attention inward and engage in a process of detailed monitoring and observation of themselves. Consistent with this model, research has shown that individuals with SAD focus their attention toward themselves when confronted with stressful social situations (Chen, Ehlers, Clark, & Mansell, 2002; Heinrichs & Hofmann, 2001; Mansell, Clark, Ehlers, & Chen, 1999). Other studies suggest that self-focused attention impairs performance in individuals in social-evaluative situations (e.g., Bögels, Rijsemus, & de Jong, 2002), possibly because focusing on the self expends important attentional resources necessary for optimal task performance (Ingram, 1990). Clinical studies suggest that under conditions of high self-focused attention, individuals with SAD experience spontaneous, recurrent, and excessively negative self-images, which they believe to be accurate at the time they occur (Hackmann, Clark, & McManus, 2000). These negative self-images are causally related to social anxiety (Hirsch, Clark, Mathews, & Williams, 2003). Moreover, individuals with SAD report fewer negative self-statements as a result of therapy (Hofmann, 2000; Hofmann, Moscovitch, Kim, & Taylor, 2004) and report less anxiety and negative beliefs when instructed to focus their attention on aspects of the external environment rather than on themselves (Wells & Papageorgiou, 1998).

In summary, these studies suggest that negative self-perception is an important maintaining variable of SAD. In addition, there is a large body of literature on individual differences in self-consciousness, which is closely associated with the term "self-monitoring" (for a review, see Gangestad & Snyder, 2000). This construct is related to measures of self-esteem, social anxiety, shyness, and sociability (Hofmann, 2006; Wolf, Lennox, & Cutler, 1986).

Submissiveness

Humans have a basic need to maintain their membership and status in their social groups (e.g., Barkow, 1989; Baumeister & Tice, 1990). To maintain this status, the individual displays behaviors, including submissive behaviors, which decrease the likelihood of rejection from the social group (Gilbert, 2001; Hofmann, Moscovitch, & Heinrichs, 2002). For example, blushing and other signs of embarrassment have been viewed as involuntary remedial displays that occur when the individual's standing in a social hierarchy is threatened (Walters & Hope, 1998; Trower & Gilbert, 1989). The literature suggests that many individuals with SAD display more submissive behaviors during social interactions than nonsocially anxious individuals. These behaviors vary in nature, degree, and number, and appear to reflect important within-group differences (Gilbert, 2001; Walters & Hope, 1998). Some theorists conceptualize these submissive behaviors as safety and avoidance behaviors. Similar to other avoidance strategies, such behaviors probably contribute to the maintenance of the disorder (Wells et al., 1995).

Anger

Some individuals with SAD show behavioral tendencies in social situations that can be described as angry and hostile, rather than submissive. Although research examining the link between anger and social anxiety is relatively scant, the literature suggests that anger may arise in vulnerable individuals under conditions that threaten their sense of self-worth (Edmondson & Conger, 1996). Anger has been closely linked to social anxiety in early theories. For example, Novaco (1976) posited that an anger outburst may serve the perceived function of bolstering one's public self-image by channeling feelings of anxiety, insecurity, and vulnerability into a more "socially acceptable" presentation of self, thereby increasing one's sense of personal control. Anger outbursts are more likely to occur among individuals who lack assertiveness skills in social situations (Allan & Gilbert, 2002; Novaco, 1976), a premise that underscores the rationale for including social skills training in therapy for anger management problems (see Edmondson & Conger, 1996). Erwin, Heimberg, Schneier, and Liebowitz (2003) reported that individuals with SAD exhibited greater anger and poorer anger expression skills than nonanxious control participants. The analyses further examined attrition and response to cognitive-behavioral group therapy in a subset of patients treated for SAD. The results showed that patients were less likely to complete a 12-session course of therapy if they experienced anger frequently, perceived unfair treatment, and were quick tempered. Treatment completers showed significant reductions in the experience of anger to perceived negative evaluation. Furthermore, individuals who suppressed anger responded less favorably to the intervention.

Some researchers have argued that the link between social anxiety, aggression, and anger may occur through the experience of shame (Gilbert & Miles, 2000). Socially anxious individuals may chronically fear both *feeling* ashamed and *being* shamed, leading to feelings of "brooding resentment" and anger as a result. Tangey, Wagner, Fletcher, and Gramzow (1992) examined shame and anger in a correlational study in which undergraduate students completed various self-report questionnaires. They found that experiencing shame was strongly correlated with becoming angry and externalizing blame for negative events. Moreover, the experience of shame was associated with a tendency to express anger and hostility in an indirect rather than straightforward manner (Tangney et al., 1992).

Empirical evidence in support of anger and dominance as an independent factor that is distinctive of some individuals with SAD comes from a study by Kachin, Newman, and Pincus (2001). These authors used a modified version of the Inventory of Interpersonal Problems (IIP; Horowitz, Rosenberg, Baer, Ureno, & Villansenor, 1988) to assess the prevailing interpersonal styles of individuals with SAD (Interpersonal Problems Circumplex Scales [IIP-C]; Alden, Wiggins, & Pincus, 1990). A cluster analysis of the IIP-C revealed two distinct subtypes with discriminating core interpersonal features. One cluster was characterized by anger, hostility, and mistrustfulness, whereas the other was characterized by difficulties with unassertiveness, exploitability (i.e., susceptibility to coercion and inability to express anger), and overnurturance. The two subtypes were labeled "hostile dominant" and "overly friendly submissive." This study also demonstrated that generalized SAD was associated with more severe interpersonal problems, but did not differentiate the two clusters in any other meaningful way.

In sum, there is preliminary support for the notion that anger and anger expression is an important dimension that distinguishes individuals with SAD. An important area for future research is to examine the nature of the anger expression in more detail (i.e., anger focus, and the variables that moderate and mediate its expression).

Summary and Discussion

Individuals with SAD fear a wide range of social situations. Some individuals fear a large number of different types of situations, whereas others fear some or only a few social situations. The *DSM-IV* includes a generalized subtype specifier based on the number of feared situations and also permits the comorbid diagnosis of APD. Because the generalized subtype of SAD is defined as "most or all social situations," researchers were left to devise their own definitional criteria, which probably contributed to the inconsistencies found in the literature. As a result, it is difficult to compare results across different studies.

Given that APD and generalized subtype of SAD are highly overlapping constructs, there may be an unnecessary redundancy in the *DSM*. In fact, there is little empirical support for retaining both diagnoses as separate clinical entities on two separate Axes. Because of the large degree of overlap between APD and the generalized subtype of SAD and the lack of any notable differences between the two constructs, we suggest that APD should be eliminated from the diagnostic system.

To develop an alternative and heuristically more useful classification system for SAD subtypes, we reviewed the clinical, developmental, personality, and social psychological literature. Instead of a categorical typology, we propose a dimensional classification system based on the individual's emotional response and behavioral tendencies. A dimensional system is more compatible with the existing empirical literature and less restrictive than a categorical system. We identified anxiousness, fearfulness, shyness, self-perception, submissiveness, and anger as possible dimensions.

Our review suggests that the *DSM-IV* category *social anxiety disorder* refers to a heterogeneous group of individuals that may differ in several dimensions, including fearfulness, anxiousness, shyness, self-perception, submissiveness, and anger. Future research is needed to further isolate the characteristics that distinguish individuals in their expression of SAD, and to determine whether individuals with SAD differ in kind or degree. From our perspective, a dimensional approach to classifying intrapersonal and interpersonal characteristics of individuals with SAD seems to be more clinically useful as well. An assessment of the idiosyncratic manifestation of these characteristics in patients with SAD (rather than simply assigning the specifier of generalized or nongeneralized) would provide valuable information for therapists that may help to optimize treatment success.

References

Aron, E. N., & Aron, A. (1997). Sensory-processing sensitivity and its relation to introversion and emotionality. *Journal of Personality and Social Psychology, 73,* 345–368.

Alden, L. E., & Capreol, M. J. (1993). Avoidant personality disorder: Interpersonal problems as predictors of treatment response. *Behavior Therapy, 24,* 357–376.

Alden, L. E., Wiggins, J. S., & Pincus, A. L. (1990). Construction of circumplex scales for the inventory of interpersonal problems. *Journal of Personality Assessment, 55,* 521–536.

Allan, S., & Gilbert, P. (2002). Anger and anger expression in relation to perceptions of social rank, entrapment and depressive symptoms. *Personality and Individual Differences, 32,* 551–565.

American Psychiatric Association (1980). *Diagnostic and statistical manual for mental disorders* (3rd ed.). Washington, DC: Author.

American Psychiatric Association (1987). *Diagnostic and statistical manual for mental disorders* (3rd ed. Revised). Washington, DC: Author.

American Psychiatric Association (1994). *Diagnostic and statistical manual for mental disorders*. (4th ed.). Washington, DC: Author.

Baker, S. L., Heinrichs, N., Kim, H. J., Hofmann, S. G. (2002). The Liebowitz Social Anxiety Scale as a self-report instrument: A preliminary psychometric analysis. *Behaviour Research and Therapy, 40,* 701–715.

Barkow, J. H. (1989). *Darwin, Sex, and Status: Biological Approaches to Mind and Culture.* Toronto: University of Toronto Press.

Barlow, D. H. (2002). *Anxiety and Its Disorders* (2nd ed.). New York: Guilford Press.

Baumeister, R. E., & Tice, D. (1990). Anxiety and social exclusion. *Journal of Social and Clinical Psychology, 9,* 165–195.

Boone, M. L., McNeil, D. W., Masia, C. L., Turk, C. L., Carter, L. E., Ries, B. J., et al. (1999). Multimodal comparisons of social phobia subtypes and avoidant personality disorder. *Journal of Anxiety Disorders, 13,* 271–292.

Brown, E. J., Heimberg, R. G., & Juster, H. R. (1995). Social phobia subtype and avoidant personality disorder: effect on severity of social phobia, impairment, and outcome of cognitive behavioral treatment. *Behavior Therapy, 26,* 467–489.

Bögels, S. M., Rijsemus, W., & de Jong, P. J. (2002). Self-focused attention and social anxiety: The effects of experimentally heightened self-awareness on fear, blushing, cognitions, and social skills. *Cognitive Therapy and Research, 26,* 461–472.

Borkovec, T. D., & Hu, S. (1990). The effect of worry on cardiovascular response to phobic imagery. *Behaviour Research and Therapy, 28,* 69–73.

Borkovec, T. D., & Inz, J. (1990). The nature of worry in generalized anxiety disorder: A predominance of thought activity. *Behaviour Research and Therapy, 28,* 153–158.

Borkovec, T. D., Ray, W. J., & Stöber, J. (1998). Worry: A cognitive phenomenon intimately linked to affective, physiological, and interpersonal behavioral processes. *Cognitive Therapy and Research, 22,* 561–576.

Borkovec, T. D., & Roemer, L. (1995). Perceived functions of worry among generalized anxiety disorder subjects: Distraction from more emotionally distressing topics? *Journal of Behavior Therapy and Experimental Psychiatry, 26,* 25–30.

Chavira, D. A., Stein, M. B., & Malcarne, V. L. (2002). Scrutinizing the relationship between shyness and social phobia. *Journal of Anxiety Disorders, 16,* 585–598.

Chen, Y. P., Ehlers, A., Clark, D. M., & Mansell, W. (2002). Patients with generalized social phobia direct their attention away from faces. *Behaviour Research and Therapy, 40,* 677–687.

Clark, D. M. (2001). A cognitive perspective on social phobia. In W. R. Crozier, & L. E. Alden (Eds.), *International handbook of social anxiety: Concepts, research, and interventions relating to the self and shyness.* (pp. 405–430). New York: John Wiley & Sons.

Davey, G. C. L., Jubb, M., & Cameron, C. (1996). Catastrophic worrying as a function of changes in problem-solving confidence. *Cognitive Therapy and Research, 20,* 333–344.

Dreessen, L., & Arntz, A. (1998). The impact of personality disorders on treatment outcome of anxiety disorders: Best-evidence synthesis. *Behaviour Research and Therapy, 36,* 483–504.

Edmondson, C. B., & Conger, J. C. (1996). A review of treatment efficacy for individuals with anger problems: Conceptual, assessment, and methodological issues. *Clinical Psychology Review, 16,* 251–275.

Eng, W., Heimberg, R. G., Coles, M. E., Schneier, F. R., & Liebowitz, M. R. (2000). An empirical approach to subtype identification in individuals with social phobia. *Psychological Medicine, 30,* 1345–1357.

Erwin, B. A., Heimberg, R. G., Schneier, F. R., & Liebowitz, M. R. (2003). Anger experience and expression in social anxiety disorder. *Behavior Therapy, 34,* 331–350.

Feske, U., Perry, K. J., Chambless, D. L., Renneberg, B., & Goldstein, A. J. (1996). Avoidant personality disorder as predictor for severity and treatment outcome among generalized social phobics. *Journal of Personality Disorder, 10,* 174–184.

Gangestad, S. W., & Snyder, M. (2000). Self-monitoring: Appraisal and reappraisal. *Psychological Bulleting, 126,* 530–555.

Gilbert, P. (2001). Evolution and social anxiety: The role of attraction, social competition, and social hierarchies. *The Psychiatric Clinics of North America, 24,* 723–751.

Gilbert, P., & Miles, J. N. V. (2000). Sensitivity to social put-down: Its relationship to perceptions of social rank, shame, social anxiety, depression, anger, and self-other blame. *Personality and Individual Differences, 29,* 757–774.

Hackmann, A., Clark, D. M., & McManus, F. (2000). Recurrent images and early memories in social phobia. *Behaviour Research and Therapy, 38,* 601–610.

Heimberg, R. G., Hope, D. A., Dodge, C. S., & Becker, R. E. (1990). DSM-III-R subtypes of social phobia: Comparison of generalized social phobics and public speaking phobics. *The Journal of Nervous and Mental Disease, 176,* 172–179.

Heinrichs, N., & Hofmann, S. G. (2001). Information processing in social phobia: A critical review. *Clinical Psychology Review, 21,* 751–770.

Heiser, N. A., Turner, S. M., & Beidel, D. C. (2003). Shyness: relationship to social phobia and other psychiatric disorders. *Behaviour Research and Therapy, 41,* 209–221.

Hirsch, C. R., Clark, D. M., Mathews, A., Williams, R. (2003). Self-images play a causal role in social phobia. *Behaviour Research and Therapy, 41,* 909–921.

Herbert, J. D., Hope, D. A., & Bellack, A. S. (1992). Validity of the distinction between generalized social phobia and avoidant personality disorder. *Journal of Abnormal Psychology, 101,* 332–339.

Hofmann, S. G. (2000). Self-focused attention before and after treatment of social phobia. *Behaviour Research and Therapy,* 38, 717–725.

Hofmann, S. G. (2006). The emotional consequences of social pragmatism: The psychophysiological consequences of self-monitoring. *Biological Psychology, 73,* 169–173.

Hofmann, S. G. (2007). Cognitive factors that maintain social anxiety disorder: A comprehensive model and its treatment implications. *Cognitive Behaviour Therapy, 36,* 195–209

Hofmann, S. G., & Barlow, D. H. (2002). Social phobia (social anxiety disorder). In D. H. Barlow (Ed.), *Anxiety and its disorders: The nature and treatment of anxiety and panic,* (2nd ed., pp. 454–476). New York: Guilford Press.

Hofmann, S. G., & Bitran, S. (2007). Sensory-processing sensitivity in social anxiety disorder: Relationship to harm avoidance and diagnostic subtypes. *Journal of Anxiety Disorders, 21,* 944–954.

Hofmann, S. G., Ehlers, A., & Roth, W. T. (1995). Conditioning theory: A model for the etiology of public speaking anxiety? *Behaviour Research and Therapy, 33,* 567–571.

Hofmann, S. G., Heinrichs, N., & Moscovitch, D. A. (2004). The nature and expression of social phobia: Toward a new classification. *Clinical Psychology Review, 24,* 769–797.

Hofmann, S. G., Moscovitch, D. M., & Heinrichs, N. (2002). Evolutionary mechanisms of fear and anxiety. *Journal of Cognitive Psychotherapy, 16,* 317–330.

Hofmann, S. G., Moscovitch, D. A., Kim, H. J., & Taylor, A. N. (2004). Changes in self-perception during treatment of social phobia. *Journal of Consulting and Clinical Psychology, 72,* 588–596.

Hofmann, S. G., Newman, M. G., Ehlers, A., & Roth, W. T. (1995). Psychophysiological differences between subtypes of social phobia. *Journal of Abnormal Psychology, 104,* 224–231.

Hofmann, S. G., & Roth, W. T. (1996). Issues related to social anxiety among controls in social phobia research. *Behavior Therapy, 27,* 79–91.

Holt, C. S., Heimberg, R. G., & Hope, D. A. (1992). Avoidant personality disorder and the generalized subtype of social phobia. *Journal of Abnormal Psychology, 101,* 318–325.

Holt, C. S., Heimberg, R. G., Hope, D. A., & Liebowitz, M. R. (1992). Situational domains of social phobia. *Journal of Anxiety Disorders, 6,* 63–77.

Hook, J. N., & Valentiner, D. P. (2002). Are specific and generalized social phobias qualitatively distinct? *Clinical Psychology: Science and Practice, 9,* 379–395.

Hope, D. A., Herbert, J. D., & White, C. (1995). Diagnostic subtype, avoidant personality disorder, and efficacy of cognitive-behavioral group therapy for social phobia. *Cognitive Therapy and Research, 19,* 399–417.

Horowitz, L. M., Rosenberg, S. E., Baer, B. A., Ureno, G., & Villansenor, V. S. (1988). Inventory of interpersonal problems: Psychometric properties and clinical applications. *Journal of Consulting and Clinical Psychology, 56,* 885–892.

Ingram, R. E. (1990). Self-focused attention in clinical disorders: Review and a conceptual model. *Psychological Bulletin, 107,* 156–176.

Kachin, K. E., Newman, M. G., & Pincus, A. L. (2001). An interpersonal problem approach to the division of social phobia subtypes. *Behavior Therapy, 32,* 479–501.

Kagan, J. (1994). *Galen's prophecy.* New York: Basic books.

Kagan, J. (2001). Temperamental contributions to affective and behavioral profiles in childhood. In S. G. Hofmann & P. M. DiBartolo (Eds.), *From social anxiety to social phobia: Multiple perspectives* (pp. 216–234). Needham Heights, MA: Allyn & Bacon.

Kessler, R. C., Stein, M. B., & Berglund, P. (1998). Social phobia subtypes in the National Comorbidity Survey. *American Journal of Psychiatry, 155,* 613–619.

Kollman, D. M., Brown, T. A., Liverant, G. I., & Hofmann, S. G. (2006). A taxometric investigation of the latent structure of social anxiety disorder in outpatients with anxiety and mood disorders. *Depression and Anxiety, 23,* 190–199.

Leary, M. R. (2001). Social anxiety as an early warning system: A refinement and extension of the self-presentation theory of social anxiety (pp. 321–334). In S. G. Hofmannn & P. D. DiBartolo (Eds.), *From social anxiety to social phobia.* Needham Heights, MA: Allyn & Bacon.

Levin, A. P., Saoud, J. B., Strauman, T. J., Gorman, J. M., Fyer, A. J., Crawford, R., et al., (1993). Responses of "generalized" and "discrete" social phobics during public speaking. *Journal of Anxiety Disorders, 7,* 202–221.

Liebowitz, M. R. (1987). Social phobia. *Modern Problems in Pharmacopsychiatry, 22,* 141–173.

Mannuzza, S., Schneier, F. R., Chapman, T. F., Liebowitz, M. R., Klein, D. F., & Fyer, A. J. (1995). Generalized social phobia. Reliability and validity. *Archives of General Psychiatry, 52,* 230–237.

Mansell, W., & Clark, D. M. (1999). How do I appear to others? Social anxiety and processing of the observable self. *Behaviour Research and Therapy, 37,* 419–434.

Marks, I. M., & Gelder, M. G. (1966). Different ages of onset in varieties of phobias. *American Journal of Psychiatry, 123,* 218–221.

McNeil, D. W. (2001). Terminology and evolution of the constructs. In S. G. Hofmann & P. M. DiBartolo (Eds.), *From social anxiety to social phobia: Multiple perspectives* (pp. 8–19). Needham Heights, MA: Allyn & Bacon.

McNeil, D. W., Vrana, S. R., Melamed, B. G., Cuthbert, B. C., & Lang, P. (1993). Emotional imagery in simple and social phobia: Fear versus anxiety. *Journal of Abnormal Psychology, 102,* 212–225.

Meehl, P. E. (1992). Factors, taxa, traits, and types, differences of degree and differences in kind. *Journal of Personality, 60,* 117–174

Meehl, P. E., & Yonce, L. J. (1996). Taxometric analysis: II. Detecting taxonicity with two quantitative indicators in successive intervals of a third indicator (MAXCOV procedure). *Psychological Reports, 78,* 1091–1227.

Mersch, P. P. A., Jansen, M. A., & Arntz, A. (1995). Social phobia and personality disorder: Severity of complaint and treatment effectiveness. *Journal of Personality Disorders, 9,* 143–159.

Novaco, R. W. (1976). The functions and regulation of the arousal of anger. *American Journal of Psychiatry, 133,* 1124–1128.

Öst, L. G., Jerremalm, A., & Johansson, J. (1980). Individual response patterns and the effects of different behavioural methods in the treatment of social phobia. *Behaviour Research and Therapy, 19,* 1–16.

Pollard, C. A., & Henderson, J. G. (1988). Four types of social phobia in a community sample. *The Journal of Nervous and Mental Disease, 176,* 440–445.

Rapee, R. M., & Heimberg, R. G. (1997). A cognitive-behavioral model of anxiety in social phobia. *Behaviour Research and Therapy, 35,* 741–756.

Reich, J. (2001). The relationship of social phobia to avoidant personality disorder. In S. G. Hofmann, & P. M. DiBartolo (Eds.), *From social anxiety to social phobia: Multiple perspectives.* (pp. 148–161). Needham Heights, MA: Allyn & Bacon.

Safren, S. A., Heimberg, R. G., Horner, K. J., Juster, H. R., Schneier, F. R., & Liebowitz, M. R. (1999). Factor structure of social fears: The Liebowitz Social Anxiety Scale. *Journal of Anxiety Disorders, 13,* 253–270.

Schneier, F. R., Spitzer, R. L., Gibbon, M., Fyer, A. J., & Liebowitz, M. R. (1991). The relationship of social phobia subtypes and avoidant personality disorder. *Comprehensive Psychiatry, 32,* 496–502.

Schwartz, C. E., Snidman, N., & Kagan, J. (1999). Adolescent social anxiety as an outcome of inhibited behavior in childhood. *Journal of the American Academy of Child and Adolescent Psychiatry, 38,* 1008–1015.

Stein, M. B., & Chavira, D. A. (1998). Subtypes of social phobia and comorbidity with depression and other anxiety disorders. *Journal of Affective Disorders, 50,* S11–16.

Stemberger, R. T., Turner, S. M., Beidel, D. C., & Calhoun, K. S. (1995). Social phobia: An analysis of possible developmental factors. *Journal of Abnormal Psychology, 104,* 526–531.

Stöber, J. (1998). Worry, problem elaboration, and suppression of imagery: The role of concreteness. *Behaviour Research and Therapy, 36,* 751–756.

Tangney, J. P., Wagner, P., Fletcher, C., & Gramzow, R. (1992). Shamed into anger? The relation of shame and guilt to anger and self-reported aggression. *Journal of Personality and Social Psychology, 62,* 669–675.

Thayer, J. F., Friedman, B. H., & Borkovec, T. D. (1996). Autonomic characteristics of generalized anxiety disorder and worry. *Biological Psychiatry, 39,* 255–266.

Tillfors, M., Furmark, T., Ekselius, L., & Fredrikson, M. (2001). Social phobia and avoidant personality disorder as related to parental history of social anxiety: A general population study. *Behaviour Research and Therapy, 39,* 289–298.

Tran, G. Q., & Chambless, D. L. (1995). Psychopathology of social phobia: Effects of subtype and of avoidant personality disorder. *Journal of Anxiety Disorders, 9,* 489–501.

Trower, P., & Gilbert, P. (1989). New theoretical conceptions of social anxiety and social phobia. *Clinical Psychology Review, 9,* 19–35.

Turner, S. M., Beidel, D. C., & Townsley, R. M. (1992). Social phobia: A comparison of specific and generalized subtypes and avoidant personality disorder. *Journal of Abnormal Psychology, 101,* 326–331.

Van Velzen, C. J. M., Emmelkamp, P. M. G., & Scholing, A. (1997). The impact of personality disorders on behavioural treatment outcome for social phobia. *Behaviour Research and Therapy, 35,* 889–900.

Walters, K. S., & Hope, D. A. (1998). Analysis of social behavior in individuals with social phobia and nonanxious participants using a psychobiological model. *Behavior Therapy, 29,* 387–407.

Wells, A., Clark, D. M., Salkovskis, P., Ludgate, J., Hackmann, A., & Gelder, M. (1995). Social phobia: The role of in-situation safety behaviors in maintaining anxiety and negative beliefs. *Behavior Therapy, 26,* 153–161.

Wells, A., & Papageorgiou (1998). Social phobia: Effects of external attention on anxiety, negative beliefs, and perspective taking. *Behavior Therapy, 29,* 357–370.

Wolfe, R. N., Lennox, R. D., & Cutler, B. L. (1986). Getting along and getting ahead: Empirical support for a therapy of protective and acquisitive self-presentation. *Journal of Personality and Social Psychology, 50,* 356–361.

Woodward, S. A., Lenzenweger, M. F., Kagan, J., Snidman, N., & Arcus, D. (2000). Taxonic structure of infant reactivity: Evidence form a taxometric perspective. *Psychological Science, 11,* 296–301.

17

Classification of Hypochondriasis and Other Somatoform Disorders

Kelsey C. Collimore
Gordon J. G. Asmundson
Steven Taylor
Jonathan S. Abramowitz

Introduction

There is general dissatisfaction and growing debate regarding the conceptualization and classification of the somatoform disorders. Some researchers and clinicians believe that the category of somatoform disorders needs to be extensively revised (e.g., Kroenke, Sharpe, Sykes, 2007; Noyes, Stuart, & Watson, 2008) or perhaps even deleted altogether (e.g., Mayou, Kirmayer, Simon, Kroenke, & Sharpe, 2005) because they do not seem to form a coherent category (Mayou et al., 2005). The common feature of the various somatoform disorders described in the *Diagnostic and Statistical Manual of Mental Disorders, 4th edition, text revision* (*DSM-IV-TR*) (American Psychiatric Association [APA], 2000) is physical "symptoms" (i.e., bodily changes or sensations that the person finds distressing) in the absence of a general medical condition; however, many other diagnostic categories are characterized by such physical sensations (e.g., mood and anxiety disorders). The focus of this chapter is on those somatoform disorders within the current *DSM* classification that overlap with one or more of the anxiety disorders. We begin with a brief review of the history of the classification of somatoform disorders. We then discuss current approaches and alternatives for classifying hypochondriasis, body dysmorphic disorder (BDD), and pain disorder. We then conclude by offering suggestions regarding the reclassification of these disorders as well as a number of future directions to consider as we move toward *DSM-V*.

History of the Classification of Somatoform Disorders

The somatoform disorder classification first appeared as a speculative category in *DSM-III* (APA, 1980). However, hysteria—the precursor of somatization disorder—and hypochondriasis were recognized well before *DSM-III*. Indeed, the term hypochondria dates back to approximately 350 BC, with the first contemporary description of the condition appearing in the 1863 edition of Forbes Winslow's *Obscure Diseases of the Brain and Mind* (see Ladee, 1966). Early definitions of hysteria and hypochondriasis characterized both of these conditions as comprising several somatic and psychological symptoms, with the former related to a "wandering uterus" and the latter linked with anxiety about health status stemming from disturbances of the upper abdominal organs (e.g., Ladee, 1966; Noyes, Stuart, & Watson, 2008). Toward the end of the 19th century, Breuer and Freud hypothesized that psychological distress might result in a manifestation of physical or *conversion* symptoms (Breuer & Freud, 1956). Accordingly, conversion reaction was included in *DSM-I* (APA, 1952), and *neurotic* conditions characterized by somatic symptoms but not explained by a general medical condition, (i.e., hysterical and hypochondriacal neuroses) appeared in *DSM-II* (APA, 1968). Hypochondriacal neurosis was defined in *DSM-II* as a disorder dominated by preoccupation with the body and with fear of presumed diseases of various organs. . . [that] persist despite reassurance. . . [and for which] there are no actual losses or distortions of function (APA, 1968, p. 41).

As mentioned previously, the category of somatoform disorders was introduced in *DSM-III* (APA, 1980), with the core feature of these disorders being physical symptoms suggesting physical disorder (hence, somatoform), for which there are no demonstrable organic findings or known physiological mechanisms; and for which there is positive evidence, or a strong presumption, that the symptoms are linked to psychological factors or conflicts (APA, 1980, p. 241). Somatoform disorders included somatization disorder, conversion disorder, psychogenic pain disorder, hypochondriasis, and atypical somatoform disorder (APA, 1980). Somatization disorder was characterized by recurrent and multiple somatic symptoms (i.e., 14 symptom complaints for women and 12 for men) lasting for several years, whereas the other somatoform diagnoses included somatic symptoms but were otherwise a heterogeneous group of conditions.

In *DSM-III-R* (APA, 1987) and *DSM-IV/DSM-IV-TR* (APA, 1994, 2000), undifferentiated somatoform disorder (characterized by somatic symptoms that fall below the threshold of somatization disorder), BDD, and somatoform disorder, not otherwise specified, were added to the category. Revisions in *DSM-III*, *DSM-III-R*, and *DSM-IV* also included modifications to the criteria for somatization disorder, conversion disorder, psychogenic pain disorder (referred to as somatoform pain disorder in *DSM-III-R* and pain disorder in *DSM-IV* and *DSM-IV-TR*), and hypochondriasis. Table 17.1 illustrates the various changes throughout the history of the *DSM* as it pertains to the conditions currently classified as somatoform disorders. In the sections that follow, we focus on current debate regarding the classification of hypochondriasis, BDD, and pain disorder.

Hypochondriasis

Hypochondriasis, as defined in the *DSM-IV-TR*, is characterized primarily by severe health anxiety or, more specifically, by the preoccupation with fears and beliefs about having a serious disease based on misinterpretation of benign (i.e., harmless) bodily sensations (criterion A). The focus of concerns can range from highly specific bodily sensations or perturbations, such as dizziness and stomach pain to vague and diffuse complaints (e.g., bodily aching). Preoccupation with the bodily concerns must persist despite appropriate medical evaluation

17.1 Somatoform Disorders Categories from *DSM-III* to *DSM-IV-TR*

DSM-III	*DSM-III-R*	*DSM-IV/DSM-IV-TR*
• Somatization disorder • Conversion disorder (or hysterical neurosis, conversion type) • Psychogenic pain disorder • Hypochondriasis (or hypochondriacal neurosis) • Atypical somatoform disorder	• Somatization disorder • Undifferentiated somatoform disorder • Conversion disorder (or hysterical neurosis, conversion type) • Somatoform pain disorder • Hypochondriasis (or hypochondriacal neurosis) • Body dysmorphic disorder • Somatoform disorder not otherwise specified	• Somatization disorder • Undifferentiated somatoform disorder • Conversion disorder • Pain disorder • Hypochondriasis • Body dysmorphic disorder • Somatoform disorder not otherwise specified

and reassurance of good health (criterion B), and the disease-related beliefs cannot be of delusional intensity or restricted to concerns about defects in appearance (criterion C). The concerns must also cause significant distress or impairment in important areas of functioning (criterion D) and last at least 6 months (criterion E). It is very common for people with hypochondriasis to resist the idea that they are suffering from a mental disorder; although in their calmer moments they may be able to acknowledge that their concerns are excessive. Hypochondriasis *with poor insight* is diagnosed when, for most of the time during the course of the disorder, the person does not recognize that his or her concern about having a serious disease is excessive or unreasonable.

The term *abridged hypochondriasis* has been used to refer to presentations of severe health anxiety that are missing one or more of the requisite *DSM-IV-TR* diagnostic criteria for hypochondriasis (Gureje, Üstün, & Simon, 1997). Abridged hypochondriasis might be diagnosed when a person is preoccupied with fears of having a serious disease, but eventually responds to medical reassurance (i.e., criterion B), if he or she is still able to function reasonably well (i.e., criterion D), or if he or she has significant but transient anxiety lasting less than 6 months (i.e., criterion E). We (Abramowitz & Braddock, 2008; Taylor & Asmundson, 2004) and others (Marks, 1987; Pilowsky, 1967) also conceptualize disease phobia—a *DSM-IV*-defined specific phobia characterized by the fear of being exposed to contagions or contracting a disease—as an abridged form of hypochondriasis. Like other specific phobias, it is accompanied by distress, apprehension, avoidance of situations that are associated with disease (e.g., hospitals, sick people, public washrooms), and somatic symptoms of anxiety (Côté et al., 1996). Disease phobia is commonly a feature of full-blown hypochondriasis; yet, it can exist on its own, without the other features of hypochondriasis.

Severe health anxiety also frequently occurs as a feature of other disorders, particularly panic disorder (PD) (e.g., worry about dying during panic attacks), obsessive–compulsive disorder (OCD) (e.g., intrusive thoughts about contamination from germs), generalized anxiety disorder (GAD) (e.g., worry about one's general health and safety), and mood disorders (e.g., worry that weight loss is a symptom of an undiagnosed physical condition). This has garnered controversy as to whether hypochondriasis is best conceptualized as a somatoform disorder or as an anxiety disorder, or a form of depression, or a personality disorder. The alternatives to the current classification of hypochondriasis are discussed below.

Alternatives to the Current *DSM* Classification

Several investigators have suggested that hypochondriasis may be better conceptualized as a form of anxiety and, as such, propose that it be moved to the anxiety disorders classification. Some theorists have noted the phenomenological similarities among hypochondriasis and many of the existing anxiety disorders, including specific phobia, PD, OCD, and GAD (Noyes, 1999). Mayou et al. (2005) reported that hypochondriasis overlaps with other forms of anxiety, but maintain that the focus on disease and medical diagnosis has important clinical implications, particularly related to treatment. The resemblance of hypochondriasis to PD has led some researchers to question whether or not these disorders represent distinct nosological entities (Hiller, Leibbrand, Rief, & Fichter, 2005). The main difference between the two disorders appears to concern the immediacy of catastrophic consequences (Hiller et al., 2005; Noyes, 1999); during panic attacks the person with PD often believes that death or some other calamity is imminent (e.g., cardiac arrest), whereas in hypochondriasis the feared consequences are typically perceived as lying in the future (e.g., progressive cancer). Likewise, some investigators have questioned the distinction between hypochondriasis and GAD, because both disorders involve excessive worry (Noyes, 1999).

Taking a somewhat different perspective, it has been suggested that hypochondriasis is related to OCD (Hollander, 1993; Noyes, 1999; Stein, 2000; Yaryura–Tobias & Neziroglu, 1997), primarily because its features include repetitive thinking and ritualistic or "compulsive" behaviors (e.g., repeated reassurance-seeking, checking of one's body). Others have commented on the similarity in the content of the thoughts and behaviors characteristic of hypochondriasis and specific presentations of OCD (e.g., intrusive thoughts about illness and checking behavior) (Fallon, Javitch, Hollander, & Liebowitz, 1991). It is noteworthy, however, that Hollander et al. (2008) have recently omitted hypochondriasis from their list of obsessive–compulsive spectrum disorders (OCSDs) (see chapter 18 for a discussion of the proposed OCSDs).

The *DSM-V* Conceptual Issues in Somatoform and Similar Disorders (CISSD) working group, involving 24 experts, recently released preliminary recommendations regarding the classification of hypochondriasis (Kroenke, Sharpe, & Sykes, 2007). First, it was recommended that the label hypochondriasis, be changed to *Health Anxiety Disorder* because the current name has become pejorative and unacceptable to patients. Notably, other writers (e.g., Abramowitz & Braddock, 2008; Noyes, Stuart, & Watson, 2008; Taylor & Asmundson, 2004) agree that hypochondriasis should be renamed health anxiety disorder.

Despite consensus to rename the disorder, there remains disagreement among the members of the CISSD working group as to whether hypochondriasis should be moved from the somatoform disorders to the anxiety disorders. Within the group suggesting that hypochondriasis remain a somatoform disorder, there also is disagreement as to whether it should be kept as a separate disorder or become a subclassification of somatization disorder, since both disorders are characterized by medically unexplained bodily changes or sensations. Many authors have suggested that hypochondriasis and somatization disorder are actually the same disorder (Cloninger, Sigvardsson, von Knorring & Bohman, 1984; Escobar, Swartz, Rubin–Stipec, & Manu, 1991; Vaillant, 1984).

It has also been proposed that, rather than a somatoform or anxiety disorder, hypochondriasis represents a masked form of depression (Goodstein, 1985; Lesse, 1980) Like mood disorders, hypochondriasis is often associated with difficulties with sleep and appetite, lack of energy, and pessimism about the future (Taylor & Asmundson, 2004). Still others have favored a dimensional rather than categorical view of hypochondriasis and, as such, proposed that it is a personality trait or disorder (Tyrer, Fowler–Dixon, Ferguson, & Kelemen, 1990). As we discuss below, however, there is little empirical evidence supporting these two assertions.

Body Dysmorphic Disorder

BDD is characterized by the preoccupation with either an imagined or exaggerated defect in one's physical appearance (criterion A; APA, 2000). Complaints might involve imagined or slight facial flaws (e.g., wrinkles, scars, facial asymmetry), preoccupations regarding the size or shape of a facial feature (e.g., nose, eyes, ears) or head, preoccupations regarding other parts of the body (e.g., arms, sexual organs, breasts), or concerns regarding overall body size or shape (APA, 2000). The preoccupation must cause significant distress or functional impairment (criterion B), and must not be better accounted for by another disorder (criterion C).

Alternatives to the Current *DSM* Classification

Several investigators have questioned the placement of BDD within the somatoform disorder category and, as with hypochondriasis, have suggested that it be reclassified within the anxiety disorders. Alternatively, BDD might be reclassified as one of the OCSDs (Hollander, Braun, & Simeon, 2008; Noyes et al., 2008; Phillips et al., 2007). Clinical similarities between BDD and OCD include unwanted intrusive thoughts (Frare, Perugi, Ruffolo, & Toni, 2004) and repetitive, compulsive-like behaviors (e.g., ritualistic checking of one's appearance, reassurance-seeking). Moreover, the comorbidity between BDD and OCD is relatively high (Perugi et al., 1997). Despite these overlaps, consistent differences between BDD and OCD have been reported. For instance, individuals with BDD tend to have poorer insight into the senselessness of their symptoms than do individuals with OCD (Phillips et al., 2007). BDD is also associated with greater levels of comorbidity (Phillips et al., 2007), greater social and occupational impairment, and a higher prevalence of suicidal ideation, as compared to OCD (Frare et al., 2007; Phillips et al., 2007).

It has been suggested that the functional relationship between intrusive, anxiety-provoking thoughts and strategies to reduce the resulting anxiety may be especially important in determining which disorders are characterized as OCSDs (Abramowitz & Deacon, 2005). BDD was not discussed in detail by the CISSD working group; however, preliminary recommendations were to either move it to the anxiety disorders and classify it as a subtype of OCD, or keep it in the somatoform disorders category providing the category was reconceptualized to become better defined (Kroenke, 2007; Kroenke et al., 2007; Noyes et al., 2008).

In Eastern cultures, BDD is similar to a subclassification of *taijin kyofusho*—a disorder that is conceptually similar to social anxiety disorder (SAD) (Coles et al., 2006; Kleinknecht et al., 1997). Taijin kyofusho is a syndrome characterized by social-evaluative concerns regarding the belief that the individual makes others uncomfortable (Stein & Stein, 2008), and BDD is similar to the subclassification of taijin kyofusho called *shubo-kyofu* (i.e., "the phobia of a deformed body"; Suzuki, Takei, Kawai, Minabe, & Mori, 2003). Despite this Eastern conceptualization, few studies have explored the relationship between BDD and SAD. Most studies have investigated the co-occurrence of BDD and SAD, with a specific focus on comorbidity rates (Coles et al., 2006). In general, there appear to be higher rates of SAD among BDD populations than vice versa. Among persons with BDD, lifetime prevalence rates of SAD range from 12% to as high as 69% (Hollander et al., 1993, Zimmerman & Mattia, 1998). Studies including larger BDD samples have found SAD prevalence rates of 34% to 36% (current) and 37% to 39% (lifetime) (Coles et al., 2006; Gunstad & Phillips, 2003). High rates of Avoidant Personality Disorder (believed to be a severe, chronic form of generalized

SAD; Stein & Stein, 2008) are also found among individuals with BDD (Phillips & McElroy, 2000; Veale et al., 1996), with current prevalence rates ranging from 8% to 12% (Wilhelm, Otto, Zucker, & Pollack, 1997; Zimmerman & Mattia, 1998).

BDD and SAD also share several clinical and descriptive features. Notably, BDD is associated with high levels of social anxiety (including social avoidance), fear of embarrassment, and fear of rejection and scrutiny from other people (Phillips et al., 1998; Wilhelm et al., 1997). There is also some evidence that social anxiety severity is comparable among persons with BDD and those with generalized SAD (Veale et al., 1996). Additional research is warranted to increase our understanding of phenomenological and mechanistic similarities between these two conditions.

Pain Disorder

In *DSM-IV-TR*, pain disorder is characterized by pain in one or more parts of the body that is severe enough to warrant clinical attention (criterion A). There must be significant distress or impairment in important areas of functioning (i.e., social, occupational; criterion B), and evidence suggesting that psychological factors are involved in the etiology, severity, exacerbation, and maintenance of pain (criterion C). Psychological factors may include other Axis I or II conditions (also diagnosed, but which do not fully account for the individual's pain experience) or subclinical symptoms (i.e., symptoms that do not reach the threshold for a disorder). The pain must not be intentionally produced or feigned (criterion D), and must not be better accounted for by another disorder (e.g., mood, anxiety, psychotic disorder, or dyspareunia; criterion E). Subtypes of pain disorder are defined according to associated factors (i.e., pain disorder associated with psychological factors, pain disorder associated with a general medical condition, or pain disorder associated with both psychological factors and a general medical condition; APA, 2000).

Alternatives to the Current *DSM* Classification

Several clinicians and researchers have noted that the diagnosis of pain disorder is both problematic and of limited clinical utility (e.g., over-inclusiveness, requiring a value judgment by clinicians while offering limited guidelines; e.g., Fishbain, 1995). However, relative to hypochondriasis and BDD, very little has been written on alternatives to the current classification. The CISSD working group recommended that pain disorder be deleted from the somatoform disorders category (Kroenke et al., 2007). It was recommended that pain condition(s) be coded on Axis III, with psychological factors concurrently coded on Axis I as either a specified condition or as psychological factors affecting a general medical condition (for subclinical symptoms) (Kroenke et al., 2007). While some researchers and clinicians (e.g., Mayou et al., 2005) agree that pain conditions would be better classified on Axis III, not all hold this view (e.g., Mailis Gagnon, Nicholson, & Zurowski, 2008). Gagnon and colleagues identified a limitation with listing all pain conditions on Axis III; specifically, categorizing all pain conditions (e.g., circumscribed pain problems such as low back pain, nonspecific pain symptoms such as fibromyalgia, pain associated with definable pathology such as diabetic neuropathy) on Axis III could complicate the treatment of chronic pain. In their view, the pain disorder diagnosis helps clinical decision-making in the treatment of chronic pain (e.g., specialized medical interventions for pain associated with discrete pathology, psychological and multidisciplinary treatment for pain associated with psychological factors), and eliminating the diagnosis would negatively impact the allocation of treatment resources.

Another consideration is that there are many psychological factors that are now well understood as contributing to and maintaining various chronic pain conditions (e.g., Depression; Alschuler, Theisen-Goodvich, Haig, & Geisser, 2008; Keogh, McCracken, & Eccleston, 2006). Of particular note, the constructs of fear and anxiety have been indentified as important individual difference among variables that not only exacerbate chronic pain, but may predispose one toward its development (Asmundson, Norton, & Vlaeyen, 2004; Vlaeyen & Linton, 2000). As outlined by Asmundson and Carleton (2008), there are currently no diagnostic entities or criteria for clinically significant and debilitating levels of pain-related fear and anxiety. However, significantly elevated levels of pain-related fear and anxiety are experienced by approximately one third of those with chronic pain. The available data indicate that these very specific concepts of pain-related fear and anxiety, which may or may not be considered by clinicians in assessing psychological factors, play important roles in the development and maintenance of chronic pain. As such, they may warrant specific consideration in the classification of psychopathology associated with chronic pain conditions.

Conceptual similarities to *DSM-IV-TR* specific phobias have also been noted, which the fear of nociception (i.e., pain sensations) promotes behavioral avoidance and other negative pain behavior (e.g., Letham, Slade, Troup, & Bentley, 1983; Vlaeyen & Linton, 2000). This suggests that pain disorder characterized by severe pain-related fear and anxiety might be reclassified as a subtype of specific phobia. However, unlike individuals with a diagnosis of specific phobia, people with pain complicated by high pain-related fear and anxiety are often convinced that their fears are protective rather than excessive or irrational (Vlaeyen, de Jong, Leeuw, & Crombez, 2004). A considerable and growing body of research has documented elevated levels of health anxiety among patients with chronic pain (Hadjistavropoulos, Owens, Hadjistavropoulos, & Asmundson, 2001), suggesting that the concerns of these individuals may be more similar to those with preoccupation with other benign bodily sensations (i.e., those diagnosed with hypochondriasis). As such, it may be prudent to consider classifying these individuals within the health anxiety disorders.

Classification

The sections above illustrate that there has been considerable debate on where hypochondriasis, BDD, and pain disorder belong in current diagnostic classification systems. The following points summarize questions regarding classification that have been raised in this chapter:

- Should hypochondriasis, BDD, and pain disorder be reclassified as anxiety disorders? Are the phenomenological similarities and high levels of comorbidity with anxiety disorders (particularly for hypochondriasis and BDD) sufficient to warrant this change?
- Should hypochondriasis and BDD be reclassified as OCSDs? Are their similarities with repetitive thinking and compulsions sufficient to warrant this change?
- Is there sufficient evidence to support the reclassification of hypochondriasis or BDD as either an anxiety disorder or as an OCSD?

- Should hypochondriasis be reclassified as an Axis II (personality) disorder?
- Should pain disorder be eliminated from the somatoform disorders category such that pain conditions are coded on Axis III, with psychological factors concurrently coded on Axis I?
- Should pain-related fear and anxiety be considered in the classification of psychopathology associated with chronic pain conditions?
- Should hypochondriasis, BDD, and pain disorder remain somatoform disorders?

The answers to these questions are far from simple. Decisions regarding the most appropriate category are largely dependent on the type of classification system that is used. If a phenomenologically based classification system like the *DSM-IV-TR* or *International Classification of Diseases, tenth revision* (*ICD-10*) is used, then location is determined based on clinical features such as symptom similarity and patterns of co-occurrence with other disorders. However, if etiologically based classification systems are used, then disorders with similar underlying mechanisms (i.e., biological, cognitive) should be grouped together.

Reclassify or Not?

Hypochondriasis

The conceptualization of hypochondriasis as an extreme form of health anxiety has been recognized for over two decades now (e.g., see Barsky & Klerman, 1983; Salkovskis & Warwick, 1986). In the last decade, we have been collectively referring to hypochondriasis, in its full and abridged forms, as a health anxiety disorder (e.g., Asmundson, Taylor, & Cox, 2001). It is, therefore, not surprising that our recommendation is in line with several others (e.g., Kroenke et al., 2007; Mayou et al., 2005; Noyes et al., 2008), to rename hypochondriasis as health anxiety disorder. We have also proposed that hypochondriasis may be moved from the somatoform disorder category and be reclassified as one of the anxiety disorders. There are several reasons for this. Hypochondriasis is placed within the somatoform disorder category in *DSM-IV* because of the presence of somatic "symptoms;" however, somatic symptoms are also characteristic of the anxiety disorders and so the presence of such symptoms is insufficient to justify classification one way or the other.

Hypochondriasis is also phenomenologically similar to several anxiety disorders (i.e., PD, GAD, OCD; Abramowitz & Braddock, 2008; Deacon & Abramowitz, 2008; Taylor & Asmundson, 2004), which further supports its reclassification as an anxiety disorder. Specifically, anxiety is a prominent feature of hypochondriasis (APA, 2000). criterion A for hypochondriasis highlights that the essential feature of the disorder is a preoccupation with *fears* of having, or the idea that one has, a serious disease based on a misinterpretation of benign bodily sensations (APA, 2000). Similarly, health-related fears, like other forms of fear, are multifaceted and characterized by cognitive (e.g., beliefs that one has a serious disease), somatic (e.g., benign bodily sensations), and behavioral features (e.g., reassurance seeking behavior, recurrent bodily checking). Hypochondriasis is also commonly comorbid with anxiety disorders (APA, 2000). Although there are several different approaches for disorder classification (as noted above), currently the disorders are classified according to their clinical features (e.g., signs, symptoms, and course) in the *DSM-IV-TR*. Accordingly, if the classification of disorders in *DSM-V* follows a similar approach, then hypochondriasis would be well suited within the anxiety disorders category based on symptom similarity and patterns of comorbidity with other anxiety disorders.

There are other reasons for moving hypochondriasis to the anxiety disorders section of *DSM-V*. Specifically, the mechanisms of hypochondriasis bear a close resemblance to anxiety disorders in terms of etiologic models and treatment (see Taylor & Asmundson, 2004). The cognitive–behavioral model of hypochondriasis has received the most empirical support and has provided guidance for treatment (Salkovskis, Warwick, & Deale, 2003; Taylor & Asmundson, 2004). The key tenet of this approach is that excessive health anxiety arises from and is maintained by catastrophic beliefs about health, sickness, and disease, including beliefs that lead to the misinterpretation of benign bodily changes and sensations. Although bodily sensations are common in healthy people (Pennebaker, 1982), individuals with hypochondriasis overestimate the dangerousness of these sensations and believe that they indicate some pending catastrophic consequence in the future (Warwick & Salkovskis, 1990; Taylor & Asmundson, 2004). Empirical findings suggest that, relative to nonanxious controls, individuals with severe health anxiety are more likely to report experiencing a lot of somatic symptoms (Barsky, Brener, Coeytaux, & Cleary, 1995) and misinterpret these symptoms as indicators of disease (Haenen, Schmidt, Schoenmakers, & van den Hout, 1998). Moreover, individuals with severe health anxiety are more likely to overestimate the likelihood of contracting a disease (Ditto, Jemmot, & Darley, 1988). There is also evidence that people with excessive health anxiety selectively attend to and are better able to recall health-related information (e.g., Owens, Asmundson, Hadjistavropoulos, & Owens, 2004; Pauli & Alpers, 2002). This etiological model (i.e., the cognitive–behavioral model of health anxiety) is conceptually similar to the models of other anxiety disorders and suggests that the disorders share similar underlying mechanisms.

Support for the reclassification of hypochondriasis as an anxiety disorder based on etiology would be further strengthened by investigating genetic mechanisms. Previous research using twins has shown that facets of health anxiety (e.g., disease conviction, fear of illness, injury, and death), like anxiety disorders, have a heritable component (Taylor, Jang, Stein, & Asmundson, 2008). However, whether or not hypochondriasis shares biological (i.e., genetic) mechanisms with other anxiety disorders warrants additional investigation.

Body Dysmorphic Disorder

Concrete recommendations regarding the reclassification of BDD cannot be made at this time; however, it may be appropriate for the *DSM-V* working group to consider that BDD be placed into a newly formed OCSD category—if such a category ends up in *DSM-V*—or into the anxiety disorders classification, since BDD is phenomenologically similar to both OCD and SAD. Hollander and colleagues (2008) have suggested that, given similarities with regard to intrusive anxiety-provoking thoughts and repetitive behavior, BDD should be reclassified as an OCSD. Others (Kroenke, 2007; Kroenke et al., 2007; Noyes et al., 2008) are more tentative, and recommend possible movement to the anxiety disorders (as a subtype of OCD) or pending improvements to overall conceptualization of the somatoform disorders category, leaving it in its current place. There have been no suggestions to reconceptualize BDD as a subtype of SAD, although emerging evidence (e.g., Coles et al., 2006; Phillips et al., 1998; Veale et al., 1996) indicates this may be a worthwhile consideration. The diagnostic features section of the current *DSM* indicates that individuals with BDD are embarrassed about their defect and that feelings or self-consciousness about their defect might lead to behavioral avoidance of public situations (e.g., work, school). This seems very similar to the difficulties experienced by individuals with SAD. Persons with SAD fear that they will act in a way that might be humiliating or embarrassing, and persons with BDD fear that something about their physical appearance specifically will be humiliating or embarrassing (APA, 2000).

Overall, the existing data suggest that clinically significant levels of anxiety are characteristics of BDD, whereas somatic complaints (other than anxiety and worry) are not prominent features. Emerging evidence that BDD is similar to both OCD (e.g., Frare et al., 2004; Perugi et al., 1997) and SAD (e.g., Coles et al., 2006; Phillips et al., 1998; Veale et al., 1996) provides additional support for moving BDD to the anxiety disorders classification, rather than to the putative categorization of OCSDs. It may be that BDD represents an anxiety disorder characterized by both OCD and SAD features. Future research may yield more definitive data on the classification of BDD.

Pain Disorder

Definitive recommendations regarding the reclassification of pain disorder cannot be made at this time because very little has been written on alternatives to the current classification. In fact, pain disorder is a classification that, with few exceptions, is not often used by pain clinicians or researchers. A literature search (using the Science Direct database) of research from 1999 to 2009 of the terms "pain disorder" and "somatoform pain disorder" in the titles of journal articles revealed little use (70 and 11 articles, respectively) compared with the term "chronic pain" (2,301 articles). Likewise, on the PsycINFO database, a literature search of research from 1986 to 2009 yielded 66 and 31 titles using "pain disorder" and "somatoform pain disorder", respectively, and 2055 articles using the term "chronic pain." Nevertheless, in line with the CISSD recommendations, it may be worthwhile for the *DSM-V* working group to consider coding pain conditions on Axis III, while also permitting psychological factors to be listed on Axis I (e.g., depression, clinically significant fear of pain). Coding psychological factors on Axis I may increase the degree of specificity of factors influencing the etiology, severity, exacerbation, or maintenance of pain, and may also serve to inform treatment.

Conclusions and Future Research Directions: Have We Come Full Circle?

In this chapter we have discussed diagnostic and conceptual dilemmas that confront the classification of three somatoform disorders: hypochondriasis, BDD, and pain disorder. An historical overview suggests that a return to older conceptualization of these problems might be in our best interests. Indeed, some of the earliest descriptions of these problems emphasized their phenomenology (e.g., Gillespie, 1928). Behavioral psychologists propagated this tradition by calling attention to the antecedents and consequences of attaining excessive medical reassurance (Dollard & Miller, 1950). The precision afforded by these functional and theory-driven approaches to understanding what are now called somatoform disorders, however, has been undermined by the imposition of discrete diagnostic criteria such as those of the *DSM*, which emphasize disorders comprised of lists of signs and symptoms. The *DSM's* medical model is a superficial, observational approach that merely collects behaviors according to form or topography, as opposed to considering their function or underlying etiological or psychological processes. Such an approach, inaugurated with the *DSM-III* operational criteria, may have made good sense in terms of resolving the major problem of *DSM-II*, namely diagnostic unreliability. However, the emphasis on improving diagnostic reliability has stifled, rather than aided, progress in understanding and treating these somatoform disorders.

Hypochondriasis provides, perhaps, the best example. Attempts to classify this condition on the basis of its overt topography led to its being moved from the "neuroses" (anxiety states) in *DSM-II* to the newly formed somatoform disorders category in *DSM-III*, and *DSM-IV*. As a result of this (mis)classification (within a questionable diagnostic category), the field has only recently begun to develop therapies and apply the relevant research paradigms to understanding hypochondriasis (e.g., Abramowitz & Braddock, 2008; Taylor & Asmundson, 2004).

As we have discussed in this chapter, clinical observations, theoretical conceptualization, and empirical research concerning the psychological mechanisms and emotional experiences in these conditions suggest that hypochondriasis, BDD, and pain disorder may essentially be anxiety disorders (i.e., "health anxiety") with phenomenology that is quite similar to that of other anxiety disorders (e.g., OCD, GAD, PD). It is clear, however, that additional empirical research is needed. Perhaps, for example, field trials such as those conducted in advance of *DSM-IV* would be helpful in examining questions related to the overlaps between somatoform and anxiety disorders. Such research, however, should examine not only the superficial symptom profiles of these conditions, but also the psychological and biological mechanisms associated with these symptoms. For example, a large field trial could be undertaken to compare the presence and severity of cognitive variables, anxiety symptoms, insight/overvalued ideation, comorbid signs and symptoms, and perhaps response to behavioral challenges among samples of individuals with somatoform disorders and those with anxiety disorders. Factor and cluster analyses of these data might be employed to shed light on issues of dimensionality and categorization. Such empirical work, however, has lagged behind clinical observation in this regard. We hope that researchers will continue to investigate these important diagnostic, conceptual, and theoretical questions so that they may inform future iterations of our classification systems.

References

Abramowitz, J. S., & Braddock, A. E. (2008). *Psychological treatment of health anxiety and hypochondriasis: A biopsychosocial approach. Cambridge, MA: Hogrefe & Huber*.

Abramowitz, J. S., & Deacon, B. J. (2005). The OC spectrum: a closer look at the arguments and the data. In J. S. Abramowitz & A. C. Houts (eds.), *Concepts and controversies in obsessive–compulsive disorder* (pp. 141–149). New York: Springer.

Alschuler, K. N, Theisen-Goodvich, M. E., Haig, A. J., & Geisser, M. E. (2008). A comparison of the relationship between depression, perceived disability, and physical performance in persons with chronic pain. *European Journal of Pain, 12,* 757–764.

American Psychiatric Association. (1952). *Diagnostic and statistical manual of mental disorders*. Washington, DC: Author.

American Psychiatric Association. (1968). *Diagnostic and statistical manual of mental disorders* (2nd ed.). Washington, DC: Author.

American Psychiatric Association. (1980). *Diagnostic and statistical manual of mental disorders* (3rd ed.). Washington, DC: Author.

American Psychiatric Association. (1987). *Diagnostic and statistical manual of mental disorders* (3rd ed. rev.). Washington, DC: Author.

American Psychiatric Association. (1994). *Diagnostic and statistical manual of mental disorders* (4th ed.). Washington, DC: Author.

American Psychiatric Association. (2000). *Diagnostic and statistical manual of mental disorders* (4th ed. text rev.). Washington, DC: Author.

Asmundson, G. J. G., & Carleton, R. N. (2008). Fear of pain. In M. M. Antony & M. B. Stein (Eds.), *Handbook of anxiety and the anxiety disorders*. New York: Oxford University Press.

Asmundson, G. J. G., Norton, P. J., & Vlaeyen, J. W. S. (2004). Fear-avoidance models of chronic pain: An overview. In G. J. G. Asmundson, J. W. S. Vlaeyen, & G. Crombez (Eds.), *Understanding and Treating Fear of Pain* (pp. 3–24). Oxford: Oxford University Press.

Asmundson, G. J. G., Taylor, S., & Cox, B. J. (Eds.) (2001). *Health anxiety: Clinical and research perspectives on hypochondriasis and related disorders.* Chichester, UK: Wiley.

Barsky, A. J., Brener, J., Coeytaux, R. R., & Cleary, P. D. (1995). Accurate awareness of heartbeat in hypochondriacal and non-hypochondriacal patients. *Journal of Psychosomatic Research, 39,* 489–497.

Barsky, A. J., & Klerman, G. L. (1983). Overview: hypochondriasis, bodily complaints, and somatic styles. *American Journal of Psychiatry 140,* 273–283.

Breuer, J., & Freud, S. (1956). *Studies in hysteria*. New York: Nervous and Mental Disease Publishing.

Cloninger, C. R., Sigvardsson, S., von Knorring, A. L., & Bohman, M. (1984). An adoption study of somatoform disorders: II. Identification of two discrete somatoform disorders. *Archives of General Psychiatry, 41,* 863–871.

Coles, M. E., Phillips, K. A., Menard, W., Pagano, M. E., Fay, C., Weisberg, R. B., et al. (2006). Body dysmorphic disorder and social phobia: Cross-sectional and prospective data. *Depression and Anxiety, 23,* 26–33.

Côté, G., O'Leary, T., Barlow, D. H., Strain, J. J., Salkovskis, P. M., Warwick, H. M. C., et al. (1996). Hypochondriasis. In T. A. Widiger, A. J. Frances, H. A. Pincus, R. Ross, M. B. First, & W. W. Davis (Eds.), *DSM-IV sourcebook, Vol. 2* (pp. 933–947). Washington, DC: American Psychiatric Press.

Deacon, B. J., & Abramowitz, J. S. (2008). Is hypochondriasis related to obsessive–compulsive disorder, panic disorder, or both? An empirical investigation. *Journal of Cognitive Psychotherapy, 22,* 115–127.

Ditto, P. H., Jemmott, J. B., & Darley, J. M. (1988). Appraising the threat of illness: A mental representational approach. *Health Psychology, 7,* 183–201.

Dollard, J., Miller, N. E. (1950). *Personality and psychotherapy: An analysis in terms of learning, thinking, and culture.* New York: McGraw-Hill.

Escobar, J. I., Swartz, M., Rubio-Stipec, M., & Manu, P. (1991). Medically unexplained symptoms: distribution, risk factors, and comorbidity. In L. J. Kirmayer & J. M. Robbins (Eds.), *Current concepts of somatization: Research and clinical perspectives* (pp. 63–78). Washington, DC: American Psychiatric Press.

Fallon, B. A., Javitch, J. A., Hollander, E., & Liebowitz, M. R. (1991). Hypochondriasis and obsessive–compulsive disorder: Overlaps in diagnosis and treatment. *Journal of Clinical Psychiatry, 52,* 457–560.

Fishbain, D. (1995). *DSM-IV:* Implications and issues for the pain clinician. *American Pain Society Bulletin, 6,* 18.

Frare, F., Perugi, G., Ruffolo, G., & Toni, C. (2004). Obsessive–compulsive disorder and body dysmorphic disorder: A comparison of clinical features. *European Psychiatry, 19,* 292–298.

Gillespie, R. (1928) Hypochondria: Its definition, nosology, and psychopathology. *Guy's Hospital Reports, 8,* 408–460.

Goodstein, R. K. (1985). Common clinical problems in the elderly: Camouflaged by ageism and atypical presentation. *Psychiatric Annals, 15,* 299–312.

Gunstad, J., & Phillips, K. A. (2003). Axis I comorbidity in body dysmorphic disorder. *Comprehensive Psychiatry, 44,* 270–276.

Gureje, O., Üstün, T. B., & Simon, G. E. (1997). The syndrome of hypochondriasis: A cross-national study in primary care. *Psychological Medicine, 27,* 1001–1010.

Hadjistavropoulos, H. D., Owens, K., M., B., Hadjistavropoulos, T., & Asmundson, G. J. G. (2001). Hypochondriasis and health anxiety among pain patients. In G. J. G. Asmundson, S. Taylor, & B. J. Cox (Eds.), *Health anxiety: Clinical and research perspectives on hypochondriasis and related disorders* (pp. 298–323). London: Wiley.

Haenen, M. A., Schmidt, A. J. M., Schoenmakers, M., & van den Hout, M. A. (1998). Quantitative and qualitative aspects of cancer knowledge: Comparing hypochondriacal subjects and healthy controls. *Psychology and Health, 13,* 1005–1014.

Hiller, W., Leibbrand, R., Rief, W., & Fichter, M. M. (2005). Differentiating hypochondriasis from panic disorder. *Journal of Anxiety Disorders, 19,* 29–49.

Hollander, E. (1993). *Obsessive–compulsive related disorders*. Washington, DC: American Psychiatric Press.

Hollander, E., Braun, A., & Simeon, D. (2008). Should OCD leave the anxiety disorders in *DSM-V?* The case for obsessive–compulsive-related disorders. *Depression and Anxiety, 25,* 317–329.

Hollander, E., Cohen, L., & Simeon, D. (1993). Body dysmorphic disorder. *Psychiatric Annals, 23,* 359–364.

Keogh, E., McCracken, L. M., & Eccleston, C. (2006). Gender moderates the association between depression and disability in chronic pain patients. *European Journal of Pain, 10,* 413–422.

Kleinknecht, R. A., Dinnel, D. L., Kleinknecht, E. E., Hiruma, N., & Harada, N. (1997). Cultural factors in social anxiety: A comparison of social phobia symptoms and Taijin Kyofusho. *Journal of Anxiety Disorders, 11,* 157–177.

Kroenke, K. (2007). Somatoform disorders and recent diagnostic controversies. *Psychiatric Clinics of North America, 30,* 593–619.

Kroenke, K., Sharpe, M., Sykes, R. (2007). Revising the classification of somatoform disorders: Key questions and preliminary recommendations. *Psychosomatics, 48,* 277–285.

Ladee, G. A. (1966). *Hypochondriacal syndromes*. Amsterdam: Elsevier.

Lesse, S. (1980). Masked depression—the ubiquitous but unappreciated syndrome. *Psychiatric Journal of the University of Ottawa, 5,* 268–273.

Letham, J., Slade, P. D., Troup, J. D. G., & Bentley, G. (1983). Outline of a fear-avoidance model of exaggerated pain perception-I. *Behaviour Research and Therapy, 21,* 401–408.

Mailis Gagnon, A., Nicholson, K., Zurowski, M. (2008). The future of the *DSM* pain disorder category [Letter to the editor]. *Psychosomatics, 49,* 362.

Marks, I. M. (1987). *Fears, phobias, and rituals*. New York: Oxford University Press.

Mayou, R., Kirmayer, L. J., Simon, G., Kroenke, K., & Sharpe, M. (2005). Somatoform disorders: Time for a new approach in DSM-V. *American Journal of Psychiatry, 162,* 847–855.

Noyes, R. (1999). The relationship of hypochondriasis to anxiety disorders. *General Hospital Psychiatry, 21,* 8–17.

Noyes, R., Stuart, S. P., & Watson, D. B. (2008). A reconceptualization of the somatoform disorders. *Psychosomatics, 49,* 14–22.

Owens, K. M. B., Asmundson, G. J. G., Hadjistavropoulos, T., & Owens, T. J. (2004). Attentional bias toward illness threat in individuals with elevated health anxiety. *Cognitive Therapy and Research, 28,* 57–66.

Pauli, P., & Alpers, G. W. (2002). Memory bias in patients with hypochondriasis and somatoform pain disorder. *Journal of Psychosomatic Research, 52,* 45–53.

Pennebaker, J. W. (1982). *The psychology of physical symptoms*. New York: Springer.

Perugi, G., Giannotti, D., DiVaio, S.,Valori, E., Frare, F., Cassano, G. B., et al. (1997). Prevalence, phenomenology and comorbidity of dysmorphophobia (body dysmorphic disorder) in a clinical population. *International Journal of Psychiatry in Clinical Practice, 1,* 77–82.

Phillips, K. A., & McElroy, S. L. (2000). Personality disorders and traits in patients with body dysmorphic disorder. *Comprehensive Psychiatry, 41,* 229–236.

Phillips, K. A., Gunderson, C. G., Mallya, G., McElroy, S. L., & Carter, W. (1998). A comparison study of body dysmorphic disorder and obsessive–compulsive disorder. *Journal of Clinical Psychiatry, 59,* 568–575.

Phillips, K. A., Pinto, A., Menard, W., Eisen, J. L., Mancebo, M., & Rasmussen, S. A. (2007). Obsessive–compulsive disorder versus body dysmorphic disorder: A comparison study of two possibly related disorders. *Depression and Anxiety, 24,* 399–409.

Pilowsky, I. (1967). Dimensions of hypochondriasis. *British Journal of Psychiatry, 113,* 89–93.

Salkovskis, P. M., & Warwick, H. M. C. (1986). Morbid preoccupations, health anxiety and reassurance: a cognitive behavioural approach to hypochondriasis. *Behaviour Research and Therapy, 24,* 597–602.

Salkovskis, P. M., Warwick, H. M., & Deale, A. C. (2003). Cognitive–behavioral treatment for severe and persistent health anxiety (hypochondriasis). *Brief Treatment and Crisis Intervention, 3,* 353–367.

Stein, D. J. (2000). Neurobiology of the obsessive–compulsive spectrum disorders. *Biological Psychiatry, 47,* 296–304.

Stein, M. B., & Stein, D. J. (2008). Social anxiety disorder. *Lancet, 371,* 1115–1125.

Suzuki, K., Takei, N., Kawai, M., Minabe, Y., & Mori, N. (2003). Is Taijin Kyofusho a culture-bound syndrome? *American Journal of Psychiatry, 160,* 1358.

Taylor, S., & Asmundson, G. J. G. (2004). *Treating health anxiety: A cognitive–behavioral approach.* New York: The Guilford Press.

Taylor, S., Jang, K. L., Stein, M. B., & Asmundson, G. J. G. (2008). A behavioral-genetic analysis of health anxiety: Implications for the cognitive-behavioral model of hypochondriasis. *Journal of Cognitive Psychotherapy, 22,* 143–153.

Tyrer, P., Fowler–Dixon, R., Ferguson, B., & Kelemen, A. (1990). A plea for the diagnosis of hypochondriacal personality disorder. *Journal of Psychosomatic Research, 34,* 637–642.

Vaillant, G. (1984). The disadvantages of the *DSM-III* outweigh its advantages. *American Journal of Psychiatry, 141,* 542–545.

Veale, D., Boocock, A., Gournay, K., Dryden, W., Shah, F., Willson, R., et al. (1996). Body dysmorphic disorder: A survey of fifty cases. *British Journal of Psychiatry, 169,* 196–201.

Vlaeyen, J. W. S., de Jong, J., Leeuw, M., & Crombez, G. (2004). Fear reduction in chronic pain: Graded exposure in vivo with behavioural experiments. In G. J. G. Asmundson, J. W. S. Vlaeyen, & G. Crombez (Eds.), *Understanding and Treating Fear of Pain* (pp. 313–346). Oxford: Oxford University Press.

Vlaeyen, J. W. S., & Linton, S. J. (2000). Fear-avoidance and its consequences in chronic musculoskeletal pain. *Pain, 85,* 317–332.

Warwick, H. M., & Salkovskis, P. M. (1990). Hypochondriasis. *Behaviour Research and Therapy, 28,* 105–117.

Wilhelm, S., Otto, M. W., Zucker, B. G., & Pollack, M. H. (1997). Prevalence of body dysmorphic disorder in patients with anxiety disorders. *Journal of Anxiety Disorders, 11,* 499–502.

Yayura-Tobias, J. A., & Neziroglu, F. A. (1997). *Obsessive–compulsive disorder spectrum.* Washington, DC: American Psychiatric Press.

Zimmerman M., & Mattia, J. (1998). Body dysmorphic disorder in psychiatric outpatients: Recognition, prevalence, comorbidity, demographic, and clinical correlates. *Comprehensive Psychiatry, 39,* 265–270.

18

Classification of Anxiety Disorders: Treatment Implications

Amy E. Lawrence
Anthony J. Rosellini
Timothy A. Brown

Since the publication of the first *Diagnostic and Statistical Manual of Mental Disorders* (*DSM*), there have been substantial revisions to our diagnostic nosology. Revisions to the classification system have been accompanied by equally dramatic shifts in the nature of treatment, including the advent of disorder-specific, psychological treatments. In this chapter, we review the influence of nosology on the treatment of anxiety disorders. The steady increase in anxiety and mood disorder diagnoses across editions of the *DSM* led to the development of disorder-specific treatments. However, the well-documented high overlap among anxiety and mood disorders (e.g., extensive comorbidity, shared features such as neuroticism or behavioral inhibition) has subsequently prompted the emergence of transdiagnostic interventions. Finally, we will briefly discuss the limitations of a purely categorical nosology, and how the incorporation of dimensional components in the *DSM* could foster classification and treatment.

Proliferation of Anxiety Disorder Diagnoses in *DSM* and its Consequences

In the second edition of the *DSM* (*DSM-II*), mental disorders were collapsed into two broad categories: *neuroses*, which included the precursors to the current anxiety disorders, and *psychoses* (American Psychiatric Association [APA], 1968). In the third edition of *DSM* (*DSM-III*; APA, 1980), the term *neurosis* was replaced by more fine-grained categories and the number of these categories increased further in *DSM-III-R* (APA, 1987). Moreover, a major revision introduced in *DSM-III-R* was the elimination of most hierarchical exclusionary rules (e.g., anxiety disorders could now be assigned in context of co-occurring mood disorder). With the publication of the fourth edition of the *DSM* in 1994 (*DSM-IV*, APA, 1994), the steady increase in the number of anxiety disorder categories was perpetuated. Twelve anxiety disorder categories now exist in the formal nomenclature: panic disorder, panic disorder with agoraphobia (PDA), agoraphobia without a history of panic disorder, social phobia (SOC), specific phobia, generalized anxiety disorder (GAD), obsessive–compulsive disorder (OCD), posttraumatic stress disorder (PTSD), acute stress disorder, anxiety disorder due to a general medical condition, substance-induced anxiety disorder, and anxiety disorder not otherwise specified (NOS) (see Table 18.1). A 13th category (mixed anxiety–depressive disorder) was considered for inclusion in *DSM-IV* but currently resides in the appendix of disorders in need of further study as a possible addition to the fifth edition of the *DSM* (cf. Zinbarg et al., 1994). More recently, a text revision of *DSM-IV* was published that did not revise the diagnostic criteria of disorders, but provided updated empirical reviews for each diagnostic category regarding associated features, cultural, age, and gender features, prevalence, course, familial patterns, and differential diagnosis (*DSM-IV*: Text Revision; *DSM-IV-TR*, APA, 2000).

18.1 Proliferation of Anxiety Disorders over Editions of the *DSM*

DSM-II	*DSM-III*	*DSM-III-R*	*DSM-IV*
Phobic neurosis	**Phobic disorders**	**Phobic disorders**	**Anxiety disorders**
	Agoraphobia with panic attacks	SOC	PDA
	Agoraphobia without panic attacks	Simple phobia	Panic disorder without agoraphobia
	SOC	Agoraphobia without history of panic disorder	Agoraphobia without a history of panic attacks
	Simple phobia	PDA	Social phobia
Anxiety neurosis	**Anxiety states**	**Anxiety states**	GAD
	Panic disorder	Panic disorder without agoraphobia	OCD
	GAD	OCD	Specific phobia
		OCD	PTSD
			Acute stress disorder
Obsessive–compulsive neurosis	**OCD**		Substance-induced anxiety disorder
	PTSD	**PTSD**	Anxiety disorder due to a general medical condition
	Atypical anxiety disorder	**Anxiety disorder not otherwise specified**	Anxiety disorder not otherwise specified

Bold font denotes that *DSM* identified these labels as unique categories.
Adapted from: Brown, T.A. & Barlow, D.H. (2002). Classification of anxiety and mood disorders. In D.H. Barlow (Ed.), *Anxiety and its disorders: The nature and treatment of anxiety and panic* (pp. 292–327). New York: Guilford Press.

The substantial increase in anxiety disorder categories across editions of *DSM* could be viewed as corresponding to expanding cumulative knowledge of the nature of psychopathology and in the classification of disorders. However, researchers (e.g., Andrews, 1996; Brown & Barlow, 2002; Tyrer, 1989) have expressed concern that the expansion of our nosology has come at the expense of the failure to consider the shared features o f emotional disorders that, relative to "unique" features of specific disorders, may have far greater significance in the understanding of the prevention, etiology, and course of disorders, and in predicting their response to treatment. Moreover, this expansion has led to questions of compromised discriminant validity; namely, whether our current classification system is erroneously distinguishing symptoms and disorders that in reality are inconsequential variations of broader syndromes.

Comorbidity

Consistent evidence of high comorbidity among anxiety and mood disorders is frequently cited in support of skepticism about the distinguishability of the emotional disorders (Andrews, 1990; Brown & Barlow, 2002). Comorbidity studies based on *DSM-III-R* criteria routinely indicated that at least 50% of patients with a principal anxiety disorder have one or more additional diagnoses at the time of assessment (e.g., Brawman–Mintzer et al., 1993; Brown & Barlow, 1992; Kessler et al., 1994; Pirkola et al., 2005; Sanderson, Di Nardo, Rapee, & Barlow, 1990). Similar findings were obtained in a large-scale study ($n = 1{,}127$) of patients with *DSM-IV* anxiety and mood disorders (Brown, Campbell, Lehman, Grisham, & Mancill, 2001). Specifically, 55% of patients with a principal anxiety or mood disorder had at least one additional anxiety or depressive disorder at the time of the assessment; this rate increased to 76% when lifetime diagnoses were considered. The principal diagnostic categories of PTSD, major depression, dysthymia, and GAD had the highest comorbidity rates, whereas specific phobia is the lowest (see Table 18.2). By far, the most common additional diagnosis was major depression followed by SOC. Concordant findings attesting to the high rate and patterns of comorbidity among anxiety disorders have been obtained in studies of population-based samples (e.g., Kessler, Chui, Demler, & Walters, 2005).

As we and others have discussed at length elsewhere (e.g., Brown & Barlow, 2002; Frances, Widiger, & Fyer, 1990), there are numerous conceptual explanations for diagnostic comorbidity. Some of these accounts would challenge the current *DSM* system, including explanations that disorders co-occur because they share overlapping definitional criteria (e.g., the associated symptom criteria for *DSM-IV* GAD overlap almost entirely with defining features of major depression and dysthymia) or because the diagnostic categories reflect trivial variations of a broader underlying syndrome that has been erroneously separated by the classification system. The latter account is in accord with conceptual models positing a "general neurotic syndrome" (cf. Andrews, 1990; Tyrer, 1989) which would correspond to the *DSM-II* nosology.

On the other hand, high diagnostic comorbidity may occur for other reasons, including the possibility that the features of one disorder act as risk factors for another disorder (e.g., severe agoraphobia leads to mood disorder due to hopelessness, restricted mobility, etc.) or because disorders emerge from shared diatheses (e.g., genes, personality). As a potential example of the first explanation, findings from Brown, Campbell, et al. (2001) indicated that the presence of PTSD was associated with a significantly elevated risk of PDA. Temporal sequences analyses indicated that PDA rarely (28%) preceded PTSD. This association is noteworthy because PTSD and PDA are the only two emotional disorders characterized by high levels of autonomic arousal (Davidson & Foa, 1991; Jones & Barlow, 1990). Although this aggregation may be due in part to feature overlap, temporal sequence analyses raise the interesting possibility that PTSD serves as a risk factor for PDA; that is, the high autonomic arousal and low perceptions of personal control associated with PTSD, perhaps coupled with a preexisting trait such as anxiety sensitivity, give rise to PDA.

Hierarchical Models of Anxiety and Depression

The latter general account for comorbidity, that a common diathesis underlies anxiety and mood disorders, is intriguing because of its alignment with leading conceptual models which posit that these conditions emanate from shared biological and psychological vulnerabilities (e.g., Barlow, 2002; Clark, Watson, & Mineka, 1994). These models assert that while emotional disorders co-occur in part because they arise from core diatheses, this common vulnerability is manifested heterogeneously (i.e., as different *DSM* disorders)

18.2 Overall Percentage Rates (and Relative Risk Ratios) of Current Additional Diagnoses in Patients with Current Principal Anxiety and Mood Disorders

	DSM-IV principal diagnosis *(n)*											
Current additional diagnosis	PD (36)	PDA (324)	PD/A (360)	SOC (186)	GAD (120)	OCD (77)	SPEC (110)	PTSD (13)	MDD (81)	DYS (21)	MDD/ DYS (102)	Overalls[a]
Any Axis I	42 (.73)	62 (1.14*)	60 '(1.09)	46 (.78*)	68 (1.24*)	57 (1.01)	34 (.56*)	92 (1.64*)	69 (1.25*)	76 (1.36*)	71 (1.28*)	57
Any anxiety/ mood	42 (.75)	60 (1.16*)	59 (1.12)	45 (.79*)	65 (1.21*)	53 (.96)	33 (.56*)	92 (1.69*)	68 (1.26*)	76 (1.40*)	70 (1.30*)	55
Any anxiety disorder	36 (.84)	47 (1.17*)	46 (1.14)	28 (.61*)	52 (1.25*)	39 (.91)	27 (.61*)	62 (1.45)	64 (1.58*)	57 (1.35)	63 (1.56*)	43
Any mood disorder	17 (.58)	33 (1.28*)	31 (1.19)	29 (1.04)	36 (1.32*)	32 (1.17)	10 (.34*)	77 (2.79*)	11 (.37*)	38 (1.36)	17 (.56*)	28
Anxiety disorders PD	—	—	—	1	3 (.28)	1 (3.25)	0 (.86)	0 (—)	4 (—)	0 (3.25)	3 (—)	1 (2.48)
PDA	—	—	—	3 (.24*)	15 (2.09*)	8 (.88)	5 (.58)	23 (2.75)	15 (1.90*)	14 (1.68)	15 (1.96*)	9
PD or PDA	—	—	—	3 (.24*)	18 (2.24*)	9 (.88)	5 (.49)	23 (2.33)	19 (2.08*)	14 (1.42)	18 (2.03*)	10
SOC	8 (.37)	15 (.58*)	15 (.53*)	—	36 (2.33*)	26 (121)	9 (.38*)	15 (.70)	41 (2.07*)	48 (2.25*)	42 (2.24*)	22
GAD	19 (1.59)	16 (1.50*)	16 (1.64*)	13 (1.10)	—	12 (.93)	5 (.40*)	23 (1.87)	5 (.37*)	5 (.38)	5 (.36*)	13

GAD: No hierarchy	22	22	22	21	—	16	7	38	67	90	72	25
	(.87)	(.79)	(.78*)	(.78)		(.59)	(.26*)	(1.52)	(3.16*)	(3.80*)	(3.73*)	
OCD	6	7	7	8	4	—	3	23	9	5	8	7
	(.83)	(1.12)	(1.08)	(1.29)	(.59)		(.38)	(3.62*)	(1.35)	(.71)	(1.21)	
SPEC	8	15	15	8	12	12	15[b]	15	15	10	14	13
	(.65)	(1.36)	(1.28)	(.58*)	(.91)	(.91)	(1.17)	(1.21)	(1.18)	(.75)	(1.09)	
PTSD	0	4	4	3	1	0	0	—	6	0	5	3
	(—)	(2.30*)	(1.95)	(1.09)	(.30)	(—)	(—)		(2.84*)	(—)	(2.20)	
Other anxiety	3	4	4	3	1	3	3	0	2	0	2	3
	(.92)	(1.86)	(1.81)	(1.10)	(.25)	(.86)	(.90)	(—)	(.81)	(—)	(.63)	
Mood disorders	8	24	23	14	26	22	3	69		33	—	20
	(.41)	(1.41*)	(1.28)	(.66*)	(1.39)	(1.14)	(.12*)	(3.67*)	—	(1.73)		
DYS	8	7	7	13	6	10	4	23	11	—	—	8
	(.99)	(.73)	(.74)	(1.75*)	(.66)	(1.26)	(.40)	(2.80*)	(1.36)			
Other mood	3	3	3	5	6	4	4	0	0′	5	1	4
	(.74)	(.87)	(.84)	(1.40)	(1.71)	(1.05)	(.98)	(—)	(—)	(1.29)	(.24)	
Other disorders	0	2	1	1	4	1	0	0	2	0	2	2
	(—)	(.99)	(.84)	(.65)	(3.53*)	(.83)	(—)	(—)	(1.68)	(—)	(1.31)	
Other Axis I	3	2	2	1	6	6	2	0	6	0	5	3
	(.92)	(.63)	(.64)	(.31)	(2.25)	(2.41)	(.58)	(—)	(2.28)	(—)	(1.77)	

Note. DSM-IV = *Diagnostic and Statistical Manual of Mental Disorders*, fourth edition (American Psychiatric Association, 1994); PD = panic disorder; PDA = panic disorder with agoraphobia; PDIA = PD or PDA; SOC = social phobia; GAD = generalized anxiety disorder; GAD: No hierarchy = GAD ignoring *DSM-IV* hierarchy rule with mood disorders; OCD = obsessive–compulsive disorder; SPEC = specific phobia; PTSD = posttraumatic stress disorder; MDD = major depressive disorder; DYS = dysthymia; MDD/DYS = MDD or DYS. Dashes in parentheses indicate that the odds ratio is inapplicable.

Overall frequency category was assigned as an additional diagnosis.

* Significantly increased or decreased risk of co-occurring disorder (95% confidence interval).

From: Brown, T.A., Campbell, L.A., Lehman, C.L., Grisham, J.R., & Mancill, R.B. (2001). Current and lifetime comorbidity of the *DSM-IV* anxiety and mood disorders in a large clinical sample. *Journal of Abnormal Psychology, 110*, 585–599.

due to exposure to differing environmental influences, other genetic/biologic agents, and so forth (e.g., Barlow, 2002; Clark, 2005; Hettema, Prescott, Myers, Neale, & Kendler, 2005). For example, whereas a genetically based trait such as neuroticism may underlie SOC and depression, whether or not one or both conditions becomes manifest may depend on environmental determinants such as direct experiences with social humiliation, rejection, or vicarious exposure (e.g., parental modeling of ineffective coping). Accordingly, despite the considerable overlapping features among anxiety and mood disorders, differentiation is thought to be useful because it has important implications for understanding clinical course, complications, and treatment.

These models posit two genetically based core dimensions of temperament that are instrumental in the etiology and course of the emotional disorders: *neuroticism/negative affectivity* and *extraversion/positive affectivity*. Whereas neuroticism/negative affectivity is etiologically relevant to all anxiety and mood disorders, the influence of extraversion/positive affectivity is more specific to depression and SOC (e.g., Brown, Chorpita, & Barlow, 1998; Mineka, Watson, & Clark, 1998; Watson, Clark, & Carey, 1988). Although the theoretical frameworks were developed independently (cf. Eysenck, 1981; Tellegen, 1985), neuroticism/negative affectivity and extraversion/positive affectivity are closely related to Gray's (1987) constructs of behavioral inhibition and behavioral activation, respectively at both the conceptual and empirical levels (e.g., Campbell–Sills, Liverant, & Brown, 2004; Carver & White, 1994; Clark et al., 1994; Kasch, Rottenberg, Arnow, & Gotlib, 2002). A growing literature attests to the heritability of these constructs (e.g., Fanous, Gardner, Prescott, Cancro, & Kendler, 2002; Hettema, Prescott, & Kendler, 2004; Viken, Rose, Kaprio, & Koskenvuo, 1994), and their roles in accounting for the onset, overlap, and maintenance of anxiety and depression (e.g., Brown et al., 1998; Gershuny & Sher, 1998; Kasch et al., 2002; Watson et al., 1988). For instance, in a sample of outpatients, Brown et al. (1998) found that virtually all the considerable covariance among latent variables corresponding to the *DSM-IV* constructs of unipolar depression (DEP), SOC, GAD, OCD, and panic disorder/ agoraphobia was explained by the higher-order dimensions of negative affect and positive affect. Although the results were consistent with the notion of neuroticism/negative affect as a broadly relevant dimension of vulnerability, the *DSM-IV* disorder constructs were differentially related to negative affect, with depression and GAD evidencing the strongest associations. In accord with a reformulated hierarchical model of anxiety and depression (Mineka et al., 1998), positive affect was predictive of depression and SOC only (see Figure 18.1). Comorbidity and structural genetic findings (e.g., Brown, Campbell, et al., 2001; Kessler, Stang, Wittchen, Stein, & Walters, 1999) also reveal a differential

18.1

Structural model of the interrelationships of *DSM-IV* disorder constructs and negative affect, positive affect, and autonomic arousal.

PA = positive affect; NA = negative affect; DEP = mood disorders; GAD = generalized anxiety disorder; PD/A = panic disorder with or without agoraphobia; OCD = obsessive–compulsive disorder; SOC = social phobia; AA = autonomic arousal.

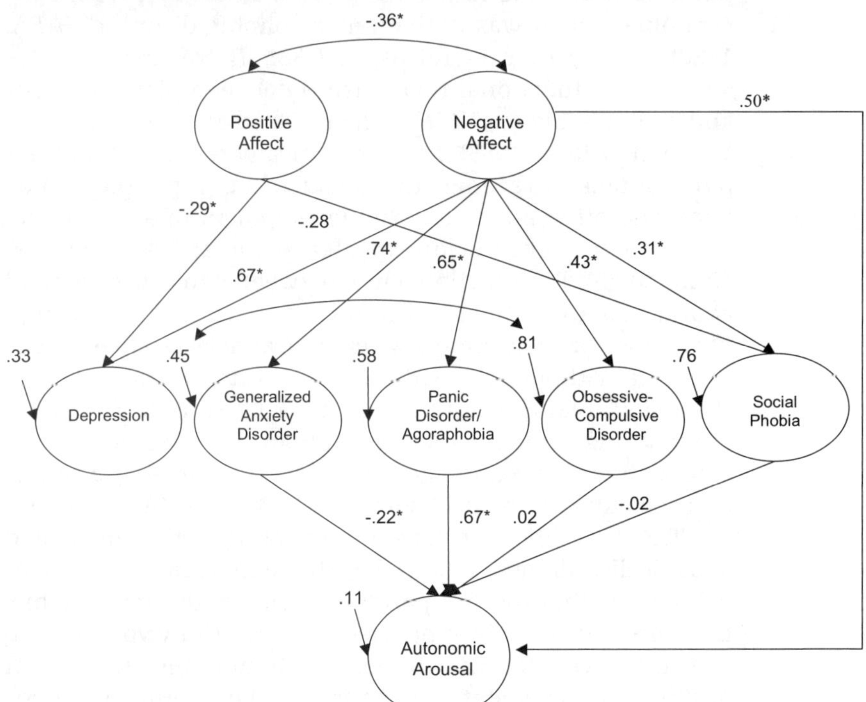

Figure reproduced from Brown, T. A., Chorpita, B. F., & Barlow, D. H. (1998). Structural relationships among dimensions of the DSM-IV anxiety and mood disorders and dimensions of negative affect, positive affect, and autonomic arousal. *Journal of Abnormal Psychology*, 107, 179–192.

relationship between mood disorders and SOC, which could be seen as consistent with the existence of a temperamental vulnerability dimension specific to these two disorders.

Development of Disorder-Specific Treatments

Despite the aforementioned issues pertaining to a possible compromise in discriminant validity, another consequence of the steady rise in anxiety disorder categories across *DSM* editions has been the development and evaluation of psychological interventions tailored specifically for each disorder. The redefinition of agoraphobia and GAD serve as good examples of the influence of classification on the development of novel treatments. Panic attacks were first recognized as distinct from other "anxiety neuroses" in *DSM-III* and panic disorder was initially regarded as distinct from agoraphobia, which was defined as a "phobic disorder" (APA, 1980). Shortly after the release of *DSM-III*, treatment studies suggested a functional relationship between panic disorder and agoraphobia (e.g., Liebowitz & Klein, 1981; Zitrin, Klein, Woerner, & Ross, 1983). Patients typically reported that their panic attacks preceded the onset of agoraphobic avoidance, and often attributed the development of agoraphobia to their experience of unexpected panic attacks (Thyer & Himle, 1985). The functional link between panic disorder and agoraphobia was further reinforced by the relatively high prevalence of agoraphobia with panic attacks relative to agoraphobia without panic attacks (Di Nardo, O'Brien, Barlow, Waddell, & Blanchard, 1983; Garvey & Tuason, 1984). In light of mounting evidence that agoraphobia was usually associated with fear of panic, agoraphobia was defined as a condition secondary to panic disorder in *DSM-III-R* (APA, 1987).

The reclassification of agoraphobia as functionally related to panic disorder was followed by the refinement of cognitive-behavioral therapy for panic disorder with agoraphobia. Evidence had already supported the use of in vivo exposure (e.g., direct contact with the feared stimuli) and subsequent positive reinforcement (e.g., praise) in the treatment of phobias (Mathews, 1978). Because of the reconceptualization of agoraphobia as apprehension about situations in which panic attacks might occur, clinical researchers began developing protocols that included exposure to anxiety-provoking situations and physical sensations (e.g., Barlow's (2002) panic control treatment (PCT); Barlow & Craske, 2000; Mitte, 2005).

The redefinition of GAD also led to the development of more targeted treatment protocols. Relegated to "residual" status in *DSM-III*, GAD could not be diagnosed if an individual met criteria for another mental disorder. GAD was redefined in *DSM-III-R* to include excessive and/or unrealistic worry about two or more areas not related to another Axis I disorder, as well as 6 of 18 symptoms of motor tension, autonomic hyperactivity, and vigilance and scanning. The criteria for GAD were revised again in *DSM-IV* to define pathological worry as "excessive" and "uncontrollable" and to require the presence of three of six associated symptoms. Most significantly, the redefinition of GAD from a residual condition to a formal diagnostic category resulted in the development of treatment protocols targeting the disorder's key feature—excessive and uncontrollable worry (e.g., Borkovec, Newman, Pincus, & Lytle, 2002; Craske & Barlow, 2006).

There now exists at least one disorder-specific psychological treatment protocol for each major anxiety disorder. However, it could be argued that, as with the anxiety disorders themselves, the similarities of these interventions outweigh their differences. In addition to shared diatheses (e.g., neuroticism), the "specific" features of anxiety disorders are *processes* (e.g., apprehension of situations or objects, protective or anxiety-reducing actions) that differ primarily (or solely) at the descriptive level in terms of the *content* or *focus* of apprehension (e.g., worry about rejection or embarrassment in SOC; worry about contamination in OCD; worry about several daily matters in GAD) or in the *form* of protective action (e.g., situational avoidance in agoraphobia, specific phobia, and SOC; compulsions in OCD; safety behaviors in all anxiety disorders). Consequently, most cognitive-behavioral treatments (CBT) for anxiety disorders contain the elements of exposure (situational, imaginal, interoceptive) and cognitive restructuring, modified for each disorder to match the specific features of that condition. Although differentiation may be helpful in conveying information about the nature of the disturbance, the question arises as to whether these manifestations are sufficiently distinct (e.g., beyond variations in content) to warrant diagnostic separation and distinct treatments.

Have Treatments Become Too Specific?

Evidence from various sources might suggest that anxiety disorder treatments have become too focused on the specific features of these conditions. For instance, the fact that numerous disorders respond similarly to the same psychological or drug treatment could be viewed as countering the need for disorder-specific treatments, as well as lend further evidence of the questionable discriminant validity of the anxiety and mood disorders (e.g., Hudson & Pope, 1990; Tyrer et al., 1988). It is well known, for example, that the serotonin selective reuptake inhibitors are efficacious for a variety of conditions including panic disorder (Michelson et al., 1998), GAD (Pollack et al., 2001), SOC (Stein et al., 1999), OCD (Hohagen et al., 1998), and PTSD (Brady et al., 2000). Similar evidence has also been obtained with benzodiazepines, tricyclic antidepressants, and monoamine oxidase inhibitors (Bandelow, Zohar, Hollander, Kasper, & Moller, 2002). In another large study bearing on this issue, Tyrer et al. treated 210 outpatients with GAD, panic disorder, or dysthymia with one of the following five interventions: diazepam, dothiepin, placebo, cognitive-behavioral therapy, or a self-help program. Although some treatment condition differences were noted at post-treatment (e.g., diazepam was less effective than dothiepin, cognitive-behavioral therapy, and self-help), no diagnostic group differences were obtained. In view of the lack of diagnostic group treatment response differences, Tyrer et al. concluded that differential diagnosis of anxiety and mood disorders did not provide a sound basis for treatment prescription.

In addition, there is consistent evidence that psychological treatment for a given anxiety disorder produces a significant decline in other anxiety or mood diagnoses that are not addressed in treatment (e.g., Borkovec, Abel, & Newman, 1995; Brown, Antony, & Barlow, 1995; Craske et al., 2007; Tsao, Lewin, & Craske, 1998). For instance, Brown et al. (1995) examined the course of additional diagnoses in a sample of 126 patients who were enrolled in a short-term psychological treatment program for panic disorder with minimal agoraphobic avoidance. At pretreatment 40% of patients had an additional diagnosis, but comorbidity decreased significantly at posttreatment to a rate of 17%. A similar decrease in comorbidity has been found in other studies that entailed the treatment of patients for panic disorder (Craske et al., 2007; Tsao et al., 1998) and GAD (Borkovec et al., 1995). None of these studies provided evidence that comorbidity existing at pretreatment had a deleterious impact on the treatment response of the targeted disorder. Thus, at least in the short-term (i.e., immediately following the active treatment phase), diagnostic comorbidity seems to have no relevance to the prediction of treatment outcome but declines significantly with treatment of another condition.

Although the aforementioned findings might suggest that disorder-specific treatments are irrelevant because various conditions respond favorably to the same intervention, there is some evidence, although less compelling to date, that these treatments are overly specialized because they do not generalize in a manner that fosters favorable long-term outcome. For instance, in an evaluation of the long-term efficacy of PCT, Craske, Brown, and Barlow (1991) found that a considerable portion of patients who attained panic-free status at 2-year follow-up did not meet criteria for high endstate functioning due to lingering agoraphobic avoidance. Thus, despite the functional relationship between panic attacks and agoraphobia now acknowledged in *DSM*, these findings indicated that in many patients, treatment focused specifically on the amelioration of panic attacks did not generalize to the alleviation of panic-related situational avoidance. This led the authors of this study to conclude that regardless of the level of agoraphobic avoidance, interventions for PDA should target all features of this disturbance (i.e., PCT for panic attacks and fear of panic attacks, situational exposure for agoraphobia). In addition, a subsequent study found that patients successfully treated for panic disorder exhibited no improvement in comorbid depression (Woody, McLean, Taylor, & Koch, 1999).

In fact, the impact of psychological treatment on comorbid disorders may be less appreciable when long-term outcome is considered. In the Brown et al. (1995) study noted previously, overall comorbidity declined substantially from pretreatment to posttreatment (i.e., 40%–17%). At 2-year follow-up, however, the rate of comorbidity increased to a level (30%) that was no longer significantly different than pretreatment. This was despite the fact that in the aggregate, patients maintained or improved upon gains for panic disorder across the follow-up interval, indicating considerable independence between panic disorder symptoms and overall comorbidity. Although speculative, these findings could be interpreted in accord with the explanation for comorbidity and theoretical models stating that disorders emerge from shared vulnerabilities. Specifically, that PCT is effective at treating the symptoms and maintaining processes of panic disorder, but does not result in substantial reductions in general diatheses (e.g., dimensions of temperament such as neuroticism) that leave patients vulnerable to the emergence or resilience of other disorders (see also Tsao, Mystkowski, Zucker, & Craske, 2002).

Longitudinal Course of Putative Dimensions of Shared Vulnerability

These conclusions are highly speculative and await future research (i.e., measures of vulnerability were not administered in these studies of the short- and long-term outcome of disorder-specific treatments and their impact on comorbidity). Given their conceptualization as trait vulnerability dimensions, it might be expected that neuroticism or negative affect and extraversion or positive affect are temporally stable in clinical samples, and are relatively less responsive to treatment. Kasch et al. (2002) examined the temporal stability (8 months) and predictive utility of self-reported levels of behavioral inhibition and behavioral activation in 41 individuals with major depression (most of whom received treatment during the follow-up interval). Lower time 1 behavioral activation predicted poorer clinical outcome of depression at the 8-month reassessment. Moreover, the self-report measures of behavioral inhibition and activation (i.e., BIS/BAS scales; Carver & White, 1994) were remarkably stable over time and clinical state. In fact, while over a third of participants were classified as no longer depressed at the 8-month follow-up, BIS/BAS scores displayed the same high level of temporal stability in this group (e.g., time 1 and time 2 BIS $M = 24.2$ and $M = 23.3$, respectively) as in a subgroup of participants who were depressed at both assessment points (e.g., time 1 and time 2 BIS $M = 24.0$ and $M = 23.9$, respectively).

Brown (2007) examined the temporal course and temporal structural relationships of latent dimensions of temperament (neuroticism/behavioral inhibition, N/BI; behavioral activation/positive affect, BA/P) and selected *DSM-IV* disorder constructs (DEP, GAD, SOC). Patients ($N = 606$) were reassessed at 1-year (t2) and 2-year (t3) follow-ups with structured clinical interviews and the same questionnaire battery used at intake (t1). As the majority (76%) of patients received treatment after intake, the overall rate of anxiety and mood disorders declined significantly over follow-up (e.g., 100% to 58% for T1 and T3, respectively). Despite the marked decline in *DSM-IV* diagnoses by T3, test–retest correlations of the factors and unconditional latent growth models (LGMs) indicated that BA/P evidenced a very high degree of temporal stability, consistent with its conceptualization as a trait vulnerability construct that is relatively unaffected by treatment.

However, of the five constructs examined, N/BI evidenced the *greatest* amount of temporal change (Cohen's $d = .70$) and was the dimension associated with the largest treatment effect ($d = -0.98$). Although perhaps at odds with conceptual speculations that core dimensions of temperament are resilient to psychological treatment (cf. Kasch et al., 2002), this result may be reflective of the fact that self-report assessment of temperament is prone to mood–state distortion (cf. Clark, Vittengl, Kraft, & Jarrett, 2003; Widiger, Verheul, & van den Brink, 1999). That is, it is likely the measurement of N/BI consists of some combination of stable temperament variance (i.e., vulnerability) and variability attributable to generalized distress (i.e., more prone to mood–state distortion, subject to greater temporal fluctuation). The considerable covariance between N/BI and the emotional disorders is not only partly due to a temperamental component (N/BI acts as vulnerability, is relatively stable) but also because of the distress associated with having a disorder. Presumably, the latter aspect is less temporally stable and more apt to covary with temporal fluctuations in the severity of disorders.

With the exception of Kasch et al. (2002), the prevailing result is that scores on measures of temperament change significantly from pre- to post-treatment (e.g., improvement in depression is accompanied by a reduction in neuroticism; Boyce & Parker, 1985; Clark et al., 2003). In attempt to reconcile these findings, Clark et al. employed multivariate statistical procedures to separate the variance of their measure of temperament into trait and state components. These authors found that changes in depression severity correlated with state changes in temperament measurement, but not with stable trait scores.

In addition, the findings of Brown (2007) indicated that N/BI operated differently than the *DSM-IV* disorder constructs in several ways. For instance, unconditional LGMs of each *DSM-IV* disorder construct revealed inverse relations between the Intercept and Slope (rs = –.42 to –.48); that is, higher initial disorder severity was associated with greater change over time. However, the intercept and slope of N/BI were positively correlated (r = .47) indicating that patients with higher initial levels of N/BI showed less change in this dimension over time; and conversely, patients with lower initial levels of N/BI tended to prove greater change. Thus, unlike the *DSM-IV* disorders, the stability of N/BI increased as a function of initial severity. This may indicate the influence of mood–state distortion/general distress on the measurement of N/BI is most pronounced at the lower end of its continuum. It is the lower range of N/BI that is less temporally stable and presumably more apt to covary with temporal change in disorder severity.

Given that dimensions of temperament are construed as risk factors for emotional disorders, studies have also examined whether pretreatment levels of these constructs are associated with poorer treatment response and long-term course. In the depression literature, results have been mixed with some studies showing that pretreatment levels of temperament predict poorer treatment outcome (e.g., Geerts & Bouhuys, 1998; Joyce, Mulder, & Cloninger, 1994; Kasch et al., 2002) whereas other studies reported no such effects (e.g., Boyce & Parker, 1985; Clark et al., 2003; Sato et al., 1999). In Brown (2007), parallel-process LGMs were conducted to examine the directional effects among temperament and psychopathology constructs over 2-year follow-up. Higher initial levels of N/BI were associated with less improvement in the *DSM-IV* constructs of GAD and SOC. Moreover, lower BA/P predicted poorer outcome of SOC, although this effect only approached statistical significance (p = .07) when N/BI was in the analysis. Although no temporal relations were obtained for DEP, these results are in line with in earlier work and theory that N/BI and BA/P have directional temporal effects on Axis I psychopathology (cf. Gershuny & Sher, 1998; Kasch et al., 2002; Meyer, Johnson, & Winters, 2001). Consistent with prediction and theory, initial levels of the *DSM-IV* disorders did not predict increases in temperament over time (i.e., the *DSM-IV* disorders did not have directional effects on dimensions of temperament).

Moreover, Brown (2007) found that temporal change in DEP, SOC, and GAD was significantly related to change in

N/BI. Of particular interest is the finding that all the temporal covariance of the *DSM-IV* disorder constructs was accounted for by change in N/BI; that is, when N/BI was specified as a predictor, the temporal overlap among disorder constructs was reduced to zero. The correlational nature of these findings precludes firm conclusions about the direction of these effects. Although counter to earlier initial evidence and conceptualization (Brown et al., 1995; Kasch et al., 2002), N/BI may be therapeutically malleable and this in fact mediates the extent of change in the emotional disorders. Alternatively or additively, a reduction in disorder severity is associated with a decrease in generalized distress; a feature shared by the emotional disorders and is partially reflected in the measurement of N/BI. Finer grained methodologies are required to explicate the nature of these relationships (e.g., therapy outcome-based designs entailing multiple assessments of temperament and disorder features over the active treatment phase). Yet, these findings further underscore the role of N/BI as a unifying construct accounting for the covariance among the emotional disorders (cf. Brown et al., 1998).

Transdiagnostic Treatments

The recognition of the similarities among emotional disorders and their treatments as well as the limitations of disorder-specific approaches led to the emergence of transdiagnostic approaches. These therapies combine elements of empirically supported treatments and apply them to a variety of disorders. Transdiagnostic treatments have been developed for several classes of diagnoses (e.g., eating disorders; Fairburn, Cooper, & Shafran, 2003). Researchers have noted that most manualized treatments for anxiety disorders consist of psychoeducation, cognitive reappraisal, and exposure. Although there are disorder-specific variations among manuals, these typically involve the adaptation of the same principle to different presenting problems. Furthermore, the observation that CBT for one disorder often results in improvements in comorbid diagnoses (e.g., Borkovec et al., 1995; Brown et al., 1995; Tsao et al., 1998) led to speculation that emotional disorders share an underlying mechanism which itself may be a worthwhile focus of treatment. Informed by several lines of research (e.g., comorbidity studies, latent structural analyses, laboratory studies of emotion regulation), these treatments offer a promising alternative to disorder-specific manuals and reflect the field's movement toward an integrative approach to classification and treatment.

Several transdiagnostic treatment approaches are based on hypotheses about the processes common to the emotional disorders. For instance, in their unified protocol for the treatment of anxiety and depression, Barlow, Allen, and Choate (2004) posit that maladaptive emotion regulation strategies (e.g., suppression, avoidance) underlie all emotional disorders. Accordingly, the focus of treatment is on acceptance of emotional experience and the modification of rigid, emotion-driven behaviors. Exposures are an essential component of treatment, as they are in traditional CBT approaches. However, in Barlow et al.'s protocol they are conceptualized as "emotion exposures" and are not designed to target a single Axis I disorder. Rather, a patient might complete exposures that target situational avoidance related to panic attacks, avoidance of social situations due to fear of negative evaluation, and excessive hand washing due to fears of contamination. The focus of treatment is the broad construct of emotional avoidance rather than the relief of symptoms associated with a particular disorder.

Hayes, Wilson, Gifford, Follette, & Strosahl (1996) argue that experiential avoidance or unwillingness to remain in contact with particular experiences (public and private) underlies many forms of psychopathology and that syndromal classification (the identification of clusters of signs and symptoms, as in *DSM-IV-TR*) fails to adequately inform treatment. Acceptance and Commitment Therapy (ACT), the therapeutic approach developed by Hayes, Strosahl, and Wilson (1999), was not developed solely for anxiety disorders and has been used to treat psychotic disorders (Bach & Hayes, 2002; Gaudiano & Herbert, 2006), substance abuse (Hayes et al., 2004), and trichotillomania (Woods, Wetterneck, & Flessner, 2006). The focus of treatment is acceptance of emotional experience and behavior that is in accordance with one's values. ACT techniques, which include experiential exercises and the use of metaphor, diverge considerably from traditional CBT. Although ACT has been adapted for anxiety disorders (e.g., Eifert & Forsyth, 2005), there is a paucity of controlled trials examining its efficacy.

Other transdiagnostic approaches have been developed with the primary goal of enhancing treatment effectiveness rather than offering a unifying theory to explain the emergence and maintenance of anxiety disorders. These approaches have typically been delivered in a group format with modifications to individual CBT protocols. Erickson (2003) found medium to large effects sizes in his small, uncontrolled trial of group CBT for heterogeneous anxiety disorders. Norton and Hope (2005) found mixed evidence for the efficacy of broad-spectrum group CBT applied to patients with heterogeneous anxiety disorders. Although decreases in clinician-administered severity ratings for primary anxiety diagnoses were observed among individuals in the treatment group, no differences were evident on self-report measures. In a benchmarking study examining the effectiveness of group CBT for diagnostically heterogeneous groups, McEvoy and Nathan (2007) concluded that the effects of group treatment on outcome measures (including the Beck Depression Inventory and the Beck Anxiety Inventory) were comparable to those found in previous studies. Overall, these studies provide partial support for transdiagnostic CBT for anxiety disorders. Unlike Barlow's (2002) unified protocol and Hayes et al.'s (2004) ACT, these approaches do not offer a unified theory about the psychopathology of anxiety disorders. Additional research is necessary to determine if these approaches are equally efficacious across diagnoses and if they offer any benefit in therapeutic value or cost-effectiveness over disorder-specific protocols.

Transdiagnostic approaches to the treatment of anxiety disorders offer several advantages over the use of multiple, disorder-specific manuals. First, they reflect advances in our understanding of the relationships among anxiety disorders. Converging evidence from various lines of research suggests that anxiety disorders emerge from a shared vulnerability and are maintained by similar mechanisms. Viewing disorder symptoms as manifestations of this underlying vulnerability, some approaches attempt to address the vulnerability directly. Second, transdiagnostic treatments may facilitate dissemination by condensing empirically supported interventions into more widely applicable approaches. Although these approaches offer several benefits, the efficacy of these protocols in relation to disorder-specific intervention awaits controlled investigation. In addition to the evaluation of the differential outcome for the presenting disorders, it will be of interest to ascertain whether these transdiagnostic interventions are more efficacious in promoting long-term reductions in putative dimensions of shared vulnerability (e.g., neuroticism).

Toward a Dimensional Classification System

As noted above, the *DSM* classification system does not recognize the common features of emotional disorders that may be germane to long-term outcome and which perhaps should be targets of treatment in addition to, or instead of, disorder-specific features. The current nosology does not foster treatment planning in several other ways. Owing to its purely categorical approach to classification, the *DSM* does not capture individual differences in disorder severity and does not provide adequate coverage for clinically significant symptom presentations that deviate from the definition of a formal diagnostic category. Moreover, diagnostic hierarchy rules that remain in *DSM-IV* obscure comorbidity patterns that may be relevant to treatment planning and outcome. Most of these limitations could be addressed by incorporating dimensional elements into the *DSM* (cf. Brown & Barlow, 2005).

We have encountered many problems with *DSM*'s categorical diagnostic system in our work with the anxiety and unipolar mood disorders (see Brown & Barlow, 2002, for a review). A diagnostic reliability study of the *DSM-IV* anxiety and mood disorders (Brown, Di Nardo, Lehman, & Campbell, 2001) found that for many categories (e.g., SOC, OCD), diagnostic disagreements less often involved boundary issues with other formal disorders but were primarily due to problems in defining and applying a categorical threshold on the number, severity, or duration of symptoms. This threshold problem is manifested in various ways. It can be seen in diagnostic disagreements where both raters concur that the key features of a disorder are present, but disagree as to whether these features cause sufficient interference or distress to satisfy the *DSM-IV* threshold for a clinical disorder (common with social and specific phobia). The problem is also evident in the high rates of disagreements involving NOS diagnoses (both raters agree on the presence of clinically significant features of the disorder, but one rater does not assign a formal anxiety or mood disorder diagnosis due to subthreshold patient report of the number or duration of symptoms; common with GAD and major depression). A similar problem is at the root of diagnostic disagreements involving major depression versus dysthymia (DYS; core features of clinically significant depression are observed by both raters, but disagreement occurs with regard to the severity or duration of these symptoms). Finally, whereas dimensional ratings of the severity of major depression symptoms are reliable (r = .74), the *DSM-IV* categorical severity specifiers for this disorder are not reliable (e.g., κ = .30; Brown, Di Nardo, et al.,).

Imposing categories on dimensional phenomena leads to a substantial loss of potentially valuable clinical information. As noted by Widiger and Samuel (2005), the *DSM* does not provide adequate coverage for clinically significant symptom presentations that fail to meet criteria for formal diagnostic categories (as reflected by the high rate in which NOS diagnoses are assigned as current and lifetime conditions; cf. Brown, Di Nardo, et al., 2001; Stein, Walker, Hazen, & Forde, 1997; Zinbarg et al., 1994). Given the array of possible presentations of anxiety disorder NOS, the diagnosis provides clinicians with little information and does not lend itself to a disorder-specific, manualized treatment. Moreover, the *DSM* does not provide a sufficient mechanism to record the severity of disorders (e.g., the severity of depression rather than the presence/absence of comorbid mood disorder per se may be more relevant to the prediction of the treatment outcome or natural course of a principal anxiety disorder). Salient information is also lost by adherence to the *DSM*'s elaborate set of hierarchical exclusions and differential diagnostic decision rules. These rules are in place to foster diagnostic reliability and to avoid excessive comorbidity (i.e., two separate categories should not be assigned if one diagnosis is deemed to be "due to" the coexisting disorder that occupies a higher position in the hierarchy). For example, *DSM-IV* criteria indicate that GAD should not be diagnosed if its features occur exclusively during the course of a mood disorder. Adherence to diagnostic rules of this nature leads to considerable information loss and misleading findings about the overlap of various disorders. In our comorbidity study of *DSM-IV* anxiety and mood disorders (Brown, Campbell, et al., 2001), the comorbidity rate of GAD and DYS was found to be a mere 5% when *DSM-IV* diagnostic rules were strictly followed. This result is strongly at odds with the wealth of evidence indicating substantial phenotypic and genetic overlap of GAD and the mood disorders (e.g., Brown et al., 1998; Kendler, Neale, Kessler, Heath, & Eaves, 1992). When this diagnostic hierarchy rule was ignored, the GAD–DYS comorbidity estimate rose to 90%. Thus, if adhering strictly to *DSM-IV*, an individual may be diagnosed only with major depressive disorder despite also meeting full criteria for GAD. This potentially obscures important information about the phenomenology of the patient's symptoms and their level of functioning and overall psychopathology (Zimmerman & Chelminski, 2003). Artifacts of *DSM-IV* differential diagnostic rules are evident in other comorbid patterns, including lower estimates of the co-occurrence of PDA with SOC and specific phobia (Brown & Barlow, 2005; Brown, Campbell, et al., 2001).

Developers of *DSM-V* will "grapple" with the prospect of incorporating dimensional elements into the classification system. Although the utility of dimensional classification has been recognized for over three decades (e.g., Kendell 1975), no strong proposals have emerged with regard to how dimensional classification could be accomplished in the *DSM*. An entirely dimensional classification system, First (2005) has argued, might impede communication among mental health professionals and lead to cumbersome clinical assessments. Elsewhere (Brown & Barlow 2005), we have suggested that movement toward this goal could begin with basic research systems whereby dimensional ratings of severity are introduced to the extant *DSM* diagnostic categories and constituent symptom criteria (akin to the methods in the Anxiety Disorders Interview Schedule for *DSM-IV*; cf. Brown 2007; Brown et al., 1998). If ultimately adopted in clinical practice, this seems to be a relatively practical alternative, because the categorical system would remain intact and the dimensional rating system could be optional in settings where its implementation is less feasible (e.g., primary care). Although not directly addressing the problem of high comorbidity, this strategy would address some of the chief complaints with *DSM-IV*, such as the poor reliability of categorical disorder specifiers (e.g., mild, moderate, severe major depression; cf. Brown, Di Nardo et al. 2001), and the failure to capture individual differences in disorder severity as well as other clinically significant features that are either subsumed by other disorders (e.g., GAD in mood disorders and PTSD) or fall just below conventional thresholds because of a *DSM* technicality (e.g., subclinical or NOS diagnoses where the clinical presentation is a symptom or two short of a formal disorder). Because dimensional ratings would simply be added to the current diagnostic categories, this approach would have several other advantages including: (a) its basis on a preexisting and widely studied set of constructs (cf. APA, 1994, p. xxii); and (b) the ability to retain functional analytic and temporal (duration) aspects of diagnosis that are difficult to capture in a purely psychometric approach. Moreover, it would provide a standardized assessment system that fosters across-site comparability in the study of dimensional models of psychopathology. Thus, this approach might be a prudent "first step" that would assist in determining the reliability and feasibility of more ambitious dimensional systems (e.g., quantifying higher-order dimensions of temperament that convey disorder risk or prognosis).

References

American Psychiatric Association. (1968). *Diagnostic and statistical manual of mental disorders* (2nd ed.). Washington, DC: Author.

American Psychiatric Association. (1980). *Diagnostic and statistical manual of mental disorders* (3rd ed.). Washington, DC: Author.

American Psychiatric Association. (1987). *Diagnostic and statistical manual of mental disorders* (3rd ed., rev.). Washington, DC: Author.

American Psychiatric Association. (1994). *Diagnostic and statistical manual of mental disorders* (4th ed.). Washington, DC: Author.

American Psychiatric Association. (2000). *Diagnostic and statistical manual of mental disorders* (4th ed., text revision). Washington, DC: Author.

Andrews, G. (1990). Classification of neurotic disorders. *Journal of Royal Society of Medicine, 83,* 606–607.

Andrews, G. (1996). Comorbidity in neurotic disorders: The similarities are more important than the differences. In R.M. Rapee (Ed.), *Current controversies in the anxiety disorders* (pp. 3–20). New York: Guilford Press.

Bach, P., & Hayes, S. C. (2002). The use of acceptance and commitment therapy to prevent the rehospitalization of psychotic patients: A randomized controlled trial. *Journal of Consulting and Clinical Psychology, 70,* 1129–1139.

Bandelow, B., Zohar, J., Hollander, E., Kasper, S., & Moller, H. J. (2002). World Federation of Societies of Biological Psychiatry (WFSBP) guidelines for the pharmacological treatment of anxiety, obsessive–compulsive, and posttraumatic stress disorders. *World Journal of Biological Psychiatry, 3,* 171–199.

Barlow, D. H. (2002). *Anxiety and its disorders: The nature and treatment of anxiety and panic* (2nd ed.). New York: Guilford Press.

Barlow, D. H., Allen, L. B., & Choate, M. L. (2004). Toward a unified treatment for emotional disorders. *Behavior Therapy, 35,* 205–230.

Barlow, D. H., & Craske, M. G. (2000). *Mastery of your anxiety and panic (MAP-3): Client workbook for anxiety and panic* (3rd ed.). San Antonio, TX: Psychological Corporation.

Borkovec, T. D., Abel, J. L., & Newman, H. (1995). Effects of psychotherapy on comorbid conditions in generalized anxiety disorder. *Journal of Consulting & Clinical Psychology, 63,* 479–483.

Borkovec, T. D., Newman, M. G., Pincus, A. L., & Lytle, R. (2002). A component analysis of cognitive-behavioral therapy for generalized anxiety disorder and the role of interpersonal processes. *Cognitive Therapy and Research, 22,* 561–576.

Boyce, P., & Parker, G. (1985). Neuroticism as a predictor of outcome in depression. *Journal of Nervous and Mental Disease, 173,* 685–688.

Brady, K., Pearlstein, T., Asnis, G. M., Baker, D., Rothbaum, B., Sikes, C. R., et al. (2000). Efficacy and safety of sertraline treatment of posttraumatic stress disorder: a randomized controlled trial. *Journal of the American Medical Association, 283,* 1837–1844.

Brawman-Mintzer, O., Lydiard, R.B., Emmanuel, N., Payeur, R., Johnson, M., Roberts, et al. (1993). Psychiatric comorbidity in patients with generalized anxiety disorder. *American Journal of Psychiatry, 150,* 1216–1218.

Brown, T. A. (2007). Temporal course and structural relationships among dimensions of temperament and *DSM-IV* anxiety and mood disorder constructs. *Journal of Abnormal Psychology, 116,* 313–328.

Brown, T. A., Antony, M. M., & Barlow, D. H. (1995). Diagnostic comorbidity in panic disorder: Effect on treatment outcome and course of comorbid diagnoses following treatment. *Journal of Consulting and Clinical Psychology, 63,* 408–418.

Brown, T. A., & Barlow, D. H. (1992). Comorbidity among anxiety and mood disorders: Implications for treatment and *DSM-IV*. *Journal of Consulting and Clinical Psychology, 63,* 408–418.

Brown, T. A., & Barlow, D. H. (2002). Classification of anxiety and mood disorders. In D.H. Barlow, *Anxiety and its disorders: The nature and treatment of anxiety and panic* (2nd ed., pp. 292–327). New York: Guilford Press.

Brown, T. A., & Barlow, D. H. (2005). Categorical *vs* dimensional classification of mental disorders in *DSM-V* and beyond. *Journal of Abnormal Psychology, 114,* 551–556.

Brown, T. A., Campbell, L. A., Lehman, C. L., Grisham, J. R., & Mancill, R. B. (2001). Current and lifetime comorbidity of the *DSM-IV* anxiety and mood disorders in a large clinical sample. *Journal of Abnormal Psychology, 110,* 585–599.

Brown, T. A., Chorpita, B. F., & Barlow, D. H. (1998). Structural relationships among dimensions of the *DSM-IV* anxiety and mood disorders and dimensions of negative affect, positive affect, and autonomic arousal. *Journal of Abnormal Psychology, 107,* 179–192.

Brown, T. A., Di Nardo, P. A., Lehman, C. L., & Campbell, L. A. (2001). Reliability of *DSM-IV* anxiety and mood disorders: Implications for the classification of emotional disorders. *Journal of Abnormal Psychology, 110,* 49–58.

Campbell–Sills, L. A., Liverant, G., & Brown, T. A. (2004). Psychometric evaluation of the Behavioral Inhibition/Behavioral Activation Scales (BIS/BAS) in large clinical samples. *Psychological Assessment, 16,* 244–254.

Carver, C. S., & White, T. L. (1994). Behavioral inhibition, behavioral activation, and affective responses to impending reward and punishment: The BIS/BAS scales. *Journal of Personality and Social Psychology, 67,* 319–333.

Clark, L. A. (2005). Temperament as a unifying basis for personality and psychopathology. *Journal of Abnormal Psychology, 114,* 505–521.

Clark, L. A., Vittengl, J., Kraft, D., & Jarrett, R. B. (2003). Separate personality traits from states to predict depression. *Journal of Personality Disorders, 17,* 152–172.

Clark, L. A., Watson, D., & Mineka, S. (1994). Temperament, personality, and the mood and anxiety disorders. *Journal of Abnormal Psychology, 103,* 103–116.

Craske, M. G., & Barlow, D. H. (2006). *Mastery of your anxiety and worry* (2nd ed.). New York: Oxford University Press.

Craske, M.G., Brown, T.A., & Barlow, D.H. (1991). Behavioral treatment of panic disorder: A two-year follow-up. *Behavior Therapy, 22,* 289–304.

Craske, M. G., Farchione, T. J., Allen, L. B., Barrios, V., Stoyanova, M., & Rose, R. (2007). Cognitive behavioral therapy for panic disorder and comorbidity: More of the same or less of more? *Behaviour Research and Therapy, 45,* 1095–1109.

Davidson, J. R., & Foa, E. B. (1991). Diagnostic issues in posttraumatic stress disorder: Considerations for the *DSM-IV*. *Journal of Abnormal Psychology, 100,* 346–355.

Di Nardo, P.A., O'Brien, G. T., Barlow, D. H., Waddell, M. T., & Blanchard, E. B. (1983). Reliability of *DSM-III* anxiety disorder categories using a new structured interview. *Archives of General Psychiatry, 40,* 1070–1078.

Eifert, G. H., & Forsyth, J. P. (2005). *Acceptance and commitment therapy for anxiety disorders: A practitioner's treatment guide to using mindfulness, acceptance, and values-based behavior change strategies.* Oakland, CA: New Harbinger Publications.

Erickson, D. H. (2003). Group cognitive behavioural therapy for heterogeneous anxiety disorders. *Cognitive Behaviour Therapy, 32,* 179–186.

Eysenck, H. J. (1981). *A model for personality.* New York: Springer.

Fairburn, C. G., Cooper, Z., & Shafran, R. (2003). Cognitive behaviour therapy for eating disorders: A "transdiagnostic" theory and treatment. *Behaviour Research and Therapy, 41,* 509–528.

Fanous, A., Gardner, C. O., Prescott, C. A., Cancro, R., & Kendler, K. S. (2002). Neuroticism, major depression, and gender: A population-based twin study. *Psychological Medicine, 32,* 719–728.

First, M. B. (2005). Mutually exclusive versus co-occurring diagnostic categories: The challenge of diagnostic comorbidity. *Psychopathology, 38,* 206–210.

Frances, A., Widiger, T., & Fyer, M. R. (1990). The influence of classification methods on comorbidity. In J.D. Maser & C.R. Cloninger (Eds.), *Comorbidity of mood and anxiety disorders* (pp. 41–59). Washington, DC: American Psychiatric Press.90

Garvey, M. J., & Tuason, V. B. (1984). The relationship of panic disorder to agoraphobia. *Comprehensive Psychiatry, 25,* 529–531.

Gaudiano, B. A., & Herbert, J. D. (2006). Acute treatment of inpatients with psychotic symptoms using Acceptance and Commitment Therapy: Pilot results. *Behaviour Research and Therapy, 44,* 415–437.

Geerts, E., & Bouhuys, N. (1998). Multilevel prediction of short-term outcome of depression: Nonverbal interpersonal processes, cognitions, and personality traits. *Psychiatry Research, 79,* 59–72.

Gershuny, B. S., & Sher, K. J. (1998). The relation between personality and anxiety: Findings from a three-year prospective study. *Journal of Abnormal Psychology, 107,* 252–262.

Gray, J. A. (1987). *The psychology of fear and stress* (2nd ed.). Cambridge, England: Cambridge University Press.

Hayes, S. C., Strosahl, K., & Wilson, K. G. (1999). *Acceptance and commitment therapy: An experiential approach to behavior change.* New York: Guilford Press.

Hayes, S. C., Wilson, K. G., Gifford, E. V., Bissett, R., Piasecki, M., Batten, S. V., et al. (2004). A preliminary trial of 12-step facilitation of and acceptance and commitment therapy for polysubstance-abusing maintained opiate addicts. *Behavior Therapy, 35,* 667–688.

Hayes, S. C., Wilson, K. G., Gifford, E. V., Follette, V. M., & Strosahl, K. (1996). Experiential avoidance and behavioral disorders: A functional dimensional approach to diagnosis and treatment. *Journal of Consulting and Clinical Psychology, 64,* 1152–1168.

Hettema, J. M., Prescott, C. A., & Kendler, K. S. (2004). Genetic and environmental sources of covariation between generalized anxiety disorder and neuroticism. *American Journal of Psychiatry, 161,* 1581–1587.

Hettema, J. M., Prescott, C. A., Myers, J. M., Neale, M. C., & Kendler, K. S. (2005). The structure of genetic and environmental risk factors for anxiety disorders in men and women. *Archives of General Psychiatry, 62,* 182–189.

Hohagen, F., Winkelmann, G., Rasche–Ruchle, H., Hand, I., Konig, A., Munchau, N., et al. (1998). Combination of behaviour therapy with fluvoxamine in comparison with behaviour therapy and placebo. Results of a multicentre study. *British Journal of Psychiatry, 35,* 71–78.

Hudson, J. I., & Pope, H. G. (1990). Affective spectrum disorders: Does antidepressant response identify a family of disorders with a common pathophysiology? *American Journal of Psychiatry, 147,* 552–564.

Jones, J. C., & Barlow, D. H. (1990). The etiology of posttraumatic stress disorder. *Clinical Psychology Review, 10,* 299–328.

Joyce, P. R., Mulder, R. T., & Cloninger, C. R. (1994). Temperament predicts clomipramine and desipramine response in major depression. *Journal of Affective Disorders, 30,* 35–46.

Kasch, K. L., Rottenberg, J., Arnow, B. A., & Gotlib, I. H. (2002). Behavioral activation and inhibition systems and the severity and course of depression. *Journal of Abnormal Psychology, 111,* 589–597.

Kendell, R. E. (1975). *The role of diagnosis in psychiatry.* Oxford: Blackwell.

Kendler, K. S., Neale, M. C., Kessler, R. C., Heath, A. C., & Eaves, L. J. (1992). Major depression and generalized anxiety disorder: Same genes, (partly) different environments? *Archives of General Psychiatry, 49,* 716–722.

Kessler, R. C., Chui, W. T., Demler, O., & Walters, E. E. (2005). Prevalence, severity, and comorbidity of 12-month *DSM-IV* disorders in the National Comorbidity Survey replication. *Archives of General Psychiatry, 62,* 617–627.

Kessler, R. C., McGonagle, K. A., S. Zhao, S., Nelson, C. B., Hughes, M., Eshleman, S., et al. (1994). Lifetime and 12-month prevalence of *DSM-III-R* psychiatric disorders in the United States. Results from the National Comorbidity Survey. *Archives of General Psychiatry, 51,* 8–19.

Kessler, R. C., Stang, P., Wittchen, H. U., Stein, M., & Walters, E. E. (1999). Lifetime comorbidities between social phobia and mood disorders in the U.S. National Comorbidity Survey. *Psychological Medicine, 29,* 555–567.

Liebowitz, M. R., & Klein, D. F. (1981). Differential diagnosis and treatment of panic attacks and phobic states. *Annual Review of Medicine, 32,* 583–599.

Mathews, A. M. (1978). Fear-reduction research and clinical phobias. *Psychological Bulletin, 85,* 390–404.

McEvoy, P. M., & Nathan, P. (2007). Effective of cognitive behavior therapy for diagnostically heterogeneous groups: A benchmarking study. *Journal of Consulting and Clinical Psychology, 75,* 344–350.

Meyer, B., Johnson, S. L., & Winters, R. (2001). Responsiveness to threat and incentive in bipolar disorder: Relations of the BIS/BAS scales with symptoms. *Journal of Psychopathology and Behavioral Assessment, 23,* 133–143.

Michelson, D., Lydiard, R. B., Pollack, M. H., Tamura, R. N., Hoog, S. L., Tepner, R., et al. (1998). Outcome assessment and clinical improvement in panic disorder: Evidence from a randomized controlled trial of fluoxetine and placebo. *American Journal of Psychiatry, 155,* 1570–1577.

Mineka, S., Watson, D., & Clark, L. A. (1998). Comorbidity of anxiety and unipolar mood disorders. *Annual Review of Psychology, 49,* 377–412.

Mitte, K. (2005). A meta-analysis of the efficacy of psycho- and pharmacotherapy in panic disorder with and without agoraphobia. *Journal of Affective Disorders, 88,* 27–45.

Norton, P. J., & Hope, D. A. (2005). Preliminary evaluation of a broad-spectrum cognitive-behavioral group therapy for anxiety. *Journal of Behavior Therapy and Experimental Psychiatry, 36,* 79–97.

Pirkola, S. P., Isometsa, E., Suvisaari, J., Aro, H., Joukamaa, M., Poikolainen, K., et al. (2005). *DSM-IV* mood, anxiety, and alcohol use disorders and their comorbidity in the Finnish general population: Results from the Health 2000 study. *Social Psychiatry and Psychiatric Epidemiology, 40,* 1–10.

Pollack, M. H., Zininelli, R., Goddard, A., McCafferty, J. P., Bellew, K. M, Burnham, D.B., et al. (2001). Paroxetine in the treatment of generalized anxiety disorder: Results of a placebo-controlled, flexible-dosage trial. *Journal of Clinical Psychiatry, 62,* 350–357.

Sanderson, W. C., Di Nardo, P. A., Rapee, R. M., & Barlow, D. H. (1990). Syndrome comorbidity in patients diagnosed with a *DSM-III-R* anxiety disorder. *Journal of Abnormal Psychology, 99,* 308–312.

Sato, T., Hirano, S., Narita, T., Kusunoki, K., Kato, J., Goto, M., et al. (1999). Temperament and character inventory dimensions as a predictor of response to antidepressant treatment in major depression. *Journal of Affective Disorders, 56,* 153–161.

Stein, D. J., Berk, M., Els, C., Emsley, R. A., Gittelson, L., Wilson, D., et al. (1999). A double-blind placebo-controlled trial of paroxetine in the management of social phobia (social anxiety disorder) in South Africa. *South African Medical Journal, 89,* 402–406.

Stein, M. B., Walker, J. R., Hazen, A. L, & Forde, D. R. (1997). Full and partial posttraumatic stress disorder: Findings from a community survey. *American Journal of Psychiatry, 154,* 1114–1119.

Tellegen, A. (1985). Structures of mood and personality and their relevance to assessing anxiety with an emphasis on self-report. In A.H. Tuma & J.D. Maser (Eds.), *Anxiety and the anxiety disorders* (pp. 681–706). Hillsdale, NJ: Erlbaum.

Thyer, B. A., & Himle, J. (1985). Temporal relationship between panic attack onset and phobic avoidance in agoraphobia. *Behavior Research and Therapy, 23,* 607–608.

Tsao, J. C. I., Lewin, M. R., & Craske, M. G. (1998). The effects of cognitive-behavior therapy for panic disorder on comorbid conditions. *Journal of Anxiety Disorders, 12,* 357–371.

Tsao, J. C. I., Mystkowski, J. L., Zucker, B. G., & Craske, M. G. (2002). Effects of cognitive-behavioral therapy for panic disorder to comorbid conditions: Replication and extension. *Behavior Therapy, 33,* 493–509.

Tyrer, P. (1989). *Classification of neurosis*. Chichester, England: John Wiley & Sons.

Tyrer, P., Seivewright, N., Murphy, S., Ferguson, B., Kingdon, D., Barczak, B., et al. (1988). The Nottingham study of neurotic disorder: Comparison of drug and psychological treatments. *Lancet, 2,* 235–240.

Viken, R. J., Rose, R. J., Kaprio, J., & Koskenvuo, M. (1994). A developmental genetic analysis of adult personality: Extraversion and neuroticism from 18 to 59 years of age. *Journal of Personality and Social Psychology, 66,* 722–730.

Watson, D., Clark, L. A., & Carey, G. (1988). Positive and negative affectivity and their relation to the anxiety and depressive disorders. *Journal of Abnormal Psychology, 97,* 346–353.

Widiger, T. A., & Samuel, D. B. (2005). Diagnostic categories or dimensions: A question for *DSM-V*. *Journal of Abnormal Psychology, 114,* 494–504.

Widiger, T. A., Verheul, R., & van den Brink, W. (1999). Personality and psychopathology. In L.A. Pervin & O.P. John (Eds.), *Handbook of personality: Theory and research* (pp. 347–366). New York: Guilford Press.

Woods, D. W., Wetterneck, C. T., & Flessner, C. A. (2006). A controlled evaluation of acceptance and commitment therapy plus habit reversal for trichotillomania. *Behaviour Research and Therapy, 44,* 639–656.

Woody, S., McLean, P. D., Taylor, S., & Koch, W. J. (1999). Treatment of major depression in the context of panic disorder. *Journal of Affective Disorder, 53,* 163–174.

Zimmerman, M., & Chelminski, I. (2003). Generalized anxiety disorder in patients with major depression: Is *DSM-IV*'s hierarchy correct? *American Journal of Psychiatry, 160,* 504–512.

Zinbarg, R. E., Barlow, D. H., Liebowitz, M., Street L., Broadhead, E., Katon, W., Roy-Byrne, P.P, Lepine, J.P., Teherani, M., & Richards, J. (1994). The *DSM-IV* field trial for mixed anxiety–depression. *American Journal of Psychiatry, 151,* 1153–1156.

Zitrin, C. M., Klein, D. F., Woerner, M. B., & Ross, D. C. (1983). Treatment of phobias. *Archives of General Psychiatry, 40,* 125–138.

19 Classification of Anxiety Disorders for *DSM-V* and *ICD-11*: Issues, Proposals, and Controversies

Steven Taylor
Gordon J. G. Asmundson
Jonathan S. Abramowitz
Dean McKay

Introduction

"Endless forms most beautiful and most wonderful have been, and are being evolved."

—Charles Darwin, *The Origin of Species*

Except for the reference to "most beautiful," Charles Darwin's famous concluding statement could be readily applied to the systems developed by creators of psychiatric classification systems. Endless forms, most wonderful indeed, have been proposed. One of the best examples is the elaborate system proposed by the eminent German Psychiatrist Karl Leonhard (see Fish, 1974). Leonhard's influence is reflected, to some extent, in classificatory systems today. And now, the time has come to reconsider the classification of anxiety disorders.

Our goal in preparing this book was to provide in-depth coverage of issues and critical discussion related to the classification of anxiety disorders. This is an important endeavor, given that the fifth edition of the Diagnostic and Statistical Manual of Mental Disorders (*DSM-V*) is currently in preparation, with publication scheduled for 2012. The World Health Organization is also in the process of revising its diagnostic manual, the *International Classification of Disease* (*ICD*). The 11th edition is planned to be ready in 2014.

In the years since the publication of the current editions of *DSM* and *ICD*, a wealth of research has accumulated on the classification of anxiety disorders, making it time to consider whether the current classification schemes should be altered. The chapters in this volume amply show that there many concerns with the current classification schemes. The purpose of this concluding chapter is to take a broad perspective on the classification of anxiety disorder by providing a critical review of the issues and proposals raised in the chapters in this volume and in the broader literature on proposals for *DSM* and *ICD*. We begin by examining important issues concerning the classification of mental disorders in general, and highlight the relevance of these issues for the classification of anxiety disorders. We then consider issues specific to the anxiety disorders, including the organization or grouping of disorders and proposals for refining the criteria for specific disorders. We conclude by examining the progress to date, as indicated by published reports, of the relevant *DSM-V* and *ICD-11* committees.

General Issues Concerning Revisions to the Classification of Mental Disorders

Conceptual Issues in Classification

The difficulty involved in identifying discrete types of mental disorders has long been recognized. In 1922,

Kraepelin made the following observations, which remain relevant today:

> *Innumerable have been the attempts to classify . . . cases, and so to arrive at types. But again and again it has been found that the diversity of the phenomena makes mock of such imprisonment, that the mixed and indefinite forms thickly overgrow the simple types artificially stripped of their bark, and that a close examination leaves but few cases that will go unmistakably into this or that pigeon hole. (p. 117)*

Today, it is widely believed that *DSM* and *ICD* are not carving nature at its joints, as originally planned (Hen & Hyman, 2005). Several possible approaches to reclassifying disorders have been considered, such as the following: (a) classification by clinical features, such as signs, symptoms, and course, as attempted by Kraepelin and used in the current versions of *DSM* and *ICD*; (b) classification on the basis of treatment response, which, as noted by Hen and Hyman (2005), is a questionable approach given some treatments (e.g., serotonergic medications) are efficacious for a range of disorders; (c) classification by etiology, which was Kraepelin's unfulfilled ambition, such as classification in terms of genes or gene-environment interactions that confer risk for a given pattern of psychopathology; and (d) classification by pathophysiology; that is, by neural, cognitive, and emotional processes that give rise to signs and symptoms.

Each of these approaches has its difficulties, and it may be necessary to integrate multiple perspectives in order to develop adequate classification (and explanation) of the disorders (Kendler, 2008). Several of the above-mentioned approaches may need to be used in the forthcoming editions of *DSM* and *ICD*; specifically, diagnoses based on clinical features combined with what little firm evidence there is on etiology. The purpose of diagnosis (i.e., primarily for research, treatment, or both) also shapes the form that an optimal classification system should take, as we discuss in more detail later in this chapter.

All these considerations suggest that one of the first steps in revising the classification system for mental disorders in general, including anxiety disorders, is to carefully examine the important conceptual issues involved in classification. Accordingly, Kendler and colleagues (2008) proposed that, for the preparation of *DSM-V*, there should be a conceptual issues workgroup for examining problems that cut across disorders. (Presumably the same recommendation would apply to *ICD-11*.) Kendler et al. identified the following issues as important:

- What is the definition of a mental disorder? If disorder X is proposed for *DSM-V*, how will we decide whether it represents a legitimate psychiatric condition?
- What should be the criteria for revising diagnostic criteria?
- What are the organizing principles for classification? Should disorders be classified by symptomatic resemblance, etiological relationships, or other criteria?
- In validating alternative criteria sets, which validators (e.g., signs, symptoms, clinical course, functional impairment) should be given priority? What do we do if different validators yield different answers?
- As we introduce laboratory values or other etiological criteria into *DSM*, what guidelines should be established regarding their inclusion?
- How should we relate dimensional models for mental disorders to traditional, symptom-based categories?
- What should be the mechanisms for setting priorities for all these questions?

These are unquestionably important issues for consideration. Before discussing them in detail, we will consider the important question of *how* the issues will be addressed. That is, the process of decision making in revising *DSM* and *ICD*.

Concerns with Committee-Based Classification

In his commentary of the process of developing *DSM-IV*, Spitzer (1991), one of the architects of *DSM-III*, observed that it is likely that when final decisions are made about *DSM-IV*, the decisions will still be based primarily on expert consensus, rather than on data, as was the case with *DSM-III* and *DSM-III-R* (p. 294). Will the same be the case for *DSM-V*?

An important question is how the workgroups will arrive at their decisions. Will decisions be based on committee vote, informed by their review of the scientific literature, as in previous *DSM*s? This is likely. But, what if the nature of the vote (recommendation) varies with the composition of the workgroup? In other words, would a vote by one workgroup be different from that of a workgroup composed of different individuals? This question of reliability may be an important issue, given that it is not uncommon for one group of investigators to arrive at different conclusions from another group. To illustrate, two workgroups reviewing the efficacy of treatments for posttraumatic stress disorder (PTSD) arrived at quite different conclusions. Various expert reviewers and workgroups (e.g., National Institute of Clinical Excellence, 2005) concluded that behavior therapy and selective serotonin reuptake inhibitors were effective treatments. In contrast, a workgroup assembled by the Institute of Medicine concluded, on the basis of reviewing essentially the same data as the other workgroups, that the only treatment with sufficient evidence of efficacy was behavior therapy (Institute of Medicine, 2007).

In addition to these concerns, there is the problem of what to do if the recommendations of the conceptual issues workgroup differ from those of the other workgroups. At the heart of the problem is the reliability (as noted above) and validity of committee-based decisions. A partial solution might be to treat the proposals for revisions to *DSM* and *ICD* as if they were journal articles; the proposals would be sent out for peer review to multiple reviewers and then an independent group of experts would synthesize the reviews and highlight the important issues to be addressed, say, in field trials, before the proposals would be accepted for publication.

Workgroup decisions are likely to be influenced, at least in part, by sociopolitical and financial pressures. For example, committee members might tend to make decisions about the structure of *DSM* in accord with the best interests of their own funded research or clinical practice agendas, even if such conclusions are controversial or contested in the empirical literature. Insurance companies and other third parties that pay for mental health treatment also have a stake in the architecture of the next *DSM* because reimbursement for services is tied to diagnosis. Likewise, the pharmaceutical industry is a stakeholder in the emerging revised taxonomy. More than 50% of *DSM-IV* and *DSM-IV-TR* committee members had financial ties to this industry, including being funded for research, consultation, and participation on speaker bureaus (Cosgrove, Krimsky, Vijayaraghavan, & Schneider, 2006). One might imagine it would be difficult for those shaping the diagnostic criteria to ignore the interests of the pharmaceutical companies to which they have such ties.

Mechanism-Based Classification

Complexity of causal mechanisms. Classification systems serve several functions, one of which is to organize phenomena and thereby facilitate research into underlying mechanisms. Thus, a good classificatory system is important for understanding the etiology of the myriad forms of psychopathology. The current classification systems define and diagnose disorders largely on the basis of descriptive features (signs, symptoms, and their course) rather than on the basis of etiology.

Several investigators, including some of those in this volume, have called for a mechanism-based classification system. They argue that, instead of using a purely descriptive system, a more useful approach for defining and grouping the disorders would be on the basis of their underlying mechanisms, as is done in other areas of medicine. Clinically, the treatment (and prevention) of anxiety disorders might be improved if diagnosis was based on mechanisms. The purpose of diagnosis would be to identify mechanisms that need to be targeted with clinical interventions.

A mechanism-based system would rely on either etiology (genes, environmental factors, and their interactions), pathophysiology (brain circuits and structures and their associated cognitive and emotional processes), or some combination of both. Few investigators appear to have considered what such a mechanism-based classification system would look like, and fewer still have considered the implications of such a system. Notable exceptions are Hyman (2007), Kendler (2008), and a handful of others.

Hyman (2007) explored the possibility of a neuroscience-based system, and arrived at the following conclusions:

> *It is probably premature to bring neurobiology into the formal classification of mental disorders that will form the core of the DSM-V. However, it is not too early to use neurobiology as a central tool to rethink the current approach to mental disorders, and to begin some careful experiments that could liberate science from the unintended consequences of reifying the current diagnoses that probably do not mirror nature. (p. 731)*

Even the comparatively simpler task of using laboratory tests (e.g., data from blood tests) as proxy measures of any neurobiologic measures is not feasible, at least at present. As noted by First and Zimmerman (2006), "despite widespread acceptance that most psychiatric disorders are 'diseases of the brain' . . . the field of psychiatry has thus far failed to identify a single neurobiological marker that is diagnostic of a mental disorder" (p. 2041). First and Zimmerman went on to suggest that "embedding laboratory tests with less-than-perfect diagnostic sensitivity and specificity parameters in polythetic criteria sets may finally allow the inclusion of objective laboratory tests into *DSM-V* diagnostic definitions" (p. 2042). Such a recommendation seems misguided, at least at the present time. Diagnostic criteria are unlikely to be improved by making a diagnosis on the basis of objective tests that have dubious or unsubstantiated reliability and validity.

Kendler (2008) considered what would be required for a comprehensive understanding of the mechanisms underlying mental disorders, which has implications for classification. Multiple explanatory perspectives would probably be required, including neurobiology, cognitive processes, and other social or environmental factors. Kendler highlighted the complexity likely to be involved—causal networks consisting of multiple subsystems with multiple nonlinear interactions and causal loops. Adding to the complexity, multiple etiologies may produce similar pathophysiologies that are not perfectly coupled to symptoms, signs, and impairment (Hen & Hyman, 2005). All of this raises the question of the feasibility of developing a mechanism-based classification system. But if one were to attempt to devise a mechanism-based classification of anxiety disorders, based on the current state of knowledge, what would it look like? In the following section we will consider some possibilities and their implications, based on leading models of anxiety disorders.

Mechanism-based classification of anxiety disorders. In the years since *DSM-IV* was published (American Psychiatric Association, 1994), great strides have been made in understanding anxiety disorders, and many models of these disorders have been proposed. However, such models are typically limited to a particular domain or level of understanding. The models are typically based entirely on either biological dysregulations or cognitive and behavioral factors. There has yet to be a widely accepted comprehensive biopsychosocial model for any anxiety disorder.

But even if we took one of the leading models of the anxiety disorders as a basis for mechanism-based classification, would the resulting classification system be any better than the current one? Consider, for example, the leading cognitive models of anxiety disorders, such as those proposed by Beck and Emery (1985), Clark (1986), or Salkovskis (1996). Classification based on these models would be unsatisfactory for at least five reasons. First, these models are based on the current *DSM*; for example, each cognitive model is tied to a specific disorder, such as the cognitive models for panic disorder, social anxiety disorder, obsessive–compulsive disorder (OCD), and so forth. So, the structure of a cognitive-based classification would be quite similar to the current system, with the possible exception that particular sorts of dysfunctional beliefs or appraisals might become explicit diagnostic criteria. For example, catastrophic misinterpretation of bodily sensations, which currently appears in the descriptive text of *DSM-IV-TR*, might become one of the criteria needed to diagnose panic attacks in panic disorder. But such changes would be relatively minor; the content and structure of the classification of anxiety disorders would remain essentially unchanged.

Second, the cognitive approach does not have any advantages over the current system in terms of treatment implications. The current system of anxiety disorders has no explicit implications about which treatments would or would not be effective. Although the cognitive approach does have the advantage of predicting that cognitive-behavior therapy would be an effective intervention, the cognitive approach fails to predict that various drug treatments would be effective.

Third, the cognitive approach neglects many important etiologic factors, such as genetics. In other words, a mechanism-based diagnostic approach based on the cognitive model would be biased to highlight some mechanisms (e.g., learning experiences and dysfunctional beliefs and appraisals) while neglecting other mechanisms (e.g., genetic, epigenetic, and other biological factors).

Fourth, the cognitive approach fails to explain all cases of anxiety disorders. For example, contemporary cognitive models of OCD (e.g., Frost & Steketee, 2000; Salkovskis, 1996) fail to account for the findings that many people with this disorder do not have abnormally elevated scores on measures of the types of dysfunctional beliefs that cognitive models regard as central to the disorder (Taylor et al., 2005). It is unclear how a cognitive classification system would diagnose such people. If dysfunctional beliefs were part of the mechanism-based criteria for OCD, then these patients would not be diagnosed as having this disorder, even though they had comparable obsessive–compulsive symptoms to the patients who had dysfunctional beliefs.

Fifth, mechanisms of the anxiety disorders may differ across cultures (Hinton, Hsia, Park, Rasmussen, & Pollack, this volume). Very little is known about cross-cultural differences in the anxiety disorders, and there is no guarantee that the cognitive models of anxiety disorders—developed to account for these disorders as they arise in Western culture—apply to other cultures.

PANDAS as a mechanism-based classification? Perhaps the best case for an etiologically-based classification concerns a class of disorders known as pediatric autoimmune neuropsychiatric disorders associated with streptococcal infection (PANDAS; Williams, Grant, & Kim, 2008), in which a specific agent (streptococcal infection) causes a specific dysfunction (inflammation of the basal ganglia and associated structures), which leads to a characteristic pattern of symptoms (e.g., rapid onset of childhood OCD and other disorders or symptoms that abate if the infection is treated in the acute phase). Although the PANDAS concept is not without its critics and conceptual problems (e.g., Kurland & Kaplan, 2004; Singer et al., 2008), it remains a promising candidate for an etiologically based classification of a subgroup of people who would be currently diagnosed as having OCD. However, PANDAS makes only a modest contribution to an etiologically based classification because PANDAS accounts for no more than 10% of OCD in children (Trifiletti & Packard, 1999).

Practical implications of mechanism-based diagnosis. There is one way in which mechanism-based diagnostic classification would be radically different from *DSM*—different in such an extreme fashion that the current generation of mental health practitioners might have difficulty adjusting to the new system, and insurance companies would be reluctant to adopt. A mechanism-based system would not require signs, symptoms, impairment, distress, or disability to diagnose a disorder; all that would be needed to be present would be the psychopathological process. This is analogous to some areas of general medicine, where "silent" (symptom free) diseases can be diagnosed. Examples include arteriovenous malformations, hypertension, hypercholesterolemia, and the hyperlipidemias.

Under a mechanism-based classification system, panic disorder (or a related, etiology-defined construct, perhaps called the anxiety sensitivity syndrome or panic-prone personality), for example, could be diagnosed simply by the presence of elevated scores on measures of etiologically related constructs (e.g., on a measure of the tendency to catastrophically misinterpret bodily sensations), which would serve as markers of the underlying psychopathologic process. Many seemingly healthy, well-adjusted people have elevated scores on such measures (Taylor, 1999). They may not be suffering from panic attacks but are at risk for developing panic disorder (Schmidt, Lerew, & Jackson, 1997). All of this suggests an unintended consequence of mechanism-based diagnosis: It would vastly inflate the prevalence of diagnosed disorders, with important consequences in terms of the economic burden carried by insurance companies and healthcare system in general.

The Place of Clinical Significance in Psychiatric Classification

Several investigators (e.g., McCabe, Swinson, & Jacobs, this volume) have argued for the refinement of the clinical significance criterion, noting that some disorders may be associated with minimal distress or interference in functioning. On this basis one would diagnose, say, a snake phobia, when a person lives in a place where real snakes are never encountered and the person rarely, if ever, encounters snake-related stimuli, and therefore rarely experiences clinically significant distress or impairment. But if the clinical significance criterion is dropped, then this opens the floodgates for labeling ordinary misery or daily hassles as pathological problems. Eliminating the criteria for clinical significance can also lead to absurdities, as illustrated by Bentall's (1992) provocative proposal for classifying happiness as a mental disorder:

> *It is proposed that happiness be classified as a psychiatric disorder and be included in future editions of the major diagnostic manuals under the new name: major affective disorder, pleasant type. In a review of the relevant literature it is shown that happiness is statistically abnormal, consists of a discrete cluster of symptoms, is associated with a range of cognitive abnormalities, and probably reflects the abnormal functioning of the central nervous system. One possible objection to this proposal remains—that happiness is not negatively valued. However, this objection is dismissed as scientifically irrelevant. (p. 94)*

Subclinical Conditions

Over the years researchers have defined subclinical forms of various disorders in which the afflicted individual meets some but not all criteria required to diagnose a given disorder. Examples include abridged hypochondriasis (e.g., Gureje, Üstün, & Simon, 1997) and partial PTSD (e.g., Kulka et al., 1990). The argument is that it is important to recognize these clinical conditions because they are associated with significant impairment in social and occupational functioning, and these conditions can be effectively treated with interventions used for the full-blown versions of the disorders.

In our view it is unnecessary to create new diagnostic categories for subclinical conditions. Under the *DSM-IV* classification system, these clinical conditions can be classified as adjustment disorders if they arise in the context of an identifiable stressor—whether it be a traumatic or nontraumatic stressor—and went into remission within 6 months of the termination of the stressor. If the symptoms last more than 6 months after the termination of a relevant stressor, or do not arise in the context of a stressor, then the diagnosis would be anxiety disorder not otherwise specified (anxiety disorder NOS). A limitation with this proposal is that, like the diagnosis of adjustment disorder, the NOS classification is problematic because it is vague. It conveys very little information about the nature of the symptoms and does not represent a homogeneous clinical construct.

A further problem with defining subclinical syndromes as either adjustment or NOS disorders is they blur the distinction between *normal* and *abnormal*. The distinct is blurry even without considering subclinical conditions. It has been argued, for example, that social anxiety and unipolar mood disorders are over diagnosed; that is, some people meeting full criteria for these disorders may be simply suffering from normal anxiety (shyness) or dysphoria (Horwitz & Wakefield, 2007; Lane, 2007; Wakefield, Horwitz, & Schmitz, 2005).

Issues Specific to the Classification of Anxiety Disorders

Grouping of Disorders

Distress disorders, fear disorders, and the OCD spectrum. A number of investigators, including contributors to the present volume, have argued for the regrouping of anxiety disorders for *DSM-V*. Three major classes of disorders have been proposed: (a) distress disorders, consisting of generalized anxiety disorder (GAD), PTSD, major depressive disorder, and dysthymia (Emmelkamp & Powers, this volume; Gamez, Watson, & Doebbeling, 2007; Watson, this volume); (b) fear disorders, consisting of panic disorder, agoraphobia, social anxiety disorder, and specific phobia (Emmelkamp & Powers, this volume; Gamez et al., 2007; Watson, this volume), and (c) obsessive–compulsive related disorders (OCRDs), consisting of OCD and various other disorders (Gamez et al., 2007; Hollander, Braun, & Simeon, 2008).

In our view, such a regrouping would have little, if any, clinical significance. That is, the regrouping would have no impact on either diagnostic practices or treatment. However, the regrouping may have greater significance on research into the disorders because the regrouping carries the implicit assumption that disorders within groups have greater similarity, in terms of clinical features and perhaps etiology, than disorders between groups. The distinction between fear disorders and distress disorders is supported by factor analytic research (Watson, this volume) in which fear disorders and distress disorders load on separate factors. If one assumes that each factor represents a distinct set of causal mechanisms (Cattell, 1978), then the regrouping will encourage researchers to look for common mechanisms between particular types of disorders; for example, common mechanisms in fear disorders. The concept of OCRDs is much more controversial.

Is OCD an anxiety disorder? Hollander and colleagues (e.g., Bartz & Hollander, 2006; Gamez et al., 2007; Hollander et al., 2008) have argued that OCD should be moved out of the anxiety disorders category and into a newly formed OCRD category. The composition of this category is currently unclear. Hollander et al. (2008) proposed that the category should include OCD, obsessive–compulsive personality disorder, Tourette's syndrome, "grooming disorders" (trichotillomania, skin picking, nail biting), body dysmorphic disorder, and eating disorders. In other publications, Hollander and colleagues have argued that OCRDs should include a substantially broader range of disorders, including hypochondriasis, pathological gambling, depersonalization disorder, a wide range of tic disorders (including Tourette's syndrome), and autism (e.g., Bartz & Hollander, 2006). The omission of hypochondriasis from Hollander et al.'s (2008) list of OCRDs is surprising, because of all these disorders, hypochondriasis bears the closest resemblance to OCD in terms of clinical features (e.g., obsessional doubting, compulsive checking; Abramowitz & Moore, 2007; Neziroglu, McKay, & Yaryura–Tobias, 2000), etiologic models (e.g., cognitive-behavioral formulations; Taylor & Asmundson, 2004), and treatment (e.g., cognitive-behavioral approaches; Taylor & Asmundson, 2004).

In addition to the vagueness of the concept of OCRDs, there are several other problems (Abramowitz et al., this volume; Storch, Abramowitz, & Goodman, 2008). The concept was initially conceived on the basis of the supposed similarity of symptoms among various disorders (e.g., repetitive thinking and repetitive behavior). Yet the phenomenology of these repetitive symptoms varies considerably across the proposed

OCRD conditions; for example, repetitive behaviors in OCD (i.e., compulsions) are distress-reducing activities that do not produce pleasure, whereas repetitive behaviors in trichotillomania (e.g., pulling hair from the scalp) or pathological gambling (e.g., persistent betting) are pleasurable activities (Nestadt et al, 2001). Repetitive behaviors in tic disorders are more akin to dysregulated, reflexive muscle movements than to anxiety-reducing or pleasure-seeking behaviors.

In an effort to garner support for the concept of OCRDs, Hollander and colleagues asserted that the various disorders also overlap in terms of patterns of comorbidity, familial patterns, neurobiology, and treatment (Hollander et al., 2008). Patterns of comorbidity, however, fail to provide strong support for a distinct category of OCRDs (Bienvenu et al., 2000; Jaisoorya, Reddy, & Srinath, 2003). In fact, OCD is more commonly associated with mood and anxiety disorders than with the putative OCRDs (Nestadt et al, 2001).

The link between OCD and putative spectrum disorders is also unsupported in terms of neurobiological correlates (e.g., O'Sullivan et al., 1997; Stein et al., 1997), familial aggregation (Bienvenu et al., 2000), and response to pharmacologic and psychosocial interventions. Treatments that are effective for OCD, serotonergic reuptake inhibitors (SRIs) and exposure and response prevention (ERP), are quite different from the empirically supported treatments for some of the OCRDs. For example, studies of trichotillomania have shown no beneficial effect of SRIs relative to placebo (Christenson et al., 1991; Ninan et al., 2000; van Minnen et al., 2003). To our knowledge, there is no evidence that ERP is effective for some of the putative OCRDs, such as obsessive–compulsive personality disorder, trichotillomania, and autism.

Is hypochondriasis an anxiety disorder? *DSM-IV* considers hypochondriasis to be a somatoform disorder because of the prominence of bodily complaints. Yet, empirical evidence shows that hypochondriasis shares many symptom similarities with anxiety disorders, particularly panic disorder, GAD, and OCD (Taylor & Asmundson, 2004). As noted above, some investigators have emphasized a particularly close association between hypochondriasis and OCD (Abramowitz & Moore, 2007; Neziroglu et al., 2000). Based on these data, and contrary to the idea that hypochondriasis be included as an OCRD, several investigators have suggested that hypochondriasis be renamed "health anxiety disorder" and, accordingly, should be moved into the anxiety disorders category (Asmundson et al., this volume; Kroenke, Sharpe, & Sykes, 2007; Mayou, Kirmayer, Simon, Kroenke, & Sharpe, 2005). This proposal is consistent with the fact that anxiety is a prominent feature of hypochondriasis, and that this disorder is commonly comorbid with anxiety disorders (APA, 2000). However, hypochondriasis is also commonly comorbid with other somatoform disorders, such as somatization (APA, 2000). Accordingly, the proposal that hypochondriasis is an anxiety disorder remains to be further investigated.

One test of the proposal would be to compute genetic correlations from behavioral-genetic (twin) studies. Previous twin research has shown that hypochondriacal facets, such as disease conviction and fear of illness, injury, and death, have a genetic component (Taylor, Jang, Stein, & Asmundson, 2008). Genetic correlations, which represent the correlation between the genetic components underlying two different phenotypes, therefore can be computed to determine the strength of etiological relationship between different disorders. Thus, one could conduct twin research to determine whether the genetic correlations between facets of hypochondriasis and features of anxiety disorders are larger than the genetic correlations between hypochondriacal facets and features of other somatoform disorders. Environmental correlations could be similarly computed to determine whether hypochondriasis is etiologically more similar to anxiety disorder than to somatoform disorders. Here, etiology would be defined in terms of environmental factors such as learning experiences, which have been implicated in hypochondriasis (Taylor & Asmundson, 2004).

Dimensional Approaches to Classification

It is difficult to adequately investigate the etiology of a disorder without an accurate description of its phenotype (signs and symptoms). The current *DSM* and *ICD* classification systems assume that anxiety disorders, defined phenotypically, are categorical (present versus absent). Yet, research using taxometric methods suggests that many disorders represent the extremes of a continuum of phenotypic severity (Ruscio, Haslam, & Ruscio, 2006). Similarly, the symptoms within these disorders (e.g., the severity of worry in GAD or the severity of avoidance in PTSD) can be defined dimensionally. Accordingly, a major theme to emerge from this volume and from the empirical research in general is that the classification of anxiety disorders may be improved if dimensional classification is used (Emmelkamp & Powers, this volume; Hofmann, Richey, Sawyer, Asnaani, & Rief, this volume; Shear, Bjelland, Beesdo, Gloster, & Wittchen, 2007; Watson, this volume).

The distinction between categorical and dimensional diagnosis has important implications for theory and research, as each implies a different set of causes. A categorical approach assumes that a disorder arises from a small set of causal factors (e.g., the presence versus absence of some critical factor or set of factors). A dimensional approach assumes that a disorder is the result of incremental effects of a multitude of factors; for example, numerous genetic factors, each making a small but important additive contribution to the risk of developing some anxiety-related problem. Dimensional approaches are consistent with current thinking about the role of genes in psychiatric disorders. Investigators are increasingly interested in identifying the many genes that appear to make only small (e.g., 1%–2%) contributions to phenotypic variance (Plomin, Defries, Craig, & McGuffin, 2003). Thus, the assumption that the facets of anxiety disorders are dimensional will focus research efforts differently than the assumption that the phenomena are grouped into one or more categorical entities.

Dimensional quantification of disorders, or features of disorders is likely to be of more value to researchers than clinicians. For clinicians, it will remain necessary to define (e.g., for managed care reimbursement) whether a given patient passes the threshold for qualifying for a given disorder. Accordingly, it has been argued that dimensional classification, if used at all, should be subsumed within a categorical classification system, rather than replace the categorical system (Helzer, Kraemer, & Krueger, 2006; Shear et al., 2007).

Refining Criteria for Specific Disorders

In the following sections we will critically examine various proposals for revising specific anxiety disorders. Not all disorders have been slated for substantial revision. Accordingly, we will discuss only the four disorders for which substantive revisions have been proposed; specific phobia, panic disorder and agoraphobia, PTSD, and GAD.

Specific phobia. Several investigators, including Emmelkamp and Powers (this volume), have noted that the current *DSM* classification of specific phobia subtypes requires revision because it is not fully consistent with the research literature. That is, there is a lack of empirical support for the distinction between animal, natural environment, and situational subtypes. Blood-injury–injection (BII) phobia, however, can empirically be distinguished from animal and situational phobias on the basis of factor analytic data and physiological patterns of response.

Based on observed patterns of comorbidity, Emmelkamp and Powers proposed an alternative scheme for subtyping phobias: (a) simple subtype (i.e., only one specific phobia), and (b) generalized subtype (more than one specific phobia). This mirrors the current distinction between specific and generalized types of social anxiety disorder; however, the merits of this subtyping scheme remain to be demonstrated. A further problem is that the generalized subtype may blur the distinction between specific phobia and agoraphobia. The latter is characterized by multiple phobias (e.g., excessive fear of heights, enclosed spaces, open spaces, being alone, bridges).

An alternative subtyping could be based simply on distinguishing BII versus other phobias. BII differs from other phobias in a number of ways, including the characteristic patterns of physiological reactions. On exposure to phobia stimuli, BII involves an initial heart rate acceleration followed by bradycardia, a drop in blood pressure, and fainting. Other phobias are characterized by increased heart rate without subsequent bradycardia (APA, 2000). These potential subtypes also differ in their treatments; applied tension is the treatment of choice for BII, whereas various forms of exposure therapy are the most efficacious treatments for other phobias (Barlow, 2002).

Panic disorder and agoraphobia. Emmelkamp and Powers (this volume) suggested that the symptoms for defining panic disorder be expanded to include blurred vision, headache, diarrhea, and polyuria. The merits of this revision remain to be empirically examined. One problem with this proposal is that the added symptoms, as diagnostic criteria, may undermine the distinction between panic disorder and other disorders because symptoms such as headache, diarrhea, and polyuria are nonspecific stress reactions present in many disorders, particularly GAD and PTSD (APA, 2000). Emmelkamp and Powers (this volume) also observed that agoraphobic avoidance is sometimes motivated by *fear of symptoms* such as headache, diarrhea, and polyuria because of their perceived consequences. For example, fear of losing bowel or bladder control in public places, or the fear of having migraines in brightly lit outdoor spaces. Accordingly, the authors propose that such fears should be part of the diagnostic criteria. It is unclear whether this is necessary; instead, it could be simply mentioned in the body of the descriptive text on agoraphobia, as is done in *DSM-IV-TR*, noting that agoraphobic avoidance is motivated by the fear of having panic attacks or panic-like experiences such as migraine attacks or sudden urges to void one's bowels. The notion of panic-like experiences could be clarified in the descriptive text in *DSM-V* to include such things as the fear of losing bowel or bladder control; however, there seems to be no need to modify the actual diagnostic criteria.

Posttraumatic stress disorder. When the diagnostic criteria for PTSD were formally introduced in *DSM-III* (APA, 1980), traumatic stressors were defined as being those events outside of the realm of usual human experience. If an event did not meet this criterion, a person could not be diagnosed with PTSD, regardless of whether the person had PTSD-like symptoms. If the person did have such symptoms in the absence of a qualifying event, he or she might receive some other diagnosis, such as a relatively minor diagnosis of adjustment disorder or a vague diagnosis such as anxiety disorder NOS.

The criteria for defining traumatic stressors became more liberal, in terms of defining more commonplace events as traumatic, in subsequent editions of the *DSM*, including the current version. The criteria were modified in light of epidemiologic research showing that highly stressful events, such as sexual assault or serious road traffic collisions, were hardly rare and not outside the realm of usual human experience. A further modification in *DSM-IV* was that PTSD could be diagnosed if a person witnessed or learned that a significant other had experienced a trauma. In *DSM-III* and *DSM-III-R*, it was necessary that the person directly experienced a trauma in order to diagnose PTSD. According to *DSM-IV* criteria, a traumatic stressor is defined as an event in which (a) the person experiences, witnesses, or is confronted with an event or events that involve actual or threatened death or serious injury, or a threat to the physical integrity of self or others, and (b) the person's response involves intense fear, helplessness, or horror. Once the more liberal criteria for traumatic events were adopted, the number of eligible cases of PTSD increased by 20% (Breslau & Kessler, 2001).

Given the current diagnostic criteria, some clinical investigators have claimed that even seemingly minor events could qualify as traumatic stressors. For example, it has been claimed that traumatic stressors may consist of exposure to offensive remarks by coworkers (Avina & O'Donohue, 2002) or the loss of a farmer's cows because of foot-and-mouth disease (Olff et al., 2005). Other purported examples include various forms of vicarious exposure to trauma such as watching atrocities on television. McNally (2003) referred to this increasingly liberal definition of the concept of traumatic stressor as the *criterion bracket creep*. According to McNally, bracket creep is something that seriously imperils the credibility of the diagnosis of PTSD; "the more we identify noncatastrophic events as stressors deemed capable of producing PTSD, the less likely it is that we will ever discover any common mechanisms that mediate PTSD symptoms" (p. 280). Other investigators have expressed similar sentiments (Rosen, 2005) and have objected that the liberal criteria for trauma trivialize the experiences of genuine trauma victims (Elhai, Kashdan, & Frueh, 2005).

Not all investigators share this view (Brewin, 2003; Taylor, 2006). In fact, the liberal definition of a traumatic stressor (for diagnosing PTSD) is consistent with a diathesis-stress conceptualization of the disorder; the greater the person's diathesis (predisposition) for developing PTSD, the smaller the amount of stress required to trigger the disorder. Consistent with this conclusion, research indicates that PTSD varies along a continuum of severity rather than being a categorical (present or absent) entity (Ruscio, Ruscio, & Keane, 2002). Research also shows that even nontraumatic stressors can give rise to PTSD-like symptoms such as nightmares, insomnia, avoidance, and exaggerated startle (Horowitz, 2001; Mol et al., 2005). This may be especially true for highly vulnerable individuals. To illustrate, when the film *The Exorcist* was released in 1973, there were reports of people developing PTSD-like symptoms after seeing the film. After watching the movie, one person became frightened that the devil might possess him because of all the bad things he had done in life. He suffered from this fear for about 4 weeks, along with insomnia, irritability, decreased appetite, and inability to remove scenes of the film from his mind. Eventually, his problems resolved after receiving treatment at a local hospital (Bozzuto, 1975).

Given these considerations, there is ongoing debate about how traumatic stressors should be defined in order to diagnose PTSD. Because PTSD-like symptoms occur in people who have been exposed to nontraumatic stressors, perhaps the traumatic stressor criterion should be dropped, and PTSD should be renamed "stress disorder." Or perhaps we should return to the *DSM-I* label of "gross stress reaction." Regardless of label, the disorder would be diagnosed on the basis of the number and severity of symptoms, along with the associated degree of impairment.

A further proposed revision to the criteria for PTSD is to separate the symptoms of effortful avoidance and numbing into separate clusters, because the two groups of symptoms can be distinguished in terms of factor analytic studies, hypothesized underlying mechanisms, and treatment response (Asmundson, Stapleton, & Taylor, 2004).

In a provocative editorial, Rosen, Spitzer, and McHugh (2008) argued that PTSD is simply a meld of major depressive disorder and specific phobia. The implication is that the category of PTSD is superfluous. This view is inconsistent with the fact that PTSD can be diagnosed in the absence of major depression (e.g., Blanchard, Buckley, Hickling, & Taylor, 1998). Moreover, some features of PTSD, particularly reexperiencing and hyperarousal symptoms, are not characteristic features of either major depression or specific phobia. Despite the overlap in numbing symptoms, PTSD and major depressive disorder are factor-analytically distinct from one another. This was demonstrated by Blanchard et al. (1998). Using structural equation modeling, they found that a two-factor model in which PTSD symptoms defined one factor and major depressive symptoms defined another factor had a better fit to the data than a model in which all these symptoms loaded on a single "general distress" factor.

Generalized anxiety disorder. When GAD was introduced in *DSM-III*, it was considered a residual category to be diagnosed only if some other disorder, such as panic disorder or major depressive disorder, was not present. When another disorder was present, GAD symptoms were simply regarded as associated features. In subsequent editions of *DSM*, this requirement was dropped so that GAD could be diagnosed even when another disorder was present. From *DSM-III* to *DSM-IV* the number of requisite symptoms was also reduced so that there was less emphasis on somatic symptoms and more emphasis on uncontrollable worry.

Given that GAD commonly co-occurs with major depression, the question arises as to whether GAD is simply an associated feature of depression. If this is the case, then GAD plus major depression could simply be relabeled as "major depression, agitated subtype." This issue was examined in two recent reviews (Hettema, 2008; Mennin, Heimberg, Fresco, & Ritter, 2008). The similarities and differences between GAD and major depression were examined in terms of symptoms, comorbidity, etiology, pathophysiology, and treatment. Both reviews concluded that although the two disorders have a lot in common, they also have significant differences and so GAD should be retained as a distinct disorder. This conclusion has sound empirical justification.

It may be asked whether GAD should be merged with some other anxiety disorder. Watson (this volume) observed that factor analytic research shows that GAD and PTSD are more closely related to one another than they are to other anxiety disorders. Recall that Watson groups GAD, PTSD, dysthymia, and major depression into a category called distress disorders. If GAD and PTSD can be distinguished from depression, the question remains as to whether GAD and PTSD are distinct from one another. Is GAD, for example, a milder form of PTSD, where GAD is characterized primarily by PTSD hyperarousal symptoms? If this is the case, then Watson's category of distress disorders could be classified into an anxiety subtype (i.e., what we currently call PTSD and GAD) and a depressive subtype (major depression and dysthymia).

A problem with merging GAD and PTSD is that the two differ in important ways, including their characteristic symptoms (e.g., uncontrollable worry about minor things for GAD versus intrusive trauma recollections for PTSD). They also differ in terms of empirically supported treatments (e.g., stimulus control for GAD versus prolonged exposure for PTSD) (Barlow, 2002).

Progress of the *DSM*-V and *ICD-11* Workgroups

DSM-V Prelude Project

Planning for *DSM-V* began in 1999 (Kupfer, First, & Regier, 2002). This led to the *DSM-V* Prelude Project, which comprised a series of conferences organized under the auspices of the American Psychiatric Association in order to discuss issues for *DSM-V*. Summaries of the presentations have been published on the Internet (http://www.psych.org/MainMenu/Research/DSMIV/DSMV/DSMRevisionActivities/ResearchPlanningatHigherMagnification.aspx). Presenters were established experts in the area, many of whom later became members of various *DSM-V* workgroups (and some are contributors to this volume). A goal of each conference was to arrive at recommendations concerning important issues. We will consider the recommendations concerning the anxiety disorders.

The June 2005 conference was called "Stress-Induced and Fear Circuitry Disorders Conference," the title of which suggests an interest in etiology-based classification. Rather than recommending specific changes, the workgroup called for more research into the nature and etiology of anxiety disorders (e.g., neuroimaging studies).

The June 2006 conference concerned OCD-related disorders. It was concluded that in order to classify a given disorder as being OCD-related, there should be strong evidence from at least three out of the following five domains—phenomenology, comorbidity, family history, fronto-striatal brain circuitry (e.g., caudate hyperactivity), and treatment response—with either family history or fronto-striatal brain circuitry required. Based on this criterion, it was concluded that the strongest evidence for a relationship with OCD was for Tourette's syndrome, body dysmorphic disorder, and hypochondriasis. Curiously, as noted above, the latter disorder was omitted from Hollander et al.'s (2008) classification of OCRDs.

The conference summary also concluded that many other disorders could be classified as OCRDs: obsessive–compulsive personality disorder, Sydenham's chorea, PANDAS, trichotillomania, and eating disorders. It was concluded that there was the least support for skin picking and nail biting. Note that skin picking and nail biting were included in Hollander et al.'s (2008) classification. The various inconsistencies highlight the uncertainty about what qualifies as an OCRD.

Possible subtypes of OCD were also considered, including tic-related, childhood-onset, symmetry type, hoarding type, postpartum, poor insight, impulsive type, inattentive type, and PANDAS. Research is needed to investigate whether OCD can be fruitfully divided into these subtypes. Based on the available evidence, the subtyping scheme is questionable because many patients are likely to belong to more than one subtype. For example, childhood-onset OCD may be associated with tics. Similarly, hoarding can be associated with poor insight.

The July 2006 conference concerned dimensional aspects of psychiatric diagnosis, including the diagnosis of anxiety disorders. It was recommended that the categorical approach to diagnosis should be retained, but supplemented with dimensional ratings. For example, ratings could be made about the severity of disorders or symptoms. It would not be practical to do this for all the symptoms of anxiety disorders, and so it was suggested that dimensional ratings be made for symptoms that cut across most or all of the anxiety disorders (e.g., anticipatory anxiety, fear, avoidance). It was noted that dimensional ratings may facilitate research into the etiology of anxiety disorders, and that such ratings supposedly have clinical value because disorder severity often predicts treatment outcome. That is, people with more severe anxiety disorders, compared to those with mild disorder, may require a longer period of treatment in order to reach remission.

The last of the conferences relevant to the anxiety disorders took place in June 2007, where issues concerning the comorbidity of GAD and depression were considered. There was general agreement that GAD and major depressive disorder were closely related but not identical disorders. Accordingly, it was recommended that they be retained as distinct disorders. Some conference participants also suggested that the close relationship between the two could be emphasized in the text descriptions of both disorders in *DSM-V*.

DSM-V Task Force

In November 2007, the American Psychiatric Association Task Force on *DSM-V* was officially assembled, consisting of 12 work groups and four "cross-cutting" study groups. The mandate of the task force is to thoroughly reconsider the diagnostic system rather than "tinkering around the edges" (Oldham, 2007, p. 350). At the time of writing this chapter (October 2008), little information about the progress of the work groups was publically available, and the nature of the major revisions remains unknown.

International Advisory Group for *ICD-11* Mental and Behavioral Disorders

The activities and recommendations of the Advisory Group (AG) for producing the *ICD-11* section on psychiatric disorders have been presented in a series of minutes, available at http://www.who.int/mental_health/evidence/en. We reviewed all posted minutes available at the time of writing this chapter. The minutes concerned three meetings, from January 2007 to March 2008. They focus on the classification of psychiatric disorders in general, without specific reference to revisions to the anxiety disorders. Nevertheless, the recommendations have relevance to the classification of anxiety disorders.

The AG recommended that any revisions should be limited to whatever changes can be justified by the available empirical literature. Accordingly, literature reviews were conducted and a database of relevant empirical studies will be assembled. In revising the *ICD*, the AG recommended that the diagnostic classification manual should not function as a textbook. This is in contrast to the current edition of the *DSM* (APA, 2000), which is very much a textbook on psychopathology, containing background information for each disorder concerning associated features, demographic features, clinical course, prevalence, family history, and other pertinent disorder-related information. The AG also recommended against the inclusion of multi-axial classification, as is used in the *DSM*. Despite the difference between *ICD* and *DSM*, the AG considered it important that, as far as possible, the classification scheme in *ICD-11* should be similar to *DSM-V*. The AG even formed a Harmonization Coordinating Group to facilitate this goal. This suggests that proposed revision of *ICD* may resemble a stripped-down version of *DSM-V*; that is, lacking background text and multi-axial diagnoses. If an important goal is to make *ICD-11* as similar as possible to *DSM-V*, then why do we need two classification systems? One would surely suffice, whether it is *ICD-11* or *DSM-V*.

An important point raised by the AG, which has been largely overlooked in previous discussions about the revision of diagnostic manuals, concerns the differing needs of clinicians and researchers. The AG observed that *ICD-10* contains approximately 150 diagnoses, with each requiring 10 to 30 pieces of information. (There are more than 290 diagnoses listed in *DSM*-IV). The AG noted that the number of *ICD-10* diagnoses and the amount of information required to establish each diagnosis "substantially exceeds the level of information that the human brain can easily process" (p. 3 of the September 2007, minutes). The AG further noted that more than half of all diagnoses in clinical practice are assigned to NOS categories, thereby indicating that residual categories were more often used than specific disorder categories. This is entirely opposite to what a good classification system should do; specific disorders should be more often diagnosed and residual categories should be reserved for rare clinical presentations. The AG proposed that two versions of *ICD-11* be produced, one for clinicians containing a simplified (prototype-based) classification scheme, and a more detailed version for researchers containing more specific sets of classifications. This proposal highlights an interesting issue concerning the different and sometimes competing goals of a classification system, and one that should be considered further. Both *ICD* and *DSM* aim to be relevant to clinicians and researchers, but perhaps there needs to be separate versions to better serve clinical and research purposes.

The AG also recommended that it is important to classify disorders in terms of their level of severity. This is a point that has been raised by contributors to this volume. The AG conceptualized their recommendation (according to the September 2007, minutes) largely on the basis of treatment recommendations; "one option would be to identify those disorders for which there is specific evidence of differential treatment effectiveness based on severity, so that levels of severity or a dimension of severity can be developed for these categories as a part of the diagnostic system" (p. 4). This is a pragmatic approach to the use of dimensional classification; that is, using groupings on a given dimension when they have practical consequences. Finally, the AG has also begun to examine the value of regrouping disorders, similar to the proposals discussed above.

Conclusions

Is it premature to revise *DSM-IV* and *ICD-10*? Despite the large amount of research published since these manuals were introduced, it seems premature to move to mechanism-based classification systems. Similarly, we believe it is premature to use the results of laboratory tests as diagnostic criteria. The time seems ripe, however, for reorganizing some disorders into empirically defined subgroups, such as the groups of fear disorders and distress disorders identified by Watson (this volume). This regrouping of disorders will, however, likely be of more use to researchers than clinicians. It remains debatable as to whether OCD should remain in the anxiety disorders section or be moved into a newly defined section composed of OCRDs. Further research, including studies of whether the OCRDs share basic mechanisms, such as common genetic factors, is needed. It is unclear whether such studies can feasibly be conducted before the scheduled publication of *DSM-V* and *ICD-11*. It also remains to be determined whether hypochondriasis should be classified as a somatoform disorder, an OCRD, or as an anxiety disorder.

Regarding the revision of the diagnostic criteria for specific disorders, there appears to be a consensus that GAD should remain as a distinct disorder, rather than being reconceptualized as an associated feature of major depression. There is also evidence to challenge the *DSM-IV* subtyping for specific phobia, but the most robust (replicable) set of subtypes remains to be established.

So far, there is consensus that the categorical classification scheme should be retained, but supplemented by dimensional ratings, such as ratings of the severity of symptoms and disorders (e.g., ratings of mild, moderate, and severe). Ample research indicates that the various features of anxiety disorders, and the global severity of these disorders, can be reliably rated on dimensional scales when structured interviews are used (e.g., see Hunsley & Mash, 2008). However, clinicians typically don't use such scales; they generally use unstructured interviews. Field trials are required to determine whether dimensional ratings are reliable and clinically useful when assessed in this way.

There have been proposals to develop two kinds of diagnostic manual (e.g., two forms of *ICD-11*), consisting of a detailed manual suitable for researchers and a simplified or streamlined version that would be more efficient to use in clinical settings. Field trials are needed to compare the research and clinical versions of such manuals in order to establish their respective reliabilities and to ensure that there is acceptable concordance between versions for each disorder. In other words, it is important to ensure that the versions are diagnosing the same disorders.

As presently defined, anxiety disorders are among the most prevalent forms of mental illness. There can be no doubt that the way anxiety disorders are classified has played an important role in how we have conducted research to improve our conceptualization and management of these problems. Moving forward, the exciting challenge, or perhaps the *gamble*, for the field of mental health is to decide how, or *whether*, we might do an even better service to science and our patients by embarking on reclassification.

References

Abramowitz, J. S., & Moore, E. L. (2007). An experimental analysis of hypochondriasis. *Behaviour Research and Therapy, 45,* 413–424.

American Psychiatric Association (1980). *Diagnostic and statistical manual of mental disorders* (3rd ed.). Washington, DC: Author.

American Psychiatric Association (1994). *Diagnostic and statistical manual of mental disorders* (4th ed.). Washington, DC: Author.

American Psychiatric Association (2000). *Diagnostic and statistical manual of mental disorders* (4th ed., text rev.). Washington, DC: Author.

Asmundson, G. J. G., Stapleton, J. A., & Taylor, S. (2004). Are avoidance and numbing distinct PTSD symptom clusters? *Journal of Traumatic Stress, 17,* 467–475.

Avina, C., & O'Donohue, W. (2002). Sexual harassment and PTSD: Is sexual harassment diagnosable trauma? *Journal of Traumatic Stress, 15,* 69–75.

Barlow, D. H. (2002). *Anxiety and its disorders* (2nd ed.). New York: Guilford.

Bartz, J. A., & Hollander, E. (2006). Is obsessive–compulsive disorder an anxiety disorder? *Progress in Neuropsychopharmacology and Biological Psychiatry, 30,* 338–352.

Beck, A. T., & Emery, G. (1985). *Anxiety disorders and phobias: A cognitive perspective*. New York: Basic Books.

Bentall, R. P. (1992). A proposal to classify happiness as a psychiatric disorder. *Journal of Medical Ethics, 18,* 94–98.

Bienvenu, O., Samuels, J., Riddle, M., Hoehn-Saric, R., Liang, K., Cullen, B., et al. (2000). The relationship of obsessive–compulsive disorder to possible spectrum disorders: Results from a family study. *Biological Psychiatry, 48,* 287–293.

Blanchard, E. B., Buckley, T. C., Hickling, A. E., & Taylor, A. E. (1998). Posttraumatic stress disorder and comorbid major depression: Is the correlation an illusion? *Journal of Anxiety Disorders, 12,* 21–37.

Bozzuto, J. C. (1975). Cinematic neurosis following "The Exorcist": Report of four cases. *Journal of Nervous and Mental Disease, 161,* 43–48.

Breslau, N., & Kessler, R. C. (2001). The stressor criterion in DSM-IV posttraumatic stress disorder: An empirical investigation. *Biological Psychiatry, 50,* 699–704.

Brewin, C. R. (2003). *Posttraumatic stress disorder: Malady or myth?* New Haven, CT: Yale University Press.

Cattell, R. B. (1978). *The scientific use of factor analysis in the behavioral and life sciences.* New York: Plenum.

Christenson, G., Mackenzie, T., Mitchell, J., & Callies, A. (1991). A placebo controlled, double-blind crossover study of fluoxetine in trichotillomania. *American Journal of Psychiatry, 148,* 1566–1571.

Clark, D. M. (1986). A cognitive approach to panic. *Behaviour Research and Therapy, 24,* 461–470.

Cosgrove, L., Krimsky, S., Vijayraghavan, M., & Schneider, L. (2006). Financial ties between DSM-IV panel members and the pharmaceutical industry. *Psychotherapy and Psychosomatics, 75,* 154–160.

Elhai, J. D., Kashdan, T. B., & Frueh, B. C. (2005). What is a traumatic event? *British Journal of Psychiatry, 187,* 189–190.

First, M. B., & Zimmerman, M. (2006). Including laboratory tests in DSM-V diagnostic criteria. *American Journal of Psychiatry, 163,* 2041–2042.

Fish, F. J. (1974). *Fish's clinical psychopathology*. Bristol: Wright.

Frost, R. O., & Steketee, S. (2002). *Cognitive approaches to obsessions and compulsions: Theory, assessment, and treatment*. Oxford, UK: Elsevier.

Gamez, W., Watson, D., & Doebbeling, B. N. (2007). Abnormal personality and the mood and anxiety disorders: Implications for structural models of anxiety and depression. *Journal of Anxiety Disorders, 21,* 526–539.

Gureje, O., Üstün, T. B., & Simon, G. E. (1997). The syndrome of hypochondriasis: A cross-national study in primary care. *Psychological Medicine, 27,* 1001–1010.

Helzer, J. E., Kraemer, H. C., & Krueger, R. F. (2006). The feasibility and need for dimensional psychiatric diagnoses. *Psychological Medicine, 36,* 1671–1680.

Hen, R., & Hyman, S. (June 2005). [Untitled paper.] Presented at the Stress-Induced and Fear Circuitry Disorders Conference. Arlington, VA: Headquarters of the American Psychiatric Association. Extracted September 24, 2008, from http://www.psych.org/MainMenu/Research/DSMIV/DSMV/DSMRevisionActivities/ConferenceSummaries/StressInducedandFearCircuitryDisordersConference.aspx.

Hettema, J. M. (2008). The nosologic relationship between generalized anxiety disorder and major depression. *Depression and Anxiety, 25,* 300–316.

Hollander, E., Braun, A., & Simeon, D. (2008). Should OCD leave the anxiety disorders in DSM-V? The case for obsessive compulsive-related disorders. *Depression and Anxiety, 25,* 317–329.

Horwitz, A. V., & Wakefield, J. C. (2007). *The loss of sadness: How psychiatry transformed normal sorrow into depressive disorder.* New York: Oxford University Press.

Horowitz, M. J. (2001). *Stress response syndromes* (4th ed.). Northvale, NJ: Aronson.

Hunsley, J., & Mash, E. J. (2008). *A guide to assessments that work.* New York: Oxford University Press.

Hyman, S. E. (2007). Can neuroscience be integrated into the DSM-V? *Nature Reviews Neuroscience, 8,* 725–732.

Institute of Medicine. (2007). *Treatment of posttraumatic stress disorder: An assessment of the evidence.* Washington, DC: National Academies Press.

Jaisoorya, T., Reddy, Y., & Srinath S. (2003). The relationship of obsessive–compulsive disorder to putative spectrum disorders: Results from an Indian study. *Comprehensive Psychiatry, 44,* 317–323.

Kender, K. S. (2008). Explanatory models for psychiatric illness. *American Journal of Psychiatry, 165,* 695–702.

Kendler, K. S., Appelbaum, P. S., Bell, C. C., Fulford, K. W. M., Ghaemi, S. N., Schaffner, K. F., et al. (2008). Issues for DSM-V: DSM-V should include a conceptual issues work group. *American Journal of Psychiatry, 165,* 174–175.

Kraepelin, E. (1922). Ends and means of psychiatric research. *Journal of Mental Science, 281,* 115–143.

Kroenke, K., Sharpe, M., & Sykes, R. (2007). Revising the classification of somatoform disorders: Key questions and preliminary recommendations. *Psychosomatics, 48,* 277–285.

Kulka, R. A., Schlenger, W. E., Fairbank, J. A., Hough, R. L., Jordan, B. K., Marmar, C. R., et al. (1990). *Trauma and the Vietnam war generation.* New York: Brunner/Mazel.

Kupfer, D. J., First, M. B., & Regier, D. A. (Eds.) (2002). *A research agenda for DSM-V.* Washington, DC: American Psychiatric Press.

Kurland, R., & Kaplan, E. L. (2004). The pediatric autoimmune neuropsychiatric disorders associated with Streptococcal infection (PANDAS) etiology for tics and obsessive–compulsive symptoms: Hypothesis or entity? Practical considerations for the clinician. *Pediatrics, 113,* 883–886.

Lane, C. (2007). *Shyness: How normal behavior became a sickness.* Newhaven, CT: Yale University Press.

Mayou, R., Kirmayer, L. J., Simon, G., Kroenke, K., & Sharpe, M. (2005). Somatoform disorders: Time for a new approach in DSM-V. *American Journal of Psychiatry, 162,* 847–855.

McNally, R. J. (2003). *Remembering trauma.* Cambridge, MA: Harvard University Press.

Mennin, D. S., Heimberg, R. G., Fresco, D. M., & Ritter, M. (2008). Is generalized anxiety disorder an anxiety or mood disorder? Considering multiple factors as we ponder the fate of GAD. *Depression and Anxiety, 25,* 289–299.

Mol, S. S. L., Arntz, A. Metsemakers, J. F. M., Dinant, G. J., Vilters-van Monfort, P. A. P., & Knottnerus, J. A. (2005). Symptoms of post-traumatic stress disorder after nontraumatic events: Evidence from an open population study. *British Journal of Psychiatry, 186,* 494–499.

National Institute of Clinical Excellence (2005). *Posttraumatic stress disorder: The management of PTSD in adults and children in primary and secondary care.* London: Gaskell and the British Psychological Society.

Nestadt, G., Samuels, J., Riddle, M., Liang, K., Bienvenu, O., Hoehn-Saric, R., et al. (2001). The relationship between obsessive–compulsive disorder and anxiety and affective disorders: Results from the Johns Hopkins OCD Family Study. *Psychological Medicine, 31,* 481–487.

Neziroglu, F., McKay, D., & Yaryura-Tobias, J. A. (2000). Overlapping and distinctive features of hypochondriasis and obsessive–compulsive disorder. *Journal of Anxiety Disorders, 14,* 603–614.

Ninan, P., Rothbaum, B., Marsteller, F., Knight, B., & Eccard, M. (2000). A placebo-controlled trial of cognitive-behavioral therapy and clomipramine in trichotillomania. *Journal of Clinical Psychiatry, 61,* 47–50.

Oldham, J. (2007). Launching DSM-V. *Journal of Psychiatric Practice, 13,* 350–351.

Olff, M., Koeter, M. W. J., van Haaften, E. H., Kersten, P. H., & Gersons, B. P. R. (2005). Impact of a foot and mouth disease crisis on posttraumatic stress symptoms in farmers. *British Journal of Psychiatry, 186,* 165–166.

O'Sullivan, R., Rauch, S., & Brieter, H. (1997). Reduced basal ganglia volumes in trichotillomania measured via morphometric MRI. *Biological Psychiatry, 42,* 39–45.

Plomin, R., Defries, J. C., Craig, I. W., & McGuffin, P. (2003). *Behavioral genetics in the postgenomic era*. Washington, DC: American Psychological Association.

Rosen, G. M. (2005). Traumatic events, criterion creep, and the creation of posttraumatic stress disorder. *Scientific Review of Mental Health Practice, 3,* 39–42.

Rosen, G. M., Spitzer, R. L., & McHugh, P. R. (2008). Problems with the posttraumatic stress disorder diagnosis and its future in DSM-V. *British Journal of Psychiatry, 192,* 3–4.

Ruscio, A. M., Ruscio, J., & Keane, T. M. (2002). The latent structure of posttraumatic stress disorder: A taxometric investigation of reactions to extreme stress. *Journal of Abnormal Psychology, 111,* 290–301.

Ruscio, J., Haslam, N., & Ruscio, A. M. (2006). *Introduction to the taxometric method.* Mahwah, NJ: Erlbaum.

Salkovskis, P. M. (1996). Cognitive-behavioral approaches to the understanding of obsessional problems. In R. Rapee (Ed.), *Current controversies in the anxiety disorders* (pp. 103–133). New York: Guilford.

Schmidt, N. B., Lerew, D. R., & Jackson, R. J. (1997). The role of anxiety sensitivity in the pathogenesis of panic: Prospective evaluation of spontaneous panic attacks during acute stress. *Journal of Abnormal Psychology, 106,* 355–364.

Shear, M. K., Bjelland, I., Beesdo, K., Gloster, A. T., & Wittchen, H. U. (2007). Supplementary dimensional assessment in anxiety disorders. *International Journal of Methods in Psychiatric Research, 16(S1),* S52–S64.

Singer, H. S., Gause, C., Morris, C., Lopez, P., and the Tourette Syndrome Study Group. (2008). Serial immune markers do not correlate with clinical exacerbations in Pediatric Autoimmune Neuropsychiatric Disorders Associated with Streptococcal Infections. *Pediatrics, 121,* 1198–1205.

Spitzer, R. L. (1991). An outsider–insider's views about revising the DSMs. *Journal of Abnormal Psychology, 100,* 294–296.

Stein, D., Coetzer, R., & Lee, M. (1997). Magnetic resonance brain imaging in women with obsessive–compulsive disorder and trichotillomania. *Psychiatry Research, 74,* 177–182.

Storch, E. A., Abramowitz, J., & Goodman, W. K. (2008). Where does obsessive–compulsive disorder belong in DSM-V? *Depression and Anxiety, 25,* 336–347.

Taylor, S. (1999). *Anxiety sensitivity*. Mahwah, NJ: Erlbaum.

Taylor, S. (2006). *Clinician's guide to treating PTSD: A cognitive-behavioral approach*. New York: Guilford.

Taylor, S., Abramowitz, J. S., McKay, D., Calamari, J. E., Sookman, D., Kyrios, M., et . (2005). Do dysfunctional beliefs play a role in all types of obsessive–compulsive disorder? *Journal of Anxiety Disorders, 20,* 85–97.

Taylor, S., & Asmundson, G. J. G. (2004). *Treating health anxiety: A cognitive-behavioral approach.* New York: Guilford.

Taylor, S., Jang, K. L., Stein, M. B., & Asmundson, G. J. G. (2008). A behavioral-genetic analysis of health anxiety: Implications for the cognitive-behavioral model of hypochondriasis. *Journal of Cognitive Psychotherapy, 22,* 143–153.

Trifiletti, R. R., & Packard, A. M. (1999). Immune mechanisms in pediatric neuropsychiatric disorders: Tourette's syndrome, OCD, and PANDAS. *Child and Adolescent Clinics of North America, 8,* 767–775.

Van Minnen, A., Hoogduin, K., Keijsers, G., Hellenbrand, I., & Hendriks, G. (2003). Treatment of trichotillomania with behavioral therapy or fluoxetine: A randomized, waiting-list controlled study. *Archives of General Psychiatry, 60,* 517–522.

Wakefield, J. C., Horwitz, A. V., & Schmitz, M. F. (2005). Are we overpathologizing the socially anxious? Social phobia from a harmful dysfunction perspective. *Canadian Journal of Psychiatry, 50,* 317–319.

Williams, K. A., Grant, J. E., & Kim, S. W. (2008). The PANDAS subgroup of obsessive–compulsive disorder. In J. S. Abramowitz, D. McKay, & S. Taylor (Eds.), *Clinical handbook of obsessive–compulsive disorder and related problems* (pp. 95–108). Baltimore, MD: Johns Hopkins University Press.

Index

A

B

C

D

E

F

G

H

I

J

K

L

M

N

O

P

T

U

V

W

Y